SEXUAL CHOICES
An Introduction to
Human Sexuality
Second Edition

SEXUAL CHOICES
An Introduction to Human Sexuality

Second Edition

GILBERT D. NASS
University of Connecticut, Storrs

ROGER W. LIBBY
University of Massachusetts, Amherst

MARY PAT FISHER
Storrs, Connecticut

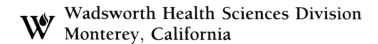 Wadsworth Health Sciences Division
Monterey, California

Sponsoring Editor: James Keating
Production Services Coordinator: Marlene Thom
Production: Greg Hubit Bookworks, Larkspur, California
Manuscript Editor: Jerilyn Emori
Interior Design: Langfeld Design Associates
Cover Art: Auguste Rodin (1840–1917), *The Kiss;* bronze, dark brown patina, with traces of green and rust color; 23¼ × 14¼ × 14⅛ inches. The Fine Arts Museums of San Francisco, Alma de Bretteville Spreckles Collection. Photo by Schopplein Studios.
Cover Design: Nancy Benedict
Typesetting: Boyer & Brass, San Diego, California

Wadsworth Health Sciences Division
A Division of Wadsworth, Inc.

Printed in the United States of America
10 9 8 7 6 5 4 3 2 1

Library of Congress Cataloging in Publication Data

Nass, Gilbert D.
  Sexual choices.

  Includes index.
  1. Sex. 2. Sex (Biology) 3. Sex (Psychology)
4. Hygiene, Sexual. I. Libby, Roger W. II. Fisher, Mary Pat, 1943–   . III. Title.
HQ21.N26 1984   613.9′5   83-25951

ISBN 0-534-03039-4

Photo/Cartoon Credits

1, © Paul Fusco/Magnum; 3, © Bennett Hall; 6, © Peter Simon; 8, © Charles Harbutt/Archive Pictures; 10, © Robert Burroughs/Jeroboam; 16, Courtesy of the Naturist Society/Oshkosh, Wisconson; 21, © Dave Patrick; 40, from *Two Guys Fooling Around with the Moon and Other Drawings,* © by B. Kliban 1982. Reprinted by permission of Toni Mendez, Inc.; 47, © Bob Clay/Jeroboam; 53, © Dianora Niccolini/Phototake; 54, © John Pearson; 55, Mad Magazine, © 1970 by E. C. Publications, Inc.; 60, © Robert Foothorap; 64, Betty Dodson; 71, © Peter Simon; 76, David Ballard; 77, © Erika Stone; 83, © 1981 Anne Dorfman/Jeroboam; 89, © 1975 Hank Lebo/Jeroboam; 92, © Erika Stone; 95, © Gilles Peress/Magnum; 100, © Jane Scherr/Jeroboam; 109, © Mary Ellen Mark/Archive Pictures; 111, © Jim Ritcher/Stock Boston; 114, © 1981, Rick Winsor/Woodfin Camp; 116, © 1983 King Features Syndicate, Inc. World Rights Reserved; 117, © Bernard Pierre/Wolff/Magnum; 120, © 1982, Jules Feiffer; 124, copyright © 1983 by Playboy, and reprinted by permission of *Playboy;* 129, © Peter Simon; 132, © Frank Siteman/Jeroboam; 145, © Robert Foothorap; 149, © Optic Nerve/Jeroboam; 154, © John Picatti/Jeroboam; 159, Courtesy Spencer Collection, NY Public Library; 164, © Dave Patrick; 165, © Susan Ylvisaker/Jeroboam; 173, © Hella Hammid; 175, © Hella Hammid; 177, reprinted courtesy of Penthouse Publications, © 1983; 179, © 1980, Joani Blank; 182, © 1980, Donald Dietz/Stock Boston; 183, © 1978, Bruce Kliewe/Jeroboam; 187, © Hella Hammid; 191, © Peter Simon; 195, © Henri Cartier-Bresson/Magnum; 197, © 1982, Laimute E. Druskis/Jeroboam; 200, © Gilles Peress/Magnum; 205, © Peter Vandermark/Stock Boston; 206, © Owen Franken/Stock Boston; 219, © Phiz Mezey; 223, © Arthur Grace/Stock Boston; 229, © Don Ivers/Jeroboam; 231, © Mitchell Payne/Jeroboam; 234, © 1978, Karen Preuss/Jeroboam; 237, © Patricia Hollander-Gross/Stock Boston; 244, © John P. Cavanagh/Archive Pictures; 248, © 1979, Kent Reno/Jeroboam; 250, © 1975, Betty Lane; 255, © Betty Lane; 259, © Tom Forma; 263, © Hap Stewart/Jeroboam; 267, © Robert Foothorap; 272, From *I'm in Training to be Tall and Blond,* by Nicole Hollander. © 1979 by Nicole Hollander, St. Martin's Press; 275, © 1982, Constance S. Lewis/Woodfin Camp; 280, © Bob Adelman; 282, © Harold Chapman/Jeroboam; 283, © Dave Patrick; 285, © Peter Simon; 300, © Bennett Hall; 305, © John Pearson; 311, copyright © 1983 by Playboy, and reprinted by special permission of *Playboy;* 329, © 1983, Art Rogers; 332, © Phiz Mezey; 334, © Mary Ellen Mark/Archive Pictures; 346, © Art Rogers; 359, © Suzanne Arms/Jeroboam; 361, © Steve Hansen/Stock Boston; 367, © Bennett Hall; 382, © Kit Hedman/Jeroboam; 387, © Peter Simon; 388, © Peter Simon; 389, © 1982, Thomas Hopker/Woodfin Camp.

/ Contents in Brief

/ Contents in Detail

12. Sexual Assault   237

13. Sex for Sale   263

14. Enhancing Sexual Health   283

Sex is not a four-letter word. Our sexuality is an integral part of our humanity that colors many of our thoughts and behaviors. Yet even in the midst of seemingly liberating changes in sexual behaviors, some of us are still reluctant to talk openly about sex.

Concerned about social problems such as teenage pregnancy, abortion, exploitative sex, rape, sexually transmitted diseases, sexism, and divorce, some groups are seeking cures by denying others sexual choices. We reject this approach in favor of providing people with information to make caring sexual choices. This textbook is a tool for informed sexual choices—for understanding all aspects of our sexuality and making choices that are wise, responsible, satisfying, and joyous.

Sex can be fun, funny, loving, life enriching, joyful. But we may not experience it in these positive ways if we make poor sexual choices. In order to make informed sexual choices, we need some insights from research, the arts, and philosophy and from our own experiences with friends, parents, and lovers. Choices needn't be laborious. In fact, choices include emotional and sexual desires and not just rational decisions. We cannot quantify and computerize the pros and cons of a particular choice about sex. Considering our gut feelings along with our developing values about sex must lead to a holistic blend of our emotions, our beliefs, our thinking, and our unique experiences.

Unlike most people who write textbooks on sex, we believe humor is compatible with a scholarly approach to sex. There are many sexual humor books and many dry texts, but there is a third alternative: to present scientific information in a humanistic and joyful way. This approach is what we've intended in this book. We *are* accepting of alternative sexual lifestyles, and we are committed

on some subjects. We don't expect all readers to agree, and we hope this book will stimulate many lively and informative discussions in and out of the classroom. We don't assume everyone should have sex with just anyone; we see celibacy as one legitimate choice. But we are open to choices that affirm dignity and support healthy views of ourselves and our partners as deserving, loving people.

FEATURES OF THIS BOOK

The second edition of *Sexual Choices,* like the first, includes these special features:

■ Chapter opening vignettes that serve to ground our book in real-life sexual experiences.

■ "Language of Sex" boxes appearing throughout the text to examine verbal attitudes about sex and, where appropriate, offer sex-positive alternatives.

■ A second color used throughout to highlight specific concepts and nontext elements and to enhance the illustration program.

■ Extensive illustrations to visually describe sexual anatomy and depict factual information, and specially commissioned artwork, to portray variations in sexmaking.

■ A broad photo program to complement the major themes in each chapter.

■ A comprehensive bibliography (over 1,000 entries) indicating the breadth and depth of research brought to this work and directing the reader to further readings and resources.

■ Two bonus features at the end: an innovative discussion of the do's and don'ts of sex research—

"A Brief Look at Sex Research" (Appendix A), and a resource guide—"The Yellow Pages for Informed Sexual Choices" (Appendix B)—to provide our readers with names and addresses of national organizations dedicated to sexual well-being.

■ A subject index to guide the reader to definitions or key discussions of specific topics and issues.

For the second edition, we have also added chapter outlines and chapter summaries to help readers assimilate information, and an author index to help locate the work of specific researchers. In extensively revising the book for this second edition, we have included new research and scholarship in every chapter. For instance, we have incorporated new information on conception control (such as news of health benefits of the Pill) and the latest sexually transmitted disease concerns, including in-depth coverage of herpes, nongonococcal urethritis (NGU), and the Acquired Immune Deficiency Syndrome (AIDS). Discussions of many topics have been enriched, including sections dealing with love, commercial sex, pornography, political issues, marital rape, and teenage sex education. To broaden and pull together our discussion of the anatomy and physiology of sex, we have created a new chapter: "Our Bodies" (Chapter 2). In Chapter 1, we've developed a new section on sexual ethics, including information on historical and cross-cultural variations in ways of looking at sexual morality.

The breadth and depth of this book reflect our combined experiences and academic backgrounds in child and family relations, human development, sociology, and psychology: Nass's strong background in sociology and social psychology; Libby's scholarly work in sex roles and sexuality, human development, sociology, and social psychology; and Fisher's humanistic, feminist perspective and experience in writing readable textbooks for undergraduates. We have enjoyed working together to create this book; we hope that it reflects our joy.

/ Acknowledgments

In gathering materials for *Sexual Choices,* we have talked to and corresponded with people all over the country—people who are researching the physiology of sexual response, people who study sexual opportunities for the aged, people who are concerned with the relationship of sex to intimate bonds, and so on. In every case, we've found them unusually interested and helpful.

We would like to thank all whose suggestions and assistance guided the development of this second edition of *Sexual Choices*. In particular, health educator Ron Mazur was ever ready with resource materials and ideas. Nursing educator Joellen Hawkins answered numerous questions about physiological and medical aspects of our sexuality. G-spot researcher John Perry has continued to explain the latest understanding of the physiology of orgasm. Psychologist Barry Singer contributed perceptive writings about the sociobiology of sex. Al MacDonald, Jr., Will Mahoney, Robert Athanasiou, Jacqueline Boles, Charles Marshall, Carol Radzik, and Jeanette Ames McIntosh generously shared resources and ideas. Marian Willard, M.S.N. (College of Nursing, University of Kentucky) and Rodney M. Cate, Ph.D. (Department of Human Development and Family Studies, Oregon State University) provided thoughtful and useful reviews of the manuscript. We are pleased to thank our photo editor, Monica Suder, for her enthusiastic contribution to this edition of *Sexual Choices*.

Many teachers who used the first edition of the book have contributed suggestions for its revision. We are grateful to all who have done so, with particular thanks to Rikke Wassenberg, who has also prepared an excellent new instructor's manual to accompany this edition. Many thanks also to Barbara Keating for suggestions about the instructor's manual.

Student helpers Beth Maltzen, Patty Maltzen, Jay Nass, Craig Nass, Lenore Azaroff, and Marcelle Muller were of tremendous assistance in the mechanics of researching and preparing the manuscript. Lydia Zwirz and Ethel Krapf offered generous office assistance.

We would also like to thank again the many people who were acknowledged in the first edition as contributors to the original framework of *Sexual Choices*. The sensitivity of all who helped has broadened our awareness of the factors to be thoughtfully considered in making our sexual choices.

Gilbert D. Nass
Roger W. Libby
Mary Pat Fisher

1

Our Sexual Identity

After years of being taught that my body is to be hidden and that sex is sinful, I'm just beginning to accept my sexuality. It's hard for me to reject the values my parents taught me, but it helps me to think that they did what they did thinking it would protect me as a female. I'm starting to realize that I can think for myself.

To me, sex is a very special part of myself—so special that I'm saving it for when I get married to the man I love. Both of us want to hold and kiss each other often, and we do, but we feel that to have intercourse is a deep commitment that we choose only within the sacred bond of marriage. I think it will mean more that way.

Maybe there's something wrong with me. Everyone else seems to be fucking their brains out, but not me. Other guys I know seem to score almost every night, but I can't even get to first base. Partly I don't know what to say to a girl, and partly maybe it's my looks. I've been working out to build up my chest and biceps, and once they look good I'll get some sexier clothes. Maybe that will help.

I don't know quite what I am sexually. I've had some wonderful experiences with women, but I can't ignore the fact that some men turn me on, too, or that I love them. I feel pretty weird about that because I grew up thinking you were only supposed to make love with women. I like my body, especially when I have a tan and am in good shape. It gives me and other people a lot of pleasure. But I really don't know at this point whether I could ever feel okay about having sex with another man.

My wife says I'm a great lover—and who am I to argue? I'm in good shape from my lumberyard work, and my vital parts really do the job. That's a good thing, because we like to have sex often and a guy has to be up for it, you know?

I love sex! I love getting myself off and I love being in bed with men, too. I've had a lot of lovers. Most of them have been friends in other ways, too. I'd like to keep it that way, but one of the men I love wants to keep me to himself. He sees sex as something very romantic and special—which it is—but he thinks you should have it with only one person and then commit yourselves to live together forever. I really do like him, but I don't agree with him. To me, sex is a way of having fun and expressing affection, and I feel happy and affectionate with lots of people.

The statements at the beginning of this chapter illustrate aspects of the *sexual identities* of six unique individuals. Their sexual identities are a composite of their personal morals, whether they are male or female, how they define masculinity or femininity, whether they prefer males or females as sexual partners, how they feel about their bodies, and the meanings and plans of action for sex that they've learned.

In this chapter we'll explore the various aspects of sexual identity in order to set up a framework for defining who we are sexually. Most people don't automatically try to define their sexuality. But to make sense of what's going on right now in our sexual lives will help us to develop a good background for making decisions about what will happen next.

THE SOCIAL NATURE OF IDENTITY

We were not born with our sexual identities. They develop as we interact with other people.

We humans are symbol-using creatures. As such, we exist in a world of meanings that we have created. Take breasts, for instance. They are simply protuberances on the chest that are large or small depending on how much fatty tissue and/or milk they contain. They feel good when they're licked, sucked, or caressed. In females they also have a biological function: providing milk for babies. But beyond this, any ideas we have about women's breasts involve not only their biological properties but also the social meanings attributed to them. We usually learn these meanings from others whose opinions we value—our family, our peers, our teachers, our favorite media personalities, our subculture, our society. In the United States female breasts are defined by most of these sources as extremely erotic objects. People are therefore sexually aroused by looking at them. But in those few societies in which breasts are not given any erotic significance, women go about bare-chested in public and no one is turned on.

Through social interaction we learn that people have definitions for *us* and expectations for how people in our role should behave. We pick up these messages both verbally and nonverbally. Kindergarteners, for instance, are expected to

Our society has traditionally defined women's breasts as sexually erotic—and considered sex something to be controlled. Women are therefore expected to cover their breasts in public, even when the weather is hot. They rarely have the freedom to enjoy the feeling of sun, wind, and waves on their chests. By contrast, men are often allowed to take their shirts off in public since their breasts have not been defined as sex objects.

answer when their name is called, sit "nicely" in a circle, and enjoy listening to stories—rather than whistling, feeling their crotches, or writing on the walls. They get approving messages—smiles and praise—if they behave as expected, disapproving messages—frowns and scoldings—if they don't.

Although the way we see ourselves is molded to a large extent by lessons learned in childhood, it changes throughout life partly in response to changes in whom we listen to. As teenagers we may be influenced more by what our friends think of us than by what our parents think. At various points in our adult lives we may incorporate ideas gleaned from intimate friends, marital partners, books, magazine articles, television programs, therapists, or religious advisers. Their judgments are not always explicit. Often how we think they see us—and our emotional reaction to *that*—is what shapes the way we feel about ourselves.

As we take on different social roles—student, lover, friend, spouse, political activist, parent,

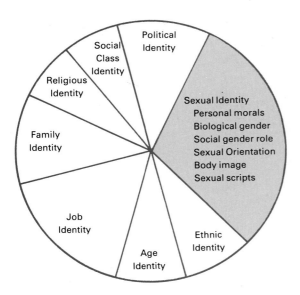

Figure 1-1. Identity Pie. The relative importance of various pieces of our self-concept varies from person to person. And within our own lifetime, the size of the "slices" in our "identity pie" may change considerably. At this point in time for the person represented by this pie, sexual identity is even more important than job or family identity.

manager—and internalize the social expectations that seem to accompany these roles, some parts of ourselves become more important to us than others. These parts of ourselves can be considered varying *identities*. The degree to which they color our overall self-concept can be represented as a pie with wedges of different sizes. For instance, the female represented in Figure 1-1 by the "identity pie" views her sexual identity as a major factor in her self-concept. For many other people sex may not be nearly so important.

SOCIAL ETHICS AND PERSONAL MORALS

One major facet of our sexual identity is our system for determining what is "right" and "wrong" for us sexually. Most cultures have established informal social expectations, religious pronouncements, or even formal laws in an attempt to control sexual behavior because of its potential effects on social cohesion. However, ideas about what would best serve society have varied widely across cultures and during the history of our own society.

Anthropological Variations in Sexual Ethics

Cross-culturally, attitudes toward sexual behavior range from expectations of strict celibacy in monastic orders to relative sexual freedom in certain small-scale foraging and farming groups. Some societies' views restrict sex to the absolute minimum needed for propagation. Among the Maring of New Guinea, for instance, work and living arrangements and religious beliefs all promote extreme hostility between men and women. Males are taught to avoid intercourse by the engendering of fear that intercourse will cause wrinkling, wasting away, stunted growth, loss of hair, weakness, ugliness, fuzzy thinking, and perhaps spitting up of phlegm.

Many cultures are less restrictive in their view of sex, but try to restrict it to marriage and to limit the number of potential partners in a lifetime. In such groups proof of virginity in females is highly valued.

Freer and more open views of sexual morality are favored in certain small-scale tropical island cultures. Among the Trobriand Islanders of Melanesia, parents do not hide their lovemaking from their children. It is assumed that young children will fondle their own and others' genitals and eventually will play at having intercourse. Adolescent couples share beds in special houses; those who are regular lovers may also have other occasional sex partners. After marriage, however, sex outside the relationship is seen as such a serious offense to the reputation of individuals and families that murders and suicides are not uncommon among offenders.

By contrast, some other societies do not treat extramarital sex as threatening to the social order. Among the Mundurucu of Amazonian Brazil, sexually exclusive marriages are the exception rather than the rule, and divorce is common, partly because women have considerable personal autonomy. Among the Toda of India, a man who tries to keep his wife from having sex with other men is considered immoral. In this and other societies, extramarital sex is seen as a way of expanding or strengthening social ties (Howard and McKim 1983).

Historical Variations in Western Sexual Ethics

During the history of our own Western industrial society, the pendulum has swung back and forth between restrictive and open attitudes toward sexual morality, depending on circumstances of the times. Among the early Old Testament Jews, Mosaic laws forbade adultery—considered a property offense because females were thought to belong to their father or husband. But sex among the unmarried was not forbidden, unless it was against the girl's father's wishes. Prostitution was common. Within marriage sex was encouraged as a means of increasing the size of the tribe. Celibacy was treated as a crime.

In the ancient mother religions of the Near East, sex was seen as a sacred mystery. Ishtar, Assyrian and Babylonian goddess of love and fertility, referred to herself as a "prostitute compassionate," a mother offering her tenderness to all of her sons (Taylor 1970). Temple priests and priestesses made their bodies sexually available to worshippers as a source of mystical contact with the divine. Greeks worshipping Dionysus incorporated sacramental sexuality into their ceremonies. The Greek city-states treated sex as an enjoyable pleasure, regarded the celibate with pity, and idealized loving homosexual relationships. The Greek physician Galen prescribed intercourse and masturbation as cures for hysteria (Sussman 1976).

Around 500 B.C. these positive attitudes toward sexuality began to change. Among the Greeks, and then the Jews, the feeling grew that the body was impure and that all pleasure, particularly sexual pleasure, was sinful. Homosexuality and masturbation were condemned, virginity elevated to a virtue, and contact between the sexes strictly limited. Although Jesus did not say much about sex, the early Christian church held celibacy as the ideal for those immediately expecting his Second Coming. Sex was seen as worldly pleasure, a sin to be kept in proper perspective to one's love of God. At the same time, the institution of monogamous marriage was upheld by the early Christian church and was cherished by its writers, whose works nevertheless reflected tension between these various views of sexuality.

Similarly, the medieval church had varying and complex attitudes toward sex. Many church writers were obsessively antisexual. Pleasure derived from sex—even within marriage—was considered so damnable that the *chemise cagoule*, a men's heavy nightshirt with a hole for the penis, was invented so that couples could reproduce the species with a minimum of physical contact. A series of "penitential books" described every imaginable sexual variation in detail, with bans and punishments for all forms of sex other than marital intercourse for purposes of procreation. Even having thoughts of sex with a nonspouse was grounds for forty days of penance (Taylor 1970). Although many people apparently ignored such prohibitions in the frankly sexual early Middle Ages, the neuroses inspired by the Church's attempts at repression eventually led to hysterical witch trials in which women were condemned as agents of the devil because they inspired lust in men.

During the Renaissance Europeans began to reject such rigid moral controls, seeing themselves as free individuals with natural, acceptable desires. However, after the freely sexual Elizabethan period, John Calvin's teachings again swung back the pendulum. Calvin's work formed the basis of Puritan morality: Any form of pleasure was unacceptable because it interfered with serving God. Despite official proscriptions, however, church records from the end of the Puritan era reveal that in one Groton, Massachusetts, church at least a third of the brides were pregnant before they walked down the aisle (Calhoun 1945).

In early nineteenth-century America an intervening period of relatively sex-positive protest movements advocating free love, birth control, equality for women, and marriage reform gave way to the rigid ethics of Victorianism. Women were presumed to have no sexual desires, and men were counseled to repress theirs. Even married couples were encouraged to desexualize their union, restricting intercourse to no more than once a month (Degler 1980). In 1873 moralist Anthony Comstock convinced Congress to pass the Comstock Law prohibiting the mailing of material considered "obscene," a label that was stretched to include birth control information.

Victorian, Puritan, and Judeo-Christian moral codes still linger in twentieth-century America. However, influences such as psychoanalytic, sociological, and biological studies of sexuality;

availability of effective contraceptives; increasing social and economic equality for women; mass communication; and faster transportation have promoted greater freedom in sexual behavior. Despite periodic swings of the pendulum back toward repressive views of sexual morality, we are influenced today by the "sexual revolutions" of the 1920s and '60s and '70s. In portraying sex as normal, healthy, and desirable, crusaders of these periods helped establish a new set of social expectations: that one *should* experience sex frequently and skillfully or else be considered unusual. During the 1980s groups with varying positions are still involved in struggles regarding sexual ethics, resulting in conflicting statements that "We are morally right, and you are morally wrong!"

Personal Morals

Heirs to all these conflicting traditions, many of us are morally confused today. It is helpful to examine our own behaviors not by this confusing mixture of rules and expectations but by the relevance of such prescriptions to our present realities.

The sexual pendulum has swung back and forth between restrictiveness and openness throughout human history. Today many are again enjoying the sensual pleasures of hot tubs, but they are nothing new. In medieval Europe, for example, couples stayed many hours in the tubs at public bathing houses and enjoyed music, food, and drink supplied by the bathing house owners.

In general the most sexually restrictive periods have been times of great economic hardship or have followed periods of social chaos. Under such circumstances many see the family as the only stable institution in society and strive to hold it together by supporting monogamous marriage and limiting nonmarital sexuality—thereby presumably decreasing potentially disruptive factors such as sexual jealousy, unwanted births, and paternity confusion. In some cases restrictive attitudes may also have been motivated by a desire to protect women from unwanted pregnancies and male domination (Degler 1980).

Today, sex need not be inhibited by these concerns, for contraception and abortions have made it possible to avoid unwanted pregnancies. Freedom of choice need not be socially disruptive if we choose to grow beyond sexual jealousy, to assert our personal freedom to say either "yes" or "no,"

6

depending on the circumstances, and to accept our sexuality so that we can make rational, responsible, and caring—instead of crazy—choices.

People are increasingly beginning to apply the same question to sex that they apply to other areas of behavior: "Does it harm anyone?" If a sexual experience does not seem to harm anyone—including themselves—and is perhaps even growth-enhancing and joyful, many people are beginning to see it as okay. At the same time behaviors that *do* harm others—such as rape and manipulative, exploitative relationships—are being judged more harshly than in the past (Singer 1980).

Today we still see evidence of attempts to apply historical ideas about sexual ethics to changing realities. We're still faced with groups trying to impose their values on others—through censorship of sexually explicit materials and with lingering repressive but unenforceable laws punishing choices such as oral sex, homosexuality, and abortion. But there is a growing feeling that we each have the right—and the responsibility—to make our own sexual choices.

In developing our own moral code for personal sexual conduct, we can think in terms either of absolutes or of situation ethics. *Moral absolutes* are established rules about what we should or shouldn't do that are supposed to apply to every situation. By contrast, in *situation ethics* we may view our choices as moral or immoral according to the specific social situation. What's moral in one situation may be defined as immoral in another.

Sexual attraction to certain persons—or sexual arousal in general—just happens. Usually it is not a matter of conscious choice. Our choices lie in recognizing our feelings and physical sensations and in deciding what—if anything—to do with them. Ethicist John Crosby (1981) asserts that we should act as individuals making personal choices, rather than subjecting those choices to social laws. Individuality of choice does not automatically mean that we will choose open sexual relationships—nor does it automatically mean monogamy.

Crosby asserts that in making sexual choices, we should operate from feelings of self-respect and wholeness, judging our options by three imperatives. One is *equality*—sharing rights, obligations, and power equally rather than assuming different standards for one gender than for the other. The second is *responsibility*—the affirmation that we each are responsible for our own feelings and behaviors, especially as they touch the lives of others. Crosby's third imperative is *honesty*—trying to discover our inner motivations, needs, feelings and expectations. As Crosby puts it, this means recognizing that "we each perceive reality in our own way and that honesty is our attempt to see ourselves clearly, the other clearly, and the situation clearly—even though others may see these differently" (1981, p. 51). To share truth, to take responsibility, and to relate as equals means avoiding manipulation, deception, and game playing and opening our potential for personal integrity and humanity in our choicemaking.

GENDER AND GENDER ROLES

In addition to the ideas about sexual morality we choose or inherit, our sexual identity involves our *biological gender*—whether we are male or female—and the *social gender roles* we associate with "masculinity" or "femininity."

Our culture is struggling with what it means to be male or female. Traditionally the label "masculinity" has carried connotations such as assertiveness, independence, lack of emotions, rationality, insensitivity, and roughness. By contrast, "femininity" has carried different connotations—nonassertiveness, dependence, emotionality, sensitivity, and gentleness. These distinctions are thought to follow us to bed, where men traditionally have been seen as aggressive initiators and women as passive receivers.

To what extent are these perceived differences caused by biological differences between the

The Language of Sex

Many men and women refer to each other as the *"opposite"* sex. We suggest avoiding that common phrase because it suggests that confrontation is inevitable and that the sexes are so different that they can be seen as opposites. The simple phrase the *"other"* sex should do.

"Masculine" and "feminine" gender roles may be acted out from an early age. Are they caused by biological differences between males and females or by differences in how we are culturally shaped?

sexes? To what extent are they the result of social learning? To what extent are they totally nonexistent? These questions are part of one of the hottest debates in the social sciences today. The answers are still evolving. Some say that it's mostly biology, some that it's mostly social learning, and some that it's a combination of biology and social learning.

Biological Influences

As we'll see in Chapter 2, males and females are both similar and dissimilar in anatomy, physiology, brain structure, hormones, and so forth. These biological factors do not automatically translate into behavioral patterns. However, one finding that may have relevance for sexuality concerns the capacity for aggression. Studies show that males tend to be more aggressive than females, in terms of willingness to hurt others (Maccoby and Jacklin 1974). Experiments with animals suggest that high levels of the "male" hormones may be responsible for this difference (Money and Ehrhardt 1972). This biological difference in potential for physical aggression—coupled with the male's generally

greater strength—may underlie the traditional definition of males as sexual aggressors and females as passive recipients: There is more threat of violence behind the males' interest in females than vice versa. This power differential is reflected in many aspects of male/female relationships, as we'll see throughout this book.

Sociobiologists speculate that social differences between the genders are the inborn results of natural selection, just as they are in animals. In most animal species that have been studied, the male tends to be the sexual aggressor, competes with other males for access to females, has a seemingly higher sexual need than does the female, tends to show off and court the female, is quicker to mate and less choosy about his choice of mate, and displays a greater inclination toward sexual variety than does the female. In nature it just doesn't happen that females fight over sexual access to a male; it is almost always the other way around. Animals have "gender roles" too, in other words (Singer 1982).

In the past decade researchers have formulated a theory to explain such "gender roles" in animals. It is called the parental investment theory. Simply put, female mammals have more of an "investment" in a sexual act than do males, because females risk a long, taxing pregnancy if they conceive and a long demanding period of lactation and child rearing afterward. It would be to a female's advantage, in propagating her genes, to be careful about who fathers her children. Females should look for potential fathers who have "good genes" or who display status and commitment, so that they will be more likely to care for their offspring. Accordingly, female animals often put male suitors "through their paces" during courtship, choosing the male who expends the most effort in building a nest or in gathering food. Male animals, on the other hand, invest only a small quantity of sperm in each sexual act. They don't necessarily have to stay around or be involved with pregnancy or child rearing. The female carries out these responsibilities. Thus it is in the male's genetic interest, in order to propagate as many descendants as possible, to be opportunistic, unfaithful, sexually driven, quick to mate, willing and eager to have sex with a wide range of females, and to compete with other males for sexual access to females. Because of these male characteristics of fighting and competing for control of females, male animals usually are larger than females (Singer 1982).

Does the foregoing description sound familiar? Sociobiologists tell us that all of these tendencies are in our genes, as they are in most mammalian genes. Other social scientists say that we have no evidence for this notion, that it's speculation, that humans are socially trained rather than biologically inclined toward male or female gender roles. A third possibility—one that is not necessarily dismissed by sociobiologists—is that our behaviors reflect a blending of socialization and biology. Which influence is strongest in a particular situation is not always clear.

Social Influences

Our social cues to how males and females should behave are called *gender role expectations*. Perhaps even more than our biological tendencies, they direct our options and channel us into ways of behaving that are defined as "natural" and "appropriate" for males or females.

Every society tries to teach its young the gender roles considered appropriate. Children are assigned to a gender role as soon as they're born: "It's a boy!" or "It's a girl!" From then on people tend to react to them according to the culture's gender role expectations. Mothers and fathers may influence their children by the things they say, their subtle nonverbal cues, the behaviors they reward or punish, the toys they provide, and the models they set. Peers, teachers, other adults, and the mass media contribute to the role-learning process, too. These sources may offer contradictory messages. According to one evolving theory, rather than absorbing them all, children usually choose from these social resources the opinions of persons they consider the best advisers (McDonald 1980).

Anthropologists have found that male and female gender roles differ considerably among cultures depending on local expectations. Margaret Mead (1935) located one culture in which everybody acted gently "feminine"; another in which everybody acted fiercely "masculine"; and another in which men learned delicate dances, tried to look and act charming, and swapped gossip, while women held the power and initiative in the community. And when cultures allow sexual expression relatively free rein, the sex drive of males and females appears to be equally strong. On the Polynesian island of Mangaia, for example, everyone seems to love sex. Intercourse begins for both boys and girls when they reach puberty, with no disapproval from the community. Girls expect sexual satisfaction, and boys learn from older females how to help girls orgasm again and again. Both boys and girls are expected to experience a number of partners (Marshall 1971).

"I can't help it—it's in my jeans!"

Social scientists and sociobiologists have engaged not only in hot intellectual debate over gender differences but in personal and ethical arguments as well. Some social scientists contend that sociobiological speculation, in addition to being inaccurate, is unethical and dangerous. Saying that sexist behavior is "in our genes" implies to many that "biology is destiny," that women and men were meant to be different, and that it's no use fighting that biological fact. This sort of thinking can be and has been used to support our society's present power structure and to justify male sexist and oppressive behavior (Tiefer 1978). Attributing emotions and behaviors to "involuntary" biological causes may also be a way of lessening the burden of guilt from reactions our society would otherwise find unacceptable.

Sociobiologists would reply that if in fact men and women have biological differences in their personal makeup, knowing that fact is especially important, because our efforts at "androgyny" are thereby doomed to failure. It would not be enough, they assert, to attempt to be nonsexist. We would need to account for the strong innate gender differences as well, either by giving men an extra heavy dose of socializing toward parenting, for example, or perhaps by some sort of biological or genetic intervention. Evolution can be conquered, this thinking goes, but only if we first recognize it and take it into account. Interestingly enough, some of the strongest advocates of this position are women (Konner 1982).

In our society males traditionally have been expected to be independent and assertive; they have not been expected to have "soft" feelings, such as sorrow and empathy. Just the reverse has been expected of females. Some social scientists see these gender role expectations as training for the assumption of power by males, of powerlessness by females.

In the past women in our society were trained to believe that they had little sexual desire in order to curb their expression of sexual power. They were expected to submit passively to males' desires, and then only within marriage. By contrast, males were socialized to the idea that they were lusty sexual aggressors who were allowed to seek sex in a variety of situations. This difference in sexual expectations for males and females is called the *double standard*.

These gender role expectations linger today, limiting our growth as whole persons and our ability to be intimate with others. For instance, counselor Tom Marino (1979, p. 103) admits, "I fear softness as a snowman fears sunshine." So long as power is expected of men and denied to women, assertiveness in females and sensitivity in males will continue to meet with social disapproval. And so long as power—rather than love and recognition of our common humanity—is thought to be a reasonable basis for human interaction, different roles will be expected of those on top and those below, regardless of gender.

Beyond Gender Roles

Today the differences in the ways males and females are socialized in our culture are being challenged. Some people are now raising children to be simply human, rather than "masculine" or "feminine," and tend to accept a wider range of sexual expression in both genders.

In place of separate gender roles, some persons support what has been called *androgyny*. Interpreted literally, this word means being both male (*andros*) and female (*gyno*). If by "maleness" we mean instrumentality (the ability to be assertive and get things done) and by "femaleness," communality (warmth), the combination of these two aspects does yield exceptional competence in human interaction (Baumrind 1982). However,

Some of us do not confine ourselves to behaviors traditionally considered appropriate for our gender; instead, these people grow towards full expression of their humanity.

these traits are not necessarily linked with biological males or biological females but are simply two complementary sides of our common humanity. Therefore it's possible to define androgyny as flexibility in gender role, as moving beyond femininity and masculinity toward an individual level of well-being. This approach means choosing from the whole range of human behaviors those that suit our individual personalities or that seem most appropriate in a given situation, rather than only those that match the old notions of what is appropriate for our gender.

Some people of both genders are learning to express parts of themselves once thought appropriate only for the other gender. For instance, some women are beginning to initiate sexual encounters and to seek pleasure for themselves—behaviors once reserved for males. And some men are allowing themselves to be more sensitive and emotionally expressive in intimate relationships—traits once associated only with "femaleness." At the same time some are reaffirming their comfort and sense of appropriateness with traditional gender role behaviors.

Cross-Gender Identities

Biological gender and gender identity coincide for most of us. If we have a female body, we tend to see ourselves as women. But for some there is disparity between biological gender and gender identity. For instance, a number of biological males are convinced that they are women imprisoned inside male bodies (*male transsexuals;* female transsexuals are far less common). Some consider their problem so central to their identity that they have undergone "sex-change" operations to bring the self they present to the public into line with the gender identity they perceive within themselves. After hormone treatments to enlarge their breasts and surgery to replace penis and testicles with an artificial vagina, many are said to express profound relief at having resolved their "identity crisis" (Benjamin 1967; J. Morris 1975). But follow-up information suggests that some may have severe psychiatric problems if their physical gender is changed (Stoller 1976).

There is evidence that transsexualism may be related to an unusual biochemical or neuroendocrine pattern in the brain, but which is cause and which is effect is unknown (Boyar and Aiman 1982). Feminist Janice Raymond (1979) suggests that we focus on a different issue: transsexualism as an extreme result of gender role stereotyping. If we were all truly free to be ourselves, people who wished to express aspects of themselves socially associated with the other sex would not need to undergo sex-change operations. Raymond encourages transsexuals to become gender role critics rather than gender role conformists.

The term *transvestism* refers to a different cross-gender pattern: erotic arousal from dressing in the clothes of the other sex. Transvestites do not see themselves as members of the other sex; they find the pretense and the exaggeratedly "feminine" or "masculine" cross-dressing sexually exciting. A third category—*drag queens*—are male homosexuals whose costumes are caricatures of the artificially made-up and corseted woman (Ackroyd 1979).

The Language of Sex

Is the female's part in heterosexual intercourse truly passive? Our labels make us think so: a woman gets "balled," "screwed," "fucked," "humped," "banged." But by changing these labels, we could redefine the woman's role as the active one. How about images in which the vagina actively envelopes the penis?

It's also possible to use labels for sex that avoid connotations of power. "Getting laid" carries ambiguous power connotations—it's not clear who's on the bottom. "Going to bed with" and "sleeping with" someone have no power implications, but they skirt the issue of what's actually happening. "Doing it" and "making it" reveal a similar reluctance to specify what "it" is. "Lovemaking" is a favorite traditional label for what goes on in affectionate intimate relationships. But what unambiguous label can we use for mutually shared sexual pleasure that is not necessarily based on love? "Sexmaking"? "Sexual encounters"? "Sexual activity"?

SEXUAL ORIENTATION

In addition to the influence of our biological gender and our social gender roles, our sexual identity is influenced by whom we eroticize as sex partners. Some of us are turned on by people of the other sex (*heterosexuals),* some of us are turned on by people of the same sex (*homosexuals),* some of us are turned on by both sexes (*bisexuals),* and some of us aren't turned on by anybody at all (*asexuals).*

Kinsey and his associates (1948, 1953) devised a scale to cover the range of sexual orientations. Amusingly enough, he called true heterosexuals (people who respond sexually only to the other sex) "zeros." "Ones" and "twos" have varying degrees of responsiveness to same-sex acquaintances but are largely heterosexual. "Threes" are true bisexuals, equally attracted to both sexes. "Fours" and "fives" are more attracted to their own sex than to the other sex, but they can be aroused heterosexually to some extent. "Sixes" are exclusively homosexual, and "Xs" don't respond sexually to anyone. "Xs" may simply have a low level of

The Language of Sex

Many people use the phrase *sex object preference* in talking about which gender they prefer
as partners. But to view others as "objects" denies
their humanity. Instead, we can call this dimension of our sexual identity our *sexual orientation*.

interest in sex or a strong learned aversion to sex.

We differ not only in our orientations but also
in how public we make them. For instance, some
men who have eroticized other men as sex partners nonetheless contract heterosexual marriages
and go to great lengths to keep their sexual
orientations secret. Their sexual identities differ
considerably from those of gay males who have
"come out" publicly.

Since many of us do not make our sexual
orientations publicly known, others have a tendency to typecast us according to common assumptions about what heterosexuals and homosexuals
are like. With heterosexuality as the dominant expectation, males who fit the "masculine"
stereotype—the physically strong and emotionally
tough types—are presumed to be heterosexual.
"Effeminate" males are commonly presumed to be
homosexuals. Females who fit the "feminine"
stereotype are assumed to be heterosexual; those
who don't are suspected of being homosexual. But
these popular assumptions don't hold true. Some
burly male football players are gay; some brusque,
athletic females are straight.

We'll explore sexual orientations more extensively in Chapter 8. The point here is that social
definitions—of homosexuality and bisexuality as
"abnormal" (instead of just different) compared
with heterosexuality, which is defined as "normal,"
and of "effeminate" men and "masculine" women
as gay—have a tremendous amount of influence
over how others see us and therefore over how we
see ourselves.

According to one study children whose identities cross gender role boundaries—boys who see
themselves as having "girlish" traits and girls who
see themselves as "boyish"—are more likely than
other children to define themselves as "bad" or
"wrong" (Burke and Tully 1977). This self-concept
is largely the result of negative labeling that begins

in childhood, according to one current theory. As
children effeminate boys are branded as "sissies"
and excluded from more masculine play groups.
As adults people defined as "queers" may lose their
jobs, their status in the straight community, and
their heterosexual friends. As long as society defines cross-sex behaviors and homosexuality as
wrong, people who recognize these tendencies in
themselves may have a hard time maintaining their
self-esteem.

Gay rights advocates are gradually decreasing
the extent to which homosexuals and bisexuals are
defined as weird people doing immoral, abnormal
things. For instance, pressure from the gay rights
movement led the American Psychiatric Association to change its definition of homosexuality from
a mental disorder that should be cured to a choice
that need not be changed unless the person with a
same-sex orientation finds it disturbing (Lyons
1973). As we make the transition to defining
homosexuality somewhat differently, more
homosexuals should be capable of having positive
self-identities. If homosexuality is not stigmatized
socially, homosexuals won't have to worry about
building strong walls to resist negative labels by
others. Instead, they can use their energies to grow
as individuals.

BODY IMAGE

How we feel about our own bodies also plays a
large part in how we feel about ourselves sexually.
When we're feeling healthy and agile, we're more
likely to feel sexually enthusiastic than when we
are sick or in poor shape. But this natural response
to physical well-being may be overlaid with an
obsessive concern about how we think other people are reacting to our appearance. We often try—
consciously or unconsciously—to shape their
reactions by the way we dress and move.

Concern for Appearance

In our society many of us are so self-conscious
about how we look to others that a slight roll of fat
or another outbreak of pimples may make us feel
unappealing. Advertisers cater to—and probably
promote—hyperawareness of physical appearance
to sell products that are defined as coverups for

natural "defects." We are bombarded with messages that we will gain sexual approval if we disguise our underarm scents with deodorants; if we rinse our mouths with potions that will make others want to kiss us because we taste so good; if we reshape our bodies with foundation garments, platform shoes, or workouts to approximate the "ideal" masculine or feminine shape. Human definitions of the ideal figure vary, though, for they are based on socially learned notions. Our affluent, youth-oriented and health-conscious society values slenderness; other cultures value heaviness as a symbol of wealth.

How many of us take these messages to heart? The cosmetics industry is making $10 billion a year from people who think they enhance their sex appeal by altering their appearance ("Cosmetics: Kiss and Sell" 1978). Frederick's of Hollywood does a multimillion dollar business in retail and catalog sales of undergarments that push the female figure up and out at the breasts, pull it in at the waist, and drape it suggestively with black lace (Klemesrud 1978). From health clubs to running shoes the physical fitness industry reported sales of over $30 billion in 1981 ("America Shapes Up," Nov. 2, 1981). Plastic surgeons are besieged with requests for facelifts, hair transplants, breast enlargements, and eyelifts by people who want to look more like the national ideal. Psychiatrists report that "those who do have such changes made almost always feel happier, more attractive, and often enjoy better sex lives" afterward (Cook and McHenry 1978, p. 181).

Asexuals Come Out of the Closet

Newspaper columnist Art Hoppe, writing in the *San Francisco Chronicle*, probably brought glee to millions when he conducted a fictitious interview with a guy who came out of the closet to become president of the militant asexual liberation movement:

Question: You are an avowed asexual, Mr. Gates?

Answer: Yes, and proud of it, although I should add that we asexuals prefer being called "A's" or, even better, "straight A's."

Question: And have you been an A all your life, sir?

Answer: Oh, no. No one is born an A. Our members come from all walks of sexual preferences. In each case, he or she comes to realize that the fleeting pleasures of sex are scant rewards for the constant hassles it entails. Or, as our patron saint, Dorothy Parker, put it so long ago, The screwing you get isn't worth the screwing you give.

Question: And so they retire into sexual closets?

Answer: Yes. But now they are coming out in droves. There are two reasons for this: First, it really isn't much fun doing nothing in a closet. And second, being a secret A arouses all sorts of suspicions among one's friends. Strange he's never married, they'll whisper behind your back. And the fellows still start avoiding you in the locker room.

Question: But you're out to change all that?

Answer: You bet. We members of A Lib are stressing A pride. When we are asked our sexual preference on employment forms, we boldly write down, none.

Question: Are you discriminated against nevertheless?

Answer: We sure are. We're presently fighting a case against the Marine Corps. They're trying to dishonorably discharge a young private who admitted to being a practicing asexual when they caught him reading War and Peace.

Question: I suppose you A's tend to hang around together?

Answer: Naturally. There's hardly a community in the land these days that doesn't have its A restaurants, A bars, and A motels.

Question: And what do you do in these places?

Answer: Eat, drink, and sleep.

Question: Well, I admire your honesty in bringing this problem out in the open. But do you think society is ready to meet it head on? Could an admitted asexual, for example, ever rise to the top of his profession?

Answer: Is the pope Catholic?

*From "A New Sex Fad," by A. Hoppe, *San Francisco Chronicle*, October 10, 1979, p. 57. Copyright © 1980 Chronicle Publishing Company. Reprinted by permission.

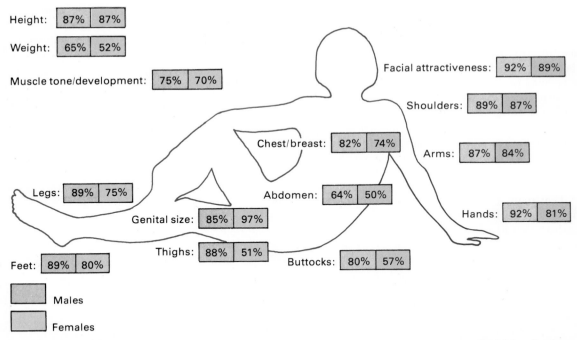

Height: 87% 87%

Weight: 65% 52%

Muscle tone/development: 75% 70%

Facial attractiveness: 92% 89%

Shoulders: 89% 87%

Chest/breast: 82% 74%

Arms: 87% 84%

Legs: 89% 75%

Abdomen: 64% 50%

Genital size: 85% 97%

Hands: 92% 81%

Thighs: 88% 51%

Feet: 89% 80%

Buttocks: 80% 57%

Males

Females

Note: Based on a survey of 62,000 *Psychology Today* readers (reduced to a subsample of 2000 approximating the national age and sex distributions).

Figure 1-2.   Satisfaction with Body Appearance.
Judging from the sample of *Psychology Today* readers, most of us are fairly satisfied with our bodies. Dissatisfaction tends to be greatest with areas that we can change by healthy diet and exercise.

A number of studies show that these people are responding to real, rather than imagined, emphasis on the importance of physical appearance in our culture. On being shown pictures of attractive males and females, both men and women judge these people to be warmer, stronger, and more sexually responsive, interesting, friendly, and considerate than people who are less attractive (Dion, Berscheid, and Walster 1972; Huston and Levinger 1978).

Many of us are generally satisfied with the way we look. A poll of *Psychology Today* readers revealed that most of them (77 percent of the females, 85 percent of the males) were satisfied with their overall body appearance. However, as one respondent pointed out, there's no way of knowing what people meant by checking the "satisfied" response. She wrote, "Does this mean that I am very good-looking and know it—or could it mean that I'm sick of so much emphasis on physical appearances and that I just don't give a damn about a trivial thing like being 'pretty'?" (Berscheid, Walster, and Bohrnstedt 1973, p. 120).

Despite general satisfaction with what cannot be changed—such as penis size and facial structure—about half the women and a third of the men said they were dissatisfied with their weight. Our culture's emphasis on slenderness seems to have been internalized by many as a hard-to-achieve ideal. Much of the concern for "overweight," as well as dissatisfaction with parts of the face, apparently stemmed from childhood taunting by peers.

Clothing and Body Language

We often try to shape others' reactions to us by the clothes we place between them and our naked selves. How long we wear our hair or skirts, how tight we wear our pants and shirts are often messages about how we want to be perceived sexually. A low-cut shirt that reveals a male's chest hair or the cleft between a female's breasts is usually meant—or construed—as a symbol of sexual availability. The person in the shirt seems to be saying, "I consider myself sexy and want you to see me that way, too."

Skin-tight clothing that reveals the bulge of the genitals or the outline of the nipples seems to invite glances and touches. Loose-fitting clothing may leave more to the imagination but suggests a readiness to cuddle. Even our foot coverings may be chosen with sex appeal in mind. According to William Rossi (1976), who's devoted a whole book to *The Sex Life of the Foot and Shoe,* sandals suggest sensuousness, boots a macho or sadomasochistic bent. High heels give women a "leggy" look and make their walk a sexy come-on.

These messages are not always clear, though, to either the sender or the receiver. One difficulty is that motives for wearing sexy clothes may vary. If a twelve-year-old male chooses to wear skin-tight hip-huggers, he may be acting on a desire to imitate his friends (who in turn are imitating media stars) rather than a desire to look sexy by emphasizing the erotic sway of his hips and the bulge of his crotch. The braless, pantyless look that men read as sexy may have been chosen by women who are more interested in their own comfort than in their sex appeal. We might also wear tight clothes when we're uptight about sex, trying to base our appeal more on our outer selves than on inner qualities such as warmth and intelligence. Sometimes we dress as the person we'd like to be—but aren't. And sometimes we may wear clothing considered erotic in order to be approved of and appreciated as sexually desirable—without necessarily wanting to become sexually involved with our admirers. As we'll see in Chapter 5, this confusion over who people are behind the clothes they wear complicates the business of sexual communication.

Another reason our clothes may not give clear messages about our sexual identity is that what we wear is not altogether a matter of free choice. Some observers see political implications in clothes. Power differences between males and females are a good example. Historically, women's clothes have been most restricting during periods when women have had the least power. During periods of relative equality of the sexes, women are far more likely to be accepted in clothes, such as pants, that allow them the male's freedom of movement. According to this theory, gradual progress toward equality between the sexes was mirrored in the increasing acceptance of unisex clothing in the 1960s and early 1970s (Horn 1975).

The "hooker look" in female clothing—heavy makeup, teetering heels, and clingy outfits slit to the waist from above or below—therefore puzzles social observers. Some see it as a regression to old gender patterns. For instance, some explain it as a backlash against the women's liberation movement by females who claim to enjoy their traditional role as sex objects. Others see it as a ploy by males to sabotage women's growing power by turning them back into "dumb pinup girls." But some view it as a symbol of a new kind of liberation—an indication that women are now comfortable with the idea that they can both initiate and enjoy sex as participants, rather than as objects. And to Norma Kamali, who designs figure-hugging disco dresses, it reflects women's new pride in keeping fit and in knowing that they can do a lot of things well: They can be bright, successful, and sexy, too (Klemesrud 1978).

The sexual politics expressed in clothing may also affect the subtle differences in body language that distinguish the powerful from the less powerful. Psychologist Nancy Henley (1977) speculates that women act out feelings of inferior status by holding their arms close to their body and their legs together, as if to allow males more space. They cock their heads, toy with their hair, and smile a lot to indicate their submission and desire for sexual approval.

Are our body language and sexual behaviors affected by the clothes we wear? For instance, do women tend to move and behave more assertively when they wear pants than when they wear skirts? Do we behave more seductively when we're wearing bikini underwear? While we often choose our clothes for the effect we have on each other, what we wear probably affects *us* as well. To a certain extent, we may *become* what we wear.

Nudity

For some of us clothing may be so essential to our sexual selves that we feel—and think we look—

A guide to places where clothes-free enjoyment of natural settings is accepted.

less sexy without it. Psychotherapist Albert Ellis (1962) tells of one woman who, though tremendously attracted to men, couldn't undress before them. Her problem: Accustomed to being admired for beautiful clothes, she was embarrassed to reveal that beneath them lay only a run-of-the-mill body.

Although this attitude may seem a bit extreme, it reflects an ancient truth: We eroticize body parts by concealing them. Imagination is one of the greatest sexual stimulants. In nudist camps where nothing is left to the imagination, men are surprised to find that their fears of having public erections over seeing so much nakedness simply don't materialize. With no clothes to heighten their sensuality, bodies become simply another part of the social scene. Modesty typically is maintained not by clothes but by a strict set of social rules: no staring, no sex talk, no body contact, no alcohol

(Weinberg 1965). In these settings attempts to *conceal* parts of the body are considered erotic and therefore taboo (Friedrichs 1972).

Outside of nudist camps, though, taboos over revealing parts of the body still persist. Some people are reluctant to reveal their entire naked selves except in a few carefully defined social situations. For example, a study of nude beaches in California indicates that even though friends may be nude together all day at the beach, their roommates may not tolerate nudity in the kitchen or living room at home (Douglas, Rasmussen, and Flanagan 1977). And when showering after gym, people usually feel that it's okay to be naked in front of others but only those of the same gender.

Social scientists believe that despite the universality of some form of bodily modesty, it is socially learned rather than innate. They point to its variability as proof. In our culture, for instance, females are taught to keep their legs together when they wear skirts to avoid letting men see their underpants, which are socially defined as erotic garments. Females will suffer great discomfort and loss of bodily freedom to preserve this taboo—by never bending over in a short skirt, by crossing their legs tightly to keep the thighs together, and so on. But since this taboo does not extend to outer garments, the same females will spread their legs and move about freely when wearing bikinis or shorts, readily displaying their crotches (Levin 1975).

Resisting such distinctions as unnecessary and unnatural, some people are opting for a "clothes-optional" lifestyle. They are freeing themselves to be comfortably nude at home and to enjoy the sensual pleasures of full skin contact with sun and sand and water in natural recreational settings. As one clothes-optional organization, The Naturists, explains,

Body fear is dwindling. It's not so scary to accept one's body as a temple of the spirit, suitable for viewing and living in without fear or needless prudery. Discretion, tact, consideration for those who might be offended, yes. But we're more and more inviting our good friends to join us in the hot tub, on a camping trip, a day at the free beach, or on vacation, where we know that nudity is realistic and desirable experience part of the time. [Naturists, 1982, p. 2]

SEXUAL SCRIPTS

The final pieces of our sexual identity—*scripts*—enable us to translate our notions of who we are into actual behaviors. Scripts consist of *meanings* for what we'll do and *plans of action* for how, when, where, and with whom we'll do it. An example of scripted behavior is the rather predictable chain of events through which a young, middle-class couple manage to have intercourse for the first time (Gagnon 1973). From the setting (alone in a private, darkened place) to what they do about removing their clothes (usually hers come off first) to what they say to each other afterward (reassurances that there is a bond of affection, as well as sex, between them), much of what goes on is preprogrammed rather than totally spontaneous. They have learned the scripts that guide their first attempt not from experience but from fragments they have picked up from others.

Some Common Scripts

In our culture many different general scripts have developed historically and are shaping sexual behavior today. We may internalize one script as children but switch at least partially to another as we grow up and are subject to different social influences. Scripts may be combined, switched, or even made up to fit different situations. Just which of the scripts we're following is therefore hard to tell, for they rarely exist in any pure form and are often combined. At any one time the script mixture might include the following basic types.

1. *Traditional script,* in which sex is acceptable only within marriage. Sex means reproduction, though it may also have something to do with affection. People are expected to commit themselves to a single mate for life, with strong community support for this choice (as in the golden wedding anniversary).

2. *Romantic script,* in which sex means love. According to this script, if we grow in love with someone, it's okay to "make love," either in or out of marriage. Without love sex is a meaningless animal function. The eligible actors are two people who are in love, the ideal emotional state is uncontrollable loving passion, the words exchanged are assurances of affection, and all activities should appear to be spontaneous expressions of love (Gecas and Libby 1976). Despite the stereotyped notion that women are more likely to feel this way than men, males in fact are often found to be deeply emotionally involved in relationships and to suffer severe trauma if the relationships break up (Wassenberg 1982). They may actually grow in love more quickly and out of love more slowly than women (Rubin 1973).

3. *Sexual friendship script,* in which people who are friends can also have an intimate sexual relationship. Although the association of the actors in this script is usually ongoing, typically it's not sexually exclusive.

4. *Casual/mutual desire script,* increasingly publicized by the mass media, in which sex is defined as recreational fun. In this script the actors are casual acquaintances who are mutually sexually aroused. Qualities that are looked for in sexmaking may include joy, playfulness, abandon, variety, and, increasingly, good technique. Because there's no ulterior reward for sex, the sex itself must be highly satisfying (Long Laws and Schwartz 1977).

5. *Utilitarian-predatory script,* in which people have sex for some reason other than sexual pleasure, reproduction, or love. In this script the reasons for sex might include economic gain (as in prostitution), career advancement, or power achievement. For example, to achieve power, some male groups see sex as "scoring" and believe they enhance their status within the group by boasting of their sexual exploits.

For each of these general scripts there are many short scripts for what to do in specific situations. People who use the traditional script, for example, may have situational scripts covering petting (above the waist? below the waist? with or without clothes?), while the casual script may include a situational script for picking someone up in a bar.

Problems with Scripts

Sexual scripts can be useful if they help us to make sense of our own and others' behaviors. But they can cause problems, too. Some of us follow our scripts too rigidly, rather than adapting them to various situations. And some of us don't have clear scripts to work from. Sometimes scripts are incompletely learned because sex is such a taboo area that it's not talked about directly. As Lillian Rubin points out, many of us aren't brought up with *any* well-defined script:

Girls generally learn only that it's "wrong" before marriage. But what that "it" is often is hazy and unclear until after the first sexual experience. As for the varieties of sexual behavior, these are rarely, if ever, mentioned to growing children, let alone discussed in terms of which are right or wrong, good or bad, permissible or impermissible. [Rubin 1976, p. 139]

Even if the whole script is learned, it may not fit the person or the person's experiences. Judith Long Laws and Pepper Schwartz (1977) point out that individuals who form coherent, solid sexual identities are those whose personal experiences fall in line with the script they've been socialized to. But for others matching script to experience is more difficult. Sometimes there's simply no social script available for the things we experience. For instance, until recently there was no script for female masturbation. It was as though this behavior simply didn't exist. Likewise, today there's no social recognition of the possibility that a male may not want sex when presented with an opportunity for it. Reluctant men who are approached by sexually aroused females have no script for saying "no" or even "not now." Scripts that women have used hardly seem appropriate for men. What can a man say? "No thanks, dear, I have a headache tonight"? "I have my reputation to think of"? "I don't want to be seen as an easy lay"? "Will you respect me in the morning"? It doesn't occur to many of us that we can write our own scripts for sexual behavior—but we can.

If the lack of a script can be a problem, so can working from too many scripts at once. Individuals who are socialized to two or more conflicting scripts may feel confused and dissatisfied with their sexual activities. Females who have grown up with the romantic script, for instance, but who as adults are exposed to the casual script by friends whose judgment they value may come out with a scrambled set of motives and behaviors. And as we

will see in Chapter 5, conflicts may arise when two people with different scripts try to negotiate a sexual relationship. Their actions and the meanings they read into what's going on simply don't mesh.

SEX AS A LIFETIME CAREER

The scripts we have in our heads today need not be stuck there for life. It's helpful to regard our sexuality as a career of sorts, one that will continue to grow and change over our lifetime. This concept is not so obvious as it may seem. Most of us are very here-and-now oriented. To look at our sexual expression as a career—defined optimistically by *Webster's Third International Dictionary* as "a course of continuous progress"—gives us a different perspective on the present. Our sexual identity today may be different from what it was ten years ago, and it's possible that it may change considerably in the next ten years.

Much of what will happen to us in the future will be unexpected. People and events that we can't possibly foresee will pass through our lives and leave us changed. But some changes are rather predictable, for they happen to most people in a given culture as they reach certain stages. Puberty, for instance, brings predictable biological changes and often some form of sexual experimentation. At some time during young adulthood, many people begin to develop intimate sexual relationships. During the twenties and thirties, careers, marriage, pregnancy, and parenthood for some bring new influences to bear on sexuality. Middle age promises a new set of concerns for people in this society, as does old age.

For some this progression may follow the typical traditional path—from dating to monogamous marriage to parenthood to growing old together. For others clusters of episodes will occur that don't lead in any particular direction—periods of marriage, for instance, may alternate with periods of singlehood, some of which are celibate, some of which involve an active sex life. Either way, each stage brings opportunities for making new choices, revamping old scripts, and reexamining routine behaviors. It's possible to rethink and perhaps change our ideas of who we are sexually.

The ability to change the unsatisfying parts of our sexual identities may make a difference in how fully we live each day. As Stanley Cohen and Laurie Taylor (1976) point out in their book *Escape Attempts: The Theory and Practice of Resistance to Everyday Life,* the major problem many of us face is simply how to get through the boredom, despair, and disappointments of everyday life. A way out? "Identity work"—that is, struggling to free ourselves from routines and stereotyped roles, figuring out who we want to be, and then trying to actualize that identity. Outer change is not the whole answer, Cohen and Taylor say. Moving to a new city or finding a new partner will get us nowhere if we lapse into the same old routines built on the same old stultifying identity. Instead, Cohen and Taylor recommend that we step back and take a look at our inner selves to see whether any changes can be made there. Sex itself can make our lives more satisfying and rewarding, although some people do not find it so.

To help us step back, look at our inner selves, and consider possible changes, the next seven chapters will encourage individual exploration of the processes by which we become sexually experienced. We will first explore our biological selves and then look at how we behave sexually, both with ourselves and in relationships with others.

SUMMARY

As sexual individuals we are multifaceted composites of assorted traits. The degree to which some of these aspects of our identity are biologically or socially caused is controversial. One facet that is clearly influenced by what we have learned within our society is our sense of what is moral in sex. A second facet of our sexual identity is our gender and the social roles we have learned to play as persons of that gender. A third facet is whether we find erotic the same or the other sex or both. Fourth is our body image—how we feel about our naked selves and the lengths to which we may go to alter our appearance in the quest of "sex appeal." Fifth is the sexual script or scripts that guide and explain our sexual experiences. These facets of ourselves may not be static; rather, they may grow and change over our lifetime, sometimes as a result of our conscious choices.

2

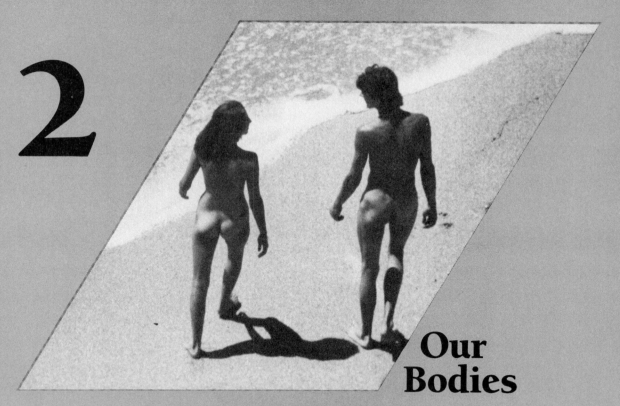

Our Bodies

The Anatomy and Physiology of Sex

My partners hardly ever pay any attention to sensitive places like my nipples or ears, or anus, or the insides of my elbows when we're making love, but I wish they would. Everybody thinks a man consists mainly of his cock. Sure, my cock feels great and does great things, but it's not all there is to me.

I feel so horny sometimes; other times I could care less about sex. I think it has something to do with my periods. I get really turned on right before my periods start, but my lover doesn't want to have sex because he feels funny about the blood. I wish he could get over that, because I feel so high then and really want him inside me. I can get myself off and that helps some, but it's not the same.

Around the time when my breasts started growing, I began to notice white stuff in my vaginal area when I went to the bathroom. I didn't know what it was. I tried to wash it away, but more kept appearing. It didn't seem to cause any problems, but I wish somebody had told me then what it was. There was a lot I didn't know about my body—and I'm still learning. When you're a female, you have to be a contortionist to see all that stuff.

I really love my body. The more I get to know it, the more amazed I am at the things it does, without my having to think about it at all. I've learned, though, that if I breathe a certain way or tense certain muscles I can make myself come faster or slower if I want to. Mostly I just enjoy being along for the ride—and when I come, what fireworks!

Our body's sexual responses are often a mystery to us. Even the latest scientific understanding of the anatomy and physiology of sexual responses is still in its infancy, with many areas only partially mapped out.

What is known begins with embryonic gender differentiation: the sexual similarities and differences between males and females as they develop before birth. Adolescence brings further sexual differentiation. After surveying these periods, we will explore female and male adult sexual anatomy, the physiology of sexual responses, and hormonal influences on sexual behavior. Although we must examine these topics separately, they are unified by the brain as a complex system of interrelated physical factors, which are further influenced by the complex of psychological and sociological factors discussed throughout this book. Sex is not a simple reflex phenomenon.

PRENATAL GENDER DIFFERENTIATION

For the first weeks of life all embryos are visibly identical, though they differ in genetic makeup. Fetuses that will become females usually have received from each parent what is called an X chromosome as part of the hereditary package that will shape their biological development. Males-to-be have received an X chromosome from their mother and a Y from their father. The presence of these chromosomes determines whether the undifferentiated *gonad* (reproductive organ) will become a pair of *ovaries* (if the child is female) or *testes* (if the child is male).

The apparent vehicle for this differing development is the *H-Y antigen,* a protein whose appearance is induced by a gene on the Y chromosome, found only in males (Therman 1980). The H-Y antigen causes the testes to develop. As they do, they begin to secrete *androgens,* or male hormones, of which the best known is *testosterone.* In the presence of a high level of androgens, the basically "female" plan of the undifferentiated genitals become the *penis* and *scrotum* characteristic of males. The female fetus produces a lower level of androgens. In the absence of a certain level of androgens, the bump earlier called the *genital tubercle* becomes the female's sexually sensitive *cli-*

toris, analogous to the penis; the folds and swellings beneath become the inner and outer lips (*labia minora* and *labia majora),* analogous to the male's scrotum. Differentiation of the sexes is complete by the fourteenth week of fetal life. This sequence is actually the reverse of our male-oriented myth that woman was created from Adam's rib as an afterthought. As medical psychologist Robert Athanasiou (1979) puts it, "God created Eve first and then created Adam with a shot of testosterone."

Disorders in gender differentiation are surprisingly common. One in every 400 males and one in every 650 females has a chromosomal gender disorder (Thompson and Thompson 1980). For example, people with Klinefelter's syndrome have an abnormal XXY chromosomal makeup; as adolescents they may develop small breasts but usually have been regarded as males because they have a penis and small testes. Some genetic (XY) males produce normal levels of androgens but have a genetic defect that makes them insensitive to male hormones. They may therefore develop as females and are assumed to be girls until, as adolescents, they fail to begin menstruating because they have no internal female organs. Others with this defect may be born with ambiguous genitals that are surgically altered to a male or female appearance. Prenatal exposure to androgens taken by the mother during pregnancy may also result in masculinized genitals in female fetuses.

Such abnormalities provide one of the few ways of assessing the effects of biological gender on behavior patterns in humans. However, surveys of people of uncertain biological gender indicate that their gender identity and behaviors are strongly influenced by the social expectations of the gender to which they are assigned at birth. The extent to which this social influence outweighs the "male" or "female" chromosomal and hormone pattern is controversial (Hines 1982).

In addition to prenatal differentiation of the external genitals, certain areas of the brain develop differently in males and females before birth, as indicated by recent research with mammals. This prenatal development appears to be influenced by the levels of male or female hormones present (Hines 1982). The degree to which such animal findings can be applied to humans is uncertain, for

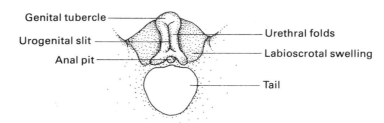

Undifferentiated

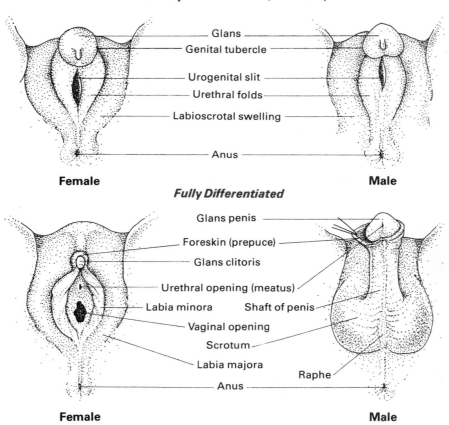

Figure 2-1. Differentiation of the External Genitals. At first the external genitals of male and female embryos are identical in structure. The genitals shown in the top drawing could thus belong to either a male or a female. But seven or eight weeks after conception, androgen stimulates male genitals to develop differently from those of females. By the time fetuses are nine or ten weeks old, the genitals of males and females look somewhat different, as shown in the middle drawings. In their final forms—shown in the lowest set of drawings—female and male genitals differ markedly. For example, the shaft of the female clitoris lies solidly against the body; though it had the same origin, the shaft of the male penis protrudes from the body. But similarities persist: Both clitoris and penis have a shaft, a glans, and a foreskin.

much of human behavior is organized and monitored at a higher cognitive level.

THE CHANGES OF PUBERTY

After a child is born, its reproductive cells secrete low levels of hormones until some unknown factor triggers the final development of the reproductive system. This process—known as *puberty*—usually begins between the ages of eight and thirteen in girls and nine and fourteen in boys (Ganong 1981) and may take several years.

The unknown factor seems to send chemical messages to a part of the brain that is important to sex hormone regulation: the *hypothalamus*. The hypothalamus then apparently sends a chemical-releasing factor to the *pituitary gland,* which lies just below the brain. The pituitary in turn secretes two *gonadotropins* (gonad-stimulating substances): FSH (follicle-stimulating hormone) and LH (luteinizing hormone). They stimulate the development of sex hormones in the female's ovaries and the male's testicles. These sex hormones prepare the body for reproduction by creating numerous physical changes.

In females the ovaries secrete *estrogens,* which are "feminizing" in their effects, and *progesterone, a* hormone that prepares the uterus for pregnancy. Females also receive small amounts of androgens ("male hormones") from their ovaries and adrenal cortex, but it is the estrogens that cause most of the *secondary sex characteristics* that develop at puberty. These include enlargement of the breasts, uterus, and vagina; broadening of the hips; development of fat deposits on the breasts and buttocks; an increase in vaginal secretions; and the onset of menstruation *(menarche).* Hair also begins to grow in the pubic area and armpits, a change that is triggered chiefly by androgens.

In males large amounts of androgens and a small amount of estrogens are secreted by the testes; more androgens and perhaps estrogens are secreted by the adrenal cortex. The androgens have a "masculinizing" effect, creating the male secondary sex characteristics. These include changes in hair distribution, body shape, and genital size; maturation of the internal reproductive structures; and thickening of skin gland secretions that may lead to acne. Because the reproductive organs have matured, ejaculation is now possible—and may happen spontaneously, as "wet dreams" (nocturnal emissions). These ejaculations during sleep may be associated with erotic dreams or simply may occur as a release of sexual tensions built up during the day. Females may experience orgasm during sleep, too, for the same reasons but may not be aware of it because their sheets are not sticky in the morning.

These changes of puberty may be a source of embarrassment or fear to those who don't know that the new things their bodies are doing have a natural, expected biological base. In the past girls who were not taught about menstruation feared that they were "bleeding to death." Because they had learned to regard their genital area as taboo, they were afraid to tell anybody and instead secretly suffered, worried, and tried to hide the blood. Even today, young women who do not know that it is natural for lubricating fluids to appear in their vaginal area when they are sexually aroused may worry that they are "wetting their pants," something they were trained from infancy to avoid. It is possible that in trying to inhibit this natural flow of fluids, some may develop holding-in (or tensing) patterns that later interfere with free enjoyment of sex.

For boys, too, absence of talk within the family about sex (see Chapter 9) may lead to embarrassing attempts to conceal the evidence of wet dreams. The spontaneity of erections—which begin to happen at socially awkward times—may also lead to embarrassment in those who see no humor in their penis's surprising behaviors. Nevertheless, early pubertal development enhances boys' self-esteem. By contrast, girls who experience the physical changes of puberty early and have begun "dating" are typically but perhaps temporarily lower in self-esteem than sixth- and seventh-grade girls who have not (Simmons et al. 1979). Girls whose breasts swell early may try to hide them, disturbed by the attention from others who perceive them, on the basis of their changed physical appearance, as being mature and sexually interested.

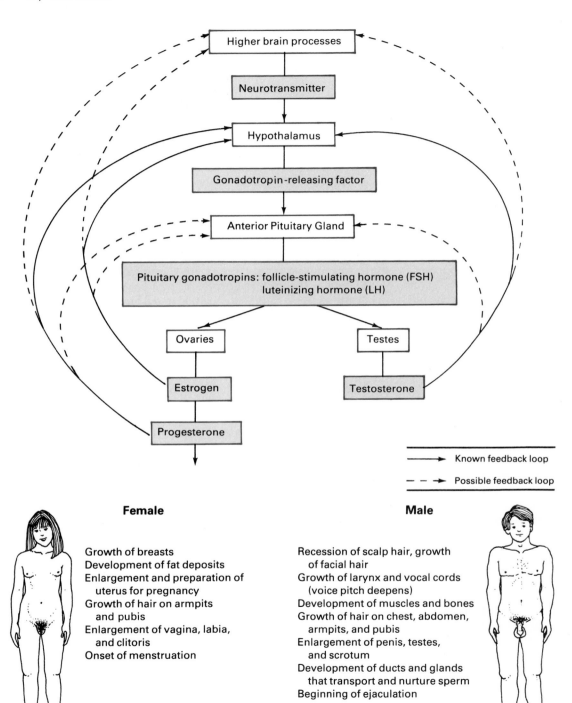

──────▶	Known feedback loop
─ ─ ─▶	Possible feedback loop

Female

Growth of breasts
Development of fat deposits
Enlargement and preparation of
   uterus for pregnancy
Growth of hair on armpits
   and pubis
Enlargement of vagina, labia,
   and clitoris
Onset of menstruation

Male

Recession of scalp hair, growth
   of facial hair
Growth of larynx and vocal cords
   (voice pitch deepens)
Development of muscles and bones
Growth of hair on chest, abdomen,
   armpits, and pubis
Enlargement of penis, testes,
   and scrotum
Development of ducts and glands
   that transport and nurture sperm
Beginning of ejaculation

Figure 2-2.   Male and Female Changes of Puberty.

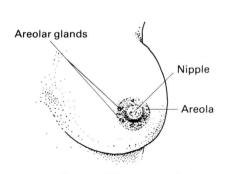

Areolar glands

Nipple

Areola

External Structure of the Breast

Female Breast

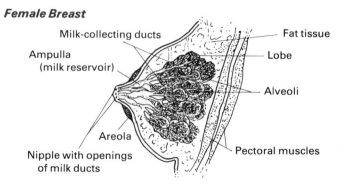

Milk-collecting ducts

Fat tissue

Ampulla (milk reservoir)

Lobe

Alveoli

Areola

Nipple with openings of milk ducts

Pectoral muscles

Internal Structure of the Breast

Figure 2-3.   Female Breast.

FEMALE SEXUAL ANATOMY

Puberty, whether it is greeted with embarrassment or celebration, often draws our attention to the sexually sensitive parts of our body. Actually we are exquisitely sensitive to gentle touches almost anywhere, but our cultural focus centers on the breasts and genitals. In this chapter we will look at the anatomy of these areas and how they become sexually excited; in Chapter 16 we will examine their reproductive functions.

Breasts

The breasts house the *mammary glands,* as well as protective fat tissue and ligaments that attach the glands to underlying pectoral muscles, helping to support the weight of the breasts. The mammary glands themselves consist of fifteen to twenty *lobes,* each of which consists of small glands called *alveoli, ducts* to collect the milk the alveoli produce after a child is born, and an opening in the nipple. The nipple contains nerve endings that are extremely sensitive to temperature and touch. The nipple is surrounded by the *areola,* or area of nerve and muscle fibers that can make the nipple erect when it is stimulated.

Breasts vary considerably in size and shape from one woman to another and may not even match exactly on the same woman. According to *Playboy*'s survey of over 100,000 of its readers, only 28 percent of the men and 26 percent of the women consider breast size important to a woman's sexual attractiveness. However, breasts

were cited as an extremely sexually sensitive area by 75 percent of the women (Petersen et al. 1983a).

Vulva

The external structures of the female genitals collectively are known as the *vulva.* They are protectively enclosed by the *labia majora,* or outer lips. These folds of fat tissue merge at the front to form the *mons pubis,* a rounded, hair-covered mound of fatty tissue sometimes referred to as the "mound of Venus." Within the labia majora lie the *labia minora,* or inner lips. These flattened folds of skin overlie connective tissue that is so richly supplied with blood that the inner lips usually appear reddish.

The inner lips merge to form the *hood* covering the *clitoris,* a small projection at the front of the vulva. The *shaft* is hidden under the hood; the small tip is called the *glans.* Like the male's penis, the clitoris is composed of erectile tissue; the glans is so richly supplied with nerve fibers that it is highly sexually sensitive.

The space within the labia minora is called the *vestibule.* Structures a woman can find here if she looks in a mirror include the *urethral opening* and the *vaginal opening,* partially covered by a membrane called the *hymen.* The degree to which the hymen covers the vaginal opening depends on many individual factors, only one of which is sexual activity. The *vagina* is a potential (rather than

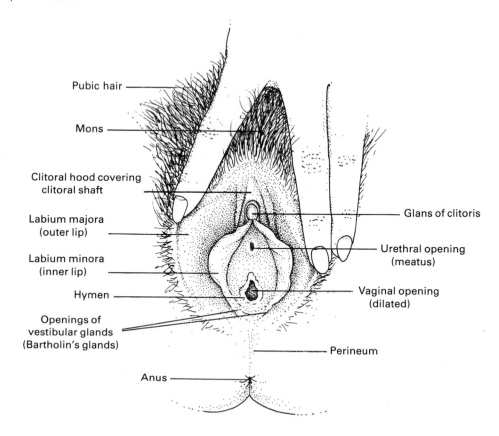

Pubic hair

Mons

Clitoral hood covering
clitoral shaft

Labium majora
(outer lip)

Labium minora
(inner lip)

Hymen

Openings of
vestibular glands
(Bartholin's glands)

Anus

Glans of clitoris

Urethral opening
(meatus)

Vaginal opening
(dilated)

Perineum

Figure 2-4.   Female External Genitals.   In females, the major structures in the external genitals are the pleasure-sensitive clitoris, inner and outer set of lips (shown parted here), and the opening to the vagina. Women can best see these structures in themselves with a mirror. This is a simplified drawing; the structures are actually far more complex in form.

actual) cavity, so the sides of the opening normally touch. Below the vagina on either side of the labia minora, the small openings of the *vestibular glands* (or Bartholin's glands) may be seen. These secrete a small amount of mucus during sexual excitement, which may help to lubricate the area for intercourse. Between the vestibule and the anus is a hairless area called the *perineum* that, like the *anus,* may be erotically sensitive.

Like breasts genitals differ considerably in shape from person to person. Few of us look exactly like the generalized diagrams in sex and anatomy books. Not knowing this, artist Betty Dodson (1974) writes that she was horrified and disgusted when she first inspected herself "down there" with a mirror at age twelve. What she saw looked like a chicken's wattles, for her inner lips were the extended kind. Although hers was one of many common variations in vulva shapes, Dodson considered herself deformed and ugly. Her body loathing lasted until she was thirty-five, when a new

lover convinced her that her genitals were beautiful. Her stylized drawings of vulval patterns as beautiful forms have helped many women take a more positive view of their own genitals.

Internal Sexual Organs

Most of a female's sexually sensitive areas are on the outside of her body. Two inner structures involved in her sexual responses, the vagina and uterus, also may have a degree of sexual sensitivity. The *vagina* is a tubular, muscular structure several inches long. Its walls are usually collapsed together, but the stretchable potential cavity can

Internal Female Reproductive System (side view)

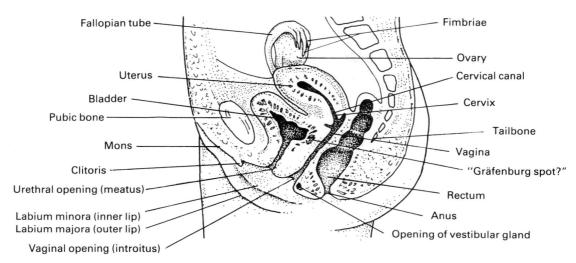

Fallopian tube

Uterus

Bladder

Pubic bone

Mons

Clitoris

Urethral opening (meatus)

Labium minora (inner lip)
Labium majora (outer lip)

Vaginal opening (introitus)

Fimbriae

Ovary

Cervical canal

Cervix

Tailbone

Vagina

"Gräfenburg spot?"

Rectum

Anus

Opening of vestibular gland

Figure 2-5. Internal Female Reproductive System (Side View).

expand considerably during sexual excitement or childbirth.

Sex researchers William Masters and Virginia Johnson (1966) have long maintained that the inner vagina has little sensitivity to touch or pain, but researchers John Perry and Beverly Whipple (Ladas, Whipple, and Perry 1982) have identified in many women a sexually sensitive area deep within the vagina. They call it the *Gräfenburg spot,* after the physician who first described it. The spot has been medically overlooked, they believe, because it cannot be found in a cadaver and because it responds only to deep pressure on a certain area, pressure that normally would not be exerted during a vaginal exam, particularly when there is no permission for the doctor to excite the woman sexually or even to ask if the touches feel good.

Perry and Whipple believe that the G spot is comparable to the male's prostate gland and probably is composed of blood vessels, paraurethral glands, and nerve endings surrounding the urethra near the neck of the bladder. It is usually found halfway between the pubic bone and the cervix, near the urethra, about a centimeter beneath the surface of the vagina wall. The area may feel like a small bean to a partner or examiner (it is too deep to be located manually by the woman herself), which swells during sexual excitement to the size of a dime or even a half-dollar. There is some spec-

ulation that the swelling in this area prevents a penis from bumping into the urethra during intercourse.

The existence of the Gräfenburg spot—or any other sexually sensitive area within the vagina—has been denied by some critics. The only true expert on the sensitivities of a woman's body is each woman herself, paying close attention to her own body's responses. To a certain extent, sexual responses are learned; being aware of subtle sensations can help a woman learn how to augment them, if she chooses.

The vagina leads to the *uterus,* with the cervix in between. The *cervix* is the rounded base of the uterus, and it has a small opening *(os)* into the *cervical canal* for the passage of semen (during intercourse) and menstrual fluids. The cervix usually is not erotically sensitive but can experience pain during intercourse if some form of cervicitis (see Chapter 14) is present. The *uterus* is a hollow organ that can expand to house a growing fetus and has muscular walls that may be involved in sexual response. If its position relative to the vagina is inflexible because of scarred or inflamed tissue, the woman may experience pain during intercourse. This condition can be corrected surgically.

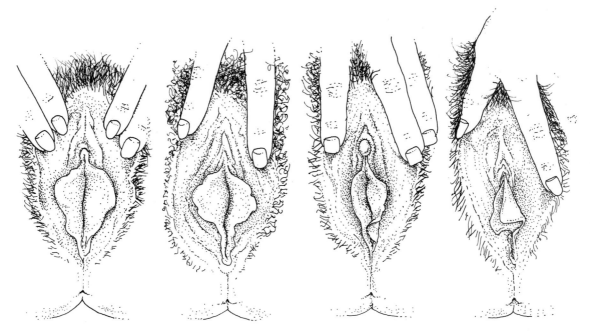

Figure 2-6.   Variety in Female Genitals. Female genitals come in a great variety of shapes, a few of which are shown here. Some women link their vulva patterns with natural shapes—shells, flowers, petals, caves, leaves. Betty Dodson (1974) even sees vulva "styles"—Baroque, Danish Modern, Gothic, Classical, and so on.

On either side of the uterus are the *ovaries*. These oval structures, which house the egg cells for reproduction and also secrete sex hormones, are not erotically sensitive. *Fallopian tubes* lead from each ovary to the uterus, providing a pathway and transport for the egg cells, one of which is released during each menstrual cycle.

MALE SEXUAL ANATOMY

Men are usually more aware of their external genital structures than are women, for men's genitals are more easily seen—and touched. But men's knowledge of their internal structures may be more limited than women's. Most young females are taught the anatomy and physiology of menstruation.

Penis

The most visible—and celebrated—part of the male's external sexual organs is the *penis*. Like the clitoris, it consists of a cylindrical *shaft* and a highly sensitive rounded head called the *glans,* which may be partially covered by a *foreskin*. In males

who have been *circumcised* (usually at birth), this soft, pliable, open-ended fold of skin has been surgically removed.

When it is present, the foreskin has an outer layer that is an extension of the skin of the penile shaft and an inner layer that is attached to the shaft just below the sensitive *coronal ridge*. The foreskin is highly sensitive itself, and men may find that its natural drawing back during erection is an erotic sensation. The foreskin may also help to keep the glans more sexually sensitive; in a circumcised penis the skin of the glans may toughen to tolerate continual rubbing against clothes. However, differences in sexual sensitivity and responsiveness between circumcised and uncircumcised men have not been documented (Wallerstein 1980).

Smegma may accumulate behind the foreskin. This substance consists partly of oily, lubricating

A. Flaccid state

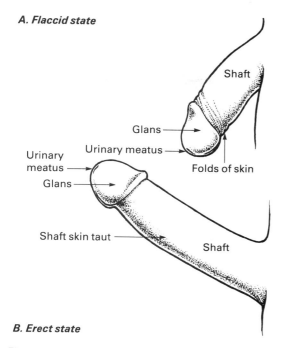

B. Erect state

Figure 2-7.   The Circumcised Penis.

secretions from small glands in the foreskin and coronal ridge. When allowed to accumulate and combine with dead skin cells, these secretions form the cheesy substance known as smegma. It is found in the genital area of women as well. In both sexes it can and should be removed by regular washing of the area to avoid irritation and bacterial growth.

Circumcised or uncircumcised, the penis houses the *urethra*, a tube that conveys urine and semen to the outside of the body. The penis also contains three columns of specialized erectile tissue: two *cavernous bodies* (corpora cavernosa) on top and a single *spongy body* (corpus spongiosum) below that allow the penis to enlarge and stiffen during sexual arousal. These erectile tissues contain networks of small blood vessels, shut off from the body's normal blood flow by tiny valves (Silber 1981). During sexual excitement these valves relax and open, allowing the erectile tissue to swell with blood. As the blood pressure in the penis increases, it elongates and becomes more stiffly erect. After ejaculation the pressure drops and the penis returns to its normal *flaccid* (limp) state.

Scrotum and testicles

At the base of the penis is the *scrotum,* a sac containing the *testicles.* The scrotum seems to regulate the temperature of the testicles, helping to protect them from external and internal temperatures that would interfere with sperm production. During cold weather or sexual excitement, the muscular covering of the scrotum wrinkles and tightens against the body.

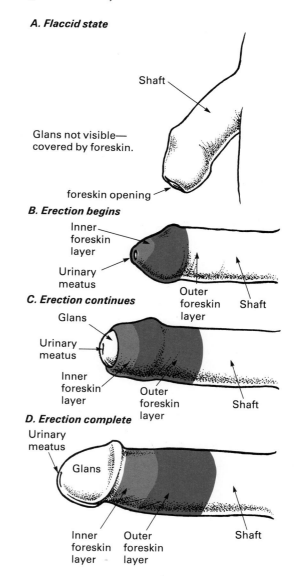

A. Flaccid state

B. Erection begins

C. Erection continues

D. Erection complete

Figure 2-8.   The Uncircumcised Penis.

Penis Size: Women's Views

Men have long assumed that a large penis is highly desirable because of its erotic effect on women. Concern for penis length may affect men more than women, however. Masters and Johnson (1966) found that during erection short penises enlarge more than long ones. A vagina can adjust to fit almost any size of penis snugly, especially if vaginal muscles are in good shape. And many women say that if they have any preference, it is for girth rather than length. Of 100 sexually active women surveyed by *Forum* magazine (Nobile 1982b), 64 said they did prefer penises of a certain size. To 51 of these women, a medium-size penis was preferable to a large or small one. Some comments:

I am afraid big men will hurt. Also, big men think all they have to do is ram and bam. Small ones usually make for more considerate lovers.

Naturally, it's nice to have a big cock, but I like all cocks so it really doesn't matter. Actually, I prefer a small to medium when giving head. I feel I can do a better job and really get into it.

Small cocks offer no friction during sex, large causes too much pain and takes away from the pleasure. A medium-size cock allows both tight fit without the pain and permits close body contact. A man with a large cock is no good at all if I want to have anal sex. [Nobile 1982b, pp. 25, 28]

Despite their general preferences, 75 percent of these women stated that penis size did not affect their relationships with their partners. As one woman put it, "A man's character is far more important than his penis size." The differences in size are not great, anyway. According to recent tabulations of Alfred Kinsey's measurements of 2500 American men's erect penises, almost 90 percent are within an inch of the average six-inch erection (Nobile 1982a).

Suspended within the scrotum by the *spermatic cords* are the two *testicles,* or *testes.* Each cord contains a *vas deferens,* or sperm-transporting tube. Because the left cord is usually longer than the right one, the left testicle hangs somewhat lower than the right one in most men, giving the scrotum an asymmetrical appearance. Within the testes sperm are produced by the convoluted *seminiferous tubules* and stored in the *epididymes.* Hormones are secreted from the *interstitial* (or Leydig) *cells* between the tubules.

Internal Sexual Structures

The fluid that squirts out of the urinary meatus during ejaculation consists only partially of sperm cells produced in the testicles. Other specialized fluids are contributed by the *seminal vesicles* that join the vas deferens at the base of the bladder, the *prostate gland* that surrounds the urethra below the bladder, and the *bulbourethral* (Cowper's) *glands* below the prostate gland. During sexual arousal, about two to six milliliters of the resulting mixture —*semen,* or seminal fluid—is accumulated and then forcefully expelled through the urethra. The *sphincteric band* at the base of the bladder constricts during this process, preventing urine from mixing with the semen. The *urethral sphincter,* below the point where the vas deferens, seminal vesicle, and prostate gland pool their secretions, remains constricted until the time of ejaculation. A few drops of fluid from the bulbourethral glands may appear at the tip of the penis before ejaculation, for this lubricating secretion is not held back by the urethral sphincter. Contractions of the vas deferens, seminal vesicles, and prostate gland create the inner sensation of *emission,* or orgasm; relaxation of the urethral sphincter and contraction of the urethral bulb and various pelvic muscles cause the ejaculation of semen that usually follows.

The intricate sequence of events is probably partially orchestrated by the *pudendal nerve,* which carries sensations from the penis to the spinal cord and thence back through motor nerves to the penis (in which case erection is a simple reflex reaction to physical sexual stimulation), and partially by psychological inputs to the brain, which then sends motor impulses down the spinal cord to the penis (in which case erection involves mental arousal). The reflexive and mental pathways to orgasm usually work together, but psychological factors such as guilt or hostility can block the erectile reflexes (de Groat and Booth 1980).

Male Reproductive Organs

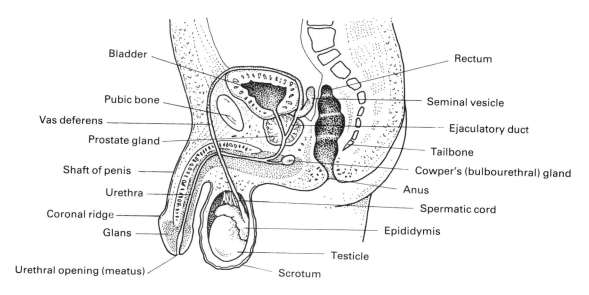

Longitudinal Section of Penis

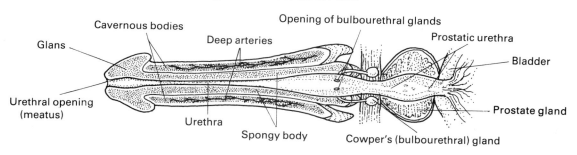

Cross Section of Scrotum and Penis

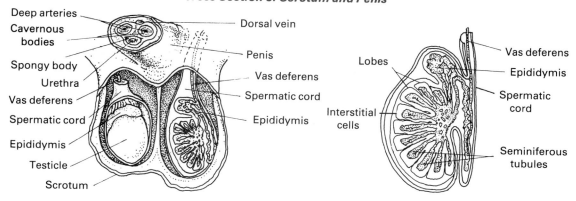

Figure 2-9. The Male Reproductive System. Our genital areas are not our only sexually sensitive parts, yet their complex structures are often of interest. In males the penis houses the *urethra* and three cylinders of spongelike tissues that fill up with blood during sexual arousal. The scrotum houses the two *testicles*. Sperm from the testicles and fluid from the *seminal vesicles* and *prostate gland* all combine during orgasm to form semen, which is then ejaculated through the urethral opening.

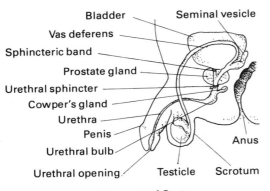

Bladder
Seminal vesicle
Vas deferens
Sphincteric band
Prostate gland
Urethral sphincter
Cowper's gland
Urethra
Penis
Anus
Urethral bulb
Urethral opening
Testicle
Scrotum

Unaroused State

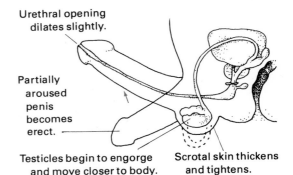

Urethral opening dilates slightly.

Partially aroused penis becomes erect.

Testicles begin to engorge and move closer to body.

Scrotal skin thickens and tightens.

Excitement Phase

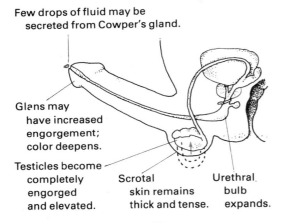

Few drops of fluid may be secreted from Cowper's gland.

Glans may have increased engorgement; color deepens.

Testicles become completely engorged and elevated.

Scrotal skin remains thick and tense.

Urethral bulb expands.

Plateau Phase

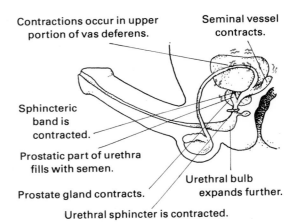

Contractions occur in upper portion of vas deferens.

Seminal vessel contracts.

Sphincteric band is contracted.

Prostatic part of urethra fills with semen.

Prostate gland contracts.

Urethral bulb expands further.

Urethral sphincter is contracted.

Orgasm Phase, Stage 1: Sensation of Orgasm

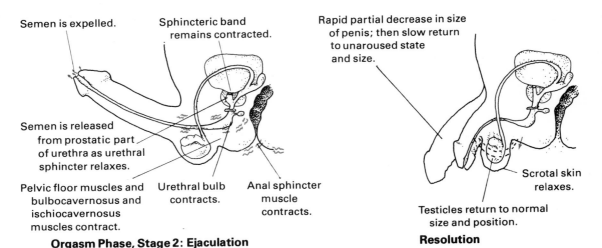

Semen is expelled.

Sphincteric band remains contracted.

Semen is released from prostatic part of urethra as urethral sphincter relaxes.

Pelvic floor muscles and bulbocavernosus and ischiocavernosus muscles contract.

Urethral bulb contracts.

Anal sphincter muscle contracts.

Orgasm Phase, Stage 2: Ejaculation

Rapid partial decrease in size of penis; then slow return to unaroused state and size.

Scrotal skin relaxes.

Testicles return to normal size and position.

Resolution

The *parasympathetic* and *sympathetic* nerves operate below the level of consciousness to activate the muscular and glandular responses after sexual stimulus messages are received at the spinal cord or brain level. Scientists are not yet certain exactly how these nerves help to create the changes. We do know, however, that although erection is not fully subject to conscious control, it is influenced by higher as well as lower parts of the central nervous system—by thoughts, emotions, and memories, as well as by direct physical stimulation of sexually sensitive parts of the body.

STAGES OF SEXUAL RESPONSE

Research has shown that the buildup of sexual tension to orgasm follows typical patterns that are similar in both sexes. According to current thinking ("Understanding 'Transition' Phase" 1981), arousal begins with a *desire* (or *transition*) *phase*— the process of moving from nonsexual to sexual attitudes. This initial period of sexual awakening was overlooked by William Masters and Virginia Johnson (1966) in their classic description of the sexual response cycle, but it is highly significant. If we approach sexual situations without first quieting our minds, shifting our attention from the hassles of everyday life to enjoying our own and our partners' bodies, we are unaware of the rich sensations of the moment and may not fully enjoy what happens.

The Response Cycle according to Masters and Johnson

Masters and Johnson's *Human Sexual Response,* drawn from their laboratory studies in the 1960s of 7500 female and 2500 male orgasms, has long

been considered the definitive statement on the physiology of sexual response. But there is much that we don't yet know and much that was inconclusive in Masters and Johnson's pioneering research.

One of Masters and Johnson's main findings was that buildup to orgasm follows a regular pattern, with four rather distinct phases. In both males and females it begins with the *excitement phase:* Sexual stimuli cause partial erection in the male and vaginal lubrication and swelling of the clitoris and vaginal lips in the female. All are the result of *vasocongestion:* More blood flows into these organs than out of them. Vasocongestion in surface blood vessels may create a "sex flush" all over the body. The first phase includes muscle responses, too. In females the inner two-thirds of the vagina involuntarily balloons up and out, lengthening the vaginal barrel. In males the scrotal skin tightens and thickens and the whole sac draws closer to the body. Nipples may contract and become "erect" in both genders. Voluntary muscles, such as those in the buttocks, tend to be tensed as well.

During the *plateau phase,* many of these responses increase in intensity. Penis and nipples erect further, the inner vagina balloons more, and voluntary and involuntary muscle tension mounts. A few drops of moisture from the bulbourethral glands may seep from the penis. They may contain active sperm cells and thus can cause pregnancy. In women the outer third of the vagina swells dramatically as its tissues fill with blood. The opening of the vagina narrows and provides a tighter grip for the penis, increasing pleasurable sensations for both partners during intercourse. The uterus lifts and enlarges, and the clitoris disappears beneath the clitoral hood. The clitoral area will still respond to stimulation, though.

Figure 2-10. Physical Changes in Male during Sexual Response Cycle. In males sexual stimulation causes the arteries of the penis to dilate and fill erectile tissues with blood. The same happens in females' sexually responsive tissues, too, but in males' the result is more visible: The penis may double in size as it stiffens and rises in an erection. Orgasm occurs in two phases: (1) There is the rushing inner sensation of orgasm as the vas deferens, seminal vesicles, and prostate gland contract and fill the enlarged prostatic part of the urethra with semen. (2) During ejaculation the sphincter that has held this fluid back relaxes and allows the semen to flow into the urethral bulb. The urethral bulb and muscles surrounding the base of the penis all contract, sending semen out of the urethral opening. Contraction of the sphincteric band at the base of the bladder prevents urine from mixing with the semen.

When muscle tension and engorgement of blood vessels reach a peak, the genital area may be rocked by the rhythmic contractions that Masters and Johnson labeled the *orgasm phase*. In females contractions occur in the outer vagina, uterus, and anal sphincter muscle. Males may experience a two-stage reaction. The feeling of orgasm—or emission—occurs in the first stage, as the organs containing sperm and the other seminal fluids contract and force their contents into the enlarged area of the urethra next to the prostate gland. During the second stage, or *ejaculation,* the urethral bulb and muscles at the base of the penis contract, forcing the semen out of the penis. While all this is going on, pulse rate, blood pressure, and breathing rate peak, and various muscles spasm. Abdomen and buttock muscles may contract, hands and feet clench, faces contort. Although these sensations may be extremely pleasurable, we're more likely to grimace than smile when we orgasm.

The fourth phase Masters and Johnson identified is *resolution*—that is, a subsiding of muscle tensions and release of blood from congested vessels. Return to an unstimulated, deeply relaxed state may happen faster for the male than for the female, who may still be somewhat aroused half an hour after orgasm. Whereas some women can be stimulated to further orgasms at this point, Masters and Johnson wrote that men typically need a breather before they start up again. They labeled this interval during which further stimulation may lead nowhere the *refractory period.*

Other Descriptions of the Elusive Orgasm

Sexual excitement and orgasm can be described from several points of view other than that of Masters and Johnson.

The Language of Sex

*O*rgasm can be used as a verb as well as a noun. Most people in our culture speak of "achieving orgasm" instead. But to do so clearly sets up orgasm as a performance goal for sexmaking, rather than a delightful thing our bodies happen to do sometimes. We don't speak of "achieving urination." We just urinate. Similarly, we just orgasm.

Mental Orgasm.   For one thing, it's possible to see orgasm as something that develops in our thoughts, not just in our genitals. Carmen Kerr points out that as physical sensations and tensions increase:

The mind gets a little fuzzy, devil-may-care spacey. Either quite suddenly or very gradually this tension ends, to be replaced by a feeling of well-being, relaxation, and satisfaction. If you've had this feeling, you've had an orgasm.   [Kerr 1977, p. 149]*

The clinical focus on measurable genital responses has led us to ignore what's happening in our mind. But our brain plays an extremely important part in sex. We can turn ourselves on with fantasies that we concoct or turn ourselves off with anxieties or subconscious refusal to allow ourselves to orgasm. And once we know what orgasm feels like, we can consciously create it. Some people who have no sensation in their genitals because of spinal cord injuries can even create totally mental orgasms for themselves, just by remembering what an orgasm once felt like and then recreating and intensifying that feeling in their minds.

As Carmen Kerr points out, having an orgasm is not just an automatic genital response. It is "an aggressive, assertive, conscious decision. . . . That decision is what carries you over the edge from excitement to orgasm. It's not magic—it's you!" (Kerr 1977, p. 149).

Individual Variations.   Even in physiological terms it's possible to describe orgasm differently than Masters and Johnson did. Sex researchers and therapists William Hartman and Marilyn Fithian (1979) have found that not everyone follows the pattern Masters and Johnson described. Hartman and Fithian consider sexual responses highly individual, like fingerprints. Hartman says he can look at an orgasm chart and tell whose it is by its pattern. The research that he and Fithian are doing at their Center for Marital and Sexual Studies in Long Beach, California, indicates that there are at least four general patterns, with many individual variations. They find that some people orgasm as

*From *Sex for Women Who Want to Have Fun and Loving Relationships with Equals,* by Carmen Kerr. Copyright © 1977 by Carmen Kerr. This and all other quotations from this source are reprinted by permission of the publisher, Grove Press, Inc.

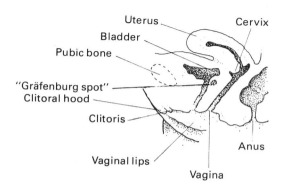

Uterus
Cervix
Bladder
Pubic bone
"Gräfenburg spot"
Clitoral hood
Clitoris
Vaginal lips
Vagina
Anus

Unaroused State

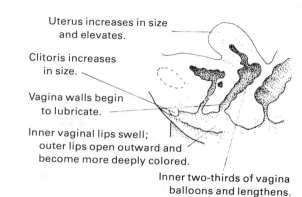

Uterus increases in size and elevates.

Clitoris increases in size.

Vagina walls begin to lubricate.

Inner vaginal lips swell; outer lips open outward and become more deeply colored.

Inner two-thirds of vagina balloons and lengthens.

Excitement Phase

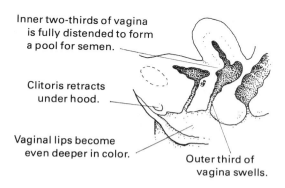

Inner two-thirds of vagina is fully distended to form a pool for semen.

Clitoris retracts under hood.

Vaginal lips become even deeper in color.

Outer third of vagina swells.

Plateau Phase

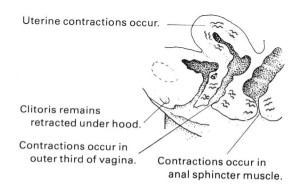

Uterine contractions occur.

Clitoris remains retracted under hood.

Contractions occur in outer third of vagina.

Contractions occur in anal sphincter muscle.

Orgasm Phase

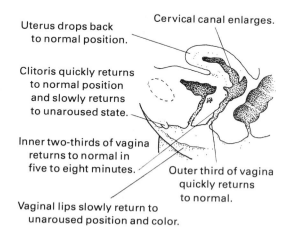

Cervical canal enlarges.

Uterus drops back to normal position.

Clitoris quickly returns to normal position and slowly returns to unaroused state.

Inner two-thirds of vagina returns to normal in five to eight minutes.

Outer third of vagina quickly returns to normal.

Vaginal lips slowly return to unaroused position and color.

Resolution Phase

Breast Changes

Unaroused State

Excitement State
Breast size increases; nipples become erect; veins become more visible.

Plateau and Orgasm Phase
Breast size increases more; areola increases in size (making nipples appear less erect); skin color may become flushed from vasocongestion.

Figure 2-11. Physical Changes in Female during Sexual Response Cycle. The sequence of events shown here is based largely on generalizations from Masters and Johnson's research. Individuals vary considerably, and some women may experience "upper" orgasms involving contractions of deeper muscles than those surrounding the outer part of the vagina. Some researchers feel that such orgasms may be triggered by stimulation of the Gräfenburg spot, which seems to swell when deeply stroked. What this area looks like—in unaroused and aroused states—is not yet known.

they're approaching the peak of heartbeat and breathing, some as they hit the peak, some on the way down. And some orgasms are so gradual that the researchers can't tell when they start, although it's obvious when they end.

Laboratory research using an anal probe to measure anal contractions in men (Bohlen, Held, and Sanderson 1980) has verified that each male has his own orgasmic pattern. Three general types have been found: regular contractions in a short, simple series; a series of regular contractions, followed by numerous irregular contractions; and a series of preliminary contractions, followed by a series of regular contractions. Furthermore, the male orgasm need not end in a turned-off refractory period. Some men have learned how to orgasm again and again, experiencing multiple orgasms with the same erection. Others can keep their erection after they ejaculate and continue to enjoy sex for a while before the erection subsides. There's even some evidence that males can learn to consciously control their erections, long assumed to be totally involuntary responses. Wilhelm Reich (1968) insisted long ago that males might ejaculate without experiencing orgasm, which he defined as a total release of psychological and physiological energies. This distinction has been largely overlooked because of the prevailing cultural notion that orgasm is simple and inevitable in the male. Most attention has been focused on the female orgasm, with the notion that it is the "different" experience to be analyzed and explained.

As for the elusive female orgasm, Hartman and Fithian have found that a number of women who think they're not orgasmic actually are. One thought that orgasm meant shaking, seeing lights, and feeling violent contractions in her uterus and vagina. These reactions, it turned out, were part of her *sister's* pattern (Easton 1977).

Barbara Erickson (1977) has found that lengthy and intense stimulation of the clitoris plus erotic fantasies lead to orgasm for 93 percent of the 108 women she has studied. But the cultural goal is orgasm during intercourse for both partners. Estimates of how many women are orgasmic with intercourse range from 70 percent down to only 25 percent (Tavris and Sadd 1977). These disparities can probably be accounted for partly by differing definitions of orgasm and partly by how the woman is being stimulated. Masters and Johnson had strict physiological standards for what constitutes orgasm. On their charts if peaks of physical response weren't different enough from what came before and after, it wasn't orgasm (Ayres 1979). This standard may have been a valid distinction for research purposes, but it may mislead a lot of women into thinking that what they experience cannot be defined as orgasm.

The "Vaginal Orgasm" Controversy.   The matter of vaginal contractions is especially troublesome. According to Masters and Johnson, if there are no contractions, it's not orgasm. But many women have noticed that with intercourse they experience a peak of sexual tension followed by total relaxation, without any sensation of involuntary contractions in their vaginal area. Some therapists think that such women are having vaginal contractions but just aren't aware of them because muscles all over their bodies are contracted (Kerr 1977; Ayres 1979). Others think there may be something different going on. For instance, many women surveyed by Shere Hite (1976) note a subjective difference between orgasms with a penis inside and those without a penis—from masturbation or oral sex, for instance. In general they experience the intercourse orgasms as more "diffuse" and whole-body-involving, the nonintercourse ones as more "intense" and "localized." Some find the former more satisfying, some the latter.

According to Masters and Johnson, all female orgasms are triggered by rubbing of the clitoris and are expressed as contractions in the vagina, uterus, and anus. If a woman orgasms during intercourse, they speculated, it is probably either from direct rubbing against her clitoris or indirect traction on the clitoral hood as the penis moves the vaginal lips attached to it (Masters and Johnson 1966). But Hite suggested that indirect traction is as ineffective as pulling our ear back and forth in order to move the skin on our cheek. She insisted that most women need direct clitoral stimulation to orgasm. Each respondent who could orgasm with intercourse said she did so by gently grinding the mons area against her partner's pubic bone, or by positioning herself so that his penis lay against her clitoris and barely or seldom entered her vagina, or by using hand stimulation of her clitoris during intercourse, or by getting to the brink of orgasm before beginning intercourse and climaxing just as intercourse started (Hite 1976).

Josephine and Irving Singer (1972) also threw some ideas into the controversy. They suggested that all this effort to stimulate the clitoris might be unnecessary and might detract from emotional intimacy for some couples. They think that many women easily orgasm in a different way during intercourse and find it extremely pleasurable without being aware that what they're experiencing can be labeled "orgasm." Once identified, these sensations can be consciously amplified.

The Singers suggest that there are three general kinds of orgasm. The first they call *vulval orgasm.* It is characterized by involuntary, rhythmic contractions in the genital area and can be experienced during either intercourse or stroking of the clitoris. This kind of orgasm seems to be the one that Masters and Johnson described. The second is a possibility mentioned by a few researchers outside the Masters and Johnson tradition. The Singers call it *uterine orgasm,* which may be a misnomer because some women who've had their uteruses surgically removed have the same sensations. An alternative label: *upper orgasm.* Instead of involuntary vaginal contractions, the Singers say, the "upper" orgasm is characterized by breathing changes: tension in the diaphragm, which lies above the abdomen; a few strangling gasps, leading to involuntary breath holding because of a strong contraction in the muscle at the back of the throat; and then explosive exhalation. This pattern seems to be triggered not by the slow, gentle thrusting that Masters and Johnson (1970) recommend, but by deep, accelerating, but relatively brief thrusting in which the penis contacts the cervix, jostling the uterus and perhaps the pleasure-sensitive lining of the abdominal cavity (which we can also feel when a car swoops over a bump or an elevator drops quickly). This kind of orgasm usually occurs only with intercourse, and it may bring the woman great sexual and emotional pleasure, followed by total relaxation. But for reasons we don't yet understand, some women find deep penetration painful and are afraid of it. Some possible causes for this pain are displacement, infection, or tumors of the uterus; ovary problems; infections of the cervix; or injury to the vagina from childbirth or operations. Many of these conditions can—and should—be treated by health care professionals.

The third kind of orgasm identified by the Singers is what they call *blended orgasm:* a mixture of the first two. It occurs during intercourse and is characterized by both interrupted breathing and a sensation of contractions in the vagina. These contractions may be experienced subjectively as "deeper" than those of the "vulval" orgasm. This third kind of orgasm seems to result from thrusting that begins slowly and then works up to a strong and deep climax. Women report that like "upper" orgasms, "blended" orgasms are both emotionally and physically satisfying, leaving women feeling "loving" and satiated. The "vulval" orgasm, on the other hand, may sometimes leave a woman hungry for more, no matter how often she climaxes. The Singers speculate that this reaction may be the basis for Mary Jane Sherfey's (1972) claim that women are inherently insatiable. They conclude that different kinds of orgasm may bring different kinds of satisfaction. "None of them," they write, "is necessarily preferable to any other" (Singer and Singer 1972).

The Singers' ideas may be supported by findings that there are two distinct major nerves serving the female genital area. One (the pudendal nerve) serves the outer region—clitoris, lips, and outer third of the vagina, including the PC (pubococcygeus) muscle. The deeper areas—the inner two-thirds of the vagina, bladder, uterus, and nearby supporting muscles—are served by the pelvic nerve. It's possible that the Singers' three types of orgasm are actually points along a continuum. "Vulval" orgasm might be an extreme that involves only the pudendal nerve; "upper," an extreme that involves only the pelvic nerve; and "blended," various degrees of involvement of both sets of nerves (Perry 1979, 1980; Perry and Whipple 1980).

The "Gräfenburg Spot" and Female "Ejaculation." In addition, intriguing new research by John Perry and Beverly Whipple (1981) suggests that the "Gräfenburg spot" beyond the vaginal wall may trigger upper orgasms when it's stimulated. Using a special electronic detection device attached to the cervix during intercourse, these researchers have found that some women experience intense upper orgasms without substantial contractions of the PC

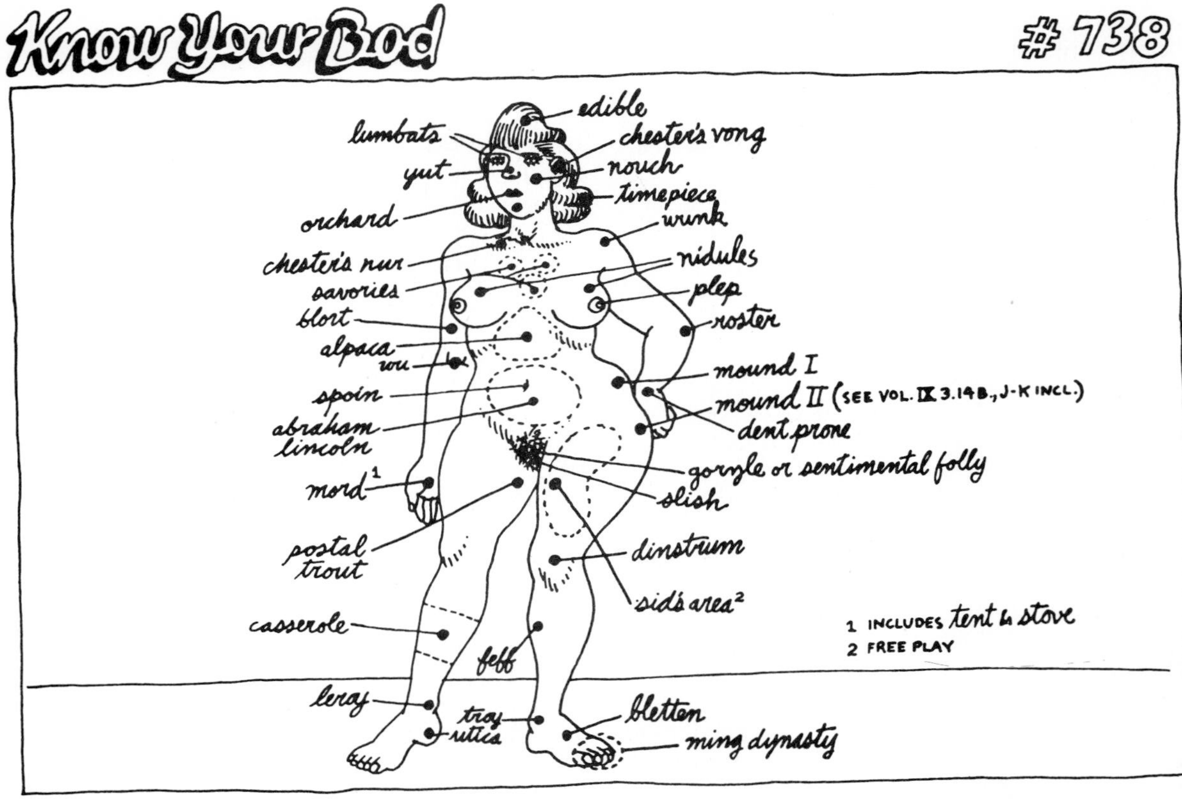

Know Your Bod   # 738

A diagram of a female figure with humorous labels:

edible
chester's vong
lumbats
yut
nouch
orchard
timepiece
wrunk
chester's nun
nidules
savories
plep
blort
roster
alpaca
vou
lex
mound I
spoin
mound II (SEE VOL. IX 3.14B, J-K INCL.)
abraham lincoln
dent prone
mord[1]
gornyle or sentimental folly
slish
postal trout
dinstrum
sids area[2]
casserole
1 INCLUDES tent & stove
2 FREE PLAY
leray
feff
troy rutica
bletten
ming dynasty

muscle surrounding the vagina. The researchers link these orgasms to stimulation of the Gräfenburg spot, which seems to be especially sensitive to sexual contact. Examinations of over 400 women showed that every one was unusually sensitive in this area. Although the strength of their responses varied considerably, in general the sensitivity of the Gräfenburg spot seemed to differ as much from that of other areas of the vagina as the clitoris differs in sensitivity from areas surrounding it.

When doctors can locate and press on the spot, women who've never been contacted in this area before at first interpret the sensation as a need to urinate. The spot lies close to the bladder, and the sensations may be confused because women are not accustomed to making fine spatial distinctions in this part of their body. They may be frightened by the feeling until they recognize that it's not a urinary sensation but, rather, a pleasurable sexual sensation (Perry 1980).

Far from avoiding such contact, women who've long known that they can orgasm during intercourse without any clitoral stimulation may do so by bracing themselves and thrusting against their partners to increase the depth of penetration. This apparently forces the penis against the Gräfenburg spot far within. The result may sometimes be almost immediate—exciting upper orgasms and perhaps even "ejaculation" of fluid from the urethra (Ladas, Whipple, and Perry 1982). Because this "ejaculated" fluid chemically resembles the secretions of the male prostate gland rather than urine, Whipple and Perry speculate that the Gräfenburg spot is the female homologue of the male prostate. Some sex researchers deny the existence of either the Gräfenburg spot or female ejaculation and claim that if any fluid does come out of the woman's urethra during orgasm, it is probably urine (Wolfe 1982). However, researchers using immunological techniques have de-

The Uniqueness of Human Female Sexuality: A Sociobiological View

The human female has the most dramatic and intense orgasm of any species. There may be a few primate species whose females experience orgasm, but their orgasms are pale and infrequent compared with a female human's (Symonds 1979). Also, in human females alone is the fertile ovulatory period of the menstrual cycle "concealed." Usually there are no overt body changes that signal either the woman or the man that the woman is in her fertile period. In other animals coitus tends to be confined to these ovulatory periods, when changes in the female's body signal and excite the male. In gorillas, for instance, coitus takes place only two or three times per year, during the female's infrequent ovulatory periods. This pattern is quite sufficient to ensure conception. In humans, by contrast, conception is relatively difficult. A couple must have intercourse repeatedly over an extended period to make conception likely. In humans sexual behavior occurs often and rather uniformly over the menstrual cycle and can be intensely pleasurable to both parties. The human female is the most sexually potent and active female of any species on earth.

Sociobiologists figure that an evolutionary story must lie behind all of this. That the unique facets of human sexuality have developed accidentally, as a by-product of something else, is just not plausible. To conceal ovulation and make conception difficult is such a counterindicated evolutionary strategy that it would not have occurred without a compelling, overriding evolutionary reason. The unanswerable question lies in the fact that any number of plausible evolutionary scenarios can be constructed to explain the facts; at present there is no way to choose a favored scenario. As sociobiologists continue to study primate behavior in the field, to learn more about the ecology of primitive humans, and to understand better the universals of human sexuality, gradually they will be able to construct the most plausible answer. For now it is not too speculative to say that human sexuality serves different evolutionary purposes from the sexuality of other animals and that those unique human purposes probably have to do with pleasure, emotional bonding, and family.

tected prostate glands surrounding the female urethra ("G Spot/Female Ejaculation . . ." 1983).

Despite such controversies research may revolutionize our understanding of female orgasms and perhaps free many women to enjoy sex more. At the same time, if each woman's pattern is a little different, it is also helpful for each woman to be sensitive to her own responses and to share what she learns about herself with her partner.

HORMONAL EFFECTS ON SEXUAL PROCESSES

Sexual processes are controlled to a certain extent by *hormones*—chemical secretions that move directly from ductless glands into the bloodstream to act on certain target organs. The sex hormones are secreted largely by the testes in males and the ovaries in females; the adrenal glands also contribute. Sex hormones regulate our reproductive processes and may have some bearing on our "sex drive."

Basic Hormonal Patterns

Secretion of sex hormones is regulated by the *hypothalamus*, located in the brain. The hypothalamus releases *gonadotropin-releasing factors* that in turn relay a chemical message to the *pituitary gland* to secrete *luteinizing hormone* (LH) and *follicle-stimulating hormone* (FSH). LH triggers ovulation (release of an egg from an ovary) and development of the corpus luteum (the progesterone-producing remains of the ovarian follicle left after an egg has been released) in the female ovaries, as well as production of androgens in the male testes. FSH stimulates development in females of an egg-bearing ovarian follicle and production of estrogens in the ovaries; in males it triggers sperm cell development in the testes. The resulting levels of androgens, estrogens, and progesterone circulating in the bloodstream signal the hypothalamus to lower the levels of gonadotropin-releasing factor until the hormones drop below a certain level, at which time more gonadotropin-releasing factor is sereted. This *negative feedback system* keeps hormone production within bounds.

Men's Patterns.   In males LH is released in pulses, with levels rising several times every six hours; testosterone levels are more constant but seem to be highest in the morning and lowest in the evening in young boys, an effect that levels off in older men. In addition cycles of eight to thirty days have been noted in the testosterone levels of many men, an effect that might possibly contribute to variations in sex drive (Williams 1981).

Women's Menstrual Cycles.   Compared with males, females' sex hormone levels fluctuate more dramatically. These changing levels, with concomitant stages in monthly preparation for pregnancy, are known as the *menstrual cycle.*

From puberty until menopause somewhere between the ages of forty and fifty-five, a woman's body prepares for possible pregnancy 300 to 500 times. These menstrual cycles last an average of twenty-eight days. The cycle length varies in each woman and from one woman to another, from as few as twenty days to as many as forty. In athletes undergoing intense training, the cycles may be irregular, lacking ovulation or menstruation, or delayed in onset, though these effects are neither universal nor clearly understood (Baker 1981; Baker et al. 1981; Bonen et al. 1981; "The Joy of Running . . . " 1980).

Each menstrual cycle prepares an egg, or eggs, for fertilization by a male's sperm cell. If fertilization does not occur during any given month, the preparations are cancelled and then begun again. A cycle has no beginning or end, but the common practice is to call the first day of menstrual bleeding day one of a twenty-eight-day cycle.

The Menstrual Phase.   On "day one" the *menstrual phase* of the cycle begins—if the woman has not become pregnant that month. For an average of four to five days the uterus sloughs off, through the vagina, the lining that had been prepared to receive a fertilized egg. When fertilization has not taken place, the tissue that lines the uterus (the *endometrium*) releases four to sixteen tablespoons of blood, cells from the endometrium, and uterine mucus. A greater flow of menstrual fluids may signify some physical problem.

Sometimes women find menstruation uncomfortable—accompanied by cramps, nausea, headaches, and pelvic pain or a feeling of heaviness. Extremely painful or difficult menstruation is called *dysmenorrhea.* Cramps occur when the uterus contracts too hard and fast, constricting blood circulation and causing pain; the suspected cause is an overabundance of *prostaglandins.* These powerful chemicals have many important functions, such as regulating blood pressure, reproduction, and blood clotting. Those produced by the uterus trigger the contractions that are needed for menstruation and childbirth. But when produced in excess, prostaglandins may cause cramping of the uterine muscle and other discomforts. For women who find dysmenorrhea severely debilitating, drugs that inhibit prostaglandin production often provide significant relief. Although less effective, oral contraceptive pills may relieve cramps and reduce the volume of menstrual bleeding. Orgasm from self-pleasuring or two-person sex may relieve menstrual cramps, too. Although some couples prefer to avoid intercourse during the female's menstrual periods, it does no known medical harm.

The Estrogen Phase.   After the menstrual phase only a thin layer of endometrial cells is left in the uterus. As this lining again begins to grow, or *proliferate,* during the *estrogen* (or *proliferative*) *phase,* a new egg is prepared in one of the two *ovaries.* When a female is born, these small oval organs together house 300,000 to 400,000 tiny, round egg-bearing *follicles.* After the female starts menstruating, a number of these follicles will cooperate each month to prepare a single egg for fertilization.

As the menstrual phase ends, decreased levels of estrogen from the ovaries alert the hypothalamus to release a chemical that in turn triggers release of follicle-stimulating hormone (FSH) from the pituitary gland. This hormone makes ten to

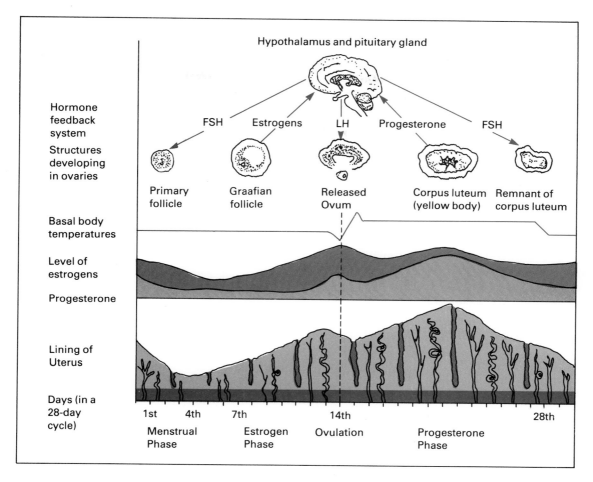

Hypothalamus and pituitary gland

Hormone feedback system

FSH   Estrogens   LH   Progesterone   FSH

Structures developing in ovaries

Primary follicle   Graafian follicle   Released Ovum   Corpus luteum (yellow body)   Remnant of corpus luteum

Basal body temperatures

Level of estrogens

Progesterone

Lining of Uterus

Days (in a 28-day cycle)

1st   4th   7th   14th   28th

Menstrual Phase   Estrogen Phase   Ovulation   Progesterone Phase

Figure 2-12. Hormone-Regulated Changes during the Menstrual Cycle. In a complex feedback system the hypothalamus and pituitary gland both create and respond to changing levels of estrogen and progesterone in the bloodstream by raising and lowering FSH and LH secretions. In the ovaries FSH from the pituitary stimulates growth of follicles, which in turn secrete estrogen. When the estrogen level in the bloodstream therefore rises, the hypothalamus signals the pituitary to send out more LH. This hormone causes the follicle to rupture, turn into a "yellow body," and secrete progesterone. As the estrogen level drops, FSH secretion is raised again and the cycle starts over.

twenty of the follicles in the ovaries start growing. As they grow, they secrete estrogen, which signals the lining of the uterus to proliferate. Most of the follicles then begin to degenerate; usually only one continues growing to become a mature *Graafian follicle.*

Estrogen from the follicles also circles back in the bloodstream to the brain, stimulating the hypothalamus to signal the pituitary to send out more luteinizing hormone (LH), named for the yellow pigment "lutein." This increment causes the Graafian follicle to rupture, releasing the egg through the wall of the ovary 13 to 15 days before the next menstrual period. This event is *ovulation.* Some women know when ovulation happens, for they can feel it as a cramp on one side of their

lower abdomen or their lower back or they may see a slight discharge—perhaps bloody—from their vagina. Those who are familiar with what their cervix normally looks like may be able to see with a speculum and mirror that the cervical mucus is thinner and stretchier than usual.

The Progesterone Phase.   The third set of events in the menstrual cycle is known as the *progesterone (or secretory) phase.* After it releases the egg, the ruptured follicle is called a *corpus luteum,* or "yellow body." From inside the ovary, this yellow, fat-filled follicle produces progesterone that signals the hypothalamus and pituitary to lower production of FSH and LH. Progesterone also helps to nourish the fallopian tubes and uterus for maintenance of a pregnancy.

Once the egg leaves the ovary, it is drawn into the nearest fallopian tube. If enough sperm cells from a male are waiting in the upper fallopian tube or appear while the egg is viable (usually for about twelve to twenty-four hours after ovulation), conception could take place. Fertilized or not, the egg gradually moves toward the uterus through the fallopian tube, a short but slow journey that takes three to seven days. Should the egg not be fertilized, it gradually disintegrates. The corpus luteum also becomes inactive, and estrogen and progesterone levels drop rapidly. This change signals the hypothalamus to signal the pituitary to start the cycle again, with release of the built-up uterine lining.

Premenstrual Syndrome.   During the days just before the menstrual phase begins, many women experience what is now called *premenstrual syndrome* (PMS). Their breasts and abdomen may become tender and swollen; their faces may break out with acne; they may have migraine headaches; they may be bloated with retained water; and they may feel irritable, tired, or depressed. In severe cases they may be accident-prone, violent, or suicidal. As one woman who considered her premenstrual symptoms "not severe enough to bother seeking medical help" described her body's response:

I feel so brittle before my periods—it's like if there's one little flick, I'm going to crack. I'm less able to cope with stress, since I'm already down. I get clumsier—if I'm going to break things, it will be right then. The main thing I feel is anger, and it is so incredibly not all in my head. It's like this foreign element taking over my personality. I feel cross for no reason at all, and it's nothing I can control. As soon as my period starts, it's like a weight has lifted.   [from the authors' files]

Many women find that their relationships with others temporarily deteriorate. The changes of PMS have been blamed for marital strife, child abuse, and criminal behaviors, and are sometimes claimed as legal defense for uncharacteristically violent actions. An estimated 70 to 90 percent of all menstruating women have recurring premenstrual problems of some degree; 20 to 40 percent say they are temporarily mentally or physically incapacitated by PMS (Reid and Yen 1981).

No one yet knows for sure what causes these symptoms. Causes may include a decreased level of progesterone, an insufficient amount of the brain chemicals that trigger release of hormones from the pituitary gland, a vitamin deficiency, an underactive thyroid gland, ovarian cysts, stress, or an expectation of feeling bad during this time.

Working from the premise that PMS is a health problem that deserves medical attention, a special Premenstrual Syndrome Program has been set up in Reading, Massachusetts. Treatment may include dietary changes, vitamin supplements, biofeedback, hypnosis, counseling, diuretics to curb water retention, advice to cut back on caffeine, sugar, alcohol, and salt, and perhaps progesterone supplementation (Henig 1982).

Some feminists are expressing concern over the attention given to PMS and dysmenorrhea. They fear that publicizing the fact that some women are debilitated by these problems for several days each month may fuel sexist arguments that women are biologically unfit for important work. On this issue it should be noted that while rates of crime, accidents, and suicide are highest for women during the premenstrual days, these rates are nevertheless lower than those found in men (Reid and Yen 1981).

On the other hand medical aid that does not consider a woman's symptoms "all in her head" has been welcomed by women who previously suffered severe menstrual problems. And as the social taboo on talking about menstruation is being lifted, some women are learning to define their monthly changes in more positive terms. A majority of college women find menstruation somewhat bothersome but not disruptive (Brooks-Gunn and Ruble 1980). Some women recognize menstruation as the time when they feel most psychically open, powerful, and creative (Henig 1982).

Hormones and "Sex Drive"

Sexual arousal and orgasm develop in response to a variety of physical and psychic stimuli. But the responses of different people to the same stimuli, or of the same person to the same stimuli at different times, vary considerably. We may be tremendously turned on by a certain song or scent or touch at one time but feel "nothing" at another time.

This is so because our thresholds for responding to physical or psychic stimuli seem to depend on many variables. Some are culturally influenced: Breasts and biceps are given greater turn-on value in some cultures than in others. Some variables are individual experiences that cause us to associate memories of shame, anxiety, rejection, or joy with sex. Some are feelings of the moment: our delight or disgust with the other person, our preoccupation with nonsexual matters. And some variables seem to be biologically determined. If we are rested, relaxed, feeling well, and have high androgen levels, we tend to turn on readily. If we are tired, hungry, depressed, or taking certain drugs, it will be harder for our bodies to be sexually aroused (Lief 1981). Of this list the hormonal effects on sexual responsiveness have received particular attention from researchers.

Androgen levels may be one of the biological factors in the complex interplay of biology, individual experience, and social learning that we call "sex drive." Experiments with animals and humans show that injections of minute amounts of testosterone increase a male's interest in sex. Injections of estrogen, on the other hand, inhibit androgen production and decrease sexual desire (Money and Ehrhardt 1972). In men who have been injected with the gonadotropin-releasing factor that triggers LH production, and therefore androgen production, erections develop somewhat faster, larger, and longer than usual (Evans and Distiller 1979).

Androgen seems to have something to do with female sexual responsiveness, too. When female rhesus monkeys are injected with testosterone, they are more likely to present themselves sexually to males (Money and Ehrhardt 1972). In a study of the hormone levels and sexual behaviors of 11 human couples, women who had experienced the greatest sexual satisfaction were those whose average androgen levels were relatively high (Persky et al. 1978). Particularly during the luteal phase of their menstrual cycles, women with high levels of testosterone have higher levels of sexual arousal and vasocongestion in response to erotic stimuli than do women with low testosterone levels (Schreiner-Engel et al. 1981). Interestingly, although women have lower blood levels of testosterone than do men, women have significantly more than men of another androgen in their blood. This is *androstenedione* (an androgen made of the combined secretions of the adrenals and the gonads), which has been shown to have equal or greater effects than testosterone on sexual behavior in animals (Purifoy, Koopmans, and Mayes 1981; Williams 1981).

Although some studies show no significant monthly patterns in female sexual interests (Schreiner-Engel et al. 1981), many studies do indicate that women's sexuality changes somewhat with their menstrual cycle. Changing levels of estrogen and progesterone—as well as of androgen—may therefore be involved in women's sexual desire. Two peaks in desire have been noted—one at ovulation (when androgen and estrogen seem to reach their highest levels) and one right before and during menstruation. This second peak in desire occurs as estrogen and progesterone levels seem to be dropping, while androgen levels remain more constant (Speroff, Glass, and Kose 1978). Another way of relating women's sexual desire to their hormone levels is to study the frequency of intercourse throughout the menstrual cycle. Intercourse is most frequent at ovulation, in midcycle (Udry and Morris 1968). This relationship is true even when only female-initiated sex is measured, except for women who use birth control pills, which artificially control their hormone levels (Adams, Gold, and Burt 1978). However, women say they feel the most sexually aroused near the time of menstruation and are most likely to masturbate then (Kinsey et al. 1953). A second peak in intercourse frequency occurs on the night after menstruation ends, an effect that may be more a reaction to doing without intercourse than to hormone levels (Gold and Adams 1981).

Hormonal effects are obscured by social influence. For example, intercourse frequency may be held down during menstruation by a learned taboo against "unclean" menstrual blood. Even though women often feel especially "horny" during their periods and may masturbate to relieve their sexual tensions, both they and their partners may feel squeamish about two-person sex at this time—or they simply may not feel well enough to share sex. How much of what we call "sex drive" is based on hormones is therefore unclear. A welcoming attitude toward sexual pleasure is usually essential for arousal. As we'll see throughout this book, such an attitude may be encouraged or discouraged by a great variety of social and personal influences.

Some studies suggest that our hormone levels may even reflect our behavior patterns, rather than vice versa. For instance, women who enjoy sex regularly have more stable menstrual cycles than women with sporadic, less frequent sexual activity (Cutler, Garcia, and Krieger 1980). Biology and social learning and activity are so closely intertwined that often it's hard to distinguish cause from effect.

SUMMARY

Understanding our sexual biology is one aspect of understanding our sexuality. As females and males we are initially similar as embryos, and these similarities in anatomy and physiology persist throughout our lives. The factor thought to cause the differences in our developmental patterns is androgen, a group of hormones that have a "masculinizing" effect during fetal development and again at puberty as boys develop secondary sex characteristics. Estrogens have "feminizing" effects on females at puberty.

The female's breasts, inner and outer vaginal lips, clitoris, vagina, and uterus all respond to erotic stimuli, though the degree to which the vagina and structures behind it are sexually sensitive is variable and controversial. Males' most visible sexual organs are the penis and scrotum, backed up by a network of organs providing fluids that combine with sperm to form semen. In both sexes the erectile tissues, muscular structures, and nerve pathways involved with these organs are critical to sexual response, though scientific understanding of their anatomy and physiology is still limited. They seem to respond to erotic stimuli by a process that can be divided into five stages: desire, excitement, plateau, orgasm, and resolution. We each have our own way of experiencing this cycle, and our patterns may change with experience and learning.

Our reproductive readiness—and therefore our potential for enjoying sex—is partially regulated by our sex hormones. The complex feedback system involves the hypothalamus, pituitary gland, and gonads (ovaries and testes) in producing estrogens, progesterone, and androgens, among other hormones. In males hormone levels are relatively constant; in females they change regularly to create the menstrual cycle. Attention recently has been focused on two aspects of the menstrual cycle that some women have found difficult: premenstrual syndrome and dysmenorrhea. Attempts to find relationships between hormone levels and sex drive suggest that people with high androgen levels are more likely to feel "sexy." However, links between such biological factors and our social behaviors are often unclear, for what we do is heavily influenced by what we have learned as social, thinking beings.

3

Turning On

The first thing that turns me on is the physical appearance of a man. I go for tall, well-built, and attractive men. The smile is very important.

The second thing is the way the man speaks. If he is well spoken and intelligent, I am definitely intrigued. After that it is his personality. I like a man to be sensitive and kind to everyone. I like a man with patience.

In a sexual way I like a man to be again, patient and sensitive. Turn-ons are a quiet and softly lit room, well decorated with a nice big bed. I like classical music and a clean smell. I also like pillows all over, and a plush carpet.

I like to be hugged and touched all over before actual sexual intercourse. Afterward, I like to relax, have a glass of wine, and fall asleep in my lover's arms.

What turns me on? Hah! I wish I knew! Because of losing a great deal of weight (80 pounds), I'm only just beginning to go through what others went through at sixteen. Let me tell you, puberty at twenty-one is no fun! The limited things and experience that I know turn me on are related to the one semirelationship I've had, and the one fling I've had. I believe you begin to realize what turns you on only after you've experienced different situations.

There is no set "thing" or "action" that arouses me; rather, it is a series of them. The most basic form of sexual arousal for me is when my boyfriend/lover is holding my hand. While doing this, he caresses my hand—with his thumb in a circular motion.

My current lover knows what I enjoy. I love to be scratched (not too hard but enough to leave a mark) down my back and over my stomach, breasts, and inner legs. He also knows my fetish for being bitten. Sound crazy? Not really. The best places for being bitten are my entire neck/chest area, my back, and especially near the undersides of my ear.

Any hand manipulation of my breast I find <u>extremely</u> arousing (pinching my nipples, arousing them to where they become pointed and hard). Even more, I like the feel of his tongue on my breasts, stomach, and thighs.

The most arousing thing for me is when my wife comes on to me directly—when she initiates sex. In lots of ways she lets me know what she wants but still gives me a choice. Then her excitement as she gets more and more into it really turns me on!

Each of these people has identified some preference for what turns them on. Turning on is a complex process with many exciting variations. The scent of musk is exciting for some. Others are aroused by well-defined muscles, gapped teeth, gentle caresses, fantasies of sexually enthusiastic partners, tender ballads, or direct sexual overtures. The nature and strength of our arousal is determined in part by our sexual identity. But which specific cues turn us on involves many additional factors, some of which we'll explore in this chapter.

AROUSAL AND THE BRAIN

Sexual arousal is orchestrated between our ears, making our brain our most important sexual organ. The brain is the center from which all sexual thoughts and actions begin. Although physiologists measure sexual arousal in terms of quantifiable genital responses—penis erection in males, lubrication and swelling in the vaginal area in females—these reactions are the result of a complex interplay of conscious and unconscious processes that are organized in the brain. Its control centers receive inputs from sensory receptors—eyes, ears, nose, tongue, skin, and perhaps other nerve and chemical receptors within the body—and combine them with memories, associations, emotions, and conscious thoughts, from fears to fantasies. Once this information is processed, the control centers apparently send out chemically transmitted messages that either stimulate or inhibit the sensations and changes that we perceive as sexual excitement.

Certain areas of the brain are thought to be especially important in the arousal process. The area most often linked with sensations of sexual pleasure is the *limbic system,* a name sometimes given to a collection of structures that lie deeply buried in an old, rather "primitive" part of the brain. In humans this area is now covered by the *cerebrum,* the convoluted area that we associate with "higher" conscious-thought processes.

Although it operates at a subconscious level, the limbic system still plays an important part in sexuality. It seems to be a control center for certain

sensory perceptions, "drive"-related behaviors, involuntary body responses (including sexual responses), and the expression of emotions. It can be stimulated not only by sensory inputs but also by memories, associations, and thoughts that carry strong emotions. Researchers have also found that it can be stimulated electrically or chemically to produce sensations of sexual arousal.

When electrodes were experimentally implanted in the limbic systems of rats, these laboratory animals repeatedly chose to push levers to turn on the current until they fell asleep or dropped exhausted. On waking they started pushing the "turn-on" lever again. Offered other levers that they knew would bring food and water, the rats often ignored them, choosing instead to stimulate their "pleasure centers" again and again (Olds 1956).

Humans have shown somewhat more restraint in their responses to such experiments, but stimulation of certain areas of the human limbic system does seem to be linked to sexual arousal. For instance, a man whose septum (part of the limbic system) was stimulated by electrodes reported that he felt sexually aroused, alert, and goodwilled and that he wanted to masturbate. When the same area was monitored during sexmaking, it showed patterns of activity that largely ceased after orgasm (Heath 1972). When pleasure-inducing drugs were applied directly to an area in the limbic system of a woman's brain, she first reported that she felt mildly euphoric and then began thrashing about with multiple orgasms. Another man so stimulated reported that he had never felt such intense pleasure (Jones and Jones 1977).

Our understanding of how the human brain works is still too limited for us to make direct connections between our complex experiences and how our brain perceives and acts on them. There is a large element of conscious choice involved—if we choose to feel turned on, we often are. Certain cues from our environment or even from our brain itself also tend to create the sensations we perceive as sexual arousal. These include emotions that predispose us to feeling sexual; certain sights, sounds, smells, tastes, and touches; mood-modifying drugs; erotic materials; and our own fantasies and dreams.

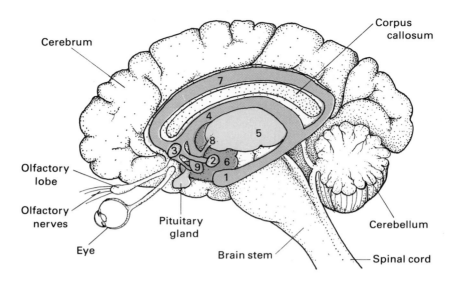

Major structures of the limbic system:

1. Hippocampus	4. Fornix	7. Cingulate gyrus
2. Amygdala	5. Thalamus	8. Mammillothalamic tract
3. Septum	6. Hypothalamus	9. Mammillary body

EMOTIONAL READINESS FOR SEX

Although we're often unaware of the connections, our own emotions predispose us to eroticism—or to avoidance of sexual feelings. Among these are love, fear, rage, and an assortment of other emotions that initially seem to have nothing to do with sex. If we tend to be sensation seekers, we may also tend to be emotionally ready to turn on.

Relabeling Nonsexual Emotions

Many life situations stimulate a feeling of generalized excitement. Interviews for college or jobs, near accidents while driving, anticipation of meals at fine restaurants, the frustration of trying to hammer a nail into solid oak—such events trigger our adrenalin flow and make us feel restless, ready for action. But how we interpret this restlessness and what we do about it depend on our social environment.

In our culture social cues to sexual excitement are everywhere. Ads with sex appeal are used to sell everything from mouthwash to cars. Novels

Figure 3-1. Limbic System of the Brain. Buried deep within the human brain, some parts of the limbic system are thought to organize responses that are perceived by higher parts of the brain as sexual pleasure. Limbic system structures are linked with each other by a network of interconnecting nerve trunks; they also communicate with the rest of the body through the bloodstream and spinal cord and with other parts of the brain by chemically transmitted messages. Many different bits of information may thus be brought to bear on whether we feel sexually aroused in a particular situation. Sometimes sexual response is a set of simple reflex actions that respond to physical stimulation and are coordinated below the level of consciousness. At the opposite extreme sexual arousal can be triggered totally by conscious thought.

and magazines and television shows are full of erotic reminders. Because we're surrounded by sexual cues, many of our emotional stages lead to sexual responses, especially if a partner who satisfies our learned notions of "sexy" is present. This may be a loved partner, an attractive person, or, for some of us, just about anything that moves!

Many kinds of excitement are commonly translated into sexual desire. When we're exuberantly happy, we may easily shift into sexual enthusiasm if an acceptable partner is on the scene. Even our negative emotions may be reinterpreted as sexual desire. For instance, hatred, jealousy, and pain all have been linked to sexual arousal (Dutton and Aron 1974). Fright can be a turn-on of sorts, too. The Kinsey researchers (1948) found that young boys had erections as a result of everything from being chased by police to having to recite in front of their classes. And psychological experiments have shown that anxiety can create a heightened readiness for sex (Hoon, Wincze, and Hoon 1977; Dutton and Aron 1974).

Even anger may lead to arousal. Psychologist Andrew Barclay (1969) angered University of Minnesota students by exposing them to an insulting assistant. Participants were then shown ambiguous pictures and asked to make up a story about what was going on. The stories invented were far more sexually oriented in the angered group than in a nonangered control group. In addition tests of the angered males' urine showed a marked rise in acid phosphatase, a chemical indicator of sexual arousal.

In trying to explain how strong emotions like anger or anxiety might excite sexual arousal, Dutton and Aron (1974) came up with several suggestions. One is the theory that we may *relabel* strong emotions as sexual arousal if an acceptable sex partner—or a fantasy—is present, so long as the circumstances that have made us emotional do not require our full attention. White, Fishbein, and Rutstein (1981) found that college men misattributed their state of arousal to romantic attraction. Compared with those not emotionally aroused, emotionally aroused men will heighten their interest and critical attention to the attractiveness of a potential dating partner. According to this misattribution theory, when we are aroused by any exciting event, we can without knowing it readily turn that arousal toward another person and relabel it romantic attraction.

Relabeling an emotion with negative social connotations (anger, for instance) into one considered more positive in our culture (such as love) may help us to cope with it. Another possibility is that strong emotions may help us drop our learned inhibitions against expressing sexual feelings. Sequence is critical, though. Studies have shown that if we're made anxious *after* we've already been sexually aroused, our anxiety will *inhibit* our sex-

ual responses: Men will tend to lose their erections, and vaginal blood volume will decrease in women (Hoon, Wincze, and Hoon 1977).

Some emotions are turn-offs at any time. Sex therapist Helen Singer Kaplan (1979) has found that some people's sexual desire and excitement are inhibited by fear of intimacy or fear of romantic success. Fear of intimacy is the inability to trust. It probably results from negative and disappointing experiences with parents, friends, or others. Avoiding intimacy is a way to keep from being hurt or made to feel guilty again. This coping style leads people to avoid being turned on. When a situation becomes too intimate, their sexuality shuts off.

A similar avoidance pattern occurs in people who unconsciously fear success. In childhood they may have been assigned a script in which to succeed or have fun was defined as wrong—often by competitive or sexually repressive parents. If such values are never questioned, pleasure and success may bring feelings of guilt and shame rather than of satisfaction. To avoid these negative self-judgments, when such people near a goal—such as becoming intimate with someone they desire—they sabotage themselves. By irritating their partner, overeating to keep from looking "too sexy," getting anxious, or simply avoiding sex, they ensure that they won't succeed (Kaplan 1979).

Love

For those of us who do not fear intimacy, desire for close emotional and physical contact with someone we love may be a strong pull toward sexual pleasuring. A nursing baby caresses its mother's breast and smiles with "love" and sensual delight. New lovers touch in public as much as their subculture will permit, for their joy in each other and their feeling of togetherness seem to demand physical expression.

Although our society frowns on some forms of affectionate public touching, generally it supports the linking of love and sex. We learn to expect to be sexually aroused by people who excite our romantic passions—and to love people who turn us on. Our expectations don't necessarily reflect reality, however. We may have been primed to think this way by our culture's traditional tendency to base marriage on love and to consider sex okay only for married partners or for those who plan to marry. Ideas of sex and love are thus linked because of their common association with marriage. Traditionally, sex was thought to be an expression of deep love; without love sex was considered a meaningless, vulgar activity. Although many people today have discarded the notion that sex should be reserved for marriage, some people still need to feel love or at least affection in order to be sexually aroused.

Complicating this issue is the fact that what we think of as a single, natural emotion actually takes many forms. As we'll see in Chapter 5, different sets of historical circumstances have shaped numerous versions of what "love" means. These definitions range from a burning desire to possess a partner whose charms and virtues we've idealized to caring so much for someone that the distinction between giving and receiving pleasure is blurred. Despite vast differences in how love is defined, people feel it is a trigger to sexual arousal.

Sensation Seeking

Some of us are motivated to find situations sexually stimulating simply because we have a low tolerance for the absence of stimulation. While some define freedom from stimulation as a positive goal ("inner peace"), others define it as a negative state ("boredom").

To measure this difference in people, psychologist Marvin Zuckerman (1978) devised a test of sensation-seeking levels. Those who score high on this test tend to crave stimulation of all sorts, from hallucinogenic drugs to variety in sex partners. By contrast, low-sensation seekers find such stimuli disturbing or dangerous rather than pleasurable. Seymour Fisher (1973) administered this test to young married women and found that the high-sensation seekers reported more frequent masturbation, intercourse, multiple orgasms, and plentiful vaginal lubrication with intercourse. In fact they turned on so easily that they even became sexually aroused in the course of a lab session that didn't include any erotic touching. Zuckerman notes that for such people sexual arousal is triggered by a desire for *increase* in sensations rather than by a desire for release from tension.

SENSUAL TURN-ONS

Our emotional states may predispose us to being turned on by sensual stimuli. But not everything we sense is defined as erotic. For instance, plenty of things we smell don't turn us on in the least. The scent of condoms is arousing for some who've had great sex with them, but it may do nothing for others. Nudity may be stimulating, but the sight of a nude person who violates our definitions of physical beauty might turn us off rather than on. Many of these distinctions between sexual turn-offs and turn-ons are socially learned, either from cultural shaping or from our unique experiences with others.

Sight

The first sense that comes into play in sexual arousal is typically sight. Recognizing the importance of visual turn-ons, ancient peoples blinded those suspected of sexual crimes. The inability to see the objects of one's desires was apparently considered a fate worse than death (Kirtley 1975).

The Importance of Physical Attractiveness. The value our culture places on looks gives the beautiful some advantage. First impressions tend

The Language of Sex

Many of us tend to use the words *sensual* and *sexual* interchangeably. To do so obscures an important distinction. *Sexual* refers specifically to sexmaking activities. A highly sexual person is one who thinks about or engages in them often. *Sensual* refers to the senses—touch, smell, taste, sound, sight. A highly sensual person is one who is richly responsive to pleasures of the senses—perhaps someone who savors the sound of an English horn, the colors and flavors of fine food, the textures of fur and leather, the heady perfume of tropical flowers, the bubbly warmth of a whirlpool bath. These pleasures do not necessarily include sexual joys, though for many sensual people they do.

Women have not traditionally "checked out" men, but there are indications of women's growing interest in men's sexuality—and men's willingness to display it.

to be based on the assumption that physical beauty correlates with warmth and strength. As we noted in Chapter 1, persons who were asked to describe strangers' personalities just by looking at their pictures asserted confidently that the attractive people would be sexually warmer, more responsive, kind, sensitive, strong, poised, sociable, outgoing, nurturing, and exciting than the more ordinary-looking people (Dion, Berscheid, and Walster 1972). Other experiments show that the attractive are more likely to be chosen as college counselors, to influence an audience, to be given directions when they're lost, to be preferred for jobs and promotions, even to have their lost letters mailed (Cook and McHenry 1978).

Study after study has shown that physical attractiveness is a major factor in our evaluation of potential sex partners. But caution is raised by one recent study showing that attractive females don't necessarily have a clear path to social success (Reis et al. 1982). Unlike attractive males they may have fewer social contacts with the other sex, for a variety of reasons: (1) They are less assertive and no more socially competent than less attractive females (having learned that people will come to them); (2) they have less trust of the other sex; and

(3) less-attractive males are unlikely to seek them out because the males tend to assume they will be turned down.

Situational differences may also be important to the effect of physical attractiveness on sexual arousal. In settings that don't allow other kinds of evaluation, looks are all we have to judge others by. At dances, for instance, music is often so loud that we can't learn anything about others by talking to them. In such public arenas status concerns are foremost anyway—an attractive partner enhances our own status. But in a quieter, more private setting, where communication about each other as interesting personalities can occur, attractiveness loses some of its importance.

In a laboratory study each of 40 male and 40 female psychology students was left in a room sitting face to face with either an extremely unattractive or an extremely attractive person of the other sex. The pretext given for this forced togetherness was that the machinery for a supposed experiment in music listening had broken down. But what researchers Bryant Crouse and Albert Mehrabian

Our bodies come in assorted shapes and sizes. Which ones are considered most beautiful varies from one society to the next.

(1977) were really studying—through hidden microphones and one-way mirrors—was whether the looks of the stranger (actually the experimenters' stooge) would affect the subjects' inclination to talk warmly with her or him. It didn't. However, questionnaires administered afterward revealed that both men and women were more likely to consider *dating* the stranger if she or he was attractive.

Participants were also asked how well they *liked* the stranger. Males who'd been found to be highly empathic—that is, able to sense and care about others' feelings—liked unattractive stooges as well as the attractive ones. By contrast, low-empathy males liked attractive stooges more than unattractive ones. This finding suggests that our own personality may determine whether we use physical attractiveness as the major criterion for turning on or whether we respond to less superficial traits.

Standards for Visual Arousal. Within each society people tend to agree on which individuals are more attractive than others. In the United States, for instance, youthfulness is generally considered more arousing than elderliness. Gross fatness and bad complexions are thought to detract from sex appeal. Height, broad shoulders, strong jaws, and slim hips are valued in men; figures that curve out at breasts and hips and in at the waist are valued in women. But individual preferences for hair length, beards, breast size, buttocks, leg shape, and other specific features vary considerably. After studying 190 societies around the world, anthropologist Clellan Ford and psychologist Frank Beach (1951) concluded that there are almost no universal standards for physical beauty. Cleanliness is one of the few exceptions. Personal filthiness is almost universally considered a turn-off. Some cultures view a clean body as the greatest of all possible turn-ons.

Almost all human groups pay more explicit attention to women's looks than to men's. But definitions of female beauty vary. In many cultures fat women are considered more arousing than thin ones. In some societies a beautiful woman should not only be plump but also tall and strong.

There are also great variations in which parts of the body have the strongest turn-on power. Some people focus on the shape and color of eyes.

For some the ears are more important. Thighs, buttocks, skin color, head and body hair, noses, mouths, and navels all receive special attention somewhere. And in some cultures females stretch the *labia,* or lips of their genital region, to increase their sex appeal, for large labia are considered an arousing sign of heightened sexual responsiveness.

Revealing of Sex-Related Body Parts. Whether or not they're considered beautiful, the genitals often carry strong stimulus value. In some soci-

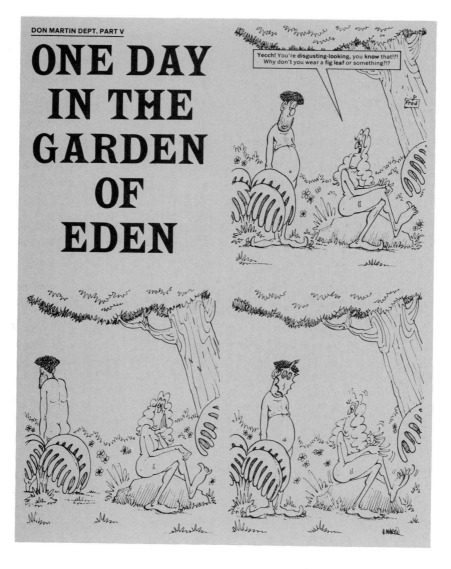

eties women deliberately reveal their genitals to turn on potential sex partners. To avoid giving off this powerful invitation inadvertently, women everywhere are expected to cover their genitals or at least keep their legs together. Men are not subject to the same restriction (Ford and Beach 1951). Often they're encouraged to exaggerate the visual impact of their genitals. For instance, men of fifteenth- and sixteenth-century Europe wore codpieces that reached enormous proportions. And males of some tropical cultures wear long penile shafts—and nothing else—to create the intimidating impression of perpetual massive erection in order to ward off enemies (Eibl-Eibesfeldt 1970).

The physical symptoms of sexual arousal may be exciting to viewers. Facial blushing is often construed—rightly or wrongly—as part of the glowing skin of a sexually aroused person. Contemporary males who place their penises upright in tight underwear beneath close-fitting pants and females whose nipples are revealed by figure-hugging shirts give off a sexually exciting "erect" look. And as we'll see later, the enlarged pupils of an aroused person's eyes can be a strong subliminal turn-on.

Actual baring of parts of the body that have previously been covered may be tremendously exciting at first. But as newcomers to nudist camps soon discover, continued exposure lessens desire. The German magazine *Der Spiegel* reports that as European women are increasingly going topless on beaches, their breasts are losing power as super sex signals to men ("More Bare Breasts . . ." 1978, p. 23).

Ogling. In enjoying the sight of another person, some of us glance at them discreetly, while others stare openly. This ogling can be disturbing to the "oglee" if it's unwanted. For instance, at nude beaches the regulars often resent clothed voyeurs as unfair intruders. Nevertheless, natural body beauty is appreciated among the regulars, and "all nude beachers are into voyeurism themselves" (Douglas, Rasmussen, and Flanagan 1977, p. 113).

A better-known example of ogling is the attention many women receive as they walk past groups of males: overt visual scanning and suggestive remarks. Some women find this attention flattering and amusing; others find it frightening or disgusting.

One woman notes that her reactions tend to vary according to how many men are involved. If one or two men make a "stray comment" as she passes, she is "amused and somewhat flattered." But if she has to pass a group of men lined up at lunchtime to check out passing females, she feels as though she were "running a gauntlet." In this situation she says, "I feel foolish and annoyed. I feel like an unwilling player in or object of someone else's game. The interesting thing here is that I do not feel that I am being appraised sexually, but rather that I am being ridiculed" (O'Connell 1977, p. 63).

Psychiatrist James Mathis (1977) suggests that men's participation in this group behavior is a form of exhibitionism. He notes that many ways of calling attention to oneself are considered normal in our society—gaudy cars, flamboyant clothes, public appearances. A form of male exhibitionism that is considered far less acceptable—showing one's penis to an unsuspecting female to provoke a reaction from her—may be motivated by hostility toward women or insecurity about one's masculinity. In group ogling, Mathis suggests, females may be mere pawns in a game designed to impress the other men in the group with one's sexual prowess and daring. The fact that females may find these attentions disturbing is no deterrent. It's the male group's approval and support that encourage this "adolescent-like" behavior (Mathis 1977, p. 64).

Overt female ogling of males is far less common. All-female construction crews are rare, and occasional incidences of whistling at passing males are often playful or angry put-downs of the male pattern. There is, however, an international group of 4000 females who call themselves Man Watchers, Inc. Their activities include male beauty contests, "Take a Man to Lunch Day," and "Copious Compliments Day." But these activities are intended partly to poke fun at male ways of relating to women by reversing the roles. According to one spokeswoman, these women's interest in men is actually based more on their "charisma" than on their visual similarity to Robert Redford (*US* 1979, p. 8).

Eye Contact. Although many of us are turned on by visually surveying a potential sex partner's body, simply catching the other's eye can be tremendously stimulating, too. The locking of gazes can be a powerful turn-on when it reflects an understanding of mutual sexual desire.

Unbeknown to us, our pupils tend to dilate considerably when we look at something that arouses a strong and pleasant emotion, such as a baby or a lover. Psychologist Eckhard Hess (1975) found that we respond more warmly to people with dilated pupils. He speculates that large pupils turn us on because they signal the intensity of the other's interest in us. But this attraction operates at a subliminal level. Experimental subjects never mentioned pupil size as a reason for choosing the picture of a person whose pupils had been re-touched to make them appear larger in preference to a picture in which the pupils had been made smaller. Hess notes that centuries ago, Italian women doused their pupils with belladonna (a medicinal extract) to dilate their eyes artifically, thereby making themselves more attractive. To-day, advertisers who know of Hess's finding touch up photographs with black ink to make the mod-els' eyes more appealing.

Even at a distance where pupil changes cannot be seen, our eyes can subtly stimulate desire. At a Yale "mixer" dance Lever and Schwartz (1976) noted that eye contact was often used to signal attraction. Sometimes eyes of strangers locked; sometimes one person merely glanced briefly but "meaningfully" at the other. Either way, the mes-sage seemed to be, "I find you attractive. Come here," or "May I come over?" One male reported that this device was used intentionally to lure females away from other men: "You try to meet eyes with a girl who doesn't look happy with the person she's with, in the hope that she'll say she has to go to the bathroom [a common ploy]. Then you pick her up on the return trip" (Lever and Schwartz 1976, p. 332).

The intensity of mutual erotic arousal evident from direct eye contact is virtually like enjoying sex—the excitement is communicated through what some call "eye fucking." But some recipients find the intense stare an invasion rather than a shared pleasure.

Sounds

Animals often turn each other on with special vo-cal invitations to sex. The alligator's bellow, the gecko's chirp, the porcupine's whine, the baboon's dental clicks, and the macaque's lip smacking are considered highly erotic by their intended part-ners. And as baboons copulate, they utter deep grunts that turn on all the other baboons within earshot (Ford and Beach 1951). We humans re-spond erotically to sounds, too. Although we usually don't bellow or chirp at each other or smack our lips in anticipation, we are aroused by music, songs, and language that we interpret as sexual.

We often use music to shape social situations. By our choice of music, we try to set the mood for the kind of interaction we want. In general we seem to choose fast music with an accentuated beat when we want to create a feeling of excite-ment and activity. We choose slower music with lighter rhythmic accents when we desire calm, re-laxed social interaction. Which kinds of music arouse us most probably depends on how we pre-fer sex—wild and vigorous, slow and mellow, or somewhere in between.

Popular music lyrics are often highly erotic, sometimes thinly veiled with nonsexual images: "Light My Fire!," "Let My People Come," "Help Me Make It through the Night," "Mama's Got a Squeeze Box, Papa Can't Sleep at Night" (osten-sibly about a woman with an accordion). The abil-ity to allude to sex through clever use of puns, metaphors, and double meanings is warmly appreciated from church socials to business con-ventions.

Indirect sex talk pervades certain social scenes—such as drinking places—and may even be quite ritualized. Strangers will go through a conversational pattern that tests the other's availa-bility without asking explicitly (Cavan 1976). Comments about the weather and the place are interspersed with questions such as "Do you live/ work around here?" and expressions of availability ("I'm celebrating the first anniversary of my di-vorce" or "I'm new in this city—it seems hard to meet people here"). Often such talk—and sugges-tions that they adjourn together to another, perhaps more private, setting—leads to sex with-out ever explicitly having discussed this possibil-ity. Cavan speculates that to verbalize sexual in-vitations as direct requests—"Let's go to my place and fuck"—robs sex of its "poetry." She thinks that indirect verbal maneuvering not only protects us from the embarrassment of overt rejection but also provides a titillation that many find pleasurable.

Nevertheless, many people do issue direct verbal invitations to sex. Whether we find such invitations turn-ons or turn-offs depends partly on their content and wording. Some of us might be far less aroused by "Let's screw" than by "I want so much to make love with you." A remark that might seem innocuous or arousing to a man might be a real turn-off for some women, and vice versa. Even the words used in sexual invitations may convey different meanings for males than for females. In 1974 sociologists Robert Walsh and Wilbert Leonard polled 248 Illinois State University students to find out which terms for intercourse were most familiar and which ones they preferred to use. Both males and females listed "fuck," "screw," and "ball" as the most familiar terms. But females tended to cite less taboo technical words ("copulate" and "coitus") and the romantic euphemism "make love" more often than men. And in actual use males were far more likely than females to think it okay to say "fuck" and "screw." In the years since 1974 many women have become freer in their use of sexual words. But Walsh and Leonard's analysis of why the genders differ in sex-word use is still relevant: In many words used for sex, women may perceive the unwanted connotation that something is being done *to* rather than *with* a woman. Such connotations may make a big difference in whether we respond erotically to verbal invitations. As Benjamin Whorf has suggested, words may not only express our attitudes but also *shape* them (Fearing 1954).

Smells and Tastes

Many of us think we can turn others on by changing the way we smell or taste. Men may splash themselves with scents considered "masculine"— Pierre Cardin, Brut, English Leather. Women may rub musk, sandalwood, and patchouli oil into pulse spots to enhance their sensuality. And teenage women may use flavored lipsticks to make themselves "deliciously kissable." Although our society emphasizes such artificial smells and tastes as turn-ons, many of us are nonetheless aroused by more natural stimuli: the smell of clean skin and of armpits, the taste of the mouth and the vulva. Some cultures teach an appreciation of these natural body scents and tastes. For instance, in one group men tuck handkerchiefs under their arms to soak up their sweat as they dance. These odor-laden cloths are then used to entice women who have learned to define them as tremendously erotic. And in the South Pacific lovers eschew kissing on the lips in favor of the "oceanic kiss"—touching nose to cheek or cheek to cheek in order to sense gently the other's scent (Davenport 1977).

We know that smells and tastes are essential to sexual arousal for many animals. The odor from the scent gland behind a male goat's horns excites a female goat if she's in heat. Males of many species commonly smell the female's perspiration, urine, and vaginal secretions to see if she's in heat. Presumably they smell and taste different while the female is in her sexually receptive period (Beach 1977).

Unlike these animals human females don't have a clearly marked "heat" cycle. But the fact that human intercourse frequency goes up when estrogen levels are highest in the female—at midcycle—has led some researchers to speculate that women may smell or taste "sexier" at this time. Studying our closest relatives, the primates, Richard Michael (1975) has found that males are not very interested in females whose ovaries have been removed. But when the genitals of these estrogenless females are smeared with vaginal secretions from normal females in heat, males immediately try to mount them. Michael has isolated the *pheromone,* or chemical signal, that seems to be responsible for the males' interest. He calls it "copulin." When he examined 47 human females, he found that copulin was present in their vaginal secretions, too, and that it reached peak levels around the time of ovulation. But in women whose hormonal cycles were artificially controlled by oral contraceptives, copulin levels were lower and unchanging. Scent attraction is apparently a mutual process, for some women find the male's scents highly erotic. On the average women have a keener sense of smell than do men, especially during ovulation. At ovulation some women are a hundred times as sensitive to musk—a hormone-related secretion from the male musk deer—as

Touching and Sex—Some Women's Opinions

General body touching is more important to me than orgasms. . . . A good hug—an-I-love-you-and-always-will-and-care-so-much-for-you-and-here-is-my-heart-and-soul-and-I-am-taking-you hug is worth the world. It is so much more than words. A really good hug will take over an orgasm any day.

You can't love sex without loving to touch and be touched. It's the very physical closeness of sex that is the main pleasure. With my present lover we spend anywhere from two to six hours caressing, touching, cuddling and hugging, kissing, and just resting against one another. It feels marvelous!

There's something very warm and intimate and very beautiful about lying in the dark with someone, holding them close and talking softly. Frankly, I enjoy it more right now than genital sex, but that could be due to my rather limited experience.

I feel affection is very important. How nice it is to know someone is hugging you, because they really care about you as a person, instead of a cunt. If a partner is not very physically affectionate at times when sex is not involved, I resent being touched later just to prime me for sex. Too many men act this way.

I long to embrace and be embraced; just to stretch out next to a man and feel the contours of his body. I certainly do not do as much of this as I would like to, because it would only be accepted as part of sex and I really am not ready for that yet.

I crave physical affection. I don't get it at home, and have gone out and taken a lover because he will hug me. I require hugs and in exchange give sex. This is all right with me because I enjoy sex; however, I want to stress that often all I really am seeking is for a man to touch me.

I would like to touch some people, but hesitate because they are aware of my "sexual preference," and this makes me and them uncomfortable. It's awfully hard to explain to an old friend that I only want to hug her because she is an old friend and not a potential bed partner.

From *The Hite Report*, by Shere Hite, pp. 556–63. Copyright © 1976 by Shere Hite. This and all other quotations from this source are reprinted by permission of Macmillan Publishing Company, Inc.

most men, who can barely detect it. Many women are also excited by the substance in urine called "exaltolide." Twice as much of it is secreted in men's urine as in women's ("Men's Fragrances . . ." 1979).

Smell—whether conscious or unconscious—is probably more central to human sexual attraction than most of us realize. Scientists are beginning to discover more human pheromones that may be bona fide aphrodisiacs for attracting people to each other. Men are said to be irresistible if they use sprays containing alpha androstenol, a compound derived from androstenone—a pheromone that is part of human sweat. The house of Jovan, Inc., is marketing perfumes containing alpha androstenol with the promise that they will attract others to us (D. White 1981).

Vaginal and other odors are also a turn-on for what some of us *taste*—as in oral-genital sex.

Women often say they are amazed to hear their partners exclaim, "You really taste good!"

For all the erotic excitement of eyes meeting across a crowded room, the appeal of some smells may bring the attraction to a sexual culmination that sight alone may not induce. Perhaps we emphasize what we like in smells and tastes as much as what we prefer in physical appeal ("I'd love to meet someone who smells like . . . tastes like . . . looks like . . . and touches like . . .").

Touching

Although all the senses bring us erotic messages, the one we most often associate with sexual arousal is touch. Perhaps because touch is so commonly linked with sex—which many consider acceptable only in certain realtionships—our society generally disapproves of touching outside of those relationships. People who are not lovers normally

Loving massage is a pleasure at any age.

touch only by shaking hands. Those of the same sex walk arm-in-arm in other cultures but typically not in ours. Friends and relatives sometimes kiss but in a nonerotic manner. Those with license to touch—barbers, tailors, hairdressers, doctors—do it impersonally so that their intentions will not be misconstrued. Touching by psychotherapists and sex therapists is usually carefully limited by professional guidelines. And caressing between adults and older children is sometimes inhibited by incest taboos as well as by fears of making homosexuals of the young.

These learned inhibitions against freely touching are unfortunate, for some holistic physicians are now saying that touch is essential to our health (Shames and Sterin 1978). And anthropologist Ashley Montagu (1971) speculates that a lack of loving touching in childhood leads to self-touching substitutes—such as thumb sucking—and to roughness, lack of response to touching, or a desperate craving for it in adult sexual expression. Montagu notes that among children girls have traditionally received more tactile stimulation than boys. He suggests that this helps to explain why women of all ages are more responsive to sensual caresses than are men.

Women also seem more open about desiring touching, a feeling that some men have perhaps learned to repress. Shere Hite (1976) reported that the desire for more touching is almost universal among women she surveyed. Many complain that

men use touching solely as a means of arousal for intercourse. By contrast, these women deeply enjoy touching for its own sake. Anthony Pietropinto and Jacqueline Simenauer (1977) countered this complaint by pointing out that over a third of the men they interviewed said that kissing and caressing were their favorite kinds of "foreplay." But they didn't ask men how they'd feel about touching if it didn't lead to intercourse.

One of the few areas in which our society is beginning to distinguish sensual touching from genital sexmaking is massage. A skillful or loving massage can be a deeply sensual experience, but it need not be interpreted as sexually arousing. In other cultures, such as Japan, massage is considered normal for everybody. Until recently, North Americans have defined massage as acceptable only as therapy for stiff or sore muscles. Massage parlors carry taboo sexual connotations and have been banned in many communities. But here and there, individuals are learning that they can give great pleasure to their children, friends, and parents—as well as their lovers—with their hands.

Sex educator Jessie Potter has long held that we need more touching. She concludes that if people would value each other as individuals, it is important to avoid the fundamental error of believing that touch serves as only a means to an end. In fact, it is a primary form of communication, a silent voice. It avoids the pitfalls of words while expressing our feelings. Touch bridges physical separateness from which none of us is spared: It establishes a sense of solidarity between two individuals. Touch carries its own message. It can be sexual, or used to convey feelings or emotions, or to give comfort, or to reassure. It can be a sensual thing, exploring the texture of the skin, the suppleness of the muscle, the contours of the body, with no further goal than the enjoyment of touch and being touched (Potter 1982).

FANTASIES

Thoughts of sex may turn us on even in the absence of sensory stimulation. Some of us can even fantasize to orgasm.

Sometimes our thoughts drift to sex as we're daydreaming; sometimes we intentionally concoct fantasies to turn ourselves on. Our own sexual fantasies are even more arousing than erotic pictures or stories. Two social psychologists asked married people to read some sexy stories, look at erotic photographs, or imagine the sexual activities that the others had seen or read about. Those asked to fantasize became twice as aroused as those shown pictures or given stories (Byrne and Lamberth 1971).

Sexual fantasies may be romantic (falling in love with a beautiful stranger, complete with music and flowers) or they may be explicitly erotic. Using sophisticated physiological measuring devices as well as self-reports, Julia Heiman (1977) found that for sexually experienced males and females, erotic images are much more arousing than romantic ones. But her subjects found even neutral images somewhat arousing, perhaps because they defined and fantasized the experiment as a sexual situation.

As we might expect from people who are socialized differently, males and females seem to differ in their fantasy patterns. Kinsey and his associates (1953) found that midcentury men more often had been aroused by sexual thoughts than had midcentury women. Almost a third of the nearly 6000 females interviewed said they'd never been turned on by thinking about sex, not even by thoughts of sex with their husbands or lovers. But by 1971 Byrne and Lamberth found that married women were as turned on by erotic images as were married men, and perhaps even more so. And in

1973 Barbara Hariton polled 141 conservative middle-class women and found that only 7 percent had never experienced sexual daydreams or fantasized during masturbation or intercourse.

As inhibitions on female sexuality are increasingly lifted, researchers are discovering that many women have a rich fantasy life. Women's fantasies tend to include arousing images that involve all the senses—touches, tastes, smells, sounds, and sights. Men's tend to be imitations of hard-core pornography, with emotionless but sexually driven characters and visual depictions of who-does-what-to-whom.

The activities we conjure up differ somewhat by gender, too. In a sample of 421 midwestern college students (Sue 1979), fantasies of a former lover and of being found sexually irresistible were common among both females and males. Among other often-cited fantasies, males were somewhat more likely than females to fantasize about oral-genital sex, forcing others to have sex with them, and others' giving in after initially resisting. Males were also far more likely than females to fantasize about an imaginary lover. For their part females were far more likely to fantasize about being forced or overpowered into having sex. Few of either gender fantasized about someone of the same sex (only 3 percent of males and 9 percent of females) or sex with animals (1 percent of males and 4 percent of females). Even in our fantasies we tend to use the scripts handed to us by our society.

How we feel about our own fantasies is greatly influenced by social opinions. When Nancy Friday (1973) published *My Secret Garden,* a compilation of women's sexual fantasies, many people defined fantasy as sickness. The opinion was that even if men sometimes fantasized about activities that fell outside the narrow range of behaviors defined as normal, sane women certainly didn't. Women who secretly carried on this taboo mental activity therefore felt guilty and abnormal. As we began to discover that many other people fantasize too, public and private opinions shifted dramatically. Now a rich fantasy life is widely defined as a normal form of sexual exuberance—an acceptable way to sample and enjoy erotic possibilities that might be dangerous or guilt producing if acted out. We now know that fantasizing is not related to marital maladjustment (Hariton 1973).

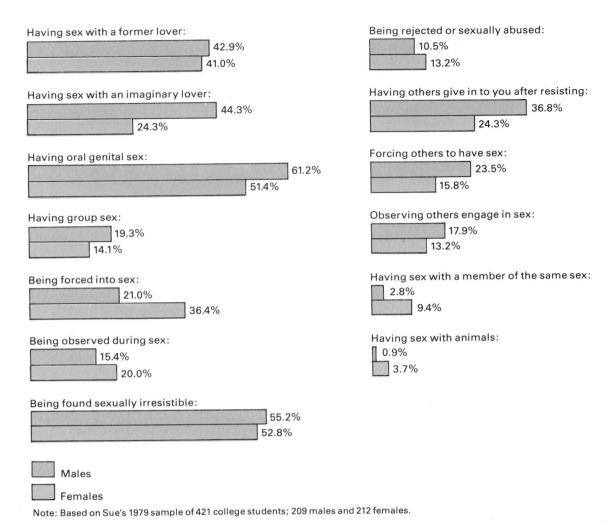

Having sex with a former lover:
42.9%
41.0%

Having sex with an imaginary lover:
44.3%
24.3%

Having oral genital sex:
61.2%
51.4%

Having group sex:
19.3%
14.1%

Being forced into sex:
21.0%
36.4%

Being observed during sex:
15.4%
20.0%

Being found sexually irresistible:
55.2%
52.8%

Being rejected or sexually abused:
10.5%
13.2%

Having others give in to you after resisting:
36.8%
24.3%

Forcing others to have sex:
23.5%
15.8%

Observing others engage in sex:
17.9%
13.2%

Having sex with a member of the same sex:
2.8%
9.4%

Having sex with animals:
0.9%
3.7%

Males

Females

Note: Based on Sue's 1979 sample of 421 college students; 209 males and 212 females.

Figure 3-2. Fantasies during Intercourse. According to a sample of college students, oral-genital sex and being found sexually irresistible are the most common fantasies for both males and females. Note that males and females differ considerably in some fantasies. For instance, women are more likely to fantasize about being forced into sex, while men are more likely to fantasize about forcing others to have sex. Even in our fantasies we tend to act out traditional gender role expectations.

Whether actually acting out these forbidden desires is good for us and for society is heatedly disputed. Some therapists and religious leaders see kinky sexual acts as perversions to be cured. Some feel that they're okay so long as participants are willing and don't hurt anyone. And some openly encourage making fantasies realities. For instance, there's a theater group in New York City that invites people to write scripts from their favorite fantasies and then publicly star in them. A nightclub in Boston encourages transvestites to dress in the clothes of the other sex within the club's supportive, protected atmosphere. And many therapists are now encouraging rich fantasizing to help people get in touch with their sexual selves and to give themselves permission to explore hidden desires in fact as well as in fantasy.

Fantasies encourage us to experiment with a wider variety of sexual pleasures—to savor our sex partners in ways we had never thought of or had been too inhibited to try. Sharing fantasies ("I fantasized that we were making love in an abandoned cabin on a fur rug in front of a warm fire") can enrich our sex lives and help us to explore our erotic potential instead of letting sex become boringly routine. On the other hand, if we let our fantasies become our expectations, our real sex lives may suffer. What we actually do may seem too tame in comparison with the erotic activities we imagine. And if we focus on fantasies too much during sex, we may lose touch with our body's own sensations and the warmth of contact with one another.

DREAMS

Some of us continue our imaginary sex lives far into the night. Freud insisted that our dreams are symbolic attempts to resolve sexual conflicts that date back to our childhoods. But many contemporary analysts of dreams see them as subconscious reflections of daily concerns, which may or may not be sexual.

Dreams are not always what they seem. Sometimes we use sexual imagery in dreaming about nonsexual concerns. Dream analyst Ann Faraday (1974) suggests that if we dream of being nude in public, we may be feeling unusually vulnerable (rather than sexy) in our waking lives. Dreams of vigorous sexual activity may reflect feelings of excitement about what's happening in our daily lives.

For many of us, of course, dreaming about sex mirrors thoughts of sex. The late psychologist Abraham Maslow found that among women, overtly sensual dreams occur almost exclusively in those who are high in self-esteem. Their dreams reflect the desire for abundant and varied sexual experience, which they already express in their everyday lives (Maslow 1942). Faraday (1974) encourages paying attention to dreams. She suggests writing them down on waking and then trying to figure out what they mean, for they may reveal important things about ourselves and our problems that we otherwise ignore or repress.

Whether openly or symbolically sexual, dreams may be extremely arousing. Kinsey (1953) found that almost all males and about three-fourths of all females have had erotically stimulating dreams. For 83 percent of the males Kinsey studied and 37 percent of the females, dreams were sometimes such a turn-on that they led to orgasm. For males these "nocturnal emissions" were most common during the late teens and early twenties. For females sexual dreams including orgasm were most frequent during the forties.

While Kinsey's findings were based on volunteers' self-reports, we also have physiological measures indicating that sexual responses to dreams are common. Men have been wired to erection detectors or simply watched by researchers as they slept in the nude. They seem to have full or partial erections 95 percent of the time that they are in the rapid-eye-movement state, which indicates dreams are in progress. Some of these dreams last over half an hour, yet the erections are maintained. They tend to slack off a bit with age, but the only significant difference is between adolescents and men sixty years and older. Even newborn babies have erections during rapid-eye-movement sleep. The only thing that seems to inhibit erections is anxiety-producing elements in the dreams themselves. For instance, one subject who suddenly lost his erection while dreaming later reported that he'd dreamed of being attacked by sharks (Greenhouse 1974).

Because of technical problems, only a few women have been studied for sexual arousal while sleeping. But those studied have clitoral erections as often as men have penile erections with most occurring during dreaming periods (Greenhouse 1974). Perhaps this is why we're so annoyed when awakened before our dreams have ended!

EROTICA

Some of us are turned on by pictures of beautiful nude bodies and by erotic books and films. Others of us find them embarrassing or downright disgusting. Erotica are not just pleasing or displeasing: We also see erotic materials as intrinsically good or bad (Byrne et al. 1974). People who have

Betty Dodson's sex drawings are examples of erotica rather than pornography, for they portray mutual sensual pleasures rather than exploitative sexual situations.

been socialized to less positive views of sex—people high in sex-guilt, sexually inexperienced people, and some females—tend to rate erotic films as more pornographic, disgusting, and offensive than others (Mosher 1973). Since many people see a need for government protection from erotic materials they consider harmful, there are now legal as well as personal definitions of pornography.

Legal Definitions

Late in the 1960s public concern over pornography led to the creation of a blue-ribbon group charged to investigate whether obscene materials pose any danger to the public. The scientists, lawyers, clergy, and antipornography representatives on this panel—the Commission on Obscenity and Pornography—funded and reviewed millions of dollars worth of research. The majority recommendation: Government should not interfere with the right of adults to see or read sexually explicit materials. The commissioners pointed out that according to a study they ran, the majority of people in the United States agree that this should be an area for individual decision making rather than for government intervention. They also noted that exposure to explicit sexual materials does not lead to increases in sex crime or to changes in attitudes. (These potential effects had been major concerns of antipornography groups.) The commission noted that erotic stimuli may actually have a slightly beneficial effect on sex among the married and that people soon tire of erotica anyway (Commission on Obscenity and Pornography 1970).

Both our U.S. Congress and president rejected the commission's advice and opted instead for laws restricting the sale of erotic materials deemed unacceptable by local standards. This decision has been hard to put into practice, because public standards of what is undesirable are difficult to pin down. The courts have tried to define unacceptable material as that which the average person using contemporary community standards would think appeals mostly to prurient interest, with little artistic, political, scientific, or literary value. "Prurient interest" has been defined as a sick interest in nudity, sex, or excrement, as opposed to a normal, healthy, erotic interest in such matters. But the thoughts of this mythical "average" person are hard to trace, for value judgments as to what is sick and what is normal vary by sensate capabilities, educational level, income, location, age, religion, political leanings, gender, and other variables.

Gender Differences in Response to Erotica

To explore just one of these variables, males and females do seem to differ somewhat in their responses to explicit sexual materials. But just how they differ seems to be changing with time.

At midcentury, Kinsey (1948, 1953) found that men were more aroused by visual erotica and sex stories than were women. He noted that men were much more likely than women to be exposed to and interested in erotic materials. Yet, in 1975 Julia Heiman reported that in her sample of sexually experienced American college students, females were as aroused by erotic tapes as males were. It's quite possible that women did not respond much to erotica in the past because it was created by and for men, with content that simply may not have been a turn-on for women. Heiman's students were most aroused by a tape that described a female-initiated sexual encounter and focused on the woman's perceptions. Wondering why *both* sexes preferred this female-centered tape, Heiman (1975, p. 93) speculated that they may have differed in their reasons for being turned on: "Perhaps this particular fantasy gives women a sense of sexual control that they do not have usually, while it allows men a chance to lie back and enjoy it, without having to worry about performance."

Women as well as men find sexual explicitness exciting. In Candice Osborn and Robert Pol-

lack's (1977) sample of female graduate students from the University of Georgia, vaginal blood-volume responses showed that these women reacted far more to "hard-core pornography" stories than to stories of "erotic realism." Compared with the latter, hard-core pornography was defined as material with more sexual terms, more exaggerated superlatives, and fewer references to situations and feelings that didn't contribute to sexual arousal. This ability to respond erotically without romantic cues has been demonstrated even in a sample that includes women with negative attitudes toward sex and erotica (Fisher and Byrne 1978).

Although males and females don't seem to differ in their general responses to explicit sexual materials, just what is being explicitly portrayed does make a difference to them. Both sexes seem to be aroused by scenes of the other gender engaging in some taboo sexual activity but are turned off by watching an actor of their own sex doing the same thing. For instance, when Elaine Hatfield and her associates (1978) showed an introductory human sexuality class a film of a male masturbating, a number of male students left the room. When they showed a film of a female masturbating, women left. During a different semester, they asked a class of 58 students to watch the same two films and then fill out questionnaires about their feelings, physiological arousal, and sexual behaviors after watching the films. Results were the same: Both sexes were moderately aroused by watching someone of the other sex masturbate and moderately turned off by watching someone of their own sex masturbate. When the experiment was repeated with scenes of heterosexual and homosexual sex, shown to a class of 556 students, these results were even more marked. The males found female homosexuality "extremely arousing," but male homosexuality "extremely unarousing." Women's reactions to these films were much less intense in both directions. The researchers speculated that the students were identifying with those of their own sex on the screen and feeling uneasy because the activities depicted still met with social disapproval.

Another way in which females' assessment of erotic contents may differ from males' may be women's dislike of situations that seem to exploit their own sex. Psychologist James Herrell (1975) had 32 males and 32 females read a passage from the book *Eternal Fire,* in which the female was clearly sexually exploited, and an erotic passage from *Lady Chatterley's Lover,* in which the female clearly enjoyed herself and grew psychologically. He noted that *both sexes* were aroused by the second but angered by the first.

It's possible, though, that women are more sensitive to subtle forms of exploitation than are men. Gloria Steinem, for instance, feels that nude pictures of women displaying their genitals for male viewers are exploitative. She and other writers in a special issue of *Ms.* (November 1978) voice concern over what they see as an increasingly sadistic slant in male-oriented pornography and chic advertisements. Steinem (1978, p. 54) holds that distinctions should be made between depictions of "mutually pleasurable sexual expression between people who have enough power to be there by positive choice" and sex used as a weapon of violence and dominance against the less powerful—usually women and children. She defines the former as erotica, the latter as pornography. What Steinem (1978, p. 78) finds truly obscene is the humiliating idea that sex means male domination: "Our spirits . . . break a little each time we see ourselves in chains or in full labial display for the conquering male viewer, bruised or on our knees, screaming a real or pretended pain to delight the sadist, pretending to enjoy what we don't enjoy." Robin Morgan (1978) fears that the more men see of sexual brutality in films, ads, and magazines, the more they'll define it as acceptable behavior.

Erotica for both sexes still seems to be patterned on traditional male models—look at the genitals, look at the breasts, see who does what to whom. For instance, an analysis of current "adults only" paperbacks (Smith 1976) shows that great attention is paid to descriptions of women's bodies. Men are characterized only by the giant size of their genitals. Character development and emotional involvement are shallow or nonexistent. The male typically dominates sexual activities, often by physical or mental force. Women are depicted as responding erotically to being overpowered.

There have been a few erotic books written by women that do not follow this pattern. But as Gloria Steinem (1978, p. 78) has written, women's "bodies have too rarely been enough our own to develop erotica in our own lives, much less in art and literature." As women increasingly find acceptance for their richly sensual sexual fantasies, and as men learn that sex can mean more than intercourse, the emerging genre of erotic art may come to mirror a broader, deeper, and more sensitive view of sexuality than most pornography has in the past.

CHEMICAL MOOD MODIFIERS

Sexual desire can be stimulated by altering our physiological state as well as our perception of what turns us on. Establishing an erotic mood can be sensitive, requiring the cooperation of both participants. An untimely joke, interruption, expression of disgust, or feeling or embarrassment can redefine the mood and decrease sexual interest. For those who have learned to associate negative messages with sex ("Repress your sexuality," "Don't enjoy yourself") or who have memories of unpleasant sexual experiences, letting go of inhibitions to sexual feeling may be especially difficult.

In order to keep erotic feelings from being waylaid by distractions or sex-negative learning, some of us use artificial mood modifiers. They range from music that creates a sexually arousing atmosphere to alcohol and other drugs that are thought to induce pleasure. Researchers have found that one of the chief ingredients in successful mood modifiers is our *expectation* that they will work. Pleasure-inducing chemicals may have actual physiological effects, too. In the short run some seem to create the desired effect; in the long run some may endanger our health.

Alcohol

Alcohol depresses the central nervous system, and although it may initially lower sexual inhibitions, it ultimately detracts from sexual arousal and sexual potential. Alcohol also lowers testosterone levels (Gordon et al. 1976), with the usual effect of lowering sexual desire and arousal. Male orgasm and ejaculation were adversely affected by alcohol in a study by Malatesta, Pollack, Wilbanks, and Adams (1979). With higher levels of alcohol the men took longer to ejaculate while masturbating and they reported decreased sexual arousal, decreased pleasure, decreased intensity of their orgasms, and increased difficulty in experiencing orgasm.

Nevertheless, using alcohol to promote sexual arousal is quite common. Lever and Schwartz (1976) note that at a college mixer drinking a lot of beer seems to "allow" people to do whatever they please. They can withdraw, or really let go, and have an excuse for their actions. Many of the men they spoke to said they felt that getting a little drunk ahead of time was necessary "to loosen inhibitions and numb sensitivities for the personal tests that were to come" (p. 324).

Some observers feel that a loosening of inhibitions is actually only part of the set of expectations that surround alcohol use. Dennis Brissett (1978) interprets heavy drinking as a pattern that carries certain apparent psychological benefits for the user. Heavy drinkers often see alcohol as a means to redefine social situations and how they fit into them. Their drinking pattern gives them a clear identity ("heavy drinker") and a feeling of apparent self-worth that comes from consistently acting out this "solid identity." Getting drunk regularly lends their lives an illusion of continuity and order, thereby providing a way to deal with a seemingly insane world.

The expectation that alcohol also increases one's sexual powers is apparently widespread among males. A study of this expectation was conducted by a team of psychologists from Old Dominion University (Briddell et al. 1978). It showed that merely *believing* we have consumed alcohol is more likely to enhance sexual arousal than actually consuming it.

In a thorough and recent study, Malatesta, Pollack, Crotty, and Peacock (1982) use physiological, behavioral, and cognitive indexes to determine the effect of alcohol levels on female orgasm. Female orgasmic responsiveness decreased physiologically and behaviorally with increased alcohol consumption, but women still *perceived* greater sexual enjoyment and became more sexually aroused after consuming alcohol. It may be that

women believe they are more satisfied with alcohol because they need alcohol more than men to overcome sexual inhibitions and guilt feelings. As with other drugs, alcohol is often used to compensate for sex-negative beliefs.

For some chronic alcoholics impotence is permanent. Researchers blame damage to the nerve centers involved in erection—parts of the brain, spinal cord, and sensory nerves in the genitals. As one alcoholic bemoaned, "I drank Early Times, but the result was Old Grand Dad" (Lemere and Smith 1973, p. 212).

Continued heavy alcohol use actually diminishes sexual capabilities in both genders, according to a number of studies. Although the desire for sex may remain high, the ability to "perform" decreases. But in one of the studies that verified this statement (Wilson, Lawson, and Abrams 1978), the eight chronic male alcoholics tested insisted at the beginning of the experiment that alcohol would not have a negative effect on their sexual functioning. They parroted the prevailing social expectation that alcohol either increases sexual arousal or at least leaves it unaffected. But under higher and higher doses of alcohol, their erections in response to erotic films dropped off to the point that they might have been too limp for sexual action.

Pleasure-Inducing Drugs

People have long searched for some substance that would make them better lovers. This has been especially true for men because of the notion that sexual interaction cannot take place unless the man has an erection. Reputed *aphrodisiacs*—substances thought to increase sexual frequency, performance, and drive—have ranged from oysters, ginseng, and powdered rhinoceros horn to hallucinogenic drugs. A common medical opinion is that if they seem to enhance sex, it is only because we expect them to.

Frank Gawin (1978) points out, however, that research into the effectiveness of various drugs may be focusing on the wrong effects and using shoddy methods. If the definition of aphrodisiacs is expanded to include perceived enhancement of sexual *pleasure,* then some substances may qualify. Actually, there have not been careful "placebo" studies of drugs that parallel those studies done with alcohol. In other words research is needed that compares the sexual responses of people who are (1) given a reputed aphrodisiac and told that's what is is, (2) given a placebo—a similar-appearing but chemically neutral substance—and told that it's an aphrodisiac, (3) given a reputed aphrodisiac but told that it's not an aphrodisiac, and (4) given a placebo and told that it's a placebo. For valid results such tests should be double-blind: The researchers handing out the "aphrodisiacs" should not know whether they are placebos or "the real thing."

We do have evidence of increased sexual *pleasure* from self-reports. These reports may be valid measures in this area, for what is being analyzed goes beyond the basic biological level to what Gawin (1978, p. 109) calls "the sensual-aesthetic, emotional-interpersonal, and even the mystical or spiritual" levels. But on the biological level there is considerable evidence that pleasure-inducing drugs are dangerous. As we'll see, the documented hazards range from nose tissue damage and hair loss as a result of sniffing cocaine to brain cell damage and death from overdoses.

In general the various drugs that produce temporary sensations of pleasure—stimulants, depressants, intoxicants, and hallucinogens—do so by entering the brain through the bloodstream. Within the brain they seem to alter the normal functioning of the subconscious limbic system and/or the areas of conscious thought by upsetting chemical patterns of communication and response. Processing of information about the outside environment or the user's own body is distorted. Sights, sounds, smells, and touches may be intensified or dulled; equilibrium may be upset, senses confused with each other, memory impaired, or sense of time distorted. At the same time sensations and emotions that may be regarded as pleasurable are artificially created: a sense of well-being, loss of inhibition, alertness or relaxation or light-headedness, illusions, and in some cases a feeling of sexual excitement or orgasmic release that seems to come from the brain rather than from the genitals. These effects—and their potential hazards—vary depending on the type of drug.

Marijuana.   Many users of marijuana claim that it increases their enjoyment of sex. Specifics:

Touches seem more intensely stimulating, skin feels warm and tingly, emotional warmth between partners is greater, sex seems to last longer, people feel more relaxed and free, personal involvement in the experience of intercourse increases, and orgasms seem more intense. This feeling that marijuana increases sexual pleasure is most common among those who use pot frequently. Perhaps they've learned better how to meet subcultural expectations of what being "stoned" feels like.

According to a study of 251 students from eight major universities across the United States, more females attribute a *desire*-enhancing effect to pot than do males (Koff 1974). Researcher Wayne Koff speculates that marijuana's relaxing effect may be especially significant for women because it loosens their learned inhibitions against experiencing and expressing sexual desire. But more males than females feel that marijuana increases their sexual *enjoyment* and think their partners enjoy sex more while high.

Marijuana has helped some people to overcome blocks to sensual feeling. And some have learned through marijuana to experience sexual responses in their whole bodies, not just in their genital areas (Gawin 1978).

Just as with alcohol, however, increased marijuana use may bring diminished sexual returns. People who smoked one joint or less in an experiment Koff ran (1974) were more likely to report that pot increased their sexual enjoyment than those who smoked two or three joints per session. While the quality of marijuana generally available varies greatly, Koff's results were based on precisely measured amounts of THC, the most active chemical in pot. While high doses of pot have resulted in lowered sexual drive and an inability to perform sexually (Hollister 1975; Chopra 1969), moderate doses enhanced the quality of orgasm for 40 percent of females and 68 percent of males in a study by Halikas, Weller, and Morse (1982). These researchers also found that sexual pleasure and satisfaction were increased for 75 percent of the males and 90 percent of the females. But these effects were only true of *moderate*—not heavy—use of pot. As the pot user becomes more intoxicated, he or she may tend to withdraw into inner experiences or simply get sleepy and dizzy, lessening the sexual focus of the occasion.

In addition to this short-term effect of diminishing sexual returns, long-term use of marijuana may depress the release of FSH and LH by the pituitary gland, thereby impairing messages to the ovaries and testicles to produce the sex hormones. Production of testosterone and sperm may drop in males; pregnant females who use marijuana run the risk that their babies will be deprived of hormones during critical periods in their fetal development (Jones and Jones 1977).

Other Drugs. Whereas marijuana acts as a relaxant, certain drugs affect sexual pleasure by *stimulating* the central nervous system. Cocaine and amphetamines ("speed") act directly on the brain to produce a feelng of euphoria. Users report that such substances make any kind of sexual stimulation feel more intensely pleasurable, probably because they increase blood pressure and muscle tension in the genital area and enable the genitals to swell abnormally for long periods of time. But high doses of these central nervous system stimulants seem actually to decrease interest in sexual activity (Woods 1975), and repeated heavy use increases the possibility of brain damage, physical deterioration, and psychosis. The marathon sex sessions that stimulants sometimes allow may also become painful, for orgasm may not relieve the artificially created blood congestion and muscle tension (Jones and Jones 1977).

Cocaine may inhibit ejaculation, thus prolonging sexual excitation (Wesson 1982), but there are no controlled studies of the effects of cocaine on sexual arousal (Buffum 1982). Amphetamines in low doses may stimulate sexual desire in both sexes, as well as delaying ejaculation in males, while females report a higher probability of orgasm (Smith, Buxton, and Dammann 1979). Parr (1976) found that multiple orgasms were more common in both sexes, but men were more favorable toward amphetamines than were women.

· Heroin has been found to cause decreased sexual desire, retarded ejaculation, and failure to have an erection (Buffum 1982). Mirin and others (1980) found that heroin results in acute suppression of release from the pituitary gland and a resulting drop in testosterone level. Experiences with hallucinogenic drugs, such as LSD and mescaline, vary considerably. Most people find that these drugs don't enhance sex. But some experi-

enced users say they've had extraordinary sexual sensations and insights while intoxicated. Sensory perceptions may change considerably, partners may feel they're "truly merging" during intercourse or getting to know each other on a "deeper level," and individuals may experience "new insights" into sex. Whether or not this warping of normal perceptions is valued depends on individual judgment (Gawin 1978). The possible hazards of LSD use include personality change, frightening hallucinations, impairment of short-term memory and the coding of new information, lack of motivation, altered attention span, and nerve cell disturbances (Jones and Jones 1977).

Barbiturates and tranquilizers may produce a relaxed sense of well-being and a lessening of inhibitions. But as dosage increases, interest in sex drops. At high, continued doses these drugs are highly addictive. As tolerance builds, the risk of overdosing to achieve the desired effects increases. Overdose or combination of these drugs with alcohol may be fatal. But whether or not tranquilizers or barbiturates are combined with alcohol, their usage relaxes muscles that must be tensed for orgasm to occur.

Sleeping pills, or sedatives, may also inhibit sexual arousal and orgasm. But one such drug has a street reputation for being an aphrodisiac—methaqualone (Quaalude). As Buffum (1982) concludes, increased sexual desire from methaqualone and other drugs is probably a function of decreasing inhibitions. As with alcohol and other supposed aphrodisiacs, we can assume the perception of increased sexual arousal is largely because users expect that the drug will have such an effect.

Amyl nitrate supposedly magnifies the intensity and pleasure of orgasm by dilating blood vessels. Nitrates are inhaled just before orgasm to enhance orgasm (Sigell et al. 1978). But when nitrates are inhaled too soon, men lose their erections. Nitrates are used by some male homosexuals to relax the anal sphincter muscle to facilitate anal intercourse, but there are no known studies on the effectiveness of the drug, and the way the drug works is not well known. For some nitrates cause headaches, dizziness, and fainting.

Many other drugs may affect sexual arousal; some appear to have a negative effect. For example, high doses of certain antipsychotic agents may decrease sexual desire or inhibit ejaculation; oral contraceptives decrease some women's sexual interest; diuretics may cause impotence; and centrally acting antihypertensives may decrease sexual desire, cause erectile impotence, and inhibit orgasm (Kaplan 1979).

Cigarette smoking may also have negative sexual effects. Hagan and D'Agostine (1982) showed erotic movies to three groups of men—those smoking two high-nicotine cigarettes, or two low-nicotine cigarettes, or those consuming no nicotine. They reported that as few as two high-nicotine cigarettes have a significant negative effect on male sexual response. Nicotine restricts vasocongestion of blood necessary for full erection and arousal.

Considering the potential for serious side effects from use of pleasure-inducing drugs, some people who want to enhance their sexual feelings choose a safer route: exercise, rest, good diet, and sex-positive thinking.

SUMMARY

What turns us on—or off—varies. Sensory inputs, emotions, and conscious thoughts all are considered by our brains, which orchestrate the physical responses of sexual arousal. To enter the desire phase, we must be emotionally ready to feel sexual, but many seemingly nonsexual emotions will do. Sensory inputs to which we may respond include sights, sounds, smells, tastes, and touches. Within our own heads fantasies and dreams may waken our desires. Erotic materials are prized by some as excitement or art; sexually explicit materials are condemned by others as pornography. Many people use alcohol or drugs to induce an inhibited, relaxed, or high state that helps them to enjoy sex, but the actual or long-term effects of chemical mood modifiers may actually diminish sexual responsiveness.

4

Sex
With
Ourselves

It happened the first time when I was 9 and was climbing the rope in gymnastics. On my way down I had the rope between my legs and I had my first orgasm.

Ann, 12 years old*

When I was 10 years old my best friend Jim, who was two years older, showed me his penis and how to masturbate. We are still doing it together.

Robert, 14 years old*

We were more than six of us from 8 to 13 years of age, and Bill instructed us how to do it. A bunch of boys lined up jerking off; it is funny to think about it now.

Arthur, 18 years old*

I had my first orgasm when I was 14 years old. I borrowed my girlfriend's bike and all of a sudden I felt a tickling between my legs. That was the way it started. I did not know what it was until my girlfriend told me all about it, but that was two years later.

Christine, 18 years old*

I was taught that masturbation was bad, and that there were only a thousand orgasms doled out to each person and not to waste them. I have found both to be untrue. On the average I masturbate two or three times a week, and have even all during my married life for twenty years.

Adult Male†

When I discovered my clitoris at age eighteen, I thought I was queer and I alone had one. I left home and masturbated a lot and thought I was the only woman in the world who did it. Now I know that is ridiculous, but my first lover [for four years] didn't either.

Adult Female‡

*Langfeldt, 1981a.

†Hite, 1981.

‡Hite, 1976.

We experience our first sexual sensations and awarenesses without adult-sanctioned scripts. The ambiguity and privacy of the early experiences involve considerable individual creativity as we try to make sense of them. Discovering new body sensations and potential pleasures should have positive outcomes. Yet teachers and researchers point out that self-pleasuring is one of the most difficult topics to discuss in class, let alone to research.

One recent study of children's sexuality chose to omit interview questions about masturbation because the pilot study interviews caused the children too much embarrassment. The masturbation questions were also judged too sensitive for parents and school officials (Goldman and Goldman 1982). Another study of eighth graders showed that even though exposure to sex education increased their awareness that masturbation is a normal experience, such awareness did not decrease their worry about their own self-pleasuring. The researchers concluded that eighth graders are still getting negative messages about masturbation (Parcel and Luttman 1981).

Why are these negative reactions expressed by children, teenagers, and even college students today? To understand these responses, we need to consider the social-psychological aspects of early sexual pleasuring, as well as the historical definitions of masturbation that still influence our attitudes.

MASTURBATION IN HISTORICAL PERSPECTIVE

For most of the history of Western civilization, masturbation has been viewed in a negative light. Many religions linked it with damnation. When science and medicine were thought to hold the answers to life, it was associated with a multitude of physical problems. And when psychoanalysis became popular, it was seen as a cause of neurotic disorders or at least a sign of immaturity. Although opinions have begun to change, this heritage of negative thinking still taints our attitudes toward having sex with ourselves.

Early Judaic and Christian Definitions

The ancient Jews valued reproduction highly, for it enhanced tribal survival and supplied sons to perpetuate the patriarchal system. Sexual activities that wouldn't increase the population were therefore strongly tabooed. The story of Onan, in Genesis 38:8–10, reflects this taboo. Onan's brother had died, leaving his widow with no male offspring. Onan's father commanded Onan to have sex with his sister-in-law (a practice called "the levirate," which was expected in such cases) so that sons could be raised in his brother's name. For some reason Onan refused to fulfill his obligation to his brother—either by masturbating or by withdrawing from intercourse just in time to avoid sharing his sperm (Lewinsohn 1958). According to the story, the Lord was so displeased that he killed Onan, and masturbation came to be called "onanism" and regarded as a serious sin in Judaism. Those of a strict orthodoxy held that it was even to be punished by the death penalty.

Christian sex codes, influenced by Jewish abhorrence of all nonprocreative sex, taught that masturbation was an "unnatural" use of the sexual organs. Because the male sperm was believed to contain all the essentials of a human person, masturbators were thought to be murderers doomed to hell unless they received forgiveness.

The Language of Sex

What can we call this thing we do with ourselves? The word *masturbate* carries heavy negative connotations from the past. Its Latin roots are negative, too—they mean "to pollute with the hand" (Hamilton 1978). *Onanism* is linked with the idea of sin, and its meaning is unclear, anyway. "Playing with ourselves" sounds like a childish activity. Some more positive alternatives: "self-love," "self-pleasure," "jollification," "self-stimulation," "sex with ourselves."

Medical Influences

Adding to religious definitions, the medical profession began to teach that masturbation caused a long list of diseases. Foremost among these alarmists was a Swiss doctor named Tissot. His 1758 treatise on the dangers of masturbation claimed that men waste away as they lose semen. Tissot advised saving it carefully for reproductive acts, because loss of too much semen would lead to bodily decay, headaches, numbness, pimples, blisters, impotence, premature ejaculation, venereal disease, bladder tumors, intestinal disorders, and fogging of the mind, perhaps to the point of madness. For females masturbation would cause many of the ills listed for men, and more: hysteria, jaundice, stomach cramps, sore noses, cervical ulcers, and tremors of the uterus that would turn females into unthinking, indecent, lustful brutes and cause them to prefer women as lovers (Bullough 1975).

These claims were not based on controlled studies. Instead, they seemed to leap quickly from selected observation to presumed cause. The notion that masturbation could lead to insanity, for instance, stemmed from observations that many people in insane asylums masturbated (Brecher 1969). The possibilities that they might be masturbating because they had no other sexual options, or that their insanity might be attributed to any number of other factors (such as eating: they all ate) rather than to masturbating, or that many sane people also masturbated were overlooked. Instead, the old religious teachings were given the ring of scientific truth and tightened their grip on people's views of masturbation.

The idea of insanity through masturbation soon became a self-fulfilling prophecy as fear of masturbation reached epidemic proportions. According to Alex Comfort (1967, p. 78), Tissot's treatise unleashed "one of the most astonishing floods of psychologically damaging medical nonsense in history." Medical "experts" added to Tissot's list of the dangers of masturbation such infirmities as epilepsy, asthma, memory loss, paralysis, blindness, and even death by suicide. The *Boston Medical and Surgical Journal* warned in 1835 that "the victim of masturbation passes from one degree of imbecility to another, till all the powers of the system, mental, physical, and moral, are blot-

ted out forever!" ("Insanity . . ." 1935, p. 109). In 1886 Richard von Krafft-Ebing pushed the hysteria a step further by citing masturbation as one of the main causes of all deviations from "normal" intercourse, from fetishism to homosexuality to lust murders (Brecher 1969). All the ills that would befall a masturbator were said to be passed on to his or her innocent offspring as well.

Preventive Measures

To avoid letting their children fall prey to a habit that was now considered extremely dangerous as well as immoral, mothers were exhorted to watch their children closely. They were to be taught from infancy that their genitals were only for excretion, that touching them would cause terrible sicknesses. Parents were urged to keep track of what their servants were doing, too. As one doctor wrote in 1874, "Nurses are not long in finding out that titillation of the genital organs is the surest way of keeping even babies quiet. Thus the mischief is begun, and infants not yet two years old are frequently found repeating the lesson" (Lewis 1874, p. 183).

If watchfulness and warnings didn't work, many bizarre and sadistic "cures" were available. Hands were tied or chained to walls. Genitals were desensitized with a hot iron, locked into chastity belts, or encased in spiked cages. Surgical intervention—such as circumcision or implantation of a steel ring in the penis for boys and surgical removal of the clitoris for girls—was the preferred method of treatment between 1850 and 1879 (Spitz 1975).

The Tide Turns (Somewhat)

Paranoid reactions to masturbation began to wane by the beginning of the twentieth century. As medical science became increasingly objective, more and more physicians dared to point out that there seemed to be no proof for the claims of the scaremongers. After reviewing the research, Havelock Ellis concluded in 1905 that "there appears to be little reliable evidence to show that simple masturbation, in a well-born and healthy individual, can produce any evil results beyond slight functional disturbances, and these only when it is practiced in excess" (1942, p. 250). Ellis reported that self-stimulation is common among animals and that it had been found in almost all cultures then known. For instance, among the Nama Hottentots "masturbation is so common that it is regarded as a custom of the country; no secret is made of it, and in the stories and legends of the race it is treated as one of the most ordinary facts of life" (p. 167). In Ellis's own Victorian England masturbation was "inevitable," especially as marriage rates declined and "illicit sexual relationships" were openly discouraged (p. 164).

In 1912 Freud and his followers proposed that masturbation should be considered normal, though somewhat disgusting, in the young. The Freudians introduced a new fear, though: If a person continued masturbating "to excess" in adulthood, he or she might get stuck at the "infantile" self-oriented level of sexual development and be unable to form good sexual relationships with others. For instance, Freudians viewed masturbation as a practice that would not allow women to learn how to experience a vaginal orgasm—the kind of orgasm Freudians considered "mature"—because females were learning to respond only to clitoral stimulation. The view that masturbation is a form of sexual expression that we should outgrow is still evident among psychoanalysts today (for example, see Marcus and Francis 1975).

Despite the Freudian view that masturbation among the young was to be expected, many sectors of society kept trying to prevent it. A 1930 Roman Catholic manual emphasized that parents should make sure their children have no chance to masturbate. For instance, "they should not be sent to bed unsupervised when they are excited and not tired enough for immediate sleep. . . . Children should be trained to sleep on either side, rarely in the unnatural position on their back" (Kirsch 1930, p. 263). A poll of 360 priests showed that preventive measures most often recommended against the "solitary sin" of "self-abuse" were frequent confessions, prayer to avoid temptation, development of strong willpower, accurate instruction on what practices were to be avoided, prudent choice of the child's companions, checkups by doctors to make sure there were no mental or physical defects, control of the child's thoughts

and reading material, and "plenty of interesting work and wholesome play" (Kirsch 1930, p. 265).

Up to 1940 a male could be discharged from the navy if medical examiners found "evidence" that he masturbated. And until 1945 the Boy Scout handbook described the genitals as organs that "secrete into the blood material that makes a boy manly, strong, and noble. Any habit which a boy has that causes this fluid to be discharged from the body tends to weaken his strength, to make him less able to resist disease, and often unfortunately fastens upon him habits which later in life can be broken only with great difficulty" (quoted in Gordon 1968, p. 24).

At the same time, more tolerant definitions of masturbation continued to reach the public. Kinsey (1948, 1953) made masturbation seem more "normal," for he found that the majority of his 12,000 volunteers had done it. Instead of portraying masturbation as a moral evil or a physical danger, Kinsey saw it as an effective release from built-up sexual tensions. Without this release, Kinsey (1953, p. 166) wrote, people may become "nervous, irritable, incapable of concentrating on any sort of problem, and difficult to live with." The only problems Kinsey linked to masturbation were feelings of guilt and anxiety. He viewed these reactions as inevitable results of over two thousand years of antimasturbatory socialization. Kinsey noted that experience gained in masturbation seemed to help women orgasm with intercourse. He even gave the practice some snob appeal by reporting that it was most common among better-educated and higher-class males.

After recording over 10,000 male and female orgasms in their St. Louis sex clinic, William Masters and Virginia Johnson (1966) gave masturbation another public boost. They noted that at least for women self-induced orgasms seemed to be stronger than those resulting from intercourse. By 1968 masturbation had such a good name that one of Kinsey's associates, Wardell Pomeroy, advised boys and girls to masturbate as often as they liked (in *Boys and Sex,* 1968, and *Girls and Sex,* 1969). In 1978 distinguished sex educator Eleanor Hamilton recommended self-pleasuring in her young person's guide to sex as a release for sexual tension and a way to become "pleasantly at home with

"Hey, you better cut that out! If you keep doing that, your hand will go bald!"

your own sexual organs" (p. 33). And many therapists are now advising their adult clients to masturbate to improve their sex lives. Albert Ellis recently commented, "Many years ago when I first started therapy, almost all of my clients would be ashamed of masturbating. Now they'd almost be ashamed *not* to" (Clanton, 1979, p. 244). As Carol Tavris and Susan Sadd (1977, p. 135) summed it up: "The activity once thought to cause warts is now recommended to do all but cure them. . . . Masturbation is the all-purpose tonic. And, as the wag said, you don't have to look your best." Although masturbation has been widely redefined as good rather than bad, the messages of the past still shape our attitudes and our behavior.

SELF-PLEASURING PATTERNS

Young children evidence considerable sexual interest and behavior. They are curious about their own and playmates' sexual anatomy, and they play sex-exploring games, learn available terminology, and explore their own sexual capacities. Childhood is not a quiet or "latent" sexual time but one of sexual adventure.

Self-stimulation among infants only a year old has been observed by parents and caretakers. Recall by older children and adults also suggests that by ages three and four many remember having experienced sexual feelings. Martinson (1981)

concludes that by age five any child is capable of erotic feelings. Although young children have this potential, wide differences exist in individuals' early sexual patterns.

Gender and Learning

It is a common observation that the penis has more consequences for young boys than the clitoris has for young girls. Langfeldt (1981b) contends that boys learn and readily label the relation between visible penis and sexual pleasure, while girls do not readily label and connect the less visible clitoris to sexual pleasuring. In addition boys' arousal and erection provide focus for jokes and sex talk among boys themselves and lead to the establishment of a "boys' sex culture."

Although young girls can masturbate and have heard sexual words, they do not easily connect the words to their sexual activity. They also tend to masturbate alone, reducing sexual sharing with peers, while boys will invariably be involved with groups of other boys and will explore and display sexual capacities. They get advice and encouragement to masturbate from older boys during secret meetings centering on sex play. Boys' groups encourage masturbation within the context of what Gagnon and Simon (1973, p. 57) call the "heroic sexual contest." For example, one male tells of the neighborhood "jerking-off" contests that took place in his mother's greenhouse. First it was only himself and his brothers, aiming for their favorite target, a sickly cactus:

We'd try to plant our come squarely on one of the broad, fleshy scales. News of this sport spread through the neighborhood and there were often waiting lines to get in. Some of the older boys could do all sorts of wonderful things, such as backward, upward, and sideward variations.   [Preterm Institute 1975, p. 68]

By contrast, Ruth Clifford (1978) concludes from interviews with 100 women from State University of New York at Stony Brook that masturbation usually began for these females as an "accidental discovery." This stumbling on an experience and continuing it, usually between ages ten to fifteen, involved no definitive labeling or social validation by others. They were aware that the behavior had sexual meaning, but they had no definitions that gave it clear self-meaning. This left masturbation somewhat vague, at best something done when feeling anxious or to help in getting to

It is not uncommon for children to discover and explore their genitals—but some parents feel such behaviors should be inhibited.

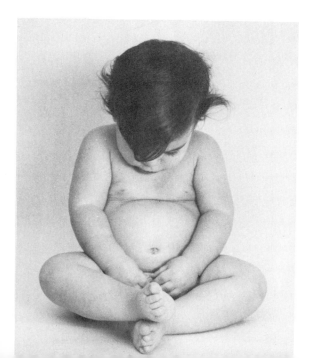

sleep. The lack of a script or even a label for females' early masturbation experience is evident in these comments:

In high school I never masturbated with a goal.

There was a negative feeling before it, so it was more for an equilibrium than enjoyment.

It took me about a year to figure out what was going on. Then I realized, this must be what is mentioned about climax.   [Clifford 1978, p. 565]

A similar description is novelist Alix Kates Shulman's childhood puzzlement:

Between my legs I had found an invisible button of flesh, sweet and nameless, which I knew how to caress to a nameless joy. I was pretty sure no one else had one, for there was no joy button in the hygiene book, and there was not even a dirty name for it. Though I listened carefully, I never heard anyone, boy or girl, so much as allude to it, nor was it pictured on the diagram in the Kotex box. Once, my anxiety overcoming my embarrassment, I had tried to ask my friend Jackie about it. But lacking a name or description for it, I couldn't even present the subject. When Jackie simply looked at me blankly, little beads of shame dampened my forehead, and I shut up. . . . Evidently, only starfish like me had joy buttons. [Shulman 1973, pp. 45–46]

Later on, through an extended process of talking to friends and reading, females come to define their masturbatory behavior as sexual and pleasurable. However, information from friends and from reading often depicts masturbation as an activity of males, or even animals, rather than females and leaves women to draw indirect parallels with their own behavior. One-fifth of Clifford's women so lacked a personal script for self-pleasuring that their first masturbation experiences were actually copies of their male partners' petting techniques.

Lifetime Rates and Frequency

Since masturbation is usually done privately, kept secret from adults, and rarely discussed, solid data are difficult to obtain. Yet most men and a solid majority of women have experienced some self-pleasuring.

Kinsey (1948, 1953) estimated that 92 percent of the males he studied had masturbated to orgasm at some time, or would within their lifetime if patterns were projected ahead. In contrast, only 62 percent of the females he studied had masturbated, and only 58 percent of them had masturbated to orgasm. The gap between males and females remains. In Morton Hunt's (1974) national sample of 2026 people from twenty-four United States cities, 94 percent of the males but only 63 percent of the females said they'd masturbated at some time. In Cody Wilson's (1975) national probability sample of 2468 adults, 53 percent of the females said they'd never masturbated, compared with 14 percent of the males. Similarly, Arafat and Cotton (1974) surveyed 600 students chosen at random from three New York universities. They found that over 89 percent of the male students masturbated *at that time,* whereas only 61 percent of the females did.

A *Playboy* survey of 65,396 male readers and 14,928 female readers reported that 88 percent of the men and 74 percent of the women masturbated. The relatively higher percentage reported for women in this survey compared with others may reflect the sex-positive nature of *Playboy*'s readership (Petersen et al. 1983a).

Males who masturbate also do so more often than females do. A study of introductory sociology students in Washington showed that the 132 women who currently masturbated did so once a week on the average. For the 116 men in the study, two times a week was the average frequency (Mahoney 1980).

The *Playboy* survey (Petersen et al. 1983a) reported that among the men 50 percent masturbated at least a few times a week, with a median frequency of 140 times a year. Among the women 28 percent masturbated at least a few times a week; the median frequency for females was 44 times a year. The greater frequency of masturbation in the early learning patterns of boys, combined with peer learning and encouragement, seem to continue to make masturbation an important sexual expression in adult life. The frequency of women's patterns has been more restrained.

Age

In addition to gender, age influences masturbation patterns. Kinsey (1948) found that single males masturbated most between puberty and age

twenty; married males, between twenty-one and twenty-five. For both groups the numbers who were masturbating and how often they did so dropped steadily after this peak. This trend had changed somewhat by the time of Hunt's (1974) survey. Whereas over one-fifth of Kinsey's single men had stopped masturbating by the time they were thirty, only a tenth of Hunt's thirty-year-olds had done so. In fact, those who were masturbating at all at this point were doing so more often than males aged sixteen to twenty-five.

Kinsey had assumed from his data that there was a natural biological decline of the male's sexual powers after young adulthood. But the fact that this trend is changing suggests that its origin was not biological but social. As we noted, Freud and his followers had defined masturbation in adulthood as a sign of immaturity. Although this idea still lingers, its hold over our attitudes is being counteracted by a newer message: Masturbation is acceptable and normal at all ages.

In contrast to males, females' masturbation frequencies, although lower, never dropped off after their twenties. On the contrary: Kinsey's (1953) females, both married and single, were most likely to masturbate when they were in their forties. At all ages the average frequency of masturbation remained fairly constant—about once every two and a half to three weeks for single women and once a month for married women.

Hunt's (1974) study indicates that single females are now masturbating more on the average at all ages than in Kinsey's time. But even now, women reach their peak later than men. About 60 percent of Hunt's women masturbated between the ages of eighteen and twenty-four; by their late twenties and early thirties, over 80 percent were doing so.

Kinsey (1953) suggested four possible explanations for why female rates rise with age rather than drop off as men's do: (1) Women's physical erotic capacity may somehow increase with age; (2) the number of other sexual outlets may dwindle for them as they grow older, prompting them to have sex with themselves; (3) females often shed their learned sexual inhibitions as they get older; and (4) as women gain more experience with two-person sex, they learn that they can produce the same results through masturbation.

TECHNIQUES

Although we learn to masturbate more by chance than by design, eventually we figure out what methods of self-stimulation seem most reliably to produce pleasurable sensations.

Males

Males have a varied repertoire of masturbation techniques. The standard techniques are hand stroking of the penis from the head (glans) to the base, rapid stroking of the head only, or rubbing and kneading of the whole organ. A few stimulate their anuses at the same time; some use their free hand to caress their thighs, breasts, stomach, or scrotum, and some rub against something such as a T-shirt rather than using their hand (Otto and Otto 1972). A survey of *Forum* magazine's sexually liberated readership (Africano 1979) indicates that a number of men have found ways to elaborate on the pleasure of masturbation. Three-fourths of the 20,000 respondents use erotic literature to turn on while masturbating. (At one time even Kinsey's

books were stolen from libraries for this purpose.) Others mention using vibrators, dildos (artificial penises), clothing, sheets, blankets, pillows, tubes, bottles, velvet or furs, shaving cream, vegetable oil, massage oils, and even banana peels.

Bernie Zilbergeld (1978), a specialist in sex therapy for men, suggests making masturbation a time for sensitive and leisurely personal exploration rather than the traditional speedy orgasm. He's found that because males tend to be ashamed of a behavior they have learned to regard as "childish," they usually masturbate as fast as they can. Kinsey (1948) found that most of his males climaxed within a minute or two after they started masturbating. For some orgasm occurred after only ten to twenty seconds of self-stimulation. Zilbergeld points out that this hurry tends to develop a habit of climaxing quickly in two-person sex, in which prolonging pleasure might be more satisfying for both partners. Hurrying also reinforces men's tendency to ignore arousal sensations that are more subtle than orgasm. To undo this learned pattern, Zilbergeld prescribes a number of "sensate focus" exercises that help men delay climax and pay attention to the subtleties of their responses.

Females

The majority of women masturbate by lying on their back and rubbing their vulval area—particularly the clitoris—with one hand. Variations on this basic pattern are common: inserting something into the vagina and/or anus (fingers, cucumbers, bananas, ice cubes, hot dogs, pickles, dildos, stuffed condoms, brass "ben-wa" balls [which jiggle in the vagina], bottles, hairbrush handles, candles, douche nozzles, teddy bears, and flashlights), using a vibrator, watching in a mirror, caressing breasts, using saliva or other lubricants to avoid painful friction and to increase sensual pleasure, sucking on a rubber penis, teasing the skin with feathers, holding legs apart or tightly together, lying on the stomach, squeezing thighs together rhythmically to build muscle tension, thrusting against a soft object, using faucets or removable shower heads for water flow over the genitals, and pressing against a vibrating washing machine (Hite 1976; DeMartino 1974).

Despite their interest in exploring any sensa-

tions that seem pleasurable, some creative masturbators are concerned about imagined social reactions to their private practices. For instance, one woman who likes to use something like a hairbrush handle to stimulate her vagina says she does so because it's tiring and difficult to reach that far with her hand. But she's defensive about vaginal stimulation with objects because she thinks it's considered "unfashionable" and "unnatural" (Hite 1976, p. 101). Unfashionable because some feminists frown on the idea that women need anything that resembles a penis to orgasm. Unnatural because sex aids are not defined as a normal part of sex in our culture. The point here is that social definitions of what is acceptable and normal and even pleasurable not only influence whether we masturbate, but they even affect how we do it and what sensations we are aware of.

Vibrators

Although vibrators are increasingly purchased as gifts for oneself or for lovers, some women feel anxious about using vibrators. They've learned to define the technological orgasm as "unnatural," "artificial," an insult to their partner, or a crutch they might get hooked on. But they consider it okay to use other electrical appliances to make life easier or more pleasant--irons, toasters, hair dryers, clocks. A vibrator allows a woman to stimulate herself faster, steadier, longer, and more intensely than she can with her hand. For some women this kind of stimulation is essential if they are to orgasm, especially when they're first learning how. Although most can eventually switch to less intense hand-stroking (sometimes preferred for more sensitive, leisurely self-pleasuring), many continue to enjoy a vibrator's quick touch. And males' fears that they've been replaced by a machine may be unfounded. If a vibrator has helped their partner learn to be more sexually alive, this is to both partners' advantage. Since some men enjoy a vibrator's sensations themselves, many couples have added vibrator pleasuring to their mutual sexual activities.

Transferring Orgasm from One- to Two-Person Sex

Many think that one of the advantages of masturbation is learning how to orgasm, knowledge that can be carried over to two-person sex. But for some people this transfer doesn't happen. Some men and women who orgasm readily on their own can't seem to orgasm with a partner. When Toni Ayres and Bernie Zilbergeld questioned patients at the Sex Advisory and Counseling Unit of the University of California Medical Center, they concluded that the weak link was *how* people masturbated.

Ayres (1979) explains that men classified as "premature ejaculators" in two-person sex typically masturbate quickly. They've trained their bodies to a response pattern that may be dysfunctional in a two-person situation. On the other hand those who can't orgasm at all with a partner may have patterns of masturbating that bear no resemblance to the kind of stimulation they receive during intercourse. Most men wrap their whole hand around the shaft of their penis and stroke up and

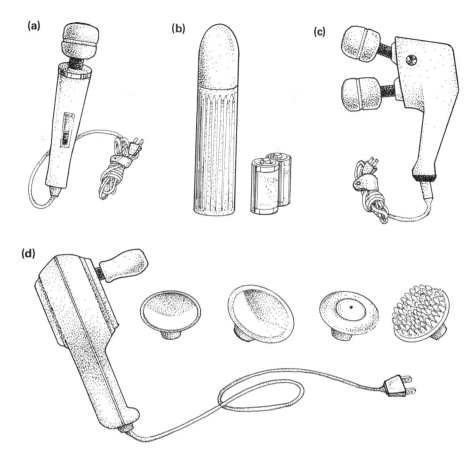

Figure 4-1. Types of Vibrators. Using a vibrator is one of the surest ways to orgasm for females; many males enjoy a vibrator's sensations, too. Styles of vibrators vary. Those shown here are (a) an electric model that produces strong vibrations that are good for sore muscles as well as for genital massage, (b) a portable, battery-powered vibrator that can be played over the external genitals or inserted into the vagina, (c) a two-headed vibrator for males that massages both sides of the penis at one time, and (d) an electric model with an assortment of attachments, including a special one for the clitoris.

Vibrator Sales: Out of the Closet

Once sold mostly out of sleazy porno shops, mail-order catalogs that also feature crotchless panties and the like, or department stores (as "body massagers"), vibrators are now sold openly as sexual pleasure-enhancers by a few special boutiques. Interviews with Bryce Britton, sex therapist and part owner of "Eve's Garden" in New York City, and Joani Blank, sex educator, author of *I Am My Lover* and other candid booklets on sex-uality, and owner of "Good Vibrations" in San Francisco, provide a handle on who patronizes these stores and what they're looking for. Both women report that vibrator sales are booming.

Bryce: Our East Side brownstone boutique is designed to make a person feel comfortable. We have beautiful murals, artwork, sensual items other than vibrators, and a catalog that's very permis-

sion-giving. We couch vibrator use in very positive terms: You have a right to your own sexuality, this is okay. We're getting away from the old "naughty, naughty, dirty" type of sneaking-around sexuality.

The average age of our buyers is between twenty-five and thirty-five. Most of the traffic in the store is women, buying something for themselves. However, the most money is spent by men. Although some men want a vibrator for their own use, in about 75 percent of cases they are buying one to encourage a female partner in her sexuality. If there are men in the store and a woman comes in, usually she won't speak up about what she wants. She feels inhibited and rather shy. Sometimes people pretend that they want something for a sore neck. We automatically speak about how a particular vibrator can be used all over your body, including your genitals, to help bring this subject into the open. But usually if people are open and aggressive enough to even come in, then they've already made the commitment to talking about vibrators and vaginas and clitorises and pleasures.   [Britton 1979]

Joani: *My store is not in a bustling commercial area—it's in a neighborhood area of San Francisco—so almost everybody who is coming in is coming there on purpose. They're not seeing it on the street, walking in, and saying, "Oh, isn't this weird?" or "Isn't this funny?" or "Isn't this neat?"*

The vast majority of vibrators are bought by women who are buying them for themselves. Right now I would say we're seeing a few more lesbians than straight women. Once something like this gets started in the tight lesbian community, word spreads pretty fast. I think it's just a matter of who knows my store more. I don't think it's because lesbians are more interested in using vibrators than straight people. Women come into the store alone, or with a friend, or sometimes with their lover—male or female.

The second most common people who actually purchase vibrators are men buying them for their women partners. The third most common—this is something I really enjoy seeing—is couples who will say they are buying them to use together or for both of them to enjoy either together or separately. Very few men buy vibrators for themselves. Gay men who come in are usually buying them for themselves, or themselves and their partners.

It's important to debunk the myth that when you say "vibrator," you're talking about dildo battery vibrators (as opposed to some of the large electric vibrators). I find the most persistent, hard-to-deal-with myth that men and some women are suffering from is that the way a woman uses the vibrator is as a penis substitute. She not only has a vibrator shaped like that, she also uses it like that, moving it in and out of her vagina, just like a "real person" enjoys sex. Men are very attached to that idea. They typically walk right over to the counter where the battery-operated dildo-type vibrators are.

If there's any one thing that needs to be said about vibrators, it's that they are not really a substitute for anything—a penis that won't work, or a lover who can't quite make it with her fingers. Vibrators aren't a substitute for anything—they're just vibrators.   [Blank 1979]

down and around the testicles. But those who can't orgasm with a partner tend to use different techniques, such as stroking only the glans with their fingertips, or twisting their penis down toward their feet, or crossing their legs and rubbing against the bed. After drawing these descriptions out of their patients, Ayres and Zilbergeld suggested that they expand their ways of masturbation to resemble intercourse more closely: stroking up and down the whole shaft, with lubrication.

Clifford (1978) speculates that women who masturbate while lying on their stomachs orgasm in intercourse more readily because of the easy transfer of their masturbatory techniques to partner sex. She observes that the diffuse stimulation the entire front of a woman's body receives while she is masturbating on her stomach resembles face-to-face contact during intercourse. However, transfer from masturbation to partner sex is far from automatic. Ayres (1979) says she's run across many women who say they are "stuck" on one way to have orgasm that is not easily transferred to sex with a partner. One somehow climaxed by rubbing her genitals against a door jamb. She was too embarrassed by this unusual method to say to her partner in the middle of sex, "Excuse me, I have to use the door." Some used overstuffed chairs, shower heads, or faucets and couldn't seem to climax without them. None felt they could say to their partner, "Excuse me, I have to go get the chair," or "Okay, let's get in the tub." Ayres's cure: teaching them to masturbate by using their hand, an aid that is more readily available for help during two-person sex.

The Role of Fantasy

Many of us increase our sensual pleasure by fantasizing while masturbating. What function do fantasies serve? Many use them as attempts to partially fulfill unmet needs. For instance, husbands and wives who've never had extramarital affairs but long for variety may get vicarious enjoyment from fantasies of sex with other partners, something they don't permit themselves in real life. Sometimes fantasy is used as an escape from a situation that doesn't meet physical or emotional needs. For instance, people who define intercourse as the only "normal" way to enjoy sex may pretend that they are having intercourse instead of masturbating.

Needs dealt with in fantasies may not necessarily be sexual in nature. For example, a male who's been socialized to value achievement and dominance may fantasize about performing like a stud and dominating a whole harem of women. But some of us do use fantasies for explicitly sexual purposes. For those who find it hard to orgasm, focusing on erotic fantasies helps distract attention from the fear of letting go or from attempts to control physical responses consciously. Fantasizing about exciting sensations may even help us "feel" them.

Favorite fantasies for both men and women are most likely to involve intercourse with an attractive or loved partner, the activity most commonly linked with the idea of sex in our culture. But fantasies sometimes deviate from this standard script, especially among the young. Thoughts of intercourse with strangers are fairly common, having occurred in fantasy form to 47 percent of males and 21 percent of females in Hunt's (1974) study. Less typical fantasies include sex with several people of the other gender (mentioned by 33 percent

Many of us create romantic images of two-person lovemaking in our fantasies while we are actually self-pleasuring.

A Sampling of Fantasies

My most common fantasy is of the assertive stranger, the female that I just meet somewhere and she initiates sex. It's more direct than anything that usually happens in real life. She unzips my pants, shuts the shades and doors, sucks me off. I keep wishing I'd meet more women like that.

My favorite fantasy is finger-fucking a continuous line of women, playing each one as an instrument of passion and rhythm. Each one shall teach me a new song of love as I bring her to a crescendo of ecstasy with my musical fingers of rhythmic lust, only then to begin the song anew. Ah, sweet funky finger-fucking.

Besides being deep-throated by Linda Lovelace, . . . I have always wanted to have two women at the same time.

While walking in the park or museum, to make eye contact only with a smashingly sensuous person, take hands, and walk to a secluded grove or office and make love slowly and spontaneously.

I like to fantasize that I'm standing at the top of the globe, masturbating next to a master switch. I could produce current which would go out to thousands of women holding electric vibrators ready to use them on their clitorises. They would all get off at the same time and they would all hear each other (and also me making sexual comments on the same closed circuit). It would be the orgasm sent around the world.

Lying in deep grass high on a hill—my body naked and the sun splashing down on me—feeling its warmth penetrate me. My lover stands before me, blocking out the sun. I look at his beautiful smile and the nakedness of his body. He comes down on me, his body on top of mine—gentleness—kissing touching licking penetrating, our arms and legs entwined in one another—and we roll down the hill together. [Collected by Bryce Britton and the authors]

of males and 18 percent of females), sexual activities one would "never" act out in reality (19 percent of the males and 28 percent of the females), being forced to have sex (10 percent of the males and 19 percent of the females), forcing someone into sex (13 percent of the males and 3 percent of the females), and sex with someone of the same gender (7 percent of the males and 11 percent of the females).

CONTEMPORARY PERSPECTIVES

Although many of us masturbate and have built a rich fantasy life to accompany sex with ourselves, the remnants of thousands of years of antimasturbatory teaching are still evident in some of our social institutions. In the medical profession adult masturbation is sometimes viewed as regression to a childish level. One study of graduate medical students and residents showed that 16 percent believe that masturbation causes "certain conditions of mental and emotional instability" (Miller and Lief 1976).

Many religions also maintain a "hands-off" attitude toward masturbation, although some are edging toward a more positive approach. For instance, in 1970 the United Presbyterian Church issued a paper on sexuality that included this sentence: "Since masturbation is often one of the earliest pleasurable sexual experiences which is identifiably genital, we consider it essential that the church, through its teachings and through the attitudes it encourages in Christian homes, contribute to a healthy understanding of this experience which will be free of guilt and shame." (*Minutes of the General Assembly . . . 1970*, p. 902).

In many ostensibly sex-positive publications for males, however, masturbation is never mentioned. Magazines whose centerfolds cater to the male masturbator skirt the subject in both their articles and their cartoons. Masturbation is also conspicuously absent from the lusty novels that help shape male sexual identity. In everyday life men who regularly brag and joke about sex rarely speak of masturbation, for it's not considered something to be proud of. Edgar LeMasters (1975, p. 97) has heard blue-collar bar patrons admit that masturbation is "better than no sex at all," but "I jerked off five times today!" simply isn't heard. Calling a guy a "jerk" always carries negative connotations. As Morton Hunt (1974, pp. 66–67) points out, "It is far easier to admit that one does not believe in God, or was once a Communist, or was born illegitimately, than that one sometimes fondles a part of his own body to the point of orgastic release."

In families, too, masturbation is rarely talked about but silently discouraged. Several studies indicate that only 7 to 18 percent of parents talk to their children about masturbation at all. But 40 percent of parents say they disapprove of the practice (Wilson 1975; Roberts, Kline, and Gagnon 1978). Some of this disapproval is probably expressed in their earliest nonverbal training of the child—by slapping or removing hands as they touch genitals or by anxious attempts to distract the child's attention from its body. Also, parents happily teach their children names for everything nongenital. As sex counselor Diane Brashear (1979, p. 84) notes: " 'Where's your eye! Your nose?' is a favorite parent-child game which aids the child's cognitive development as well as communicating positive value about the named body parts. . . . But, how many parents say, 'Where's your penis? Your vagina? Vulva? Clitoris? Testes?' " Perhaps parents hope that these parts will be unused and forgotten if they are left nameless and unmentioned. Many girls therefore grow up with no labels for their genitals other than "down there" (from "Don't touch yourself *down there*") and no idea of what parts they've got "down there."

Nevertheless, there is a trend in our society toward optimizing experiences. An emerging ethic is that sensations should be maximized and that everyone has a right to sexual pleasure and gratification of some sort. Suddenly a number of institutions are saying that masturbation is okay and even good for us.

In 1974 the Sex Information and Educational Council of the United States (SIECUS) announced that sexual self-pleasuring is "a natural part of sexual behavior for individuals of all ages" (Brashear 1979, p. 83). According to the SIECUS statement, masturbation can be defined as a way of learning that our bodies are part of ourselves and that it's acceptable to enjoy them. It can also be seen as a tension-releaser that's harmless to us and others, a preparation for sexual activities with a partner, and an aid to seeing ourselves as full and vibrant human beings.

The Language of Sex

Many researchers claim that masturbating makes a woman more "responsive." This label for female sexuality makes woman sound like a passive—or at best, willing—receptacle for male sexual advances. To portray a more equal involvement in initiating and enjoying sex, we can use words that describe individual feelings, such as sexually "alive," "aroused," "vibrant," "enthusiastic"—for both genders.

Many sex therapists are now promoting masturbation as a learning tool. For instance, Van Wyk (1982) reports that masturbation therapy exercises help women who have never orgasmed. He contends further that women spending more time on the masturbation therapy exercises are better able to develop orgasmic responses than women who spend little time doing the exercises.

Therapist Robert Kohlenberg (1974) had several couples in which the woman hadn't become orgasmic after thirteen weeks of the standard Masters and Johnson program for nonorgasmic women. Kohlenberg added "directed" masturbation to what they were doing already. Within a few weeks the women were having orgasms with intercourse as well as with masturbation and were more sexually aroused in general.

Sex therapist Helen Singer Kaplan (1974) encourages nonorgasmic women not only to masturbate—with a vibrator if necessary—but also to fantasize if they are blocking orgasm by thinking about it too much. And Julia Heiman and Leslie and Joseph LoPiccolo (1976) find that they must often add other elements to their masturbation therapy for nonorgasmic women to undo the anti-sex training many grew up with. Among these are pelvic-rocking exercises (to loosen learned inhibitions that stiffen this area) and "role-playing orgasm"—pretending to have a wildly exciting orgasm in order to confront learned fears of moving or feeling that may be holding orgasm in check.

Women's publications are now encouraging masturbation. In the popular self-help book *Our*

Bodies, Ourselves, the Boston Women's Health Book Collective (1976) recommends masturbation as "a special way of enjoying ourselves" that need not be limited to pleasuring of clitoris, vagina, and breasts. Since "masturbation allows us the time and space to explore and experiment with our own bodies, . . . we are learning to enjoy all parts of our bodies" (p. 47). And the heroine of Erica Jong's novel *How to Save Your Own Life* is so casual about masturbation that she describes it as mundane:

I rolled over on my back once more, studied the ceiling, reached down to fondle my breasts, . . . then reached lower down to fondle my cunt. I began to masturbate again desultorily, but quickly lost interest. Nothing so mundane would tranquilize me on this particular night. [Jong 1977, p. 16]

Encouraged by such openness, women in some circles talk freely to each other about masturbation. Therapists now prescribe self-pleasuring to women who want to be more easily orgasmic and to men who take orgasm too seriously. Bernie Zilbergeld (1978), for instance, recommends masturbation exercises to help free his male clients from the old performance expectations and to introduce them to the pleasures of just relaxing and enjoying whatever sensations come along.

In her sex guide for teenagers, therapist Eleanor Hamilton (1978) describes masturbation as a practice that has no dire consequences except the "unnecessary" feeling of guilt. From birth to death, she writes, self-pleasuring can be seen as one of several ways of expressing sexuality. It is especially useful for teenagers as a way to release sexual tension and learn the "pathway to orgasm" before intercourse starts. Hamilton warns, however, that unenlightened parents may not be so happy with the practice. For the time being she recommends self-pleasuring in a locked bedroom for "privacy, safety, and leisure."

OUR CHOICES IN PLEASURING OURSELVES

Despite more positive messages, many of us still feel uneasy about masturbating. There's a real split between attitudes and behavior here. In *Forum's* liberal male readership, 99 percent masturbated but only 28 to 30 percent said they felt happy after masturbating (Africano 1979). Although 81 percent of DeMartino's "highly intelligent" women (1974) masturbated, only 68 percent approved of the practice. And of the 435 university students questioned by Arafat and Cotton (1974), over a third had negative feelings after masturbating: guilt, depression, feeling of perversion, even fear of becoming insane. And some consider masturbation "second best," seeing it as a poor substitute for two-person sex.

Despite these dilemmas, most of us find that masturbation simply feels so good that it's worth continuing. It's highly effective in producing orgasm, for we know better than anyone else precisely how we like to be stimulated. For Kinsey's women (1953) masturbation was the number one source of orgasms. According to Masters and Johnson's laboratory studies (1966), masturbation affords the most measurably intense orgasms for both sexes.

In addition to satisfying our arousal by giving sensual pleasure, masturbation rewards in nonsexual ways. It's seen by some as a release for tensions built up through work or personal problems, an escape into fantasy, a comfort when we're feeling lonely or rejected, a bright spot in a sometimes drab existence, a relief for menstrual tension or cramps, and a good way to get to sleep. And for those who don't like to feel dependent on a partner, self-pleasuring can provide a sense of autonomy.

The sexual dividends of masturbating often extend beyond the pleasure of the moment. Learning how to stimulate ourselves to sexual arousal and orgasm—without an audience and without having to mesh with a partner—can be transferred to two-person sex as knowledge that can be shared with our partner about what kind of stimulation we find most effective and as heightened interest in sexuality. The more orgasms we have—by whatever method—the more we can have, for frequent use increases our capacity for pelvic blood congestion, the biological basis for sexual excitement.

Some lovers enjoy masturbation during two-person sex. Released from the old embarrassments and inhibitions about masturbation, they can touch themselves as easily and as fondly as they touch each other, thereby enriching the spontaneous erotic possibilities of their encounters.

Self-pleasuring is always available, even if our partner isn't feeling sexual or even if we don't have a partner. Learning to know and enjoy our bodies intimately can help us build and maintain a solid and positive self-concept at any age. Self-pleasuring can be a rich part of our sexual lives—neither better nor worse than intercourse, just different—from the cradle to the grave. As Betty Dodson (1974, p. 1) puts it, "It got me through childhood, puberty, romantic love, marriage and it will happily see me through old age."

SUMMARY

From childhood through adulthood, many of us derive at least occasional sexual satisfaction from self-pleasuring. Yet traditionally many have felt guilty or awkward about this common behavior. Throughout much of Western history masturbation has been castigated by social institutions, and parents have passed the negative attitudes on to their children. Today, somewhat more positive messages are appearing.

At all ages males are more likely to masturbate than females. But whereas men's rates of masturbation decline with age, women's rates rise as they get older. While masturbation is a pleasure unto itself, it can also help people better enjoy sex with a partner. Techniques vary, some being more easily transferred to two-person sex than others. For many, fantasies and vibrators enhance self-pleasure. As social messages that masturbation is okay and even potentially good for us appear, we can choose to free ourselves from the guilt long associated with self-pleasuring.

5

Developing Sexual Relationships

I'd really like to find a man but I don't want to be hurt again. Twice now I've fallen in love with beautiful men, had sex with them, and then lost them because I seemed to care more about keeping the relationship going than they did. Both times I let myself be open and vulnerable, let them know how very much I wanted them, but they seemed to be scared away by the intensity of my feelings. I don't want to hide the way I feel—but I don't want to be hurt again either. I love being in love, and I love touching and being touched, but I don't know if it's worth the pain.

"Do you want to do it?" Angie asked at 7:30 Saturday morning, her hand wrapped around my stiff rod. "You always want to do it twice, you know" (by which she meant both evening and morning, and then only at times when one of us didn't have to rush off). I said, "No," followed by her "Why not?" and my "It just doesn't feel right." My wife's trouble is she tunes in to my tremendous interest in sex, but she herself could usually take it or leave it. When she's in that disinterested mood I pick it up immediately, and it's a real turn-off. Sometimes I'll try to get her excited, but other times I just give up. It's just too much hassle to try to be warm and loving with a person that is only doing her duty. Sex can be a bummer when it's like that. But when you really love your wife, you accept it, and just wait till she is really ready.

We met fifteen years ago—love at first sight—and have been together ever since as friends, lovers, and husband and wife. It hasn't all been a bed of roses. I've loved—and made love with—other men from time to time, and it's been hard for him to deal with his jealousy and hurt pride. He has tried to be philosophical, though, no matter what his emotions have been. We've had to keep reworking our ground rules for outside relationships as things change. For instance, for several years he's had a sexual friend himself and he enjoys seeing her more often than the once-a-month rule we agreed to long ago, so that one has now been relaxed. Sometimes he's been so upset about things I've done, or ways I've done them, that he's almost left. But I'm so grateful that he hasn't, for we come out of each difficult time closer and appreciating each other more. We don't keep coming back to the same place—it's more like a spiral, stretching always higher and wider into the infinite dimensions of love.

As Erica Jong (1973, p. 14) notes in *Fear of Flying*, the "zipless fuck"—in which strangers meet, immediately sense the sexual electricity between them, and slip easily into sex with no complications, no stuck zippers, no embarrassments, no interpersonal problems—is "rarer than the unicorn." Sex cannot be isolated from the rest of a relationship, and making a relationship work is not always easy. Developing a sexual relationship and keeping it alive and healthy usually involve continuing sensitive negotiations.

We tend to define sex as extremely significant activities loaded with symbolic meanings. To get together sexually with another person, we need to understand not only our own ideas about what sex means but theirs, too. Developing these understandings can be complicated by our unwillingness to talk about sex openly and directly. With varying degrees of success, couples often try to make up their own rules for sexual "bargaining" as they go along.

The private nature of most sexual encounters makes it difficult to get valid research data. Data gatherers have had to eavesdrop at singles bars and other places to get some idea of what goes on. Public unwillingness to explore the mysteries of love has been another major obstacle. Senator William Proxmire, for instance, presented his infamous Golden Fleece Award to professors Elaine Walster (Hatfield) and Ellen Berscheid for a grant they'd received from the National Science Foundation (NSF) to study passionate and companionate love. His rationale: "I believe that 200 million other Americans want to leave some things in life a mystery, and right at the top of things we don't want to know is why a man falls in love with a woman and vice versa" (Walster and Walster 1978). After that the NSF withdrew further support of the research.

Our understanding of the extremely important area of sexual relationships continues to be sketchy. We know a good bit more about how vaginas and penises work than about how they find each other. Many social scientists think that these relationships operate like the economic marketplace. That is, we form and maintain intimate relationships through a bargaining process in which we each try to maximize our rewards and minimize our costs. Much of our social interaction is guided by socially learned definitions. Sexual exchanges are complicated by the fact that some of us have learned different symbolic definitions of the costs and rewards of sexual relationships.

PARTNER SEEKING

The initial step in two-person sex is finding a partner. Weighing of costs and rewards here involves our motives for sex, our socially shaped notions about monogamy versus more open sexual lifestyles, our distrust of or friendship toward the other gender, our willingness to take risks, and our embarrassment over looking for partners and communicating our availability.

Motives for Sex

A number of current self-help books encourage us to free ourselves from dependence on others—that is, to be autonomous, self- rather than other-directed persons. This line of argument assumes that we can satisfy our own needs to some extent. But Robert Thamm (1975), author of *Beyond Marriage and the Nuclear Family*, disagrees. We humans are *inter*dependent creatures, he claims. We have certain needs that can best be met through relationships with others rather than through experiences with ourselves.

According to psychologist Richard Centers (1975), the most important of these needs are probably a longing for sexual gratification, a yearning for affectionate intimacy with another human, and a desire to see our socially defined gender role enhanced—that is, to feel more "manly" or "womanly." Touching, caressing, emotional closeness, and sexual sharing are powerful antidotes to the sense of loneliness we may feel as independent adults. We are therefore strongly attracted to persons who might provide these enriching experiences.

Family studies specialist Gerhard Neubeck (1972) speculates that beneath these socially approved motives for sex are other hidden motives. Some we define as sexual; some we consider nonsexual. Neubeck's motives for sex include:

■ **Affection**—longing for love, closeness, and the physical and emotional union that can be satisfied through sex

A sexual relationship may satisfy a variety of needs, only one of which is sexual gratification.

■ **Hostility**—for those of us who are taught that sex is dirty and degrading, using it as a way to degrade people we feel hostile toward

■ **Anxiety**—using sex as temporary relief from nonsexual frustrations or worries

■ **Boredom**—using sex to enhance a dull environment, routine activities, or even less "intimate" forms of touching

■ **Duty**—feeling that it's our responsibility to have sex on schedule or to keep a partner from being uncomfortably frustrated (typically a female feels that she can't leave a male unsatisfied. The notion that he could masturbate or that she might feel equally uncomfortable if highly aroused but not satisfied is missing from traditional scripts)

■ **Mending wounds**—using sex as a way to make up after an argument or even to avoid dealing with it

■ **Accomplishment**—wanting to have sex as often as we think everyone else does, in every conceivable position

■ **Adventure**—desiring to explore beyond the bounds of our previous experiences

■ **Recreation**—having sex for fun or for creating pleasant sensations for each other

■ **Lust**—having passion for increasing and then gratifying sexual desires with a focus on sensual arousal, fantasies, and delight in touching and being touched

■ **Self-affirmation**—acting out our perceived sexual identity so that the other will notice and approve of it

■ **Altruism**—feeling that we give others sexual pleasure and enjoy doing so

Other social scientists have accepted Neubeck's list of motives but have added more of their own. For instance, Gail Fullerton (1972) asserts that some of us seek sexual relationships to substitute for other needs we cannot satisfy. One of these needs is the desire to feel powerful. From the barrios to rural filling stations, young males who are poor flaunt the only power they have—sexual prowess—just as powerless women find a sense of power in their ability to turn men on.

Another possibility: Sex may be motivated by a desire for spiritual experience. This notion rarely occurs to Westerners who've been taught to associate sex with sin. But in certain Eastern religious traditions, sexual ecstasy is prized as an experience of universal love, a level of awareness that transcends the usual conscious, inhibited ways of thinking (Moffett 1974).

Dennis Brissett (1972) notes that it's not enough merely to identify and list motives for sex seeking. He thinks it may be equally important to explore how specific motives influence the sexual relationships that result. Some motives seem more likely to lead to enjoyment; others, to problems. Changes in motives are worth examining, too. Over a lifetime sexual career one person's motives might change from adventurousness to intimacy seeking to pleasure seeking to accomplishment. Even during a single encounter boredom may be replaced by lust, or a sense of adventure may be supplanted by a sense of duty. Brissett thinks it would be helpful for partners to discuss their motives openly with each other before, after, and even during sex.

Cultural Assumptions about Sexual Attraction

Our motives for partner seeking are acted out within a socially structured framework. In the past the expected pattern was to seek sexual partners only within the framework of marriage—or at least of progression toward marriage. Today feelings of economic and social insecurity are again encouraging support for an increase of exclusive pairing, with or without marriage. Such partnerships hold out the promise of stability in unstable times. We have, however, no evidence that this belief has resulted in more monogamous behaviors. And since many intimate relationships do not last, this pattern has been called *serial monogamy*—one partner at a time, replaced by a new one after breakup, divorce, or death.

At the same time a set of counter assumptions about sexual relationships has been emerging. This trend assumes that there is an eternal, erotic, emotional attraction between people and therefore a permanent availability of people to each other for emotional and sexual expression, regardless of marital or living arrangements or gender. Relationship choices other than monogamous marriage—such as singlehood, living together, and multiple relationships—are increasingly visible and accepted, widening people's options. In many communities people can privately do as they wish without negative social sanctions, so long as they are discreet. And since women's status is increasingly independent of husbands, women no longer need to be so cautious about withholding sex for its exchange value. Instead of a scarce good to be bargained over, sexuality has become something women enjoy for its own sake.

Some of us interpret these emerging realities as encouragement for more sex with more people for more reasons. For instance, Robert Thamm (1975) asserts that if we were truly rational about this matter, we'd see that the best thing to aim for is commitment and interdependence with several partners. Too many, he thinks, limits the possibility for depth of involvement with each person. Too few—as in the monogamous model—increases our risk of having our needs unmet. If that single resource fails to provide us with gratification and security, we are unhappy or even fall apart.

On the other hand, establishing a new relationship requires a lot of time, effort, and psychological risk. After investing all these things in one partner, some of us find it more profitable and comfortable to maintain and deepen that relationship than constantly to look for others. Some people define loyalty and commitment as sexual exclusiveness. Others, whether they agree with this definition or not, still find great sexual and emotional satisfaction in a single sexual relationship, perhaps augmented with other close friendships. This monogamous path is increasingly seen as a choice, though, rather than what is solely expected of everyone.

One phenomenon that is becoming increasingly common in our fast-paced, transient society is the brief but rich intimate relationship. Coleman and Edwards (1979) devote an entire book to these "brief encounters." They emphasize the spontaneity and fun of short-term, temporary relationships:

A temporary alliance . . . can be a contract to be devilish together—to eat hot fudge sundaes, jaywalk, shop for unnecessary clothes, use profane words, and laugh a lot. It can be a contract just to have oodles of playful, lusty sex but not to talk of problems or have heavy discussions. . . . [Coleman and Edwards 1979, p. 10]

Brief sexual encounters may be valued for their intimate potential, rather than devalued because they are different from long-term relationships. John Wilson describes past attitudes toward short-term relationships:

With sex, casual relationships must *somehow be wrong, simply because they are not deep or "grave" relationships. So they are described with loaded terms, like "superficial," "shabby," "neurotic," and "inadequate.". . . The fallacy lies in passing a value-judgment against them merely because they are not something else.*   [Wilson 1965, p. 72]

We can choose to enjoy both short- and long-term relationships, as they need not be incompatible.

Scripts for Being Together

In the past it was difficult for males and females in our culture to be together as friends, or to enjoy brief encounters rather than relationships, for these ways of relating did not fit into the traditional courtship script. Rather than encouraging people to feel comfortable and friendly with each other, the traditional script sometimes created an atmosphere of mistrust and misunderstanding between the sexes. Females were trained to guard their sexual expression because it was all they had to bargain with. The idea was to find the best match and to interest him sexually without giving him "too much," in which case he would no longer respect or desire the woman. The goal: to make him want her for his wife. Males, on the other hand, were expected to be the competent, confident initiators in the relationship—arranging dates, paying the tab, driving the car, making explicit sexual overtures. The typical exchange: his status and economic security for her sex appeal and domestic services. There was no accepted script for sexual attraction to one's own gender.

Boys and girls were expected to act out their presumed attraction to each other in prescribed stages of exclusive "dating." By fifth or sixth grade they were expected to have one boyfriend or girlfriend; in junior and senior high school they were to progress from group dates to double and single dates and to "going with" or "going steady" with a person after several dates together. These stages were supposed to lead eventually to monogamous marriage. Although there was an expectation of exclusivity, "cheating" on the side was not uncommon. Relationships tended to be characterized by traditional gender role expectations and by the assumption of permanence. They sometimes broke up anyway, for partners often blamed each other, rather than the form of their relationship, when they were unhappy with it. The goal—living

happily ever after as a married couple—was realized by some but not all.

As a result of the traditional courtship script, men distrusted women for their learned eagerness to please without truly giving in. Women distrusted the lines—"You're beautiful, I love you"—men traditionally used to get them to agree to greater sexual intimacies than women were supposed to want. Sex was thus socially structured as a battlefield. As psychologist Albert Ellis wrote of the situation prevailing back in 1962:

Maybe if we were willing to devote millions of dollars and years of research effort to devising a set of courtship customs and mores which were specifically designed to lead to exceptionally low-level . . . sex satisfaction for both males and females, we could actually devise a more sexually sabotaging set of dating procedures than we now have. Maybe.   [Ellis 1962, p. 66]

The mutual feeling was that persons of the other sex were too treacherous to be trusted with control of the situation but so attractive and so essential to social status that one couldn't live without them. This set of expectations was hardly conducive to trusting, openness, intimacy, and spontaneity.

Although this dating script still shapes much of our heterosexual behavior, traditional expectations are being replaced to some extent by a more flexible "getting together" script. The new approach is characterized by egalitarian activities with friends of both sexes and by simply being together rather than having structured dates in which the male pays and drives the car. When close relationships evolve, whether to have sex and whether to be sexually open or exclusive may be open to ongoing negotiations. Partners may encourage each others' growth as individuals, viewing their being together as a continually changing process and a conscious choice rather than a static set of promises.

Sexual Politics

As the sexes raise their consciousness of themselves as whole people, they develop the potential for more honest and freely loving relationships with each other. However, some have chosen a different path: Either from anger at becoming fully aware of what the other sex has "done to them" or from joy at discovering the strengths and depths of their own sex, some have tried homosexual relationships. Others have opted out of the battle between the sexes by choosing to be celibate.

Women's Liberation and Sexuality. A major complaint that has emerged from the women's movement is that women's roles have been oppressively limited by society as a whole and by men in particular. In sex women traditionally have been held to stricter standards than have men. Some observers speculate that it was to women's evolutionary advantage to be more selective than males in mating (Symonds 1979); some note that women themselves have tried to limit their sexuality in the interest of not getting pregnant when and with whom they didn't choose, or in the interest of maintaining some autonomy within marriage (Degler 1980); some feel that men, as the dominant sex, took enjoyment of sexual freedom for themselves and denied it to their wives and daughters (Reiss 1981). Whatever the reason, many women have felt that they have been denied control of their own bodies.

In addition to the double moral standard women's sexual biology in the past has been defined largely by men. Men wrote most of the books describing female orgasm, prompting Barbara Seaman (author of *Free and Female*) to threaten to write a book entitled *Sore Balls* describing "how it feels to be kicked in the testicles by a horse" (Seaman 1973, pp. 35–38).

The medical establishment given responsibility for women's sexual health is still predominantly male. Only about 12 percent of physicians in the United States are women; of those only 7 percent are obstetrician/gynecologists (Fee 1978). Male doctors sometimes apply traditional sexist assumptions about women to their female patients and dismiss them with fatherly pats as weak, hysterical, neurotic complainers rather than intelligent persons describing real symptoms and deserving direct answers. Men are not the only ones creating this unequal doctor-patient relationship. In the past women trained to want someone else to play the "daddy" role often liked this setup and worshiped doctors who appeared kindly and Godlike (Corea 1977).

Economically, men have maintained power by controlling most of the money and holding the most economically and socially rewarding occupations. If anything, the inequity between women's and men's salaries has increased. Although 43 percent of the workforce in the United States now consists of women, women earn only 60 percent of what men earn, and this figure has actually dropped by 4 percent during the past quarter century (Hendrick 1982). Most of the women who work are in stereotypical female occupations, such as nursing and school teaching. Low-paying and low-status positions are more often held by women than by men (*Current Population Reports* 1980).

Women's liberation has freed some women from images of females as childish sex objects.

The result is a shaping of women's love as subordination. With an unequal balance of power, love and intimacy become difficult to attain because they can develop better between trusting people who have no desire to control each other. To the extent that women are dependent on men for their economic survival, they are subject to men's control over all aspects of their lives—including the sexual.

The so-called sexual revolution, although it has had some positive spin-offs for both sexes, has largely benefited men. But even men may not have gained so much from the revolution. The sexual revolution has developed a new set of "shoulds" and "don'ts," with people straining to live up to rigid expectations rather than being liberated from past restrictions. Carmen Kerr laments that the revolution is based on a male model of performance and conquest:

We valued quantity or quality in lovers, we tried to come in five minutes, as we attempted to isolate our genitals from our hearts. Like men, we tried to turn our bodies into high performance machines—and soon had no idea what we ourselves were, sexually. All the sex revolution seemed to do was release us from women's sex-role oppression and "liberate" us into men's oppression. [Kerr 1977, pp. 14–15]

Feminist Linda Phelps (1975, p. 16) contends that the sexual revolution has alienated women sexually by detaching them from their own desires. She believes that women have accepted men's sexual fantasies. Women remain objects of men's desire, while men initiate and define sexual relationships for women. These rigid roles don't allow men to become sexually arousing to women—men's bodies are not defined as erotic and often are viewed as ugly. Thus a sexual script is created in which women are always passive—sex is something *done* to women rather than a mutual expression where both sexes are free to say yes or no—to be honest about their feelings.

Women have organized to increase their social power and to bring about change in some of these areas of contention. In issues such as economic opportunity, legal equality, women's sexual health, sexual harassment, rape, and commercial exploitation of sexuality, their collective voice is being heard. But as Pepper Schwartz (1977a, p. 230) has pointed out, many men still define women as "sexually inexperienced persons who achieve sexual maturity in a 'committed relationship' and who then settle down to the primary roles of wife and mother." Such men are confused and threatened by assertive women whose behaviors don't fit this pattern. And many men and women still see sex according to the old battlefield model, in which both persons are competing for control of the sexual bargaining process. Relationships between men and women might be improved not only by egalitarian roles but also by a new way of looking at sex: as an opportunity to cooperate for mutual pleasure and fulfillment rather than as competition.

Liberating Men's Sexuality.   Mutually beneficial partnerships and true humanity require that men be willing to change, too—to relate to both women and other men more flexibly in intimate rather than exploitative ways. Our sexual pleasure ultimately depends on the quality of these partnerships. The total surrender of spontaneous, thoroughly involving sexual joy is impossible if partners don't trust and feel comfortable with each other.

Beginning male-liberation efforts will probably focus on sexual relationships between men and women and between men and men. Men often desire closeness, cuddling, and intimate communication, and many are frustrated by the social restrictions on meeting these needs. Marc Feigen Fasteau recognized the importance of sex to changing concepts of masculinity in his book *The Male Machine*:

The sex act is the only intimate contact many adult men ever have with women: it is as close as they come to crossing the barrier between the sexes. "As close as they come" because men take all their conditioning, all their ingrained ideas about how they should act and feel, to bed with them, where they tend to stifle the freedom and spontaneity that make sex personal and give it meaning. [Fasteau 1974, p. 20]

Men's liberation books have been published for a decade or more and have strongly argued for the following changes: talking between men on deeper levels than shoptalk, touching and hugging between men and between women and men without any necessarily sexual implication, not competing and overworking at work and in sports, accepting women as colleagues, disowning violence, and loosening stereotypes about what it means to be a man.

No one knows how long it will take for men to recognize they are missing intimacy and sexual satisfaction because of their unwillingness to risk change and to experiment with sensitive and loving role definitions. Backlash to both women's and men's liberation has surfaced as "new macho." But in 1980, feminist Betty Friedan asserted that the "he-man mystique" was already dead and that men in the United States were entering a "tidal wave" of radical change in what it means to be male. She predicted that men's liberation will affect males' identity as powerfully as women's liberation has affected the way women see themselves. Referring to changes in both sexes, Gloria Steinem observes that "underneath the current landscape of backlash, transitional ills, and confusion, there is an earthquake of changed hopes—and some of them belong to men" (Steinem 1981, p. 45).

Willingness to Take Risks

In addition to the traditional gender roles that twist expression of our attraction to each other, attitudes we've learned from our experiences and our culture often get in the way. These barriers include guilt, embarrassment, playing "cool," and preserving "virginity." And as self-help guru Wayne Dyer (1976) has pointed out, most of us have been trained not to explore our potential. Parents and then teachers encourage us to stay in a safe groove: Memorize the right answers, don't get lost, prepare for a lifelong job, find one partner and then cling to him or her as long as you both can stand it. But Dyer contends that never choosing uncertainty, spontaneity, exploration, or new experiences is risky, too:

You are not going to collapse or fall apart if you encounter something new. In fact, you stand a much better chance of avoiding psychological collapse if you eliminate some of the routine and sameness in your life. Boredom is debilitating and psychologically unhealthy. Once you lose interest in life, you are potentially shatterable. [Dyer 1976, p. 127]

One form of sexual risk taking is exploring

deeper within a relationship—allowing ourselves to be increasingly open about what we want and how we feel and encouraging our partner to do the same. Although greater openness makes us more vulnerable to being rejected for what we reveal, it is a path to knowing ourselves and our partner more intimately and to richer enjoyment of sex.

Some of us explore outward as well as inward, seeking new experiences with new people. On the other hand, some of us are so shy that we find it hard to present ourselves sexually to people who attract us. As social psychologist Philip Zimbardo (1977, p. 92) has written, "Sex may make the world go around, but the trip usually makes the shy person nauseous. Virtually all the things that bring on an anxiety attack fuse to ignite a shyness time bomb when sex is concerned." According to Zimbardo, these sources of anxiety include the extraordinary ambiguity of encounters that may or may not be sexual, the lack of explicit guidelines for what to do, the loss of protection from clothes if the participants manage to get them off, lack of knowledge and practice of sexual techniques, unrealistic media-fed expectations for one's own performance, and traditional uneasiness with the other sex. However, it may be that shy people are better at expressing themselves *sexually* than verbally. Their trouble may be in initiating a relationship.

In the past shyness in making sexual overtures was mostly a man's problem. In heterosexual encounters he was expected to try to turn social interaction into sexual interaction, whether through a switch in the conversation or through a tentative touch. Men who were too shy to take these initiatives got nowhere sexually. Although many women now feel free to initiate sex within a relationship that is already sexual, few will take the risk of beginning sexual overtures from scratch. This means that the burden of risk taking—and rejection—is still carried mostly by men, to the disadvantage of both sexes. Feminist Paula Webster observes that the women's movement encouraged women to feel victimized by traditional sexual scripts but did not replace these scripts with feelings of choice and pleasure. Many women have not yet learned to define themselves as people with natural erotic desires who can consciously seek pleasure. Acceptance of sexual initiative by women need not mean social chaos, Webster asserts:

Sexuality is under our control; we can pursue it, refuse it, mold it, and generate it in our lives. . . . We will not perish if we challenge the taboos that domesticate our desires. It is clear from the experience of other women that we will not eat up our sexual partners, even though our hunger is real, and that we will not fall from grace. We will not step out of our gender category by having feelings that are "not appropriate to our sex," we will not become a "bad girl" instead of the good one we were trained to be. The longer we refuse our imagination and our sexual interests, the farther away we remain from knowing ourselves.   [Webster 1982, p. 263]

Looking for Partners

In America we've been socialized to think that sex and romance will magically bloom when we meet "the one and only." We therefore have difficulty in thinking of sex in other ways—that is, in recognizing that we may not experience rewarding sex if we just wait for it to happen, that there might be many people with whom we could form satisfying intimate relationships, or that it's okay to search for such people.

We are embarrassed to admit that we sometimes *do* try to widen our circle of acquaintances in the hope of finding potential sexual friends: As love researchers Elaine and William Walster (1978, p. 29) have written, "Because of this reluctance to be candid about their need for love and sex, men and women interested in contacting a desirable mate adopt a somewhat devious strategy. They must search for mates while pretending to be doing something else"—such as walking the dog, riding a bike, participating in club activities, using the library, traveling. A more direct partner-seeking strategy is frequenting singles bars and settings that expedite casual sexual matches. The most direct approach: ads for partners, in which terms of the desired relationship are usually spelled out quite explicitly.

The Walsters (1978) recommend an honest, friendly approach to partner seeking: saying hello to people we pass on the street, starting conversations with approachable strangers, being an attentive listener. They point out that it's not good looks, or money, or personality that is most important in determining popularity. The most crucial factor is how relaxed we are with others: "The people who do best socially are those who are pleased if others like them—but aren't particularly concerned if they don't. The people who do worst are those who are sensitive to rejection" (Walster and Walster 1978, p. 34).

Relationship facilitators Emily Coleman and Betty Edwards offer some additional advice on locating and enjoying partners: We can be gently aggressive by sending clear and honest signals of our availability for emotional and sexual sharing with new people. Eye contact, smiles, and other gestures indicating we are interested without pushing the issue may lead to playful and exciting new encounters. This gently assertive, honest approach "de-escalates the war between the sexes and puts both on the same team" (Coleman and Edwards 1979, p. 68).

There are limits to what friendliness can do for us, though. Sometimes when we're open and honest with others, they exploit us instead of responding in kind. If we're naive about what's going on, we may be vulnerable to feeling hurt, used, or even hostile. To perceive accurately the intentions of others is a skill that allows us to meet our own objectives in sexual exchange as well as in other social encounters.

Communicating Our Availability

There may be a big gap between wanting sex and getting it. How to present ourself as a potential sex partner can be a real puzzle. How should I act? What should I say? Should I be direct? Should I be subtle? How can I protect myself from embarrassment?

Other animals seem to know just what to do. To signal their sexual availability to potential partners, mallard ducks go through a ten-step sequence of gestures, birds of paradise display their colorful feathers and do a special dance, and male bowerbirds build courtship cabins and present passing females with red fruits. There are many elaborate displays of this sort in the animal world. According to German ethologist Irenäus Eibl-Eibesfeldt (1970), they are apparently designed both to attract and to appease. They seem to be saying both "I want you—come to me" and "I won't hurt you."

Advertising for Partners

Share my farm, view of the mountains, wood-splitting, animal chores, and bed. 28-year-old Taurus female seeks equal partnership with gentle, hard-working male. Your animals welcome.

Intelligent, peace-loving, reasonably good-looking male, 33, with secure income seeks honest female companion for exploration of life's joys. No drugs, smoking, or religious fads, please.

Gay white female, warm and loving, looking for affectionate, feminine gay female for potential relationship, ages 25–35.

Extraordinary lady, early 30s, highly intelligent, very attractive, discriminating tastes, incurably romantic, seeks scintillating Jewish professional. No man who likes polyester suits or discos, has dependents, or wears toupee need apply.

Gay white male, 32, 6', 190, strong build, wants small, cuddly, young gay lover.

Film producer, mature male, harassed but successful, seeks quiet, intelligent, slender, athletic young woman for fun and whatever.

Very shy male artist, age 27, seeks to meet warm female for companionship.

Exuberantly sensual 35-year-old female with open marriage seeks enthusiastic daytime partners. Prefer masculine types with good build. Any race.

Gay father, 32 with two preschool children, seeks to share home, parenthood, and companionship with compatible gay father. I'm considerate, quiet, athletic, into cross-country skiing, hiking, nature photography, and classical music.

Professional black female, 27, tall and aristocratic, desires to meet educated, expressive, proud black male.

Personal ads fill pages of certain newspapers and often spell out the desired exchange in great detail. Do people write them for kicks? Does anyone answer? Carole Goldberg (1979) ran an informal survey of people who have taken out personal ads in the *New Haven Advocate*. One finding: Ads placed by females draw far more responses than ads placed by males. Goldberg encountered one man who had done a little research on his own. He placed an ad seeking a female companion for himself, as well as a phony one by "an attractive female wishing to meet men." His ad got one reply. The fake female ad drew 100 responses.

What kind of people answer the ads? According to one male, the women who responded to his ad were "nice, . . . high-class, quality people" except for one who was "a little crazy." Women who place these ads seem pleased with their experiences, too. One woman had met her spouse through a personal ad, and so had her brother met his.

What kind of people place personal ads? Goldberg found that motives vary from loneliness to lust to playfulness. Those placing ads seem willing to take the initiative in looking for partners. But they want to maintain some kind of buffer between themselves and utter strangers. Placing an ad gives them a chance to be selective without risking their self-esteem, as they would if they were trying to meet people by going to bars, discos, or "new age" workshops. As one gay male pointed out, it's a relatively safe way to explore the unknown, "a romantic, almost quaint, old-fashioned way to meet. . . . If you get a lot of letters it's like having your own harem. You get to pick and choose by your own criteria" (Goldberg 1979, p. 42).

Even though we humans could accomplish the same thing with the unique capacity for language we've evolved, many of us don't use it directly. Instead, we clothe and arrange our bodies in special ways to make veiled references that are supposed to signal our readiness for sex without exposing us to ridicule if our overtures are rejected.

Nonverbal Signals. In Chapter 1 we looked at ways in which some of us advertise our sexual availability by the clothes we wear: the see-

Eye contacts and gestures are highly expressive in communicating wordless messages such as "I like you" and "Please."

through blouse, the unbuttoned shirt, the clingy dress or pants. How we use our bodies heightens the message. Men, for instance, may sit with their legs spread apart so that potential partners can check out the size of their genitals. Women may straighten clothing bulges and pull in their stomachs to make their bodies look sleeker and may breathe deeply to accentuate their breasts. If we're interested in someone sitting next to us, we tend to form a "loving circle" with our bodies—turning, crossing our legs, and perhaps opening our arms toward each other.

We often flirt with our eyes. The knowing wink, for instance, signals a feeling of emotional intimacy. In a common sequence that conveys the tension of arousal, we may look directly at each other, smile and briefly raise our eyebrows, lower our gaze as if in embarrassment, and then reestablish full eye contact. This form of flirtation is apparently universal, for it has been captured on film in cultures all over the world (Eibl-Eibesfeldt 1970).

Touching someone for a bit longer than "just being friendly" is as expressive as eye contact that is sustained slightly longer than usual. So is subtle violation of another's personal space—moving slightly closer to that person than he or she would

normally allow. Sometimes we betray a feeling of sensual arousal without even meaning to—absent-mindedly stroking a bottle, caressing ourselves, licking our upper lip with the tip of our tongue. These same gestures are sometimes used consciously. Deliberately licking the lips can be an invitation to sex that includes oral pleasure.

If we have no intention of getting sexually involved—and are not in the least bit aroused by the people around us—we may try to avoid giving off such signals. In a crowded elevator, for instance, people stiffen their bodies to make it clear that they aren't enjoying the physical contact, look away to signal their disinterest, and avoid talking to each other. When seated next to someone we'd rather avoid, we may cross our legs away from the person, lean back rather than forward, fold our arms across our chest, and perhaps hold something—such as a drink—as a barrier between ourselves and the other.

For those of us who are homosexual, presenting ourselves as sexually available to someone who doesn't want to reciprocate carries even greater risks than it does for those of us who are heterosexual. To avoid exposing their sexual preferences to heterosexuals, homosexuals have therefore developed elaborate signaling systems. Prolonging eye contact—meeting and holding the other's glance—often signals sexual interest between males. If they meet on the street, look at each other longer than men normally do, and then look back after they've passed, the signal is even stronger. In a gay bar standing alone next to a wall so that they can see and be seen also signals availability.

To reinforce these "cruising" cues, some gay males wear symbols of their sexual preference. A single earring or a bunch of keys clipped to the belt may mean "I'm gay." According to one code, if placed on the right side, they also signal "I'm passive"; on the left, "I'm aggressive." The earring signal is no longer a secret from the "straight" world, though, and some heterosexual men wear keys, too. Signals are sometimes changed to keep ahead of straight understanding. For instance, a newer signal in some areas is a handkerchief in the back pocket. Choice of right or left pocket indicates preferred sexual role, and the handerkerchief color indicates preferred sexual activities.

Gay women don't seem to use such elaborate signals for recognizing each other. One partial explanation: As we'll see in Chapter 8, gay women are less likely than gay men to "cruise" for brief, impersonal sexual relationships (Bell and Weinberg 1978). Another explanation: Women are more sensitive to body language than men are. Experiments show that women—and men in helping professions—are more accurate in their reading of facial expressions than most men are (Fast 1977).

Figure 5-1. Verbal and Nonverbal Methods of Displaying Interest. According to the self-reports of 22 female and 22 male sexually experienced students, touching signals are the most common ways of indicating interest in sex. Directly asking is somewhat less common, but females are no less likely to use this direct verbal approach than are males. (Data reprinted by permission from Clinton J. Jesser, "Male Responses to Direct Verbal Sexual Initiative of Females," *Journal of Sex Research* 14, no. 2, May 1978, pp. 118–28.)

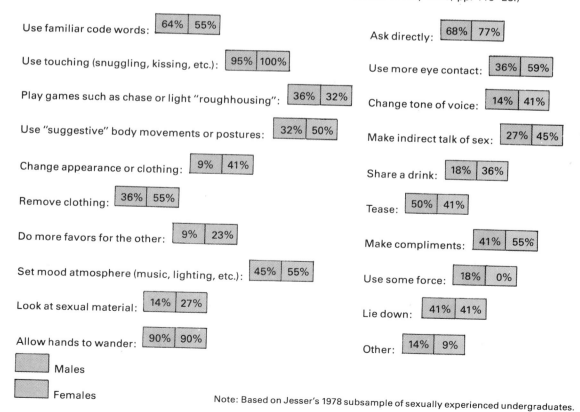

Use familiar code words: 64% 55%

Use touching (snuggling, kissing, etc.): 95% 100%

Play games such as chase or light "roughhousing": 36% 32%

Use "suggestive" body movements or postures: 32% 50%

Change appearance or clothing: 9% 41%

Remove clothing: 36% 55%

Do more favors for the other: 9% 23%

Set mood atmosphere (music, lighting, etc.): 45% 55%

Look at sexual material: 14% 27%

Allow hands to wander: 90% 90%

☐ Males

☐ Females

Ask directly: 68% 77%

Use more eye contact: 36% 59%

Change tone of voice: 14% 41%

Make indirect talk of sex: 27% 45%

Share a drink: 18% 36%

Tease: 50% 41%

Make compliments: 41% 55%

Use some force: 18% 0%

Lie down: 41% 41%

Other: 14% 9%

Note: Based on Jesser's 1978 subsample of sexually experienced undergraduates.

We are not nearly so circumspect when the risks of being rejected are reduced. In unambiguously sexual settings—"meat markets" such as singles bars and discos—we can safely assume that many others we encounter share our objective of finding a sexual partner. If we are at all attractive, we can use more overt sexual come-ons—dancing that suggests the movements of intercourse, erotic touching, mutual eye signaling, direct verbal invitations—with less fear of rejection than usual. Here, the "over-stare" and "over-touch," taboo in everyday American life, are considered appropriate behavior. But even here, coming on too strong can be a turn-off. Anthropologist David Givens has found that aggressive macho behavior is much less appealing to women in singles bars than more tentative, friendly signs of interest (Esser 1982).

In the gay male S/M (sadomasochistic or slavemaster) subculture risks of physical injury, venereal disease, and exploitation from engaging in sex with strangers are reduced by consensual guidelines or ground rules. Such arrangements are also evident in heterosexual clubs designed for quick sex with strangers. Whether with strangers or with friends, when we follow the etiquette of not forcing ourselves on others, and when we agree to take "no thank you" as a polite response to a sexual overture, we contribute to a more relaxed atmosphere where we are not as likely to be put down or truly "rejected."

Verbal Signals.   When we try to initiate sex verbally, we often talk around the subject. Instead of saying simply, "I'd like very much to have sex with you," we tend to talk about the weather or something equally irrelevant until one person finally takes the plunge with a remark that can be interpreted as "Let's go to bed." Cartoon character Doonesbury's Joanie, for instance, implies that she'd like to spend the night with her friend Rick by mentioning that she's good at cooking breakfast. She hasn't really "gone for broke" with this remark. If he were not interested in a sexual relationship with her, Rick could save face for both of them by saying, "That's nice," and talking about something else as though he were unaware of what she really meant.

The ambiguous remark, then, is one common verbal ploy. Another is explicit sex talk that does not refer directly to the intended partner. Telling sexual jokes is sometimes used as a way to signal readiness for sex, to get the subject on the agenda without revealing one's intentions before being sure of a positive response. Another seemingly explicit form of sex talk that nonetheless doesn't commit anyone to anything is flattery. Giving the other verbal strokes—"Your eyes are beautiful"—tests the other's response without getting oneself in too deep if the other is not aroused. Suggesting "Let's have a drink," "Let's have lunch together," or "How about going to my place for a while?" accomplishes the same thing. For those who share our symbol system, such an invitation signals our desires without compromising our self-esteem.

Some people are far more direct. Sociologist Clinton Jesser (1978, p. 120) recently asked sexually experienced undergraduates at a large midwestern university, "When you think your

DOONESBURY   **by Garry Trudeau**

partner can be persuaded to have sex, even though s/he has not yet become aware of your desire, what do you usually do?" Of the twenty possibilities suggested, touching signals ("snuggling, kissing, and the like" and "allow hands to wander") were checked by an overwhelming majority of the students. "Ask directly" was the next most common ploy.

These findings indicate a shift away from tentative indirectness and also from the traditional expectation that only males will initiate sex. Using limited data provided by the rest of his questionnaire, Jesser concluded that in this student population, females who ask directly for sex tend to be involved with males who also ask directly for sex and who regard females as people with equal rights. These women also tend to feel that men can cope with sexual ups and downs, and they are more assertive and less conventional than the women who don't ask. Parroting traditional expectations, over a third of the females thought that men would be turned off by an assertive woman. But only 16 percent of the men said that this assumption was true.

Despite some increase in the willingness of women to take the sexual initiative, a recent study of college students (LaPlante, McCormick, and Brannigan 1981) indicates that both males and females are still following the traditional script in which the male does everything he can to initiate sex and the woman does everything she can to avoid it. Both still tend to regard the female as the one who sets the limits—who either actively tries to prevent sex or passively goes along with it.

Embarrassment and Self-Understanding

Whether we're circumspect or direct, in any encounter or series of encounters it eventually becomes obvious whether the other person accepts the idea of being a sexual partner. If not, we may feel painfully embarrassed at having made the attempt.

We tend to think of embarrassment as a loss of self-esteem. But what's really happening is that we feel we've lost public esteem. It's the knowledge that our ineptness has been observed by another—and the assumption that the person will think less of us because of it—that makes us feel so awkward. Having "lost face"—having been unable to

Face-Saving Maneuvers

To study how individuals try to save face in partner-seeking encounters, Bernard Berk (1977) and his assistants watched the goings-on at over seventy singles dances. In these settings people were repeatedly sought out, ignored, accepted, or rejected as partners. A number of patterns for managing the pain of being ignored or turned down emerged. Among them were:

- **Enhancing presentations**—trying to present information that "upgrades" the self. For instance, many of the research assistants felt compelled to present themselves as such, against orders to blend anonymously into the crowd they were watching, in an effort to put a better face on why they weren't dancing.

- **One-downing others**—trying to even the score with remarks like "If you're so good, what are you doing here anyway?"

- **Controlling visibility**—moving around as if "checking out the action" to avoid being seen as a partnerless wallflower.

- **Withdrawing**—quickly leaving the scene of the rejection. Over 85 percent of the males who asked a female to dance but were refused beat a hasty but dignified retreat. Some went to the bar for a drink, some retired to a dark corner, some left the dance entirely.

- **Limiting involvement**—pretending to be disinterested in the search for partners as an explanation for why one isn't dancing. A number of people settled in inaccessible places or acted as though they were engrossed in other activities, such as watching the band.

- **Redefining**—trying to view rejection in a more favorable light. When one man was turned down, he and his buddy managed to talk away the hurt by deciding she wasn't worth his trouble, so he should never have asked her to dance in the first place.

pull off the image we wanted to present—we may then do whatever we can think of to repair the damage to our self-esteem.

Although trying to get rid of our temporary embarrassment seems to be a natural response, a more useful approach might be to use embarrassment as a signal for self-examination. It's one of the best clues we have as to whether our presentation meshed with the identity we meant to communicate. Somewhere along the line, something— our objectives, how we present ourselves, our reading of others' reactions—isn't working. For instance, Elaine and William Walster tell of a young divorcee who frequents a singles bar in the hope of getting remarried. Desperate for a partner, she tries to figure out what men want and then acts that way: "She tries to be coolly beautiful, yet display a certain gypsy quality; to be aloof, yet passionate; to be nurturant, yet vulnerable" (Walster and Walster 1978, p. 24). No bites. She finds her experiences humiliating—and expensive, for she has to pay someone to stay with her small children—but she keeps going back. Instead of repeating the same pattern, and being repeatedly embarrassed, she would probably do better to take a good look at her attempts. Possible trouble spots: her efforts to falsify her identity, her search for a long-term partner in a setting designed for superficial relationships, her apparent inability to initiate a relationship herself. These behaviors are all things she could change.

ASPECTS OF THE NEGOTIATION PROCESS

Once we've sensed a connection with another, we have to decide—both on our own and together— what we want to do about it. Matters to be negotiated include whether we choose to have sex with each other, whether sex will mean some sort of future commitment or purely present pleasure, how much time we'll spend together, who will contact whom for getting together, whether sexual attraction to others can be acted out and under what circumstances. Unless we squarely face these issues, we each may resent our partners for not fulfilling the unexpressed expectations each brings to the relationship.

We're rarely sure how we feel about such matters ourselves, and it's even more difficult to discover what the other person wants and then try to

mesh the two sets of desires. As we saw in Chapter 1, we may be operating from different scripts. In this section we'll explore other factors that complicate this process: our need to find approval in the other's eyes, the difficulty of discovering what the other expects of us, communication problems, recognizing attempts at manipulation, and knowing what to make of teasing.

We could see these matters as problems that make the negotiations hardly worth our while. But we prefer to view them as dynamic tensions that may make our relationships more vibrant and intimate, for they provide us with material for deeply personal and challenging discussions that keep a relationship thriving and growing.

Attraction and Validation

What is it that attracts us powerfully to some people but not to others? Over the years many scholars have tried to pin down the mysteries of interpersonal attraction. As we saw in Chapter 3, they've found that physical attractiveness is one of the main things that draw us to others (Bar-Tal and Saxe 1976). But so far, researchers have been unable clearly to identify interpersonal factors that are most important.

One major theory is that similarity of attitudes is the key: We like people who agree with us. Another is that it's complementarity of needs: People who have opposite traits, such as a nurturing person and a dependent person, are drawn to each other by what Freud would call their complementary neuroses. Richard Centers (1975) suggests yet another way of looking at this question. What probably attracts us to others, he thinks, is whether they *validate* (recognize and approve of) the identity we would like to present. This behavior is reciprocal, for we also choose people who have the traits we prefer, thereby validating *their* identity.

A brawny male athlete, for instance, might be strongly attracted to a certain woman by her warmth and intelligence (traits he values in others) and by the fact that she compliments him for being soft, caring, and understanding. Her appraisal is especially meaningful to him, for he considers these aspects of his identity important. Everyone else he's met gives him approval for his brawn, but that's not the only thing he likes about himself. For her part she's gratified to find someone who is attracted to her warmth and intelligence, traits that are as important to her identity as the physical beauty others have always complimented. And she's happy to have found a man whose overt physical masculinity doesn't prevent him from being soft and caring, traits she values in a partner. So long as these two persons continue to validate each other in areas that are important to them, the expenditure of energy needed to work out differences—such as conflicting scripts—will be worth their while.

And yet our need to find approval in another's eyes prevents us not only from knowing our own feelings but also from knowing or understanding the other's feelings. The other person may express things we like and "need," which then tend to complicate our open and honest discussion and exploration. We may be afraid to say things we think the other can't accept or deal with. For a healthy, honest relationship we must ultimately move beyond a need for approval.

Discovering the Other's Expectations

Another important aspect of cooperative bargaining is figuring out what the other person expects of us. Rarely is this expressed as a direct statement; usually we get the picture from a series of small cues. If they look pained when we talk animatedly to attractive strangers, we might infer that our partners expect us to limit our affection to them alone. Or if they hug and kiss us after sexual sessions that we've initiated but seem to lose interest if we repeatedly leave initiation of sex up to them, we might infer that they expect and approve of our taking responsibility for starting sexual encounters.

Our interpretation of others' expectations is often inaccurate. Some years ago, Jack Balswick and James Anderson (1969) found that college students tended to misread each other's sexual expectations. Men typically tried for more sex than they actually expected to get. Unaware of the limited expectations behind the man's "line," women pretended to be sexually more willing than they actually felt. They did so with the expectation that to behave otherwise would cost them a partner. Men then misread the woman's seeming willingness for sex as a demand that they be even more

aggressive sexually. The result: more sexual expression than either had bargained for.

Remnants of this dating game may still be blocking open sexual negotiations. Traces of the old double standard sometimes get in the way, too. We may discover, for instance, that our partner feels that multiple sexual relationships are okay for males but not for females, or that initiation of sex is a male role, not a female one. We too may hold such attitudes. It's important to recognize that these expectations are not immutable "facts of life" but socially learned rules for sexual conduct. As such, they can be renegotiated within each relationship.

Contemporary questioning of traditional gender role expectations logically should be replacing the double standard with increasing acceptance of others' unique identities. But some men and women feel that they're now subject to a new set of social expectations that are just as burdensome as those of the past. Many women, for instance, think that men now expect them to have sex more often and with less emotional commitment than before (Hite 1976). A number of men feel that women are laying unwanted expectations on them, too. The college men studied by Mirra Komarovsky (1976) thought their female friends wanted them to be not only more sensitive and more expressive of their emotions, but also more "masculine"—self-assured, independent, strong, and responsible. As they see it, yesterday's expectations are still with us, and new ones have been piled on. Both sexes report that such expectations are making them feel inadequate or rebellious. Because these feelings are not conducive to high-quality relationships, we may have to confront and reconsider the expectations that both we and our partners bring to bed.

Understanding Sexual Communications

To understand what the other wants from us sexually, we may have to read meaning into a maze of ambiguous gestures. Was that brush accidental or should I make more of it? Is this foreplay or just a friendly pat? Did that remark mean she'd like to be friends, touch, kiss, have intercourse, or none of the above? Our reading of ambiguous sexual gestures is complicated by several factors: our tendency to see what we want to see, our lack of empathy, confusion between sexual and nonsexual cues, and gender differences in interpreting touches.

Seeing What We Want to See.   When we try to read meaning into social signals, we first tend to see what we're looking for, according to a number of experiments. For instance, males who have been aroused by reading something sexually stimulating are more likely than others to see a potential date as attractive and sexually receptive (Stephan, Berscheid, and Walster 1971). Our perceptions are colored by our own desires. Just as food looks tastier to a hungry person, potential partners look sexier to someone hungry for sex (Rubin 1973).

Lack of Empathy.   The tendency to see others as we want them to be may lead to mistakes in reading their signals. For instance, a sexually excited man who finds himself seated next to an attractive businesswoman on a plane may misread her attempts to concentrate on her work as shyness or playfulness. Expecting her to feel as he does, he is insensitive to the possibility that she may prefer to be left alone. *Empathy,* then, is an important feature of understanding others' communications. Empathy means getting out of our own skin and temporarily disregarding our own needs in order to sense what the other is feeling.

Sexual versus Nonsexual Gestures.   Another barricade to understanding is the difficulty of distinguishing sexual from nonsexual cues. A sexual cue is a signal designed to show interest in sexual activity. It can be intended or unintended by someone sending the cue. The intention is not easy to determine unless we know the person and his or her pattern of communicating; even then it may be a guess. For instance, signs of embarrassment—looking away, nervous hand movements, a feeling of electric tension in the air—might indicate arousal or might mean something else.

Just as nonsexual gestures such as these may or may not indicate sexual arousal, some seemingly sexual acts may have nonsexual motives. Psychologist Nancy Henley found that men's touching of women does not necessarily mean sexual desire. "In this male-dominated society," she proposes, "touching is one more tool used to keep women in their place, another reminder that women's bodies are free property for everyone's use" (Henley 1977, p. 123). In our society high-status people (usually men) are allowed to touch low-status people

(usually women) *first* (but if the female is in a higher status position, *she* can touch *him* first!). Thus a boss puts his or her hand on an employee's shoulder, not vice versa. Perhaps perceiving the power implications of being touched by men, women report being angry or resentful about what they consider inappropriate or excessive touching more often than men do. For their part many women find it hard to touch men. There is little social support for this behavior in women, and many fear that it may be interpreted as readiness for instant sex. Perhaps they are right.

Gender Differences in Interpreting Touch. Gender still strongly influences how we interpret touches. Men are more apt to respond sexually to touch than women are. For example, a study by Tuan Nguyen, Richard Heslin, and Michele Nguyen (1975) reveals that men and women differ considerably in the ways they interpret touch. The researchers asked students how they would interpret squeezes, pats, brushes, or strokes from others on various parts of their bodies. Answers revealed that women responded differently to areas where they were touched, interpreting touches in some areas as not sexual and others as sexual. However, men saw touch almost anywhere on their bodies as a sign of sexual desire. Furthermore, to a male the same touch can signify pleasantness, warmth and love, and sexual desire—but not friendship. For a female, on the other hand, the more a touch seems to symbolize sexual desire, the less she reads it as warmth, love, friendship, pleasantness, or playfulness. According to the research, this pattern seems to change with increased sexual experience and social approval of female sexuality. Nonetheless, the point is that people interpret touches differently. If we naively assume that our partners react to touches as we would, the potential for misunderstanding snowballs.

Manipulation versus Cooperation

Another problem we may encounter in trying to work out a satisfying relationship is the other's attempts to force us to act in ways that will benefit her or him more than us. We may find ourselves doing the same thing, which sets up a struggle for control in the relationship that ultimately benefits neither of us.

For instance, a 1966 study of female student nurses and their dates revealed that the woman typically equated sex with love and the wish for marriage, while her male date typically saw sex as recreation (Skipper and Nass 1966). Each tried to manipulate the situation to his or her own script. The female tried to tempt her date into sexual arousal but stalled on satisfying his desires in order to force him into a long-term relationship or at least a declaration of love. The male's part in this game was equally manipulative: He would use a "line"—flattery or false commitments—to force the female into sex. These relationships usually fell apart, for neither males nor females found them satisfying. If we discover such patterns in our own relationships, we might be able to salvage them by honest verbal attempts to define what sex means to us and by negotiating our differing sexual goals.

Many people approach their differences with a fighting spirit—that is, with the idea that if one partner wins an argument, the other must lose. By contrast, *conflicts may be "managed" rather than "resolved"* (Sprey 1971). The emphasis here is on cooperation rather than on power. Instead of "winning" by destroying each other or their bond, partners may negotiate continually in an ongoing effort to allow both the relationship and the individuals in it to grow and change.

Use of Humor

One way to keep a relationship from being destroyed by changes is to handle them with a sense of humor. But sometimes what may *appear* to be humorous teasing may be hurtful and destructive to a partner.

In a healthy relationship much of what sounds like fighting is only playfulness. Some of this seems to drain tension away from potential danger areas. For example, when outside relationships seem to threaten one partner's identity or the bond itself, little jokes that exaggerate and poke fun at fears may restore a sense of perspective. The one ready for sex might holler to the one who's dawdling in the bathroom, "Hurry up or somebody else might take your place!" Sometimes negotiations themselves work better in a playful atmosphere than in a serious one.

Teasing in fun also gives us a chance to define ourselves as sexual creatures and to learn and practice our parts in the sexual exchange. The everyday flirtations we carry on with each other can be seen as trial runs that help us feel more comfortable with our sexuality. Many of us start practicing these roles in childhood through pseudosexual teasing with our parents and other grown-up friends. Fathers and daughters are especially likely to play at flirting with each other.

Although teasing helps us to be relaxed and comfortable with sexual partners, it can cause problems of its own. One is how it's received. A woman who feels that many old patterns of interaction degrade women may be infuriated rather than amused by a male co-worker's playful remarks bout her body. It's also possible that someone may mistake teasing for the real thing and try to make a sexual encounter out of what we thought was only a game. We usually assume that others read our messages as we mean them. But as we have seen, in the cloudy area of sexual communications, it's better not to assume anything. To avoid trouble, we must be perceptive and sensitive to each other's reactions and make it clear that neither intends to insult or carry the exchange beyond the play-acting stage.

The opposite possibility may be a problem, too: Some people seem to get stuck at a more serious teasing stage. Accustomed to setting limits in teasing relationships and to treating sex as something of a joke or a form of manipulation, they may have trouble relaxing their guard and letting themselves be vulnerable and emotionally involved in a deeper relationship. Sociologist Constantina Safilios-Rothschild (1977) feels that some women enjoy the socially learned role of sexual teaser. Dressing and behaving seductively but then refusing to have sex gives these women a sense of power over men. But this kind of manipulation tends to prevent women from enjoying sex for its own sake and from developing an honest understanding of themselves and their partners.

LOVE AND SEXUAL EXCHANGE

For many of us love and sex are intertwined: Sex is an expression of love, and without love sex is meaningless and dehumanizing. Journalist George Leonard observes that our society is growing tired of sex without love:

Most people today enjoy the freedom of the sexual revolution. But indiscriminate, obligatory "getting-it-on" is losing its charm. The best-kept secret of the sexual revolution is at last coming out of the closet: What people want most of all (though sometimes they can hardly bear to say it) is a return to the personal in all things—especially in erotic love. [Leonard 1982, p. 74]

Social Definitions of Love

If we were to ask other people to define love, we'd probably discover that their definitions differ from the one we take for granted. The various definitions of love seem almost to contradict each other: caring for the other's well-being more than for our own, a relationship in which both people's development is optimized, a selfish passion, an unselfish passion, dispassionate caring, romantic attraction to an ideal partner we can't bear to be separated from, owning another, being owned. The ancient Greeks distinguished six kinds of love and gave a different label to each: love of beauty (*eros*), obsessive love (*mania*), playful love (*ludis*), companionate love (*storge*), altruistic love (*agape*), and realistic love (*pragma*).

The reason we have so many definitions for what we tend to assume is a basic human emotion is that this feeling is culturally defined. Each definition of love—and accompanying scripts for how we behave when we're in love—developed historically within a particular set of social circumstances. Romantic love, for instance, was idealized in the courtly love tradition of twelfth-century Europe. Troubadours sang of imaginary love affairs in which a handsome knight would fall helplessly in love with a beautiful woman of royal blood. Since she was inevitably married to someone else, they could only long chastely for each other. Her beauty and noble character would inspire him to greatness in battle and to acting the part of her humble servant at home. Since their love was never consummated by sex or marriage, it could supposedly exist indefinitely on a spiritual plane above the humdrum of everyday life. This literary scenario proved so popular that men of the courts started trying to act it out: idealizing women, opening doors for them, and performing feats in their honor.

Historians have suggested a number of explanations for the appearance of this courtly definition of love. Among them are boredom with confining castle life, obsessive worship of virginity, unconscious rebellion against the prevailing Christian view of women as temptresses and of sex as sin, sublimation of adulterous desires, a desire to make human relationships seem more noble in times of brutal political realities, an answer to the chronic shortage of noblewomen in castles teeming with knights, and status seeking by lower-born males (Kaufman 1973; Moller 1959). Even though such historical situations have changed, the effects of past ways of looking at love color sexual relationships even now.

Mixed Emotions in a "Love" Relationship

Historical definitions of love often shape our ideas of what it feels like to be in love. According to the romantic tradition, when we're in love we can't eat, we can't sleep, we can't concentrate on anything except our beloved; yet we feel blissfully, glowingly alive. Elaine and William Walster point out, however, that this happy fog is only one of the ways we experience love. The feelings that trigger passion for another seem to run the gamut from the desire for security to anger. Passion ultimately can be reduced to adrenalin flow, they point out, and adrenalin flow can be increased by a number of emotional states, many of them considered negative: frustrated longing, loneliness, insecurity, jealousy, anger.

When we're deprived of emotional closeness and sex, we long for them more than usual. We crave physical contact with someone soft and warm to make the uncertainties of life more bearable. Instead of loneliness, many of us long for at least one person who understands us. Some of us derive great pleasure from serving another. We want security and we want excitement, whichever we don't have at the moment. We enjoy the novelty of getting to know a new person intimately. Jealousy may make us want our partner more than ever. And some people are turned on to each other by their anger. The Walsters conclude that what we call love is really a melange of emotional states. Loving relationships, they write, are at their zestful best when many of these emotions are allowed to

come into play: "Love flourishes when it's nurtured by a torrent of good experiences—and a sprinkling of unsettling, irritating, and even painful experiences. . . . A love affair fares best when lovers are relaxed and act naturally with one another" (Walster and Walster 1978, p. 104).

Learning to Love

Robert Thamm (1975) suggests that we should try regarding love as the result of an eight-step social process. It develops only when people are exposed to a loving environment. The process begins with ourselves. The first step is to know what our own needs are, recognizing when they are frustrated, and learning how to satisfy them. The second step is to behave in such a way that we meet our needs. The third is to develop close relationships with enough people that the loss of one friend will not mean that our needs are unmet. Thamm believes that we deceive ourselves when we think we need a specific person. What we really seek are social rewards—understanding, touching, emotional closeness, validation. These rewards could be provided by a network of intimates rather than by an exclusive lover whose approval is so critical to our self-esteem that we cannot truly relax with her or him.

Many different kinds of love may be present even within one relationship.

Thamm's next three steps involve a concern for others. Step 4 is accepting others—assuring them that we will not reject them for any private feelings they might reveal to us. Step 5 is empathy—trying to understand their revelations about themselves from their point of view. Step 6 is being as concerned for the other's security as we are for our own.

The final two steps in Thamm's model concern acts of loving. Step 7 is gratifying the loved one's needs. Step 8 is the "loving feeling"—being personally rewarded by gratifying the other's needs since we have empathized with him or her. We deeply enjoy giving a loved partner sexual pleasure, for his or her happiness makes us happy.

As Coleman and Edwards (1979, p. 50) have pointed out, few people recognize that "the building of a loving relationship is an act of continuous creation." In place of the old model of "falling in love," we can substitute a new model: *growing in love*. If we approach each other with caring, honesty, and a commitment to trying to understand and work things out—rather than with anger, games, and stereotyped expectations—we may in-

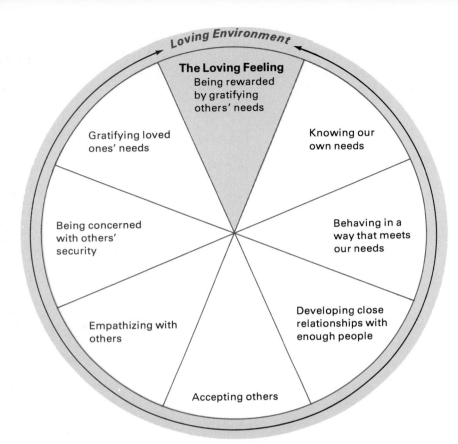

Loving Environment

The Loving Feeling
Being rewarded by gratifying others' needs

Gratifying loved ones' needs

Knowing our own needs

Being concerned with others' security

Behaving in a way that meets our needs

Empathizing with others

Developing close relationships with enough people

Accepting others

Figure 5-2. Eight-Step Social Process Resulting in Love. Thamm suggests that we grow in our ability to love through a continuous eight-step process. It develops only within a loving environment.

creasingly love what we see and feel. There will be changes in our relationships, unless we are not growing as individuals. But willingness to continually explore and reconsider our feelings and agreements can help our relationships to flex and grow and deepen.

Summary

Whether it's part of a brief encounter or a long-term association, sex does not occur in isolation from the rest of a relationship. Lovers' lives touch on many levels, sometimes inharmoniously. We may have different motives for seeking sex, different assumptions about the kind of relationship in which sex is socially acceptable, and learned gender-based differences in attaching meanings to sex. In addition to these potential snags, our efforts to develop satisfying sexual relationships may be hindered by our own unwillingness to take risks, by embarrassment about openly looking for partners, and by confusion over the subtle signals of sexual availability.

In actually shaping a sexual relationship, we must reconcile conflicts in the sexual scripts we have learned, grow beyond the need for approval toward greater honesty, figure out what expectations may stand in the way of simply accepting each other as we are, understand each others' means of sexual communications, and learn to cooperate with rather than try to manipulate each other. A humorous perspective on our own foibles may help lighten this ongoing process. And as we continually try to work things out, we may come to know and appreciate each other more and find that despite—and perhaps because of—the difficulties we face together, we are growing in love.

6

Beginning Sex with Others

I had loved him ever since we were in kindergarten together. Year after year I dreamt about holding hands with him and kissing him, but we were never alone together. Finally one night, the summer after seventh grade, I asked him to meet me at the big tree. I got there first and waited in the moonlight for what seemed like hours. Finally I heard him coming. My heart was racing, I was so excited. I had no words. Instead, I walked to him, took his hand in mine, led him to the tree and started climbing it, motioning for him to follow. We sat very close in a wide limb next to the trunk, watching the stars and not saying much. What I was feeling for him was so strong. I touched his cheek softly, explored the lines of his face with my fingertips, kissed my finger and placed it on his lips, drew his mouth toward me. When we kissed it was even better than in my dreams, even though we almost fell out of the tree trying to do it.

At the drive-in movie I felt really warm toward him. When he kissed me for the first time, I thought I'd burst I was so happy. He kept on kissing me and touching my breasts, and he pulled me down so that we were lying together on the seat. That felt good, too. But then he took my hand and tried to place it between his legs, just below his crotch. I'd never done that before and I really didn't want to. It didn't seem right somehow. I said, "No—I'd rather not." When he asked why, I couldn't explain it. Maybe I was afraid that having my hand there would turn him on so much that he'd want to go all the way with me—and I knew I didn't want that. For the rest of the evening he kept telling me how much he loved me and trying to get me to put my hand there; I kept telling him he probably didn't mean it and trying to pull my hand away. Those hassles really spoiled the friendly feeling between us.

I still remember the poignancy of the first time. . . . It was twilight and we thought of leaving the beach for home. . . . I said something, teasing her, and she pushed me off the blanket. We tussled, entangling our bodies with arms and legs. . . . Suddenly we were quiet, a bit breathlessly. I moved my hands quietly and softly over her body. She smiled. . . . The air was sweetly electric. Before dark we both left our virgin life and tentatively explored a new world for lovers. I wish I could still have that tender naive quality in my lovemaking today.

[From the authors' files]

112

Somewhere between prepuberty and middle age, most of us begin having sex with others. As we tentatively kiss, touch, and contact genitals, we may have the feeling that what we are doing is special, unique, natural, and spontaneous. It may seem special to us, but largely because we've been taught to isolate sex from the rest of our daily life. It's not unique—other people do the same things. It's not even as "natural" or "spontaneous" as our romantic myths suggest.

What we initially experience in shared sex is shaped by social concepts such as intimacy, virginity, and celibacy. The ways we touch each other follow a standard cultural pattern. Typically we begin with kissing and holding hands. More "advanced" activities are added according to cultural definitions of how "intimate" they are. Even the age at which we begin this pattern and the speed at which we progress through it are affected by the ways gender role expectations influence sexual decision making. Interest in shared sex, attitudes, and personal weighing of the pros and cons of sexual involvement all may differ along gender lines.

In this chapter we'll explore factors in actually beginning sex, as well as our reactions to what's considered a milestone event—first intercourse. We'll also look at how the process of sexual intimacy development is repeated when we begin new sexual relationships. In Chapter 7 we'll focus on patterns of body blending—that is, the specifics of the sexual experience. We'll examine homosexual and bisexual patterns separately in Chapter 8, for sexual relationships differ somewhat when both partners have learned the same gender role.

IDEAS ABOUT INTIMACY

Dictionaries define *intimacy* as interacting with another on a deeply personal level. Our society has sometimes tended to equate intimacy with skin-to-skin contacts. This was true as far back as 1926, when physician Theodore Van de Velde wrote *Ideal Marriage,* a manual for improving sex. Three hundred ten pages were devoted to physiological aspects of sex, but only ten to psychic and emotional aspects of optimal sexual "adjustment." Even today, sex manuals devote a lot more space to

the "how tos" of physical acts than to the quality of the relationship in which they are embedded.

Physical Intimacy

It's true that physical contacts do establish a kind of intimacy. In a society where nonsexual touching is largely limited to handshaking, a stroke on the cheek can be construed as an intimate gesture. Socialized to cover ourselves with layers of clothes, we feel exposed and vulnerable when we bare our skin to a new lover. When we engage in oral sex, we're allowing the other to smell and taste parts of ourselves that we're not even sure we like. And in intercourse and anal sex our most secret orifices are being shared.

Accepting social notions as ultimate truths, many assume that the more "secret" the areas contacted, the more "intimate" a sexual activity is. In sex research sexual events are commonly listed as a progression from "less intimate" to "more intimate" acts. Holding hands, hugging, and kissing are typically at the bottom of the list, as "least intimate" acts. Proceeding up the intimacy hierarchy are fully clothed horizontal embraces, caressing of the female's breasts from outside her clothes, ditto from inside her clothes, "petting" each other's genitals, nude embraces, and intercourse. Lovers are expected to go through this series in this order as they become "more intimate." Whether oral and anal sex and "dry humping" (imitating intercourse without penetration) are more or less intimate than intercourse is not spelled out so clearly in our culture as is the ranking of these other activities.

Emotional Intimacy

Despite widespread social agreement on this intimacy hierarchy, it's quite possible to go through all the levels with a partner and never feel close to him or her. Even with extremely "intimate" skin contact, we may feel that something is missing. To distinguish this from physical closeness, we could perhaps call it "emotional intimacy." It's not necessarily linked to sex, though some of us do find it with sex partners. We're referring here to emotional sharing: revealing our innermost feelings to each other, including those that we don't feel good about, and reaching out to receive the other's communications about herself or himself. Crying, or

The emotional intimacy many of us desire can be met in relationships that are not sexual, as well as in those that are.

hugging, or talking, or even a warm handshake can be expressions of deep emotional intimacy. Sex can be too, but not automatically. Some lovers communicate very little to each other. Instead of ecstatic or affectionate involvement, their interaction may be worklike and impersonal.

Impersonal sex in some cases may be a defense against the pain of being rejected or exploited while emotionally open. This pain is often interpreted as a sense of personal inadequacy, especially among the young. Rather than choosing between the risks of vulnerability or the hunger for intimacy, some people compromise with a "safely" impersonal version of sex. As Bernie Zilbergeld has observed, sex provides a semblance of personal contact that's more easily come by than emotional intimacy:

Many people these days seem to have sex rather than shaking hands or talking. In some ways, sex is easier, because talking and shaking hands can be risky. They invite contact and sharing. . . . It often seems safer to hop into bed where, one can hope, the bodies will do their part and it won't be necessary to deal with silly and annoying things like communication and vulnerability. . . . In a world where constant happiness is considered a reasonable expectation and where there is much pressure to experience everything, the complexity, responsibility, and pain of intimacy or personal sharing seem somehow out of date and not worth the trouble. [Zilbergeld 1978, p. 302]*

If we like sex because it's easier than talking, we may be choosing a painless way to avoid feeling lonely—painless because we withdraw emotionally as a defense against intimate involvement. By contrast, others see sex as a *vehicle* for emotional intimacy, an excellent way to get beyond the usual barriers between people. For some the sense of connection is almost mystical. As one woman put it, "Sex is beautiful because such a complete contact with another person makes me feel my being is not solely confined to my own body. It is one of the most direct ways to get beyond the barriers between 'them' and 'me'" (Hite 1976, p. 283).

*From *Male Sexuality: A Guide to Sexual Fulfillment,* by Bernie Zilbergeld. Copyright © 1978 by Bernie Zilbergeld. This and all other quotations from this source are reprinted by permission of Little, Brown and Company.

IDEAS ABOUT VIRGINITY AND CELIBACY

If intimacy equals sex, as some believe, then people who don't engage in sex are automatically defined as leading pretty bleak lives. Virginity is then a category we want to get out of, and celibacy is thought to be a meaningful state only for those with religious allegiances. This view is too simplistic, but pressures on people to initiate sexual relations are strong.

Social Influences

According to one national survey of college students, about half of these males and females have felt pressure from their friends to be more sexually active ("How College Men and Women . . . " 1980). Boys report pressure not only from their peers and from magazines such as *Playboy* but even from their fathers to "get it on" with some girl, even if they don't feel ready for partner sex. When formerly sexually active men choose to be celibate for a while, friends wonder how they can stand it. But as one such man remarked:

At times I was lonely, but it wasn't as difficult as I anticipated. Sometimes I was aware of missing something, but it usually wasn't sex. What I missed most was sleeping next to someone and the cuddling and playing around in bed. [Zilbergeld 1978, p. 153]

For women a lack of sexual relationships seems to be a somewhat more socially acceptable option. At certain points in their careers, it is even expected. Mary Latham (1972) has argued that many women are often rewarded for being celibate, just as prostitutes are paid for being sexual. Divorced mothers are granted custody of their children, alimony and child support from their ex-husbands, and legal respect often only so long as they stay away from new sexual relationships. Even some married women may find themselves paid *not* to have sex with their husbands—some of whom are saving their energies for outside affairs. The bargain: She services his health, status, appearance, property, and ego, suggesting that it's *she* who's lost interest in sex, in return for his continued financial support and status.

The concepts of "virginity" and "celibacy" thus are often given social meaning for women as means of controlling what they are expected to do with their scarce resource—that is, their power to gratify male sexual desires and ego needs. So defined, the concepts make sense only within the context of a system in which men are thought to have "property rights" to women.

In addition to the traditional male-controlled wages of celibacy, women are now finding their own rewards in avoiding physical intimacy. Some prefer no sex when the only available partners don't meet their standards. Periods of celibacy are valued by some as times for getting back in touch with their own feelings. Sexual frustration need not be a problem, for masturbation can be used. And according to a group of Dominican nuns who wrote an article on celibacy, avoidance of genital relationships need not mean a loss of human warmth. Sister Helen points out that although some nuns fit our society's stereotype of the cold celibate, she and her associates "perceive each other mostly as unusually vital, deeply human, understanding women whose whole purpose in life is to love not less than we would have in another lifestyle, but more" (Dominican Sisters 1978, p. 35).

The Great Divide

We've been using the word *celibacy* to mean a voluntary and perhaps temporary avoidance of sex with others and *virginity* to mean never having reached a certain level of physical intimacy. But where is the cutoff point between virgin and nonvirgin, celibate and noncelibate, monogamous and multipartnered?

The old physiological standard for female virginity was an intact hymen. Brides in some cultures were expected to produce physical evidence of their virginity on their wedding night: to bleed in order to prove that their hymen was being ruptured by first intercourse. Emphasis on the hymen is diminishing, though. We now know that hymens vary considerably, may be stretched or broken through activities other than intercourse, and may be totally lacking in some females. Such variation helps to leave the virginity question wide open to varying social interpretations.

In contrast to older generations who "knew" what virginity was, 41 percent of all males and 47 percent of all females in a study of 312 college students felt that female virginity was a meaningless or unimportant concept. Even more—56 percent of the males and 57 percent of the females—felt that it makes no sense to say that a man has lost his virginity (Berger and Wenger 1973). These people may feel that letting down sexual barriers is a gain in freedom and honesty in a relationship rather than a loss of anything. Among those who thought the idea of virginity represented something real, there was fairly strong agreement on only one criterion for females: 81 percent felt that full penetration of the vagina by a penis would constitute "loss of virginity" for a woman. But other possibilities got a few votes, too: a woman's bringing herself to climax, rupturing of the hymen, a male's bringing her to climax, full penetration of the vagina by something other than a penis, her bringing a male to climax, and partial penetration of the vagina by something other than a penis. Most of those who thought the concept of male virginity made sense seemed to define it as full penetration of the vagina, plus ejaculation. These varying definitions of virginity revealed a clear double standard: Both males and females applied more rigid standards to females than to males.

There are even more possible definitions of "loss of virginity" these researchers didn't think to explore. For instance, are people who've only had sex with partners of their own gender considered virgins since they've never joined penis to vagina? What about anal sex in heterosexual relationships? Does this preserve "virginity"? Some people seem to think so. One male interviewed by Pietropinto and Simenauer (1977, p. 337) saw nothing peculiar about his statement that his first in-female orgasm occurred in the anus of a girl who insisted on this activity because she "did not want to lose her virginity."

Interestingly, the major studies of sexual behaviors have not taken into account the variations in ways people define virginity. Researchers have apparently assumed that it is a clear, universally agreed-on concept. For instance, surveys tend to ask for simple agreement or disagreement with statements such as "A girl should stay a virgin until she meets the person she wants to marry." What the researcher means by "virgin" is not usually spelled out, nor is the question repeated with the genders reversed.

However we define it in physiological terms, the concept of virginity has tremendous social-psychological impact. One act among many forms of sex—usually the joining of penis to vagina in first intercourse—is defined as a major rite of passage. It marks a symbolic leap from "innocence" to "experience," from childhood to adulthood, from being "out of it" to being "with it" in one's peer group, and perhaps from affection to greater intimacy or commitment in a relationship.

HAGAR THE HORRIBLE

The Language of Sex

Concern with the social value placed on virginity—especially female virginity—has prompted over fifty years of extensive research into what is usually termed *premarital sex.* This term ties the sexual activities of young people directly to progression toward marriage. However, this assumption does not necessarily describe what young people actually do or think. For many, marriage is not the goal of their sexual activities. It is more accurate to say "sex among young singles," "teenage sex," or simply "singles sex" when age is not a factor.

APPROACHING OR AVOIDING SEXUAL INTIMACIES

In sexual decision making our definitions of intimacy, virginity, and celibacy are interlaced with other factors. These include our interest in sex, our socially shaped attitudes toward it, and our personal reasons for seeking or avoiding sexual intimacy. In this section we'll also look at how partners influence making a relationship sexual.

Interest in Sex

Interest in sex is often referred to as "sex drive." The usual assumption is that sex drive is a simple biological urge that is naturally stronger in some people than in others. It's not this simple, though. As we've seen, the biological variables in sexual responsivemess—such as hormone levels—are closely interwoven with our social and psychological environments. For instance, we're more likely to want sex if we've enjoyed it in the past. How supple, healthy, and attractive we feel may influence our interest in sex, too. People who like their bodies typically enjoy sex more, have sex more often, and have it with more partners than do people who don't like their bodies.

Another critical factor: our gender. In study after study males show more interest in sex than females, on the average. For instance, in one col-

In our culture men are expected to be interested in sex.

How Important is Sex?

Some individual male opinions:

I can't imagine anyone who doesn't enjoy sex, who doesn't want sex all the time. It's the best thing ever invented. But if I meet a girl and I like her, and she's just interested in conversation, well, hell, I can still enjoy being with her. And, sometimes, it turns out that the point spread was wrong, that I should have been a favorite all along. [Joe Namath, quoted in Firestone 1975, p. 141]*

The question of sex is really a very serious problem for a sensitive person. It's bad because when a guy gets to college he's going to feel inadequate as a man if he doesn't have a certain amount of experience. He is going to be different from other guys and they all make such a to-do about it. [Undergraduate quoted in Komarovsky 1976, p. 108]

In sexual experience, one has the answer to a very great deal of human anxiety and uncertainty. For one thing, sex is certain; it is a quick clean and total release, and as therapy for a great many human conditions it has the utmost possible importance. [James Dickey, quoted in Firestone 1975, p. 135]*

I think sex is part of everything, I don't think of sex as just something that happens now and then. . . . Sex is diffused with love and affection and only once in a while it comes to the hard-on point. The feeling is always there, but there isn't necessarily always an erection. [Nelson Algren, quoted in Firestone 1975, p. 148]*

It feels like work some of the time, like a duty, but I try my best because I want to keep my wife happy. [Quoted in Zilbergeld 1978, p. 7]

Some individual female opinions:

[I love] the feeling of crazy friendliness it gives, sometimes falsely. And the reassurance, however momentary, of being held. The closeness, intimacy, honesty—and after when you feel alive and happy in a way you never do at any other time. [Quoted in Hite 1976, p. 344]

The closeness gives me a sense that I am not alone, and that life is not all rough edges after all. It makes me feel loved and special. [Quoted in Hite 1976, p. 344]

I have gone for long periods without sex (up to one and a half years), but not recently. During those periods, I felt a sense of spiritual growth and independence and increased self-confidence. [Quoted in Hite 1976, p. 342]

I really didn't have a good time with sex until after my first marriage. It was a very gradual thing with me, as I'm sure it is with a lot of ladies. [Joan Rivers, quoted in Fleming and Fleming 1975, p. 230]

I love to make love, I love my lover. I love the lover before him. I love romance and mush. And I even enjoy a good clean hostile fuck. But sometimes I absolutely loathe myself. I tell myself, "Linda, baby, love is an art, not a marathon." [University of Minnesota senior, quoted in Greene 1964, p. 157]

[Without sex] I miss feeling wanted and needed, and the body warmth when I wake up. I usually start feeling unattractive and undesirable too—mentally depressed, bored, low-energy. I lose my sense of humor. [Quoted in Hite 1976, p. 343]

*From *The Book of Men*, by R. Firestone (Ed.). Copyright © 1975 by Stonehill Publishing Company. Reprinted by permission.

lege sample of 134 men and 90 women with a mean age of 19.8 years, 42 percent of the men but only 11 percent of the women had urges to have sex at least once a day or more (Mercer and Kohn 1979).

Another study of 229 unmarried students at the University of California, Los Angeles, revealed clear expectations that males are more likely to be interested in sex than females are (McCormick 1979a). Given a list of strategies for initiating or avoiding sex, both profeminist and more traditional students described all the initiating strategies as things males were most likely to do and the avoiding strategies as things females were most likely to do. This distinction was as true of their memories of their own past behaviors as it was of their perceptions of other people's behaviors. The researcher, Naomi McCormick (1979b), has concluded that these students really lived the gender-stereotyped scripts our society has handed them: "Men did everything they could to have sex, and women did everything they could to avoid having sex. There's so little permission for out-of-role behavior that even though we might be inclined to do something expected of the other sex, we don't often give ourselves the chance." For example, even though women tend to believe that men are turned off by sexually assertive females, a majority of men report instead that they are excited and glad to participate when women take the sexual initiative (Jesser 1978; Friday 1980).

Attitudes toward Sex

Traditional male/female differences in opinions on the morality of sexual activities still persist. Even though women are moving toward more liberal attitudes, they are on average still more conservative than men.

Although sex-positive attitudes tend to be the norm among college students, even in these groups women tend to have less positive feelings about sex than do men. For instance, among 138 students from two universities—one in a mid-Atlantic state and one in the Southwest—males were more approving than women of every sex-related behavior questioned, from young singles intercourse to communal living (Laner, Laner, and Palmer 1978). Differences between males and females in acceptance of intercourse among young singles remain strong in some areas. At the University of Nebraska in Lincoln, for instance, males and the non-church-going were far more liberal in their opinions of singles sex than were females and the church-going (Medora and Woodward 1982).

According to other studies, however, females' views of singles intercourse as immoral have dropped as loss of "virginity" before the age of twenty has become the norm rather than the exception (Bell and Coughey 1980). Men seem to be changing, too. In contrast to earlier generations who expected their wives and daughters to meet more restrictive sexual standards than themselves, one survey of today's men indicated that only a quarter preferred a virgin as a marital partner. Most said they simply did not care what a woman had done sexually before they met (Friday 1980).

Opinions on singles intercourse may no longer be an accurate gauge of sexual attitudes in general, anyway. General Social Surveys conducted by the National Opinion Research Center during the 1970s revealed that attitudes toward extramarital relationships became somewhat more restrictive, whereas attitudes about "premarital" intercourse became far more permissive. This increasing acceptance was especially noticeable among people with no religious affiliation, Jews, young adults, and those with more than twelve years of education (Glenn and Weaver 1979). At the University of Georgia, although sexual behaviors are increasing, the opinion that sex with many partners is immoral and sinful is now more common among both men and women than it has been in fifteen years (Robinson and Jedlicka 1982). Changes in attitudes toward sex therefore seem to be selective, with the ideal of committed pairing increasingly seen in attitudes, if not behaviors.

Personal Reasons for Avoiding or Seeking Sex

Even if we accept singles sex in general, we are not automatically compelled to do it ourselves. The decision to become more intimate with a partner is sometimes spontaneous and irrational. Usually, though, it involves previous weighing of costs and rewards.

FEIFFER

Individual Restraints. A common reason young singles give for not having intercourse is that they simply have not met a person they want to have intercourse with or who wants to share that experience with them. Others say they aren't ready yet. A study of females who were high school juniors and seniors or college students (Herold and Goodwin 1981a) revealed a large number who were defined as "potential nonvirgins" because they had nothing against singles intercourse— they simply hadn't experienced it yet. Unlike most of the nonvirgins, the potential nonvirgins were usually not involved in a committed relationship. And unlike both virgins and "adamant nonvirgins," they were more interested in careers than in marriage.

Religious prohibitions against sex without marriage are strong guides for some young people. Although most universities have stopped trying to patrol and limit students' sex lives and young people have open opportunities to be alone together, internalized "committed sex only" norms from church and parents may still be powerful internal censors.

Both males and females often avoid intercourse for fear of causing pregnancy. Although rel-

atively reliable contraceptives have long been available, the contention of sexually restrictive groups that readily available contraception will increase the incidence of intercourse among the young is not borne out by research (Reiss and Furstenberg 1981). Instead, many teenagers leave things to chance, causing a significant increase in teenage pregnancies as the incidence of teenage intercourse has increased.

To some the idea of singles intercourse is undesirable because it might make a relationship worse rather than better. Sometimes this notion stems from the fear of surrendering too much of oneself. For instance, Zilbergeld (1978) notes that some males have preserved their "virginity" out of fear of being trapped by a sex partner. They seem to think that sex inevitably leads to marriage, loss of autonomy, forfeiture of personal space, and lifetime obligations. Females, too, may feel that in agreeing to sex they are allowing a male to constrict them. But sex can instead be seen as shared pleasure. And whether it carries future obligations may be seen as negotiable rather than inevitable.

Some people are also held back by fears that their partners will expect them to be sexual experts

Strategies for Initiating or Avoiding Intercourse*

How do we encourage each other into or out of sex? Naomi McCormick (1979b) asked 120 single male and 109 single female college students to imagine that they were alone with someone with whom they had "necked" but not had intercourse. They were asked first to describe how they would try to influence this person to have intercourse and then to describe what tactics they might use to avoid having sex. Responses fell into ten categories. All of the following strategies could be used either as "come-ons" or as "put-offs," except for the last one:

■ **Reward**. The come-on: saying how much we like or admire the other. The put-off: using our hands or mouth to bring the other to orgasm to avoid intercourse.

■ **Coercion**. The come-on: trying to have sex and getting angry if the other balks. The put-off: getting angry if the other tries anything ("It's my apartment—leave!").

■ **Logic**. The come-on: trying to convince the other that it's natural to have these sexual desires. The put-off: reasoning that one should think of the consequences, such as pregnancy or venereal disease.

■ **Information**. The come-on: directly asking the other if he or she wants to have sex. The put-off: simply saying that we don't feel like it.

*Adapted from Naomi McCormick, "Come-ons and Put-offs: Unmarried Students' Strategies for Having and Avoiding Sexual Intercourse," *Psychology of Women Quarterly* 4, no. 2 (Winter 1979): 194–211. Reprinted by permission of the author and Human Sciences Press.

■ **Manipulation**. The come-on: setting up a sensuous atmosphere with soft lights, mood music, a drink, or some pot. The put-off: trying to distract the other into some nonsexual activity—making popcorn or watching TV, for instance.

■ **Body language**. The come-on: touching the other in subtle ways, moving closer, listening attentively. The put-off: not touching, moving and looking away, talking.

■ **Deception**. The come-on: telling the other we love him or her and have contraceptives ready, when we don't. The put-off: lying that it's our period or that we don't have any contraceptives.

■ **Moralizing**. The come-on: telling the other that it's unfair to turn us on and then leave us hanging. The put-off: insisting that intercourse should be saved for marriage.

■ **Relationship conceptualizing**. The come-on: telling the other that our relationship is now so strong and close that we're ready for intercourse. The put-off: telling the other that our relationship is just beginning and that intercourse might spoil things if it occurs before we know each other better.

■ **Seduction**. Used only as a come-on: setting up an elaborate strategy that might include a number of techniques mentioned already—perhaps a candlelit dinner with much eye-contact, moving closer, touching, "You really excite me," "Your hair is beautiful," "I'd love to give you a slow massage and then kiss you all over and then make love to you for hours. . . ."

and that they'll fail the test. In the past this notion has been especially problematic for men. In some other cultures, experienced older women are expected to teach young men the arts of sex when they reach puberty. But in our society the male has traditionally been expected to be older or at least more experienced than the woman and to play the role of sexual teacher. Even with widespread singles sex, the idea of the male as sexual expert and teacher still lingers. It's awkward for a male brought up with this notion to admit that his partner may know a lot more than he does. But if he's honest about his lack of experience, she is likely to enjoy "breaking him in." As one woman put it:

To tell the truth, I was shocked when he told me he never had intercourse before. I didn't think a man could reach the age of thirty-three without having sex. But the shock quickly died down and I thought, why not? I had the time of my life. It was fantastic being the teacher and breaking him in. He was so appreciative and I got everything I wanted. [Zilbergeld 1978, p. 151]

Individual Reasons for Sex.   On the prosex side of the ledger, seeking to give and receive sexual pleasure is conspicuously absent from many lists of motives for intercourse. Perhaps the reason is because pleasure giving and receiving have not been considered socially acceptable until recently. For instance, before midcentury, the only socially recognized reason for having sex outside of marriage was to *prepare* for marriage. According to a thirty-year study of the changing motives among male students at the University of Virginia in 1943 and 1944, males thought they were justified in "practicing" ahead of time because their experience might make marital sex more "successful." By 1967-68, focus had shifted to the couple. Marital success was thought to depend not only on the skills of the male but also on sexual "compatibility" between the husband and wife. This qualification should presumably be tested ahead of time so that marriage plans could be reconsidered if people found that they were sexually "incompatible" (Finger 1975).

When the surveys were repeated in 1969 through 1973, the notions of developing skill and determining compatibility before marriage again were cited by a majority as good reasons for singles sex. Those who didn't see marriage—or anticipation of marriage—as a necessary precondition for sex thought that no legal or moral barriers should be imposed on what they saw as a natural and satisfying activity. Many also stated that intercourse is a good way to increase intimacy between people. As researcher Frank Finger (1975, p. 311) put it, they felt that "anything that can increase interpersonal understanding and appreciation in a world of alienation is not only legitimate but to be encouraged." This perspective is not limited to men. As one woman who viewed sex as "the ultimate in human closeness" explained, "It brings me

The Language of Sex

Sociologists sometimes refer to positive attitudes toward sex as "permissiveness." For instance, in 1967 Ira Reiss announced that the emerging sexual ethic seemed to be "permissiveness with affection." But "permissiveness" suggests a kind of passivity. It sounds like permitting sex to happen, rather than actively shaping and sharing sexual encounters. It also suggests a certain irresponsibility. Use of "permissive" obscures the fact that sexual exploration is sometimes based on thoughtful individual or mutual decision making. Instead of "permissive," then, we can refer to people who take this approach as "sex-positive," "favoring sex," or "sexually enthusiastic."

closer in spirit to others in ten minutes than I can get in ten years to people I do not share sex with" (Hite 1976, p. 284).

Older studies have come up with other motives for beginning intercourse: "curiosity," love, "a natural outcome of the relationship," "to get it over with" so they would seem more "experienced" to future lovers, sexual satisfaction for themselves, to please their partners, the feeling that their partners would end the relationship if they didn't agree to having intercourse, rebellion against parents, proof of manhood, forcing marriage, accommodating an older partner's mores, and exploring further once "making out" became boring (Shope 1971; Martinson 1966). For some, choosing singles intercourse is a way of keeping up with peers. As one female explained, "Everyone was doing it. . . . It felt good being as sophisticated and knowing as I thought the rest of them were" (Schaefer 1973, p. 109). The degree of sexual experience among one's friends is one of the most significant predictors of nonvirginity (Herold and Goodwin 1981a).

When asked which of these strategies they had actually used, both females and males in a follow-up study cited seduction as their most common ploy in initiating intercourse, although men reported using seduction strategies somewhat more than women. In general both genders were more likely to use indirect strategies such as body language to initiate sex and direct strategies such as coercion to avoid it. McCormick speculated that we use the indirect come-ons not only to avoid embarrassment but also because our partners are more likely to cooperate if we don't seem to be forcing them into a sexual encounter. Such strategies preserve the romantic myth that sex is mutually desired. On the other hand, subtle strategies don't work so well in saying no. If we use them, we risk giving the impression that we might be persuaded to change our mind.

THE PROCESS OF BECOMING SEXUALLY INTIMATE

Although our culture tends to define the act of first intercourse as a sudden transition, for most of us it is but part of a long process of becoming physically closer to others. Along the way we are variously influenced by our parents, peers, mass media, and other cultural shapers, as we'll see in Chapter 9. Some of the things learned at one age are un-learned at another age or are coordinated into new scripts. This process of testing our capacities, learning physical and interpersonal skills, rethinking and changing old ideas and behaviors, and exploring new dimensions of physical and emotional intimacy with others does not—or need not—level off once we've reached a certain "goal," such as intercourse or orgasm. In a sexually alive person this growth process may continue for a lifetime.

Beginners' Sex

Although it seems unique and special when it happens to us, the process of becoming physically more intimate with others tends to follow a standardized pattern in our society. It typically moves from activities considered less intimate to those considered more intimate.

Early in our sexual careers, "sex" consists of holding hands, kissing, hugging, dancing close. Advancement into "more intimate" contacts usually begins with boys' attempts to touch girls' breasts. Sometimes these first tries are "disguised" as hugs that gradually creep downward, under the blouse, and beneath the bra, if any. The girl's part in this traditional script is to resist whether she likes being caressed or not; the boy's is to be the

Where It Happens

First intercourse for most is no longer a quick tumble in the back seat of a car. According to Zelnik and Kantner's research (1977), more than three out of four young unmarried women have first intercourse in a home: their own, a friend's, or their partner's, particularly the latter. Other less common sites: cars, motels, or "elsewhere"—dorms? closets? summer camps? beaches? haylofts? swimming pools? elevators? Although sex at home once carried risks of detection by parents in the next room, its growing popularity may be related to the fact that today there's probably no one else in the house or apartment. Single-person and unmarried-couple households are increasingly common. Even when teenagers live with their parents, chances are that both mother and father work, and the home is often invitingly vacant.

cool aggressor, whether he's scared and embarrassed or not.

As one girl described amateur night at the drive-in:

You'd sit close to the person and all of a sudden . . . they'd put their arms around you and they'd slowly drop it to your shoulder and slowly into your blouse. You'd jerk his hands away, and you'd smile or something like that and you'd turn back to the movie and he'd start doing it again. And you'd say, "No," "Come on," "Stop" or something like that. . . . He wouldn't actually say anything, but he'd think he was really cool, you know. . . . So it [sic] would just get around to it again. This time he'd go further, and he'd undo your bra and that would start it. You'd start kissing and he'd start feeling you. Not that many words, except if you were really a prude. [Sorensen 1973, p. 175]

In this script discussion of feelings and desires is rare. Progression to "more intimate" contacts is usually initiated by the boy, with the girl following somewhat reluctantly. Behaviors that require active participation by the female—such as her caressing his penis—appear later than those initiated by boys. Nevertheless, steady increases in the incidence of "making out"—both above and below the waist—during the past 40 years have been especially significant among females (Diepold and Young 1979).

Researcher Robert Sorensen (1973) found that most teenagers spend relatively little time in what he called the "beginner" stage. Some soon moved on to intercourse. Others explored paths of mutual pleasuring that did not include merging of penis and vagina, such as oral or manual genital caresses. He noted that some of these "advanced beginners" seemed to enjoy sex more fully and to have richer sexual repertoires than those who'd moved directly into intercourse from early petting activities. The focus in "advanced beginning" techniques is on mutual pleasuring, an approach that sometimes gets lost in intercourse that is unimaginative and orgasm-oriented.

First Intercourse

At what age people have first intercourse and how they feel about it afterward vary considerably. But some general patterns have been discerned.

Age at First Intercourse. According to a number of studies, males and females are converging statistically, as well as bodily. Females are typically younger at first intercourse than they were several decades ago, but males are typically *older*. In Kinsey's time 73 percent of the males surveyed but only 23 percent of the females had coital experience by age twenty (Kinsey, Pomeroy, and Martin 1948; Kinsey et al. 1953). By contrast, in a 1975 survey 61 percent of all males and 64 percent of all females had had intercourse by the age of twenty (Wilson 1975). In *Playboy*'s survey of over 100,000 readers, the historical trend toward younger age of females at first intercourse is clearly demonstrated by the fact that 58 percent of women then under twenty-one had intercourse before they were sixteen, compared with about 34 percent of the twenty-one to twenty-nine year-old generation and about 14 percent of the thirty to thirty-nine year-old generation (Petersen et al. 1983a).

The First Time

I was eighteen—a freshman in college. A married friend with whom I worked part-time at a grocery store fixed me up with his eighteen-year-old sister-in-law Maria, who was visiting from Mexico. He knew that I was a virgin. He and his wife and Maria discussed it and decided this was going to be my first time. I didn't have anything to say about it really.

I went out the first time and I was making out with Maria. She was really beautiful. Didn't speak hardly any English, and I had had Spanish in high school. She said in Spanish, "I don't want your hand." Being the gentleman I've always been, I took my hands out of her pants. What she really meant of course was that she wanted to go all the way.

I went back and told my roommate what had happened. He said, "You idiot. Don't you realize that's what she wanted?" I said, "Do you really think so?" He showed me how to use condoms and stuffed my pockets with rubbers the next time I went out with her.

I went out like a nervous wreck the next time. This time she wasn't going to take no for an answer. She had dressed up in a real slinky outfit and I took her to a dance—you know, the slit up the side of the legs, and all the guys were just staring at her. She was beautiful, a beautiful woman.

We went out in the car. She had this black lace bra and black lace panties and took off her dress— she took it off as soon as I stopped the car. I couldn't even breathe, my mouth was open. I couldn't believe it. I didn't know what to do. I said, "Aren't you going to take the rest off?" I didn't even take the bra and panties off. She took everything off and laid back. I

fumbled and put my rubber on. And we had intercourse. It wasn't anything great and I'm sure she could tell it was my first time, but I enjoyed it. The first night it was three or four times. We kept driving to different places and having intercourse.

The next night we went out, it was really great. We tried several positions and I was really into it. It was just great from the beginning. It was never a disappointment. I know I improved quickly—I was a quick learner. She didn't exactly direct me directly, but she did it through nonverbal ways; her hands and her eyes would kind of assist me. She was so sensual and into oral sex and everything. What a first time! I don't care if it was in the front seat of a car—it could have been anywhere. It was just fantastic.

But I felt funny coming back to the grocery store. I thought, "Oh my God, he lined me up with this woman, and I go out and I fuck her. Oh, my God, what did I do?" But he was chuckling, saying, "Well, I understand you and Maria had a good time the other night." I said, "Yeah." He said, "Yeah. We talked about it. She said she really enjoyed it." I said, "You know?" He said, "Yeah, we talked about it. She said she really enjoyed it and you learned fast." I said, "Gee, I'm on my way, huh?" He said, "You're on your way." I said, "Thanks a lot." Nice to have friends like that, huh? [From the authors' files]

Not all first experiences are as positive as this one. Some people who have good sex lives today may look back at their first experience as a disaster. But good first experiences may be more common as we become a more healthy culture and accept our sexuality as a natural part of life.

In metropolitan areas the average age at which females first have intercourse is now about 16.4 years among whites and 15.5 years among blacks (Zelnik and Kantner 1980). In 1979 almost two-thirds of all white women had first intercourse before the age of nineteen. Black women tend to have first intercourse at a younger age. Most men have now had first intercourse by the end of their teenage years (Zelnik and Kantner 1980). From the ages of sixteen on, the incidence of singles intercourse is now the same for males and females, and for both sexes it doubles between the ages of seventeen and eighteen (Diepold and Young 1979).

Over the past twenty years not only have females closed the gap with males in the incidence of singles intercourse, they have also broadened the range of relationships within which they have intercourse. In the 1950s those women having singles sex tended to do so right before they got married, with their future spouse, and even then they tended to feel guilty afterward. Since then, there has been an increase in the number of women having intercourse at all degrees of relationship—from dating to being engaged—and a decrease in guilt (Bell and Coughey 1980).

Many social observers have speculated that women are sexually more active at younger ages because of the availability of reliable contraceptives, especially the pill. There is no clear evidence, however, that the availability of birth control devices or information has any effect on the incidence of teenage intercourse, although it does cut down on the number of pregnancies (Zelnick and Kim 1982).

A more significant factor in the decrease in females' age at first intercourse seems likely to be gender role changes. Instead of the traditional pattern in which many boys recruited a few "bad girls" for exploitative relationships, boys are now finding that more of their female peers are interested sexual partners. The fading of double-standard gender expectations also allows females to be more sexual.

In addition to gender role factors, decisions to move on to intercourse during the teenage years is related to other nonsexual tendencies, according to researchers at the University of Colorado (Jessor and Jessor 1975; Jessor et al. 1983). These researchers note that intercourse is only one of many behaviors to which social age norms are applied. Like drinking or working instead of attending school, it is considered abnormal or deviant at early ages but normal at later stages of development. A ten-year-old who drinks two beers a day is considered deviant; a nineteen-year-old who does so is not. Intercourse is considered more deviant in junior high school, more normal in college. The researchers found that certain traits were correlated with making the transition from virginity at an age when it is still socially defined as deviant. High school students showed these characteristics even before they began having intercourse. Compared with those who remained virgins in high school, these transition-oriented students placed a higher value on independence and a lower value on achievement. They were more tolerant of deviance from social norms, more positive about sex, more likely to voice social criticism, and less reli-

gious. In other words, they were less conventional in many ways than virgins. At the college level, however, this difference was less marked because intercourse was a common behavior.

Aftermath.   How do we react to The First Time? That depends on the quality of physical and emotional interaction. Physically, an estimated 20 percent of all males are "unsuccessful" at first intercourse. That is, some can't get an erection going long enough to penetrate the vagina, some ejaculate before they do, and some never have an erection at all. Rather than discussing this experience honestly or encouraging their partners to help, many lie to their friends but become anxious about "proving" themselves the next time (McCarthy 1978, p. 65). For females first intercourse may actually be painful if the vagina is too tight. Gradually stretching it by hand ahead of time or lubrication with saliva, oils, or K-Y jelly can help. Plenty of preintercourse arousal is likely to make the first penetration enjoyable.

As for the emotional quality of the relationship, relaxation, honest talk, and gentleness in coupling are beneficial. First intercourse between people who are gentle, caring, and trusting with each other may be deeply gratifying even if it is not wildly passionate or technically skillful. The experience may be frightening or dull under other interpersonal circumstances.

For some, a long-term relationship provides a sense of security and love that makes first intercourse a pleasure. In a longitudinal study of 403 students, three-quarters of the women and half of the men first had intercourse within a committed relationship (steady dating, engagement, or marriage); only 25 percent of the women and 12 percent of the men in the total sample had found first intercourse a negative experience (Jessor et al. 1983).

In addition to the immediate reactions to the first act of intercourse, many of us see ourselves in new ways afterward. We have expanded our sexual identity. Even our bodies feel different to us. We change in our approach to partners, families, and people we meet. Sometimes we feel that we are changed in a way few others would understand or suspect.

Sex with New Partners

For some the first partner in intercourse becomes a lifetime partner. Many others have sex with several or more than several partners, with varying degrees of intimacy and satisfaction. How well things go depends not only on the sexual techniques we'll discuss in the next chapter but also on how we feel about the timing of sexual intimacies and about loosening up with someone new.

How Long We've Known Each Other. We now have two contradictory cultural expectations about how the timing of sex will affect a relationship. A traditional faction holds that "instant sex" can damage a relationship by cutting short the development of emotional intimacy. A more liberal faction thinks that sex can facilitate rather than hinder emotional intimacy. To test these assumptions, researchers Letitia Peplau, Zick Rubin, and Charles Hill (1977) studied 231 heterosexual dating couples from colleges in the Boston area for a period of two years. They divided the couples into three groups: those who had had intercourse early in their relationship, those who had had it later, and those who had abstained so far.

The "early-sex" group consisted of the 41 percent who had had intercourse within a month of their first date. Women in this group were generally higher in self-esteem, more interested in singlehood and careers, and less interested in housewifery than were women who delayed intercourse. These early-sex couples tended to feel that sex without love is okay, to consider intercourse an expected part of a dating relationship, and to have sex more often and enjoy it more than other couples did. Some saw intercourse as a *means* to emotional intimacy rather than as a *result* of it.

The couples who progressed more slowly toward intercourse tended to feel that intercourse is okay if people love each other, but that it takes a while for partners to become emotionally intimate enough to be ready for it.

A third group of couples—18 percent of this sample—were dating but not having intercourse. Aside from those who were simply mismatched, these students tended to hold traditional attitudes: that commitment to marriage is necessary before intercourse begins and that avoiding intercourse is a sign of love and respect, an indication that there's more to the relationship than sexual attraction. Many such couples did everything short of "real sex," however.

Despite the different time frameworks for sex and emotional intimacy in these three orientations, the researchers found that how soon a couple had intercourse bore no relationship to their satisfaction with the relationship or how long it lasted. Couples with early intercourse, later intercourse, and no intercourse felt similarly satisfied with the quality of their relationships. And after two years individuals in each group were equally likely to have married (20 percent), kept on dating (34 percent), or broken up (46 percent). The researchers' conclusion: "We found no evidence that early sex necessarily short-circuits the development of lasting commitments, nor that sexual abstinence or moderation consistently increases or decreases the development of a lasting relationship" (Peplau, Rubin, and Hill 1977, p. 103). What is probably important is the *meaning* individuals attach to intercourse. If they see it as a vehicle for emotional intimacy, then they'll probably think they are emotionally more intimate once they've started intercourse. If they see intercourse as debasing if love has not developed, having intercourse ahead of schedule may damage their relationship.

Loosening Up. Even though it's satisfying to get to know someone better and to improve a sexual relationship over time, there's nothing quite like the excitement of the first time with a new partner. The thrill of encountering a new body and a new soul—if they *are* delights—is unique. Some long-term partners are threatened by this recognition because they know "newness" is one thing they can't offer each other.

On the other hand, many people find it hard to be loose and trusting with a new partner. Sharing sex with someone new may at first be almost as awkward as some find the first time. Before first intercourse the progression from kissing and hugging to intercourse and oral sex may last for months or years, perhaps with the same partner. This gradual process of getting to know each other sexually is often collapsed into a much briefer time frame with later partners, with no drop in expectations.

Many of us worry that a new partner will not find our body and our "performance" sexually appealing. Lengthy apologies about parts of our body that don't please us—such as scars—are common. Many men worry that they may not have an erection or that they'll perform poorly in comparison with their partner's previous lovers. Many women feel so tense with a new partner that they don't orgasm.

Bernie Zilbergeld (1978) acknowledges that first-time encounters will probably feel somewhat tense and strange. But he suggests that they can be more enjoyable if people take this simple advice: Don't have sex until you're comfortable with the other person and until your conditions for good sex are met. Our conditions for good sex are whatever makes a difference to us: perhaps our own emotional state, our physical state, our feelings about our partner, what we want and whether we can expect to find it with this person, the kind of stimulation we like, the setting, the time of day. But instead of paying attention to what's important to us, many of us operate on stereotyped assumptions about what our partner thinks. According to Zilbergeld, many of us assume a new partner will feel disappointed, undesirable, or angry or will question our sexual interest and ability if we don't propose sex. If we just compared notes, he says, we might find that we'd both prefer waiting until we're more comfortable with each other. Even if the other is interested in sex and we're not, we still have the right to say no and to have our refusal accepted with good grace.

SUMMARY

Although we are sexual beings from birth, socially patterned ways of expressing our sexuality usually become more obvious during our teenage years. We begin to crave emotional and physical intimacy and often don't make clear distinctions between the two. Spontaneous expressions of these desires for intimate contact are inhibited by our culture's ideas about virginity. But depending on our own level of interest in sex, our attitudes toward sex, our personal reasons for seeking or avoiding it, and decisions made jointly with—or influenced by—our partners, we are statistically likely to progress from activities considered less "intimate" to intercourse some time during our teens. That the majority of both males and females are likely to end their "virgin" status by the age of nineteen marks an end of the old behavioral double standard in this area. Afterward, the degree of comfort and joy we feel with new sexual partners—if any—depends partly on when we think sex "should" happen in a relationship and how spontaneous we allow ourselves to be.

7

Experiencing
Sex

It's beautiful. Two people together, naked, touching, feeling, kissing, sucking, licking, teasing, caressing . . . why shouldn't I love [it]?

[Quoted in Hite 1981, p. 338]

Even more important than the orgasm is being able to wrap your arms and legs and whatever else around another human being. It makes you feel less alone, more alive. There's just nothing like it.

[Quoted in Hite 1981, p. 338]

When I was married, my husband and I never did anything but have intercourse. We did it often, at least three or four times a week. It never lasted more than five minutes, and I never came once. Our sex life was pitiful. But I don't want to blame it all on my husband. We had married without either of us having much experience, and we were embarrassed with each other. We never tried anything new. We broke up after eight years and one child, and I started dating again. . . . But I still didn't have orgasms, and I never ever suggested ways of making love that might help me to have them. Then at last I met my present lover, a very special man. With him I can say what I want, or he just knows. With him I always have orgasms and sex is an adventure. It's different every time.

We have oral sex, and anal sex, and we make love in every conceivable position. I like them all, especially the man on top, or the woman on top. I also like him to enter me from behind, while I am on my knees. I like foreplay, and want it to last at least fifteen minutes. But sometimes I don't mind starting right out with intercourse. My lover will put his penis inside me to begin with, and he'll play around with my clitoris while he's maintaining a really relaxed kind of screwing. After a few minutes of that, I'm ready to come. And even after I do, if he just keeps on, I can come again. Sometimes I can come four or five times. My lover is gentle, considerate, and expert.

[Quoted in Wolfe 1981, pp. 94–95]*

We made love in a lot of positions, and also on the floor and the davenport, because I didn't like the afterbounce of his waterbed. I loved the feel of him inside me and there is nothing I've seen in this world so far that can compare with the look of ecstasy he got on his face when he came.

[Quoted in Wolfe 1981, p. 94]*

What we truly experience when we're with another person sexually is hard to verbalize—an assortment of indefinable emotions, mysterious physical sensations, perhaps an altered state of consciousness. Our physical actions are somewhat easier to describe, for of all the ways that two bodies can touch and fit together, we tend to choose from a rather limited repertoire. In this chapter we will review the most common forms of heterosexual body blending, discuss the emphasis on producing orgasms, and consider the interpersonal dynamics that may mean more to our satisfaction with sex than do our physical behaviors and sensations.

BODY BLENDING

Once a sexual relationship has been established, sexual encounters tend to fall into a routine pattern. Shere Hite asked females, "How have most men had sex with you?" Of those who were heterosexual, 95 percent described the following pattern: "foreplay," penetration, thrusting, and then orgasm (typically for the male, sometimes for the female). End of session. One woman commented, "I'm beginning to think there must be a sexual *Robert's Rules of Order* which every guy follows" (Hite 1976, p. 320). Blame for this routinization of sex is usually placed on men, for they have traditionally been the orchestrators of sexual activities. But if women take the lead, they can be as unimaginative as men.

This structured pattern is not the only way to have sex. Sex need not be approached like a four-course meal in which the appetizer never follows dessert. Instead, sex can be enjoyed as a smorgasbord of intimate delights. Activities that are labeled "foreplay," because they are typically used to arouse our partner before intercourse, can instead be enjoyed for their own sensual rewards at any point. Sometimes we can linger for an hour of cuddling, soft kisses, and intimate talk; sometimes there's only time for quick but satisfying oral or coital sex; and sometimes our hunger demands a hearty banquet of caresses, kisses, oral and/or anal

pleasuring, and intercourse. As one married woman described this some-of-everything approach:

What I like best about sexual activity is . . . a combination of all choices—all our mutual activities and orgasm are made more pleasurable by the extreme amount of touching involved. Feeling the closeness of my husband, in every sense: spiritual, emotional, physical; the physical drowning in each other, and total overall caressing. . . . There are not enough words for touch hunger fulfillment, but that is the ulimate in sexual activity for me. [Tavris and Sadd 1977, p. 155]

Exploring the Sensuous Body

One of the results of limiting sex to a standardized routine is that we tend to touch each other only in the so-called *erogenous zones*. These are areas known to produce sexual sensations: clitoris, vagina, breasts, testicles, penis, and perhaps anus. But if we're bored with routine sex or are otherwise turned off, these areas may "feel" nothing. And if we're sufficiently interested in being sexually aroused, every part of our body can respond to erotic touches. Gentle licks or nibbles or caresses of our eyelids, the backs of our knees, our earlobes, the nape of our neck, the arches of our feet, and the insides of our thighs can be exquisitely thrilling. Exploration of each other's bodies may reveal many such pleasure spots that are not on the standard itinerary.

Even in the known erogenous zones, guided tours of each other's bodies ("Mmmm, that feels *really* good!") may lead to discoveries of subtle sensitivity shadings that are unique to our partner. A penis, for instance, may be especially responsive to touch on the glans or on the frenulum, where glans joins shaft on the underside. Although the scrotum is sensitive to pain, it may respond pleasurably to being gently stroked or licked or sucked. Some men especially enjoy having their perineum caressed or licked. Women differ in sensitivities in their outer genitals. For instance, some women prefer direct licking and stroking of the clitoris; others, deep but indirect pressure on

Skin-to-skin touching can be highly erotic and tender, no matter where we are touched.

either side or on the fleshy mons above. Learning what pleases our partner can be one of the most exciting parts of a sexual relationship.

Kisses and Caresses

Even the activities that are considered most elementary can be endlessly elaborated for mutual pleasure by creative and caring partners. Kissing, for instance, may range from a brush on the cheek to lip-nibbling to the penetrating, sucking "French" tongue-kissing that can bring some women to orgasm. Kisses need not stop at the mouth, of course. Alex Comfort (1972, p. 129) chides men, "If you haven't at least kissed her mouth, shoulders, neck, breasts, armpits, fingers, palms, toes, soles, navel, genitals, and earlobes, you haven't really kissed her." Comfort also points out that we can "kiss" with parts other than our lips—tongue, penis, eyelashes, even vaginal lips.

The erotic potential of touching, too, is limited only by time, imagination, and interest in sensual sharing. Those who have plenty of all three may enjoy spending hours just exploring each other's body, with or without orgasm. Many of us give and receive pleasure by massaging and bathing each other. Caresses need not be limited to hands. Breasts, genitals, wisps of our own hair, and even toes can give loving touches.

Many women have noted that they don't get enough of such kisses and caresses to satisfy them. Their partners tend to rush into intercourse after a brief period of "foreplay." As one woman put it,

A lot of the men I meet are into marathon screwing. They think the longer they can do it, the better they are and the better I like them. They're so wrong. I like them when they're into marathon foreplay. [Wolfe 1981, p. 97]

In a survey by *Cosmopolitan* magazine, almost half of the women liked foreplay to last up to half an hour; another 14 percent liked foreplay that lasted an hour or more. The clitoris is most erotically sensitive, but most of these women reported also being highly aroused by stimulation of their breasts and by kissing.

Males, too, may desire—and need—kissing and caressing if they are to be erotically responsive. An erection need not be a prerequisite to sex if, instead of waiting to be turned on, the woman herself actively helps to arouse her partner. For both sexes a teasing approach or prolonged pleasuring rather than a rush to orgasm often helps build sexual excitement to ecstatic and explosive heights.

The length of time devoted to kissing and caressing may be less of an issue for some than the quality of these touches. Routine rubbing of skin

132

surfaces can be boring rather than arousing. Gentle touches that barely skim the skin surface, exciting tiny body hairs, may feel more erotic. Genitals are especially sensitive to the quality of caresses. But it's hard to know what feels best to our partners unless they tell us. For instance, many women need direct clitoral stimulation if they are to orgasm. But direct rubbing of the clitoris may be painful or numbing, blocking erotic pleasure, for others. Some different possibilities: much gentler caresses, pressing the mons area against the pubic bone, rubbing to one side of the clitoris, increasing pressure as the woman becomes more aroused.

Men sometimes have the same problem: Women don't know what feels good to a man's genitals unless they're told. To help bridge the communication gap, the National Sex Forum recently presented some especially pleasurable penis-stroking techniques at sexuality workshops for women. This group suggested rubbing warmed oil onto penis, testicles, and perineum and then including all these sensitive areas in the stroking that follows. In the "countdown," for instance, one hand starts at the top of the penis and the other under the testicles. They are slipped toward and then away from each other, accelerating from ten counts per stroke to one per stroke (Hooper 1979).

For some people who have long enjoyed sex, these warm-ups may not be necessary. For them arousal is a sort of conditioned response that can be activated quickly by the mere suggestion of sex. They can be instantly ready for the "quickies" that are sometimes enjoyed as a change of pace. But even those who can warm themselves up may like to be touched often—bathing and sleeping with a partner, sitting close, walking hand in hand, touching when they talk—whether or not the touching leads to orgasm.

Oral-Genital Sex

In an increasingly common agenda kisses and caresses are typically followed by sucking and licking of the other's genitals. The act of sucking and licking the female's genitals is called *cunnilingus*. When a male is on the receiving end, it's called *fellatio*. Cunnilingus and fellatio are pleasurable ways to lubricate genitals before intercourse. They can also be used as a particularly erotic way to initiate sexmaking, an interlude in intercourse

thrusting, a way to provide more orgasmic satisfaction for either partner before or after intercourse, a means of getting the male started on another erection, or an end in themselves. But oral-genital sex was once considered perverted and is still against the law in many states. As Carol Tavris and Susan Sadd (1977, p. 125) point out, if such prohibitions were strictly enforced, "more American adults would be in jail than out of it." Among *Playboy*'s survey respondents 95 percent of males and females used oral sex sometimes; more than half include oral-genital pleasuring every time they have sex (Petersen et al. 1983a). Also, 87 percent of the men and 77 percent of the women say they enjoy "giving head."

Variations on a Theme.   As with other forms of sex, there are a variety of ways for partners to excite each other orally. Cunnilingus may include lapping, tongue-flicking, or circling of the clitoris with the tongue; sucking or gentle nibbling of the clitoris; placing tongue to clitoris and moving one's head back and forth; tongue-caressing of the labia; penetration and exploration of the vagina with the tongue; and pressing the chin against the vagina and labia while the tongue is busy elsewhere. Strokes may be hard or gentle, fast or slow. At the same time the man's hands may be caressing the woman's body, putting pressure on the mons or sensitive spots inside the vagina, teasing or penetrating the anus.

Fellatio can be similarly varied by an imaginative partner. She can take the whole penis into her mouth and stroke it by moving her head up and down. At the same time her tongue can provide a second set of sensations by flicking or licking at especially sensitive spots as they pass by. Humming, blowing hard, or stroking with teeth as well as lips along the shaft adds yet another dimension to erotic pleasure. Sucking on the penis creates a vacuum that pulls blood into the area and rapidly causes an erection. For gentler sensations a woman may take only the glans into her mouth, licking or pressing her lips around the undersurface, or nibbling sideways along the shaft. The entire genital area, including the sensitive perineum and anus, may be licked. And if the woman is careful not to hurt her partner, she may give him pleasure by taking his testicles into her mouth and gently sucking and tongue-caressing them. Her hands can add to his pleasure by caressing his body, playing with his nipples, encircling the base of his penis with a tight grip, stroking the shaft, fondling his testicles, stimulating his anus.

Personal Attitudes.   Learning these advanced practices is more than a matter of technique. It also takes unlearning of some socially learned attitudes. If we've been taught that the genitals are dirty or that their odors are unpleasant, these attitudes must be unlearned before we can feel comfortable about taking someone's genitals into our mouth or letting someone take ours. It may be hard to believe that the other person might actually *enjoy* stimulating us this way. But many people do.

Sex manuals now reassure us that a washed penis or vulva harbors fewer bacteria than the human mouth. But the proximity of these sexual pleasure spots to excretory openings may still prompt the feelings of disgust that our culture has taught us to associate with body wastes. An appreciation of the eroticism of natural sexual scents in these areas is just beginning to be encouraged by a few voices in our culture.

For women fellatio can have other problems—gagging when the man's penis is in too far and swallowing his seminal fluid if he ejaculates. Relaxation can help overcome the gag reflex. The base of the penis can be held so that the man cannot thrust far enough to cause gagging. Breathing may still be difficult—it helps to breathe on the out-strokes. The swallowing of semen is a matter of personal preference. Some women find swallowing semen exciting; others are turned off by its consistency and taste, so they avoid swallowing and spit out the fluid afterward. For both sexes fellatio also involves trusting—for the male, trust that she won't bite; for the female, trust that he won't thrust too hard.

A symbolic meaning that may cause discomfort with oral sex is taking what some consider a "selfish" or "passive" role in sex: lying back and letting the other person give us pleasure. Some believe that sex should always involve mutual giving and taking of pleasure. One way to make oral sex fit this model is to practice cunnilingus and fellatio at the same time. This combination is commonly known as "69," because the number shapes

suggest where partners' heads are. But it may be hard to both give and receive intense oral pleasure at the same time. We may be too distracted by our own sensations to concentrate on pleasing our partner. Freedom of movement and position may also be more awkward during 69. To fully enjoy being on the receiving end of one-person-at-a-time oral sex, we must overcome the notion that we are being selfish, for our partner may truly enjoy the shapes, textures, and scents of our genitals and find great pleasure in helping build our sexual excitement and feeling us come to a climax. And we need not view our role as passive or detached, for we may be fully involved in the emotional and sensual experience. We need not be face to face to be totally immersed in each others' bodies and emotions.

Intercourse

The desire for giving and receiving pleasure at the same time has traditionally been satisfied through intercourse. For many people in our culture, sex means intercourse. But the other activities we've described can be seen as sex, too. Sexual encounters don't have to end in intercourse or even include it. However, some people find that intercourse provides the most intense orgasm; many appreciate its sensual emotional intimacy. Intercourse often satisfies women's aching longing to be filled and embraced; men speak of the vagina as "home"—"a beautiful embracing organ" (Hite 1981, p. 337), a warm and friendly place they love to enter. To be so close, vagina welcoming penis, is for many a strong mutual experience of love and acceptance. Those who don't like intercourse tend to cite social rather than physical reasons: feelings of being used as a receptacle or a mechanical stimulant, emotional distance from someone who is caught up in a solitary experience, or simply boredom.

Although liking or disliking intercourse does not depend on orgasm alone, often there is an expectation that the man and the woman both experience orgasm during intercourse. This is not always the case. Hite (1976) found that although 87 percent of the women she surveyed like intercourse, only 30 percent of them thought they regularly experienced orgasm from the stimulation of a thrusting penis. In the *Playboy* survey 40 percent

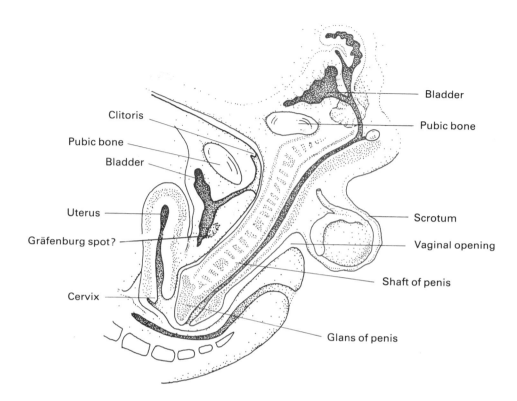

Figure 7-1. Genital Fit during Intercourse. This cross section of male-female genital interlocking during intercourse suggests that in-and-out movement of the penis would create friction on the clitoris. Some couples find that there is too little rubbing against the clitoris for the woman to orgasm easily in the male-on-top position. Other positions may increase clitoral stimulation and freedom of movement for the woman. But neither intercourse nor orgasm is essential to joyful sex—for either males or females.

of the women said they orgasm almost every time with intercourse; another 38 percent say they orgasm sometimes with intercourse (Petersen et al. 1983b). Some of the others may be experiencing "upper" orgasms with intercourse and not knowing why they find intercourse so pleasurable; some may have been socialized to ignore their lack of physical satisfaction and orgasmic release and to concentrate instead on the emotional pleasures of intercourse.

Some men may also find the stimulation of the vagina insufficient for orgasm. There are alternative paths to orgasm, and orgasm need not be the goal of sex. But if orgasm is desired, and with intercourse, there are some things partners can do to help each other.

Increasing Stimulation for the Female. Women who do note a lack of physical stimulation from intercourse tend to point out that clitoral stimulation is either too brief or nonexistent. Some women may need fifteen to twenty minutes of

thrusting for their clitoris to be aroused to the point of orgasm. Back in Kinsey's time men thrusted only about two minutes on the average before coming to a climax (Kinsey, Pomeroy, and Martin 1948). To increase the chances that their partners—or they—will orgasm, and to build their own excitement to a higher peak, 85 percent of the men in one study now try to prolong thrusting (Pietropinto and Simenauer 1977). Common tactics: being still when orgasm seems imminent, attempting to distract their attention from mounting sexual tension, or trying to tolerate greater sexual excitement before ejaculating. The female can

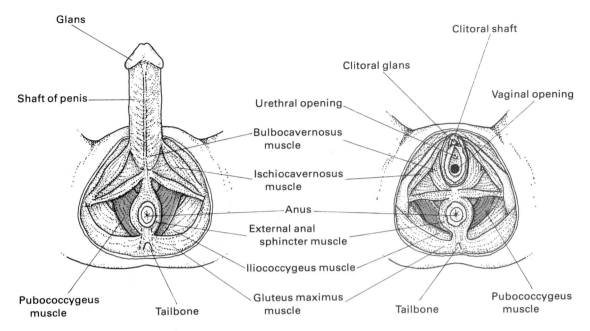

Pelvic Floor Muscles in Male

Pelvic Floor Muscles in Female

Kegel Exercises for Females

1. Insert one finger into the opening of your vagina. Contract the vaginal muscles so that you can feel them squeeze your finger. Remove your finger, contract the same muscles, and hold the contraction for 3 seconds. Relax. Repeat this sequence 10 times.
2. Quickly contract and release the same muscles 10 to 25 times. Relax and repeat.
3. While imagining what it would feel like to draw something into your vagina, contract the muscles that would be involved. Hold the contraction for 3 seconds. Relax. Repeat this sequence 10 times.

Two-Person Kegel Exercises

1. The male lies on his back; the female straddles him, penis in vagina, in female-on-top intercourse position.
2. He tightens his pelvic floor muscles, making his penis throb; she clenches her pelvic floor muscles in return. Repeat up to 50 times, remaining otherwise motionless.
3. After this exercise session, thrust slowly. If the male feels an impending orgasm, both clench their pelvic floor muslces to prevent ejaculation, and then continue gentle thrusting (Jardine 1979).

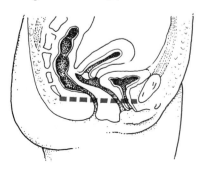

Female with Good Tone in Pelvic Floor Muscles

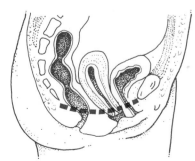

Female with Poor Tone in Pelvic Floor Muscles

help by squeezing the area below the glans of the penis with her fingers. This technique stalls the ejaculatory urge. In addition to prolonging thrusting, some men also caress or play a vibrator over the clitoral area during intercourse to help their partner orgasm. Women may take over this role themselves, for it's easier for them to tell just how they want to be touched.

Increasing clitoral stimulation during intercourse still may not bring the woman to orgasm. Even if it does, it may take a long time, longer than it does for her to orgasm with masturbation. Exercises to invigorate the muscles surrounding the vagina are often helpful in increasing muscular response and vasocongestion in the vagina. Back in the forties and fifties Arnold Kegel (1952) discovered that his treatments for inability to control urination were having surprising side effects for thousands of his female patients: They were feeling and enjoying intercourse more. Kegel's exercises consist of voluntary contractions of the *perineal muscles,* which span the pelvic floor. The *pubococcygeus,* or PC muscle, is the one of this group that is used when we try to stop the flow of urine. It also encircles the rectum and the outer half of the vagina.

Since the perineal muscles are often weak, some therapists today are prescribing up to an hour of Kegel contractions per day for those women who want to increase both feeling and muscle tone in their vaginas (Kline-Graber and Graber 1978). One theory is that the PC muscle is both the receptor of sexual stimulation and the source of orgasmic contractions of the vagina. A strong PC muscle reputedly feels more, because exercising a muscle increases its blood vessel capacity, and blood congestion is the basis for sexual arousal. Some research has shown that a strong PC muscle also facilitates orgasms more readily

and more intensely than a weak one, either with or without intercourse (LoPiccolo and Lobitz 1972).

Increasing Stimulation for the Male. Men, too, may benefit from exercising *their* PC muscle. It can be exercised by alternately stopping and starting the flow of urine, by consciously elevating the testicles, or even by lifting a washcloth draped over the erect penis. The only time men's PC muscle gets exercised otherwise is when they orgasm. After several weeks of efforts to locate and strengthen the pelvic floor muscles, men may be able to consciously prevent ejaculation and to experience orgasm by clamping down on their PC muscle just as they're about to ejaculate. They can make sexual sessions last as long as they and their partner desire, perhaps experiencing several powerful orgasms along the way (Jardine 1979).

In addition to their own muscle-building efforts, some men enjoy increased sexual stimulation with their partners' help. The idea that a male may need help during intercourse is rarely acknowledged in our culture. Much is made of women's problems; men are not supposed to have any. Some things a woman can do for a man: wrestle playfully with him to increase his muscle tension, caress or suck his penis to get it fairly hard before beginning intercourse, guide it with her hand into the vagina because it's easier for her to know where the vaginal opening is, tighten her PC muscle voluntarily to provide extra friction, encircle the base of his penis with her fingers to provide extra stimulation during intercourse, thrust actively to help build his excitement as well as hers, and suck or massage his penis again if it becomes limp.

Contrary to contemporary recommendations that the male hold off as long as he can and thrust slowly to increase the chances that his partner will orgasm, some women in Hite's survey said they said they found prolonged intercourse boring unless it involved good clitoral contact (Hite 1976). Sometimes women who experience "upper" orgasms actually prefer the old no-foreplay, hard and fast intercourse with deep penetration, which was once the male ideal, but which has since been discouraged in the search for female clitoral orgasm. Sometimes men might prefer this traditional pattern, too, and enjoy vigorous thrusting and quick ejaculation as a satisfying form of self-

◀**Figure 7-2. Pelvic Floor Muscles.** The muscles of the pelvic floor stretch across the lower pelvic region like a hammock. They hold up the internal organs and are linked in structure and function to the muscular bands that encircle structures passing vertically through this hammock: the anal canal, vagina, and urethra. One of the pelvic floor muscles—the *pubococcygeus muscle,* only a portion of which is shown in these cutaway views—seems to be involved in healthy sexual functioning.

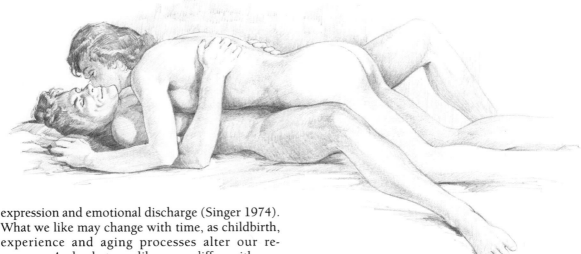

expression and emotional discharge (Singer 1974). What we like may change with time, as childbirth, experience and aging processes alter our responses. And what we like may differ with our moods. When we're feeling passionate, spontaneous thrusting may be just what we want, but sometimes we delight in slow, sensuous pleasure building.

Positioning.   Positions recommended in sex manuals now tend to be those that maximize friction on the woman's clitoris or pressure on sexually sensitive muscles and glands surrounding the vagina, allow her to move freely, and help the man delay his orgasm. One of the best for this purpose is the *female-above* position, with the woman lying or kneeling over her partner and bending forward or leaning back. So long as she doesn't thrust so vigorously that she hurts him, the male can lie back and enjoy her movements, perhaps rubbing her clitoris with his hand or a vibrator and thrusting to deepen penetration.

This symbolically passive role may be hard for men accustomed to traditional male-dominant expectations to accept. They're more likely to see the *male-above* or "matrimonial" position as the "natural" one. Although the male-above position is fine for affectionate or passionate kissing and hugging during intercourse, it may provide relatively little clitoral stimulation or freedom of movement for the female. Amused Polynesians who typically used other positions christened it the "missionary position" in honor of the benighted Western missionaries who brought it to their attention. Some women who feel pinned down by this position

aren't so amused by it—they call it the "dead bug." But Alex Comfort (1972) speaks of its quick-orgasm potential for men and notes that it can be the starting point for numerous variations. For instance, the woman can raise her legs or lock them around her partner's back to increase muscle tension, increase friction by squeezing one or both of his legs between hers, or deepen penetration by raising one leg and turning sideways as he kneels upright.

Rear-entry of penis into vagina—while standing, kneeling, sitting, or lying back-to-side—allows deep penetration, pleasurable pressure on the woman's buttocks, friction of the bed against the clitoris, and an exciting viewpoint for men.

This position is also particularly good for "upper" orgasms. It does not, however, allow face-to-face contact.

Another position used at some point by many couples: *side-by-side,* with one of her legs between his and the other above. This position is a favorite for leisurely sex: Both partners can be on their sides, and neither impedes the other's movements. For extra friction the female can wrap her legs around the one of his that lies between them.

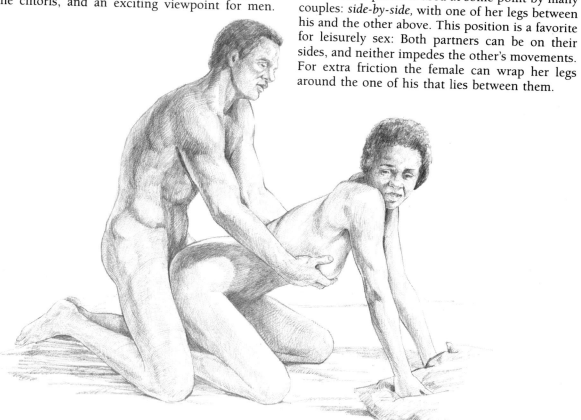

For couples who delight in variety, these basic combinations are only a beginning. Bodies can be creatively blended in hundreds of ways, especially if both partners are supple and athletic. But for some seeking variety in positions and "perfection" in techniques may seem a sterile game. Emotional intimacies and joy in giving and receiving pleasure may be more satisfying than mechanical attempts to improve sex out of the context of the relationship. Often it's the spontaneous emotional things we do—her loving his penis so much that she lays her cheek against it as she caresses it, playful wrestling, laughing together in bed—that mean the most.

Anal Contacts

One more of the endless possibilities in body blending deserves special mention because of its social implications: pleasuring the partner's anus by hand, mouth, dildo, or vibrator. Many consider the anal area taboo because of its associations with body waste. But some people find buttocks visually exciting and contact with the anal nerves erotic.

In the *Playboy* sample about 47 percent of the men and 61 percent of the women have experienced anal intercourse; over a third of both sexes have had anal-oral contact (Petersen et al. 1983a). In *Redbook*'s study of 100,000 married women, 43 percent had tried anal intercourse at least once, but only 2 percent used it often. Only 10 percent of those who'd tried anal intercourse described it as "very enjoyable"; 42 percent found it "unpleasant,"

and 7 percent found it "repulsive" (Tavris and Sadd 1977).

Enjoyment of anal contacts requires unlearning the disgust we've been trained to attach to excretion. It also requires dealing with some quite legitimate reservations. Some doctors feel that yeasts and other microscopic organisms from the intestines can cause trouble if they get into the vagina or the urethra. They caution that nothing that has been in the anus should be put in the vagina without first being washed, a rule that interferes with the spontaneous flow of erotic activities. Use of a lubricated condom that is taken off after anal intercourse is a partial solution. Anal intercourse may also be painful for the woman, for the sphincter muscle that normally keeps the anus shut is usually reluctant to relax. Men trying anal intercourse should lubricate the anal area and the head of their penis and proceed very slowly. Both partners will be most likely to find anal intercourse pleasurable if they abandon any expectations about what "should" happen, communicate what does and doesn't feel good, and be sure that neither is doing anything he or she doesn't want to do (Morin 1981).

Pleasure Enhancers

Many of us feel awkward about adding gadgets to our sexual encounters. Our romantic notion that what happens in sex is a "natural," "instinctive" expression of love rules out additions that take planning and purchasing, with the possible exception of contraceptives. But to shake off this learned inhibition opens up a world of erotic possibilities for exploration.

Some couples use vibrators in two-person as well as one-person sex. Both men and women may enjoy the buzzing sensation of a vibrator played all over their bodies, including genitals. A vibrator can be used before, during, after, or instead of intercourse to stimulate the woman's clitoris or the man's nipples, penis, and buttocks. And some males and females find that a lubricated vibrating dildo placed in vagina or anus increases muscular excitement.

Many couples have found that safflower or coconut oil, cocoa butter, or K-Y jelly liberally applied to one or both partners' genitals adds lubrication needed, especially when intercourse is prolonged or repeated. Other joys: feathers for teasing each other's skin surfaces, mirrors to reflect the sensuality of naked bodies, ribbed condoms to ripple across the vaginal muscles, rings for the base of the penis to keep an erection going and provide

extra stimulation for the clitoris, and "French ticklers" that excite the cervix with special projections and act as condoms, too. Whirlpool baths may seem too warm for active intercourse but are often considered a pleasant way to mellow out together before or after sex. Incense can add sensuality to the atmosphere, as can music. Some find the steady thumping of hard-rock records excellent to thrust by. A waterbed envelops and rocks with its own rhythmic waves. And sex on a fur rug is almost unbearably sensual, for we're caressed everywhere at once.

ORGASM ISSUES

Orgasmic release from built-up sexual tensions is usually considered the major physical goal of sex. Sessions often include the anxious question, "Did you come?" Perhaps there is some validity to this concern. Although we needn't think we have to orgasm every time we turn on, prolonged sexual stimulation without some kind of orgasmic release can be uncomfortable for both genders. A female may be sleepless, irritable and uncomfortably swollen in her pelvic area; a male may develop prostate gland trouble or painfully swollen testicles (Masters and Johnson 1966; Galton 1979).

In the past women tended to complain that men didn't care whether they orgasmed or not; now some women are stating that men are too insistent on making sure that the woman orgasms. More men cite their partner's orgasm than their own orgasm as their favorite moment in intercourse (Petersen et al. 1983a). Some may genuinely enjoy giving pleasure; some may view creation of an orgasm for their partner as their goal. Women may not appreciate the latter approach, for they may experience it as pressure to perform rather than just enjoy. One woman explained:

I like the closeness that kissing and cuddling and hugging bring. I do not think orgasms are always so important. But men think that if you do not have one, they are not the great lovers they think they are. Men see sex as some kind of athletic competition. They really want to perform so as not to dissatisfy women. So they shortchange us on cuddling and hugging and go just for the clitoris, and it turns me off, not on.   [Wolfe 1981, p. 142]

Goal Orientation

Even if we reach the cultural goal of orgasm with intercourse every time we have sex, other goals often lie beyond. One is the *mutual orgasm*: both partners climaxing at once and enjoying the excitement together. This goal, however, can block spontaneous sexual enjoyment. Arranging for the woman to have a clitoral orgasm at the same time as the man ejaculates may take twenty minutes or more of steady grinding for her and holding back for him. How this contributes to emotional intimacy is hard to imagine. The "upper" orgasm may happen to coincide with male orgasm because it's triggered by the kind of deep thrusting that typically precedes the male's climax. But to make simultaneous orgasm a goal turns sex into work rather than love or play. Irving Singer (1974, p. 149) even suggests that something may be lost if people climax at the same time, for the slight loss of consciousness that often accompanies orgasm

prevents partners from being fully aware of each other's pleasure: "For some people, to enjoy the beloved's orgasm is as deep and intimate a pleasure as the sharing of responses that are timed in perfect unison."

Multiple orgasms, too, are held up as a cultural goal. But they may be no more satisfying than single ones. When Kinsey and then Masters and Johnson revealed that some women had the capacity for climaxing repeatedly in a single sexual session, everybody wanted to do it. Many women found that they could if stimulation continued. Some men interpreted this discovery as a new performance burden: thrusting or licking or fingering until their partner had had enough. But women who want more can choose to stimulate themselves rather than expect their partners to "provide" more orgasms for them.

Another potential performance expectation now looms with publicizing of the fact that some men can orgasm repeatedly without ejaculating, or ejaculate repeatedly in a single session, or orgasm repeatedly even after all semen is gone. The ability to separate orgasm from ejaculation may involve good PC muscle control to keep semen from being ejaculated after contractions of the internal sexual organs, plus conscious relaxation at the brink of orgasm in defiance of strong desires to thrust harder. Using such techniques, one multiorgasmic male had twenty-five or thirty orgasms during a single hour of sex. He was forty-nine years old at the time (Robbins and Jensen 1978; Tavris 1976).

To realize the potential for multiple male orgasm takes concentration and unlearning of the cultural expectation that after a man has climaxed once, he's had it, at least for a while. But in publicizing the discovery of male multiple orgasms, Carol Tavris worried that she was adding yet another performance goal to our already goal-burdened sexmaking. Some reactions from her male friends: "For the good of mankind, don't publish it!" "Oh, hell" (Tavris 1976, p. 56).

Researchers Mina Robbins and Gordon Jensen point out that multiple orgasms are not necessarily more satisfying for males than single orgasms. Their subjects said there were differences between sexual sessions. Sometimes one orgasm with ejaculation was totally fulfilling; sometimes it took many orgasms before they were physically and emotionally satisfied (Robbins and Jensen 1978). Women, too, report that multiple orgasms may be no more enjoyable or no more satisfying than single ones (Clifford 1978). As one woman put it,

Orgasms are important but being close and loving is as important. My husband, knowing that I have multiple orgasms, feels the more I have . . . the better sex is. That is not true—my orgasms are purely physical and can be arrived at without much foreplay. I do not feel it is "making love" just because you have an orgasm. [Hite 1976, p. 385].

Faking Orgasms

The view of orgasm as an expected accomplishment rather than a delightful experience that sometimes happens leads some of us to pretend to orgasm when we really don't. Occasionally, men who think they've climaxed too soon or fear that they won't do it at all may make some vigorous thrusts and moan a bit to make their partner think they've orgasmed at the "right" time. Since women often can't feel semen shooting into their vaginas anyway, they can be deceived. For their part they may be faking, too: moving around a lot, making noise, and perhaps tightening their PC muscle voluntarily to pretend that they're having a knock-out of a climax. In *Playboy's* sample 28 percent of the men and almost two-thirds of the women had faked orgasms (Petersen et al. 1983a).

Some people who fake orgasm seem to be motivated either by fear of being considered "inadequate" or by concern for their partner's feelings. They may think that the other will feel hurt, inadequate as a lover, or tired of trying if they don't climax on cue. Others pretend to orgasm so their partner will stop stimulation that has become boring or painful. But to use deception to solve these problems locks a relationship into an unsatisfactory pattern. So long as the deceived partner thinks that a sexual routine is exciting for the other, there's no impetus for change. Although it may be embarrassing at first, honest talk about sexual concerns is more likely to improve a sexual relationship than is deception.

Overemphasis on Orgasm

Social observer Philip Slater charges that our tension-producing culture is responsible for this pre-occupation with orgasms and more orgasms:

In a society like ours, which perpetually bombards its participants with bizarre and dissonant stimuli—both sexual and nonsexual—tension release is at a premium. It is this confused and jangling stimulation, together with the absence of simple and meaningful rhythms in our daily lives, that makes Americans long for orgasmic release and shun any pleasure-seeking that does not culminate in rapid tension discharge. [Slater 1977, p. 10]

Slater feels that men suffer from a need to release tension because they have been socialized to inhibit emotions. Women, allowed to express their feelings, may not feel so urgent about releasing bottled-up *emotional* energies. But their *sexual* energies may be as urgent as men's, whether they recognize this or not.

Slater charges that men have wanted to force women into screaming orgasms for the male's sake—so that he can vicariously enjoy an emotional release that he is not culturally allowed to express. Slater (1977, p. 9) thinks that a favorite male fantasy expressed in popular literature— "that of the inhibited or resistant woman forced by overwhelming sexual arousal into unexpected and explosive orgasm"—is based on wishful identification with the woman in the fantasy.

In place of the male's goal-oriented script calling for explosive orgasms, especially on the part of the female, Slater suggests a mellower approach to sex. He asserts that focusing on goals distracts us from the pleasure of the moment. In the "task-free eroticism" he envisions, orgasm would be seen simply as a "delightful interruption" in the process of creating pleasurable sensations (Slater 1977, p. 10). In comfortable sexmaking, he writes, orgasm would not be the goal of every sexual encounter. It would be enjoyed when it happened, but some sex would probably be nonorgasmic.

SATIATION

Perhaps an underlying goal in our search for orgasm is a craving for the "laid-back," peaceful, loving warmth of afterglow. These are the sensations that follow truly satisfying orgasm. Not all orgasms have this effect. Many women climax again and again but are still left restless. Men, too, may ejaculate without experiencing a strong build-up and total release of emotional and physical tensions. On the other hand, some couples can reach that mellow, intimate level together without orgasm, just through affectionate, barriers-dropped, relaxed cuddling. Perhaps this reason is why so many women say they'd rather just cuddle than start on sexual stimulation that may leave them aroused and tense but not satisfied.

Instead of considering such factors, most researchers have looked at sexual satisfaction in terms of frequency counts of intercourse. For in-

stance, in *Playboy's* sample of over 100,000 of its readers, the most common pattern was to have intercourse two or three times a week. The majority of people in this sample say they are satisfied with their sex lives, but they would like to have intercourse and oral sex more often (Petersen et al. 1983a). In the *Redbook* survey of married women, Tavris and Sadd found that more sex tended to mean better sex. In their sample they wrote, "the higher the frequency of intercourse, the happier wives were with their marriages and the better they rated their sex lives. Cause and effect become circular in this case, . . . like a serpent swallowing its tail: The more you like it, the more often you do it, and the more often you do it, the better it is" (Tavris and Sadd 1977, p. 100).

The important factor here is enjoyment, though, rather than frequency. Having sex every Monday, Wednesday, and Saturday just to keep up with the national average may be pointless and unsatisfying. Instead, individual preferences should be explored. Some of us are happiest when we have intercourse several times a day, some of us prefer an occasional seven-course session, and some of us would simply like to touch and be touched more often.

INTIMACY DYNAMICS

Satisfaction with sex depends not only on how ingeniously or how often we fit our bodies together or how many times we orgasm, it also depends on the quality of emotional involvement, communication, and caring.

Involvement

Some of us become so absorbed with performing skillfully that we forget to participate emotionally. We almost become spectators—watching our performance, but not feeling it. Getting inside of the sexual experience may mean opening the door to feelings and behaviors that some of us don't allow ourselves in everyday life: tenderness, anger, fear, physical sensations so strong that they're almost unbearable, loss of conscious control of our movements, incoherence, whimpering, sobbing, overwhelming love for the other person. Such feelings provide the emotional climax to our sexmaking.

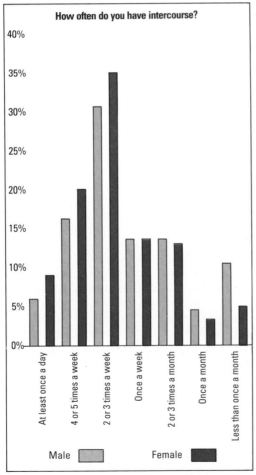

Based on *Playboy's* survey of 65,396 male and 14,928 female readers (p. 241).

Figure 7-3. Frequency of Intercourse.

In spontaneous, emotionally involved sex, there are no set patterns. For this woman, nudging her partner playfully with her nose was an impulse of the moment.

It's an extraordinary experience in being fully alive, but some people never let themselves feel it. Trained to act restrained and to subdue feelings in public, they have a hard time letting go with a sex partner. And afraid of allowing themselves to be this physically and psychologically vulnerable, they cannot let down their guard and experience an emotional climax.

In addition to cutting us off from our own sensations, "spectatoring" can cut us off from our partner. To mechanically manipulate a penis or vagina—insert A into B—and thrust to orgasm is different from just doing whatever being together makes us feel like doing: wrestling, or biting, or chewing on each other's hair, or sucking each other's fingers, or rubbing our breasts against the other's back, or giggling, or rolling over and over together, or pounding or scratching each other, or

Letting Go

As young children, we move and express ourselves with abandon. We let our excitement carry us away. But as we grow older, we learn from past hurts and social lessons to control our emotional responses and stiffen our bodies. According to Jack Lee Rosenberg, author of *Total Orgasm* (1973), we stop ourselves from feeling excitement and tension and pleasure even during sexmaking by learned defensive muscular patterns—that is, by restricting our movements and our breathing. And John Perry (1979) has found that some preorgasmic women have—instead of weak PC muscles—incredible tension in their pelvic areas.

Rosenberg has therefore compiled a series of exercises that by unlocking muscular tensions may help us to experience and tolerate greater sexual excitement. These exercises begin with deep breathing from the diaphragm, in which each exhalation is a noise-making letting go. They then progressively relax each area that we typically tense: neck, chest, hands, face, back, belly, thighs, knees, pelvis. Some examples:

To free the chest and neck, lie on your back and raise your arms perpendicular to the floor while inhaling deeply. Drop them over your head as you exhale noisily. Repeat this five times and then reverse the process: Exhale as you raise your arms, inhale as you put them down.

To free the thigh and stomach muscles that we tense in defending our genitals, lie flat on your back and draw your legs slowly over your body with knees bent. Let your legs fall apart and then slide them along the ground until they're straight again. Feel your stomach to make sure you're not tensing it. Repeat this six times. Keep breathing rhythmically, letting out any sounds that occur.

To free the pelvis, lie on your back with your knees bent. As you slowly breathe in, let your pelvis rock under, arching your back slightly. As you breathe out, allow your pelvis to return to a forward position. Don't tense your stomach—this should be a relaxed movement. As you do it, imagine that you are breathing in and out through your genitals. If your neck begins to tighten, massage the tension out of it and then slowly begin the pelvic rocking again.

*Adapted from Total Orgasm by J. L. Rosenberg. Copyright © 1973 by Random House, Inc. Reprinted by permission.

lying curled up together, or squeezing each other in a bearhug, or saying each other's name over and over, or bouncing on the bed together, or chasing each other, or gently joining penis to vagina but not thrusting much, or thrusting uncontrollably. None of these are carefully scripted, performance-and-goal-oriented behaviors. They're raw expressions of sexual energies and feelings for each other. Behaving the way we really feel may not fit our romantic or mechanical notions of what sex is supposed to be like, but it can be immensely satisfying.

Rather than watching ourselves and our partner from afar, some of us isolate ourselves from sex by fantasizing that something else is going on. In addition to escape, fantasies are often used to increase excitement. Interviews with 56 suburban housewives showed that 65 percent fantasized at least occasionally during intercourse and 37 percent did so often. The researchers concluded that fantasizing while having sex with a partner is "an adaptive normal adjustment mechanism for replacing boredom or for enhancing a routine experience" (Hariton and Singer 1974, p. 319). But if sex were neither boring nor routine, and if partners told each other what feels good and what doesn't, fully experiencing sexual sensations might be more rewarding than escaping from them into fantasy.

Psychologist Donald Mosher suggests that sexual involvement has three dimensions: enactment of sexual roles, sexual trance, and engagement with the partner. If our involvement in these dimensions stays at a shallow, surface level, the sensations we experience remain largely physical. When our involvement is moderately deep, the sexual encounter tends to be valued as an emotional rather than sensual experience. And at deep levels of involvement, lovemaking puts us in touch with eternal values such as truth, beauty, richness, perfection, and unity. Instead of being methodical and consciously chosen, our behaviors are ecstatic and involuntary; our conscious awareness of ourself is lost in a transcendent consciousness that "celebrates the spirit of life itself" (Mosher 1980, p. 25).

Communication

Another important aspect of sexual satisfaction is open communication. In the *Redbook* study of mar-

ried women, the strongest indicator of satisfaction with sex was the ability to talk about it with one's partner. The more often women discussed sex with their husbands, the higher they rated their sex lives as well as their marriages and their general happiness (Tavris and Sadd 1977).

Being open and humorously "up-front" about our feelings, desires, and needs can be fun and informative, too: "I've had so much to drink that I don't think I can get it up for heavy sex tonight. I'd love to just hug and kiss with you before I fall asleep, though." When we talk about sex, we may be at our most vulnerable, and potentially our most intimate. Sex talk can also help us deal with potential conflicts: differences in how often we want sex, what kind of stimulation we prefer, whether we feel sexier at night or in the morning, and so on.

Sex itself can be an intimate form of communication. Hugs, caresses, tender oral pleasuring, kisses soft or passionate—all may be expressions of affection as well as of sexual desire. We read the looks on our partner's face, the sighs and groans, and muscular tensions building up in the other's body as clues to what she or he is experiencing. And rather than saying, "Now do this to me," "Faster!" or "Gentler, please," we often soften these requests by making them with our hands rather than with words.

There are limits to what we can communicate nonverbally. Misreadings of nonverbal clues may lead to unnecessary resentments that can poison a relationship. Caught early, such resentments can often be undone with a few words. For instance, it took only three sentences for one couple to change a misunderstanding into a happy ending. He had come home seemingly tired from a late night of work. She was feeling lusty but was concerned about letting him sleep if that was what he wanted. He flopped into bed and turned his back to her. She waited for a sign. Nothing. After about fifteen minutes, he turned onto his back. Normally she would take this as a signal of availability; tonight she was afraid that by initiating sex she might be depriving him of sleep. Finally he sat bolt upright and snorted with disgust. She: "What's wrong? Did you want to get laid?" He: "I thought that was clear!" She collapsed into giggles in delighted relief.

Talking about sex is often hard, though. Many

women say they'd like to talk about sex, but their partners turn defensive whenever the subject is broached. The problem, Bernie Zilbergeld thinks, is in men's models, or lack of them. In the macho male image traditionally projected in men's magazines and fiction, males don't talk to their partners about sex:

Doing it is the only thing that matters, and aside from the "I'm going to do it to you" and "Do it to me harder and faster" routine, what could there possibly be to say? The superstuds in the model never feel fear or concern or tenderness or warmth, they never have problems, they never need to stop or rest. So where can a boy or man turn for an example of emotional or sexual communication? No place at all. [Zilbergeld 1978, p. 34]

Men are less socialized to admit to feelings of fear, or tenderness, or ignorance. Instead, Zilbergeld (1978, p. 34) writes, they learn to hide behind "a mask of aggressive sexuality, cool confidence, or stony silence." To communicate intimately would be to lift the mask. Despite such training, some men are now perceptively and honestly revealing themselves as feeling people.

Although women are given more approval for expressing emotions in our culture, like men they have little training in talking openly about sex. Many of us are uncomfortable with blunt sexual language—"Eat me," "Fuck me"—because we have learned to associate it with vulgarity. On the other hand, we associate clinical terms—"oral-genital sex," "coitus"—with coldness. The problem is not in the words themselves but in our reluctance to say them. The more we use them and make them suit our meanings, the more comfortable we may be with them. Many couples devise their own words and phrases to describe body parts and sexual activities.

In addition to cultural and language barriers, we may have trouble talking about sex because we haven't learned how to communicate effectively in sensitive areas. One communication skill many of us have not learned is *neutrality*—that is, accepting responsibility for our own feelings and not blaming anything on or assuming anything about the other. If we are bothered by aspects of our sexual interaction or if we want to try something

new, we should disclose our feelings by making clear, honest statements in the first-person singular: "I think," "I wish," "I'm afraid," "I need." Inferences about the other's motives and feelings—"You think," "You wish," "You're afraid," "You need"—are unwarranted.

In addition to neutral exchange of feelings, good sexual communication requires *mutual* intent to improve the relationship. It's not enough for one person to make disclosures and try to change to accommodate the other's needs. Negotiations should be reciprocal, with both partners motivated by concern for the other's happiness as well as for their own. Otherwise, the more empathic, accommodating, and concerned partner may be controlled by the selfish desires of the other (Masters, Johnson, and Levin 1975). This self-centeredness inhibits both intimacy and growth in the relationship.

Another essential ingredient in successful sexual communication is how we approach problems. Instead of taking a blunt approach—seeing the choices as your way, my way, or a compromise neither of us wants—we can view our differences as conflicts to be *managed* through ongoing communication rather than resolved once and for all. This time frame allows us to take a deeper look at what's really going on. For instance, disagreements about how often we want sex may be seen not as head-on clashes between someone who is naturally "horny" and someone who isn't, but perhaps as clues to individual or interpersonal conflicts that have not yet been aired.

Revealing negative emotions is not easy for two people who've been socialized to protect each other from uncomfortable communications. But negative feelings exist in any relationship. Rather than viewing them as unchangeable and potentially disruptive and therefore sweeping them aside and allowing them to smolder, it's possible to see them as tensions that may ultimately be good for the system. Airing differences of opinion keeps alive the dynamic processes of continuing negotiations, learning, and discovery. With such an approach partners might still disagree on how often they'd ideally like to have sex with each other, for instance, but by making thoughtful self-disclosures and rethinking their old routine, they can increase their intimacy and perhaps make sex more exciting and satisfying for both of them.

Caring

A third dynamic influencing our satisfaction with sex is how we feel about our partner. For many of us sex is best when there is strong mutual concern for making each other happy.

The most highly evolved form of love is said to be the sense that how our partner feels deeply affects how we feel. We pay attention to the other's needs and desires, balancing them against our own immediate wishes. We behave this way not because we feel we have to, but because we want to, for the other's happiness has become intimately meshed with our own. When we act in each other's best interests, even though doing so may be at odds with what we think we want for ourselves at the time, we are saying, "I care how you feel, because I am affected by your feelings. When you are happy, I am happier; when you are unhappy, it is harder for me to feel good because I feel your unhappiness as my own. Since I want to feel good, I want you to feel good."

When we think and act in this spirit, we demonstrate an emotional commitment to each other. We indicate that we can be trusted to be concerned and to try to understand even when the other reveals things that may disturb us. For many of us, true vulnerability—revealing our feelings and letting ourselves go sexually—is possible only within the context of such a relationship. To expose ourselves to someone who does not care is a misplaced act of faith. Rather than intimacy, we may find pain. For instance, revealing that we need a different kind of stimulation or that this time we'd really prefer a backrub to intercourse may earn us scorn rather than empathic understanding or attempts to work things out. Being hurt this way tends to make us retreat into a defensive shell, for the other has made it clear that she or he cannot be entrusted with our feelings. But when there is mutual caring, the continuing process of becoming closer and more open with each other may be expressed in sex that gets better all the time.

Summary

We typically blend our bodies in standardized ways: kisses, caresses, oral sex, intercourse, and perhaps anal contacts. To depart from the standard routine to simply delight in exploring and giving pleasure to each other may take some of the emphasis off reaching orgasm. By contrast, creating orgasms—especially mutual and multiple ones—is so often viewed as a performance goal that spontaneous enjoyment of the moment is blocked. Many people of both sexes sometimes fake orgasm in order to end a sexual session or to avoid disappointing their partners. Orgasm does help to relieve built-up tensions—sometimes—and people who have intercourse frequently are most likely to enjoy it. But the quality of emotional sharing may be as important to our satisfaction with sex as how often, who does what, and who orgasms. Important dimensions of intimate emotional contact are our involvement in the moment, our communication with each other, and how much we care for each other.

8

Homosexual and Bisexual Orientations

As a black woman growing up in the South in the fifties and sixties, I spent most of my life trying to deal with the racist attitudes in this country. I learned very early that a black woman was supposed to be a passionate and ever-ready bedmate and a tireless drudge. Needless to say, neither option appealed to me a great deal. . . . When I went to college . . . I began to become aware of an attraction to women, which I kept trying to suppress. Women struck me as being warmer and more open than men. I was fascinated by the idea of loving a woman but was totally turned off by what I thought lesbians were supposed to be like. . . . Though I never became active, the [women's] movement gave me support because I could see other women having the courage to change their lives. Their example gave me the courage to see that I was cheating myself by pretending I was straight, and that if I kept it up I would go on being miserable. I finally did come out sexually with a black woman I met at work. I was scared stiff at first and had to confront my own prejudices about what I thought lesbians were. For the first time, I began to feel the freedom to be whatever I needed to be at the time, and the freedom to be different. . . . My life has been much fuller since then, and a lot happier.

[From a Boston gay collective, quoted in Boston Women's Health Book Collective 1976, pp. 84–85]*

Philosophically I'm smack in the middle—. . . fifty-fifty. Though my experience is much more with men, I'm open to women just as much. If Larry and I ever split up, I think I could love and live with a woman. In fact, my therapist's remark a number of years ago had a very strong influence on me. He once said that when you want to give or get love, it makes no difference which sex you get it from.

[A bisexual woman, quoted in Klein 1978, p. 99]

I believe most people are born with a bisexual potential. No one is born gay or straight. Most of us become one or the other as we grow up, though a few remain bisexual. There is no one cause of being either gay or straight, and any attempts to find such a universal common denominator will fail. There is no reason to consider developing as a straight superior to developing as a gay. The difference is that all the factors that society can readily control are set up to crank out straights.

[A gay male, quoted in Spada 1979, pp. 281–82]†

Homosexuality has long been a puzzle to social scientists. In a society that provides only heterosexual scripts for sexual expression, while branding others as deviant, how do some people develop homosexual or bisexual orientations?

As we'll see in this chapter, we're not even sure how to label those who do. We can talk about typical patterns of developing and expressing homosexual or bisexual orientations—but we know that individual careers vary tremendously. We can talk about the joys of sex with one's own gender—but must note that homosexual sharing may have its problems, just as heterosexual sharing does. And we can list groups and places within which homosexuality is receiving increasing support as an acceptable and satisfying sexual orientation—but we can also cite contemporary examples of the risks of being gay in a predominantly straight society.

Our understanding of homosexual and bisexual orientations is limited not only by their complexity but also by several research problems. Many people have inappropriately studied homosexuality by using heterosexual models. Although much has been written about homosexuality most of this writing has dealt with males. The past tendency has been to view homosexuality as a male phenomenon. Research on female patterns is mostly new and still emerging. So is research on bisexuality. The option of having sex with both genders received less attention in the past from social scientists than from the popular media, who discovered in the mid-1970s that bisexuality is considered "chic" in some circles. But a few social scientists have started looking into bisexuality as a useful way to study what they see as the flexibility of our sexual identities. Results of such surveys paint an incomplete picture. But they still provide insights into living and loving lesbians, bisexuals, and gay men.

LABELS

It's difficult to get a handle on whom we're talking about when we say "homosexual" or "bisexual." Individuals differ in the degree to which they find people of their own gender erotic, have sex with them, are seen as homosexual by others, see themselves as homosexual, and share this perception with others. Even those who are admittedly homosexual vary in what they want to be called. And some researchers feel that we prejudice understanding by using global labels for people.

Variations in What's Labeled

Some researchers have defined homosexuality and bisexuality as *preferences* for partners of the same or both sexes—that is, preferences based on the gender of people who appear most in our fantasies, whose bodies catch our eye on the street. Since these preferences may or may not be acted out, other researchers have focused only on sexual *activities* with the same or both sexes. Kinsey suggested a compromise: Categorize people by using two separate scales—one for the degree of *preference* for partners of one's own gender and one for the degree of sexual *activity* with those of one's own gender (Kinsey, Pomeroy, and Martin 1948; Kinsey et al. 1953). As we saw in Chapter 1, zero on Kinsey's scale referred to exclusively heterosexual preferences or activities, six to exclusively homosexual preferences or activities, and one to five to varying degrees of bisexuality (attraction to or sexual activities with both sexes). Since these preferences and behaviors may vary over our life span, it would be even more accurate to use the Kinsey scale to measure four categories: (1) past preferences, (2) present preferences, (3) past behaviors, and (4) present behaviors.

Another factor to be considered is *how others label us*. In Chapter 1 we noted that others tend to confuse our overt "masculinity" or "femininity" with whom we choose as sex partners. Effeminate men and assertive women are often assumed to be gay. By the same token many people believe that only effeminate men are gay—which is far from true.

Sometimes gender orientations are confused with politics, especially the notion that females who support the women's liberation movement also choose women as sex partners. And sometimes gender orientations are confused with occupational choices: the assumption that male dancers and female mechanics are gay. These stereotyped assumptions are true for some individuals. For instance, an estimated 80 percent of male models

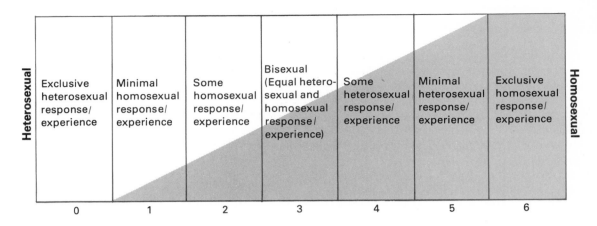

Exclusive heterosexual response/ experience	Minimal homosexual response/ experience	Some homosexual response/ experience	Bisexual (Equal hetero-sexual and homosexual response/ experience)	Some heterosexual response/ experience	Minimal heterosexual response/ experience	Exclusive homosexual response/ experience
0	1	2	3	4	5	6

Note: Based on Kinsey et al. 1948.

Figure 8-1. Kinsey's Continuum of Heterosexual-ity-Homosexuality.

and dancers are homosexual (Whitam and Dizon 1979). But actually, females and males who choose their own gender as sex partners are spread across all occupations, gender role types, and political orientations.

It's also important to note *how we see ourselves.* Many who engage in homosexual activities don't define themselves as "homosexual." For instance, women who attend "swinging" parties with their husbands often engage in enthusiastic sex with other females, but they don't see themselves as lesbians. Some men who visit public restrooms for homosexual "blow jobs" avoid viewing themselves as homosexual. Instead, they rationalize their desires as simple "genital urges" (Humphreys 1970). Such people may not even see themselves as bisexual, for this category is still largely unknown. Usually people see themselves as having either homosexual or heterosexual orientations.

There is no automatic link between a certain behavior and how those who engage in it interpret it. Social stigmatizing of a behavior gives us both a reason and a way to avoid accepting the negative connotations of its label. Taught that homosexuals are bad and strange looking, people who consider themselves okay believe that they're not homosexuals. As one man put it, "I had been told by my mother that all fairies—as she called them—were very light and small. I was big and muscular so I knew I wasn't one" (Warren 1974, p. 55). Taught that homosexuality is a sick choice, some people fail to link the good experiences they've had with the negative connotations of the label. As one male said, "As far as I knew homosexuality was a horrible thing, and I knew sex with Gerald was fantas-

tic, so I knew I couldn't be homosexual" (Warren 1974, p. 55).

It is also important to consider the *degree* to which people have "come out" publicly as gay or bisexual. Miller's study of gay fathers, for instance, makes distinctions between *trade* (men who furtively engage in homosexual acts but see themselves as heterosexual), *homosexuals* (men who engage in homosexual acts and see themselves as homosexuals but try to present a heterosexual public image), *gay* men (those who reveal their homosexual preferences to a limited public audience—perhaps others in the gay community), and *publicly gay* men (those who acknowledge to the wider community that they have sex with other men) (Miller 1979).

Label Preferences

Even those who publicly acknowledge their same-sex activities differ in the label they prefer for themselves. For instance, some people who find both genders erotic dislike the rigid fifty-fifty connotation of the "bisexual" label. They prefer the term *ambisexual,* because they feel it suggests a preference for one gender but an ability to relate sexually to both.

Among women the terms *homosexual* and *female homosexual* are used as self-labels mostly by those who adopted gay behaviors before gay liberation movements surfaced in the late 1960s. These women tend to see the label "gay" as ironic, for maintaining sexual relationships with women often meant isolation and fear rather than gaiety.

The Language of Sex

Is homosexual expression a "choice," a "preference," or an "orientation"? When it comes to gay, bisexual, and lesbian behavior, we do not always knowingly choose it. Many simply are homosexual—their behavior is an orientation. What we can choose is how we will express our sexual feelings, and whether we will be open or closed about our sexual orientation to others or whether we will wish to change it. We may prefer one sex over another when it comes to sexual arousal and emotional feelings, but such a preference is really our sexual *orientation* at any given point in time. Our sexual orientation can change as our sexual identity changes—from fantasies and from actual sexual experiences. The term "sexual orientation" is better than "sexual preference" because it does not give the double meaning of both *being* and *choice* that "preference" implies.

In feminist circles both *homosexual* and *gay* are disliked because they're considered male terms. *Lesbian* is preferred, either for its association with Sappho's beautiful poetry about love among women on the island of Lesbos or for its political connotation of a totally women-oriented lifestyle and solidarity with the women's movement. Some women who see this solidarity as more than sexual ask to be called "women-oriented women," or "women-identified women" (Wolf 1979).

Doing versus Being

A further complication in applying labels to people is the notion that it is more accurate to use them as adjectives than as nouns representing people's identity. For instance, "He is now involved in a homosexual relationship" may be preferable to "He is a homosexual." The former leaves open the possibility that gender orientations are choices that sometimes change over time. The latter treats gender orientations as permanent conditions. Sociologist Edward Sagarin (1977a) has suggested that this distinction is important. He feels that if we say we *are* homosexual or bisexual or heterosexual, we close the door on our potential for intimacy. Without what Sagarin calls the "tyranny of the label," we may feel freer to explore our emotional and

sexual attraction to *individuals* and to develop other nonsexual aspects of ourselves.

ATTITUDES TOWARD HOMOSEXUALITY

Our freedom to choose whom we prefer as sex partners is severely circumscribed by public attitudes. Although these have changed somewhat over the past decade, a majority of Americans still disapprove of homosexuality, sometimes violently. In this section we'll explore the extent of this disapproval and examine ideas about what causes it. Then we'll look at some signs that attitudes may be changing, including evidence that some homosexuals have managed to transcend negative public opinion and to turn their deviant status into a source of strength and growth.

Public Disapproval

The strong negative reaction that many heterosexuals have to open displays of gay and lesbian affection is constantly present. There have been only slight changes in public attitudes about homosexuality according to Gallup polls taken in 1977 and 1982: While 43 percent of Americans felt that homosexual relations between consenting adults should be legal in 1977, 45 percent felt the same way in 1982. There has been no change in whether a homosexual can be a good Christian or Jew: 53 percent believe they can, while 32 percent disagree. In 1982 for the first time the poll questioned if homosexuality should be considered a socially acceptable lifestyle and found that 51 percent are against this idea, while 34 percent favor it ("Public Perceptions of Gays . . . " 1982).

Negative attitudes persist even among professionals. Under pressure from the gay rights activists, a small majority of members of the American Psychiatric Association voted in 1973 to change their categorization of homosexuality from "sociopathic personality disorder" to "sexual orientation disturbance" in those who were dissatisfied with their sexual choice (Leo 1979). But according to a 1977 survey of 2500 psychiatrists, 69 percent still view homosexuality as usually a "pathological adaptation" rather than a "normal variation" (Lief 1977). Perhaps this is because homosexuals who come to them for counseling tend to be those who are disturbed about their sexual orientations.

Homophobia

Compulsive intolerance of homosexuals is sometimes known as "homophobia." Some people do have strongly negative reactions to homosexuality. Studies have shown that these attitudes are strongest in those who are authoritarian, dogmatic, sexually and intellectually rigid, intolerant of ambiguity, status conscious, guilty about their own sexuality, and generally intolerant of others. Some researchers have suggested that these people's attitudes toward homosexuals reflects anxiety about their own homosexual impulses. Other researchers see these people as anxious about sexual impulses in general. And some attribute negativity toward gays to learned notions that what homosexuals do together is "unnatural" because it's nonprocreative (although heterosexual oral-genital sex and contraception, also nonprocreative, are now generally considered okay).

Another intriguing theory is that people are intolerant of those who don't seem to fit their learned gender role expectations. Social psychologist A. P. MacDonald has found that people tend to be offended by confusion of traditional gender roles. What they disapprove of is not so much what gays do in bed but effeminacy in men and dominance in women. MacDonald thinks this is because people cling to their learned double standard: They want males to be more dominant, females to be more submissive. He's found that people who are most approving of homosexuality tend also to support equality between the sexes (MacDonald 1976).

Disapproval of homosexuals is sometimes expressed as aversion to them. Aversion to gays seems especially strong in males. Some males are even physically violent toward gays, especially when gays make sexual passes. One blue-collar worker describes a typical reaction:

We had this fairy in our outfit when I was in the Navy. One night at a bar in San Diego we got drunk together and the sonofabitch reached over and put his hand on my cock. I knocked that bastard off his bar stool and halfway across the room. The sonofabitch never bothered me again. [LeMasters 1975, pp. 107-8]

Much opposition to homosexuality may not be homophobia, a neurotically compulsive reaction. Some opposition comes from those who cherish

Some heterosexuals' negative attitudes toward homosexuality may be partially linked to unfamiliarity with scenes of same-gender affection.

traditional family life centered in heterosexual marriage; these people may define homosexuality as counterproductive and wrong because it conflicts with their own value system. For example, heterosexual college students who are particularly negative toward homosexuals include business majors, frequent church attenders, those responsive to negative peer attitudes, religious fundamentalists, and authoritarians (Larsen, Reed, and Hoffman 1980). Among those who cherish traditional heterosexual norms, most vocal in their opposition to homosexuality is the religious New Right, with groups such as the Moral Majority and Christian Voice promoting legislation that would cut off federal funds to homosexual educational and service projects.

Will antihomosexual attitudes change? Stephen Morin and Ellen Garfinkle (1978, p. 42) think that "for the vast majority of people beliefs about homosexuals are simply an unchallenged part of their socialization experiences." They have found that a single course on homosexuality dramatically altered psychology students' attitudes. Even exposure to an article on homosexuality can significantly sway people toward a more positive or a more negative view, depending on the article's tone.

In training male therapists to work with gay clients, Morin and Garfinkle have forced them to confront their own homophobia by going to gay bars. The trainees were initially embarrassed by seeing men dance together. But as the evening wore on, they became used to the idea and even danced themselves. Some typical reactions: "I was amazed at how many of the men appeared more masculine than myself," and "During the night, I moved from feeling like a voyeur to feeling like a participant" (Morin and Garfinkle 1978, p. 43). Many embraced on leaving, and most said that this single excursion into a gay setting broke down more of their prejudices than did all their readings and discussions.

Beyond Deviance

The desire to be freed from the fears and stigma of the past has prompted some homosexuals to join together in the hope of reeducating the public. Their actions have promoted greater acceptance of homosexual orientations. At the same time they've helped many gays develop a more positive self-image.

At midcentury homosexuals in the United States were largely isolated from each other, closeted, and afraid of being discovered and punished by a disapproving culture. A significant step taken to counteract their negative image was the founding in 1950 of the Mattachine Society for male homosexuals in Los Angeles. It defined homosexuals not as deviant individuals but as a discriminated-against minority group. Awareness that they might be able to make some changes if they organized spread to lesbians, and in 1955 Del Martin and Phyllis Lyon founded the Daughters of Bilitis. During this early phase the focus of homophile organizations was to encourage social acceptance of same-sex orientations. More recently, the emphasis has changed to more basic reforms: restructuring homosexuals' image of themselves and promoting education, legal change, and research favorable to gays.

The gay rights movement has made some gains. For instance, many national corporations have announced that they won't discriminate against gays in hiring. Some municipalities have voted to forbid discrimination against gays in housing and jobs, although others have voted down such proposals. Both television shows and movies are now openly and sympathetically airing gay themes. Ann Landers advises parents that they shouldn't be ashamed of their gay children. Gay

baths and bars now operate openly across the country.

Even organized religions have offered sporadic support for gay acceptance. For instance, in 1979 a religious group in Seattle asked that discussion of homosexuality be integrated into public school curricula. And the expulsion of two professed gay students from a Methodist theological seminary in Illinois prompted forty-eight professors from Northwestern University to withdraw from a doctoral program run jointly with the seminary. At a nearby Catholic school fifty-three faculty members issued this statement: "We are dismayed that a Christian academic institution seems to be de-

Dislike of Effeminacy

To many people—both gay and straight—"effeminate" behaviors in men are the most distasteful part of the gay stereotype. Perry Deane Young, biographer for gay football player David Kopay, muses about their uneasiness with effeminacy:

Both of us once cringed at the popular image of homosexuals as silly creatures. To us, the image—and the real people who backed up the stereotype—seemed to represent overt self-hatred. An effeminate man was mocking the best of what was male and taking on the manners of the worst of what was female. It was a long and difficult process for both of us to accept that we are part of a minority that includes "nelly fags."

For me, the process included the realization that as a child I had been (naturally?) effeminate. In later years I deliberately changed my behavior to become more "masculine," more acceptable to the larger society. I also had to examine the source of my discomfort over effeminacy in men. It was grounded in the myths that masculinity meant strength and seriousness, while femininity meant weakness and frivolity. Women, especially, have done a great deal to dispel these myths in the last ten years; and homosexuals are now in the process of doing the same thing. [Kopay and Young 1977, p. x]*

* From *The David Kopay Story* by David Kopay and Perry Deane Young. Copyright © 1977 by David Kopay and Perry Deane Young. Used by permission of Arbor House Publishing Co.

nying individual Christians the right and opportunity to theological educations and the free and open struggle to define their own sexuality" ("Some Happenings . . . " 1978, p. 4). Gay Catholics in Boston charge that their diocese neglects them—they want to be accepted as gays in the church. The official Catholic position is that being homosexual is not a sin so long as one commits no homosexual acts. In response to the traditional Catholic position, a national organization called Dignity has attempted to support gay Catholics (Sipress 1982).

It is almost unheard of for gay or lesbian public school teachers to be open about their preferences, but there is a Gay Academic Union nationally, with 700 members. Its purpose is to provide support and conferences for gay professors (Biemiller 1982). But even in academia it is sometimes difficult for a gay or lesbian professor to be hired or promoted after "coming out" (Huber et al. 1982).

BISEXUAL ORIENTATIONS

There are now bisexual organizations, clubs, and newsletters, and considerable media publicity has been given to the growing sentiments that it is best to be "bi" and that bisexuals are the only fully sexual people. As a new wave bisexuality is promising to create a trichotomy of sexual orientations (heterosexuality, homosexuality, and bisexuality). Yet what really constitutes a bisexual orientation may be ambiguous, both for individuals and for social scientists.

There is no clear way to define what it means to be bisexual, let alone for others to understand what this identity connotes. Bisexuals may prefer one gender over the other, or they may have no preference. Bisexuals may have several partners of both sexes, or they may be sexually exclusive (monogamous) with one sex but have more than one partner of the other sex. MacDonald (1982) further categorizes bisexuals as: those who are *transitory* and eventually return to exclusivity with a preferred gender; those who are *transitional* and change from one preference to another (usually from heterosexuality to homosexuality); those who engage in *homosexual denial* and contend they are turned on by both sexes to avoid the stigma of

homosexuality; and those who are *enduring bisexuals* and maintain permanent interest in both sexes. Blumstein and Schwartz (1975) also identify the "ideological bisexual," someone whose sexual orientation is bisexual but who has not experienced sexual activities with both genders. Support for such a separate definitional category is provided by the 1983 *Playboy* readers' survey. Nineteen percent of the male and 18 percent of the female bisexually oriented respondents stated they had been sexually active only with the other gender; these "ideological bisexuals" so far had no active homosexual experiences as adults (Cook et al. 1983). Although the definitional complexities seem imposing, the diversity of potential bisexual lifestyles suggests that mixing data about bisexually oriented people with homosexually oriented people in research reports is inappropriate and likely to muddy the waters.

Data on bisexual orientation are quite limited, but judging from the latest *Playboy* national sex survey, which included responses from 2786 bisexual men and 948 bisexual women, the sexual lifestyles are strikingly different for each gender (Cook et al. 1983). Basically, women of bisexual orientation tend to thrive, while bisexual men tend to suffer. Of the bisexual sample 70 percent of the women say they are happy with their lives; 40 percent are married. These bisexual women, whose average age is twenty-six, report that sex is frequent and of high quality. For example, 69 percent report having intercourse two or three times a week, although 40 percent experience their most intense orgasmic pleasure from oral sex. Eighty-nine percent also masturbate, a higher percentage than found among either heterosexual or lesbian women. Compared with heterosexual or lesbian women, nearly twice as many bisexual women use sexual devices in their erotic play. On almost every indicator the survey found that bisexual women were the most sexually active women.

This pattern is not reported by the men identifying as bisexual; nearly half are dissatisfied with their sex lives. They report a pattern of mostly heterosexual sexual contacts; their average age is thirty-one. Many are disappointed that they don't receive enough oral sex. Compared with heterosexual and homosexual men, they are most likely to visit prostitutes. They note serious difficulties in making adequate contacts with the gay community, for committed organized gays tend to distrust their fence-sitting (Cook et al. 1983).

Changing to bisexuality from a previously heterosexual or homosexual orientation can bring criticism from both "sides," for both genders. As Schwartz (1977b, p. 171) states: "Most lesbian women perceive bisexual women as being unable to come to grips with their true sexuality. . . . " Lesbians may be threatened by bisexuality for political reasons as well. They often want a unified front as lesbian feminists. If men are viewed as the enemy, bisexual women may not be trusted because they still sleep and share with men. Men receive even harsher criticisms for their bisexual activities. Women's same-sex lovemaking is even a part of many men's sexual fantasies; the classic ménage à trois is two women and one man, an arrangement often instigated by the man. The reverse seldom holds, for women are less likely to be turned on by male homosexuality. The general case is that becoming bisexual does not require a woman to deny her heterosexuality, whereas for previously heterosexual men to become bisexual appears to be seen as considerable denial of their heterosexuality (Cook et al. 1983). Woody Allen's contention that being bisexual doubles your chances for a date on Saturday night may not be altogether accurate.

Feminist Pressures

Today the effort to end stereotyping and oppression continues but not without some internal squabbling within the gay rights and women's movements. Long-time lesbians are suspicious of feminists who've recently begun making love to women and who call themselves lesbians. The "true" lesbians feel that these self-avowed soul mates have suffered no real oppression; they fear that the "newcomers" may go back to their men after their social experiment becomes stale.

On the other hand, some feminist literature argues that all women can *choose* to be lesbian and that the only real feminist is a lesbian because she is not as dependent on men. For example, Faderman (1981, p. 387) states: "Lesbians now see their lesbianism as a choice they make because they want to be free from prescribed roles, free to realize themselves." To view the term "lesbian" as a political choice rather than a sexual choice—as "a philosophical statement, a self-definition, a world

view" (Axelson 1981, p. 6A) may be somewhat semantically confusing, for it means redefining a sexual term ("lesbian") as a political and philosophical phenomenon.

Has feminism increased lesbian relationships and identities? No one really knows from broad-based research, but it seems that the women's liberation movement has made it more acceptable to "come out" as a lesbian or bisexual, and this acceptance may pave the way for more women to relate sexually with each other. However, being lesbian or bisexual may be as temporary as being heterosexual or celibate—that is, it may be a process that changes with time in response to personal experiences and changing social influences.

Contrasting opinions from different feminist groups about the appropriateness or necessity of lesbian relationships may be confusing to women who are unsure of their sexual identities. Carmen Kerr is concerned about the expectation that women *should* be gay because the women's movement and the sexual revolution seem to *demand* it. Kerr considers this pressure to be as oppressive as pressures from males to have sex with them:

Proving our sexual freedom by having sex with another woman because we feel we ought to, rather than because we feel turned on and want to, causes hurt feelings and can ruin good friendships. What's more, this is the same sort of adapting we have previously done with our men lovers—and it didn't feel good then, did it? We are not liberated when we respond to "should's," no matter how radical they appear to be. [Kerr 1977, p. 106]

However, the social scripting of feminism includes loving and appreciating one's sisters, and for some this includes loving women sexually. Andrea Hayes's (1979) empirical study of college women indicated that of three kinds of women (traditional, modern, and radical) the radical feminists were most likely to *call* themselves lesbian or bisexual. However, most who called themselves lesbian or bisexual had never actually *had* a sexual experience with a woman. One radical feminist said:

I consider myself bisexual but sort of a lesbian. When I call myself a lesbian it would be when I'm in a relationship with a woman. Now I'm a little confused but politically I'm a lesbian. In the future I see myself *with a woman although I've never had a relationship with a woman.* [Quoted by Hayes 1979, p. 16]*

Hayes concluded that lesbianism for some is not a sexual orientation but a political statement. She found that some of her sample fought the label "feminist" because they felt it implied being lesbian.

INCIDENCE

Although homosexuality has increased in visibility and acceptance, the numbers of homosexuals may not have increased since Kinsey's time. It's hard to know for sure, though, because of a number of methodological problems in Kinsey's gay headcounts.

Kinsey concluded that 37 percent of American males had some overt homosexual experience to the point of orgasm from the teen years on. By their middle forties 13 percent of females in the Kinsey study had experienced orgasm in homosexual contacts (Kinsey et al. 1953). But many social scientists now feel that these figures were misleading overestimates of how many people were gay, for at least three reasons: (1) Kinsey was counting everyone from one to six on his scale—thereby lumping bisexuals with homosexuals and calling them all homosexuals; (2) he sought out homosexuals in gay bars rather than having an entirely random sample; and (3) he included in his tally everyone who'd ever had sexual contact with the same gender, rather than limiting his count to those for whom homosexuality was a clear and continuous pattern.

To establish a more usable base line for comparison with today's estimates, it might be better to look at different sets of figures in Kinsey's books: his estimates that 8 percent of all males were exclusively homosexual in their responses or activities for at least three years between the ages of sixteen and fifty-five, and that between the ages of twenty and thirty-five 1 to 3 percent of single females and 0.3 percent of married females were exclusively homosexual in their responses or overt activities (Kinsey, Pomeroy, and Martin 1948; Kinsey et al. 1953).

* From Andrea Hayes, senior honors thesis at the University of Massachusetts, 1979. Reprinted by permission.

Comparison of these figures with contemporary estimates indicates that the incidence of homosexuality is still about the same. For instance, the *Redbook* survey of 100,000 married women indicated that 3 percent had experienced homosexual sex during adulthood: 1.7 percent only one time, 0.8 percent occasionally, and 0.4 percent often (Tavris and Sadd 1977). In a 1970 survey reported in *Psychology Today,* 4 percent of the males and 1 percent of the females identified themselves as exclusively homosexual, with an additional 4 percent of the males and 1 percent of the females saying they'd had frequent sexual experiences with their own gender. Another 20 percent of the women in this liberal sample said they'd "thought about" engaging in lesbian sex (Athanasiou, Shaver, and Tavris 1970).

The Institute for Sex Research defined as homosexual anyone who's had sex more than six times with partners of the same gender, and on that basis estimated that 13 percent of all males and 5 percent of all females in the United States fit this definition, although only 1 percent of these people identify themselves publicly as gay ("How Gay Is Gay? . . . " 1979). The institute's definition apparently includes bisexuals, as counts of "homosexuals" often do. Wardell Pomeroy (1975) estimates that people who fall between two and four on the Kinsey continuum—from mostly heterosexual with more than incidental homosexual experience, to the reverse—account for 10 percent of all men and 5 percent of all women in the United States.

Given the problems of conceptualizing and measuring bisexuality, no one has an accurate, current estimate of the incidence of bisexuality. Bell, Weinberg, and Hammersmith's (1981) interviews with nearly 1500 people in the San Francisco Bay Area revealed that 8 percent of the white homosexual men and 13 percent of the white homosexual women could be categorized as bisexual (a score of two to four on the Kinsey scale). Kinsey and his coauthors concluded that 4 percent of the males sampled were exclusively homosexual, while 46 percent of them engaged in sex with both sexes at some point in their lives (1948, p. 656). But it seems conceptually vague and empirically meaningless to group all men or all women who have had one sexual experience with the same sex, and to call these people "bisexuals." In the

Playboy survey most people who identify themselves as bisexuals fall into the Kinsey scale ratings from 1 to 3. They have predominantly straight experiences, even at present. Only a few fall into the higher categories (more homosexual experience than heterosexual experience) (Cook et al. 1983).

ORIGINS OF HOMOSEXUALITY

It's not at all clear how homosexual, or bisexual, orientation emerges, any more than it's clear how heterosexual orientations emerge. Efforts to find a single reason why some people develop homosexual orientations and some don't have been inconclusive. Perhaps this is because same-gender interest appears at different times, under different circumstances, and with different patterns for different people. Such interest may appear so early in childhood that it seems to be inborn, or it may first take shape in adulthood. Sometimes homosexual orientations lie dormant for years before being acted on. Sometimes same-gender sex develops as an extension of affection between people who were not initially attracted to each other by erotic desires. Sometimes it flows from consciousness-raising messages that it's okay to be close to people like ourselves. Sometimes formerly exclusive homosexuals grow in love with someone of the other sex and change their idea of their sexual "place." Sometimes people have had an unhappy heterosexual relationship and have been so hurt by it that they fear another. And sometimes people

switch back and forth between sex with women and sex with men. It would be hard to find any single theory that would account for all these patterns.

Social Factors

One body of ideas about the causes of homosexuality involves samples of homosexuals seeking psychiatric help. These theories generally assume that homosexuality is sick behavior stemming from something that has gone "wrong" in a child's early upbringing. Abnormal relationships with parents are often blamed. For instance, Irving Bieber found that of the 106 male homosexuals he studied, 73 percent had mothers who behaved seductively with them and were so overprotective that they thwarted development of traditional "masculine" behaviors. None of the 106 had a "normal" relationship with his father. Instead, fathers tended to be weak, detached, or hostile (Bieber 1962). Although this pattern may have contributed to these unhappy patients' sexual orientations, it does not necessarily describe the experiences of homosexuals who have led basically healthy emotional lives.

Some social scientists have tried to explain homosexuality as a reaction to negative personal experiences: learned fear of the other sex, bad experiences at the hands of the other sex, or disturbing childhood events such as exposure to pornography. Research based on these negative experiences has not accounted for the "Why," even though such events may contribute to some people's homosexual preferences.

Instead of trying to explain homosexuality as heterosexuality damaged by negative experiences, some researchers assert that we are not naturally heterosexual. They think we are born "omnisexual" and will respond to almost anything that feels good—our hand, a teddy bear, a cousin, a playmate, toys in the bathtub, our blanket. But we learn to channel narrowly our sexual energies as

Some contemporary efforts to find a "cause" for homosexuality tend to be based on a negative assumption: that something has gone wrong. By contrast, homosexual love was praised as being life enriching by classical artists and poets. The Greek poet Sappho, depicted here with a friend in an 1825 drawing, wrote nine books of lyric poems expressing her adoration of other women.

responses to those toward whom our culture and our own experiences steer us.

In some cultures males are encouraged to undertake homosexual activities. For example, the Siwans of Africa expect all males, including the heterosexually married, to engage in anal homosexual intercourse. Those who *don't* are regarded as peculiar. A few societies consider it normal for females to lie on top of each other, caress each other's clitoris, or excite each other's vagina with bananas, sweet potatoes, maniocs, or wooden phalluses (Ford and Beach 1951). But in the United States we learn from fragmentary clues that physical contact with those of our own gender is "queer" and to be avoided.

How then do some of us develop homosexual or bisexual orientations? Perhaps the same way that many of us learned to masturbate as children. Even though we were strongly discouraged from stimulating our genitals, some who did discovered that it felt compellingly good and continued to do so, for they considered the rewards of this behavior greater than the costs of being discovered. Those who have the opportunity to engage in sex play with someone of the same gender may discover that it feels good and want to do it again, despite learned fears of discovery.

This pattern doesn't necessarily lead to homosexuality, however. Early sex play may or may not be interpreted as sexual and may or may not be incorporated into later sex-partner orientation. As we learn to construe our physical responses as sexual, we gradually learn to turn ourselves on sexually in situations we expect to enjoy and to turn ourselves off in situations we think we won't enjoy. If experiences with the same gender continue to be positive, they may become learned sexual turn-ons for us. However, the cultural message that homosexual responses are deviant may block further sexual exploration with our own gender. Choice of same-sex partners during childhood may have been a mere expedient anyway. Often friends are simply the only people available for secret activities.

One potential problem with this theory: For many people homosexual desires and fantasies come *before* actual sexual involvement with anybody. For instance, some boys begin to find male genitals erotic before they ever touch a friend sexually. It's possible that some kind of learning may

be involved. For example, some boys learn to associate male anatomy with sexual excitement by looking at themselves as they masturbate. But if all boys who masturbate became homosexuals, heterosexuals would be a tiny minority.

Biological Factors

Homosexual leanings sometimes develop so early that some researchers believe that an innate predisposition must be involved. They've looked to biological explanations but so far haven't found much. Some suspect unusual balances of hormones or other chemicals as causes of homosexuality. But comparisons of hormone levels in homosexuals with those in heterosexuals have been methodologically shoddy and have been further hampered by the normal tendency of hormone levels to fluctuate and by little-understood interaction among a variety of body chemicals. Findings have therefore been contradictory and inconclusive. Lynda I. A. Birke (1982) and Sigusch and colleagues (1982) conclude that there is insufficient evidence to argue that homosexuality has hormonal bases. They also believe that those trying to prove a hormonal basis for homosexual orientation are interested in controlling homosexuality.

Other studies suggest that male homosexuals have less androgen than do male heterosexuals; most studies indicate, however, that there are no differences or that there is no clear cause-and-effect relationship between androgen and gender preference (Meyer-Bahlberg 1977). For instance, Green Berets about to leave for combat missions in Viet Nam were found to have lowered androgen levels, too, so this condition might be linked more to stress than to gender orientations (Bermant and Davidson 1974). One researcher testing the assumption that androgen makes a "real man" tried giving homosexuals extra androgen. All it did was to increase their sexual desire—for men (Sage 1972).

No hormones or genetic variables were measured by Bell, Weinberg, and Hammersmith (1981) in their large interview study attempting to trace the etiology of homosexuality, but they still concluded that there must be a biological basis to homosexual development. Their study, published as *Sexual Preferences,* has been widely cited by the media and by sexologists to argue that biological variables are probably more critical to sexual orientation than are socialization variables. Bell and his coauthors found little parental impact on children's sexual preference. They instead argued that gender nonconformity is more closely predictive of homosexual orientation, and that such nonconformity was particularly predictive of male homosexual development. This "explanation" was tautological, for by definition a gay or lesbian person exhibits gender nonconformity. Another flaw of the study was that Bell and his colleagues did not measure any biological variables that might be involved.

These limited research findings make clear that (1) the importance of genetic variables still needs to be determined, and (2) socialization variables need to be more adequately measured and conceptualized. When more research has been completed, it is likely that scientists will find a complex interplay between genetic and socialization variables.

IDENTITIES OVER THE LIFE SPAN

In the face of inconclusive research into the origins of homosexuality, as well as the criticism that much research is based on a heterosexual view of homosexuality as something-gone-wrong, many social scientists have changed the focus of study. Instead of trying to figure out where homosexuality comes from, they watch how it emerges, develops, and sometimes changes over the life span.

It is common to view sexual orientation as a static state—but some of us change our feelings and behaviors as we fantasize and experience a broader range of sexual possibilities. Many of us may at times be attracted to our own sex. Some of us will find ways to express feelings we have repressed because of social pressures to be heterosexual. Yet others of us will never seriously consider experimenting with the same sex because we have no conscious desires to do so, because we believe it is wrong for us, or because we believe the potential risks are too high.

The Emergence of a Gay Identity

People typically go through three steps on their way to becoming gay. First, they begin to sense that they are different from others and then they suspect that this difference involves feelings of attraction to their own gender. Second, they act on this suspicion by exploring homosexual contacts. Third, they admit to themselves—and perhaps to others—that they are gay. Homosexuals do not necessarily experience these steps in this order—or even experience all three. But actual sex is usually preceded by some foggy awareness of same-sex orientations.

Early Awareness. A study of 42 lesbians indicates that most were emotionally attracted to girl-friends or female teachers during childhood or adolescence. Girlhood crushes are common among heterosexual girls too, but lesbians-to-be tended to consider themselves somehow different. Some typical comments: "Since the age of six I felt like I didn't fit" and "I remember in the fourth or fifth grade feeling like I'd have to conform till I was out of high school—then I could be myself." In females anywhere from nine years of age to twenty-nine, this vague sense of being different began to crystallize into a sense that they were feeling more than they "should" for other females (Toomey and Beran 1979).*

Many lesbians in another study recalled a long-term process before recognition dawned: (1) attraction to a childhood playmate; (2) a heavy crush on an older female, often a teacher; (3) teenage dreams of romantic scenes—but with the "wrong" sex as a partner; (4) feelings of boredom, reluctance, not-quite-rightness in dating boys; and (5) discovery of some mention of homosexuality—usually strongly negative—and the recognition that this may be what one "is" (Wolf 1979).

While homosexuality in females usually begins with affectionate impulses that may only later be recognized as sexual, in boys it may start as nonsexual behaviors expected of the other gender. A study of 206 male homosexuals shows that "prehomosexual" males are much more likely than "preheterosexual" males to (1) play with toys considered more appropriate for girls, (2) dress up in

* From Beverly Toomey and Nancy Beran, "The Lesbian Looking-Blass: Rejection or Reinforcement," paper presented at the annual meeting of the Society for the Scientific Study of Social Problems, August 1979. Reprinted by permission.

Sex without a Script

With no guidelines for making love except those borrowed from heterosexual scripts, the heroine of Rita Mae Brown's *Rubyfruit Jungle* tries to figure out how to act on her attraction to a classmate:

Leota B. Bisland sat next to me that year in sixth grade. . . . Leota was the most beautiful girl I had ever seen. She was tall and slender with creamy skin and deep, green eyes. . . . I began to wonder if girls could marry girls, because I was sure I wanted to marry Leota and look in her green eyes forever. But I would only marry her if I didn't have to do the housework. . . .

That week I thought of how to ask Leota to marry me. I'd die in front of her and ask her in my last breath. If she said yes, I'd miraculously recover. I'd send her a note on colored paper with a white dove. I'd ride over to her house on Barry Aldridge's horse, sing her a song like in the movies, then she'd get on the back of the horse and we'd ride off into the sunset. None of them seemed right so I decided to come straight out and ask. . . .

"Leota, you thought about getting married?"

"Yeah, I'll get married and have six children and wear an apron like my mother, only my husband will be handsome."

"Who you gonna marry?"

"I don't know yet."

"Why don't you marry me? I'm not handsome, but I'm pretty."

"Girls can't get married." . . .

"Look, if we want to get married, we can get married. It don't matter what anybody says. Besides Leroy and I are running away to be famous actors. We'll have lots of money and clothes and we can do what we want. . . . Now ain't that a lot better than sitting around here with an apron on?"

"Yes."

"Good. Then let's kiss like in the movies and we'll be engaged."

We threw our arms around each other and kissed. My stomach felt funny.

"Does your stomach feel strange?"

"Kinda."

"Let's do it again."

We kissed again and my stomach felt worse. After that, Leota and I went off by ourselves each day after school. Somehow we knew enough not to go around kissing in front of everyone, so we went into the woods and kissed until it was time to go home.

There were times when I felt kissing Leota wasn't enough, but I wasn't sure what the next step would be. So until I knew, I settled for kissing. I knew about fucking and getting stuck together like dogs and I didn't want to get stuck like that. It was very confusing. Leota was full of ideas. Once she laid down on top of me to give me a kiss and I knew that was a step in the right direction. . . .

One week before school ended she asked me to spend the night with her. . . . We must have kissed for hours but I couldn't really tell because I didn't think about anything except kissing. . . . Then Leota decided we'd try lying on top of one another. We did that but it made my stomach feel terrible.

"Molly, let's take our pajamas off and do that." . . . It was much better without the pajamas. I could feel her cool skin all over my body. . . . Leota started kissing me with her mouth open. Now my stomach was going to fall out on the floor. . . .

We kept on. If we were going to die from stomach trouble we were resolved to die together. She began to touch me all over and I knew I was really going to die. Leota was bold. She wasn't afraid to touch anything and where her knowledge came from was a secret but she knew what she was after. And I soon found out. [Brown 1973, pp. 38–40]*

women's clothing, (3) join girls in their activities more often than boys, and (4) be regarded as "sissies." These behaviors occurred not only in those who remained effeminate as adults but also in many who became masculine in adult appearance and behavior (Whitam 1977). But not all homosexuals were effeminate even as children: Less than half checked any of the four behaviors.

A stronger indicator of male homosexuality is being more interested in sex play with boys than with girls: 78 percent of adult homosexuals in one study said they'd felt this way as children, whereas

82 percent of adult heterosexuals said they didn't feel that way (Whitam 1977a). Prehomosexual males first became aware that they were attracted to other males anywhere from early childhood to age thirty-five. For most this recognition occurred before age seventeen, often between the ages of ten and thirteen, when many heterosexual males are also discovering their gender preference (Whitam 1977a).

First Sexual Experiences. Since homosexual orientations deviate strongly from socially approved norms, no social script is provided for expressing them. People who do so operate without any script, feeling their way, trying out not only sexual activities but also the idea of themselves as homosexual.

For females there is often a gap of about a year and a half between recognition that one may be a lesbian and acting on that suspicion by having sex with a woman. The latter happens at an average age of twenty or twenty-one. Often, attempts at heterosexual sex are tried first. Many women "sleep around," in an attempt to prove their femininity, rather than accept a stigmatized status (Peplau et al. 1978; Toomey and Beran 1979). Women recognize that to accept a lesbian identity could mean being considered socially deviant, having to live a strange and perhaps lonely life, meeting discrimination rather than understanding, being denied a chance to bear or adopt children. Nevertheless, attempts to establish heterosexual relationships and sometimes marriage—defined for women as a major cultural goal—may prove unsatisfying.

During this "unlabeled" period, affectionate relationships with other women often become sexual relationships but may not be defined as such. Often they're rationalized as women's warm, socially acceptable way of relating: "That's just souls loving souls" (Wolf 1979). First "intercourse" with another woman is usually experienced as fun and satisfying. Disappointment, regret, and guilt feelings are rare at this point. The secrecy of sexual meetings allows exploration of pleasures without forcing a confrontation with the stigma of the lesbian label (Schäfer 1976, 1977).

For males homosexual activity usually begins earlier—often to the exclusion of any heterosexual

contact. A study of 89 male homosexuals indicated that 60 percent began mutual masturbation before the age of fourteen, 53 percent rubbed their bodies against each other during preadolescence or adolescence, and 68 percent engaged in fellatio as insertor and 73 percent as insertee by the age of nineteen (Saghir and Robins 1973). Nevertheless, many males who participate in these activities do not accept a homosexual identity. Some common patterns: maintaining what seems like a suitably "masculine" (dominant but emotionally uninvolved) role in these encounters, pretending that one is only responding to another's desires, seeing sex with males as only a temporary thing that one will outgrow, or feeling that one is expressing sexually what really is an experience of overwhelming love or special friendship (Tripp 1976).

Compared with females, males report far greater difficulties in accepting homosexual behaviors and developing a homosexual identity. Blumstein and Schwartz suggest the reason is that "masculinity" is made a major element in males' feeling of self-worth in our society. Because homosexuality is popularly defined as impaired masculinity, it threatens the self-esteem of those who practice it (Blumstein and Schwartz 1977).

Coming Out. Given the stigma attached to the homosexual label, why would anyone accept it as a personal identity? Some "closet queens" never do. Others drag their heels. Males lag an average of six years between their first awareness of being attracted to other males and finally "coming out"— that is, admitting to themselves and perhaps to others that they are gay. Over 20 percent wait from ten to fourteen years to do so (Dank 1971).

Despite understandable reluctance to assume a label socially defined as deviant, homosexuals have compelling reasons for coming out. Many find trying to pretend to themselves and others that they're heterosexual a source of anguish. The secrecy that their pretense requires isolates them from the only people who might validate their true identity: other homosexuals. Some political activists want to announce to the public their gender preference to help educate the public that homosexuals come in a variety of personalities. And some find the secret too intriguing to keep it to themselves. By coming out people can reconcile the difference between what they suspect they are, what they tell themselves they are, and perhaps what they tell society they are.

Before people will accept the gay label, they must know that this category exists and then perhaps redefine it for themselves. If they don't know that there's a category of sexual behavior known as "homosexual," then they can't fit their experiences into it. And if they have learned from society to define homosexuals as "dirty perverts," "effeminate queers," or "bull dykes," they can't see themselves fitting into any of these categories. But as increasing media exposure of homosexuality challenges these negative stereotypes and as one learns that ordinary-seeming friends are gay, it becomes easier to apply the label to oneself. As one lesbian remarked, "When I found out people I really liked a lot and were close to were gay, and that they didn't have horns, then it wasn't such a bad thing. They were functioning normally and weren't hurting anybody by it" (Tanner 1978, p. 58).

Even with a more positive self-definition of

Many gay women and men experience coming out with a great sense of relief at being able at last to get on with the business of living.

the gay label, many homosexuals carefully select their audience when they come out. Some reveal themselves only to their sex partner, some to other gays, some to selected straights, and some to society as a whole. Many try to pass as "just like everyone else" in the straight world, for public understanding and acceptance of homosexuality are limited. When in public, lesbians may refrain from embracing or even from holding hands to avoid raising suspicions. Even when there is a decision to come out to straights, admission of one's gender preferences may take the form of indirect clues rather than forthright announcements.

The typical reaction of homosexuals to coming out is a great sense of relief. The tension of not knowing and not being is replaced by a sense of being in touch with oneself and of freedom to cope with other aspects of life. As one lesbian put it, "I've settled the biggest part of my life—my identity. Now I can enjoy life more fully. Now I can deal with other things in a very positive way" (Toomey and Beran 1979, pp. 13–14). But for those who haven't learned to redefine homosexuality as okay, applying the label to themselves can be an extremely unsettling experience. One lesbian said, "I thought I'd throw up—I thought I was abnormal, weird. I was scared. It was a nightmare" (Toomey and Beran 1979, p. 12).*

Although many gays encourage coming out to help strengthen the gay community, build a positive self-image, and educate the public, some observers are not sure that identifying oneself as a homosexual is a good thing. Those who feel that we are potentially bisexual and capable of changing our choices and behaviors point out that accepting the homosexual label may close the door on relationships with the other sex. Our society tends to define "gay" as exclusively homosexual, but this definition does not accurately describe the feelings or experiences of many. For instance, one-fourth to two-fifths of the "lesbians" in one study said they'd had intercourse with men at least occasionally in the past twelve months. They also said that some of their sexual desires and desires for

* From Beverly Toomey and Nancy Beran, "The Lesbian Looking-Glass: Rejection or Reinforcement," paper presented at the annual meeting of the Society for the Scientific Study of Social Problems, August 1979. Reprinted by permission.

love and affection are directed toward men, although they are predominantly oriented toward women (Schäfer 1976).

In addition to confining identity, the gay label may isolate people from personal contact with straights and cost some their jobs and family ties. And in saying that they "are" homosexual, they prompt others to view them as primarily sexual creatures rather than as human beings who also work and play and shop for groceries and are concerned about their neighbors.

Adult Roles and Relationships

Often after people have accepted a gay identity, their lives are shaped by a more positive set of values than in the past. Before the gay rights movement, lesbians felt they had to adopt stereotyped "butch" (dominant, "masculine") or "fem" (submissive) roles, and males tended to go through a period of acting out the campy effeminate stereotype in a social environment that consisted mostly of gay bars. Studies today generally show little or no evidence of butch-fem role playing among lesbians. The emphasis is on equality and freedom of individual expression (Caldwell and Peplau 1979). And many gay men have discontinued effeminate behaviors, perhaps becauase they're frowned on by both straight society and a gay sexual marketplace that values masculinity and youth. Those who persist in effeminate mannerisms—whether straight or gay—mirror this social disapproval by being psychologically less well adjusted than those whose behavior fits masculine gender role expectations (Siegelman 1978).

In general, gay males are far more likely than lesbians to engage in brief sexual relations and to have more of them. In one study of 574 white homosexual males and 227 white homosexual females, 84 percent of the males but only 7 percent of the females had homosexual experiences with 50 to 1000 partners or more (Bell and Weinberg 1978). By contrast, according to another study, 97 percent of homosexual men have had seven or more relationships that lasted less than four months, compared to 33 percent of homosexual women (Saghir and Robins 1973). Growing fear of AIDS (Acquired Immunodeficiency Syndrome, a potentially fatal sexually transmittable disease) may have an impact on this pattern.

In general, gay men have had more lovers than gay women, but the spread and danger of AIDS is cause for alarm among gay men who have had numerous sexual partners.

This does not mean that male relationships are always impersonal or short-lived, though. A recent study of 1000 gay males of all ages and backgrounds—*The Spada Report*—indicates that 90 percent prefer sex with affection. Most consider the ideal human relationship as having a best friend with whom one can also share sex. Forty-one percent have a lover with whom they currently spend a lot of time and perhaps share living quarters. But 74 percent with steady lovers also have sex outside their primary relationship or know that their partner does. In most instances both partners know about and approve of these outside involvements. However, a quarter are unhappy about them (Spada 1979).

Some typical negotiated agreements about outside lovers: "Only at the baths when we go together," "Not in our bed," "It's okay so long as our relationship has priority," "No repeats with the same trick," "Just don't bring them home with you." The ability to work out such ground rules seems to be a feature of almost all stable, long-term male homosexual relationships (Suppe 1979).

The primary relationships themselves may be close and rather long-lasting. In one study of 128 gay males, the men had been with their current partners for a median of sixteen months. Of this sample 83 percent said they and their partners were in love, and most rated their current relationships as extremely satisfying and close (Peplau and Cochran 1979).

Despite expectations that lesbian relationships will be emotionally close, sexually exclusive, and long-lasting, there is no single pattern evident today. Women's traditional socialization toward strong love attachments has been partly countered by women's movement encouragement to be independent and by human potential movement encouragement to discover and develop one's unique identity rather than living through others. Contemporary lesbian relationships therefore vary in their degree of attachment and autonomy. In general lesbians who place high value on individual freedom tend to spend less time with their partners and to have short-term relationships (Peplau et al. 1978).

Relationships in a sample of 127 lesbians had lasted anywhere from one month to eleven years. The median duration was thirteen months—somewhat *shorter* than for gay men in the matching study just described. Another stereotype-defying comparison: Only 75 percent of these lesbians said that they and their current partners were in love, whereas 83 percent of the gay males said so (Peplau et al. 1978). Similarly, Lewis and coresearchers (1981) found that 48 percent of gay men, compared with 38 percent of lesbians, reported their relationships as long-term commitments—and 62 percent of the gay men, compared with 31 percent of the lesbians, said their relationship would probably result in a formal, recognized commitment such as a "holy union." Lewis and his colleagues also found that lesbians perceived less social support for their relationships from friends and families than did gay men. Gay men were invited to social functions more often, while lesbians preferred more time with their partners without "intrusions" from friends.

In gay communities as in straight society, marriage is sometimes approved of and sought after.

Some couples are "married" in gay churches, though these unions have not been granted legal recognition. Others hold announcement parties, exchange rings, or buy a house together to signal that they are anticipating an enduring relationship in which their primary commitment will be to each other. These unions are not strictly comparable to traditional heterosexual marriages, though. For instance, many gay males feel that sexual exclusivity is not part of the bargain in maintaining an intimate relationship, so that the straight concept of "marital infidelity" does not apply (Harry and Lovely 1979). In other words fidelity is redefined to mean following through on whatever agreement or commitment has been made—whether that be an "open" relationship or an exclusive one.

In Peplau's (1981) study a major difference between heterosexuals and homosexuals was that sexual exclusivity was more important to heterosexuals than to gays and lesbians. Feminist critiques of the restrictions of monogamy and male rewards for variety as a part of male socialization explain why homosexuals are less prone to monogamy. Peplau reported that gay men were more likely to separate love and sex and to enjoy casual sex than were lesbians. Of the gay men in Peplau's study, 54 percent said they had experienced sex with someone other than their partner in the preceding two months, compared with 13 percent of the lesbians and 14 percent of heterosexuals of both sexes (Peplau 1981). Peplau's research concludes that for gays and for heterosexuals alike the critical basis for happiness is *not* whether the relationship is open or closed—but *why* and *how* the partners "arrive at the particular pattern" (Peplau 1981, p. 38).

Gay Parents

Some of the saddest effects of straight condemnation of gays occur in the lives of homosexual parents. Many have contracted heterosexual marriages, had children, and then been afraid to divorce and live openly gay for fear of hurting their children, losing custody of them, or losing their jobs and being unable to support their kids. Although some are happily bisexual, many really prefer their own gender and carry on secret homosexual liaisons when they can.

The two great fears attached to such arrangements are that the children will become homosexuals and thereby encounter the straight world's hostility and that bigoted heterosexuals will hurt them because of the parents' sexual orientation. Surprisingly, neither prediction seems to be true for the majority of cases. Several studies have been done of the behaviors, peer group choices, toy choices, and occupational preferences of children raised by gay parents. All fall within the range considered normal for their gender. For instance, in a sample of children raised by lesbians, boys' favorite toys were such things as a hot cycle, a model shark, a truck, a racing set, cars, and a gun. The boys said when they grew up, they wanted to be pilots, football players, firemen, policemen, lawyers, artists. Parents are only part of a child's environment. A child's development is strongly affected by other aspects of the social environment: television, school, reading materials (Green 1978).

In their relationships with their kids, gay parents have many of the same concerns as straight parents. One lesbian who is also a mother insisted that being gay doesn't affect her role as a mother:

I'm not a lesbian mother, just a mother! I pay the nursery bills, and I take the baby to the doctor, and he's had the chicken pox, and he's been in the hospital. And when it all happens, you don't hold him in your arms and think, "I'm a lesbian mother." You think, "That's my child, and I love him." [Rock 1979, p. 45]

Some gay parents don't reveal their preferences to their children for fear of alienating them or burdening them with something they can't understand. Some therefore omit sexual references in explaining why they live with someone of the same sex. For instance, one mother explained to her young son that the lover who moved in with them was "a person I am very happy with and care a great deal for" (Green 1978, p. 695).

But some gay parents feel that sex is not beyond the understanding of children and that it's "immoral" to deprive them of information that might help to counteract the negative image of gays painted by straight society. Bruce Voeller, an executive director of the National Gay Task Force, says that telling kids gives them two advantages over other children: (1) They know their parent is

sexual, which helps them recognize and understand their own sexuality, and (2) they feel they can come to gay parents with their own problems, for they know their parents have learned to cope with difficulties (Voeller and Walters 1978).

Many gay parents who have come out to their children have been happily surprised that the children don't reject them (Bozett 1981). To a child the parent's sexual preference may be less important than her or his parenting qualities. For instance, one boy has chosen to live with his lesbian mother rather than his heterosexual father because she has qualities he values in a parent: She loves him, keeps their apartment clean, cooks good food, and makes him do chores rather than spoiling him. He notes proudly that when he confided in his best friend that his mother was gay, his friend said, "Gay, schmay, who gives a shit? She is a swell lady. I wish I could talk to my mother, have real rap sessions, like you have with your mother. All my mother does is nag me. I like your mother better" (Rock 1979, p. 44).

On the other hand the eighteen-year-old daughter of an old-style butch lesbian complained bitterly that her mother ruined her childhood: "I was always ashamed of her. I didn't know what was what." Noting that her mother was neurotic, she emphasized, "People shouldn't have children if they don't have their heads together to take care of them" (Rock 1979, p. 131).

Although there's no evidence that homosexuals are less effective as parents on the whole than heterosexuals, in divorce proceedings in some parts of the country courts still deny custody of children to the gay parent. However, there are other options for those who like children and want to care for them without the problems of heterosexual marriages. Gay men have often chosen parentlike occupations: teachers, scout leaders, ministers, coaches, youth workers, policemen, pediatricians, and guidance counselors (Miller 1979). Although adoption agencies tend to frown on single parents, some gays adopt children informally from people who can't care for them and then rear them with support from the gay community. Lesbians who want to be mothers sometimes choose a "father" and deliberately get pregnant. Not just any man will do, however. Some feel that a male homosexual is the best bet, because according to gay folklore he'll have "nonsexist genes" and can handle a friendly relationship without trying to regard the child or the mother as his property (Wolf 1979).

Pregnancy by artificial insemination is another possibility. Many doctors are willing to help lesbians find sperm donors. Says one, "If these people are comfortable with their lifestyle and their decision to have a child, I don't think I should withhold what I have to offer." Another says, "Frankly, I don't know what the criteria should be. But, to me, the kind of family community the child will be born into is more important than the mother's sexual preference" (Shah, Walters, and Clifton 1979, p. 61).

Gay parents now have The National Federation of Parents and Friends of Gays to look to for support groups across the country. The increased visibility of gay and lesbian families has prompted such organizations and associated grass-roots groups to become part of a national network. Such formal organizing encourages education, policies, and laws that are more sensitive to gay and lesbian parenting.

Aging: Crisis or Continuum?

Old age for homosexuals now over sixty-five may be quite different from the way today's young public gays will experience aging. Those now old have spent most of their lives struggling to develop self-acceptance and self-esteem in the face of public branding of their preferences as deviant. Most struggled in secret, never having admitted their sexual preferences publicly, for they might have lost their jobs. If their long-term lovers are institutionalized, they may be denied visiting privileges. If their lovers die, property may be taken over by families despite will provisions to the contrary.

In addition to problems with public intolerance, aging gay males may remember with considerable distaste how "old queens" were stereotyped by the gay culture in their youth. According to the stereotype, they've lost their physical appeal to the young men they crave, so they no longer frequent the bars. Although they still need sexual releases, the best they can do is to make furtive tearoom contacts as insertees. Fearful of having their "perversion" discovered, they withdraw from the gay community and compulsively mingle with heterosexuals.

However, a recent study of 241 gay males aged sixteen to seventy-nine—30 of them over sixty-five—refutes this stereotyped picture. Only 4 percent visit tearooms, and half of these are under thirty-six. Of those between fifty-six and sixty-five, 63 percent go to gay bars. Involvement of older men in the gay world ranges from low to moderate, but none have disengaged from it altogether. They tend to have many gay friends and a few heterosexual friends. Most consider their sex lives satisfactory; partners tend to be their own age. At ages forty-nine to fifty-five, 59 percent have an emotional and sexual relationship with a long-term partner. But from this point on, partnerships decrease to none through death of lovers and rejection of the idea of having a single long-term partner (Kelly 1977).

According to another study of sixty- to seventy-seven-year-old gay women and men, the males are more concerned than females over loss of their physical appearance, for they still value youth. The males are all sexually active, however; the females range from no sexual interest to active sex lives. Both sexes report that their closest friends are of the same gender. These people also maintain close contact with living family members—including children, for some—and are active in groups such as the Sierra Club, Common Cause, and Society for Individual Rights. None are interested in senior citizen centers. Loneliness is a problem for many, but perhaps no more so than for older heterosexuals in our society (Minnigerode and Adelman 1978).

EXPERIENCING THE SAME GENDER

The homosexual experience consists of far more than stigma dodging. For many it carries many positive rewards that offset the sting of being labeled "queer." Some studies indicate that homosexual relationships are even more emotionally and sexually satisfying than heterosexual ones (Freedman 1975). Others indicate that they are about the same (Peplau and Cochran 1979). But what goes on between partners tends to be different, both emotionally and sexually.

Homosexual Sharing: Roses and Thorns

Many homosexuals claim that making love with someone of their own gender far surpasses any pleasures they've experienced in heterosexual encounters. Nevertheless, the qualities that make homosexual sex seem special may also be sources of potential problems.

In a society where females and males are brought up in different symbolic worlds, it's often easier to establish quick intimacy and understanding with someone of the same sex. Physical—as well as emotional—similarity makes it easy to know how to turn the other on. There's a vicarious pleasure in knowing just what each caress feels like to the other, which increases the joy of giving and makes the giver want to do all she or he can think of to add to the other's sensual excitement. And to love those of the same sex is to accept and appreciate oneself.

Homosexuals' interest in increasing their partners' sensual pleasure—just as they would like their own pleasure increased—tends to lead away from orgasm-oriented sex. Instead, many have learned to focus on tenderness, warmth, and sensuality. Gentle, teasing, nongenital caressing lasts far longer than it does in typical heterosexual encounters. And without the barriers between the sexes built into our traditional heterosexual scripts, many homosexuals find it relatively easy to discuss what feels good and to be open about their desires to explore further.

In addition to heightened sensual pleasures, women appreciate the relative equality theoretically available in contemporary lesbian relationships. In contrast to the male-dominant/female-submissive roles traditionally prescribed for heterosexual relationships—and the old butch-fem roles based on them—women-only relationships now offer the possibility (if not always the reality) of being assertive, independent, and an equal partner in loving. If males and females were brought up as trusting friends rather than carriers for traditional antagonistic masculine and feminine roles, perhaps there would be fewer differences between homosexual and heterosexual sharing.

The very similarity between partners that brings joy to homosexual relationships may also mean thorns in the rose garden. The lack of clearly defined, unequal roles may cause peculiar problems, such as disagreements over how to decorate the apartment and whose job takes preference in relocation decisions. Many homosexuals worry that they are so close, so similar in interests, and so cut off from much of the outside world that too much togetherness will make it hard to be alone sometimes. Separation has been built into traditional male-female relationships: The man's realm is work; the woman's, home. In more nearly equal homosexual relationships, conscious agreements to be separate sometimes may have to be worked out (Krestan and Bepko 1980).

Many people picture the pleasure of sexual activity as maximum intimacy. But as C. A. Tripp (1976) points out, sexual arousal and continued interest in a partner seem also to be built on resistance to intimacy: being separated, gestures of pulling away, "not yet" teasing. To keep a relationship exciting, we may need dynamic tension between intimacy and resistance. Although it's hard to establish true intimacy in a heterosexual relationship, the resistances are built into the different ways females and males are brought up. Some long-term heterosexual relationships may be held together partly by the challenge and mystery of trying to understand and get along with someone different from ourselves. According to Tripp, the relative absence of this tension in a homosexual relationship may eventually decrease interest in it.

Another problem that seems more troublesome in homosexual relationships is coping with jealousy. In heterosexual relationships it's taken for granted that both partners will have friends of the same sex. But when the same sex is eroticized, as in homosexual orientations, any outside friendships are suspect. Unless partners negotiate some kind of agreement, they may find themselves isolated from other social contacts—or else they may break up (Krestan and Bepko 1980).

Sexual Activities

What do homosexuals do in bed? This question has intrigued and puzzled the straight world, for the assumption is that not having parts that "naturally" fit together, homosexuals must be limited in their choices or else must do some pretty unusual things. Actually, homosexuals do some of the same things heterosexuals do, although the quality of sexual sharing may be somewhat different. As C. A. Tripp (1976, p. 94) notes, "the 'main event' in most sexual contacts has much more to do with the stuff of intimacy and closeness than it does with the nitty-gritty of who puts what where." The aura of mystery and taboo surrounding homosexual acts may simply make them seem all the more exciting.

Straight myths of what homosexuals do picture lesbians banging away at each other's vaginas with dildos and gay men getting off quickly in each other's mouths or anuses. The dildo image is a phallic fantasy dwelt on at length in pornography written by and for men. The instant-sex gay myth is perhaps a result of what little homosexual activity is publicly observed—namely, hit-and-run tearoom contacts, which actually account for little of the total male homosexual activity. The myth is shared even by lesbians. For instance, one of the authors of *The Joy of Lesbian Sex* writes, "Lesbians have more in common with bowerbirds and elephants than with gay men: We prefer ritual to quick fucks" (Harris 1978, p. 2).

In contrast to these myths, a major difference between homosexual and heterosexual sex noted by Masters and Johnson (1979) in their laboratory observations is that gays make sex last longer. Both males and females appear to take their time, delighting in strokes given and received, prolonging pleasure rather than speeding toward the finish line.

For gay men fellatio and anal intercourse are favorite techniques. Partners typically share "insertor" and "insertee" roles rather than specialize in one or the other. Body caresses including the nipples—an area often ignored by females in heterosexual contact—are emphasized too. Instead of pushing for orgasm, gay males often arouse each other to heights of excitement and then teasingly back off or change activities to *avoid* orgasm. Many seem to regard arousal as more important than ejaculation.

Just as some heterosexuals practice sadomasochistic (or slave-master) sex, a significant subculture of gay men are involved in S/M sex. The typical scenario is for gay men to meet in a gay bar and then go to either of their residences for what has become highly scripted sexual behavior. These men, who are often strangers, must trust each

other enough not to become too violent in their enthusiasm—for S/M involves tension-producing activities, even tying up and beating of the "slave" by the "master." As sociologist John Alan Lee (1979) points out, there are risks to male S/M sex—a person could be harmed or even killed—but most such encounters appear to be mutually pleasurable and are viewed by the participants as acting out roles carefully scripted by the gay S/M subculture.

A behavior related to S/M scripts (or included as a part of them) is "fist-fucking" or "handballing," where the hand and forearm are pushed up another's anus. According to Thomas Lowry (1982), this activity is practiced by about 50,000 gay men and by some lesbians and heterosexuals. Damage can be done to the colon, especially since drug taking often accompanies these anal penetrations. But not all homosexuals are thrilled with "fist-fucking." For example, Lionell Mitchell argues:

A thousand Anita Bryants cannot do the devastation we are committing upon ourselves by substituting the fist, which is the most powerful symbol of aggression we have, for the penis. The act is a symbolic assault. There are no sexual sensations in that and there is no sexual response. With fist-fucking there is always a soft cock." [Crouch 1982, p. 17]

Mixtures of sexual pleasure with aggression and violence illustrate the frustration and confusion about the appropriate meanings for gender roles and for sexual expression. The complex interface between pleasure and pain, and between intimacy and aggression, is in flux as our society attempts to decipher these strongly reinforced emotions and behaviors.

Lesbian sexual activities sometimes resemble those used in heterosexual ones. Cunnilingus is the favorite of most, followed by manual clitoral stimulation and body-to-body rubbing of breasts against breasts and clitoris against clitoris (Bell and Weinberg 1978). This latter technique is somewhat hard to master, so far as creating orgasms goes. However, in cunnilingus many lesbians claim that women are far more effective and imaginative than men. Skillful, knowing use of these techniques and slow, sensual full-body caressing and kissing helps women orgasm more often than they do in heterosexual sexmaking. According to one study, 70 percent of gay women "almost always" experience orgasm with their current female partners; 14 percent usually do; 10 percent do so occasionally; and only 4 percent never do (Peplau et al. 1978). This finding supports the belief of some researchers that women who are incapable of orgasm are not overly common, but that ineffective stimulation is common.

Although sex among homosexuals is sometimes more sensual than among heterosexuals, there are unimaginative, insensitive partners of both persuasions. Homosexuals may have sexual problems—for anatomical or psychological reasons—just like heterosexuals. But for lesbians especially, the political notion that someone of your own sex can satisfy you far better than someone of the other sex may be so important that it's hard to admit to having any problems. Some lesbians have the same sexual problems as some straight women, and they can be equally uptight about enjoying sex. But because of the gay fantasy that lesbians are strong, powerful, and always orgasmic, it's hard for some lesbians to admit that they're not or that they don't enjoy sex at all.

THE SEARCH FOR COMMUNITY

Many gays and lesbians feel a need to build some kind of alternative community within which they can define and express themselves. Whereas straights can find friendly souls who validate their identity and allow them to "be themselves" almost everywhere—from school to work—persons who are secretly lesbian or gay can neither show their true feelings nor find kindred spirits in these settings. In the past they've had to look for others like themselves in cruising scenes such as gay bars and baths, which are still very popular. For instance, over 400 cities in the United States have at least one gay bar where homosexuals can meet their friends and make sexual contacts. Such bars were once limited mainly to large cities, but now they are found in suburbs and sometimes in smaller cities and towns. Community gay organizations offer activities such as skiing, hiking, or sailing, as well as a social network for gays and lesbians.

According to one report, more gays and lesbians on today's college campuses are living openly as homosexuals, with a supportive subculture that includes dances, meetings, and other social activities. The report concludes that women are more likely to experiment with lesbian relationships and return to heterosexual relationships than men are likely to experiment with men as a transitory experimentation back to women (Lubenow, Abramson, and King 1982). But whether women or men identify as lesbian or gay after college, the college environment appears to provide a better haven for same-gender experimentation and social activities than do small-town or rural environments.

For many these scattered oases of freedom to be gay still leave something to be desired. Homosexuals ideally would like to be able to behave freely in every social setting—from grocery stores to doctors' offices. Since such freedom is still not possible in straight settings, many homosexuals have moved into neighborhoods and communities with large gay populations. The largest cities in the United States have distinctly gay areas in which diverse services cater to a gay clientele—from restaurants and bars to bookstores, laundromats, real estate agents, doctors, and lawyers. In addition to the proliferation of these gay-tolerant public places, homosexuals seek lack of harassment from neighbors when they entertain at home, which many find more intimate and less competitive than socializing in bars. Again, the anonymity of big-city life and the concentrations of gays in certain urban neighborhoods provide considerable freedom.

Some people, however, prefer rural or resort life to a city atmosphere or like to sample both. They have tried to settle in small, tolerant communities with growing gay populations. In some they've found a live-and-let-live attitude; in others local residents have become resentful and alarmed as they see the growing numbers of gays in their midst. In the small Vermont town of Bellows Falls, for instance, an established gay population met with the usual name calling but was more or less tolerated for years, complete with an openly gay hotel. But when *Blueboy* magazine suggested in 1979 that Bellows Falls was a nice place for gays to live and New England gay groups scheduled a Washington rally-planning meeting there, some straight residents became upset. Fearing that the small mill town would become a "haven" for the gay community, eighty demonstrators held an antigay rally, with "Gays Stay Away from Bellows Falls" signs, brick throwing at the hotel, and some "down with gays" yelling from carfuls of young men (Longcope 1979).

Despite setbacks many gays are doggedly trying to build a positive image for themselves and to gain respect for their humanity from the public. According to a majority of the gay males who responded to *The Spada Report,* the most important change that will have to be made if gay life is to improve is educating others about the realities of homosexuality. As one of the respondents noted, if this change takes place within the framework of increased acceptance of varied sexual choices—including, but not limited to, homosexuality—everyone's life will be richer:

The best thing that could happen is for people to learn enough about human sexuality, so as to accept any

act, short of violence, as natural and beautiful. My upbringing tells me that what I enjoy and want out of life is wrong, yet my experiences tell me that it's beautiful and right. Understanding and acceptance of homosexuality and sexuality are the changes that would be of most benefit to everyone. [Spada 1979, p. 299] *

Summary

The labels "gay," "lesbian," and "bisexual" cover a wide range of degrees of preference for and experience with the same sex, as well as variations in the openness of these orientations. Although public attitudes toward these orientations have often been negative, the gay liberation movement has made some gains and helped gay people develop a more positive self-image. Some feminists have actively promoted lesbian choices. Nevertheless, the numbers of people with a homosexual orientation seem to have remained about the same since researchers first began to observe them, with perhaps an increase in the number having some sexual experience with both sexes.

Research into the origins of same-sex orientations suggests a complex interplay of social and perhaps biological factors. Gay identities may begin with early awareness of same-sex erotic preferences, perhaps progressing to homosexual activities and some degree of "coming out" publicly and forming of same-sex relationships. Many who share sex with those of the same gender find these encounters satisfying because they tend to lack the learned barriers that block friendly intimacy with the other sex. Many who prefer sex with their own gender feel social barriers to freely being who they are and freely expressing affection to their partners. Gay communities and gay social services have helped to create public spaces for this freedom.

*From *The Spada Report* by James Spada. Copyright © 1979 by James Spada. Reprinted by arrangement with The New American Library, Inc., New York, New York.

9

Early Sexual Learning

Grade One

If a boy kissed me, I would kiss him more. And I would say I like you. I like Carlos because he is very nice with me. And he took me on a date. I like Carlos more than anyone in my class. I want him to want me. And do you know what? He came to my house and gave me a big, big, big kiss. The first time he saw me I was wearing a beautiful dress and it popped his eyes out.

Migdalia

Grades Two and Three

I don't like boys because they are nasty. They look under your dress and try to kiss you. Boys are very dirty. I don't like sissies. When you go up the bus they look under your dress. They kiss the girls. They give me the creeps. They are silly. That is what I don't like about boys. They come from Mars. They asked me for a date. I said no and closed the door. Don't come back, I said. If you come back, I will scream.   *Rhonda*

I don't like boys because they look under girls' dresses sometimes. And they look silly when they play jump rope with girls. Sometimes they hit girls and girls hit back.

Daisy

Grades Four and Five

I like the legs, the waist, the breasts. I like the way they walk, the way they talk. I also like them because it's nature.   *Tony*

I would like to take my girl out someday when I grow up tall. I would get marry, and sure I will have twin babies. I will stick my dick in her pussy. I will suck her lips.

Willis

Grade Six

I think that miniskirts should be worn, but parents think that miniskirts are temptations for boys. They say that they might rape you if you walk with a miniskirt. They put down the hems of your dresses without telling you. I think that sex education should be taught, because if something happens to you, you want to know what's wrong with you. About making the baby, they think, if you learn about it you would immediately go out and get pregnant. They don't let you with boys because you'll go to lover's lane and get pregnant. If you ask questions about sex they tell you to mind your business and you'll learn someday.

Anonymous female

From "Latency: Fact or Fiction?" by S. S. Janus and B. E. Bess. In L. L. Constantine and F. M. Martinson (Eds.), *Children and Sex: New Findings, New Perspectives.* Copyright © 1981 by Little, Brown and Company. Reprinted by permission.

In their earliest years children are exploring and learning sexually. What they learn comes in hesitating bits and pieces with few organized patterns. Sexual aspects of these years that most of us spend living within some kind of family are complex and little understood. There are some statistics on how many persons engage in which sexual behaviors during these years. There is a large body of research on the *problems* of teenage sex, such as pregnancy. There are also some studies on where children pick up information about sex. But we really don't yet understand childhood sexuality from a child's point of view. We have no clear picture of what meanings children place on the things they experience.

In this chapter we'll explore what sources shape children's sexual knowledge and attitudes. We'll examine reasons why many parents are uncomfortable talking with their children about sex. We'll also look at incest—a potential battleground between those who believe that parent/child interaction should be freer sexually and those who believe that it's too free already.

SEXUAL DEVELOPMENT DURING CHILDHOOD AND THE TEENAGE YEARS

During childhood we begin to know—and perhaps enjoy—our own bodies. We may also start reaching out to others for shared emotional and physical pleasures and trying out scripts we're learning for intimate interaction. As we do so, we struggle to reconcile what we want with the many expectations society gives us.

Considerable evidence exists that children are sexually active. Chapter 4 already discussed their early masturbation activities. Children also engage in sexual experimentation with others. Martinson (1981) asserts that even in our society's restricted sexual environment preteen children find ways to explore sexual curiosities with siblings, playmates, and others. In fact, many children's play activities—whether the classic doctor/nurse games, tree-house frolicking, or swimming down at the creek—are disguised opportunities to allow sexual experimentation. Most of this exploration involves showing and fondling genitals to satisfy curiosity about the hidden.

Development of intimate relationships is part of sexual growing, too. A common script is having a few close friends of the same gender, then socializing with a larger mixed gender group that hangs out together and meets at dances. The next step for many is heterosexual dating, followed by a steady attachment to a single person. But there are other modes of seeking emotional and physical closeness. For some this period is characterized by homosexual relationships or nonexclusive, getting-together heterosexual intimacies.

These partner-seeking behaviors are dictated not only by physical urges but also by nonsexual desires and attitudes. For example, "petting" is a behavior that gratifies not only physical desires but also desires to be found adequately "feminine" or "masculine"—that is, to satisfy expected gender roles. As we develop waists and breasts or deep voices and hairy faces, both adults and peers begin

What we would call "sex play" is common during childhood, but we must make best guesses about how children define the things they do.

to view us as more sexual creatures. Although at this age we are for the first time able to create a pregnancy, reaching reproductive maturity does not mean that we become sexual overnight. Some of us have been intrigued by sex all along; some of us would just as soon ignore it until some later age.

In addition to great individual variations in interest in sex, teenage sexuality is complicated by varying social expectations about what one should do sexually. As one sixteen-year-old female put it:

Everybody's always telling us you should be this, no, you should be that. When they're not telling you one thing or another to your face, you still hear the voices in your head. . . . In my head all I hear are people's orders, and suggestions, and ideas. It's like the whole world is trying to put something into me. It makes you feel like a pincushion.   [Quoted by Cottle 1979, p. 40]

Adults often characterize teenagers as shallow because they change so often or as immature because they don't hold the same values as their parents. But instead of being thoughtless and irresponsible, teenagers are tackling a difficult develop-

mental task: experimenting with and trying to reconcile conflicting suggestions about their sexuality (Miller and Simon 1979). The task that begins during childhood but continues throughout life is to sift through all social inputs and to choose those attitudes and behaviors that make the most sense to us in building our own sexual identity and sexual relationships. In making such choices we are beginning to exercise independence and good judgment that will help us shape responsible, rewarding adult sexual careers.

Not all teenagers are successful in this task, of course. From either ignorance or denial of participation and the consequences, few teenagers use contraceptives when they start having intercourse. As a result teenage pregnancy has reached epidemic proportions: One out of every ten women in the United States now gets pregnant by

Figure 9-1. Sexual Behaviors during Childhood. The classic large-scale surveys by Kinsey and his colleagues turned up evidence that many children experience some kind of sexual exploration. Note that before puberty homosexual experiences are somewhat more common than heterosexual ones.

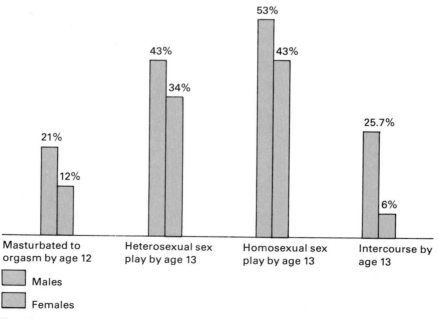

Note: Based on Kinsey et al.'s 1948 and 1953 surveys of 5,300 white males and 5,940 white females.

The Language of Sex

The term *adolescence* is still used by many adults in our society to identify the transition from childhood to adulthood and "maturity." "Adolescence" is often used as a put-down to teenagers—a way to keep them in their place. It connotes an immature state; no one likes to be called "adolescent."

"The teenage years" is a more objective and less biased way to describe the years immediately preceding the twenties. Many teenagers make exceptionally thoughtful sexual choices, whereas many adults are not at all sensible or mature in their choices. This fact raises the additional question: What is "mature" sexual behavior? Is it behavior that conforms to traditional expectations? Or can we instead define mature sexual choices as those that are situation-appropriate, mutually desired, responsible, and joyful?

age seventeen (Zelnik, Kim, and Kantner 1979). Although teenagers are now sexually more active at earlier ages than in the past, many are afraid of sex. Some are pushed into sex before they're ready for it by pressure from their peers, the mass media, and a society that dramatizes sex.

Out of curiosity, interest, and need to adapt to their own growth, children and teens do raise questions. Carol Wagner (1980) suggests three general categories of concerns that they raise. One area is the theme of what is normal: "Is it normal to masturbate?" "Is it abnormal to have thoughts about sex with people I know—even members of my family?" "Are my breasts too small?" A second set of questions involves seeking factual information: "How can I get birth control information without my parents' knowing?" "How can you tell if you have VD?" "How can I know if I have an orgasm?" A third category of questions involves sexual values: "When is it right to have sex with someone else?" "How can I say 'no'?" "How far should I go before I stop?" "Is being a virgin wrong?" For children and teenagers to answer serious questions such as these requires complex decision-making skills, self-assessment, relationship skills, and ethical evaluations. These dimensions are not easi-

ly taught in basic sex education courses (Parcel and Luttman 1981).

Analyzing children's sexual concerns in terms of their age—"too young"—is inadequate. Interestingly, in societies that consistently encourage sex and provide sexual instruction for their young—such as the Trobriand Islanders of the southwestern Pacific—people often settle comfortably into the full range of sexual intimacies before they even reach puberty (Ford and Beach 1951). Perhaps, then, we can view the sexual difficulties of our own teenagers as symptoms of the patchy, inconsistent ways children in our society learn about sex.

SOURCES OF SEXUAL INFORMATION

Our recollections of where we learned about sex are usually fuzzy. A few incidents may stand out in our minds. But when and where we picked up the rest is not so clear, for sex is ambiguously talked about in our society. For instance, developmental psychologist David Payne (1970) found that 50 percent of his college students could remember when they learned that Santa Claus wasn't real, but only 1 or 2 percent could remember when they learned that incest was not culturally acceptable. Most of the information picked up involves physical facts that are isolated from social interaction and meaning.

"Never mind the birds and bees; tell me about the moans and groans I heard in your room last night!"

Kids on Learning "All about Sex"

Judging from round-table discussions with kids across the country by *Children's Express*, many young people have the impression that they could learn everything there is to know about sex in one sitting if only someone would tell them. They differ in whom they'd really like to hear it from—and whom they think they already learned "all about sex" from. Some examples:

Tim, 12: I never told my parents my curiosity. I learned all I know about sex off the street. The basic stuff is—boys and girls kissing, have sexual intercourse, there's the baby. In sixth grade, after I'd learned most of it, then we came to the real hard stuff: what's a period, what age you go into puberty—that's down to the hard stuff. My teacher gave a full-day lesson on sex. She told us everything there was to know, and whatnot. So after that day in sixth grade I knew everything there was to tell about sex—unless they're breaking in some new health course.

Jason, 10: I don't talk about sex with my friends 'cause they always take it the dirty way. I don't talk about it with them that way, because sex is really nice. On the streets I'm always hearing bad things about it—like cursing. I just get nervous and sometimes I get confused.

Jessie, 12: If I'm curious about sex, I don't wanna get involved with my parents 'cause I don't want them to have anything to do with what I think, even though they'd be willing to tell me. My mother occasionally comes up to me and says, "You know if you wanna know anything just ask." But I never do ask, 'cause I don't think I wanna know anything from them. I don't want them to influence me in any way.

Gloria, 12: I learned almost everything I know about sex from books and from friends. . . . I wish that my parents would talk to me about sex. I know it already, but I could act like I didn't. They're waiting too long, they're waiting too long. . . . Parents think that if they don't tell you, you don't know.

Anthony, 8: My parents don't want me to learn about sex because I'm not old enough. I say, "What does that mean?" They say that I'm "not old enough to know yet." I think I'm a little bit old enough.

Kathy, 10: My baby-sitter told me, and my parents just go, "Good." My mother doesn't usually say anything unless I ask. Then she goes, "Ah . . . well. . . ." She sort of stops for a minute, and then she goes on.

Nancy, 12: I think sex education is usually most effective at home. The person is more likely to believe his mother or his father than he's going to believe a teacher at school, a teacher he barely knows. But I was doing a round table and the kids wanted to talk about sex. They said they were very embarrassed about asking their parents questions because they thought they might think they were weird or cracked. So I think it's a lot easier to pick up the stuff in school, because you don't know this person, so it isn't really going to embarrass you. [Kavanaugh 1978, pp. 145-50]*

*Copyright © 1978 by Dorriet Kavanaugh. Reprinted from *Listen to Us!* by permission of the Workman Publishing Company, Inc., New York.

Parents

Our earliest information about sexuality is implanted by parents. They give us words to use for parts of our body, although they tend to leave out those parts we haven't found or asked about (such as clitoris and vagina). When pressed for information about the function of parts they associate with sexuality, parents typically speak only of excretion at first. Erotic activities such as masturbation and sex play are usually given no labels at all. Children may therefore be punished for creating intriguing feelings they don't even have a name for, much less understand in adult terms.

This "nonlabeling" of erotic activities and body parts denies children a recognition of their own sexuality. If children are given no words for the things they notice, strange, inaccurate fantasies may accumulate around their interest in their own and others' bodies. And if parents label genitals only as organs of excretion, children's attitudes toward sexual pleasure may long be colored by a feeling that it is somehow "dirty." Such omissions create an uneasy, clandestine attitude toward sexuality through which later sex information will be filtered.

Also, much early sexual training by parents is nonverbal, extending further back into infancy than our conscious word-oriented memories stretch. Attitudes stored at this level may be especially resistant to change. If the good feeling of touching our genitals was accompanied by parental scoldings, slaps on the hand, or efforts to distract us, this mixed input probably registered and stayed with us, but at a preverbal level. Through their toilet training methods, breast or bottle feeding, willingness to be nude within the family, kisses and caresses or stiffening from bodily contact, our parents further shaped our developing attitudes toward sexuality.

Many parents at some point try to share with their children concrete information about sexual health and issues but not about sexmaking itself. Most studies indicate that the mother is far more likely to attempt this teaching than the father and that mothers are an important source of information for their daughters. For instance, Thornburg (1981) found in a study of 1152 midwestern high school students that mothers provided most of the sex information in the home and that they were especially important in teaching daughters about conception and menstruation. High-school-age daughters also credit mothers as a significant source of information about abortion and intercourse. Fathers contributed almost nothing to direct sex education.

The child usually asks questions of the parent who takes most household responsibilities. If the father shares the role with the mother or is the parent with custody after a divorce, then he may be asked questions. But according to a study of over 1400 Cleveland parents, mothers so often assume that sex education is their role—and are so uncomfortable talking about sex with their husbands—that women often don't even mention to their husbands that they've had a talk with their children about sex (Roberts, Kline, and Gagnon 1978).

Many of the parents in the Cleveland study apparently felt that once they explained where babies come from, they had finished telling their children about sex. Very few went beyond "A baby grows in its mother's tummy and then comes out of a special hole" to explain how the baby got there in the first place. Only 15 percent of the mothers and less than 10 percent of the fathers had ever told their children about intercourse. Still fewer had mentioned contraception. Although parents claim that they want their children to know about the erotic aspects of sexuality, many are afraid that if kids know about sexual activities they will "misuse" the information—that is, try the activities themselves (Libby, Acock, and Payne 1974).

By the age of nine or ten many children find their parents so embarrassed and evasive about sexual matters that they stop asking questions. "Formal" sexual education by parents, such as it is, often simply ends (Roberts, Kline, and Gagnon 1978). Even in the teenage years parents tend to

When I talk to my parents or other grown-ups about sex, they usually look like this (check one):

Parents on Talking to Children about Sex

Fifty-year-old mother of a thirteen-year-old female: "The more you talk about something, the more you think about it, and the more you think about it, the more you do it. This sex business is just like overeating and overdrinking—you've got to keep their minds off it with other activities. . . . You can't ever let your guard down, there are so many bad influences around." [Quoted in Maynard 1978, p. 84]*

A Manchester, Connecticut, parent: "I try to keep them from knowing too much; I approach it the same as my parents did. My parents did not tell me about it. I don't discuss it either. I think sex education corrupts the minds of fifteen–sixteen-year-olds! There is absolutely no communication between parents and kids about sex. Kids know too much already. I just tell them to behave and keep their eyes open." [Quoted in Libby and Nass 1971, p. 234]

Another Manchester parent: "If they know dangers, they will avoid intercourse, and have a fear of the Lord." [Quoted in Libby and Nass 1971, p. 234]

Judy Blume, mother of two teenagers and author of many teenage novels: "I hate the idea that you should always protect children. They live in the same world we do. They see things and hear things. The worst is when there are secrets, because what they imagine, and have to deal with alone, is usually scarier than the truth. Sexuality and death—those are the two big secrets we try to keep from children, partly because the adult world isn't comfortable with them either. But it certainly hasn't kept kids from being frightened of those things." [Quoted in Maynard 1978, p. 92]*

A father: "On a number of occasions, my kid would question (me) about body parts . . . he would talk about the size of my penis . . . we'd be in the bathroom together, and I'd take that as an opportunity to say a bit about that. I talked about penis sizes being variable, and that his would grow larger as he grew larger. . . . I don't know if I had a special message to deliver, just whatever I thought was appropriate." [Quoted in Roberts, Kline, and Gagnon 1978, p. 51]

A mother: "My eight-year-old daughter came in from school the other day and said, 'Hey, Mom, do you know what this means?' as she pushed a finger in and out of a circle made by the thumb and index finger of her other hand. I said I thought so, but what did she think it meant. She then proceeded to tell me that it meant making love. At that point I thought it was time to tell her more about what making love really is, just to be sure she didn't go through life thinking it had to do with fingers." [Quoted in Bell 1978, p. 85]†

* From Joyce Maynard, "Coming of Age with Judy Blume," *New York Times Magazine*, December 3, 1978. © 1978 by The New York Times Company. Reprinted by permission.

† From Ruth Davidson Bell, "The Middle Years," in Boston Women's Health Book Collective, *Ourselves and Our Children: A Book by and for Parents* (New York: Random House, Inc., 1978). © 1978 by Random House, Inc. Reprinted by permission.

use an indirect approach toward shaping sexual attitudes. Occasionally there is a passionate, direct lecture about what the child has done "wrong." But the more common indirect messages—disapproving general remarks about teenage sex, efforts to control dating (by setting curfews, for example), scare warnings about the dangers of pregnancy and VD, and vaguely worded hopes that their children can be "trusted"—often convey "don't have sex" attitudes. Females are more often the recipients of these negative messages than males. Parents worry that the potential risks of sexual exploitation, pregnancy, rape, and perhaps loss of marriage market value make females more vulnerable. According to the Cleveland study, less than 30 percent of mothers want to convey to their daughters the message that singles intercourse is okay, but nearly 60 percent want their sons to know it's okay.

Fathers are even more likely to hold this double-standard attitude (Roberts, Kline, and Gagnon 1978).

Even parents who have tried to be more open and accepting of their young children's sexuality are unsure what moral advice to give sexually active teenagers. One man who thought he'd been rational with his daughter about sex became alarmed when he learned that at age fourteen she had begun to date a twenty-year-old man. He and his wife started arguing about whether the two might be having intercourse and if so, what should be done about it. Confronted with an issue they had never before faced, they found their "rational" approach replaced by a maze of previously unexplored anxieties and prejudices:

We had always prided ourselves on how open we were about sex and had assumed that we would easily accept our children's sexual development. Now, here was the first time when we had to think about Stephanie having intercourse, and Alice and I were fighting.   (Quoted in Speizer 1978, p. 98)

Peers

In many sexual matters same-sex peers—the age group with which we identify—partially fill the void left by parents. In Thornburg's sample (1981) most people first learned about petting, contraception, intercourse, homosexuality, and prostitution from same-sex peers. Males are especially likely to share sexual information with each other. Most teenage males list peers as their major single source of sexual information; teenage females list peers as either their chief source of sexual information or else a close runner-up to their mothers (Libby and Carlson 1973; Gebhard 1977).

The things kids tell each other may be riddled with inaccuracies: "If you masturbate, your penis will fall off," "A man mounts a woman like a dog and then gets stuck there," "If you kiss a boy, you may get pregnant." Often it's a case of the blind leading the blind. For instance, kids who hear someone called a "whore" on the playground may

Figure 9-2. Parental "Sex Education." According to the Cleveland study, parents seldom discuss erotic behaviors and their social consequences with their children. Although the topic of pregnancy often comes up, few parents mention its precursor, intercourse. Fathers are especially unlikely to discuss sex with their children.

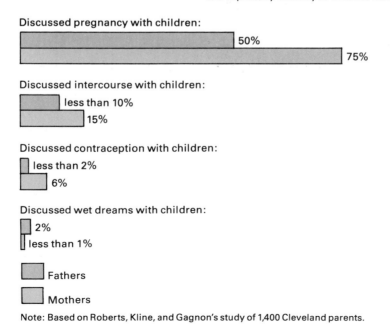

Discussed pregnancy with children:
50%
75%

Discussed intercourse with children:
less than 10%
15%

Discussed contraception with children:
less than 2%
6%

Discussed wet dreams with children:
2%
less than 1%

Fathers

Mothers

Note: Based on Roberts, Kline, and Gagnon's study of 1,400 Cleveland parents.

Peers are an important source of sexual learning, as models to imitate, as sources of "knowledge," and as partners in trials and errors.

rush together to the dictionary to find out what the word means, only to come up empty-handed because they can't figure out how to spell it. Nevertheless, talk with peers helps to satisfy curiosities left unsatisfied by parents.

Most sex information from peers is imparted during the early teen years, from twelve to sixteen, and occasionally as early as age ten (Gebhard 1977). This pattern may be part of a general shift away from parents during these years. Increasingly, peers serve as a reference group whose opinions we value and who, we think, understand us well because their experiences are similar to our own.

Siblings

A neglected area of study is the impact of brothers and sisters on our sexual learning. Most studies fail to consider siblings, yet they are tremendous influences in solving our earliest curiosities about sex. Of 796 college undergraduates studied by Finkelhor (1980), 13 percent reported having sexual experience with a sibling. These contacts were both heterosexual (74 percent) and homosexual (26 percent) and primarily included genital touching and showing off of genitals. Curiosity

and interest were seen as major factors in sibling exploration. Siblings can be actual teachers as older brothers and sisters tell about masturbation, orgasm, and other sexual delights. However, serious sex between siblings is usually not a dominant pattern because of disdain created by the familiarity of everyday living together (Bixler 1982).

Media

Studies consistently show that the mass media is becoming a more crucial source of learning about things sexual for grade school and high school students. Next to peers, it is magazines, books, newspapers, TV, and movies that provide the bulk of information (Thornburg 1981; Amonker 1980; Courtright and Baran 1980). Similarly, for college students the mass media is a prominent avenue of learning and relearning.

For 67 percent of college students in one national survey, reading was the major source of sexual information (Spanier 1977). Even at earlier ages anything written about sex may be ransacked for answers to sexual questions. Young males who can get their hands on *Playboy* or *Penthouse* study the photographs and cartoons for clues as to where they're expected to stick it in and how. Females far younger than seventeen occasionally find an article or advice column in *Seventeen* or *Glamour* introducing them to some of the mysteries and issues of sex (such as slow physical development, fears of being abnormal, doctors' examinations, first dates, breaking up, honesty in relationships, STD, pregnancy, and abortion). Novels written for teenagers with explicitly sexual passages are in such demand that it takes months to get them at libraries. Judy Blume's twelve novels for young teenagers deal candidly with the facts and emotional issues of body changes, menstruation, wet dreams, orgasm, impotence, and breaking up—and they've sold 6 million copies (Maynard 1978).

As children, we also pick up pieces of sexual information from printed matter, if we can get our hands on it.

Sex Education Programs

Sex education programs in school and church provide children with further clues to what sex is all about. These institutions are not a particularly important source of information for most. They fill in a few gaps, though. For instance, sex education programs in school are a fairly significant source of information about menstruation for males and a major source of information about STD for girls (Gebhard 1977).

The comparative failure of sex education programs to have an impact on young people is seen by some as related to confusion from the many differing voices regarding the role of school/religious/community programs. This leaves a chaotic unexamined agenda of what ought to be accomplished. Elizabeth J. Roberts (1982) has labeled this de facto national "policy" the "unwritten" sexual curriculum. These contradictory messages leave the young without solid scripts to choose for their sexual growth and conduct. As a result many sex education programs only focus on stopping pregnancies and sexually transmitted diseases, assuming that factual information will accomplish that narrow goal.

Efforts to develop guidelines acceptable to a wide range of parents and communities are actively being pursued. Sex educator Sol Gordon (1981) has proposed seven basic principles for quality sex education programs. Enhancing the self-concept is his first principle. If young people have knowledge and feel centered with themselves, they are not as likely to exploit others or to accept exploitation of themselves by the mass media or others. The second principle—preparation for marriage and parenthood—focuses on strengthening family life through communication, compromise, sense of humor, and so forth. The third principle is understanding love as a basic component of a person's sexuality. Fourth—preparation for making responsible sexual decisions—includes "owning" the consequences of one's actions and thereby valuing, rather than exploiting, others. Fifth is helping people understand the need for equal opportunities for both females and males: Sexism should not be encouraged. Sixth is developing tolerance and appreciation for those not conforming to typical norms of marriage and childbearing. Finally, seventh is contributing to knowledge and understanding of the sexual dimensions of our lives and the understanding that they involve life-long development and modification. Sex educators hope that principles such as these will unify many skeptical sectors of our society into providing a wholesome growth experience for young people.

Although sex educators advance idealistic goals, evidence exists that everyday pragmatic considerations determine how sex education is used. For instance, a 1979 restudy in Muncie, Indiana, showed that the Planned Parenthood organization's sex education programs were readily accepted as necessary, even in a conservative community such as Muncie. In particular they were becoming the accepted source of contraception information and supplies for teenagers, with an estimated one-third of the area's teenage girls using their services (Caplow et al. 1982).

Planned Parenthood has also been effective in upgrading sexual information services for young women; teenage males, however, have largely escaped their programs. High school girls score considerably higher both on birth control knowledge and total sexual knowledge compared with teenage boys, which suggests that more attention in sex education programs needs to be directed toward young men (Amonker 1980).

Criticism of public school sex education programs does not come merely from right-wing political groups or the religiously conservative. Some social scientists point out that efforts to rid junior high or high school students of sexual anxieties, fears, and guilt are destroying the development of a healthy superego, protection these young persons need against being pressured into sexual activity. From this point of view sex educators are accused of using techniques and exercises that undermine young peoples' ability to appropriately sublimate sexual feelings and to transfer them into love and tenderness. Lawrence and Ellen Shornack (1982), in a reasoned critique of the contemporary sex education movement, also raise the issues that young men are more sexually driven and therefore must be constrained while young women must be protected, and that ties between adolescents and parents must be strengthened. They support sex education programs in the school and community that accomplish these goals.

Partners

A final source of sexual information is the teenagers' sex partners. Together, teenagers may experiment with pieces of knowledge they've picked up elsewhere, often discovering together things no one else told them. For some learning how to please one another and what sex means to each is an endearing form of intimacy. This learning may also give them general feedback about their own sexuality, the sexuality of others, and about relating sexually to another person. These partner lessons may not be comfortable. One typical area of difficulty is illustrated by a Planned Parenthood study of 403 New York City teenage women. Thirty percent of these young women experienced being pressured to have sex, and of these 91 percent report that the pressure came from their boyfriends (NYC Teen Survey . . ." 1982). Similarly, if our heads carry inflated, media-fed expectations of eternal romance, passionate fireworks, multiple orgasms, or perpetual erection, our discoveries of each other may lead to disillusionment and distress rather than to tender enjoyment and understanding.

FACTORS INHIBITING SEX TALK IN THE FAMILY

Studies show that students believe that parents should have the primary responsibility for teaching young persons about sexual matters (Bennett and Dickinson 1980). Parents likewise believe that the responsibility for sex education lies primarily in the home (Wyatt and Stewart-Newman 1982). Yet actual sex education is not received primarily from parents. Why is this? Although parents may not have completely accurate information, they could provide their children with reading material and could share their personal sexual ideals, attitudes, and experiences. Sharing in this way does not require academic expertise—only an interest in communicating. Yet parents usually do not. In this section we examine a few facets creating this dilemma.

Future versus Present Orientation

While children tend to be most interested in current concerns, parents typically feel a moral imperative to worry about their children's future. Many parents regard it their responsibility to foresee and prevent future difficulties that are not apparent to their children. Parents also may believe that to engage in intercourse during the teen years may somehow spoil things later in life, especially for females. In addition to the risks of pregnancy and rape, the double-standard assumption that females should be "relatively unused" when they marry still exists, even among college students (Ferrell, Tolone, and Walsh 1977).

In general this thinking of "what's best for my child's future" leads to a more conservative set of approved activities and attitudes than parents themselves experienced. In a study of adults from West Virginia, Kentucky, and Ohio, 76 percent of the women and 93 percent of the men did heavy petting in their youth and 61 percent of the women and 84 percent of the men had intercourse before marriage. Yet these same people, when considering "acceptable and normal" teenage behavior, chose a more conservative standard than they had experienced. Only 31 percent of the women and 46 percent of the men approved of heavy petting, and only 18 percent of the women and 28 percent of the men approved of intercourse as acceptable and normal among teens (Wyatt and Stewart-Newman 1982). Likewise, another study reported that parents are reluctant to allow their own children the sexual experiences they themselves had as teenagers, for they worry about their children's future. One woman said, "Just because it was right for me doesn't make it okay for my kids" (Caplow et al. 1982, p. 171) The mothers in the study who approved of teenage sexual activity nearly always qualified their responses by asserting that contraceptive information should be readily available.

Preserving Family Calm

Although teenagers are often comfortable talking about sex with adults other than their parents, sex is usually a closed subject in the family by the time kids reach sixteen (Chess, Thomas, and Cameron 1976). Interviews with both parents and their children reveal a pattern of *mutual* evasion for the sake of family peace. Parents often will say to the dating teen, "Have a good time," but the unspoken understanding is, "Don't tell me the details of what you did." If parents don't know, then they don't have to get upset and a scene is avoided. Children also sense that much of what they think and do their parents couldn't handle well.

For instance, teenage women who have become pregnant usually don't talk to their parents about it because they view them as powerful representatives of conventional morality. From their parents' indirect messages, these women have inferred that they'd be soundly criticized for their unconventional behavior. They accept their parents' point of view as reasonable for people who grew up in a different time, but they don't expect parents to understand or support today's teenage standards. To avoid clashes over this issue, the girls typically say nothing and try to appear respectable.

Surprisingly, even when parents suspect that their daughters' behaviors don't meet conventional standards, they are reluctant to cause a scene. Although parents have certain value preferences, they are no more willing to challenge their daughters openly than their daughters are to defy them openly. They seem to be motivated not so much by naiveté or lack of concern as by a strong desire to preserve a calm family atmosphere. Even when parents finally learn of their daughters' pregnancies, their response is unexpectedly mild and supportive (Briedis 1975).

Independence Assertion

In addition to strong desires for family harmony, open discussions of sex are inhibited by children's efforts to establish their independence from the family. Whatever closeness existed when they were young may be strained as they begin to assert their autonomy during the preteen years. Many who formerly welcomed parental hugs and kisses now try to resist them, especially when their peers may be watching. They may become more private about their changing bodies and about their changing feelings as well.

Parents who are accustomed to acting as decisionmakers for their young children are often reluctant to let go and let teenagers make their own decisions and mistakes. Sex is a legitimate focus for this reluctance, for many teenagers use sex as a vehicle for trying out their freedom and their developing identity. Fearing the "worst," parents tend to take a lecturing approach if they bring up the subject of sex, rather than sensitively discussing pros and cons of specific sexual issues with their teenagers.

When parents have shown respect for their offspring all along as responsible, thoughtful humans (rather than treating them as irrational, stupid, and immoral), teenagers are more likely to weigh carefully the pros and cons of sexual involvement themselves than to act out of a desire to rebel. But even then, they probably won't want to say much to their parents about what's on their minds, for they regard their decisions and their behaviors as private (Yalom, Estler, and Brewster 1982).

Recognizing Each Other's Sexuality

Talk about sex is further limited by the fact that parents and their offspring often have a hard time seeing each other as sexual. In one study parents persistently referred to eighteen-year-olds who were having intercourse as "children." They didn't see intercourse as an experience that was appropriate or meaningful for their progeny, even at this age. And children have difficulty thinking of their parents as sexual persons. Even after experiencing intercourse themselves, young people still have difficulty perceiving their parents' sexuality. The blindness is mutual. Dad proudly says of his twenty-two-year-old daughter, "She's my baby," while children see their parents in the familial roles of "Mom" and "Pop."

One reason for this mutual blindness may be that adults see only a limited range of behaviors as sexual. For instance, when some mothers and fathers in the Cleveland study saw their infants touching their genitals, it didn't bother them particularly. Since the children's actions didn't look like what adults do, the parents apparently didn't associate them with sexuality. It was easy for them to see genital touching as "natural" and acceptable. But once self-touching became more systematic, producing recognizably sexual results, parents became more uptight about any self-touching by children, defining as sexual what may only have been random or exploratory groping.

Parents are often several years behind in their assumptions about what their children are doing sexually. Often sexual decisions have been made and acted on long before parents offer any help. Parents adjust only gradually—if at all—to the idea that their kids are having sex. As the "kids" get into their twenties and thirties, some parents open up in talking about different sexual lifestyles, once they have recognized that their now-grown "children" are no longer innocent babes and that they are sexually active and perhaps living with someone without marriage.

In some homes the tension involved with putting two active sexual partners in separate bedrooms to prevent sexmaking in the once-sacred parental home is being replaced with a more realistic and accepting approach. If two people are having sex without or with cohabitation, some parents are saying "make yourselves at home" rather than pointing their fingers toward separate bedrooms when the time comes to retire for the evening. This approach seems a healthy one—to at least give adult-aged offspring the choice of sleeping together or apart in the parents' home. In Sweden it is customary for parents to serve teenaged as well as adult offspring breakfast in bed with their sex partners long before they are either cohabitating or married. Since United States customs have tended to follow Swedish customs closely, perhaps parents in this country will not continue to be so rigid about visitation procedures.

Many parents may intentionally or unintentionally mislead their children by what they say—or don't say—about sex. Two parents who explained intercourse as the way babies are made and omitted any mention of pleasure were surprised when one of their three children drew the logical conclusion: "Oh, then you must have done it three times, right?" Given such a chance to draw their children a more accurate picture of their own sex life, few parents do. As a result of this parental reticence, most teenagers cannot imagine their parents eagerly having sex.

Many parents are even reluctant to be affectionate in front of their children. Aside from occasional public kisses and hugs, they avoid letting their children know that touching is part of their relationship. They save it for the bedroom, behind closed doors. Psychologist Barry Singer (1980) has found that about half of the students in his sex classes have never seen their parents kissing, touching, or embracing. As the researchers in the Cleveland study point out, this absence leads children to believe that touching is only sexual: "Deprived of an important opportunity to view open affection as a means of expressing themselves, [they] may grow up to feel the only way to be held, touched, or comforted is to engage in erotic behavior" (Roberts, Kline, and Gagnon 1978, p. 32).

Parents sometimes fear that if they become too close—emotionally or physically—to their children, they are jeopardizing their children's chance of developing intimate relationships with others their own age. Sometimes this is felt as a fear of making their sons and daughters homosexual.

A further problem parents and children have in openly recognizing each other's sexuality is the fear of incest. Some parents and children *are* aware of the attractions of each other's bodies, especially during the teenage years. But since sexual activity between closely related people—other than husband and wife—is heavily tabooed in our culture, recognition of each other's sexual charms may be a source of tension. Many try to steer away from potential trouble by mutual avoidance of sex talk and sexually suggestive behaviors. Some find it necessary to set new limits on family nudity and touching. One mother describes such a change initiated by her ten-year-old son:

Spontaneity is fun, but will parents feel comfortable with it? The generations often keep their sex lives in private worlds, for mutual comfort.

When Neal came home from overnight camp last summer, he no longer wanted to share a room with his younger sister, and he was much more private about his body. . . . It wasn't like he came out and said, "Now I want the door closed and to be private," but there was a feeling that I picked up that I really respected. And I had to change my behavior—instead of walking around naked I had to really be careful to put something on, because for the first time I felt like I was being provocative to him in a way that was not responsible as a parent.   [Quoted in Bell 1978, pp. 85-86]*

Although it seems okay—and sometimes even important—for parents to let children know they are sexually attractive, many find this easiest to handle when their own sexual needs are actively satisfied through other adults. Then they can respect the space between their children's sex lives and theirs and feel comfortable with touching, talking, and perhaps even sex-related joking.

INCEST

Although some degree of sexual attraction between family members is common, acting on that attraction is relatively uncommon. *Incest* is the term for sexual relationships among people who are primary relatives—other than husband and wife. There are many possible combinations among primary relatives: parent/child, grandparent/grandchild, and sibling/sibling. Some scholars also define incest to include a wider tier of "immediate" family members such as step-relatives, in-laws, uncles, aunts, nieces, nephews, and cousins. Such a broad definition is troublesome, according to sociologist Edward Sagarin (1977b). For example, if a woman enjoys sex with her brother-in-law, should that be called incest? Sagarin suggests that such a relationship is extramarital and not incestuous. Sagarin would rather define "true" incest as sexual relations between blood relatives, not "contractual" relatives such as step-

* From Ruth Davidson Bell, "The Middle Years," in Boston Women's Health Book Collective, *Ourselves and Our Children: A Book by and for Parents* (New York: Random House, Inc., 1978).© 1978 by Random House, Inc. Reprinted by permission.

relations or in-laws. With much disagreement on the exact definition of incest, it is difficult to say how frequently incest occurs. Meiselman (1979) contends that 1 to 2 million cases of incest are detected in the United States each year.

The social meanings placed on incestuous behavior are crucial to understanding why some cultures severely punish and others ignore incest. Incest is not a universal taboo. For example, Margaret Mead observed that the mountain Arapesh had no incest anxiety about brother-sister sexual relations. Instead, sibling sexual relationships were seen as somewhat foolish: better to give the sister to another man in order to gain another in-law who can be trusted and loved (Fox 1968). By contrast, United States laws punish incestuous behavior. In one case the courts invalidated a marriage between a twenty-four-year-old Massachusetts woman and her brother, who both grew up in separate adoptive families (Florescu 1979).

Sex between people who are related only by marriage may be viewed more flexibly than sex between blood relatives. Sexual relationships between a woman and her husband's brother become socially acceptable—and even required in some cultures—when her husband dies. This tradition was institutionalized in ancient Hebrew law as the "levirate." Sagarin (1977b) points out that the biological reason for prohibiting incest—that is, the enhanced possibility of birth defects when genetically similar people produce children—has no bearing on sex between in-laws and step-relatives, for they are of different genetic stock.

Another factor in how incest is perceived is the ages of the people involved. If one is a powerless young child who is coerced into sex by an adult (for example, a father or much older brother, who is supposed to be the child's protector), the relationship is usually seen as a deplorable form of child abuse. For instance, of the 200 women in one study who'd experienced incest as children—often repeatedly from age three to six on—none said they had enjoyed the experience. Feelings of helplessness and guilt were common, and two had threatened to kill their attackers if they were touched again (Armstrong 1978). A study of father-son incestuous relationships revealed that the sons, too, felt tremendous hostility toward their fathers. Some wanted to kill their fathers.

Parents Find Teenagers a Turn-On

Many mothers and fathers find themselves sexually aroused by their developing teenagers. Some worry about this reaction; others consider it natural but a reason for setting limits. A few descriptions:

Now and then I'll feel a surge of attraction to one of my teenage kids. I certainly wouldn't act on it, but I experience it as a nice, lively responding to their emerging sexuality.

Sometimes I find myself close to flirting with Sam's eighteen-year-old friends. They are so attractive and sure of themselves that they are often hard to resist.

My daughter has become sexually attractive. Until recently she kept sitting on my lap, or walking around almost naked, or cuddling up to me a lot. I found myself very aroused. I restrained myself, but often got angry with myself for responding to her this way. Now I've told her that she has to wear clothes around the house, out of respect for my limits.

When I found myself getting somewhat turned on by seeing my sixteen-year-old naked in the hallway, I took that as a signal that it was time to widen the space between us so that he could do his growing.
[Quoted in Speizer 1978, p. 99]*

Once in a while I look at my big six-foot fifteen-year-old son, nude—and think—wouldn't it be nice if part of "parenting" was to teach one's children (male or female) loving sex techniques; instead I bought him The Joy of Sex, *which he seems to peruse occasionally, as well as* Playboy, *I regret to say. I also used to have sexually stimulated feelings when nursing him and I liked it.* [Quoted in Hite 1976, p. 393]

I think perhaps I have had sexual feelings toward family members but they are hard to acknowledge usually. Like last night when my daughter was cutting my hair and her breasts and body were close to mine—it was a nice feeling—and after she was through with the haircut she bent down and kissed me—this doesn't mean we want to jump into bed together—but I think it is sexual and good and not to be feared. [Quoted in Hite 1976, p. 393]

* From Jeanne Jacobs Speizer, "The Teenage Years," in Boston Women's Health Book Collective, *Ourselves and Our Children: A Book by and for Parents* (New York: Random House, Inc., 1978). © 1978 by Random House, Inc. Reprinted by permission.

Others wanted to kill themselves and had histories of self-destructive behavior—from self-mutilation to reckless drug combinations and repeated "accidents" (Dixon, Arnold, and Calestro 1978).

Educator Valerie Pinhas (1980) believes that many young women with an alcohol problem have experienced incest (although that is certainly not a predisposing factor in the development of alcoholism). Young women, coerced in early adolescence, begin using alcohol to help relieve overwhelming guilt and anger. Pinhas suggests that in adapting, these females tend to use drinking to allow themselves to participate in sex.

Family Patterns

Despite the negative impact of many incestuous relationships, they do not usually begin with physical force or threats (Meiselman 1979). These may be brought into play later to keep children from telling anyone, but they are seldom used at first to force physical intimacies. In some cases children themselves have behaved seductively—or at least it seems this way to the adults they turn on. When an eight-year-old girl nestles into her father's lap, she may be looking only for affection. But he may interpret her behavior as seduction if he applies adult meanings to it.

Incest occurs in all sectors of society. But family constellations leading to incestuous interactions tend to follow some similar patterns. Incest has been described as a pathological way of holding things together in the face of numerous familial weaknesses (Guthiel and Avery 1977). It is important to note, however, that this observation is based on studies of those who seek psychiatric help or are legally prosecuted.

According to psychiatrists' impressions of father-daughter incest, the father is rarely psychotic. But the fact that he was often deserted or mistreated during childhood by his own father may have influenced his perception of a father's role, and he often acts the tyrant by trying to dominate and intimidate his wife and children. This tendency can be aggravated by heavy drinking, which weakens his already poor impulse control and limited conception of boundaries. That is, he tends to lack the notion that some separation between people is appropriate. His assertion of power may mask a feeling of inadequacy. He may actually want to be dependent on someone, a wish that is often directed toward his daughter as sexual desire.

The mother in this unusual family pattern is typically too depressed and passive to protect her children from their domineering father's abuse. Because she was unloved by her own mother, she is confused about her sexual identity. As a result, she tends to shirk her roles both as mother and as sexual partner to her husband. By withdrawing from them, she tacitly allows her daughter to act as her substitute.

Left with heavy household responsibilities, the daughter may seem older than her years. But she is usually confused, too. She may turn to her father for the closeness her mother has not provided. The daughter is usually an obedient, docile child who doesn't dare to oppose her father's sexual requests. But in some cases she may play the part of seductress, arousing and tempting her father (Meiselman 1979; Guthiel and Avery 1977).

Studies of father-son incest show a similar pattern. The father is typically violent and abusive, with poor judgment and impulse control. The mother usually seems overwhelmed, unwilling to satisfy her husband's sexual needs, and unable to protect her children even when she knows what's going on. For instance, one woman suspected that her husband was sexually involved with their son from the time he was ten. Although she often woke up at night and heard her husband in the son's room, she accepted his explanation that he was "just checking Richard." Six years later when her son openly told her what had been going on nightly, she filed charges with the police but then immediately withdrew them (Dixon, Arnold, and Calestro 1978).

These descriptions of typical incestuous family patterns represent a composite of cases seen by psychiatrists. In reality there are many different patterns of incestuous relationships. Not all are exploitative and abusive. Even though our society's laws make no distinction between family sexual relationships that are mutually pleasing and those that are abusive, in many cases sex among relatives is mutually acceptable.

Three studies drawing on samples not obtained from clinical or court cases report a surprisingly high rate of incest as well as a rather positive evaluation of the relationship by the respondents. Finkelhor (1980) reported that a third of his New England college sample said their sibling incest experiences were positive. Symonds, Mendoza, and Harrell (1981) indicated 80 percent of 109 California participants had "positive feelings toward the relative(s) with whom incest had occurred." Finally, Nelson (1981) solicited 100 respondents from all sections of the country, with 40 percent from the San Francisco area. In this study 25 percent of the women and 78 percent of the men evaluated their incest relationships positively. These studies call attention to the emergence of alternative data and understandings of the nature of family incest and its consequences.

The Family-Touching Controversy

Increasing awareness of the realities of incest poses the potential for a major battle between people who think there should be more sex talk and touching within the family and those who believe there's already too much. The former include groups like La Leche League, which encourages nonsexual touching, breast feeding, backrubs, and children's sleeping together or with their parents. They believe that these physical expressions of loving enhance family closeness and surround children with a feeling of warmth, security, and belonging (Thevenin 1976).

Also on the more-touching side are some scholars who'd like to increase open *sexual* expressions within the family. They claim that sexual problems, guilt, inhibitions, and inability to express affection result largely from childhood sexual repression. They'd like to do away with taboos against sex talk, nudity, and perhaps even mild forms of family sex play and children's witnessing of parents' sexmaking. Some people of this persuasion even believe that incest may be okay under certain circumstances (Pomeroy 1978).

Strongly opposed to such thinking are those who see incest as child abuse (DeMott 1980). They fear that sexual liberalization within the family may encourage parents with weak impulse control to exploit their children sexually. Such social critics would rather protect children from their elders' sexuality than expose them to more of it (Goldsen 1978). Family violence researcher David Finkelhor (1978) points out that the family-touching controversy involves four crucial questions that should be carefully researched:

First, does sexual abuse result from too much or too little repression? Freud believed that the family was riddled with incestuous impulses that had to be severely curbed. In his view taboos on incest and sex with children were necessary to prevent traumatic abuses. According to this theory, incest would be most likely to occur in families with weak social controls over impulsive behaviors. By contrast, those who want freer sexuality would expect that incest would be most common in highly repressive environments. They feel that repression shapes warped, hostile forms of sexual expression by leaving people so sexually deprived that they will exploit others to meet their needs.

Second, are there any social benefits in allowing children to express sexuality? Those who'd like sexuality to be freer assume that the potential risks—of unplanned pregnancy, emotional disturbance, and the like—would be outweighed by advantages such as fewer sexual problems, less violence, and less sexual exploitation. For instance, rapists often come from extremely repressive homes and are abysmally ignorant about sex (Delin 1978). Anthropologists have found that there is less violence in sexually open societies (Prescott 1975). Greater openness about sex doesn't necessarily mean there will be more of it. Some parents who've been extremely open with their kids about sex have found that with the "forbidden fruit" mystery removed from sexuality, children take their time in getting involved and tend to make careful decisions.

Third, what is the long-range impact on a child of sex with an adult? Those for freer sex would argue that any negative consequences are the result of society's reactions after the fact rather than of trauma implicit in the experience. Those worried about sexual abuse would disagree. They believe that the great differences in size, power, and sexual sophistication between adults and children make incest innately traumatic.

Finally, would freer sexual expression hold the same benefits for females as for males? Among people who are worried about sexual abuse, women are especially likely to see the cry for greater sexual freedom as another symptom of male domination. They see pressures for more and better sex with more people as coming mostly from men.

There's a different way of interpreting sexual freedom, though—that is, as freedom to openly

Touching and nudity within the family can either enhance or inhibit children's sexual comfort, depending on the circumstances.

Women's Attitudes toward Family Touching: Healthy or Unhealthy?

The mother who at night takes her child into her arms and comforts him, and then peacefully falls asleep with her little one touching her body, knows and feels deep down that she is not only giving but that she is also receiving something that no words can describe. It is a feeling of knowing that she is being part of the universe, a link in the chain of life. She is forming a momentary oneness with her child which, as the need diminishes, will flower into a twosome again, much like the flowering at birth. A glow fills her body, and this glow radiates to her other children and to her husband. But this feeling of total fulfillment can only exist when there is no feeling of frustration or restraint. . . . Those who sleep together touch as if to say, "You are all right. I'm all right. We remain in touch with one another." It is such a wonderful feeling to wake up in the middle of the night, and to kiss a loved one while he or she is sleeping. [Thevenin 1976, pp.48-50]*

I sometimes felt that my son derived sexual pleasure from my touching him (say, while giving him a bath). He was about four or five then. It was very confusing and embarrassing to me; I also felt guilty—clearly if I'd been a better mother this wouldn't have happened. I knew that guilt and evasiveness made everything worse, but I simply didn't know how to deal with it. [Quoted in Hite 1976, p. 393]

I touch my children a lot hoping they will grow up more attuned to it. I was raised in the "cry it out" school of child psychology by a very well-meaning but frustrated mother. Now she touches my kids a lot too. [Quoted in Hite 1976, p. 393]

My mother and I used to hug a lot when I was young. But as I got older she sort of weaned me away from that, fearing I might turn into a lesbian. As a result, it's just in the last couple of years I am beginning to feel comfortable in kissing or touching relations. [Quoted in Hite 1976, p. 393]

Sometimes I feel turned on embracing my little sister, who I'm fond of. Yet I cannot imagine actually "doing anything" with her—the thought horrifies me. I've heard that one often feels warmth and contentment in a seemingly sexual way because emotion does register in the genital area, as well as actual excitement. But I don't embrace her as often as I would like, since I am afraid it might look funny. [Quoted in Hite 1976, pp. 393]

* From Tine Thevenin, *The Family Bed* (Minneapolis: Tine Thevenin, 1976). Reprinted by permission of Tine Thevenin, P.O. Box 16004, Minneapolis, MN 55416.

explore and discuss options. Adults who try to enclose children in their own value systems and to hamper their gathering of sexual information deny the young their right to consider options thoughtfully for themselves. Only when they are given space and information for sexual decision making will they be able to develop a sense of personal responsibility and control in their own sex lives.

Summary

Children are innately sexual, yet little overt recognition is given to this fact by adults. Parents' silence about or punishment of eroticism teaches children that sexual interest should be hidden. Children may learn where babies come from if they ask, and girls are usually given information about menstruation, but most parents say nothing about the pleasures and responsibilities of sex. Information—and often misinformation—from peers and siblings helps to fill the void. So do the mass media, and, to a certain extent, sex education programs. Beyond these sources partners often explore on their own, learning as they go along.

Within the family sex talk tends to be inhibited by parents' thoughts of what's "best" for their children's future, the mutual desire to maintain a calm home atmosphere, children's need to assert their independence, and mutual blindness about each other's sexuality. On the other hand, some interaction within families may be explicitly sexual, such as incest. According to clinical accounts, these experiences are very difficult for children and arise from pathological family constellations. By contrast, some of the people who have not sought therapy for incest-related problems have had more positive responses to experiences of incest. Issues raised by the new attention to incest illustrate disagreement over whether there should be more or less touching within the family.

10

Adult Sexual Lifestyles

My sexual relations with Brett, as compared with my husband, . . . I am open, I can relax. . . . He's really into me, physically, and he's got my tempo down and what pleases me. I can tell him to stop, continue, do something new, just in response to my nonverbal clues. It amazes me how one man can be so sensitive and into a woman's being, as a woman, as compared to another man who is so completely ignorant and is very uninspired.

A thirty-one-year-old wife, quoted in Atwater 1982, pp. 111-12

I'm single and I love it. I enjoy meeting a variety of men and I absolutely am turned on by some of them. I feel great about my sex appeal—I guess that explains why I don't hesitate to initiate sex with a man who I'm really attracted to. It doesn't really matter if the man is married or not—but I prefer men who don't dwell on other women when they are with me. Sex is fun, and I enjoy sex with some male friends in addition to the new lovers I come across from time to time.

A twenty-five-year-old writer; from the author's files

I'm a happily married man, and both my wife and I really dig sex with each other. We're monogamous, but we don't expect or advise others to be as we are—it's an individual choice. We are so crazy about each other that we don't have the energy or time to pursue others.

A thirty-five-year-old married man; from the author's files

I live with Don, but I doubt we'll ever get married. For us living together is just fine—we don't treat each other as property or anything. Our sex is as fantastic as any either of us has ever had. We have an open relationship—which means once in a while Don and I enjoy sex with others we've known for years, or with someone new when we're traveling alone, but most of the time it's just sex with each other.

A twenty-two-year-old computer analyst; from the author's files

Brenda and I just broke up. Our sex life was tremendous, but we didn't share enough common values and other things that make a relationship interesting enough to last. We both agreed that we needed to look elsewhere, but it is hard for us. We're still friends, and in time I suppose we'll have sex again. But for now we aren't seeing each other at all. Neither of us has found anyone else yet, but I'm sure we both will. We were living together, but there just wasn't enough spark between us.

A twenty-three-year-old graduate student; from the author's files

Is there Life After Youth? Once we no longer live with our family, we must find ways to shape our lives to satisfy our desires for intimacy and freedom. The quest for intimacy—sexual, emotional, and intellectual—is a lifetime search. We yearn for touching, cuddling, eye contact, and other expressions of warmth. At the same time, we want to be autonomous adults, able to freely choose behaviors that make our life more fun, meaningful, and conducive to personal growth. We also need to make money to support ourselves and, perhaps, to build a sense of accomplishment. These needs are often at odds. Satisfying them all involves a lifetime juggling act—a continual sensitivity to our feelings and to those of our intimate partners, as well as repeated efforts to shape satisfying relationships and balance them against time and energies given to work.

The past assumption was that sexually exclusive marriage was the *only* way to meet all our needs. Many followed the traditional path of dating, courtship, and monogamous marriage and rarely considered getting off the beaten track. But now, living alone and having sexual friends or living with a sexual partner without marriage are attractive options for some. Some people no longer plan their sexual lives around a step-by-step progression toward marriage and parenthood. In place of the linear developmental model that assumed that we would marry, have children, and retire together to rocking chairs, some change their living arrangements, lifestyles, and intimate relationships from time to time.

The major lifestyle options are singlehood, cohabitation, and marriage. Our sexual choices among these options are complicated by other considerations, such as financial security, social status, and desire for "legitimate" children. There is some flexibility within each category, though, and each can be sexually open or sexually exclusive.

In this chapter we'll look at these choices, and we'll examine issues surrounding uncoupling. Although other people's experiences in these areas are well worth considering, it remains for each of us to deal thoughtfully with our own reactions to the joys and sorrows of the choices we make and remake.

SINGLEHOOD

Today all but the most blinkered descendants of the fabulous Mrs. Grundy would concede that for those who desire it, sexual experience in all its variations is as much the prerogative of single women and men as of their peers within the more conventional pale of matrimony. (Adams 1976, p. 148)

Singlehood is a varied experience. The realities of the years from 18 to 21 are quite different for those who go to college and those who enter the work world; singlehood at 45 is quite different from singlehood at 20.

In the past single people were ridiculed, pitied, and talked about. Singlehood was considered undesirable and certainly less appealing than marriage. Even today some singles are lonely and unhappy; few are joyous all the time. But are married or cohabiting people always in a state of bliss? Singles, much like their married and cohabiting counterparts, are likely to vary in their overall satisfaction with themselves, their careers, and their intimate relationships.

Who Is Single?

Anyone not legally married is single. A single person may be never-married, divorced, a single parent, separated, or widowed. We can be single at any age. Within the broad singlehood category there is a continuum of sexual lifestyles that people either select or drift into. A single may be sexually celibate either by choice or out of lack of opportunity to find suitable partners. Some singles have a sexually exclusive relationship with one partner. Others have sex with several or many partners, not viewing marriage as a necessary rite of passage to legitimize sexual pleasures or to provide emotional intimacies. And some singles combine sexual freedom with emotional commitment to one partner with whom they have a mutual agreement that sex with others is okay.

The continuum from being single to being bonded also includes a range of living arrangements and personal definitions of "singlehood." Some people maintain separate residences but sleep together part of the time; some have long-distance relationships. It appears that many are part-time singles and part-time cohabitants or marrieds. If singlehood is seen as a state of mind—rather than a legal status—what counts is how we live and what our lifestyle means to us.

The Trend toward Singlehood

There are no data on how many of us are socially "single." But even in strictly legal terms there is a clear trend toward spending more adult years as a single. According to census statistics, there is a definite movement away from early marriage. Whereas in the past people married at age 20 or 21, by 1981 the median age for first marriage rose to 24.8 for men and 22.3 for women. If the never-married, divorced, and widowed are combined, the number of persons living alone has risen by 75 percent since 1970 (*Current Population Reports*, June 1982).

More people are living alone because the age at marriage is rising, because divorce and separation continue to rise, and because more senior citizens maintain their own homes. The divorce ratio—the number of persons currently divorced per 1000 persons married and living with their spouses—has increased from 47 in 1970 to 109 in 1981 (*Current Population Reports*, September 1982). Our best estimate is that 50 percent or more of first marriages contracted in the mid-1980s will end in divorce. Divorces will probably continue to occur sooner—many within the first seven years of marriage—and more persons will probably wait longer to remarry if they remarry at all, with men remarrying more quickly than women. However, the slow economy also makes divorce more difficult to obtain. As the economy improves, the divorce rate will probably increase. This does not mean that marriage is not still popular. In fact, there has been a 10.2 percent increase in married-couple families from 1970 to 1981 (*Current Population Reports*, October 1981). Our best estimate is that about 90 percent of us will probably marry.

Singles Sex

Most of the research on sex among singles has been confined to "premarital sex"—usually with college student samples. But when we discuss singles sex we're talking about sex that is not necessarily a step toward marriage—and most singles sex probably isn't going to end up in marriage *to that person.*

The limited studies in recent years are magazine surveys—mainly by *Playboy* and *Cosmopolitan.* The average respondent to a mailed questionnaire published in either magazine is likely to be about twenty-five years old if single and in the late twenties to early thirties if married. Since maturing people tend to be sexually more experienced and more liberal for a variety of reasons, it is not surprising that these surveys reveal a greater acceptance of "light sex" with numerous partners.

The *Playboy* study (Petersen at al. 1983b) of 100,000 readers revealed that single people en-

Juggling Lovers

Many magazine articles are devoted to giving singles guidelines for juggling more than one lover. An article by Stephanie Egan in *Cosmopolitan* suggests that having several lovers can be healthy if it is based on positive rather than negative motives. Egan's advice: "Don't lie to your men"; "Avoid confusing discretion with dishonesty"; "Allow your men the same privacy you want for yourself"; "Defuse the issue of prime time" (so no one feels second-best); "Don't hurt or humiliate one man because of your interest in another"; "Shun comparisons"; "Never use multiple dating to manipulate or create jealousy"; "Handle your own jealousy"; "Take responsibility for having more than one sexual partner" (for example, take care about sexually transmissable diseases); and "Give your full attention to the man you're with" (Egan 1982, pp. 116-20).

gaged in as much sex as married people. Single men were somewhat *less* sexually satisfied than single women, with 33 percent of the men and 43 percent of the women saying the frequency of intercourse was satisfactory. Single women had more intercourse per week (31 percent reported four or more times per week) than single men (20 percent reported four or more times per week). These statistics may reflect the uniqueness of the women responding to a men's sex magazine survey.

Not too surprisingly, singles who had regular sex partners, whether one or more, had more intercourse—about a third of both men and women had intercourse twice a week or more if they were "dating around," while from two-thirds to three-fourths reported this frequency when they were either dating one more than others, or "going steady, engaged" (Petersen et al. 1983b).

About two-thirds of singles had intercourse two or more times per night, while only a quarter of married people reported this frequency. Petersen speculates that a variety of partners encourages having more sex with less familiar partners. As Petersen (1983b, p. 83) states: "Singles and divorced people . . . are inclined to fuck their brains out." Some singles experience a kind of "sexual burnout" from jumping from bed to bed.

Meeting Partners

Many singles want to meet others with similar interests. This wish need not be limited to sexual activities, but sexual desires are often included. Finding ways to meet other singles has long been a problem. One answer is dating services, some of which are now computerized. Some of these information services include personal advertisements. Journalist Elizabeth Ferrarini placed an ad boldly stating:

I'm looking for a man who'll be G.I.B., pay for dinner, and treat me like precious porcelain. He should also have a college degree, solid profession, good looks, weight in proportion to height, and make at least $50,000 a year. [Ferrarini 1982, p. 148].

What kind of men did Ferrarini find via computer? She reported a series of not-so-desirable men, followed by a series of very desirable men that she continued to see. She developed some genuine friendships through her computer—she considers her computer pals to be part of her relationship network. She concludes that she can "plug into an endless supply of available males . . ." (Ferrarini 1982, p. 152).

Some meet through customized dating services, at matchmaking parties, or on singles cruises. Other common meeting places include recreational and special-interest activities (such as tennis, mountain-climbing, and river-rafting clubs), singles bars, and the workplace. Whether such relationships become sexual or not, sharing common interests is one way to become close to others. Singles may meet others through friends already engaged in an activity or social group, or they may take the initiative to meet others on their own.

Sex and the Singles Bar.   Some frequent singles bars largely to meet potential partners or current sexual friends. Others enjoy socializing and relaxing. Some just like to watch the flirtations. Overcoming alienation, boredom, and loneliness and establishing self-validation are additional motivations (Allon and Fishel 1979).

Sociologists Allon and Fishel (1979) found the atmosphere was strained in the eight bars they observed. People sought companionship, but often felt they had to act out uncomfortable roles and games. Their analysis:

How long does it take for vibes to connect at a singles scene?

The main cause of . . . pressure seemed to be that many people in the singles bars were trying so hard to meet people. . . . They seemed to smile all the time so that no one would think they were bored or disinterested. They nervously lit cigarette after cigarette, and clasped their drinks for dear life. [Allon and Fishel 1979, p. 155]*

Singles bars are sometimes "meat markets," where patrons seem free to touch strangers in intimate ways. Some people enjoy this intimacy as illustrated by the following comments:

[Woman]: Forget privacy—at the bar, your body is not your own. You don't know who is going to touch you where next. Every touch is a surprise—not really expected. It is fun and scary to see who will handle you next—there is always someone new to turn you on in a body part that you never knew was so sensual. [Man]: To be in touch with others, you really have to feel their skin. If you start on the outside, then you can feel on the inside, both in terms of affection and sexual feelings. I go to a bar and touch a girl's shoulder, and I feel her tingle and quiver and that is great. We are nice to each other at the bar because we hug and kiss each other a lot, and usually we are sincere about making each other feel good by touching—it isn't phoney. [Allon and Fishel 1979, pp. 173, 175]*

*From "Single Bars," by N. Allon and D. Fishel. In N. Allon (Ed.), *Urban Life Styles*. Copyright © 1979 by William C Brown Company. Reprinted by permission.

Some people dislike being touched so freely by strangers. Since the man is often the most assertive, women are—not too surprisingly—uneasy or offended by the power moves and controlling gestures of some male bar participants. A more assertive woman is emerging, and this shift could affect interaction in public settings. No matter who does the rubbing and fondling, "a singles bar is like a massage parlor where everyone stands up" (Allon and Fishel 1979, p. 173).

Sexual Relationships at Work. Perhaps a more important arena than bars for the development of singles' sexual relationships is the work place. Many of us choose jobs with an eye toward their potential for meeting people. As a corporation personnel manager stated, "Often when I ask a young woman why she left her last job, she'll say, 'I didn't meet anyone' or 'I didn't like any of the men there'" (Adams 1979, p. 294).

Although many who become sexually involved with workmates are married or cohabiting, the never-married, separated, divorced, and widowed especially benefit from a sociable work setting. Sharing with others at work allows them to experience intimate relationships they might find difficult to develop elsewhere. At work friendships can be developed without the uncomfortable pressures and uncertainties of the heavy-dating scene. Work may be a sort of testing ground to explore and test how one fits with others. Everyday contact also makes it possible to know others without social facades. We get a more realistic idea of others' qualities when we see them in "natural" settings, both relaxed and under pressure.

An exchange of smiles on the elevator can lead to a coffee-break, lunchtime, or drink-after-work friendship; late-night or overtime weekend work together may lead to barriers-down, honest relating. Under these circumstances we learn about others in terms of their work role, not their family background or where they live. People find that their shared understanding of a specialized job world gives them plenty to talk about—and even, as in the case of computer technologies, a language all their own.

Work-place friendships may have sexual overtones, sometimes leading to sexual relationships. The results may enhance work performance as well as intimacy. For instance, people's personalities often change dramatically when they are involved in work-place romance. People who were autocratic, severe, and production-only-oriented may soften when they again become lovers in their personal lives. They mellow and begin to see other co-workers and employees as more human, competent, and worthwhile. The glow from the relationship spreads into their other activities and can soften existing colleague tensions (Quinn 1977).

Light sex can make a boring job more tolerable. Instead of being vitally involved in work, many people find their work dull. When jobs are routine, workers often try to enliven the place. Sexual banter and gestures help many a crew pass the time of day. At a certain Oklahoma factory, workers bring their campers for lunchtime sex breaks (Boles 1980). And at fast-food restaurants, employees sometimes enjoy quick sex in supply closets, on the roof—even inside walk-in freezers (Leblanc 1980).

Sex at work is not a surprising phenomenon. Work is where we spend a large part of our time. As Horn and Horn explain: "Given the strong human need for contact and affection, it is not surprising that sex rears its lovely head so regularly in the office" (1982, p. 24). But despite their potential for intimacy and fun, sexual relationships at work can cause problems. Public administration professor Robert Quinn (1977) studied the impact of romance in organizations by asking 211 persons at

Sex and the Coed Dorm

During the college years students on many campuses have the opportunity to try a unique living arrangement: the coed dorm. When some colleges first experimented with coed dorms in the late 1960s, many people assumed that these facilities would be hotbeds of casual sex. A decade later, studies of the now-common coed dorm option indicate that this assumption is not necessarily true.

According to a national survey of college students by *McCall's* magazine (Gittelson 1979), both males and females typically rate coed dorms as "wonderful!" But what they like is not so much the increased availability of sex as the opportunities for familylike friendships. Nearly 85 percent of students in coed dorms did not date anyone within their dorm; almost 54 percent had sex "never" or "less than once a month." On some campuses this avoidance pattern is referred to as "the incest taboo." But according to 80 percent of those in the *McCall's* study, coed dorms make it easier to form friendships that are not sexual.

Students contacted at one large eastern university tend to agree with these findings. For instance, one woman student reported that when she lived in an all-female dorm, "males were thought of usually in some sort of sexual-boyfriend way, whereas most males in a coed dorm were friends. The floor as a whole responded to each other in a friendly outgoing manner" (Demos 1979).

the Albany and LaGuardia airports to complete a questionnaire about a specific romance at work that they knew about. A third of the responses were characterized by serious negative features such as complaints, hostilities, and distorted communications.

If the persons involved have a supposedly exclusive relationship with someone else off the job, discovery of the intimate work relationship may damage that central bond. Maintaining secrecy is often a problem when married people get involved with someone at work without the knowledge and consent of their spouses. Work associates usually know—or assume—that people are sexually involved when they disappear together for long lunches, office visits, or joint business trips.

Even when both partners are single and unattached, sexual relationships at work can hamper their job performance. Their interest in each other may distract them from their work. It is common to lengthen luncheons, to miss meetings, to skip deadlines, to not focus on details of work. These actions draw co-workers into "covering" and doing the lovers' work. In addition bosses may give assignments to their lovers that are not within their abilities or may share inside information about other workers, sometimes threatening their job security. Resentment soon builds against such lovers' exploiting the work scene (Quinn 1977; Kent 1975).

Another sensitive situation occurs when the office romance ends. The couple may still work near each other, and friction may develop when tensions replace prior loving. The rejected person may hurt and then hang on, sulk, and display jealousy. Sharing the same work space may become difficult, embarrassing, and uncomfortable. A common solution is to fire or force out the less effective person—usually the one with the lower-ranking job, with the ex-lover sometimes doing the firing.

Although most businesses now have no official policy on sexual relationships between workers and don't try to punish or prevent them, many workers develop personal standards for work-related friendships. From their own experiences and from seeing the complications others have gotten themselves into, some people learn that sex with co-workers might interrupt either work or their personal lives. As a result they may decide to be selective about intimacies and perhaps avoid them. Many restrict sexual response to playful teasing; others feel that sexual relationships are okay only under conditions they can handle. Some possibilities: only with single people or marrieds whose mates know about and accept outside relationships, only with people with whom they don't work closely, only if it can be kept secret, only on business trips, only with people of equal job status, only if there is no heavy emotional involvement, or only if the attraction is so strong that the anticipated pleasures override any potential negative consequences.

COHABITATION

Many adults also have long-term relationships outside the work world, although they may not be married to these partners. Art Buchwald describes one such arrangement:

Being a married man, I always believed that single people living together had the best of both worlds. Whenever I met someone in a leisure suit with a gold chain around his neck and a beautiful blonde on his arm, whom he introduced to everyone as his "roommate," I must admit I was wild with envy. . . .

His "roomie" was a sweet thing named Saralee, and they shared a lovely apartment overlooking the Potomac. They had a pet dog named "Pothead," and the thing they both used to brag to me about was that they had all the benefits of being married without any of the hassles. That's the part I envied the most. [Buchwald, 1978].

Marrieds may fantasize about the freedom of singlehood, and singles may be attracted to the security of marriage. Others try a compromise: living together and sharing sex on a marriagelike basis. Despite the increasing visibility of this arrangement, we still don't have a good label to describe a live-in partner. Is a fellow cohabitant a roommate? Sexual friend? Lover? Live-with? Parents (if they know about it) may have plenty of negative ways to label their college-aged sons' and daughters' living with someone. But not all cohabitants are college students. Many are adults. How they shape this arrangement varies widely.

What Is Cohabitation?

Cohabitation is such a grab-bag term that it is difficult to pin down its meaning. We use the word to describe people who live together in a sexual relationship without being married. Some researchers include nonsexual roommates and those who spend only a few nights a week together. But having roommates is not the same as having a live-in sexual relationship. Part-time, experimental cohabitation—during college, for instance—is much different from sharing economic arrangements and living full time in a marriagelike relationship. Cohabitation is a living arrangement shared by young and old and by same-sex as well as other-sex couples, but most of the research has focused on heterosexual cohabitation among college students.

How Common Is Cohabitation?

No one really knows how prevalent cohabitation is. For college students, estimates of how many are cohabiting range from 9 to 36 percent, depending on the college, which sex is asked, and how cohabitation is defined (Macklin 1978). However, if one were to interview college graduates, the statistics would be higher, as they would include all of the college years. Dormitory and apartment rules, the sex ratio of women to men, and whether a school is private or public, conservative, or liberal also affect the rate of cohabitation.

Even more college students would like to cohabit than have actually done so. Several estimates suggest that anywhere from 50 to 80 percent of college students would live with someone of the other sex if given the opportunity.

In the United States population as a whole, 1980 census figures indicate that unrelated adults sharing a common residence represented about 2 percent of all households (*Current Population Reports*, June 1982). This figure is almost surely an underestimate of the proportion of cohabitants. The census does not distinguish between roommates and those living together in a sexual relationship. Nevertheless, census figures reveal a significant increase in heterosexual cohabitation: In 1982 there were 1,863,000 nonmarried couples cohabitating, compared with only 523,000 couples doing so in the 1970 census ("Unwed Couples Tripled . . ." 1983). Spanier (1983) notes that 4 percent of all couples living together are unmarried; half of them have been previously married.

One cohabitation survey that did not focus on college populations came up with a considerably higher figure. Of 2510 young men contacted, 18 percent had lived with a woman for six months or more, although only 5 percent were still doing so (Clayton and Voss 1977). The true rate of cohabitation for postcollege groups is probably closer to 10 percent at any one time. About 13 percent of *Cosmopolitan* readers and 5 percent of *Playboy* readers were cohabiting (Wolfe 1981; Petersen et

al. 1983b). If we were to ask adults at age sixty if they had ever cohabited, it is likely that about half would have done so, from the cumulative impact of cohabiting in the younger years with later cohabitation among the divorced and widowed.

Cohabitation and Sexual Expression

Most college students simply drift into cohabitation without consciously planning it. They simply sleep together more and more often, and then they eventually move in together. They share everyday life, regular sex, emotional intimacy, and household tasks. For most cohabitants there is only a day-to-day commitment to the relationship—with the primary commitment being to oneself (Clarke 1978a). For many cohabitants living together is a way of testing how well getting married might work. As one young woman put it, "We know we're compatible on Saturday nights; we know we can have good sex together; we know we feel we love one another; but we *don't know* how we will like one another day after day" (Clarke 1978a, p. 152).

College students may not regard cohabitation as trial marriage, though. Even though living with a partner seems to be a commitment of sorts, most college students do not feel a long-term commitment is necessary. A strong, affectionate, and sexually exclusive relationship is what most students want (Macklin 1978). One researcher found only 16 percent of seventy cohabiting couples had sexually open relationships (Huang 1974). Another found that 19 percent of cohabiting females and 31 percent of cohabiting males had sexual intercourse with one or more other persons since cohabiting began (Bower 1975). We don't know whether this openness was mutually agreed on. Cohabitation, like other intimate relationships, may be redefined several times when it comes to sex with others.

What about sexual satisfaction among cohabitants? The *Playboy* survey found that those who cohabit have the best sex lives—they had more intercourse with more satisfaction than did married and single readers. But frequency of intercourse dropped dramatically for cohabitants who were together more than four years—just as it dropped for singles and married people. Over half

DOONESBURY   by Garry Trudeau

of the cohabitants reported having intercourse four or more times per week when they had been together four or fewer years. But after four years only 28 percent of the men and 14 percent of the women reported the same frequency (Petersen et al. 1983b).

MARITAL SEX

We expect too much from life in general, and from married life in particular. When castle-building before marriage we imagine a condition never experienced on this side of heaven; and when real life comes with its troubles and cares, the tower of romance falls with a crash, leaving us in the mud-hut of everyday reality. Better to enter the marriage state in the frame of mind of that company of American settlers who, in naming their new town, called it Dictionary, "because" as they said, "that's the only place where peace, prosperity, and happiness are always to be found." [How to Be Happy Though Married 1885, p. 55]

Some of us expect great sex, warm companionship, and emotional nirvana when we marry. These expectations are unrealistic in any relationship. But in marriage as in other intimate relationships, experimenting, communicating, and caring may help us realize these goals.

Marital sex is both the most approved of and the most practiced sexual activity. Most interpersonal sex occurs in marriage. Sex used to be a major reason to marry: We were told to abstain so

we would have something to look forward to. With the near-universality of intercourse among the never-married and the prevalence of extramarital and comarital sex, marriage is not necessary to enjoy sex. Marital sex can be a joy if it is based on intimate understanding, caring, and lively interest in each other. Under other circumstances it can be unsatisfying—a duty to perform, something to endure.

Statistical Satisfaction

Contemporary surveys paint a rosy picture of marital sex. By comparing Kinsey's figures with most contemporary studies, we find that married couples now have sex more often, at greater length, with more varied activities and intercourse positions, and with more orgasms for women. Orgasm is not the only measure of sexual happiness, but it is emphasized in the media, by researchers, and, not surprisingly, by people in general. Most research on sexual satisfaction does not ask what makes for satisfaction or problems. We know *Redbook* women are pleased with marital sex: 33 percent say it is very good; 34 percent, good; 21 percent, fair; 9 percent, poor; and 3 percent, very poor (Tavris and Sadd 1975). A survey of 83,000 *Ladies' Home Journal* wives revealed that 82 percent were satisfied with sex in their marriages—47 percent said they made love from three to five times per week (Frank and Enos 1983). Similarly, nearly a fifth of married men and just over a fourth of married women in *Playboy*'s sample had intercourse four or more times per week, and 38 percent of the men and 41 percent of the women had sex two to three times per week. Fewer of *Playboy's* married men (38 percent) were satisfied with the frequency of sex than were the married women (56 percent) (Petersen et al. 1983b).

Who initiates sex seems to be related to satisfaction. In the *Redbook* study 44 percent of married women initiated sex half the time; 42 percent, sometimes; 11 percent, always or usually; and 4 percent, never. As we might guess, women who either always or never took sexual initiative were the least satisfied sexually.

In addition to initiating sex, women who take an active role during sex are much happier with their sex lives than are passive women. Three-fourths take an active part, and only 13 percent are truly passive (Tavris and Sadd 1975). The *Redbook* researchers conclude:

Women are no longer hewing to the traditional ideal of letting the man make the first move, and they are

Some couples are so burdened with the responsibilities of marriage that they lose interest in each other. Others keep their intimate relationship strong by taking time to be together in special ways, with or without children.

no longer lying in bed like ice cubes, waiting to melt. To be sure, most of them don't make their desires known by grabbing their husband's penis and shouting "Let's fuck!" and "Tally ho!" as they leapfrog into bed. But there are plenty of nonverbal ways of expressing sexual interest, and this group knows them all. (Tavris and Sadd 1975, pp. 118-19)*

Coping with Problems

Despite the positive image of marital sex presented by those who participated in these magazine surveys, a more representative sample of married couples might reveal more problems. Fifty percent of all marriages have some sexual-functioning problem, say Masters and Johnson (1970). But they have no national or random sample to justify their claim. It seems reasonable to assume that at least 25 percent of all married couples experience some sexual problems, though the problems may not be permanent. Although there can be physical reasons for problems, the dynamics of marriage are strongly related to sexual satisfaction. We cannot isolate sex from the rest of a relationship or from the rest of life.

A major problem in many marriages is that sex simply becomes boring. There are many potential barriers to continued sexual excitement in marriage. One is the tendency to let our appearance go once we've settled into a long-term relationship. A "what the hell" attitude after marriage can result in spouses' becoming overweight and out of shape.

The responsibilities of marriage may squelch active interest in sex. After working all day, there may be household chores—the lawn to mow, the laundry and dishes to wash, and a leaky faucet to fix. If there are children, they may interfere with privacy or spontaneity. There may not be much time or energy left for an exciting evening or morning of sex when the baby is crying, the phone is ringing, pressure to entertain relatives or friends is looming, and a pile of bills is waiting to be paid.

The first child is difficult for some. Pregnancy is not conducive to marital sexual bliss, although creative spouses can deal with a pregnancy while

* Excerpted from the book *The Redbook Report on Family Sexuality* by Carol Tavris and Susan Sadd. Copyright © 1975, 1977 by The Redbook Publishing Company. Reprinted by permission of Delacorte Press.

For some married couples, family life broadens and enriches their own intimate bond.

maintaining their sex life. In their study of 216 women during and after pregnancy, Tolor and DiGrazia (1976, p. 539) found a decline in sexual interest, activity, and desire.

Mismatching of body rhythms may be another problem. One spouse may be a night person who feels most alive and sexually interested in the evening, whereas the other feels that way only in the morning and simply wants to sleep at night. An example of a mismatch:

We do not seem to agree on the time for sexual activities. I am really tired at night, and go to bed for rest, not sex. In the morning, when I am rested and feeling great for the new day, is when I enjoy sexual activity the most. My husband wants to sleep in. . . . [Adams and Cromwell 1978, p. 11]

A study of graduate-student married couples (Adams and Cromwell 1978) found that biorhythmically matched couples were sexually more in tune. Also, morning couples tended to have a lower overall level of sex than night couples.

Some married couples manage to keep an exciting and rewarding sex life alive in spite of the everyday pressures of jobs, noise, differing energy levels, and children. Instead of falling into boring, unsatisfying sexual routines, some emphasize open communication, mutual planning, and a willingness to vary sexual activities. And, instead of seeing children as an excuse for avoiding sex, some couples believe that sharing children enhances their love and sexual intimacy. This new dimension in closeness may compensate for lack of privacy and spontaneity when children are around. And expressing their deep, caring feelings by being openly affectionate both with children and with each other can be healthy for the children as well as for the marriage.

Parents' inability to make love whenever the "vibes" are good can be offset by occasional trips together without the children. In motels, on deserted beaches, in the mountains they can find the privacy and spontaneity for exuberant, varied sex that are harder to come by at home. Such efforts can keep marital sex from falling into the boring, repetitive routine that is a reality for some.

Eroticism over the Years

What elements in this marriage have made sex continually exciting?

You and I are twenty years older. Your belly is a little rounder now, your waist a little thicker, the hair on your chest a lot grayer. But your ass is still small and tight, your shoulders still strong and muscular, your chest still broad and manly. The beauty of your body remains undiminished. . . .

I love it when you come to me already hard, engorged with your passion for me. And I love it when first we come together and you are still soft, and I am the one who makes you hard.

I take it in my hands and feel it spongy and squishy and formless under my fingers. I stroke it lovingly in the way you've shown me, the way that feels the best to you. I am grateful for your tutelage. Never having had a cock myself, I cannot imagine what one can feel like . . . .

You stand before me, your cock pointing straight ahead, your mouth set in a smile, pleased with yourself, pleased to be with me. I'm smiling, too. We have such fun together. Swiftly I sink to my knees in front of you and I take your hard cock into my mouth. Suddenly I don't feel like your wife of twenty years, the mother of your children, your best friend, a person I know you love and respect. I feel like a whore who loves her work, who loves to make her man happy. I want to give you the best blow job you've ever had in your life. Oh yes, I've become skilled over the years. I've learned from your cues. I've read one book after another. I've talked techniques with my women friends. Now you will reap the fruits of my labors . . . .

I feel your hands tightening on my shoulders. I feel your body tightening under my hands, I feel your hot, smooth cock bounding within my mouth. It pulsates—and I taste the salty essence of you. "More, more!" I shout inside my head. "Keep coming! Release more of you into me!" I want to cry out. I cannot speak, for my mouth is still closed firmly around you. I keep moving my tongue around, keeping time to your throbbing rhythms. Hungrily, greedily, I swallow the syrupy nectar of your passion. I feel filled by your joy. And eager for my own.

You draw me toward you on the bed, look over at me, and smile. No longer contorted by passion, your face is smooth, relaxed, content. I am content to have made the miracle happen for you once again. Part of my contentment rests on my secure knowledge that you will make it happen for me before long. (Rose 1978 pp. 64-67)*

*Reprinted by permission of the Julian Bach Literary Agency, Inc. Copyright © 1978 from Sara Rose, "Ode to Your Cock," in Charleen Swansea and Barbara Campbell, eds., *Love Stories by New Women* (Charlotte, N. Carolina: Red Clay Books, 1978).

EXTRARELATIONSHIP SEX

Another potential problem area is our attraction to many people even when we feel a central commitment to one partner. For some couples sex with others provides enriching variety, while the central bond provides continuing security and depth of involvement. This situation is extremely sensitive, though. If the extra relationship is not handled well, it may destroy the central relationship.

What Does Sex with Others Mean?

As we've seen repeatedly, physical acts are invested with symbolic meaning by the people involved. To have intercourse—still the main focus of ideas about sex—with someone outside our central relationship means quite different things to different people. To some, it's a serious infringement on a love commitment. Sex outside marriage may be viewed as a breach of a monogamous legal and/or religious contract. At the opposite extreme some people applaud any close relationship. They believe that it is good to express the warmth, love, or sexual desire they feel for others. In their minds such feelings may enhance life in the central relationship rather than detract from it.

Sometimes people in a central relationship discuss and consent to sexual encounters with others. Consent is often limited to certain conditions. Some typical negotiated agreements: only when out of town, not in our bed, only if casual,

The Language of Sex

The meanings we attach to extrarelationship sex show up in the words we use for it. If we approve of extrarelationship sex, we may use terms such as *open relationship* or perhaps *playing around*. Many who've read the O'Neills' best seller *Open Marriage*, find it chic to say, "I have an open marriage." If we disapprove, we use words as barbs and call people "unfaithful," "sinner," "adulterer," or "cheater." Some who believe any extrarelationship sex is wrong eventually have a brief "affair" (usually highly intense emotionally) and call themselves "unfaithful" out of guilt.

Rather than using these value-laden terms, some social scientists prefer the more neutral words, *extrarelationship sex* or *extramarital sex*. To distinguish outside sexmaking that is carried on with the consent of those in the central relationship, they may call this "comarital" or "corelationship" sex.

only if intimate, not with friends, only with friends, just don't tell me, always ask me first. Some agree to sex with others on one night a week—a night off from marriage. People also differ in how much they agree to tell their partner. Some agree to privacy so they do not feel obliged to "tell all" after a sexual experience. Others feel compelled to explain what happened and sometimes even provide erotic details.

Extrarelationship Attitudes and Behaviors

In our society's traditional sexual mores extrarelationship involvement is one of numerous potential pleasures that is negatively labeled. Most Americans still believe that sex outside of a central relationship—especially marriage—is wrong. Polls indicate that from 75 to 87 percent of North Americans disapprove of extramarital sex (Levitt and Klassen 1973; Glenn and Weaver 1979). Atwater (1982) suggests that when the 19- to 29-year-old group is separated out, about 40 percent of that group approve of extramarital sex under some circumstances.

What do magazine surveys tell us about extramarital sex? Of women responding to the *Redbook*

survey, 13 percent said they would definitely or probably engage in extramarital sex, and another 38 percent said they might (Tavris and Sadd 1975). A questionnaire answered by *Psychology Today*'s somewhat liberal readership over a decade ago indicated that nearly 80 percent would consider extramarital sex under some circumstances (Athanasiou, Shaver, and Tavris 1970). By contrast, only 15 percent of 321 college students at a New England state university in 1981 would accept extramarital sexual behavior of any kind (Weis and Slosnerick 1981).

Some debate may exist as to whether extramarital sexual attitudes have become more conservative or not, but there is not as much debate when we compare attitudes with reported behavior—extramarital *attitudes* seem more traditional than extramarital *behaviors*. Whether we are hypocritical, guilty, or whatever, we indulge ourselves in extramarital sex more than we believe to be proper.

More married people—particularly wives—are having more extramarital sex than in the past, and they are doing it at younger ages. In Kinsey's era over a quarter of a century ago, 26 percent of women and 51 percent of men reported extramarital intercourse (Kinsey, Pomeroy, and Martin 1948; Kinsey et al. 1953). In 1974 29 percent of the *Redbook* women had already engaged in extramarital sex—but 53 percent of those who *worked* and almost as many housewives under age twenty-five had done so, and 39 percent of women forty and older did so (Tavris and Sadd 1975). Women in the *Redbook* survey from ages eighteen to thirty are at least three times as likely to have experienced extramarital sex as females in the same group in Kinsey's research (Hunt 1974; Wolfe 1981). To be specific, 54 percent of the *Cosmopolitan* sample reported extramarital sex—with 69 percent of those 35 and older doing so (Wolfe 1981)—while 34 percent of the *Playboy* women had extramarital sex (Petersen et al. 1983b). Wives answering the *Ladies' Home Journal* survey were much less likely to have had an affair when compared with other magazine readerships—only 21 percent said they had engaged in extramarital sex (Frank and Enos 1983).

A recent survey by the Institute for Advanced Study of Human Sexuality ("Sex and the Married

Woman" 1983) revealed that 43 percent of married women had had extramarital intercourse, and half felt that their marriage vows did not govern their sexual relationships. To add fuel to the fire, 40 percent declared themselves "naturally polygamous."

What about the likelihood of married men having extramarital sex? Estimates vary, but it appears that between a half and nearly three-quarters of married men currently have extramarital sex by age 50, if not by 40. If all age groups are combined, *Playboy* found that almost 45 percent of currently married men have had an affair; by age fifty 70 percent of the men and 65 percent of the women have had an affair (Petersen et al. 1983b). Hite (1981) found that 72 percent of men married two years or more reported extramarital sex.

When all age groups are combined, husbands are more active than wives with other partners—but when married men and women in their late teens and twenties are compared, women are the most active. As these more active young married women get older, and as their younger counterparts enter marriage, it may be that women will "catch up" with men's extramarital activities. It is clear that the double standard that holds extramarital sex is okay for men but not for women does not show up in the reported behavior of many wives.

According to several studies of married people who have had sex with someone other than their spouse, about 40 to 50 percent have had one extra partner, 40 to 44 percent have had two to five, 5 to 11 percent have had six to ten, and 3 to 5 percent have had more than ten extramarital partners (Kinsey et al. 1953; Hunt 1974; Tavris and Sadd 1975). The *Redbook* study shows that most women engaged in sex from two to five or more times with each partner, only 18 percent had a one-night stand, and 19 percent saw each partner more than ten times (Tavris and Sadd 1975).

As we noted earlier, 23 percent of Huang's (1974) cohabiting couples, and 19 percent of the cohabiting females and 31 percent of the cohabiting males in Bower's study (1975) had sex with others while cohabiting. In *Cosmospolitan's* sample of somewhat older persons, 70 percent of the women who were not married but who lived with their lovers said that sexual exclusivity (called

"fidelity") should be part of their commitment (Wolfe 1981). It is difficult to estimate the proportion of singles with a central relationship who engage in extrarelationship sex.

Not all extrarelationship sex is "cheating." In a recent national study of 12,000 people involved in a couple relationship (Blumstein and Schwartz 1983), 15 percent of married couples said they had an understanding that allowed for non-monogamy under some circumstances. Nearly twice as many cohabitators (28 percent) had such an understanding with each other, while 65 percent of gay male couples and 29 percent of lesbian couples agreed to extrarelationship sex. A sample of married *Ms.* readers (Atwater 1982) indicated that one-fourth of the women discussed extramarital sex with their husbands before engaging in it, and one-third changed the rules from having affairs secretly to doing so with their husband's knowledge. If we include *tolerance* as well as agreement, it may be that 35 to 40 percent of couples have some level of awareness that their partner might have extrarelationship sex. According to Blumstein and Schwartz's (1983) survey, most people eventually find out if their partner has had outside sex.

How do we get involved with extrarelationship sex? In her interview study of 40 women, Lynn Atwater (1982) traced the stages of getting involved. The first step was awareness of the opportunity. Men typically initiated the first invitation, but knowing and talking to someone who had already gotten involved also influenced women to consider it. Three-quarters of Atwater's sample next gave a lot of thought to extramarital sex—whether they really wanted it and what its positive and negative effects might be—before getting involved. This thinking phase lasted from several weeks to several years. Atwater observes that half the women were not emotionally involved the first time. Some said they were casual friends or they liked the person. But the situation was more influential than the specific person—these women were simply ready. Once in the situation, half said the decision was mutual, with slightly more saying it was due more to the man's initiation than to the woman's (Atwater 1982).

According to Atwater, women's reaction to first extramarital sex is almost always favorable. One woman reported:

Some Views of Extrarelationship Sex

My feeling is that people come and go in your life and you can't stop this, so just love and enjoy them while you can and be grateful that you've touched each other's lives. . . . I also believe there are a lot of lonely people in this world and if we don't fool ourselves into thinking we can only love one person at a time, there would be a lot less lonely people. [Hayes 1979]

Neither one of us, so far as I know, has ever had a sexual relationship outside of marriage. I guess 'cause we just don't believe in them. When you're married, you're married.   [Gerstel 1979, p. 157]

Look, I don't like the idea of myself as an adulterous wife. But there comes a time in every woman's marriage when she just doesn't feel the bedsheets under her, the quilt over her. . . . And playing around, adultery, makes her know.   [Wolfe 1975, p. 7]

In extramarital sex, I've found the passion that's hard to maintain in our friendly marriage. But the excitement—of being found sexually attractive, of encountering a different loving style and a new intimate friend, and of giving deep pleasure to him—is something that recharges not only me but also my relationship with my husband. In giving love to another man, I find that I have more to give to my husband as well. It reawakens my love affair with life.   [From the author's files]

It was like "Why did I wait so long?" It was very satisfying. I was also having sexual problems with my husband aside from everything else. And this was really a very, very good thing for me. I saw myself as a woman and sexually satisfying to somebody. [Atwater 1982, p. 47]

Playboy men and women listed similar reasons for having extramarital sex—sexual variety and reassurance of their desirability were major motives (Petersen et al. 1983b). By contrast, *Cosmopolitan* women got involved because they felt emotionally isolated when all their husbands wanted was sex, or because they no longer shared the same goals and values (Wolfe 1981).

Effects on the Central Relationship

Sex with someone other than a marital partner may be positive or harmful to marriage, to oneself, and to any "extra" person(s). The men in Hite's (1981) sample felt there was either "no effect" or that the extrarelationship sex "helped" their marriages. The effects depend on whether the partner finds out and whether there is some agreement or at least tolerance when extrarelationship sex occurs. Some who have extrarelationship sex are satisfied with their marriages; others are dissatisfied. Engaging or not engaging in extrarelationship sex does not seem to be the most critical predictor of marital happiness—how the extrarelationship sex is handled and what it means is what counts. A negative effect can be expected if the extrarelationship sex is viewed by the partner as a breach of contract rather than part of a sexually open relationship.

There is more than one way to design and live a nonmonogamous lifestyle. Grass-roots attempts have been made to inform those who are interested in sexually open relationships about the potential pitfalls and joys. A group called Beyond Monogamy published a newsletter for several years, offering one such information base. But alternative lifestyle organizations are sometimes difficult to maintain in a society that is mostly geared to monogamy as the only "acceptable" choice.

Sexually Open Marriage.   Engaging or not engaging in extramarital sex does not seem to be the most critical factor related to marital happiness—it is how it is handled and what it means. Buunk's (1980) study of Dutch couples indicates that comarital sex agreed to by both partners on an egalitarian basis can coexist with a satisfactory marriage. Those who are secretive about their outside involvements have very different kinds of interaction with their marital partner—especially if they're "found out"—than those who have agreements about outside sex. "Tell all" couples may differ from those who simply allow each other some space. But we're not yet sure how well these degrees of candor work.

We have no large study with follow-up interviews to determine whether sexual openness is beneficial or harmful to marriage. Studies have only included those who are still together. But some satisfactions and problems can be determined from exploratory studies. Whitehurst studied both legally married and nonmarried couples but found no difference between these two groups. He concluded that women had an easier time selecting men, that relatives and friends had to be kept in the dark, and that jealousy was often a problem when one spouse felt "left out." However, most people had careers and other people to balance any loneliness. Whitehurst did not advise comarital sex unless people are able "to handle freedom, time alone, complex interrelationships, high-intensity communication, or the inevitable struggle of possessiveness versus autonomy" (Knapp and Whitehurst 1977, p. 151).

In a parallel study by Knapp, respondents felt they benefited from their sexually open marriages: They were more fulfilled personally, they liked the excitement of new experiences, their marriages were improved sexually, and in time there was a lessening of possessiveness and jealousy. Knapp reported problems too: jealousy, time-sharing problems, resentments from differing expectations, and the fear that others might be threatened or offended. But Knapp sees an increasingly important role for open marriages because more women are opting for egalitarian marriages (Knapp and Whitehurst 1977, p. 159). It is too early to tell whether Whitehurst's skepticism or Knapp's optimism is most accurate.

Atwater (1982) points out that our ability to choose the lifestyle we most want depends on how much power we have. She reasons that if one partner has more power, that person can shape the relationship and its ground rules to his or her desire. Atwater's sample of 50 women who had experienced extramarital sex supports her conclusion that women who entered other relationships after changing the rules of their marriages had the most power—which often meant having more education and more income. Atwater sees some promise in sexually open marriage, but she is not confident that this form of marriage will become popular in the near future.

Watson and Whitlock (1982) studied 19 couples involved in sexually open marriages over a three-year period and found that *all* the couples who had entered an open marriage were still married to each other, but only one couple was still

actively involved in other sexual relationships. The majority of couples were still emotionally committed to the importance of caring about others, and this commitment left reentering other sexual relationships an open issue. Some saw sexual openness as a stage in their marriage, yet most felt they might at some time sexually experience others again. No one regretted the experience. Open marriage as an ideal was still favored by all. Watson and Whitlock also interviewed "secondary" partners to the 19 couples and found that about half still were satisfied being secondary partners to a person who had another, more central relationship.

A study by Arline Rubin (1983) compared the "dyadic adjustment" of 130 sexually open married couples with the adjustment of 130 sexually exclusive married couples and found *no differences*. Rubin found that couples who were still together (regardless of the marital type) were more adjusted than those who had broken up.

What can we conclude about extramarital sex and open relationships? Atwater (1982) concludes that these relationships will become "a more obvious part of marital lives in the future" (1982, p. 204). Atwater, Watson, and Whitlock, and Rubin all see open marriage as part of the evolution of marriage—of trust, communication, and more realistic ground rules. Watson and Whitlock believe that honesty and openness "may be a necessary step for commitment of any sort, for commitment is strongest when it is founded in the awareness and experience of alternatives" (1982, p. 174).

Swinging (Partner Swapping). For those who want sexual variety but fear negative consequences, open marriage and swinging can be compared for their unique advantages and disadvantages. Those who prefer more privacy and separate sexual relationships with others may prefer open relationships, while those who feel comfortable when they are present when their partner is engaging in sex with another person may opt for swinging.

Swinging is a form of corelationship sex in which married persons swap spouses for an hour or, less often, for an evening. The few surveys that include items on swinging reveal that 2 to 5 percent of adults have tried this exchange (Tavris and Sadd 1975; Hunt 1974; Athanasiou, Shaver, and Tavris 1970).

Is swinging good or bad for marriage? Does it satisfy? Again, the data are based mostly on those still swinging, so the conclusions may be biased. Gilmartin's investigation concluded that mate sharing will not in itself benefit or harm marriage, but how partners view their behavior will. Gilmartin contended that if partners are mentally and emotionally satisfied with swinging, it is good for them. Compared with the nonswingers in Gilmartin's sample, swingers had sex more often with their marital partners, were slightly more happily married, and were generally less bored. They did not equate their activities with affairs because they were shared experiences. They were less close to their kin and neighbors than nonswinging marrieds, but felt that their nonsexual and sexual friendships made up for any social isolation (Gilmartin 1978).

There are different styles of swinging. One style is for some couples and singles to mingle in unstructured, large parties—where they may not know anyone well—and to pair off with one or more people and then to go to a vacant bedroom. Some call this recreational swinging.

Interpersonal swinging is more structured, usually happens in smaller groups, and is more likely to involve ongoing sexual interaction between the same people. Closer emotional ties are called for with this type of swinging because the sexual aspect is not the total focus, as it is with recreational swinging. Gilmartin points out a third style that attracts egotistical swingers—those who do not seek any emotional involvement (Gilmartin 1978).

Swinging parties typically include some same-sex sexual interaction between women. Gilmartin found that 68 percent of his sample of swinging wives participated in same-sex interaction occasionally at parties (Gilmartin 1978). However, same-sex interaction between men is almost unheard of. This reflects the stronger cultural bias against gay male interaction; less stigma is attached to lesbian sex.

Some swingers agree not to swing with those they meet at parties *outside* of the party context, but Gilmartin found that obedience to this rule was far from complete: Nearly half of the swinging husbands and 43 percent of the wives had intercourse with fellow swingers on their own time. Gilmartin noted that nearly two-thirds who engaged in sex with others outside of the parties had some kind of open marriage agreement.

A question that arises about open marriage and swinging is, should extrarelationship sexual experiences be explained to children? In Gilmartin's sample of 100 swinging couples, 82 percent had children. Gilmartin interviewed an additional 24 swinging couples to obtain more understanding of the children issue. Of these couples 65 percent said their children already knew about their swinging, and 81 percent already had told or planned to tell their children about their sexual activities. However, 19 percent would never tell their children about their swinging. Only 15 percent would not be happy if their children also became swingers. Gilmartin's interviews with the children led him to conclude that they were happy and well adjusted—more so than the children of the nonswinging control group studied at the same time (Gilmartin 1978). McGinley's research sharply disagrees with Gilmartin's conclusion about children. McGinley found that most swingers view their sexual lifestyle as private, and they do not tell their children (Singer 1982b, p. 71).

Swinging can have its problems. In a study of marriage counselors' experience with swingers *who dropped out*, problems included jealousy, guilt, threat to marriage, boredom, divorce, fear of discovery, and the inability of one or both to handle the experience (Denfield 1974).

Some caution should be exercised if we decide on any sexually free marriage, whether of the open-marriage or swinging variety. But then we should also be careful about entering a monogamous union where the expectation may be for all of our desires to be met in one relationship for an entire lifetime. There are no easy choices when it comes to balancing our needs for freedom and security.

Jealousy: Grounds for Negotiation. Jealousy can pose a barrier to satisfying open relationships. The reality or even the fear that an intimate partner may become sexually involved with others is a common source of anxiety. The Green-Eyed

Monster can strike any of us—even the most liberal. Some are more "with it" in what they say than in their emotional reactions. Over the years Helen Gurley Brown has advocated sexual freedom for women. As editor of *Cosmopolitan* she has shaped liberal sexual values. And yet, if her husband were to spend one night with another woman, she is quoted as saying, "I'd go absolutely crazy" (Seligson 1977, p. 249). None of us is above jealousy.

Jealousy is often seen as a destructive force. It's useful to see where jealousy comes from and how some have managed to negotiate agreements about extramarital sex that enhance, rather than threaten, the relationship. According to Gordon Clanton and Lynn Smith (1977), jealousy is a natural reaction to a fear of losing someone who gives us great delight. It is also a warning signal that there may be something wrong in a central relationship that should be attended to. In our society we *learn* to feel jealous and act possessively. We can also learn to manage and understand our jealousy. As we become more secure in our intimate relationships, we are likely to become less jealous.

Romantic jealousy follows threats to self-esteem and/or to the quality of an intimate relationship, especially when threats are caused by our perception that our partner is attracted to another person. Gregory White's (1981) study of 150 romantically involved college-student couples revealed that men valued sexual motives, while females valued permanence. A female was more likely to stress nonsexual qualities of an outside relationship—the other woman's personality and ability to communicate—as well as problems in the primary relationship as causes of the extrarelationship involvement of her partner.

Possessive jealousy may arise out of our property notion of owning another in the name of love. This possessiveness is "commitment without trust" (Mazur 1973, p. 105). If we can learn to redefine love as something other than sexual exclusiveness, then we can begin to react less defensively to our partner's needs for emotional and sexual freedom. And if we can begin to view our partner's outside friendships as experiences that may make him or her more vibrantly alive, then perhaps we can see such friendships as enriching rather than destroying our relationship.

Neither partner can create this dynamic balance alone. Jealousy over what our partner chooses to do with time away from us is not just our problem—our partner and others need to be aware of its existence and deal with it constructively through open discussion. One person's admission of feeling jealous can lead to communication and negotiations that strengthen the relationship, reduce the pain, and increase awareness and appreciation for each other and for the life we're building together. Or it can lead to recognition that the relationship is not worth saving.

Social psychologist Bram Buunk's (1982) study of 50 Dutch couples, most of whom had experienced extramarital sex, indicated that 82 percent of the women and 76 percent of the men had experienced jealousy. Jealousy was more often a problem for women than for men: 22 percent of the women said they often felt jealousy, with only 2 percent of the men saying the same (Buunk 1982).

Buunk (1982) found that the most frequent coping strategy for handling jealous feelings was open communication with partners. Similarly, Cole and Goettsch (1981) discovered that self-disclosure and communication leading to an improved relationship were most enhanced by a commitment to the relationship that transcended jealousy, and by a willingness to make changes to continue the primary relationship. Their sample included over 300 cohabiting couples, but their findings seem to apply to other intimate relationships, too. Cole and Goettsch (1981) concluded that relationship depth only emerges after partners deal with conflict over issues such as nonexclusive dating and sexual jealousy. Handling a sexually open relationship was viewed as a way to develop and validate a high degree of commitment in a central relationship.

In talking through our feelings about what's going on, we can each clarify our needs and the meanings we attach to sex with others. We can also thoughtfully question the basis and ground rules of our own relationship. Is there still an emotional commitment to each other? A deep feeling of love, concern, and wanting to be with each other? Or is there only pain on one side and a yearning to break away on the other? Are some aspects of the situation more distressing than

"You're seeing another woman, aren't you, Robert?"

Drawing by Chas. Addams; © 1980 The New Yorker Magazine, Inc.

others? If so, can these be defined and restricted by agreement, leaving each other as much freedom to grow and experience life's excitement as our relationship will allow? Or is there only a hollow shell of habits holding us together, with little emotional commitment left to justify trying to continue the relationship? These are critical questions that we rarely face—often it takes jealousy's jolt to bring them into the open.

Those who are unable to work through their jealous feelings may resort to the law to punish their partner for straying from a marriage. In one case a judge ruled that a husband didn't own his wife, so he couldn't sue for damages when she had an affair. The Washington Court of Appeals ruled that neither spouse is the other's property—that "the love and affection of a human being is not susceptible to theft. There are simply too many intangibles that defy the concept that love is property" ("You Can't Steal Love . . ." 1982, p. 2).

214

UNCOUPLING: THE BUSTED BOND

Whether we are married, cohabiting, or single, breaking up can be one of the most painful of all experiences. The agonies of waiting by the phone for a call that never comes, of thinking that we've failed or been rejected, of wishing we could somehow start all over and make things right, of coping with loneliness, anger, and sorrow may feel like tearing flesh to some of us. To others breaking up brings feelings of liberation. The burden of trying to sustain a relationship that wasn't working is lifted. In its place may be a sense of freedom to explore new opportunities. Whether we emphasize the joys or the sorrows of breaking up in our reaction, our task is to rebuild a sense of ourself as an autonomous individual rather than part of a bonded unit.

How Many Break Up?

Intimate relationships are so difficult to maintain that about 50 percent break up in time. The same seems to be true of marriages as well as of bonded single and cohabiting relationships. But hard data are not available.

It is especially difficult to estimate uncoupling rates among singles who have a central relationship. In a long-range study of college dating couples, 45 percent (103) broke up (Hill, Rubin, and Peplau 1979). Relationships ended from one month to five years after they began, with a median length of sixteen months. Although it is hard to make inferences from one study, this statistic is our best estimate of breakups among dating couples.

Breakups among cohabitants are also hard to estimate. In a longitudinal study Cole (1979) estimated that about 50 percent of couples cohabiting six months or more break up. Those living together for less than six months were more likely to split, but cohabitants do not seem to uncouple at a rate much different from that of young married couples.

In general, then, it appears that we have about a fifty-fifty chance of making it in a central sexual relationship—whether in marriage, cohabitation, or singlehood. When we combine the very rough estimates of the proportion who separate with those who divorce, the marital breakup rate may be higher than our estimates of 45 percent and 50 percent for singles and cohabitants.

Reasons for Splitting

There are a number of reasons why we break up. Some of us didn't make wise choices in the first place—perhaps we didn't know ourselves well enough, or perhaps we knew too little about our partner to have made any long-term commitment to the relationship. Some of us whimsically fall in love easily, form alliances that we expect to be lasting, and then change the rules—we may repeatedly fall in love with beautiful people, for instance, but later lay a new set of expectations on them: In addition to being attractive, they must be responsible, punctual, clean, and so forth. Sometimes external forces contribute to the split —single women who have experienced broken relationships with married men often blame external factors: his wife, his job, his new lover (Richardson 1979).

Often our reasons for breaking up are mixed. In a questionnaire and interview study Rikke Wassenberg (1982) found six general explanations for breaking up—or being broken up with: differences in what partners expected from the relationship, jealousy, differences in goals and interests, personality differences, changes in location, and inability to handle conflicts.

The Coming-Apart Process

When one or both partners begin to feel that the costs of a relationship outweigh its rewards or that there are more attractive alternative partners, the relationship may start to fall apart. The process may be fast or slow, but once it starts it often continues.

Although uncoupling may be mutual, it is typical for the person with the least interest to break off the relationship (the "dumper"), leaving the most emotionally involved person (the "dumpee") to fare for her- or himself. This differential seems related to the original reason for most breakups: One person is less involved than the other. In a study of college couples by Hill and his associates (1979), couples who said they were equally involved had fewer breakups (23 percent) than those where one person was more involved (54 percent).

More often than not, it is the woman who initiates the split. In the Hill, Rubin, and Peplau study of college breakups, the woman was more interested in breaking up in 51 percent of the couples, the man in 42 percent, with 7 percent mutual. Men have more trouble ending a relationship, in part because they get emotionally involved sooner. Women take longer to love and are more likely to evaluate their relationships critically and to fall out of love. If the woman breaks up with the man, it is much more difficult for him to accept her as a friend. Redefining the relationship is easier for her.

The process of breaking up often culminates after problems reach crisis proportions. Problems may actually be used to escalate the crisis and dissolve the intimate bond. To use a problem to precipitate divorce, one must have proof there is a problem. Trying to pin down the facts of an affair is one tactic, evidenced by behaviors such as checking for unfamiliar lipstick marks, cigarette butts, traces of perfume, or hours unaccounted for.

Experiencing the Split

Whether uncoupling happens as a shockingly rapid disintegration; a dragged-out, on-again, off-again parting; or a slow but sustained withdrawal (Richardson 1979), it may have a heavy emotional impact. We may not believe it at first, especially if it is we who are told it is over. Our initial reaction of disbelief may change to anger ("How could he [she] do this") and eventually to acceptance, allowing us to grieve the loss. It is not uncommon to cling to the thought that our loved one still loves us, that he or she is only confused, or that he or she will regain lost feelings. Mixed messages and a lack of direct feedback can result in a painful, long process of letting go.

Men have an especially agonizing time reconciling themselves to the reality that they are no longer loved and the relationship is over (Hill, Rubin, and Peplau 1979, p. 78). Since women break up with men more than vice versa, men have difficulties adjusting to the broken bond. Many people—particularly men—report an increase in depression, wandering concentration, sleeping problems, physical illness, nervousness, mood swings, and feelings of emptiness, devastation, and loneliness. Hesitation about getting involved with another person and distrust of the other sex and of one's own feelings are common (Wassenberg 1982).

Contrary to our romantic expectations, the strongest predictor of how torn up someone will be after a breakup is not the length of relationship or the degree of sexual involvement but simply how much of their free time the two had spent together while the relationship was on. Loss of the relationship leaves a large void in the lives of those who've devoted much of their leisure time to being with the other person (Wassenberg 1982).

Not all reactions to breaking up are negative, however. In Wassenberg's study of nonmarital breakups, some respondents expressed relief that an unworkable relationship had finally ended. Some increased their partying and sexual activity after the breakup. Many did not feel vindictive and said they were still friends with their ex-partners.

Love and Sex after the Split

I'm amazed at my sex drive. I'd been frigid in my marriage and didn't think I'd ever enjoy sex or miss it, but I was really surprised! I have to watch myself, because I'm just like a kid with a new toy. I've turned out to be very aggressive. I'll ask a man for a date, or a dance, and openly tell him I'm attracted to him physically. I've tickled some men to death and scared the hell out of others. An aggressive woman really separates the men from the boys!   [Hunt and Hunt 1977, p. 149]

After uncoupling most of us are wary of new involvements. We may feel lonely, rejected, and sexually unsatisfied. A typical reaction is to have casual and friendly sexual relationships with little commitment. These new relationships can polish a tarnished ego and encourage us to love again. They can even result in more satisfying sex. Women report more orgasms in postmarital relationships than in their former marriages, and they have higher orgasm rates than wives of the same age (Gebhard 1970).

In a national questionnaire study of 984 separated and divorced persons and 113 widowed persons, Hunt and Hunt (1977) report that a great majority of the formerly married become sexually active within a year. Only one man in twenty and one woman in fourteen had no intercourse. Most stay active after they start—the typical man has four partners in a year, while the average woman has two partners. Not all sex is male initiated—two-thirds of the men and a fifth of the women say that sometimes sex is female initiated. The disparity in male and female reports on who initiates sex is also obvious in the differences about how quickly sex occurs: Only one in five women say they accept sex the first time, whereas four-fifths of the men claim women accept their advances.

Hunt and Hunt believe that the formerly married are much more open and liberal about sex with new partners than their counterparts were a generation ago. Sneaking around, particularly if children were involved, was the norm. But now the divorced may be eager and more spontaneous about sexual adventures, and fewer hide their activities from their children (Hunt and Hunt 1977).

Sex and Single Parents.   Many of us will someday be single parents. Even if we are not the primary caretakers of our children after a divorce, we will have them at times. Census figures show that single-parent families accounted for 21 percent of the 31.6 million families with children in 1981, compared with 11 percent of the 28.8 million families with children in 1970. Ninety percent of single-parent families are maintained by the mother, with a large proportion of the remainder living with a relative other than the father (*Current Population Reports*, March 1981). Some newly divorced single parents quickly enter into a series of sexual relationships. For others the fear of being hurt again and the need to learn how to trust another person seem to balance out and to result in more comfort about sex in time. In a study of 36 single mothers, Goldfarb and Libby (1983) determined that the bulk of the emotional needs of the mothers was met by other women, while most sexual needs were satisfied with men. One mother who would have preferred to combine sexual and emotional needs in the same relationship commented:

I share intimacy with my female friends—we share each other's lives, every aspect of them. The sexual needs are with men. No men have offered emotional support for several years. Because I went from being a married woman, my sexual relationships have never been hidden. Sex has been a normal part of my life to my children. Casual sexual relationships aren't so intense that the kids are threatened that someone will usurp their relationships with me.   [Goldfarb and Libby, 1984, in press]

Meeting our sexual and intimacy needs while taking care of children without a partner is sometimes fraught with problems of privacy, energy, and time. In an interview study of 38 single parents, Judith Greenberg observed that most felt their sexual activity should not be known to their children (Greenberg 1979).

In a study of 127 separated or divorced fathers with full or joint custody of their children, Kristine Rosenthal and Harry Keshet (1978a) found that most of their serious relationships were with younger, childfree women. Once the father "stayed over" with a new woman, it was usually at her place rather than his. After a while serious relationships developed—routines, common friends, and a sense of being a new couple emerged. Although it was a stumbling block for most fathers, 75 percent of them eventually asked their serious new partner to sleep over (Rosenthal and Keshet 1978b). Fathers were generally uptight about having a lover sleep over when the children were present. They worried that their children might get the idea that sex should be totally free. For instance, after one child looked down at the woman sleeping at her father's side and asked him, "Which one is that?" he decided to limit his sex life to a more settled relationship (Rosenthal and Keshet 1978b).

Intimacy Reborn.   Recoupling after uncoupling is very common. A majority of the formerly married find partners they love, and they adjust to a new life together (Hunt and Hunt 1977, p. 234). Some live together, others remarry. And some of the sex and caring experiences people have after divorce are with their ex-spouses. Some who were married remain lovers (Weiss 1979).

When children are present, there seems to be more pressure to settle into marriage. About half of the divorced who live together marry if there are children involved, while only a third do so if there are no children (Hunt and Hunt 1977).

The great majority of people interviewed feel that broken love relationships were worth the pain (Hunt and Hunt 1977). As Tennyson put it, " 'Tis better to have loved and lost/Than never to have loved at all." The sex, the romance, the deep feelings, the intimate companionship of mutual love are for many of us the most satisfying experiences life has to offer.

Each time we love—even if we lose—we gain new insights into the kind of person and situation that will fulfill our dreams. We learn more about ourselves, and we become more whole, balanced, and in touch. That is, some of us do—others may never really learn, repeating old scripts in relationship after relationship. Seeing a therapist may help us understand what is defeating intimacy.

We may fear intimacy because we resist pledging ourselves to considering a lover's feelings, to staying together while we try to work out our differences. We'd rather be free to act on our own impulses. And some of us hesitate to make ourselves vulnerable to being hurt by a partner who cannot be trusted to be considerate of our feelings.

Finding the delicate balance between freedom to be ourselves and the commitment to the other's emotions that a secure relationship requires is never easy. We'd really like to have both freedom and security without giving up anything. As Jessie Bernard puts it:

Human beings want incompatible things. They want to eat their cake and have it too. They want excitement and adventure. They also want safety and security. These desiderata are difficult to combine in one relationship. Without a commitment, one has freedom but not security; with a commitment, one has security but little freedom.   [Bernard 1972, p. 81]

Trying to juggle freedom and security is a tricky feat. But to the extent that we succeed, neither life nor sex will have passed us by.

Summary

Options for sexual partners include living together, marrying each other, or maintaining separate residences but having sex together. Some who live alone have no partners; some have many. Cohabitation and marriage may be sexually open or closed to other sexual relationships. Although marriage is a popular ideal, and most adults are married at some time, the number who are single at any one time has risen.

According to magazine surveys, single people manage to have sex as often as married people, some with numerous partners. Common places of meeting others for friendships and/or sex include singles bars and the workplace.

Those who live together seem to have more sex, with more satisfaction, than either singles or spouses—until they've lived together for four years or more. Marital partners are often sexually happy too, particularly if they have found ways of keeping their relationship alive and growing.

Many with a central relationship also have sexual relationships with other people, with or without their partner's knowledge and consent. The effects on the central relationship vary. Jealousy can be either a destructive force or a stimulus to growth and depth in the central relationship.

About half of all adult relationships break up, for varying reasons. Despite the trauma of severing an intimate bond, most people try again, in the lifelong search for the perfect balance between personal freedom and relatedness.

11

Intimacy and Older People

I like lovers who are different from those I had when I was young. Sex was never a big thing for me when I was young, but I've changed. Now I enjoy sex more. I seem to understand people better, both their tougher times and their joyful times. I'm helping others and sharing with friends more, now that I've grown as a person. It has just made me better able to share my sexual side too. When we are young we waste so much of our sexual selves, because we don't first try to understand and nurture warm relationships. No, sex has been much, much better in my "vintage years." A fifty-seven-year-old never-married West Coast woman

The best damn thing we did was get married! I take a lot of teasing. It was kinda late. But when it [love] hits you—do it! You always need someone to be with. I still work our 240-acre dairy farm and now I'll never retire! A sixty-two-year-old midwestern remarried widower

Not having sex bothers me and I feel something's missing. Like I'm wasting away. I just need sex regularly. I go hiking with my husband and friends and especially enjoy our Audubon birding club activities. That helps keep me fit and I always was proud of my legs anyway. And, of course, regular stops at the beauty parlor really keep my spirits up. A seventy-year-old New England suburbanite

Getting a little honey on the stinger is still the most fun I have in life! I still can't really hug a woman without getting a bulging cock and sure I love to tell the old stories about what happened at the big dances. These younger guys think I'm stretching 'em with old history, but right away I switch to relatin' about the women I just dated the last two weekends. They eat it up. A sixty-nine-year-old retired Wisconsin roofer

The opening statements of this chapter are typical of remarks older people make about their sex lives. They come from those who enjoy themselves sexually and who have a sense that experiencing affection and sensual pleasure is a rewarding part of being an older person.

Today only some older people have rich sexual experiences. But with changes in society's concepts, a greater percentage of the elderly will enjoy sex. Appreciation for the qualities of sex in later years may even help our society move beyond the youth-idealizing, performance-oriented ethic that now inhibits full sexual joy at all ages.

One reason for stronger interest in the aged is the trend toward more older people: About 25 million, or just over 11 percent of all Americans, are over sixty-five. By the year 2020, the proportion over sixty-five will rise to 13 percent (Trippett 1980; Hall 1980). Additionally, we can expect to live longer: A man of sixty-five now can expect to live to nearly seventy-nine, and a woman to eighty-three (Hall 1980). The more old people there are, the more recognition they will get. The result of recognizing the aged is captured by Bernice Neugarten: "No one says 'act your age' anymore. We've stopped looking with disfavor on older people who act in youthful ways" (Hall 1980, p. 68).

SEXLESS LABELING

Our society negatively labels the aged as nonsexual. Just as babies are often defined as nonsexual, we as a society have typically relegated the aged to an asexual role. Labeling of the aged as neuter can itself shut off their opportunities to remain sexually active.

Even children of older people sometimes discourage them from remarrying or showing needs for intimate and sexual liaisons with others. They seem to think that their parents look foolish when they do so (McKain 1969). Negative labeling continues into the professional area. The medical–health care profession often treats the aged as sexless and does not give them credit for sexual capabilities and concerns (Schneider 1978). Such labeling means that although the aged are often effectively cared for and treated medically, their sexual needs are not considered.

Further, sex researchers are defensive in a way that may not encourage young students to study the sex lives of older persons (Berezin 1976). Often it is difficult for students to make the empathic leap to understand and appreciate the sexual realm of older persons. When researchers tell people that they are researching sex and aging, many respond with joking and laughter. Our society simply has found it difficult to accept the sexual interest and activity of aged persons (LaTorre and Kear 1977). Older people who do defy the asexual stereotype may be labeled "weird" or "dirty old men" (and women) and made to feel that they are somehow abnormal and disgusting. Whether they are defined as asexual or abnormal, older people have little social encouragement to see themselves as sexual.

PHYSICAL AGING

The notion that the old are asexual is based partly on the idea that they are falling apart physically. Physical decline does happen eventually, but slowing of the body rhythms need not mean an end to sex. And the speed of the aging process varies widely among individuals. Some of us are still young at eighty; others are already old at forty.

Changes in Older Women

In females the aging process involves genital changes that may influence sexual activity. Masters and Johnson (1966) reported that some women no longer experience swelling of the clitoral glans after age forty. Swelling of the vaginal lips during sexual excitement is also less prevalent for older women. While vaginal lubrication appears within ten to thirty seconds in stimulated young women, it may take two to three minutes in women in their fifties. The vaginal walls become thinner, smoother, and pink in color rather than the burgundy or red of younger women. Both the length and width of the vagina decrease by age sixty. Nevertheless, older women still have the capacity for sexual enjoyment and orgasm.

Menopause. The average age for menopause is fifty-one (Hammond and Maxson 1982). This cessation of menstruation signals the end of childbearing potential. It's important to consider menopause in connection with aging because many people believe it negatively influences women's sexuality. Actually there are many different patterns of menopause, and frequently the symptoms are not correctly interpreted. For example, menstrual periods may stop suddenly, gradually, or even irregularly. In addition the age can range from early forties to mid-fifties. Other menopausal symptoms vary in occurrence and intensity, depending a great deal on the woman's physical health.

Periodic hot flashes are experienced by 75 to 85 percent of menopausal women. They may feel a blush, warmth, and tingling that involves fingers, toes, and head and that moves throughout the body. Timing of hot flashes is unpredictable. They are probably caused by sudden dilating of the blood vessels and controlled by actions of the hypothalamus (Hammond and Maxson 1982). Flashes are momentary and harmless and need to be accepted by women experiencing them as part of the menopausal syndrome.

Bloating or swelling is also a common symptom of menopause. Hormonal changes can cause women to retain body fluids more readily and to experience extrasensitive swollen breasts. Some women report additional symptoms such as back trouble, bone and muscle aching, migraines, drying skin, and wrinkles. Not all these symptoms are solely and directly related to menopause; some may be related to life stress circumstances.

Reitz (1977) suggests that all aging women, whether menopausal or not, need to give extra care to their bodies by using skin and hair oils, taking vitamins, and getting body rest. The same could be said for men. Estrogen replacement therapy may be given to menopausal women because the aging ovaries produce very little estrogen. Estrogen may be advised by many doctors to relieve the hot flashes and slow down degenerative genital changes. For example, estrogen therapy will provide significant relief from hot-flash discomfort in 90 percent of treated women. Estrogen treatment also significantly increases vaginal secretions and elasticity. In addition it is extremely effective in preventing postmenopausal loss of skeletal bone mass—osteoporosis (Hammond and Maxson 1982).

Much concern has been expressed about the side effects of estrogen treatments. These side effects include possible contribution to gallbladder stones, elevated blood pressure, and uterine cancer. Women considering taking estrogen should carefully consult with health care professionals and should study and weigh the potential costs and rewards (Hammond and Maxson 1982).

With or without estrogen therapy, the experience of menopause usually is not a severe traumatic event. Most women are matter-of-fact about it and handle the experience as well or as poorly as they do their other life events (Lowenthal and Chiriboga 1972). And contrary to popular notions that women stop being sexual when estrogen production ceases, many women find they enjoy sex *more* after menopause because they are no longer bothered by menstruation and contraceptives. Some comments by postmenopausal women:

I am constantly amazed and delighted to discover new things about my body, something menstruation did not allow me to do. I have new responses, desires, sensations, freed and apart from the distraction of menses [periods].

I felt better and freer since menopause. I threw that diaphragm away. I love being free of possible pregnancy and birth control. It makes my sex life better.
[Quoted in Boston Women's Health Book Collective 1976, p. 328]

Changes in Older Men

Like women men slow down somewhat in their physical responses to sexual stimulation as they age. What excites younger men to erection in seconds requires minutes in men over fifty; often more direct touching is needed to stimulate an erection. Masters and Johnson (1966) duly note that as men grow older, their erections are less firm and full. If their penis becomes flaccid after being fully erect, older men may be unable to regain an immediate erection—even if stimulation continues. What Masters and Johnson call the plateau phase usually lasts longer in older men, and their ejaculatory demand (feeling the ejaculation coming) is much less forceful. When they ejaculate, there is less seminal fluid; it may seep out rather than being forcefully expelled from the penis. Older men also cannot repeat ejaculation as quickly a second time because of a longer refractory period; sometimes it takes a day or more before they can have another erection. Finally, on ejaculation older men tend to return quickly to a flaccid state. As with women the capacity to enjoy sexual experiences is not automatically lost by older men.

The Notion of a Male Climacteric.   Many arguments have been raised about the possibility that middle-aged males may undergo a "change of life" similar to menopause in females. Data show that some men have psychological symptoms such as nervousness and depression when entering their forties and fifties. These symptoms seem similar to those some menopausal women report. And just as women's estrogen production drops off at menopause, men's testosterone production begins to taper off around age forty, though not as suddenly as the female hormonal change. It is thought that diminishing testosterone levels are linked to males' declining sexuality. The loss of sexual interest and capacity are often cited as symptoms of the male climacteric syndrome.

Nevertheless, our abilities and activities at any age are a mixture of social, psychological, and biological factors. If some men seem to undergo a "midlife crisis," they may be reacting not only to hormonal changes but also to passing the halfway point in life without a sense of having done anything worthwhile. Life has several such transition

> ## The Language of Sex
>
> **I**n referring to the midlife changes noted in some men, many people use the term *male menopause*. This term is rather inappropriate because menopause literally means cessation of menstruation. Two alternatives: *climacteric* (meaning a period when changes supposedly take place in the body) or *metapause* (connoting a change and a time to stop and rethink one's direction).

periods that require asking different questions about our concerns and goals; midlife could be disturbing for some. For others the crisis occurs at adolescence—even kindergarten is tough for some of us.

Problems of Health

At any age our sexual options and enjoyment are clearly related to our health. Poor health does not mean sex is out, but it usually poses many limitations. Good health does not inevitably mean good sex, but it enriches our options. A sixty-nine-year-old who keeps fit with simple, nourishing foods and a daily half-hour of yoga exercises is in a much better position to enjoy varied sex than one who is burdened by backaches, indigestion, and obesity.

General health problems pose continuing hur-

Keeping physically fit at any age contributes to good health and a feeling of well-being. Throughout life, good health enhances our sexual options.

dles to some sexually interested aged. Such problems include high blood pressure, cardiac illness, hardening of the arteries, arthritis, muscle and bone weakness, diabetes, depression, and hearing and sight problems. Add to the list problems of the "organic brain syndrome"—the disorders that impair one's memory, intellectual functions, spatial orientation, judgment, and capacity to empathize with others. Just staying alive is a problem for some.

When health is poor, not surprisingly some older people lose interest in sex; it becomes a luxury rather than an issue of survival. Studies show that only 8 percent of the aged are helplessly senile (Trippett 1980). Many older people today are alert and vigorous well into their seventies and eighties—and sex may be helping them to keep going.

Sex as Exercise

Sex may be a tonic boost for people of any age. It's good muscle exercise, and it stimulates the adrenal glands and sympathetic and parasympathetic nerves. Like any other good aerobic exercise, it also helps maintain fitness by raising heart and breathing rates (Felstein 1970). The genitals especially are kept in shape. In women the contractions of orgasm help maintain muscle tone in the vagina (Butler and Lewis 1976). And for males, too, high levels of sex—whether with themselves or with a partner—make continuing sexual responsiveness possible. Sex can be seen as a way of creating sound muscle tone and mobilizing all body systems to function better—so we can enjoy sex more!

Little research has yet been done on the health benefits of sex, but it is known to be good for arthritis. In addressing the National Arthritis Foundation, noted sex educator Jessie Potter stated that arthritis patients get several hours of relief from pain through sexmaking. She suggested that perhaps the production of cortisone was stimulated during sex and provided the relief. Support for the benefits of sexual activity to soothe and relieve pain also comes from the work of George Ehrlich. He cites adrenal stimulation as an ingredient. Sex is also good for stress, as orgasm is often followed by profound relaxation (*Medical World News* 1979).

AGELESS INTIMACIES

As important as robust health is for older people, an often undervalued point involves their capacity for intimacy. If we are primarily concerned with having intercourse often, then robust health is crucial. If we believe in a "performance ethic," then the changes in older bodies guarantee a somewhat dismal comparison between youthful and aged sex. By contrast, if we consider sexual relations in terms of genital and nongenital caressing, tender gestures, love talk, empathic kissing, and spontaneous skin-to-skin fun, then intimate behavior is readily possible for both the older and the younger person, because robust health is not a necessary condition. In fact, noncoital intimate activities are more likely to peak in later years (Foster 1979). Most teenage persons have not yet experienced the range of human loving. Fortunately, the capacity to share empathic affection does not require virile muscles or perfect physical conditioning. It does not diminish with age!

The ability to move from a focus on athletic intercourse does not come easily in our society, which has competitive, performance-oriented models in every corner. But for the older person an antiperformance model for sexual activity may be more reliable and satisfying.

One such non-goal-oriented model for sex has been developed in the Far East: tantric sex. Here the emphasis is not on speeding up sex but rather on slowing things down in order to savor each moment fully. Lovers are encouraged to focus on their own touches and to imagine how it would feel to be receiving them. Orgasm is not emphasized. In fact, sensual arousal *without* orgasm is especially cherished (Moffett 1974). Since building up to orgasm is not the objective, sex that does not end in orgasm is not seen as failure (as it is in our society). Instead, it may be a most loving gesture—one that older friends can share with each other.

Seen from a tantric point of view, the quality of sex may actually *improve* with age. For example, Foster (1979) reports exploratory findings from a married sample of 100 men. On a caressing scale husbands aged fifty-seven and older scored higher in actual activity than all but husbands aged twenty-seven to thirty-six. The least caressing occurred

want sex and forget about the rest of it—the hugging and the petting and I think that's wrong. People say, what will happen to me when I get older? Well, I'm still alive! There's no thrill like that today. People try dope, they try smoking, they try drinking. This is the one thing that is good for the body.   [Vinick 1978, p. 362]

Kimmel makes a similar observation regarding males with homosexual preferences. Genital sex continues to be important, but into the forties and older they reduce their cruising of tearooms and gay clubs and have less sex. The emphasis shifts to companionship qualities. Genital sex is still important, but without the former frenzy. For example, one sixty-three-year-old is quoted as saying "less accent on the genital, more on the total person now" (Kimmel 1978, p. 119).

SEXUAL ACTIVITY

The performance-ethic frequency-count approach is often the basic research model. To ask intercourse-to-orgasm-oriented questions ("How many times have you had intercourse in the last month?" and "How many times do you orgasm with intercourse?") limits our understanding to only one dimension of intimate connection. Nevertheless, since older people, as members of our society, share its performance ethic, the dwindling frequency of intercourse and orgasm that some experience may have significant meaning for them.

Past Research

Researchers have documented the dramatic decline in sexual intercourse that occurs with age. Kinsey's (1953) data showed that marital coitus dropped from 2.8 times per week at age thirty to 1.5 per week by forty, 1.0 by fifty, and 0.6 by sixty. Similar declines were reported in a sequence of longitudinal studies at Duke University (Pfeiffer, Verwoerdt, and Davis 1972). A sample of 261 men and 241 women was studied at two-year intervals over a period of six years. The number of persons having intercourse two or more times a week decreased with age. For example, in the group aged forty-six to fifty, 33 percent of the men and 21 percent of the women reported a frequency of two

in the youngest group, aged seventeen to twenty-six.

Sociologist Barbara Vinick (1978) reported interviews with 24 elderly remarried Massachusetts couples. The husbands' average age was seventy-three and the wives' was sixty-seven. Vinick noted that for those mentioning sex in remarriage, the physical act was not the most important aspect. Rather, the emphasis was on sharing the warmth of another body—the holding and the intimacy. She quotes one seventy-three-year-old husband:

I don't know if I'm oversexed, but I'm a lover. I like to pet, kiss, hug. I have more fun out of loving somebody I love than the ultimate end. You know, some people —and this is the failure of sex, too—some people or more times a week, whereas among those aged sixty-one to sixty-five, only 7 percent of the men and 5 percent of the women reported having intercourse two or more times a week. A nationwide survey in 1970 reported by W. Cody Wilson (1975) and a twenty-year follow-up study by Ard (1977) showed similar patterns.

These studies have revealed that some older persons are sexually active into their seventies and eighties. A 1959 study of 800 of the vibrant over-sixty-five men in *Who's Who* showed that 70 percent of the married men had intercourse an average of four times a month (Beauvoir 1973). And Ed Brecher (1980) reports that his survey of older *Consumer Reports* readers shows "a very high level of sexual activity." He speculates that earlier studies have not shown much activity because people have been afraid to ask the right questions. The Duke studies showed that almost half of married women continue to be sexually active through their sixties, and about half of married men were sexually active up to their midseventies (Palmore 1981, p. 86).

Awakened Women

The assertion that women become more interested in sex during middle age is common. For example, therapist Helen Singer Kaplan (1974, p. 113) states: "Women tend to want more sex rather than less as they approach middle age and beyond, and their responsiveness becomes only slightly less rapid and intense." Barbara Harrison (1975, p. 26) similarly states: " . . . a woman becomes vividly alive sexually—experiences the fullness of her sexual nature—when she is in her late thirties or early forties." Such statements may actually be true of relatively few women. Most studies show that women's as well as men's interest and participation in sexual interaction are highly dependent on early patterns of sexual expression, and these diminish in intensity with age. Women who are "awakened" may be those who suffered sexual deprivation in early adulthood.

Sexual attitudes prevailing when people were young influence their sexual ideas. For example, men and women now fifty to eighty years of age were generally taught quite restrictive concepts about sexuality. Few women were taught to masturbate in their youth. And few women were

taught to ask for consideration of their own needs when engaging in heterosexual relations. Some women didn't even know what their needs were. It was their partners' interests that guided sex. Thus many women experienced silent deprivation.

Today more young women are experiencing and communicating their sexual desires. They are taking greater control over their sexual lives. When these women are forty and older, they will not need "awakening." But for women raised with restricted sexual codes, growth in sexual awareness sometimes occurs during middle age.

Self-Pleasuring

In addition to warm relationships with others, older people can enjoy a satisfying sex life with themselves. Masturbation and fantasizing have not always been viable sexual activities for most elderly persons, especially for women (Wasow and Loeb 1979; Kaas 1978). Their early socialization simply did not permit it, which makes it an alternative that's tough to choose when they are older. Yet whether we are sexually active and capable or somewhat restricted physically in old age, we can usually stimulate ourselves.

Masturbation plays a significant role in the sex lives of some older people and will probably do so in the lives of many more. Women can masturbate to orgasm long after their male partners have lost the capacity to have or maintain erections. Women can masturbate to orgasm even after vaginal atrophy, arthritis, or other changes that make intercourse impossible, and men can masturbate to orgasm even after they can no longer become erect. In such cases, as in those where intercourse is still possible, older people (like younger ones) sometimes discover the delights of mutual masturbation too.

In some cases of physical handicap or debility, masturbation and mutual masturbation may afford the only sociosexual possibilities. The words of one eighty-three-year-old widow illustrate the importance of masturbation to a probably increasing proportion of the aged: "To be able to masturbate successfully in the later years . . . gives one a continued feeling of being a person . . . still a man, still a woman. . . . It keeps a necessary spark burning which says, 'I'm still alive—all of me!' " (Authors' files, 1980).

Relishing Sex at Any Age

As Masters and Johnson remarked to Carol Tavris (1977), all it takes to enjoy two-person sex at any age is reasonably good health and an interested—and interesting—partner. In their survey of 100,000 *Redbook* readers, Tavris and Sadd found that many older women were enthusiastic about the quality of their sex lives. Two of the glowing letters they received:

We live way out in the country, paradise lane I call it. . . . This is such a nice place, running water all around, we made our own swimming pond. We love going naked all the time, we even work the garden, swim, saw wood naked. We both said we hoped this honeymoon would last forever and it is. We don't care what other people think. It's so much fun to put hay in the barn and lay down on it and fuck. He don't let it come but about twice a week but we fuck all the time. We are always touching. . . . This is our summer love story and I hope fall winter spring will be even better.

   [Written by a sixty-eight-year-old woman]

I am sixty years old and they say you never get too old to enjoy sex. I know because once I asked my Grandma when you stop liking it and she was eighty. She said, "Child, you'll have to ask someone older than me."   [Quoted by Tavris and Sadd 1975, pp. 107–08]*

*Excerpted from the book *The Redbook Report on Female Sexuality* by Carol Tavris and Susan Sadd. Copyright © 1975, 1977 by The Redbook Publishing Company. Reprinted by permission of Delacorte Press.

Feminist sex educator and innovator Betty Dodson has her own particular vision of the sexual potential of older women:

I have a sexual fantasy about my old age. There are thirteen feminists living together in a collective. Our ages range from seventy to ninety. Every night we gather in front of our closed circuit TV to watch our pornographic video tapes. We light incense, get stoned, put our earphones on, and plug in our vibrators for several hours of ecstasy. The rocking chairs creak, the vibrators hum, and we occasionally nudge each other, smiling and nodding, "Yes" after a particularly good orgasm.   [Dodson 1974, p. 55]

FACTORS INFLUENCING SEXUAL EXPRESSION

It is difficult to explain why for some people sexual activity continues into the eighties while for others sex continues only into the forties or fifties. Some may encounter more social labeling as asexual; some may physically age faster than others. In addition people's lifetime sexual careers differ because of social and personal factors. Many of these factors have been considered in other chapters and apply to both younger and older persons. In this section we'll look at the most prominant factors influencing the continuance or cessation of sex.

Gender Differences

Gender strongly influences sexual patterns among the elderly. Although Kinsey (1953) found that sexual activity among women did not drop off with age as it did in men, males had higher levels of sexual activity of all sorts at every age. A prominent pattern of the Duke University aging studies was both the greater sexual interest and the greater actual activity of men compared with women. For all age breakdowns after sixty, the men expressed considerably more interest. For example, one Duke report using participants over sixty who were still healthy and functioning well intellectually and socially showed that only 33 percent of the women but 80 percent of the men expressed continued sexual interest (Pfeiffer 1975). Additionally, only 20 percent of the women, compared with 70 percent of the men, reported that they were still having intercourse.

   Although studies indicate that men at all ages are on the average more apt to initiate sexual exchange and to define sex as vital to life experience, these empirical findings may be mainly a result of the time in which a person is born. For example, the Duke University men and women cited above were born about 1890 to 1930. The time during which they experienced their family and sexual socialization was much more traditional than today, and women were not encouraged to pursue sexual fulfillment over their life careers.

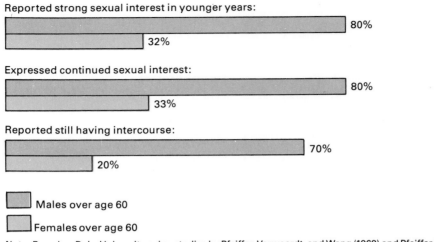

Reported strong sexual interest in younger years:

80%

32%

Expressed continued sexual interest:

80%

33%

Reported still having intercourse:

70%

20%

☐ Males over age 60

☐ Females over age 60

Note: Based on Duke University aging studies by Pfeiffer, Verwoerdt, and Wang (1969) and Pfeiffer (1975).

Figure 11-1. Early Sexual Interest and Later Interest and Behavior. Patterns of sexual interest tend to persist throughout life. If we are interested in sex when we are young, we are likely to be still interested when we are older. Continued interest in sex is somewhat more common than continuation of intercourse, but sexual activity need not be limited to intercourse at any age.

Youthful Sexual Involvement

One dominant theme that experts from many fields have cited is the positive association between our past sexual activity and the continuation of a lengthy sexual career. If sex was important early in our life, then we are more likely to continue sexual activity late into life; but if sex had little importance in our earlier years, then we are likely to be even less active as we get older (Berezin 1976). In other words, we must be active if we are to stay active. It is important to remember that even such a simplistic finding hinges on many other factors.

Degree of Erotic Motivation

Gerontologist Clyde Martin studied 188 married males aged sixty to seventy-nine who participated in the Baltimore Longitudinal Study of Aging (1981). These men were above average in health and education, were happily married, and regarded their wives as physically attractive. The participants were divided into three equal groups, from "least" to "moderately" to "most" sexually active. The average age for each group was sixty-eight. Martin's findings paralleled those previously discussed—that persons most sexually active in their earlier days were also most sexually active in old age. "Motivation" is what makes the dramatic difference between these men, Martin concluded. For example, the most active group was considerably more

aroused by things such as seeing women in a public setting and seeing their wives nude. Martin concluded that the awareness of sexual desire leads or pulls the most active group to continue their sexual activity. Those men least active did not respond sexually to visually erotic stimulation (p. 413). Martin suggests that the degree of motivation that separated these three groups of older men also played a part in their earlier sexual histories. For some the motivation for sex was not compellingly strong even when they were younger.

Availability of Appropriate Partners

A major problem for many older women is that they no longer have husbands. According to the value system they grew up with, the only appropriate intimate partner for a woman is a spouse. This lingering double-standard definition restricts older women considerably more than it does older men.

According to the Duke studies (Pfeiffer, Verwoerdt, and Davis 1972), the sex lives of women born sixty to eighty years ago depend heavily on the availability of a partner who is socially approved and sexually capable—that is, a husband who is still alive and sexually interested. Since women tend to marry men several years older and then to outlive them by seven or more years, many older women are widows. Because they have no husbands, they are sexually inactive. The starkness of this issue can be shown by the unequal ratio of persons over sixty-five—146 women for every 100 men in the United States. In raw gender figures there are 14 million older women to 9.5 million older men (U.S. Department of Health, Education, and Welfare 1978). If social ideas about the acceptability of singles and extrarelationship sex were to change, women who wished to do so could realize much more of their sexual potential.

In the Duke studies 90 percent of the women cited spouse-oriented reasons for stopping sexual activity (death of spouse, divorce from spouse, illness of spouse, spouse unable to engage in sex, spouse lost interest), whereas only 29 percent of the men noted spouse-oriented reasons for stopping. Instead, they emphasized three things about their own incapacity for sex: 14 percent cited personal loss of interest, 17 percent cited their own illness, and 40 percent thought they were unable to participate sexually (Pfeiffer, Verwoerdt, and Davis 1972).

Nevertheless, people's close ties to someone now dead cannot easily be transcended—either personally or socially. Reaching out, especially sexually, to a "new" person can evoke guilty feelings of cheating on the deceased lover. This reaction prompts reticence and perhaps impotence and makes reentry into social life difficult. As the years pass, people may even feel increasingly awkward about sex, as though it were a "skill" and they'd forgotten how to do it from lack of practice (Kohn and Kohn 1978).

In addition to their own hesitation about getting sexually involved again, widowed people may be treated as misfits if their social world consists only of paired couples. Some widowed people report feeling awkward because they are always

The sexual options of older people depend partly on the availability of partners they consider appropriate.

thought of as "the widowed person"—part of a couple—not as a single person. In addition, widows may remind "friends" too vividly of the nearness of their own husbands' death and their own possible singlehood—so they are politely shunned.

Loneliness after a partner's death is not limited to the heterosexual. For instance, aging males with a homosexual preference are also often caught up in problems of losing an intimate without many opportunities to replace their loved partners. Kelly's (1977) Los Angeles study showed that of homosexual males aged fifty to sixty-five, 50 percent reported satisfactory sex lives, but that after age fifty-five the number of lasting partnerships drastically decreased. As one participant described the impact of his lover's death, "It left me with nobody and not much chance of finding anybody at this age" (Kelly 1977, p. 330).

Apprehensive Self-Concept

Many aspects of older people's self-definitions lead them to be either asexual or less active. Two such dimensions of the sexual self are apprehensions about their ability to participate in sex and concern about their physical attractiveness. Negative build-up of apprehension and embarrassment in these areas can provide a destructive personal block to feeling sensual.

It is especially difficult for older men to maintain a positive self-concept if they worry that they are inadequate lovers. Masters and Johnson (1966) noted that the older men they observed expressed a fear of failure as their sexual capabilities lessened. Bernie Zilbergeld (1978) even points to a "cycle of retreat" from sexuality by elderly males. Unless these men can adopt a nonperformance orientation, they will become enmeshed in an anxiety cycle. As Zilbergeld comments, being apologetic about being old is not only bad for "good sex" but also bad for "good anything."

Feeling physically attractive is an important dimension of the self-concept at all ages. As such it can easily become another important aspect that troubles aging persons about themselves. They are vulnerable on this count if they accept only beauty-contest and mass-media-advertising standards of comparison. Tragically, many do just that. Nurse Merrie Jean Kaas (1978) reports that most of the nursing home elderly she studied in Detroit feel that they are not sexually attractive. As a result they say they would not enjoy sexual activity even if they had a willing partner. Wasow and Loeb (1979) reported that among residents participating in their Wisconsin nursing home study, 78 percent of the women and 58 percent of the men said they felt sexually unattractive. Their negative self-concept played an important role in their lack of sexual initiative. If people feel unattractive or embarrassed about negative physical attributes like loss of memory and other maladies, then they don't even try to engage potential intimates.

Martin (1981) suggests that we reconsider these clinical-oriented claims that an apprehensive self-concept is a major influence impeding sex among older people. None of his 188 Baltimore Longitudinal Study husbands complained about fear of failure or worried about meeting some unattainable sexual goal. Rather, the most consistent response from those sexually inactive was to accept the fact as just another sign of aging. According to Martin, all these inactive husbands accepted the loss of sex without evidence of any trauma whatsoever.

Boredom

Masters and Johnson (1966) place boredom first in their list of six reasons for the older male's loss of interest in intercourse. When not experienced as spontaneous pleasuring, sexual contact can easily become routine for partners. In addition, it may begin to seem an obligation. Kinsey (1953) remarked on the regular pattern of sex his married couples reported on their day-to-day calendars. If we are so patterned that variety, tenderness, and spontaneity are not present, then sex can quickly become dutiful and worklike.

Therapists frequently encounter this condition in marriage. Richard Kerckhoff (1976) notes that few middle-aged partners have relationships that are stimulating, challenging, and growing. Again, boredom is often the trouble; such complacency is deadly to intimacy.

Tensions and Hostilities

Built-up depression, hostility, and tensions in a long-term relationship also are devastating to arousal in older persons. Lacking buoyancy and

Continuing sexual affection requires that partners feel warmth and love, rather than unaddressed tensions and hostilities.

weighted down with a history of friction, a person with declining energies may not easily be able to activate the vibrant and compassionate feelings of the earlier days of the relationship. "When will we ever make mad, passionate love again?" can be the plaintive cry.

Over the years discord can build so that "histor-

FACTORS INFLUENCING SEXUAL EXPRESSION 231

ical anger" is established. When this happens, needs for affection cannot be met by partners because they always bring up the past hurts and these become barriers that prevent reaching out and touching each other. This historical anger leads to avoidance of intimate sexual contact. Minor peeves or annoyances are often used to vent a deep-seated rage. For example, if a husband snores, a time may come when even sleeping with him—let alone faking an interest in sex—is not worth the hassle for the wife. Separate bedrooms and physical distance can be the final distancing step. In this case it is not

Figure 11-2. Cessation of Marital Intercourse among Relatively Young Couples. Cessation of sex is not necessarily a function of aging. Many older people continue to enjoy sexual activities, while some younger couples stop having intercourse temporarily or permanently. Edwards and Booth (1976) found that a third of the 365 married people they interviewed had stopped having intercourse for a definable period (with a median of eight weeks), even though the sample was relatively young (74 percent were twenty to thirty-nine years old). The reasons given by those who had stopped are summarized in the table above.

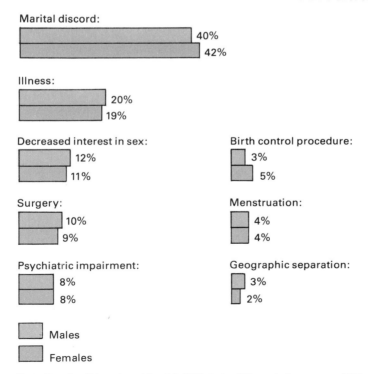

Note: Based on Edwards and Booth's 1976 study of 80 married women and 126 married men who had stopped marital intercourse for a median length of 8 weeks.

the snoring that causes the separation (one can gently roll the other over—or use ear plugs). Rather it is the accumulation of unresolved bitterness and historical anger that causes the ending of sex in a relationship.

Ending of sexual interest because of hostility is not limited to older people. Many people stop having sex permanently, or for considerable lengths of time, much before their later years. John Edwards and Alan Booth (1976) studied sexual retirement among 365 persons averaging only eleven years of marriage. Some 32 percent of the men and 36 percent of the women reported not having sex with their spouses for a lengthy period of time. Of those ending sex while young, "marital discord" was the single major cause for long-term termination of sex.

Privacy Issues

For many older people privacy is a problem. Their financial situations often make home owning unfeasible, and they have to share a residence with their children, for example. Among those who are able to maintain apartments, their health may be poor and require frequent visits from community health care personnel, neighbors, and family. Poor health can also lead to a nursing home or to hospitalization. Under these and other residence arrangements, the elderly have little privacy for themselves. Without privacy and without control over who visits at what times, they rarely have an intimate setting for sex. This lack of privacy may become a factor causing some older persons to cease sexual activity.

Much of the lack of concern for providing privacy for intimacy can be traced to the asexual labeling society has put on the elderly. Some of the lack of concern is the uneasiness sexuality itself creates for those involved in providing services for the elderly. Doctors, social workers, adult children, neighbors, and others who encounter the older person avoid raising concerns about sex. If the elderly have little or no resources to counter these hurdles of asexual labeling and ostrichlike treatment, their opportunities to continue being sexually active are greatly restricted.

The failure to consider new intimacy patterns is starkly apparent in nursing homes for the elderly.

Kaas (1978) has cited absence of privacy as a major deterrent to sexual expression in nursing homes. The problem is not merely the bother and expense of creating facilities for intimacy. The expectation of appropriate behavior for the elderly play a part in setting the "rules." The assumption is often that the elderly are sexless; thus they are treated that way. In a series of studies of Wisconsin nursing homes, Mona Wasow and Martin B. Loeb (1979) noted that administrators and others are extremely resistant to considering the elderly residents' sexual interests—even though roughly 80 percent of the residents responded yes to the question "Should older people be allowed to have sex?"

Kaas (1978) reports from a study of five Detroit-area nursing homes that nursing staff even believe that sexual activity between residents should be reported. Such a smothering policy hardly encourages a secure feeling of personal control and privacy among lovers. In this atmosphere the people who masturbate and the couples who manage to sneak an affectionate moment become the freaks. With such a definition it is difficult to advance to the level of alternatives for elderly intimacy. Would administrators and nursing staffs holding this attitude consider bringing in clinical prostitutes? Providing stimulating books? Holding sex education workshops? Offering private rooms with "Do Not Disturb" signs? Steffl and Kelley (1979) point out that even offering a conjugal-room facility does not provide the setting for ideal lovemaking. Having to sign up can take the edge off romance for anyone, not just the elderly, and doesn't allow the personal choice and control of desired settings for loving.

ENHANCING POSSIBILITIES FOR INTIMACY

Even if it were simple to change the intimate environment that has direct impact on the aged, they need improved opportunities to make their own sexmaking decisions. Social support for alternative relationships is limited, but this situation may change during the 1980s as the intimacy needs of older people receive increasing attention. A few options are presented in the following section.

Group Living

The disproportionate number of older women is one planning challenge. What possible solutions are there to this imbalance? Women could live with each other, or friends of varying ages and genders could share one residence. However, after an extensive review of such options, Paula Dressel and W. Ray Avant (1978) concluded that few older people will try such possibilities at this point in their lives. They noted that most elderly persons have been reared to view monogamy as the ideal living arrangement; for these persons it is difficult to seek intimacy outside a monogamy framework. Equally important, our social, legal, and religious institutions do not encourage polygyny (having more than one female mate at the same time) or communal lifestyles for the elderly, even though to legalize polygyny would provide opportunity for more women to marry.

House sharing may become more common at all ages if the scarce energy resources, slowed economic growth, and decreasing monies for human services of the early 1980s are continuing realities. Gerontology specialists Gordon Streib and Mary Anne Hilker (1980, p. 182) speculate that "alternative lifestyles in which older persons will share living facilities such as a house and automobile and other aspects of a common lifestyle comprise one set of realistic alternatives which can be workable, economical, energy conserving, and fulfilling in terms of the quality of life."

For the time being, older people are largely unwilling to enter such arrangements unless they are forced to do so for reasons of poor health or financial need. Some 70 percent of the people over sixty-five in the United States live in and own their own homes; 56 percent of these homeowners live alone. Most of them are widows who like it that way; they seem to relish the freedom of singlehood. They typically don't see house sharing as a vehicle for intimacy. They are especially reluctant to share a house with someone they define as old, preferring someone "middle-aged"—for this is how they view themselves, negatively stereotyping other old people (Usher and McConnell 1980).

Remarriage

Older people are more likely to find intimacy in remarriage, especially those who view sex as most appropriate within a marital relationship. Vinick (1978) reported that more than 35,000 marriages involve at least one participant aged sixty-five or older.

Loneliness is a major force pulling the elderly into remarriage—especially for men. With five widows to one widower, the opportunity for remarriage favors men under a monogamous system. Many women who adhere to a monogamous heterosexual model for intimacy must therefore adjust to being alone. Often they structure friendship groups with other women to form a sort of society of widows (Vinick 1978).

Even though remarriage sounds like a positive move, especially if neither partner is being exploited, still it is often opposed. Opposition to remarriage for the elderly can come from their middle-aged children as well as from grandchildren. Middle-aged "children" often feel resentful of the sexual overtures of their aged parents and worry that their parents are acting somewhat ridiculously. And sometimes there is selfish concern that the new partner might be willed much of the parents' money, cutting into the children's "share." In addition family members may feel the loss of attention when a grandparent invests energy in another relationship.

Interestingly, opposition to an older person's remarriage can come from the aged themselves. For instance, an older woman's friends, the society of widows, may feel deserted when she remarries. This friendship network of widows may express concern about the possible failure of their wayward friend's new marriage. Other older friends may send such subtly disparaging signals as, "Is it really what you want?" (Vinick 1978).

Since there are so few available men of their own age, remarriage is not an option for many older women. After age seventy-five only 15 percent of women are living with a spouse compared with 40 percent of the men (Streib 1978).

Older/Younger Lovers

Among the widely accepted coupling rules of our society is *age grading*—that is, the idea that intimate partners should be of similar age. Many social factors encourage the seeking of partners in age-graded fashion. The age-organized school system especially leads many of us to think of people with-

Rather than narrow age-graded groupings, we can all enjoy the richness of cross-age friendships.

in a year or two of our own age as the most appropriate friends and lovers.

This early learning blocks acceptance of the idea that lovers can be widely separated in terms of age. Many feel that it is not right to "rob the cradle," especially if the older lover is a woman. The old double standard and patriarchal habits allowed men to have the advantage in negotiating with younger women for affection. Women have only recently begun to establish their right to make a similar choice to love younger men.

Although older woman/younger man relationships among media stars receive a lot of publicity, women's right to relationships with younger men is not yet socially accepted. For example, when Bette Ziegler and Jane Seskin (1979) studied committed sexual relationships between older women and younger men, they found that the women's children expressed opposition to the involvement, especially when the younger lover was somewhat close in age to the children.

We might speculate that such a relationship would change a woman in the eyes of her own children from a caring mother into a sexual, self-oriented being, which could be difficult for the children to handle. Children could also easily think that something was being taken away from them. Perhaps only as they transcend the child role with

their mother will they accept a near-peer as mother's lover. After all, she may feel she has a right to her own life satisfaction. But the role transition could be difficult for children.

Ziegler and Seskin also noted that parents were even more resistant than children regarding older woman/younger man relationships, especially the young man's parents. Parents tend to hold on to the "my child" label for their daughters and sons even after their children become adults. This "role stretching" may be one of the factors that blind parents to accepting the love relationship of a son: "How could 'my child' love someone my age?"

If we can get away from these narrow age-graded views—and from the stereotyping of older people as wise but feeble and the young as vigorous but foolish—we may greatly enrich our own lives through intimate cross-age friendships. We may find ourselves drawn to people both older and younger than ourselves by the same attraction factors discussed in Chapter 5, for these apply to friends and lovers of all ages.

Same-Gender Relationships

Another way for older women to satisfy their intimacy needs in the face of a declining pool of male partners is to develop intimate relationships—sexual or nonsexual—with older women. Some may be developing lesbian relationships for the first time in later life, whereas others may have had homosexual orientations all along.

A study of 20 older lesbians in California reveals that sexuality continues to be important to many of these women. Unlike heterosexual women they have little trouble finding new sex partners and supportive friends of their own age. Some of these women enjoy sex even more now than when they were younger. One attributes her late sexual blooming to beginning her first lesbian relationship after being married for twenty-five years. Another, who now finds sex "happy, fulfilling, marvelous," says her sex life became much more active after she came out at age sixty-two. A third sees growing interest in sex as part of her personal growth:

Sexuality is important to me. . . . My sexual needs increase as I grow older. I think as women grow older we grow more sexual. We are getting in touch with our basic natures. I love to touch and be touched. I'm not so bothered now by what people think. Whoever I get involved with has to be very spontaneous about lovemaking. [Quoted by Raphael and Robinson 1980, p. 213]

Contrary to stereotyped notions that lesbians are lonely and isolated in later life, these women typically have strong friendships with their lovers or with others in the lesbian community. Similarly, a study of 43 older gay males in a northeastern city indicates that they continue to enjoy contacts with family and friends (Friend 1980). Faced with stereotyped expectations that to be both old and gay is doubly problematic, one of these men expressed his individual potential for a rich, satisfying life:

Everybody is afraid of aging. People think it's sad to age alone and they think it's twice as tragic if you're gay. One thing I've learned by coming out is that I'm not going to live out what they imagine about it. The older I get the more comfortable I feel. [Quoted by Friend 1980, p. 240]

Government "Solutions"

The overwhelming lack of satisfactory intimacy settings for many elderly is a disgrace in our society. In only a few communities throughout the entire country are there innovative living arrangements, such as small elderly communes and share-the-house plans. Therefore these living styles help very few and have little impact on the vast numbers of older citizens.

Change in the current fragmented government policies for older people will not come easily. One significant change the government has inadvertently created is an increase in cohabitation among older people. Elderly couples who get married lose some social security monies and are therefore penalized by the government. Cohabitation has increased as an attempt to cope with the government's social security policy that favors remaining single. This change was not planned or innovative on the government's part. But for many older people it represents a major shift away from values they grew up with and the ways in which they imagined themselves behaving.

Gerontologist Nancy Sheehan (1980) notes that government programs for the elderly exist, but they are compartmentalized. One agency does this and another does that, but no one focuses on the person as a total being. For example, there is the meals-on-wheels program, the social security check program, and the public health nurse, but not a program for anything like "sex after lunch." Sheehan believes that the lack of dealing in a unified fashion with the total person causes many elderly to feel alienated and adrift emotionally. They often feel a lack of contact with meaningful people. What exists is only a meager conveyor belt system to the elderly, and sex is not on that belt line. To effect needed change will take organized and persistent advocate groups for the aged, such as the Gray Panthers.

CONTINUED SEXUAL LEARNING

One final note regarding the varied sexual careers of the aged: Even though they may face many problems, they have the ability to learn new ideas and unlearn old attitudes and "facts." Educational programs are being developed to help energize the elderly to enjoy sex. For instance, Kay Rowland and Stephen Haynes (1978) conducted a program involving couples aged fifty-one to seventy-one in three two-week sex education sessions. Sixty percent of the participants reported improving the quality of their sexual lives. Among the changes noticed was the men's increasingly positive view of women. A main factor seemed to be the chance to explore ideas and share thoughts with others. When we can freely share thoughts about sex that were not previously out in the open, then new vitality is energized. With many elderly, that is all it takes.

It is encouraging that the elderly can be revitalized sexually through creative programs, but it should be noted that older persons continually do wish they knew more about sex. Wasow and Loeb (1979) were surprised by the nursing home residents in their Wisconsin study. Why? They wanted sex education! These older people asked such questions as "Just what is a homosexual?" and "Do normal people really masturbate?" Most of these nursing home residents said that sex was okay for the elderly, but they also said "I still need to know more." And the youngest was sixty! Sex education should not be limited to young persons. We need to make it an option for all ages and stages. Many elderly want to learn more and can and will do so.

The right to express oneself sexually should be granted to older persons, for it helps guarantee life vitality at any age. Psychiatrist Robert N. Butler states it well:

Psychologically, the sex act offers many older persons opportunities to express passion, affection, and loyalty, while providing affirmative evidence that the body is still reliable and functional. It is a means of self-assertion in a society where most traditional means of assertion are denied to older people. The sex act itself reflects a continuing commitment to life and a full participation in the human experience. Older individuals have as much right as those of any age to this form of personal expression. [Butler 1978, p. 7]

Summary

Our society has tended to label elderly people as sexless, but this is not necessarily true. Despite the physical changes of menopause, older women still have the capacity for enjoying sex. Men's sexual responses slow somewhat with age, but those in good health can continue to enjoy sex, particularly if their lovemaking is tender and affectionate rather than goal oriented.

Frequency-of-intercourse counts show a general drop in this form of sex with age. But women whose sex lives were previously limited by learned inhibitions may "wake up" sexually as they mature. For both genders self-pleasuring is always an option, even when partners are unavailable. The frequency with which people continue to have sex depends on their gender, patterns from their earlier years, their general interest in sex, the availability of partners, their self-concept, feelings between partners such as boredom or hostility, and their degree of privacy. Options such as group living, remarriage, younger lovers, same-sex friendships, and government programs could lead to enhanced opportunities for intimacy, and perhaps sex, for the aged, who are at least theoretically as available to learning and changing as are younger people.

12

Sexual Assault

237

One time he wanted to have relations and I didn't. You could say it was forceful. It was forceful enough that I did it. He had had a couple of drinks. He had me down on the bed and he was standing up. He didn't hurt me but it was a little scary. . . . He held my arms. That was it. . . . I went ahead with it. I was afraid of what might happen next, that he might become violent.   [Russell 1982, p. 92]*

We had a fight. He wanted sex and I didn't. I wouldn't say he physically forced me. It was more my fear of violence—of getting hit—that made me go along with him and have intercourse. I knew he'd hit his first wife, and I'd been pushed a couple of times by him. But I also used sex as a way of cooling down a fight. For example, a fight seemed to be getting out of hand. He threw something and it broke against a wall. I remember getting nervous. I can't really call it force—it was just the fear of it. I wasn't afraid of being hit, but of other kinds of violence. So we had intercourse.   [Russell 1982, p. 47]*

About five years ago when I lived in Chicago I awoke one night gagged with my hands pinned down by someone who was wearing leather gloves and holding a razor to my throat. I wasn't quite sure I was awake. I thought I must be in the middle of a nightmare that seemed much more realistic than usual and I couldn't break it up. I was trying to establish if there really was a person there. And then I did get my wrist cut slightly, so I realized it was real and that I was risking my life and that I'd better hold still and let the man have intercourse with me. He was very fast. He wasn't wearing any clothes on the bottom half of his body and he ran out the window in that position, just like Romeo on the balcony, onto the fire escape and down.   [Brownmiller 1976, p. 392]

*From *Rape in Marriage*, by Diana E. H. Russell. Copyright © 1982 by Diana E. H. Russell. Reprinted by permission of Macmillan Publishing Company and The Jonathan Dolger Agency.

Every day many women, children, and men are subjected—sometimes brutally—to sexual activities they don't want. These assaults violate not only their bodies but also their right to freedom and privacy. Victims of sexual assault and rape often carry emotional scars that last far longer than their bruises. And the impact of sexual aggression extends far beyond the victims. Even the fear of being sexually attacked keeps *potential* victims from enjoying life to the fullest. An ABC News–Washington Post Poll indicated that 31 percent of women worry frequently about someone raping either them or someone in their family (Alderman 1981). Many frightened women anxiously bolt their doors, fearfully investigate strange noises, avoid going out alone, and worry that their behaviors and clothes might be seen as provocative. Such constraints severely limit their capacity for exploration, growth, and personal peace. Sexual aggression is a negation of sexual choices. In this chapter we will consider the social and personal dynamics of sexual harassment and aggression.

SEXUAL HARASSMENT

Sexual harassment in work and academic environments may be defined as follows:

Unwelcomed sexual advances, requests for sexual favors and other verbal or physical conduct of sexual nature constitute sexual harassment when: (1) submission to such conduct is made either explicitly or implicitly a term or condition of an individual's employment or academic work, (2) submission to or rejection of such conduct by an individual is used as the basis for employment or academic decisions affecting such individual, or (3) such conduct has the purpose or effect of unreasonably interfering with an individual's work performance or creating an intimidating, hostile or offensive working or academic environment. [University of Massachusetts Policy, November 16, 1982, p. 1]

Work Sexual Harassment

How widespread is sexual harassment at work? In one random sample of more than 20,000 federal workers, 42 percent of all women and 15 percent of all men reported harassment ("Sexual Harassment . . ." 1981). Contrary to popular belief, women in all occupational categories are sexually harassed. Among federal workers 45 percent of the harassed women were professionals, compared with 40 percent of the clerical workers and 38 percent of the blue-collar workers. Nor are harassed women all on the low rung of the professional ladder—42 percent of federal employees who were harassed were themselves managers (Blount and Boles 1981).

Studies analyzed by Blount and Boles (1981) show that most sexual harassment is continuous and serious. The harassment is serious not just because it may lead to unwanted sex, and sometimes rape or assault, but also because it may lead to job discrimination. All of the surveys indicated that women reported negative career outcomes when they failed to go along with the demands of their harassers. The Working Women's Institute was founded in 1975 to fight sexual harassment on the job. This institute reports that as many as 25 percent of all women lose jobs, promotions, or raises because of sexual harassment.

By contrast, some women's careers have been enhanced by going along with the sexual advances of their harassers. As MacKinnon points out:

That women "go along" is partly a male perception and partly correct, a male-enforced reality. Women report being too intimidated to reject the advances unambivalently, regardless of how repulsed they feel. Women's most common response is to attempt to ignore the whole incident, letting the man's ego off the hook skillfully by underlining{appearing} *flattered in the hope he will be satisfied and stop. These responses may be interpreted as encouragement or even as provocation."* [MacKinnon 1979, p. 48]

Women in fact feel there isn't much they *can* do to stop the harassment. If they try to ignore it, their silence is often taken as acquiescence by males operating from the traditional her-no-means-yes script. If they try to decline politely, males often don't get the hint that sexual desire is not mutual. As in rape, even vigorous resistance may be interpreted as encouragement (MacKinnon 1979).

In addition to fear of reprisals, sexually harassed women report experiences that affected them emotionally or physically:

"Soured the essential delight in the work."

"Stomachache, migraines, cried every night, no appetite."

"I have difficulty dropping the emotion barrier I work behind, when I come home from work. My husband turns into just another man."

"As I remember all the sexual abuse and negative work experiences I am left feeling sick and helpless and upset instead of angry."   [MacKinnon 1979, p. 47]

The most common reaction in this study was anger. Many women also felt upset, frightened, or helpless.

A number of harassed women feel "guilty." They may wonder if there's some validity in accusations that they were willing partners, that they encouraged advances by the way they dressed or acted. Our traditional cultural patterns suggest that females are supposed to be responsible for controlling the degree of sex in relationships. If she is being harassed, a woman may guiltily dwell on her own part in the matter, as though it were her fault because she did not control the situation.

Women have begun to express publicly their fear and anger at the continual threat of being backed into unwanted sexual situations. The problem of sexual harassment is increasingly being addressed legally, with support from several national antiharassment groups. Although women sometimes sexually harass men, and gays may harass other men at work, the main focus of this protest movement is on-the-job harassment of women by men.

Much has been done to provide "due process" to those who think they have been harassed. Grievance procedures have been set up by businesses, federal agencies, and colleges. In addition many women's rights groups are encouraging women to speak up when they are sexually affronted at the workplace. But reporting sexual harassment may be extremely disturbing for a person who already feels victimized.

According to Blount and Boles (1981) the majority of harassed women do not file a grievance or take any other legal action against their harassers—out of fear or the feeling that nothing will be done anyway. Yet the federal study showed that of

the minority (3 percent of the women and 2 percent of the men) who took action, nearly 60 percent found the complaint process effective ("Sexual Harassment . . ." 1981)

A thirty-three-year-old employee of the Wisconsin Department of Health and Human Services was the first male to win a lawsuit against a female supervisor. After refusing his superior's sexual advances and asking her to refrain from making further advances, he was demoted to his old, low-er-paying job, and he filed suit—with an award for damages of $196,500 ("Role Reversal" 1982).

Sexual exploitation in the workplace can be seen not only as sexual abuse but also as an expression of dominance. MacKinnon (1979) believes that sexual harassment is "dominance eroticized." The unequal nature of the male/female relationship provides a basis for harassment of females by males. As the less powerful half of this imbalance, women are harassed by their coworkers and subordinates as well as by their superiors (Blount and Boles 1981). If people controlling the world of work consistently define women as sex objects instead of skilled and serious employees, then women may lose opportunities to get good jobs and to advance to better jobs. Such treatment of women can lead them to internalize a set of personal goals that includes submissive, compliant lifestyles. Their power has in a sense been taken away by themselves, and only a new level of consciousness will create a change encouraging women to be independent and confident persons.

Campus Sexual Harassment

"Corporate rape" is but one example of harassment. Another common place for sexual harassment is the college campus. As with the workplace most sexual harassment on campus appears to be male against female—whether the females are students, staff, or faculty.

A study by Benson and Thomson (1982) at the University of California, Berkeley, found that 30 percent of female students reported having received sexual attention from at least one male professor during their undergraduate years. In their study Benson and Thomson found less *overt* sexual bribery on the campus, compared with studies on sexual harassment in the workplace. They concluded that the direct costs of harassment to students included loss of self-confidence, disillusionment with male faculty, and an overall concern with the misuse of male power. They attribute some confusion over the appropriateness of sexual overtures to the "greater acceptance of both casual and intimate relationships between faculty and students" (1982, p. 247).

The use of legal processes against sexual harassment may cut down somewhat on its incidence. But in reference to sexual harassment of students by teachers, Sheila Tobias, associate provost at Wesleyan University, recommends another strategy. Rather than setting up special protective measures, she feels a better policy is to teach students of both sexes how to cope with their own emotions and those of their harassers—how to be more honest with each other about what's going on. Her idea is that the real world requires such coping skills; the campus can be a place to learn how to use them to avoid unwanted sex (Munich 1978).

THE MEANING OF RAPE

Like sexual harassment, forcible rape is predominantly a crime perpetrated by males. In the many studies now being done, the central concern is usually how painfully it affects victims and how they can avoid being raped. But to get at the heart of the alarming incidence of rape, it's important to study the rapist, as well as society's part in encouraging sexual aggression.

There are many kinds of rapists and many kinds of rape. But people have long tried to find a common thread running through all rapes. Three major possibilities are reflected: Is rape a sexual crime motivated by a desire for sex? Is it a political crime—a violent attempt by men to dominate women? Or is it a grotesque exaggeration of the gender roles our society has traditionally encouraged? There's no one answer, but it's helpful to consider the themes central to these questions.

Rape as an Answer to Sexual Frustration

Traditionally rape was viewed as an unacceptable way for sexually frustrated men to find sexual release. For instance, in Europe before the French Revolution, people married late and rarely risked sex before marriage or outside of it because of severe social penalties. Birth control usually consisted simply of abstaining from intercourse. Under such circumstances, writes historian Edward Shorter (1977, p. 474), we can assume that there was a "huge, restless mass of sexually frustrated men." (Shorter neglected to mention whether women, too, felt frustrated by this state of affairs.) Females were already so completely dominated by males that rape could not be seen as an attempt to assert more political power. Instead, rape was a simple expression of accumulated sexual misery—an attempt by males to forcibly release sexual tensions that had little legitimate outlet.

For the most part, however, explaining contemporary rape as the result of sexual frustration doesn't work. Studies of rapists show that their "sex drive" (however that is defined) is no stronger than anyone else's, though they do have a higher than average tendency to behave violently. Instead of grabbing just any woman for instant release, rapists tend to plan their attacks in advance and to choose as victims women they already know. Historically, rape has been no more likely to occur when there has been a shortage of women or prostitutes than at other times (Hartmann and Ross 1978). Many social scientists have therefore begun to view rape not as a sexual crime but as a political crime against women.

Rape as Violent Subjugation of Women

A most emphatic portrayal of rape as an attempt by men to dominate women is Susan Brownmiller's book *Against Our Will*. Brownmiller sees rape as "man's basic weapon of force against women, . . . the vehicle of his victorious conquest over her being." She claims that although men may get some sexual satisfaction out of forcible rape, men rape women chiefly to assert power over them. Brownmiller (1976, p. 5) goes so far as to characterize rape as "a conscious process of intimidation by which all men keep all women in a state of fear."

Brownmiller's claims have some support. A study by Menachem Amir (1971) of all rapes reported to Philadelphia police in 1958 and 1960 revealed that 85 percent involved rough pushing around, slapping, brutal beating, or choking and gagging. A few sadistic men may derive sexual

The Language of Sex

Our verbal insults mirror our tendency to see sex as an aggressive power play. "Fuck you!" and "Screw you!" suggest that the insertor in vaginal or anal intercourse symbolically dominates and humiliates his partner. If sex were instead seen as shared pleasure, we'd say "Unfuck you!" to wish someone ill, and "Fuck you" would be wishing someone pleasure.

satisfaction from such violence. But both they and other types of rapists seem to be also motivated by anger toward a specific woman or toward women in general (Burgess and Holmstrom 1974).

According to a major study of rapes in five cities by the Battelle Memorial Institute Law and Justice Study Center for the United States Department of Justice, what's done during the rape suggests a strong hostility toward women:

The sexual act or acts performed are often intended to humiliate and degrade her: bottles, gun barrels and sticks may be thrust into her vagina or anus; she may be compelled to swallow urine or perform fellatio with such force that she thinks she might strangle or suffocate; her breasts may be bitten or burned with cigarettes. [Schram 1978, p. 15]

Such sexual hostility toward women has traditionally been evidenced by their status as spoils of war: Women are frequently raped viciously during wars, but their attackers are rarely punished. As Brownmiller sees it:

War provides men with the perfect psychological backdrop to give vent to their contempt for women. The very maleness of the military, the brute power of weaponry, . . . the spiritual bonding of men at arms, the manly discipline of orders given and orders obeyed . . . confirms for men what they have long suspected: that women are peripheral and irrelevant, except as a form of booty. [Brownmiller 1975, p. 82]

Even in police and legal systems supposedly set up to protect women who have been raped, women have the feeling that they are victims of antifemale hostility. Rape victims sometimes have the impression that police are more sympathetic with the

rapist than with them. For instance, one brutally beaten and choked victim of attempted rape got angry enough to strike back at her assailant by yanking on his penis. On hearing her story, police officers first asked whether the man was hurt, not whether she needed medical assistance (Bart 1978).

Women who try to press charges in court against their attackers are often treated by defense lawyers and judges either as liars who seductively provoked an assault or as recalcitrant slaves who dared to behave as though they were free. The attitude seems to be that if a woman was in the wrong place at the wrong time—walking down a street alone at night, for instance—she deserved what she got.

In this view of rape, then, sex enters the picture only as a vehicle for control. The real effect of the threat of male sexual violence is to intimidate women into a fearful state of submission and to limit their freedom of movement.

Rape as Exaggeration of Gender Roles

It's possible to look at rape in yet another way: as an exaggerated acting-out of "normal," socially approved gender roles. In a sense we teach boys to be potential rapists and girls to be their potential victims. Our society has traditionally linked sexual assertion with masculinity, passive submission with femininity. Girls are often subtly taught that they should not actively enjoy their bodies. They learn that the only way to have sex without guilt is to be overcome: by emotion, the promise of marriage, some drinks or drugs, a man's superior force, or a romantic setting. Many do not learn to share the initiative for sex or the risk of being rejected that accompanies it.

For men exercising sexual power over women has traditionally been seen as a symbol of masculinity. But cast in the role of having to overcome a woman before she'll have sex, men are stuck with the potential burden of being rejected. To avoid the pain of being found insufficiently seductive, many tend to depersonalize their partners—that is, to see them as sex objects rather than as friends whose opinions matter.

Men also tend to read seeming rejection as coy reluctance. They may do so to protect their own egos, but this interpretation is supported by the traditional courtship script. In the traditional script when a woman says "No!" what she may mean is "Yes," "Try again," "Coax me." Anger and insecurity over actual rejections, humiliation over their inability to "perform" like studs when they make themselves vulnerable to a woman, fear of being rejected again, resentment at being placed in this awkward position, contempt for women who are still portrayed as frivolous but seductive beings in the popular media, and need to overcome resistance to have sex all add up to a rapist's mentality.

This view of rape as an exaggeration of traditional gender roles is supported by findings from several studies. Men who believe in different gender roles for males and females are more likely to thrust themselves aggressively on women and to think that women enjoy being treated this way (Griffin 1979). This mind-set inhibits the true give-and-take of loving relationships—something most rapists have been unable to establish (Rada 1978). Men who see sex as a warm, affectionate exchange are less likely to be aggressive and violent than those who define sex as an act of masculine dominance (Libby and Straus 1980).

FORMS OF SEXUAL ASSAULT

The reported incidence of forcible rape was 69 for every 100,000 women in 1981, a rate decrease of 3 percent from 1980. However, since 1977 the forcible rape rate has risen 21 percent. The 1981 total number of reported forcible rapes was 81,536 (Uniform Crime Reports 1982). Surveys of rape victims suggest that these statistics are just the tip of the iceberg, as rape is considered one of the most underreported of all crimes.

The actual number of rapes would be further swollen if variant forms were added to the statistics. The Uniform Crime Reports statistics are based on the "garden variety" of rape—heterosexual intercourse with an unwilling adult female by force or the threat of force. Homosexual rape, sexual assaults on children, sexual assaults other than intercourse, and nonforcible statutory rape with a minor are usually not included in overall rape figures. Nor is marital rape, for it is not considered a crime in most states. In this section we'll break down sexual assault into a number of types to de-

velop a broader view of its extent in our society.

Types of Adult Heterosexual Rape

The stereotyped image of rape is a stranger forcing his penis into a terrified woman's vagina in a dark alley. This is only one way rape can happen. In about one-third of all reported heterosexual rapes, the male is unable to get his penis into the woman's vagina. Either she successfully resists, or he loses his erection or gets scared and runs away. These "attempted rapes" are included in overall rape figures but usually aren't punished as severely as completed rapes—if at all. If the man uses something other than his penis (such as his fingers or a dildo) or penetrates something other than the vagina (as in fellatio), he can be accused of some lesser sexual crime but not rape, according to most states' penal codes. Since such acts can be as physically and psychologically traumatic to the woman as forced vaginal intercourse, the American Law Institute has recommended that all such acts be prosecuted under a single label: "rape and related offenses" (MacNamara and Sagarin 1977).

Rapes differ not only in physical details but also in relationships between victim and attacker. The forcible blitz attack by a stranger represents only a portion of all heterosexual assaults. But it figures high in *reported* rape statistics, for it is the only way people have traditionally learned to define rape. In the blitz attack a rapist suddenly appears, uninvited, and forces himself on a woman. Typically, he is unknown to her and tries to keep it that way by wearing a mask or by covering her face while he rapes her. He may have been following her movements for some time, singling her out as a desirable victim, or he may have struck at random. Typically, he uses considerable physical force.

Force is also typical of group rapes. Even though a gang of attackers could intimidate a victim simply by outnumbering her, they tend toward extremes of violence. Insults, beating and sexual humiliation may be prolonged and intense. Why? Perhaps the adolescents who commit the majority of group rapes (Amir 1971) are motivated by a desire to impress *each other* with their masculinity. By degrading a woman, they try to mask their feeling of inadequacy. Even the leader may feel insecure. But cast in a leader's role by the others, he may initiate violence to satisfy their expectations of him. One gang rape leader admitted, "I was scared when it began to happen. . . . I wanted to leave but I didn't want to say it to the other guys—you know—that I was scared" (Quoted in Griffin 1977, p. 54).

Certain other rape situations are initially characterized more by deceitful verbal persuasion than by physical force. For instance, in the "confidence" type of attack, there is typically some interaction between the man and woman ahead of time. They may already know each other or the rapist may use false pretenses—such as offers of assistance—to win the woman's trust. Sometimes other women act as accomplices to help win the victim's confidence. Then the man rapes her while her guard is down. In some cases the assaults are repeated over time, with the man controlling the woman by fear or force (Burgess and Holmstrom 1974).

Date Rape

Forced sex on a date is probably one of the most common forms of sexual assault and rape. However, the incidence of date rape—rape with an acquaintance or with a more intimately known person—is difficult to determine. The reason is that almost no date rapes are ever reported. Women fear that no one will believe their stories.

In one study at Kent State University, more than half the women students surveyed reported sexual aggression in the form of verbal threats, physical coercion, or violence. One in eight indicated they had been raped, but many did not use the word "rape" when they described their experiences. Only 4 percent of the men studied on the same campus admitted to the use of violence to obtain sex, but an additional 27 percent of the college men admitted to using lesser degrees of physical and emotional force when a woman was not willing to have sex (Barrett 1982).

Date rape is the most difficult type of sexual aggression for women to discuss. A woman's trust has been violated—in some cases by a man she loved or considered a friend. Victims of date rape feel a sense of self-blame—that they somehow gave the date the wrong message, or that he perhaps had some "right" to expect sex if they went to his apartment or dorm room. Because the

Where can the fine line be drawn between the sexual coerciveness some consider "normal" and unwelcome sexual assault? May friendliness be misread as a sexual green light?

rape occurs as a part of ordinary social exchange, it may *seem* less like rape to some—even to some victims.

Some college students view sexually aggressive men to be "normal." One solution might be greater assertiveness on the part of women, greater freedom to say "no" or to initiate sex when they so desire. However, asking a man out may be seen as an invitation to bed even if it is not. According to one study, college men rated intercourse against a woman's wishes as more justifiable if she initiated the date, if the couple went to his apartment rather than to a religious function or movie, or if the man paid for everything (Goodman 1982). The researchers concluded that women needed to make their initiations clear—so that no man they were interested in would misinterpret them.

In addition to rapes of current dates, sometimes a man will try to force sex on a previous partner. He may assume that he still has rights to her body, but she may no longer choose to have sex with him. A Canadian man was sentenced to three years in prison for raping a woman he'd been having sex with for some time. Her attitude in the past had been "warm and loving." When she then invited him to her house but refused to have sex, he forced himself on her anyway. The judge's decision: "Consent given on one occasion is not a continuing consent" ("Man Convicted..." 1979, p. 1).

Statutory Rape

The issue of consent is handled quite differently in cases of sex between an adult and a minor. Even if the younger person willingly agrees to sex, the adult can be charged with rape on the grounds that the other wasn't old enough to know what he or she was doing—to legally give consent.

The age of consent is set by state law. It varies from sixteen to twenty-one in most states. New Jersey has attempted to bring its laws into line with the reality of teenage sex. In 1979 the state enacted a penal code that lowered the age of consent to thirteen, except for sexual relations with relatives, guardians, or other supervisors such as teachers or employers. Both the New Jersey State Coalition Against Rape and the National Organization for Women's Rape Task Force have supported this move. They feel that the mores of increasingly sexually active teenagers "belong in the province of the family and not in the criminal justice system" (Feldman 1979, p. 20).

Sexual Assaults on Children

Much sex between adults and children is not mutually desired. But the extent of force used in interactions varies considerably. Nicholas Groth has identified two basic ways in which an adult gains sexual access to a child. In the first the offender uses nonsexual strategies to establish trust and a comfortable relationship with the child. By giving the child attention or rewards such as candy or money, the offender entices the child into a sexual encounter. Groth explains, "Such offenders appear to desire the child as a love-object and typically describe the victim as innocent, loving, open, affectionate, attractive, and undemanding. They feel safer and more comfortable with a child." ("Nick Groth on Sexual Assault" 1979, p. 2).

Whereas the first type of offender dominates his victims by seduction, the second forces himself on boys or girls by threats, manipulation, intimida-

tion, and physical strength. It is not his intention to hurt the child, so he uses only enough physical force to get the sexual attention he wants. In a sample of 175 Massachusetts men convicted of sexual assaults against children, this pattern was the most common (Groth and Birnbaum 1978).

Groth (1979) reports that child offenders are usually male and rather young. Among his Massachusetts sample of convicted offenders, 82 percent were under thirty years of age at the time of their first known offense. Some have always been sexually attracted to children; others turn to children when sexual relationships with adults become stressful. Their victims are usually prepubertal, with a mean age of ten.

Contrary to society's fears of homosexual teachers, men who eroticize sex with young boys are typically exclusively heterosexual with adults (83 percent, in Groth's sample), while 17 percent of his sample were bisexually oriented, with a preference for women. Groth believes that heterosexual adults are more of a threat to young children than are homosexual adults. Heterosexual child offenders are uninterested in or repulsed by adult homosexual relationships and find the young boy's feminine "smoothness" appealing.

Homosexual Rape

Although estimating how common it is is difficult, homosexual rape does occur, especially among males. Most of the literature on homosexual rape comes from studies of prisons, where it is common. In the Philadelphia prison system, for instance, almost every slightly built young man is approached sexually by other inmates as soon as he enters prison. Many are gang raped again and again. To avoid the terror of these brutal assaults, some find protection of sorts in continuing a single homosexual relationship with one of their attackers. Although prison authorities tend to disregard all such relationships as "consensual," they are often motivated by fear.

The politics of prison rape are similar to heterosexual rapes in the outside world. The aggressors are generally older, bigger, and in for more serious crimes than their victims. Outside prison they were powerless in their community. Unable to get good jobs, raise families, or earn the respect of other men, they used aggression and sex to bolster their sense of masculinity. Imprisoned, they do not rape out of a need for sexual release (masturbation would be easier). Instead, they seem to be satisfying frustrated desires for power by conquering and degrading a weaker person they are sure they can dominate (Davis 1977).

Marital Rape

In 1978 Greta Rideout of Oregon made national headlines by accusing her husband of raping her. The idea that there could be such a thing as marital rape took many people by surprise. By an old common law rule still upheld in most states, marriage is taken as a token of consent to sexual relations. Even wives whose husbands violently force them to have intercourse have not tended to label this act as rape. For instance, one woman's husband tore her clothes off and tried to smother her with a pillow to force intercourse when she didn't want it. But she never thought of this as rape until she was involved in a women's group discussion ten years later. She explained:

Until that time, I think I felt rape was of the stereo-typical type of the stranger leaping out of the bushes and never thought of an incident like that occurring between people who knew each other—especially husband and wife—as rape. I think this is true of many married women—they have accepted society's dictum that a man has sexual access to his wife whenever he wants, whether she does or not.
[Quoted in Gelles 1977, p. 343]

In a random sample of 930 women, Diana Russell (1982) found that "wife rape" was experienced by 12 to 14 percent of the married women. Finkelhor and Yelo (1982, p. 460) point out that forced marital sex is a "common element in the bartering situation." In their study 10 percent of women who had been married or living with someone had experienced force or threatened force to have sex. These researchers delineate three types of marital rape: (1) battering rapes, where sexual violence is a part of general abuse, (2) non-battering rapes, where violence is only a part of sexual behavior out of sexual frustration, and (3) obsessive rapes, where men are obsessed with sex in a sadistic and forceful way.

Legal action in which wives charge husbands with rape is a new alternative. But as of 1982 at least forty-seven husbands had been charged with raping their wives, and of the twenty-three cases that have come to trial, nineteen have resulted in convictions (Russell 1982). In a review of the laws on marital rape, Marianne Stecich reasoned that:

since the notion of women as property has almost disappeared, the purpose of rape laws in general has switched from protecting male interests to protecting a woman's personal safety and freedom of choice. [1977, p. 311]

Stecich concluded:

Even if the consent rationale was justified when first articulated, it is entirely inconsistent with today's concept of egalitarian sexual relationships. Consent should be given by husband and wife for each sexual act, for if women are to be equal marital partners, sexual intercourse must be mutually desired and not viewed as a wifely "duty" enforceable by threats of bodily harm and economic sanctions. [1977, p. 313]

Sadomasochism: Aggression by Mutual Consent

Although people desire protection from unwanted violent sex, some men and women derive sexual pleasure from being hurt. Coupled with partners who will take responsibility for administering pain, they willingly submit to being tied, gagged, beaten, and verbally and physically abused.

What motivates such behavior? After interviewing almost a thousand women about their erotic lives and thoughts, journalist Rosemarie Santini (1976) concluded that behaviors like "bondage and discipline" are an indirect acting out of anger and a dangerous exaggeration of traditional gender roles. On a conscious level women are fighting for their rights as free people and are encouraging men to transcend their old macho gender role. But at a deeper level, Santini has found, women are still turned on by the fantasy of being dominated by a strong man. Having at some point internalized the traditional message that to be superfeminine is to be soft and submissive, some of the strongest women seek a partner who will force them into this role. This behavior also allows them to express indirectly the anger that romantic movies and the love culture of the sixties portrayed as unloving and unlovable, especially in women. By playing the slavish, obedient masochist in response to a man cast as a domineering sadist, they are relieved of the responsibility of both unacceptable anger and the sexual initiative. This package adds up to a turn-on. As one female masochist put it:

Women feel they need a strong authority figure, and being whipped gets all the hostility out of women. It relieves their anger toward men and makes them sensual. [Quoted in Santini 1976, pp. 5-6]

In addition to anger and gender role satisfaction, there are other reasons why both men and women find sadomasochistic (S/M) roles appealing. The muscle tensions of being bound or forced may feel erotic. People bored with more common sexual practices may prefer the titillating qualities of apprehension and suspense. Turning over responsibility for what happens sexually has a strong appeal for men as well as women. Pretending to be a different kind of person allows them to experience unusual sexual pleasures without compromising their everyday identity (Weinberg 1978). And some may have had traumatic personal experiences that make it difficult for them to turn on in more conventional sexual situations.

Although scripts for sadomasochistic scenes may seem unusual, some social scientists are now insisting that they not be seen as "disturbed" behavior. For instance, Thomas Weinberg and Gerhard Falk (1978) assert that S/M aficionados have their own highly structured subculture. The fantasies they act out are not their own inventions but are instead scripts provided by our culture, such as the teacher punishing a pupil. In the S/M subculture enthusiasts contact each other through special clubs, bars, and magazines. Their initial meetings allow them cautiously to determine whether they can trust each other in what will be a potentially dangerous situation. The masochist especially wants to make sure that the other is not a "real sadist" who enjoys inflicting pain but rather someone who will act out the sadist's role within limits that the masochist finds pleasurable (Lee 1979). The boundaries for what the slave can tolerate are carefully negotiated in advance and elaborate fantasy situations organized, complete with props.

Although some suffering is willingly sought through S/M activities, it's considered bad form to let aggression go beyond agreed-on limits. In a study of several hundred S/M incidents among gay males, John Alan Lee (1979) found that although aggression was carefully controlled, a few encounters led to injuries requiring medical treatment. Gay writer Arthur Bell's assessment of the New York S/M bar scene is that many homosexuals seem to crave danger with sex ("The Gay World's Leather Fringe" 1980). Similarly, Santini notes that S/M women report their most erotic fantasy is that of dying under sexual torture. She considers it highly dangerous for women who fantasize about death to place their fate in the hands of men they may hardly know. Even if they survive heavy scenes, they may be badly hurt. Santini warns:

Although it is terribly popular in these modern times to think there are no dangers in the S/M world, that it is simply another form of preferred sexuality, I heartily disagree. My disagreement is not moral; it is simply based on human compassion. Most women in the S/M world have something physically wrong with their bodies. I have seen women's bodies covered with bruises. The women interviewed were always going into or coming out of the hospital for everything from kidney disorders, heart murmurs to internal female disorders of all kinds. [Santini 1976, p. 8]

FORCIBLE RAPE PATTERNS

Although there are many varieties of sexual assault, we'll explore one type in greater depth: adult heterosexual rape. What are the dynamics of being a rape victim? A rapist? How does the law deal with both?

Being a Rape Victim

One problem that bedevils studies and court trials of such events is the suspicion that rape is not entirely unwanted—that some women provoke their own assault. As we'll see, women as well as men have accepted this notion. But evidence on who is victimized by whom, what the experience is like, and how women react afterward clearly indicates that for the majority of victims rape is an extremely traumatic experience that is not at all of their own choosing.

Do Victims "Ask for It"?

Do women—as men often charge—somehow ask for and enjoy violent, forced sex? This question frequently underlies attempts to establish a rapist's "innocence" in court. To get a handle on this aspect, Amir studied statements by witnesses, rapists, and police to determine whether victims had encouraged their attackers to believe that they were available for sex. He used the term *victim-precipitated rape* to describe situations in which the victim had seemingly first agreed to sex then changed her mind without resisting "strongly enough" to convince her partner. He also uses the term *victim-precipitated* for "risky situations marred with sexuality, especially when she uses what could be interpreted as indecency in language and gestures, or constitutes what could be taken as an invitation to sexual relations" (Amir 1971, p. 266). Using this model, Amir determined that 19 percent of the Philadelphia rapes were victim-precipitated.

This concept has many problems, however. It assumes—as some rapists do—that a woman who is friendly, who touches a man during a conversation, who has a drink with someone she's just met, who is comfortable talking about sex, who enjoys her own sexuality and doesn't try to hide it by the way she dresses, or who doesn't act suspicious of strangers is a "bad woman" who is available to anyone for sex. The possibility that she is instead a free person who wants to have sex only with partners she chooses is ignored. And what of women whose normal activities carry them into high-risk situations? For instance, can women who must return home late at night from work or class be automatically classified as provocative?

As noted in Chapter 5, we tend to see what we want to see in potential sexual encounters. Men tend to interpret any touch as sexual desire, any attractive woman moving alone in a place where she "shouldn't be" as "asking for it." Once a woman catches on that a man has made this mistake and is trying to force sex—or sexual activities that she finds frightening, disgusting, or painful—she may try to resist. But under our outmoded "no means yes" system, the man can still assume that he's got a reasonably willing female in his grasp. How strongly must a woman resist to convince him otherwise?

A further problem in counting "victim-precipitated" rapes is that many women believe

It is inappropriate to assume that people who are warm, friendly, and comfortable with their sexuality are sexually available to anyone who wants them.

myths such as "short skirts and no-bra outfits cause rape," and "women ask for it." Many blame themselves if they are raped, whether this feeling is warranted or not. Martha Burt of the University of Minnesota's Center for Social Research found that every one of the rape victims she worked with felt this way. Every woman said, "It's my fault I was raped because . . ." ("Researcher Confirms . . ." 1978, p. 1).

Who Is Targeted?   Although many who get raped are young, pretty, and alone, these qualities hardly justify the assumption that they are "asking" to be raped. Rather than somehow choosing to be attacked, rape victims are seemingly chosen as "marks" by their attackers.

According to a survey of a quarter million people in thirteen cities (Hindelang and Davis 1977), 286 out of every 100,000 white females and 385 out of every 100,000 black or other nonwhite females aged twelve and over have been targeted for rape at some time. The age group most likely to be raped is sixteen-to-nineteen-year-olds (Hindelang and Davis 1977). Once a woman reaches thirty, the likelihood that she may be raped drops sharply. In cities surveyed by the Battelle Institute, only 11 to 21 percent of all rape victims were over thirty.

Convicted rapists typically describe their preferred victims as friendly, young, pretty, white college students or housewives. Women who are overweight, sick, pregnant, very young or middle-aged, crippled, or prostitutes are usually rejected (Schram 1978).

Women who have never been married or who are divorced or separated are far more likely to be raped than women who are married or widowed (Hindelang and Davis 1977). Women in inner-city areas are particularly vulnerable, especially in districts with parks, college campuses, or multistoried apartments. Fringe areas with concentrations of cut-rate stores, old buildings, pawn shops, and bars are high-rape districts, too (Hursch 1977). Women are most likely to be approached by rapists in their own homes (31 percent), on the street (28 percent), or in the attacker's car (12 percent). But those who are attacked on the street are often taken to a more secluded location for the rape itself (Schram 1978).

Coping with the Rape Experience.   Most women are terrified when they are raped, for they are afraid they are going to be killed. Even the minority who don't consider the possibility of death experience rape as extemely frightening, degrading, and stressful. The attack is so out of the ordinary that it severely strains their ability to cope.

Burgess and Holmstrom (1976) found that rape victims tried a variety of coping mechanisms. Before the attack many had the vague sense that something was wrong—noticed that a man was hanging around and wondered uneasily what he was up to, for instance. Reactions to this awareness of impending danger included trying to escape, memorizing what the man looked like in order to identify him afterward, talking to calm the man down or dissuade him or at least stall for time, bargaining ("I'll give you my money if you'll go away and leave me alone"), asserting their rights ("Get your hands off me!"), threatening ("My husband is a policeman and he'll be here any minute"), joking, screaming, trying to fight the man off, and blowing a rape whistle to attract attention. One-third of the victims were too scared to do anything, though. They were paralyzed by fear (especially if the man brandished a weapon), totally overpowered physically, or too shocked by an acquaintance's unexpected behavior to do anything.

Women also have varying ways of coping during the rape attack itself. Some comply with the rapist's demands, figuring it's better to be raped than killed. Others struggle to escape or to avoid penetration. But their resistance may stir their attacker to greater violence. Other strategies: trying to stay calm, recalling other people's advice about what to do if raped, praying for help, or trying to take control of the situation. Some block out recognition of what's going on. Others have involuntary physical responses such as vomiting, gagging, urinating, hyperventilating, and passing out (Burgess and Holmstrom 1976).

Continuing to Relate.   The immediate impact of rape brings about a wide range of reactions. After the extreme fear of a life-threatening situation, people may be glad simply to be alive. But they may also feel humiliated, angry, vengeful, embarrassed, or guilty. Their moods may change unpredictably. Thoughts of the attack may haunt them night and day. Many find it hard to eat and sleep, and their bodies may be sore all over.

Rape continues to disrupt victims' lives for

weeks and months afterward. Many women find it difficult to work and feel vulnerable at home. They may change their door locks, phone numbers, and apartments, but the fear of being attacked persists. Disturbing dreams, terror at being alone, and paranoid reactions to strangers and even acquaintances make it hard for victims to feel free and safe anywhere.

Sexual relationships are no comfort, for they're usually marred by associations with the rape. Sensitive partners may wait patiently until the woman's fear is gradually replaced by willing interest in sex. But some insist on asserting their own "property rights" immediately, much to the rape victim's distress. Some double-standard husbands have even subtly blamed their wives for what happened and divorced them, saying "I don't know how I could forgive her although I know it's not her fault" (Renshaw 1978, p. 12).

Rape Counseling.   The support or lack of it from people around her makes a significant difference in a woman's ability to cope with rape trauma. If she decides to report the rape and to experience the additional distresses involved in police, hospital, and courtroom procedures, she should be accompanied by an advocate to help her handle the difficulties she'll probably encounter.

Short-term rape counseling is often beneficial; it usually has two major goals. One is to help the victim gain control over stressful memories of the

Workers at rape crisis centers help rape victims deal with the emotional aftermath of their experience, as well as the complexities of pursuing criminal proceedings against their attacker.

rape. Confronting them directly by talking about what happened tends to dilute the pain and fear they cause. The second goal is to help the victim feel okay about herself again. Some women who've been raped may feel that others will reject them. They need supportive people who will reassure them of being worthwhile, loved, and appreciated. Other women need help because they feel they've lost control over their emotions. They may believe that it's wrong to express anger and want very much to be emotionally "good" again. And still others need help with feelings of weakness and insecurity. Such women are upset that they were not powerful enough to fight off their attackers, for it's important to them to feel that they are strong in any situation. For them courses in self-defense may restore a sense of physical competence, and opportunities to counsel other rape victims may give them a sense of usefulness (Burgess and Holmstrom 1974). Burgess and Holmstrom's (1979) follow-up on their 1974 sample of rape victims revealed that 74 percent of the women believe themselves to be recovered and back to normal from four to six years after the rape.

Police and Legal Responses to Rape

Many rape victims do not seek help from police or try to start criminal proceedings against their assailant. They may be inhibited by many factors: (1) fear that the rapist may take violent revenge if they tell, (2) strong need for privacy, (3) confusion and distress that delay decisions, (4) lack of knowledge of rape-reporting procedures, (5) pessimism about the chances that their attacker can be identified and caught, (6) embarrassment and shame about making their plight public, (7) refusal to be "raped" again by humiliating repetitions of their story, and (8) fear that police, lawyers, and judge will try to blame them for inviting rape (Renshaw 1978; Hursch 1977). Another possibility is that victims of some sexual assaults have not learned to define what went on as rape.

For their part police are often suspicious that women who come in claiming to have been raped may be lying. For instance, sometimes a woman who's been caught in a socially tabooed sexual situation will call it rape to shift the blame to her partner. According to a survey of police in Australia, 64 percent have the possibility of a false complaint uppermost in their minds when a woman tells them she's been raped. One explained that his department routinely shrugs off complaints they consider false, especially during holiday periods:

Over Christmas and New Year's . . . we turn them away in droves. Young girls are always complaining about being raped. What happens is they drink, have sex with the boy they're with, and feel guilty after. We just tell them to go home and forget about it. It's not even worth recording. [Quoted in Wilson 1978, p. 73]

Despite this tendency to be suspicious of rape claims, police in a Boston study were seen as polite and helpful by the majority of rape victims. Almost a third had very positive reactions, saying the police had made them feel better. Only a tenth made negative comments about police reponse, such as "Everyone just stood around staring at me" and "I felt pushed into pressing charges and they made wisecracks like 'You can't rape the willing' " (Holmstrom and Burgess 1978, p. 51).

If police are convinced that a rape did occur, they tend to urge the victim to press charges. Many victims are reluctant to do so. They feel caught in a double bind—either "It will be hell going through with it if they catch him and hell worrying if they don't" or "I'm scared to [press charges] because of what he might do to me; but I'm scared not to because he might do it again to me if he knows I won't tell" (Holmstrom and Burgess 1978, pp. 56-57).

Even if the victim doesn't want to press charges, the police can. But knowing that it's impossible to convict a rapist unless the victim will testify, few push ahead with charges when the victim is unwilling to do so. About half of the reported rapes in the Boston study (Holmstrom and Burgess 1978) dropped out of the criminal justice system at this point, either because the victim couldn't identify her assailant or because she didn't want to press charges.

Women who do press charges discover that the rape is treated as a crime against the state. They are only "witnesses" can be fined or arrested if they don't show up in court. They may watch helplessly as the police, physicians, and district attorney who question them fail to work together to build a case against their attacker. And they may be forced to appear in court again and again waiting for their case to come up, losing working hours and patience all the while. They are often kept in ignorance of what's going on and simply have to wait in the corridor without instructions.

In stark contrast to this depersonalized setting, confrontations in the corridor between the victim and the rapist may be dramatic and personal. Often interaction is hostile, with supporters of both sides slinging insults at each other. But sometimes encounters are embarrassing or loaded with pathos. Either way, these meetings are difficult.

Things may not improve when the trial begins. The district attorney (who represents the state and therefore the witness, more or less) and the defense lawyer (representing the rapist) may differ in their definition of rape. The defense lawyer's version typically prevails, in a blame-the-victim strategy that shifts attention away from the rapist and makes it seem that the victim's character is what's on trial. The defense lawyer may incessantly needle the victim, often reducing her to tears with tedious or extremely personal prodding.

If defense lawyers can establish that the woman knew her attacker, had sex with him in the past, frequented bars, was poor, was a prostitute, wore sensuous clothing, or was calm during the attack rather than resisted strongly, the rapist will often get off free. On top of an already high rate of dropped charges, this strategy is devastatingly effective in protecting the *rapist*. According to the Battelle Institute study (Schram 1978), only one out of four rape complaints results in arrest; only one out of sixty results in conviction.

Despite these discouraging results, some states are beginning to change their laws to remove barriers to rape convictions. For instance, many have adopted "rape shield laws" to prevent defense lawyers from grilling rape victims about their own sexual history, unless it involves previous sex with the accused man. In most states it's no longer necessary to prove that the victim resisted strongly, for it's now recognized that if the woman struggles, the rapist may increase the violence of his attack.

In the past most states have sentenced all rapists to twenty years or more. Now more flexible sentences that reflect the severity of the crime are being considered. For instance, under Michigan's flexible sentencing, a second-time rapist who attacked at gunpoint was sentenced to eight to fifteen years, but a man who slapped and raped an acquaintance but didn't use any other force and had never committed any other crimes was simply fined and put on probation. Given this flexibility, juries have been far more willing to convict rapists: Convictions in Michigan increased by 90 percent between 1972 and 1977 ("A Revolution in Rape" 1979).

Profiles of Rapists

What kind of person commits rape? Surveys show that rapists tend to share certain characteristics. Beyond these, they fall into several distinct motivational patterns.

Common Characteristics. Rapists are predominantly young males. In Amir's study (1971) most men arrested for rape were under twenty-five years old. One doctor who works with rapists has noticed that even older offenders seem far younger than their years, as though they've never finished the developmental tasks of growing up. She and her colleagues have repeatedly been confronted by men "who really seemed to be ten or eleven years old" (Adele Hess, in "The Rapist as Sexual Ignoramus" 1978, p. 2).

Rapists' personal histories are usually laced with barriers to maturity and self-respect. Deprivation, lack of love from parents, extreme jealousy between siblings, chaotic childhood environments, rigidly repressive religious training, abysmal ignorance about sex, and fears of women are common. Many were sexually abused themselves during childhood. Such factors seem to block fulfillment of important needs, including love and respect from those around them, positive attitudes toward sexuality, a sense of self-worth, and a feeling of responsibility for their own behavior (Delin 1978).

Immature, but wanting to fulfill social expectations of masculinity, these men try to prove their power by sexually attacking someone weaker. As one man charged with trying to rape a nurse explained:

I was seventeen. I was trying to prove that I was a man. I didn't fit in with what I saw on television. I didn't fit into that John Wayne image, so I had to do something to prove my manhood. [Quoted in "I Never Set Out . . ." 1972, p. 22]

This near-rapist noted that our society had encouraged him to believe that it's good for a man to be superaggressive and had failed to provide him with respected male models who were both gentle and sexual. And other males' reactions to his rape attempt revealed their encouragement for violence against females. For instance, police acted "as if I was a new recruit on the force." Rather than treating him like a criminal, the captain at the jail offered him a cup of coffee, cleaned the blood off his face, and said, "Damn women always causing trouble for everybody." When the near-rapist told men about his experience, they echoed macho permission to try having sex with any available female: "You should have gone ahead and done it. Every chick wants you to do it" ("I Never Set Out . . ." 1972, pp. 22-23).

Brought up to feel unworthy but to respect violence, rapists often have long criminal records. According to one large-scale study (Gebhard et al. 1965), 87 percent of rapists had already been convicted of some crime by age twenty-six. About half of these previous crimes were sex offenses. But according to Carlos M. Loredo, consultant to a Texas project on teenage sexual offenders, teenage behaviors such as incest, sexual attacks on other children, peeping, or masturbating in public are often overlooked at the time and not labeled as significant. Even when youthful sex offenders are known to police, judges, and neighbors, the prevailing attitude is that "it will just go away." For instance, a Massachusetts teenager charged with raping one University of Massachusetts student and assaulting another one had been arrested earlier in the year for raping a nine-year-old girl while forcing a nine-year-old boy to watch. Although he had been evaluated four times since that incident, it was never recommended that he be placed in a secure institution for treatment. Evaluators apparently assumed it was unlikely that he'd repeat the behavior (Kenney 1979). As a result, Loredo claims, "the prisons are filled with offenders whose problems were ignored at age fourteen" ("Judicial System . . ." 1979, p. 2).

Already deeply troubled, rapists frequently aggravate their tendencies toward violence by drinking. In one study 50 percent of rapists were drinking at the time of their rape, 43 percent of them heavily. In other words they'd had the equivalent of ten or more beers when they attacked. For most this was no isolated incident of drunkenness: 35 percent were chronic alcoholics (Rada 1975).

Differing Motivational Patterns

Aside from characteristics they have in common, rapists can be divided into four types by their motives (Burgess and Holmstrom 1974). The first wants to hurt his victim. He's angry—often at significant women in his life—but displaces this anger onto a woman who's a stranger. In his view women are hostile, ungiving, demanding, and unfaithful. His aggressiveness usually begins to show up in adolescence in exaggerated masculine pursuits—street fights, fast driving, or hyperaggressive sports. In his work, too, he chooses an occupation defined as "masculine"—such as truck driving. He usually attacks women at their home after being admitted on a false pretext, or pulls them into his car. If they struggle, he gets angrier and more violent.

Men who rape older women are usually of this type. Nicholas Groth has found that men who rape women over twice their own age tend to be motivated not by sexual desire but by an angry intent to hurt and degrade their victim. The rape is typically preceded by some particularly upsetting encounter with a woman who figures prominently in the rapist's life. His victim is usually a stranger, but she may represent an authority figure whom the rapist would like to control or an actual woman against whom he'd like to retaliate ("The Older Rape Victim . . ." 1979).

The second type of rapist is far less likely to be violent. He is motivated primarily by sexual desire and uses aggression only to achieve his aim. He usually attacks out of doors—on dark streets or in the woods. If his victim struggles, he may run away rather than use more force to subdue her. His rapes—and there may be many in his history—are neither random nor impulsive. He chooses his mark in advance, follows her, and fantasizes that her initial unwillingness to have sex with him will turn to pleading for more since he is such a great lover. During the rape, though, he may have difficulty maintaining an erection or ejaculate "too soon" or "too late"—as do about a third of all rapists ("Rape and Sexual Dysfunction" 1977).

The sex-motivated type of rapist has had sexual peculiarities for some time. From early adolescence he has expressed his sexuality through fetishism, peeping, and exhibitionism rather than through the usual development of heterosexual contacts. Some observers think that he is repressing strong homosexual tendencies. Guilty about his abnormal behaviors and his homosexual desires, he becomes increasingly lonely, shy, and inept with women. Low in self-esteem, he is plagued by feelings of inadequacy and impotence, which his fantasies of being a great lover help allay. One such man had never had intercourse with anyone but had assaulted over 100 women by trying to caress and force them to the ground until they screamed or resisted (Burgess and Holmstrom 1974).

In stark contrast to the shy, sex-starved rapist, the third type is a sexual sadist. Although he's not angry at his victim, he is turned on only by a woman who resists. To provoke her to anger and struggling, he will use playful, teasing aggression. Projecting his own sadistic desires onto her, he reads her struggling as a sign of sexual excitement, even when he's been so brutal that she's actually fighting for her life.

The sexual sadist's history is laced with aggressive behaviors toward other children and animals, as well as delinquent acts such as lying and stealing. He lacks concern for others, can't put up with frustration, and never feels bad about things he's done. To him, the world is a hostile, threatening place. He's unable to form stable relationships, for he regards other people with suspicion and views encounters as battles in which one person must win and the other lose.

In extreme cases these characteristics lead sadistic rapists to murder or mutilate their victims brutally. These rapes are the horrifying ones played up in the mass media; these are what most women fear when they are raped. Fortunately, sexual sadists are rare, and rape-murders and rape-mutilations even rarer. They account for only a fraction of 1 percent of all rapes (Delin 1978).

The fourth kind of rapist is an impulsive opportunist. Neither angry, sex hungry, nor sadistic, he sees an opportunity to rape a woman while he's committing some other crime and simply does so. Already willing to be exploitative and self-serving, he takes for himself whatever is available. For instance, one such man's principal aim was to rob an apartment, which he did. It happened also to contain a woman and her young children, so after he'd finished ransacking the place, he tied her up and raped her, unconcerned that the children were watching in horror. Little is known about what influences create this predatory type of male (Burgess and Holmstrom 1974).

COUNTERING SEXUAL AGGRESSION

What can society do to protect women from sexual assault and rape? What can women do to protect themselves against such men? What can men do to make such attacks less likely? There are no simple answers, but we'll examine a range of possibilities in this section.

Avoiding High-Risk Situations

One rape crisis center (Clement et al. 1979) recommends that as potential rape victims all women should take many precautions in their lives. For instance, if they drive a car, they should keep it in good working order, avoid running out of gas, keep doors locked and windows closed, park in well-lighted areas at night, avoid stopping to help other motorists, and never pick up hitchhikers. Women who hitchhike put themselves in an extremely vulnerable postion. At home a woman living in a high-risk area should be distrustful of any strangers who come to the door, surround herself with secure locks and curtains, avoid riding the elevator with a strange man or going alone to the laundry room, avoid giving clues to her gender on her mailbox or telephone listing, conceal from telephone callers and people who come to the door the fact that she is alone, and get a noisy dog.

This rape crisis center urges women never to walk alone at night. But if they must, they should walk quickly and look purposeful, dress for action, keep hands free, walk next to the curb, cross the street rather than pass a group of men, ignore men who try to start a conversation, change directions if a car seems to be following them, and wait only at busy bus stops.

Those who analyze high-risk situations see such advice as sheer common sense. But to what extent do fear and distrust enslave even women who've never been raped? As we've seen, what women typically fear most about rape is the possibility that they will be killed or mutilated. This fear is fanned by sensational media accounts of gruesome rape-murders. But these occur in less than 1 percent of all rapes. A woman's chances of getting killed in a car accident are far greater than her chances of being killed by a rapist. Yet most people think that to avoid being killed on the highway by not driving at all would be too great an infringement on their freedom of movement. Similarly, some women so value their freedom of movement that these restrictive suggestions would mar their view of themselves as free, brave, and trusting persons.

Strategies during a Rape

In actual rape situations a fear mentality is certainly of no help to a woman. Carolyn Hursch's (1977) study of women who were attacked but avoided being raped revealed that their ability to take the offensive quickly was an essential factor. Some calmly took psychological control over the encounter. For instance, a public health nurse was suddenly approached by a man who ordered, "Move, bitch, into the alley! I'm going to screw you!" Looking him directly in the eyes, she said in a calm yet kind voice, "If this is the only way you can get a woman, there must be something wrong with you. Why don't you come on down to our Mental Health Center in the morning and we'll help you" (Hursch 1977, p. 61). His offensive shattered, the man agreed. Hursch notes that rapists count on shock and terror to turn women into submissive victims. Women who are able to keep their fear under control or to shake up the rapist himself by screaming or fighting back with quickly mustered anger can sometimes take control out of the would-be rapist's hands.

Pauline Bart (1981) interviewed women who had been attacked more than once, successfully resisting one time but being raped another time. Like Hursch, she found that a protective offensive strategy—determining not to be raped and fighting back—distinguished the rape avoidances from the rapes. Similarly, a study by Block-Skogan found that in a stranger-to-stranger violent confrontation, women who resist reduce significantly the risk that they will be raped or robbed ("New Study Reports . . ." 1982).

In self-defense classes such as this one based on Oriental martial arts, women may learn the calmly centered self-confidence—as well as the physical skills—that may help them thwart an attempted attack.

Which offensive strategies seem to work best? Bart found that women who tried a number of things—screaming, fighting back, talking, running—were more likely to avoid rape than those who used only one strategy. Rapists themselves are likely to have only one plan, and a confident, clever woman with a variety of offenses may make them want to forget the whole thing.

Nevertheless, many women fear unwanted sex less than violence and sense that if they struggle *unsuccessfully*, they are more likely to be injured. Most people typically have little practice in fighting and are not prepared to defend themselves fiercely. Courses in oriental martial arts or "dirty street fighting" can give a feeling of power that helps women resist attack. Some common tactics taught include gouging the attacker's eyes, slamming his nose toward his brain with an open upswept palm, jerking his little finger back hard, jabbing curved clenched fingers at his throat, battering him with powerful elbow thrusts, sinking teeth into his flesh, and raking him with fingernails. The old knee-to-the-groin tactic is not recommended. It throws the woman off balance, and men expect and prepare for it, anyway.

Those who do choose to fight back must avoid the weak defenses typically associated with femininity, for they are worse than worthless. For in-stance, a woman who beats on a rapist's chest with her fists will not hurt him at all and may instead amuse or inspire him to further violence. If she chooses to resist, her main thoughts should be to cause him quick, distracting pain and then to run away fast. Sometimes just a solid, shattering Oriental type of yell suggesting black-belt abilities will unnerve the would-be assailant and give the woman a chance to escape.

There is no single good way to ward off rape or lessen its violence potential that will work in every situation. As we've seen, rapists differ in their intent. A counterattack that might frighten away a sexually motivated rapist might provoke greater brutality from a rapist who's motivated by hostility toward women. A passive victim may be violently abused if her rapist is a sadist who wants a struggle. Women differ in their strengths, too. Empathic women might cope best by seeing rapists as deeply troubled people and by encouraging them to talk and be gentle rather than hostile. Easily angered women might be better equipped to meet violence with violence.

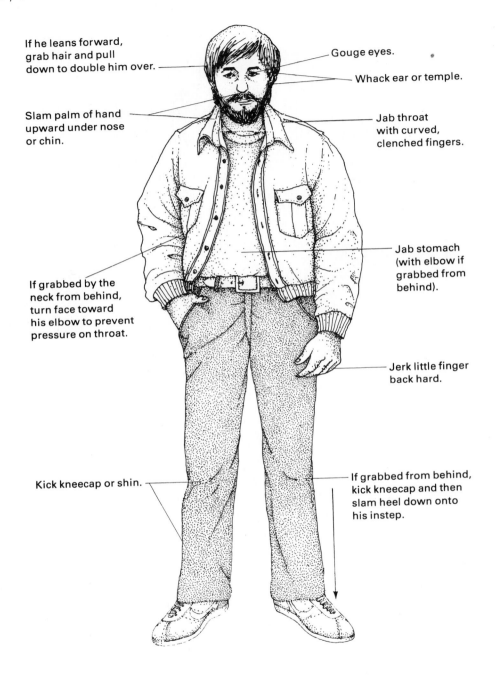

If he leans forward, grab hair and pull down to double him over.

Gouge eyes.

Whack ear or temple.

Slam palm of hand upward under nose or chin.

Jab throat with curved, clenched fingers.

If grabbed by the neck from behind, turn face toward his elbow to prevent pressure on throat.

Jab stomach (with elbow if grabbed from behind).

Jerk little finger back hard.

Kick kneecap or shin.

If grabbed from behind, kick kneecap and then slam heel down onto his instep.

Figure 12-1. Self-defense Tactics for Women. Some women learn "dirty street fighting" tactics such as these in hopes of warding off a sexual assault. If a woman chooses to use such tactics when she is attacked, speed, vigor, and the feeling of being in control of the situation are crucial to her ability to escape. If she struggles unsuccessfully, her attacker may become more violent.

Ideally, a potential victim would quickly analyze what kind of man she's up against and plan a strategy for dealing with him that emphasizes her own strengths. But in a terrifying, painful situation, this levelheadedness is exceptional. In addition it's difficult for some women to quickly shed learned scripts for acceptable public behavior and to act "aggressive" and "controlling" in the face of threat.

Stop-Rape Programs

For potential victims to have to make such choices and live with such precautions is intolerable. Some programs designed to cut down on the number of rapes do focus on such measures, however. For instance, the Boston Police Department's Stop-Rape program is based on educating women to avoid high-risk situations and to scream and run or else fight to hurt if cornered (Foreman 1979). On some college campuses police offer an escort service for women who must walk alone at night. And in West Los Angeles a group named CARE (Consultation and Rape Education) visits elementary schools to give classes in rape avoidance for children. They try to get across the message that kids have a right not to be abusively touched by others, including adults. Through stories and discussions they help children recognize conflicting values in our society. As one staff member put it, "They have to trust adults; they must not be *too* trusting. Good manners, survival techniques, and prudent behavior are often at odds. Confusion is inevitable" ("Rape Education..." 1978, p. 1).

Some victim-oriented stop-rape programs go a bit further. They focus not only on helping people avoid rape but also on helping them overcome the constant fear of victimization that so severely limits activities, independence, and life satisfaction. For instance, a guide for older women put out by the National Center for the Prevention and Control of Rape (1979) suggests ways to channel "excessive" fears into positive activities. Many programs help to create voluntary security systems of neighbors watching out for neighbors. These "neighborhood watches" are especially important in the high-crime areas in which many older women on limited incomes must live. The likelihood that criminal behaviors will then be seen and reported may act as a deterrent to rape and to other crimes as well.

Another line of stop-rape measures is aimed at men arrested for rape. The intent seems to be to make sure that they are convicted and don't rape again later when they get out of prison. Efforts at making rape sentences more flexible to reflect the severity of individual crimes have increased victims' willingness to file charges and juries' willingness to convict (Karagianis 1979).

Another factor that has made rape victims more willing to report rape is growing protection from abuse by police, medical examiners, and defense lawyers. Victims are increasingly treated with respect and sensitivity and their complaint taken seriously by police officers. Some hospitals will arrange for a victim to be examined by a female for signs of rape rather than by a male if she so requests. Rape crisis centers offer advice on where to go and what to do after a rape to increase the chances of finding the rapist and preventing him from harming other people. They also have volunteers who will accompany a victim to the hospital, advise her on police and courtroom procedures, and help her cope with any psychological and legal problems that follow the rape.

As we noted earlier, rape shield laws are being adopted by some states. These laws make a victim's own sexual history inadmissible as evidence that might help her attacker get off free and invade her right to privacy. Most states have dropped the traditional requirement of proof that the victim vigorously resisted the attack. And lawyers from the Center for Constitutional Rights are advising other lawyers how best to defend rape victims who've actually killed their attackers in self-defense. These lawyers were instrumental in a landmark decision by the Supreme Court of Washington that a woman's own perception of what she must do to save herself must be taken into account. Standards of justice that might apply to a fight between two men of equal strength are not applicable to rape of a small female by a large male, especially if she knows him to be dangerous (Schneider, Jordan, and Arguedas 1978).

Major changes could be made in the court procedure itself but have not yet happened. Since the state symbolically is seen as the aggrieved party, the real victim's hurts and needs are never addressed during the trial. Victimologist Leon Sheleff (1976) recommends a radical departure from this system. He suggests that instead of ignoring or degrading the victim and trying to punish the rapist, we should bring the two face to face to resolve their conflict. For instance, the rapist might agree to repay his victim in some meaningful way and hold to this agreement until she is restored to her original emotional and financial condition. They would both receive counseling to help them rebuild their lives. Both would then win. She'd perhaps be repaid for lost work time, and her psychological injury would be treated with serious concern. As for the rapist, he might learn and grow from being expected to take full responsibility for his own actions.

Rapists are considered the lowest of offenders in a prison population that generally elevates murderers to top status. At the bottom of this totem pole, rapists are the subjects of ridicule, sadistic acts, and homosexual attacks by other prisoners. Their hatred for women may be increased, because it was a woman who got them convicted. Their potential for violence may be fanned by their need to make up for their own humiliating prison experiences. And they learn from other prisoners how to keep from getting caught when they return to crime after their prison time is up (Hursch 1977). Rather than decreasing the number of rapists in society, such a system may actually increase it. And it costs as much to lock up and guard men this way as it would to send them to an expensive college (Delin 1978).

In contrast to this generally useless punitive setup, in the United States there are thirty-six special treatment centers for sex offenders that are sometimes more effective in returning these persons to society as healthy rather than hostile people. Here, the focus is not on punishment but on dealing with the problems that led to rape, such as alcoholism, sexual maladjustment, and feelings of inadequacy. For instance, the Treatment Program for Sex Offenders at Western State Hospital in Washington offers a guided self-help approach. Its premise is that only in a community that resembles real-life settings can a rapist learn to recognize his own deviant impulses and build a more humane and responsible way of relating to others. The usual expensive high-security restraints—such as one guard for every two prisoners—are absent. Few men escape, for they seem to recognize a need for the intense inmate-run therapy sessions, which help them drop the defensive shield that masks their feelings of guilt and worthlessness. Bart Delin

observed one particularly dramatic session:

A tall, slender man said he wanted to speak to the group. . . . "I won't see my girl for three months," he declared. "She says she's going on a trip, but I know it's all over for us. She'll never come back! I don't know how I'll live without her!" His chin trembled and tears spilled down his cheeks. Encouraging voices came from the group: "Don't hold back!" "Let it all hang out!" "Don't be afraid to cry!" "It's all right!" His static words broke through the sobs. "I've hurt so many women. I hurt so much myself. I'm no fuckin' good! I want to die!"   [Quoted in Delin 1978, pp. 53–54]

Everyone in the group—all convicted sex offenders—was moved to embrace this man and offer support.

Following the lead of therapy supervisors, inmates at this treatment center encourage each other to recognize their antisocial behavior patterns and to commit themselves to a more responsible code that is sensitive to others' feelings and rights. They leave after fifteen months of in-patient treatment, three months of work-release, and eighteen months of follow-up treatment. The result is a rate of repeat offenses five times lower than that of men discharged from "correctional" institutions (Delin 1978).

Attacking Rape at Its Roots

As valuable as these preventive measures may be, they are only Band-Aids applied after the fact. To lower the incidence of rape significantly, we must attack it at its source.

One such approach has been to assume that rape is motivated by biological abnormalities that can be "cured" biologically. For instance, in some European countries convicted rapists are castrated. The surgical removal of their testes (and their replacement with small plastic balls to retain a normal appearance) is supposed to eliminate what is viewed as an abnormally high "sex drive." The assumption here is that a high level of androgens (produced mostly in the testes) causes "criminal energy" and an unusually strong need for sexual release. According to this theory, if we remove a rapist's androgens, we remove his desire to rape.

This assumption has a number of problems. For instance, one study has shown that androgen levels in rapists and child molesters are not signifi-

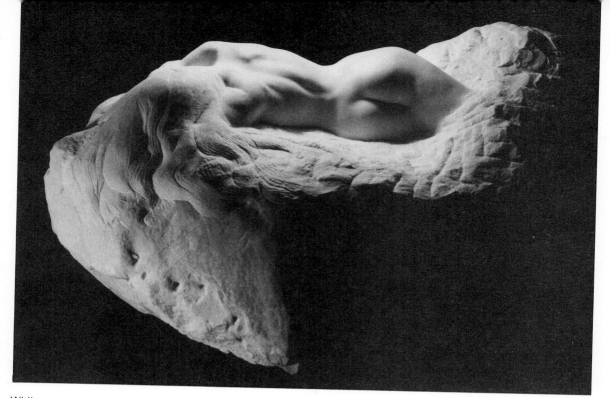

While some people oppose all sexually explicit materials, a distinction can be made between violent pornography and works that celebrate the beauty of the human body, such as this sculpture by Donna Forma.

cantly different from those in other men. Many sex offenders are actually sexually dysfunctional. Castration doesn't always put an end to sex. Even with their testes removed, many rapists are still capable of intercourse (Heim and Hursch 1979).

What we know of rapists' social backgrounds suggests many areas where changes might lower the possibility of rape. The attitudes children pick up within their families seem to be especially important. As we saw, rapists' families were typically unloving, jealous, chaotic, deprived, religiously repressive, and sexually abusive. Cross-cultural data show that this kind of pleasure-denying background breeds violence (Prescott 1975).

Neuropsychologist James Prescott (1975) believes that we can go a long way toward eliminating sexual violence simply by increasing affectionate touching within the family. For instance, he recommends that families bathe together as the Japanese do in large tubs. He notes that such behaviors have a soothing effect that inhibits violence. And nudity, openness about sexuality, and affectionate touching within the family teach chil-

dren that their bodies are not shameful but rather sources of beauty and pleasure that they can share with others. These feelings are absent in people who think that violence is necessary to solve problems.

Family problems are not the only source of encouragement to rape. From childhood on males learn not only from their families but also from society as a whole that violence is an acceptable way to solve problems. Unlike girls they are allowed and even encouraged to use their fists when someone tries to humiliate them. Competitive rather than cooperative sports are emphasized in schools and on TV. Television shows are especially violence-prone. Even in seemingly "harmless" children's shows, cartoon characters routinely flatten their opponents with steamrollers, blow up their homes with dynamite, and clobber them with baseball bats. By age sixteen the average child in the United States has watched 15,000 hours of television (Siegel 1977). Many studies have demonstrated that the aggression children see on the screen serves as a model for their own behavior

Men Organize against Male Violence

Male gender roles are the target of a number of new men's groups organized out of many men's concern over violence against women. In Santa Cruz, California, Men Against Rape characterizes itself as:

a collective of men dedicated to stopping violence against women. We feel that the roots of such aggression lie in our culture which encourages sexist and domineering behavior in men. The elimination of the problem must start by each of us monitoring our own actions. We must also challenge everything in our culture that induces violence and confront the institutions that thrive on the oppression of women. . . . Unless we come to terms with our own potential to be violent, each of us runs the risk of being paralyzed by guilt or the temptation to condescend. . . . While most men claim to be against rape, if every man accepted the responsibility for his own actions and for those of other men, there would be no rape. [Santa Cruz Men Against Rape 1983]

Such groups counsel men who are close to rape survivors, who have been sexually assaulted themselves, who have been criticized for their own violent behavior, or who are trying to outgrow their gender role training. Men Against Rape offers men who have been criticized by women for their behavior a circle of males who support these men in changing. This group also offers childcare services, helping to free women, enable men to "develop [their] lost sense of nurturing," and provide a "positive image of men for growing children." In addition Men Against Rape challenges advertisements and media that "reinforce sex role stereotypes or glamorize violence against women" and monitors legislation and "male-dominated institutions" to be sure that they recognize women's needs and that they help end rape. They conclude:

Each of us has had some experience of hurting women. Likewise each of us to some degree has been affected by the violence of other men. We do not claim to be experts. Our personal experiences of how we deal daily with our intentions is the greatest resource we can offer other men.

and increases the level of violence in their "play."

Does explicit portrayal of sex also incite sexual violence? The picture is not clear. Some women's groups claim that "pornography" (which is sometimes defined loosely as anything that is sexy and at other times as the violent abuse of women) is directly linked with rape and other sexual abuse. These women favor banning pornography, including magazines such as *Playboy,* while others simply want to stop the public display of sexually explicit materials such as exist in Times Square windows in New York City.

In his 1980 *Playboy* article, "Women at War," Robert Shea observes that no one knows whether sex crimes are increasing or the reporting is more frequent. But even if there are more sex crimes, no research has concluded that sexually explicit materials have led men to rape women. The 1970 series of studies on the effect of sexually stimulating material (Commission on Obscenity and Pornography) did not find a link between pornography and violence against women. Although some pornography has become more violent since 1970, the exact effects of even violent pornography are largely unknown.

As some feminists believe, it may be that some pornography creates a climate more conducive to the sexual abuse of women. Images on record albums of women in chains with whip marks across their backs are not positive images, and at the least they are demeaning to women. Even more likely, these negative images of women as victims are models for men to abuse women sexually.

Laboratory studies cannot prove any real-life connection between sexually explicit materials and sexual abuse of women. It is difficult, if not impossible, to control for the effect of such material on the violent behavior of men. Speculations based on existing research and some semblance of logic are the best we can do at this point in trying to understand the links between sex and aggression. As Libby and Straus (1980) found, warm, interpersonal sexual attitudes are negatively correlated with aggressive attitudes and behaviors, whereas exploitative, competitive sexual attitudes are positively linked to violent acts. The same would seem true of exposure to violent stimuli, whether on television, in the movies, or in magazines. It is unlikely that violent pornography has a benign effect or none at all (Bart and Jozsa 1979). But until more data are available, the bulk of evidence is that the availability of sexually explicit materials (*without violence*) results in *less* rape and other sexual crimes against women.

A final set of rape-encouraging attitudes built into our culture involves gender roles. The potential for hostility between the genders is built into traditional expectations that women will behave one way and men another and that they must compete for control of their intimate relationships. For instance, if men must always bear the burden of initiating sex, they are primed to despise those women who make them feel unworthy by rejecting their advances. Even in actual sexual encounters, a male who has learned to entrust his self-esteem to his ability to maintain an erection may feel humiliated if a woman witnesses his inability to do so. Such "failures" may incline men toward brutal assertion of their "masculinity."

How many rapes might be avoided if women in our society learned to share honestly the initiative—and the responsibility—for sex? If men were not taught to expect so much of themselves sexually? If women lovingly aroused them? If both genders were taught to interact as friends and equals rather than as combatants in the traditional battle of the sexes? If men did not expect to dominate women, and women to be dominated? If women learned to make honest but kind "I like you but I don't want to have sex with you" statements? If men learned to believe them and not experience such statements as personal rejection? If men learned that they, too, have the option of not expressing attraction sexually?

In short the ultimate in sexual destructiveness—rape—may perhaps best be attacked by the social changes supported throughout this book. These changes include an increase in affectionate family touching, open education about sexual pleasures and responsibilities, positive rather than repressive attitudes toward sex, honest communication about sexual feelings, linking of sex with pleasure rather than with power, and replacement of traditional gender roles with honest, caring interaction.

Summary

One disturbing aspect of sexuality that has long been with us is its potential for violent abuse of partners. In sexual harassment on the job and in academic settings, positions of power may be used to force sexual favors. Forcible rape may be seen as a release of sexual frustration, a violent effort by males to dominate women, or a distortion and exaggeration of traditional gender roles. Greatly underreported, sexual assaults range from the stereotyped stranger-in-a-dark-alley picture to date rape, statutory rape, assaults on children, homosexual rape, marital rape, and sadomasochism. Most involve people who know each other.

Women are sometimes inaccurately accused of "asking for it." Sexual attacks are usually so frightening and so unfamiliar that women's ability to cope with the situation is severely strained, both during and after the assault. Legal recourse is complicated and may increase the feeling of stress. Rapists themselves tend to be young males with personal histories that deny them a sense of mature self-respect. Some want to hurt their victims, some are sexually frustrated, some are sexual sadists, and some are simply impulsive opportunists. To avoid vulnerability to such assailants, women are advised by antirape programs to take precautions. But if they are threatened by sexual attack, an ability to quickly take the offensive may be more helpful than a fear mentality.

Attempts to lower the incidence of rape include education and protection for potential victims in high-risk areas, attempts to put rapists behind bars, rape shield laws protecting rape victims who press charges from being questioned about their own sexual histories, counseling for former rapists, counseling of men by men that promotes rethinking of violence-encouraging gender roles, efforts to stamp out violent forms of pornography, and encouragement of healthy attitudes toward sexuality.

13

Sex
for
Sale

My name is Cheryl, and I'm a call girl. I enjoy my work—because I enjoy sex. I figure most women are prostitutes of one kind or another, and so are some men. So why not get paid for what you do best? I am offering sex for a price, and I don't see why my business should be looked down on or illegal. Even though we are in an economic recession, I don't see any sexual recession when it comes to men buying sex from me.

I love to look at pictures of beautiful women's bodies, and I buy sexual devices like vibrators through a mail-order catalogue. I've been to a prostitute once, but I didn't really enjoy it. I'd rather have sex with women who like to play without pay. Fortunately, there are plenty of adventurous women around. I don't need to buy partners.

To me, sex is something private and beautiful. I don't like to see it exploited for selling things, and I don't like to have other people's sex lives thrown in my face or disturbing my children. There's too much sex on TV and in movies to suit me—I'd just rather not watch. It makes me feel uncomfortable, like a peeping Tom or something.

I run a good "massage parlor." We have nice women, and my wife and I take them all out to dinner every Sunday. I've got things set up with local officials so they don't bother us. Friends from my club love to come here for something special they can't get at home. The standard $20 fee goes to me, the women take home whatever else they can get. The way I see it, this is a community service. I love sex, and I like helping other guys get it. [From the authors' files]

Sexual experiences and sexy images are for sale in a great range of services and items, from scents, clothes, vibrators, and magazines to partners. The key is *fantasy*—sellers of sex depend on stimulating our sexual fantasies, offering an escape from everyday routine. For a brief interlude buyers can imagine themselves enjoying the sex or the sex appeal of their dreams.

Sex for sale includes prostitution, pornography, erotic materials, and advertising. Because actual bodies are negotiated as a part of prostitution, this is the most blatant example of sex for a price. Advertising and pornography affect far more people than does prostitution. People in our society differ in their acceptance or rejection of these varying commercial appeals to our sexual interests. Their differences raise the critical issue in a democratic society of whether the preferences of some should be allowed to limit the choices of others in the name of "protecting" them.

COMMERCIALIZATION OF SEXUALITY

From underwear to videocassettes, sex appeal is increasingly being used to enhance business profits. Magazines with nude photos have increasing readership among both men and women. In advertisements male shoppers are urged to indulge their lovers with gifts of sexy lingerie. Even Macy's has a "Private Lives" department with shops called "Temptations" and "For His Eyes Only" selling $23.00 sheer teddies by Blush, French Flirts bikinis for $6.50, and $47.00 breast-lifting-and-revealing bustiers by Darling (Macy's ad 1982). Female shoppers, who account for 70 to 80 percent of all sales of men's underwear, are lured by designer labels and photographs of athletic-looking models to purchase sexy bikini briefs for their partners in colors ranging from Bermuda blue to sangria (Bech 1982). As image has replaced functionalism, prices have climbed.

Erotic movies have moved from red-light districts into the home. In homes with videocassette recorders, 25 to 50 percent of prerecorded videocassettes purchased are X-rated. And when communities are wired for cable TV, 50 percent to as high as 95 percent of the subscribers are typically willing to pay the extra monthly charge for access to networks offering erotic fare. Cable subscriptions are expected to multiply by a factor of three by 1990; videocassette purchases may jump 500 percent between 1981 and 1985 (Schwartz 1981).

Objections on the Grounds of Obscenity

Some people object to certain commercializations of sexuality on the grounds that these depictions are offensively obscene. For years the courts have been trying to define "obscenity." The 1973 *Miller v. California* Supreme Court decision is used as the standard criterion for legal charges of obscenity. In this decision an object was declared obscene if a jury found that:

1. the average person, applying contemporary community standards, would find that the work taken as a whole appealed to the prurient interest, and

2. the object depicted or described in a patently offensive way sexual conduct specifically defined by the applicable state law as written or construed, and

3. the object taken as a whole lacked serious artistic, literary, political, or scientific value (Yaffé and Nelson, 1982, p. 265).

However, what is "patently offensive" or of "prurient interest" to one person may affect another differently.

Books considered literary classics by some—such as J. D. Salinger's *Catcher in the Rye*—are sometimes banned from school libraries by groups McIlvenna, head of the Institute for Advanced the video sex market some examples of sex are educational as well as entertaining, contends Ted McIllvenna, head of the Institute for Advanced Study of Human Sexuality. He believes a need exists for "sexual pleasure education" (Schwartz 1981, p. 136). Others see attacks on such materials as censorship that denies citizens rights to freedom of expression guaranteed under the First Amendment. But according to a spokesperson for Morality in Media, adult entertainment subverts Judeo-Christian values and should be regulated. Morality in Media does not view their position as censorship—their stance is that they are "protecting" the public. Peggy Charren, president of the national advocacy group, Action for Children's Television, disagrees. "If that isn't censorship, what is?" she asks (Roberts 1982, p. 21).

Objections on the Grounds of Violence

A second complaint frequently voiced about some materials considered pornographic is that they may encourage violence. It is difficult to measure the exact effects of pornography—whether pornography makes people more aggressive sexually, or more violent, or whether it simply turns them on or off sexually. Pornography's influence depends to some extent on the nature of the sexual material.

Robert Athanasiou (1980, p. 253) has noted that "the court seems to assume that within each normal average person there is a prurient maniac waiting to be released by an appropriate stimulus." By contrast, Athanasiou's review of available research on the effects of pornography and erotica concludes that the effects are more positive than negative, and that rapists report little or no discussion of sex in their homes during childhood. Actually, sexual offenders usually have had less exposure to sexual material in their formative years than have nonoffenders (Athanasiou, 1980). Laboratory studies have not demonstrated a strong link between sexual arousal and rape.

One thought is that the attempt to limit access to sexual materials may fuel an obsession to obtain such materials. We are attracted to the unknown—to that which we are not supposed to see or read. Prohibiting alcohol, drugs, and sexual materials has similar effects—people often try harder to obtain resources that are scarce.

Objections on the Grounds of Sexism

Some object to sex in advertising and to erotic displays of any kind because they believe that such materials generally exploit women as sex objects. Sometimes this is true. Women's sexuality is often controlled by men on a symbolic level, in which women are represented as objects—the subjugated—rather than as sharers of emotions and pleasure. In exploitative pornography women are pictured as slaves to men's sexual desires and demands, objects of men's often power-hungry and

A Feminist's Ambivalence toward Pornography

Some feminist groups tend to condemn all hard-core pornography as encouraging violence against women. But Ellen Willis, founder of the radical feminist group Redstockings, doubts that rape and wife-beating statistics would drop if pornographic materials suddenly disappeared. She believes that the issue of pornography is too complex to reduce it to a simplistic link with sexist violence. Pornography is about sex, some of it violent, and to forbid pornography may oppress women's sexuality as well as men's.

In two *Village Voice* columns, Willis (1979b) claims that to define as okay only those sexually explicit materials that involve romantic relationships is to deny the possibility that some women may enjoy "unladylike," erotic, powerful sexmaking—traditionally thought to be the province of men only. On the other hand, Willis does see pornography as a symptom of sexual repression—of the need to express lust in secret, forbidden ways. She points out that our society separates sex into "good" and "bad" elements—love and lust; it defines love as "a noble affair of the heart and mind, lust as a base animal centered in unmentionable organs" (Willis 1979a, p. 8). To outlaw lusty sexual materials merely reinforces this dichotomy for women as well as for men. Willis concludes:

I am quite critical of pornography and the alienated sexual attitudes it expresses, but I believe that since those attitudes stem directly from a sexually repressive culture—and are in part a rebellion against it—it is destructive and self-defeating to try to "cure" them with more repression. I also think it is particularly destructive to women to keep telling us we are, or ought to be, inherently nicer and more sexually innocent than men. [Willis 1980]*

* Reprinted by permission of Ellen Willis and the *Village Voice*.

sometimes sadistic fantasies. Erotica, by contrast, is a humanized and egalitarian representation of sex. We can be sexy without being sexist.

The increase in exploitative and even violent pornography has prompted feminist groups such as Women Against Pornography (WAP) to protest the commercial degradation of women. They are demanding that sexually explicit materials not be violent. They point out that pornography showing women in bondage to men with whips and chains and expressing an obsessive need to control women's sexual choices is dehumanizing and obscene. Another women's liberation group opposing violence in the media is Women Against Violence Against Women (WAVAW). Their focus has largely been on the violent images of women on record albums and in advertising. For instance, the Rolling Stones and other famous rock groups have been criticized and sometimes restrained in their attempts to show women in submissive poses with open cuts and bruises from abuse by men.

Many feminists also believe that women are exploited as consumers by commercial advertisements that try to convince them that they need to buy clothes, high-heeled shoes, and cosmetics to be sexual—that is, to attract a man. Feminist Dana Densmore analyzes the problems this commercial exploitation creates for women's sexual identity:

. . . Everywhere we are sexual objects, and our own enjoyment just enhances our attractiveness. We are wanton. We wear miniskirts and see-through tops. We're sexy. We're free. We run around and hop into bed whenever we please. This is the self-image we have built up in us by advertising and the media. It's self-fulfilling. And very profitable. It keeps us in our place and feeling lucky about it (the freedom to consume, consume, consume, until we swallow the world). It makes us look as if we're free and active (actively, freely, we solicit sex from men). [Densmore 1970b, p. 58]

Now that male as well as female models are being used to portray sexual images, these issues have broadened to include both sexes. But must any of us see our sexuality as defined by others? We can choose to see both ourselves and others as freely and equally human. For some of us being freely human includes enjoying eroticism. Radical feminist Shulamith Firestone asserts:

Sex objects are beautiful. An attack on them can be confused with an attack on beauty itself. Feminists need not get so pious in their efforts that they feel

Women are sometimes cast as childish sex objects in marketing that uses sex to sell things.

they must flatly deny the beauty of the face on the cover of Vogue. For this is not the point. The real question is: is the face beautiful in a human way— does it allow for growth and flux and decay, does it express negative as well as positive emotions, does it fall apart without artificial props—or does it falsely imitate the very different beauty of an inanimate object, like wood trying to be metal?

To attack eroticism creates similar problems. Eroticism is exciting. No one wants to get rid of it. Life would be a drab and routine affair without at least that spark. [Firestone 1972, p. 155]

THE SOCIAL SYSTEM PROVIDING PROSTITUTES FOR HIRE

When sexual partners are scarce or when erotic desires exceed what sex is freely available, some persons turn to practitioners of the most ancient profession: prostitution. Until recently women who prostituted themselves for money were scorned by both sexes. On the other hand, the men who visited prostitutes to satisfy their needs were accepted and even encouraged, on the assumption that men's sexuality is a strong urge that should not be denied. Because women were not supposed to have such urges, they were the targets of sexually repressive laws.

Despite expensive efforts by some groups to eliminate prostitution, the profession continues to thrive: There are still plenty of willing buyers and sellers. Only the packaging has changed. For instance, as brothels have been busted by vice squads, prostitutes and their clients have increasingly switched to posh massage parlor operations offering a variety of bodily comforts.

Today prostitutes are organizing to demand better working conditions and public respect for their therapeutic services. It has become fashionable to view prostitution as a "victimless" crime that hurts no one and should therefore be decriminalized. The total picture is more complex, though. Some prostitutes are miserable—enslaved, beaten, debt-ridden, forced onto the streets, murdered, and pushed to desperate suicide. Others—particularly call girls who service wealthy men—are happy, self-supporting, service-oriented, and professional in their work. And not all prostitutes are women. Many are teenage runaways; some are men.

A Loose Organization

At the heart of this loosely organized profession is the prostitute. Her nightly efforts may earn several hundred dollars, depending on how much she charges per "trick" and how many "johns" she services. But with the exception of some relatively independent call girls, few prostitutes get to keep everything that they are paid. Most of it is siphoned off by various peripheral people.

One of these is the pimp. He lives off the earnings of the two to ten women in his "stable," demanding that each one turn over about $200 a night to him. In exchange he offers services for which women have traditionally depended on men. These include status, protection, business management, and emotional support. The pimp may play many roles: lover, father, husband, boyfriend, agent, protector. Some pimps are brutally exploitative; some are hypnotic persuaders; some treat their women relatively well. But regardless of the nature of the relationship, a pimp is someone to come home to—someone "in the life" who understands and accepts women whose profession alienates them from straight society.

If the prostitute works out of a brothel, some management functions may be taken over by a madam who trains, oversees, and keeps peace among the women in her house and acts as a liaison with outside figures—including taxi drivers, bartenders, and bellhops who receive tips for providing information on where sex can be procured. These outside persons also include local law enforcement officials who may be paid off in money, drinks, or sex to avoid arresting prostitutes on morals charges. At the same time these officials are paid by taxpayers to suppress prostitution, upping the amounts of money spent on the profession.

Less visible—but perhaps most lucrative—are the positions at the top of this shadowy enterprise. These are the ownerships of institutions supported by prostitutes' earnings. "Prostitute-prone" hotels and massage parlors are often owned by wealthy, influential members of the community. The money to be made from prostitution has also attracted organized crime. It appears that much of the prostitution scene is too loosely organized and too bad for public relations for the Mafia to be interested (James 1976a). But through loans and intimidation, low- and middle-income racketeers seem to be taking over control of some massage parlors. This fact is not surprising, considering police tolerance of the operations and the potential for profit.

Recruitment

Women are recruited or enticed into prostitution in a variety of ways. Some women who have worked as waitresses in bars, restaurants, and nightclubs that cater to or are connected with persons involved with crime, drugs, and prostitution seem to meet pimps and other prostitutes and find themselves trying the life. Sometimes it is hard for a young woman to get out once she gets involved, especially if she has a pimp and no other means of supporting herself and, in some cases, her children.

Prostitutes face a variety of occupational hazards. Some are beaten and burned with cigarettes by their pimps and forced onto the street in all kinds of weather to earn their nightly quota. Some acquiesce out of terror and the belief that they have no alternatives. Others do it out of dependent love for a pimp. They say they'd do anything to please their man, for he's often the only person who seems to care for them. A pimp's asking them to walk the streets and bring all the money home seems a small price to pay for his support. As one prostitute put it, "What he gives me is himself. And that's much more than I can say anyone else has ever given me" (quoted by Prager and Claflin 1979, p. 103).

In contrast to the forced recruitment of some, many prostitutes enter the life by *choice*. They see prostitution as a lucrative job, a relatively easy way to earn far more than they could in other occupations available to unskilled women. Although few actually make the $50,000 to $75,000 a year that some call girls pull in, they dream of getting rich as hookers—or at least being able to pay the bills.

Researchers who have interviewed prostitutes have found a number of other reasons people choose to sell their sexual services. One is the adventure and excitement of the fast life. For instance, some prostitutes who are good at finding customers and protecting themselves from police travel all over the world, with their profession paying the way. Some enjoy contacts with men who are wealthier and higher in status than those from their own background. Some even fantasize that such contacts may lead to marriage. And some simply enjoy the adventurousness of walking the streets alone at night.

The working conditions are often seen as desirable. Aside from police roundups, beatings by pimps, and occasional encounters with dangerous customers or street people, the life offers numerous fringe benefits: To be paid for their looks and for sexual favors they once gave away for free; to wear beautiful clothes; to choose their own hours;

The Language of Sex

The word *promiscuous* is often misused. Technically, it means being nondiscriminating in sexual partners, choosing them randomly rather than by thoughtful standards of selection. But many people label as "promiscuous" any young unmarried female who has sex. This label denies the possibility that she is capable of distinguishing between relationships she wants and those she doesn't want, or that she may have a single, caring sex partner. The moral judgment behind this broad misapplication of "promiscuous" is that any sexual activity by young single women is socially unacceptable.

to make money for drugs and to deal them, too; and to do easy work that is sometimes enjoyable are positive incentives for many. In a society that links sex with power, many women also find a sense of power in having men desire them so much that they are willing to pay for access to their bodies. In such transactions the prostitute also has the satisfaction of playing the role of experienced professional (James 1977b).

Given these incentives, why don't more people sell sex for money? For one thing doing so is still so stigmatized that prostitutes find themselves largely cut off from the respect of middle-class society. Women who value their "good" reputations and who can afford to view sex as shared pleasure rather than a monetary exchange are not tempted to cross the line. But those who've already been branded as "loose" or "promiscuous" or who are left on the streets with no other way to support themselves have little to lose. As we'll see later, many who choose prostitution have such a background.

The second problem is that making the switch from free sex to paid sex takes more than wanting to. As one call girl put it:

I had been thinking . . . about wanting to do it, but I had no connections. . . . Once I tried it. . . . I met this guy at a bar and I tried to make him pay me, but the thing is, you can't do it that way because they are romantically interested in you, and they don't think it is on that kind of basis. You can't all of a sudden come up and want money for it, you have to be known *beforehand. . . . I think that is what holds a lot of girls back who might work.* [Quoted in Bryan 1972, p. 236]*

Since prostitution is illegal, "job openings" are not advertised. Entering the life requires personal contact with someone who is already in it—usually a pimp or another prostitute. This person may take responsibility for training the new recruit.

Training

Many recruits are given little or no instruction in sexual techniques except for fellatio, even though they may have had little previous experience with sex. Call girls and streetwalkers often learn new techniques from their customers. But madams may teach their house prostitutes a variety of sexual activities and specify how much each one costs and how the prostitute can avoid physical discomfort. In intercourse, for instance, prostitutes learn to prevent potentially irritating deep penetration by squeezing their inner thigh muscles together. A call girl's trainer may give instruction in the use of vibrators and pornography to excite men. Or the call girl may be introduced to special techniques for handling male sexual problems, such as the inability to have or sustain an erection.

Often the person who "turns out" a prostitute—that is, who teaches her the techniques and rules of the profession—will give her advice on avoiding sexually transmitted diseases (STD). Professionalism is most obvious in women trained by a madam. For instance, one South Dakota madam has been training prostitutes for thirty-three years in elaborate STD-prevention techniques. After choosing a woman and paying the fee for services he requests, a customer is carefully scrutinized and cleaned by the prostitute. She checks his genitals for any signs of disease and milks his urethra to check for discharge. If he doesn't pass these tests, he will not be serviced, his money will be refunded, and his name will be passed on to other houses as someone to avoid.

* From James Bryan, "Apprenticeships in Prostitution," in Robert P. Bell and Michael Gordon, eds., *The Social Dimension of Human Sexuality* (Boston: Little, Brown 1972). Originally appeared in *Social Problems* 12, no. 3 (Winter 1965). Reprinted by permission of the author and the Society for the Study of Social Problems.

Those who pass are washed both before and after intercourse with warm, soapy water. Before they leave, the prostitute bathes the outer part of the urethra with a mild solution of clear Merthiolate. Afterward, she washes her own genitals, douches with soapy water, and gargles with an antiseptic mouthwash. Once a day she also douches with a stronger product. In addition the house prostitutes trained by this madam are examined weekly for gonorrhea and monthly for syphilis by public health officials (Darrow 1979).

Such measures are thought to be extremely effective in controlling STD. So are condoms, applied by many prostitutes to all their customers. But those who enter the field without STD training and screening may be major spreaders of sexually transmitted diseases because they have sex with so many people. In Colorado Springs, for example, street prostitutes have 63 percent of the gonorrhea seen at a certain STD clinic and cause an estimated 33 percent of all the male gonorrhea cases (Potterat, Rothenberg, and Bross 1979).

Another important facet of the turning-out process is learning to hustle. To be successful at hustling prostitutes must learn to talk directly about specific sexual acts, to keep up a steady stream of verbal coaxing sensitively cued to the customer's responses, and to introduce the topic of money in a persuasive, "natural" way. A prostitute must also convince the customer that she'll be worth the money. None of these skills comes easily in a culture in which sexual negotiations are usually handled indirectly.

Finally, to make the switch from the straight world to one considered deviant, a new prostitute must learn the values of her adopted subculture. In it, hustling is defined as a reasonable occupation rather than an unacceptable behavior. The use of drugs and liquor while on the job is defined as unprofessional and dangerous. Instead of seeing men as fit objects for romantic longing, recruits are encouraged to view customers ("tricks") as corrupt and exploitative but stupid enough to be easily exploited themselves. They are taught never to be nice to men unless they are getting paid for it. Unnecessary interaction and personal sexual arousal are discouraged. The main idea is to get the trick's money and then get rid of him as fast as possible. In contrast to this disrespect for clients, a new prostitute is encouraged to see people in "the life" as intelligent and basically honest.

Some prostitutes only give lip service to these values. Some privately enjoy orgasms with their customers, some get emotionally involved, and some are high or drunk throughout their encounters (Bryan 1972).

TYPES OF PROSTITUTES

The loosely organized world of sex for sale encompasses a variety of types of prostitutes. The stereotyped image of the prostitute as streetwalker covers only a portion of the trade. Forms of prostitution change somewhat with the years, as enterprising people discover new ways to capitalize on willingness to pay for sexual favors. For instance, some women hustle the convention circuit; others pick up travelers with time to kill in airports. "Highway hookers" do a thriving business in the shadows of highway rest stops, catering to long-haul truckers whom they contact by CB radio (Knight 1977). And some make a business of moving from one wealthy person to another as lover or spouse. In this section we'll look at a few major ways in which people exchange specific sexual acts for money as a vocation.

Call Girls

The top-paying, highest-status prostitution job is that of call girl. She works in a lavishly furnished apartment and, by telephone appointments, serves relatively few men whose names she may have purchased from another call girl, pimp, or madam.

Although more money changes hands in this transaction than in any other, the paying-for-sex angle is handled discreetly. For the call girl to be tactless in the way she asks for cash in advance may spoil the fantasy the client wants. Social worker Martha Stein (1974) found by watching call girls' transactions through one-way mirrors that skill in making fantasies come to life is one of the call girl's most important assets. Depending on her reading of each client's desires, she may be called on to create an atmosphere of romance, adventure, friendship, childlike affection for a father figure, sexual openmindedness, group fun with homosexual overtones, social power, or simply instant sexual gratification.

In addition to providing illusions, call girls often act as underground therapists for their customers. Over half the men Stein observed put the call girl in a therapeutic role by using her for direct crisis intervention, expression of hidden sexual desires, explicit sexual counseling, or airing of personal problems. For many of the rest, sessions with a call girl seemed to relieve stress, enhance their feelings of self-esteem, renew their confidence in their sexual ability, and help them deal with mid-life problems.

House Prostitutes

Compared with call girls, prostitutes working in brothels—or houses of prostitution—operate under far more structured conditions and have considerably closer contact with other women in the life. Their transactions are more openly managed as a business, and in some rural Nevada counties they are even legal. Prostitutes there live in discreet but legal brothels bearing names like the Mustang Ranch, Miss Kitty's, and the Pink Pussycat. Working women are fingerprinted and checked weekly by public health officials. They are available to anyone who chooses them from pictures or an in-the-flesh "lineup." They turn over 50 to 60 percent of what they earn to the house owner and leave the place only on their monthly week off from work.

Smaller-scale houses operate illegally elsewhere in the country. Often several prostitutes share an apartment but use it only for business. One of them may act as a madam, handling referrals from taxi drivers, bartenders, and telephone clients (James 1977a).

In general house prostitutes tend to serve more clients at cheaper rates than do independent call girls. Their transactions are also more structured. Often the madam sets the rules as to what activities are permitted, for how long, and at what price. In one house, for instance, kissing and anal intercourse are prohibited, and the women are barred from "dirty hustling" practices that would hurt others in the house, such as appearing partially undressed in the lineup or performing extra services without pay. Such rules help the madam maintain control within her world and minimize problems with customers. And strict rules about who can be admitted help her avoid entrapment by police. Often only trusted old customers or friends they personally bring can enter a brothel.

Streetwalkers

Women who prefer a more independent life but who lack the class or the contacts to be call girls often work the city streets instead. They stroll around or stand in doorways or on street corners in areas known for prostitution and select passing males as marks. Many streetwalkers no longer advertise themselves by sexy clothes and heavy makeup; at night they are often recognizable simply because they are alone on the streets. To drum up business without saying anything for which they could be arrested, they make euphemistic suggestions such as, "Want a little sugar?" or "Would you like to have a party?" If the man agrees, a price is negotiated and they go to a hotel or a "trick house" that offers cheap rooms for prostitution (James 1977b).

Public solicitation is the major target of social disapproval and police arrests. Streetwalkers are therefore the most arrested of all prostitutes. To avoid being trapped by a vice squad officer into making an illegal direct sales pitch, a wary streetwalker will try to maneuver the customer into offering money for sex without verbally incriminating herself.

Prostitutes are vulnerable to violence, too. According to Merry's interviews with streetwalkers, they try to avoid violence by knowing as much as they can about the dangerous people they encounter, while giving out as little information as possible about themselves (Merry 1980).

Despite the constant risk of arrest and of being mugged or raped, streetwalkers make a fairly good living. In San Francisco, the average female streetwalker earns $36,000 a year. But about 80 percent turn what they make over to a pimp ("Enforcement of..."1979). In addition the more money a prostitute makes, the higher is her prestige with others in the life. Since stealing greatly increases the amount of money to be made, some prostitutes cooperate with pimps to steal from tricks (Merry 1980).

Women who choose streetwalking as a profession are generally less educated, lower-class prostitutes trying to earn a living. Some, however, are addicts supporting their habit. And some are enterprising suburban housewives who commute into the city to earn a little spending money during the day (Exner et al. 1977).

Massage Parlor Attendants

For those who prefer a safer indoor environment, prostitution behind a massage parlor front is an increasingly common occupational choice. Within recent years massage parlors offering "extras" have mushroomed in popularity. They give both clients and prostitutes the semblance of luxury and respectability. Services may even be charged to major credit cards, because it's hard to be sure just what goes on at any particular massage parlor. Some offer only legitimate therapeutic massages, some suggest that they offer more to lure customers, and some have women who are willing to perform sexual services if the customer knows how to ask for them.

Men seeking massages or massages-plus are first ushered into a rather elegant lounge. If several masseuses are available, they are paraded out so customers can take their pick. The masseuse then takes the customer into a small cubicle with a massage table, perhaps embellished with exotic lighting and mirrors. The massage that follows may or may not be genuinely professional. Because soliciting is illegal, sexual services probably will not be included unless the customer names them directly and offers to pay extra. The masseuse may maneuver him into the position of soliciting sex: "Is there anything else you'd like me to massage? If so put my hand there." Sexual extras include topless or bottomless massages, allowing the customer to "massage" or bathe with the masseuse, genital massage, fellatio, and intercourse.

Masseuses often set personal limits on what they are willing to do. Some want to save intercourse for their boyfriends or husbands. Others can avoid seeing themselves as prostitutes if they offer only hand or oral stimulation. One such masseuse rationalized, "There's really nothing wrong with locals; the penis is just another part of the male body and needs to be massaged too" (quoted by Rasmussen and Kuhn 1976, p. 277).

Fellatio is popular among both patrons and masseuses. Men enjoy the sensations and often say they can't get them at home. Masseuses find it convenient not to undress, and fellatio makes it easy to provide relatively quick orgasms to a succession of men. Efficiency and volume are important in this business, for masseuses typically get to keep half of the price of the regular massage and all of what they earn for sexual extras. This income can add up to $12,000 to $36,000 a year—the kind of money that even attracts college graduates to the profession (Rasmussen and Kuhn 1976).

To maintain a professional perspective, masseuses often try to avoid emotional involvement with their customers. Like call girls they are sensitive to what their clients need, both sexually and nonsexually, and are good at role playing to help meet these needs. Their services are apparently therapeutic, for clients interviewed both before and after a "complete massage" show a significant decrease in anxiety and an increase in sexual satisfaction (Simpson and Schill 1977).

Bar "Girls" and Strippers

Bars and nightclubs provide another arena for indoor hustling. At some bars all female employees are expected to offer the semblance of sexy sociability to male customers who will buy them drinks. The purpose of this repartee is not to arrange sexual encounters but simply to make more money on the sale of liquor. There are, however, bar girls who are willing to make their own arrangements for paid sex; the management may supply rooms upstairs for a portion of the fee, which usually ranges from $50 to over $100 per trick.

Because many nonprostitutes also visit bars in search of sex partners, it's sometimes hard for men to tell the difference. Like prostitutes elsewhere, bar girls no longer dress distinctively, and they avoid direct soliciting for fear of arrest. Men who want guaranteed sex rather than an expensive, possibly nonsexual date therefore learn to look for other clues: known reputation of a certain bar as a place where prostitutes can be found, the presence of unescorted girls nursing their drinks at the bar, and "the look." One bar hustler described her nonverbal message this way:

I catch his eye and hold it for a few seconds. Then I slowly drop my gaze to his zipper. I hold my eyes there for a few seconds and then slowly raise my gaze again until I meet his eyes again. He usually gets the message.   [Quoted in Atkinson and Boles 1977, p. 224]

Variations on this arrangement occur in nightclubs offering strippers or nude dancers. As in bars sometimes it's only the semblance of sexy intimacy that's on sale. For instance, strippers may bare their bodies to a tiny G-string and then give men in the audience the chance to insert tips into it in exchange for a kiss. When they're not on stage, nude dancers may receive tips in exchange for sitting in patrons' laps or for caresses at the bar. At the same time they push drinks for the management by faking an interest in flirtatious conversation. Despite an outward show of eroticism, they typically are not turned on by what they're doing (Skipper and McCaghy 1978).

Some strippers negotiate for further sexual favors; some don't. The customers' standard assumption seems to be that because they are willing to show off their bodies, all strippers are also prostitutes, so they proposition the women relentlessly. This approach may lead to hard feelings on both sides. Even women who are willing to sell further access to their bodies say they'd like at least the semblance of romantic byplay. As one put it,

They don't bother with any preliminaries. A guy just comes over to you and says, "How much?" Would it kill him to talk to me for a few minutes so we could get kind of acquainted? I'd like to be treated like he would treat women who don't work in clubs. These guys think that just because you work in clubs you don't have any feelings.   [Quoted by Boles and Garbin 1974, p. 141]

Customers feel cheated when a dancer turns them on but refuses to be fondled or adjourn to a back room. In this mutually exploitative atmosphere hostilities commonly flare into violence. Men swear at the strippers, try to grab at them, and rip their costumes. For their part dancers may insult customers, cut them with broken glass, fling drinks in their faces, have them thrown offstage by bouncers, or even shoot them (Boles and Garbin 1974).

Lesbian Prostitutes

The need for money sometimes draws lesbian women into paid sexual relationships, too. Very little is known of this activity. Since lesbian sex is more stigmatized than straight sex, it is conducted with greater secrecy. Too, women are not socialized to the role of paying for sex as men are, so their transactions may not be overtly money-based. In addition few women outside the upper-income class can afford to pay a lover, and this class is rarely studied by social scientists.

According to anecdotal reports some lesbian women pick each other up during parties in people's homes. Some hustle the all-female bars in a few large cities. And some simply live together, with the wealthier one helping to support the poorer one.

Male Heterosexual Prostitutes

Although in some states a prostitute is legally defined as a "female person who,..." many who sell peeks at or sexual access to their bodies for money are males. Some sell their services to females. As in lesbian prostitution little is known about this type of prostitution. Part of the problem is a blind spot in the perspective of social scientists. They tend to share the prevailing assumptions that unlike men, women don't want sex enough to pay for it and that at any rate there are enough men who are glad to provide it for free (Hageman 1979b).

Despite general ignorance about the subject, paid heterosexual activity is available to women who know how to look for it. Its forms are as numerous as those of female prostitution. Some tropical islands have long been known to wealthy women for their "beach boys." A new goldmine is the spectacle of nude male dancers parading their charms as sex symbols for women in nightclubs. Women patrons of all ages in these clubs yell, "Take it all off," grab at the dancers, and stuff tips in their codpieces—while behaving "more boisterously than men at a female strip show," according to one observer (White 1979, p. 10). Nude male dancers may earn up to $1500 a week from heavy-tipping females, compared with the $300 to $500 a female erotic dancer may earn (Monagan 1979).

After reviewing books written by male heterosexual prostitutes and interviewing male prosti-

Male strippers are now offering their acts as surprise gifts for women.

tutes, their contacts, and their clients, Jeannette Hageman (1979a) has described a number of ways that "gigolos" offer their services to women. At the top of the profession are those who provide amusement and pleasure for the idle rich. Some are themselves the sons of wealthy families. Middle- and upper-class women support kept men. And some males use a variety of disguises to offer their sexual services to women on a "cash-down" basis. Fronts include escort services, dance studios, studio modeling, sensory awareness centers, body-painting studios, saunas, and massage parlors. Some operate out of "boutiques" that have few clothes and no dressing rooms but offer an assortment of good-looking young males. Some have jobs that enable them to contact women—bartending, hairdressing, and even plumbing. Other men post nude photographs of themselves and their phone numbers in women's restrooms. Many run newspaper advertisements ranging from the discreet to the overt come-on.

Male Homosexual Prostitutes

Most of what is written about male prostitutes involves homosexual hustlers. These are primarily young, available males who are willing to provide sexual services to gay men in order to make money.

The ways males hustle males are similar to those used by females. Being a "kept boy" to a wealthy male offers potential prestige and an easy, luxurious life until one is replaced by a younger lover. "Call boys" who are contacted by telephone are well paid and high in status. Some run euphemistic ads for clients in prestigious newspapers by posing as "nude models."

Many of those who cruise the truck stops are homosexual prostitutes and female impersonators. They are attracted by the truck drivers' macho image; the drivers in turn find that these temporary contacts far from home in the secrecy of their cab sleeper allow them to conceal their homosexual interests from friends and relatives (Corzine and Kirby 1977).

Like females, males may operate as streetwalkers backed by an "old man." Interviews with street prostitutes in San Francisco indicate that 60 percent of the males are supporting a pimp ("Enforcement of. . ." 1979). Because homosexual soliciting is even more heavily stigmatized than heterosexual hustling, male "street hustlers" have elaborate rituals to distinguish interested potential partners from other men. In "bounding," for instance, the prostitute stands looking into a store window a few paces away from a potential client. Then he walks around the client and down the street to another location. If the man is interested, he will follow and ask the prostitute whether he'd like a beer. Having assured each other of their intentions by these actions, they then leave together (Ginsburg 1977).

Hustlers who prefer the relative security and comfort of an inside job may work in homosexual brothels that masquerade as "massage parlors." One such New York City operation is housed in an attractively furnished three-story brownstone in a fashionable part of town. To minimize the risk of vice squad raids, clients are screened by closed-circuit television as they enter. In the reception room they take their pick of the available prostitutes from a book of photographs suggesting each hustler's specialty. The book also lists which kinds of sexual activities each prostitute is willing to do. Once he has paid for the activities, the client is escorted by his prostitute to a small, dimly lit room. Heated massage oil is available if the customer should happen to want a rubdown, but the room is furnished with a bed rather than a massage table.

An intensive study of young male prostitutes reveals that there is no typical stereotype: Young gay prostitutes come from both poor and rich families; they range from being gay themselves to being heterosexual; some are effeminate, while others are masculine. One researcher was surprised to find that two-thirds to three-fourths of young male prostitutes are only part-timers, and hustling is segregated from the rest of their lives. Even their closest friends usually don't know about their sex-on-the-side (Allen 1980). Full-time young male prostitutes are more likely to be runaways—those who have left home and are forced to hustle to survive. Most of these young men are between ages sixteen and twenty-two, and they view their work as a temporary expedient. Drug use and all-night parties are part of their life as hustlers, and so are poor nutrition and the constant threat of violence (Summers 1982).

Child Prostitution

In contrast to the sometimes positive accounts of adults who choose prostitution as an occupation, stories of teenage runaways who are lured into prostitution paint a picture of desperation and victimization. People who want to abolish laws against prostitution portray it as a "victimless" crime, but justifying this position in the case of children is difficult.

Child prostitution is a social problem of alarming proportions. Every year up to a million kids in the United States run away from home (Ritter and Weinstein 1979). Some will return home. But many will not, and increasing numbers of these runaways will turn to prostitution to support themselves. In cities across the country arrests of prostitutes reveal that rapidly growing numbers of them are children, some as young as ten.

The majority of these children are running away from or thrown out of working-class or lower-class families. These families are often disintegrating in the face of poverty, alcoholism, divorce, parental neglect, or sexual abuse of the children. Some of the children, however, are middle-class kids trying to get away from parents whom they see as too restrictive, drunken, or unloving or are running away because they fear they are pregnant or from grief over a broken relationship (Ritter and Weinstein 1979; Prager and Claflin 1976).

Runaways who are girls typically have a sexually stigmatized identity added to their problems. Girls who smoke, drink, cut classes, shoplift, or return home late are often branded as impossible to handle, or "incorrigible." The underlying assumption is that they are sexually "delinquent." Turned over to juvenile authorities by parents or police, they are usually medically examined for pregnancy or lack of virginity. If either condition is found, they may be labeled "promiscuous." Young females designated as incorrigible, promiscuous, dependent, or in need of supervision may be placed in a juvenile institution until they are twenty-one. Boys are treated quite differently. Their sexual activity is typically ignored, and they are reported to police only if they have done something clearly criminal, such as burglary or car theft. The unusual harshness with which females are treated is rationalized by the double-standard arguments about the importance of protecting females by controlling their sexual behavior. Such oppressive treatment may instead be a factor pushing them over the line into running away and assuming the deviant status of prostitute (James 1977b).

Runaways typically head for a big city. New York City alone has an estimated 20,000 runaways under sixteen, plus thousands of "self-emancipated" kids who are only slightly older. They usually arrive by bus or train—hungry, lonely, and broke. As they begin wandering along the streets outside New York's transportation terminals, they are easy prey for an estimated 800 pimps ("Youth for Sale..." 1977). These opportunistic men offer food, clothing, a place to stay, and the appearance of caring. Unwilling to call their parents for help, afraid to turn to police for fear of being arrested, runaways often think they have no choice but to turn to street people.

Father Bruce Ritter, whose Covenant House in New York City annually cares for thousands of homeless and abused children, says of those who have turned to prostitution for survival:

They are not bad kids. . . . They are good kids whose only crime is, for the most part, to be cold, hungry, and homeless, with no skills, no resources, cut off from jobs or the possibility of getting medical help or public assistance. They have nothing to sell, except themselves. They keep themselves alive (or get themselves killed) committing the so-called victimless crime of prostitution.   [Ritter 1978, p. 11]

PROSTITUTES AS PEOPLE

To understand prostitution, we must take a sensitive look at the individuals behind the deviant label. In this section we'll examine family and economic factors that lead people toward the choice of prostitution. We'll also explore ways prostitutes try to maintain their self-esteem once they've adopted a deviant status.

Social Shaping

The backgrounds of prostitutes as a whole are similar to those of teenage runaways. In one study 65 percent of the streetwalkers had begun their "careers" as young runaways ("Prostitution Therapy" 1978). According to various studies, up to 80 percent of prostitutes were victims of incest, rape, or sexual or physical abuse before they entered the life. Not surprisingly, most disliked their parents. For 70 percent only one parent was on the scene during their childhood, and this parent often neglected them. Although religious training may have been emphasized in the home, sex education was not. A positive self-image was not encouraged. Instead, many of the girls were branded as "promiscuous" because they had sought in sexual relationships the affection, approval, and freedom they did not receive at home. Pregnancies and early marriages were common. Perhaps these were additional ways of seeking love, a sense of belonging, and freedom from their own unhappy homes. These marriages were usually violence-prone and short-lived, though, and the young mothers often abused their own children just as they had been abused (James 1980; Skipper and McCaghy 1978; Potterat et al. 1979).

Many who have studied prostitutes have seen this chaotic family life as the "cause" of prostitution. But the characteristics described apply to many people who grow up in poor neighborhoods. A study that contrasted prostitutes who had contracted venereal diseases with nonprostitutes who had also done so found that the two groups as a whole differed little in their early family and sexual experiences. The prostitutes, however, were far more likely to be the firstborns in their families. As such they may have had either excessive responsibilities that they wanted to escape or the strong achievement orientation often noted in first children.

Just as it's misleading to see chaotic, abusive childhood experiences as the cause of prostitution, it's also inaccurate to assume that all prostitutes have the same kind of background. Generalizations about the lives of prostitutes are drawn mostly from studies of the lower, more visible classes of prostitutes. When occupational types are analyzed separately, different patterns appear. Call girls and those who work in brothels or massage parlors are the prosperous, independent end of the spectrum. Many have bachelor's degrees; most have had at least some college experience. Compared with nonprostitutes of the same age, educational background, and marital status, they are just as well-balanced emotionally and far better off financially. They realistically expect to retire from the life by the age of thirty to thirty-five and usually have retirement plans formulated well in advance. Their entry into the profession was typically prompted not by rape, abuse, or abandonment but by recognition of the opportunity for quickly making a lot of money (Exner et al. 1977).

Maintaining Self-Esteem

Whether they are gloomy or positive about their future, prostitutes are forced to recognize that they are considered deviant by most people in our culture. They use a variety of tactics to maintain their self-esteem despite their stigmatized identity.

One is simply to deny their occupation—to try to hide it from others. For instance, strippers who don't want their families to know what they do for a living often tell people they are "legitimate" entertainers—such as dancers or singers—or pretend that they are something altogether unrelated, such as secretaries. In hotels they register under their real name rather than their erotic professional name. And outside of clubs they dress conservatively with little or no makeup in order to pass for "normal" (Skipper and McCaghy 1978).

A second and similar strategy is to earn money within the prostitutes' world but to keep one's private life entirely separate from it. Such people often live within a solidly middle-class setting—marrying, raising children, helping their relatives, going to church, avoiding swearing and sex talk, and not associating with other prostitutes or criminals.

Prostitutes who lead two lives may rationalize the deviant one as a necessary self-sacrifice in order to support dependents in their socially approved life. Rationalization—a third strategy for maintaining self-esteem—is used by other prostitutes as well. Some justify their job as a public service—that is, one that relieves tensions, loneliness, desire to rape, and fears about sexual adequacy. And some strippers define their work as just another form of visual entertainment, like movies and football games (Skipper and McCaghy 1978).

As a fourth strategy, many prostitutes set limits on what they are willing to do for money.

Masseuses, for instance, may only do "hand jobs" or "blow jobs" and refuse requests for intercourse. By defining certain acts as acceptable and others as unacceptable, they build a personal value system within which they can see themselves as okay.

Another strategy is to refuse to see themselves as making money by selling sex. Many streetwalkers seem to shift responsibility to their pimp and see what they are doing as an expression of love for him.

A sixth strategy is to depersonalize sexual interaction itself. Instead of expecting sex to be the most intimate and erotic of contacts, some prostitutes try to detach themselves emotionally and even sexually from what's going on so that its lack of intimacy and personal arousal will not bother them. This detachment also helps prostitutes view themselves as professionals who are justified in accepting money for their services.

A seventh way prostitutes elevate themselves in their own eyes is to put down their customers. Some have the attitude that having to pay for sex debases their clients and makes hypocrites of those who pretend to be "respectable." Others feel that customers exploit them and treat them as objects, so they do the same thing in return.

Feelings of being exploited, ineptly bedded, and treated crudely as objects rather than as people often create resentments toward men as a whole among female prostitutes. They may have few chances to counter this attitude by developing affectionate relationships with men outside the life. Many instead develop sexual relationships with other women in the life. These women may support their own value systems, rationalizations, and contempt for clients and may be far more sensitive as lovers than are men paying to have their own needs gratified. In a subculture that finds acceptable a range of behaviors seen as deviant by the larger society, homosexuality involves little stigma. Among strippers alone, an estimated 50 to 75 percent have had at least some homosexual contacts (McCaghy and Skipper 1969).

MEN WHO VISIT PROSTITUTES

Understanding prostitution requires knowledge of those who buy as well as those who sell. The vast majority of buyers are males. In Kinsey's time most who visited prostitutes were young, lower class, and single (Kinsey et al. 1948). Many used these occasions as an initiation to intercourse. Now, however, people are more likely to experience their first intercourse with an obliging friend. And prostitution has developed its own upper class that tends to attract older, wealthier men. Call girls, masseuses, and even streetwalkers now cater to a clientele that is largely middle-aged, middle-class, and married (Jennings 1976; Simpson and Schill 1977).

Why do these men want paid sex? Surveys have indicated that it is not sexual desire alone that motivates them. Martha Stein (1974) found that men may want sex without the risks and emotional entanglement that an affair would involve. Some want exciting variety in sex partners or sexual activities. Others are motivated by a need to impress their male group with their own masculinity and to express solidarity with "the boys." Some like the illusion of romance, friendship, fathering, or being mothered that a sensitive prostitute can provide. And others just need a place to relax and a sympathetic person to listen to their problems. For them the therapeutic benefits of going to a prostitute may not even include sexual contact.

In addition to these needs, men may visit prostitutes out of sheer curiosity. There are some who pay prostitutes to help them act out unusual sexual fantasies that their regular partners consider perverted. And others may want to escape the loneliness and sexual frustration of having no sex partner available. For instance, many seek a "woman in every port" while traveling. Others have no partner because they feel too unattractive, physically handicapped, or simply shy to endure and succeed in the intimidating process of developing a relationship. Men with erection problems, too, may prefer the expense of guaranteed, impersonal sex to the personal risks of unpaid sex. A skillful prostitute will help them relax and use techniques that may make some form of sexual release possible. Even if nothing works, a good prostitute will protect a client from seeing the encounter as a personal failure.

With the possible exception of needs labeled "freakish," the desires that lead men to prostitutes are all considered "normal." Males in general are expected to have a variety of sexual interests and to pursue them actively. By contrast, women are not expected to have any of these needs—for example, to desire a man in every port while traveling or to visit male brothels with their female friends in order to demonstrate group solidarity and femininity.

It's strange that women who cater to men's accepted needs are themselves labeled deviant. As social anthropologist Jennifer James (1977b, p. 195) has pointed out, "males break few social rules in patronizing a prostitute; females break almost all the rules of their sex role in becoming prostitutes." They openly suggest sex, request money for it, have sex with anyone available rather than with a single loved partner, walk the streets alone at night, and feel sexual in their own right rather than being turned on only by persuasive men. These characteristics are considered so unacceptable in a woman that they can be arrested for them. But even though women are stigmatized for engaging in prostitution, it is part of the traditional female role to please a man and get favors in exchange.

PROSTITUTION AND THE LAW

Prostitution is currently illegal in the United States except in a few Nevada counties, where it is permitted by local option. Elsewhere, prostitutes are frequently arrested and fined or jailed on a variety of charges. These arrests are now under criticism on many grounds: (1) They discriminate against women and the poor; (2) their advocates are often hypocritical; (3) they make prostitutes' lives more dangerous; (4) they turn people into criminals; (5) they deny rights to private sexual choice; (6) they interfere with prostitution's therapeutic effects; (7) they don't stop prostitution; and (8) they cost a lot. Alternative ways of handling this ancient profession are to legalize it, decriminalize it, or make it unnecessary.

Problems in Outlawing Prostitution

A major argument against defining prostitution as illegal is that enforcement of such laws has traditionally discriminated against women. The vast majority of arrests involve female prostitutes rather than their male clients or male prostitutes. In San Francisco, for instance, antiprostitution arrests in 1977 netted 2101 female prostitutes, 512

Being picked up by the police is a recurring reality for prostitutes, but not for their customers.

male prostitutes, and only 325 customers. Poor women are especially likely to be discriminated against. Of the 2938 San Francisco arrests the majority of the 414 people sent to jail were Third World women, even though 60 percent of the women initially picked up were white (Lynch and Neckes 1978).

Occasional efforts to arrest male customers or at least expose their names have met with howls of protest, for these are often "respectable" men whose lives, they claim, would be ruined by such exposure. This protective attitude is rarely extended to the women whom they pay to meet their needs. Prostitute union organizer Margo St. James charges that women are made the "scapegoats for society's guilt," while some men who privately enjoy their favors publicly call for an end to prostitution (Koughan 1979). Some police charged with arresting prostitutes are notoriously cozy with those in the life, having sex with prostitutes, collaborating with brothel owners, and even being involved in the prostitution rings that shift hustlers from city to city to keep ahead of local cleanup campaigns (Bode 1978). Margo St. James claims that the politicians, lawyers, and judge who were responsible for her arrest on prostitution charges approached her for sexual services afterward.

Treating people as criminals for the nonviolent consensual act of prostitution may indeed make criminals of them. Prostitution typically rates a jail sentence or a delayed fine, for which one must work the streets again to pay (Koughan 1979). These penalties force prostitutes into contact with other kinds of criminals, both in jail and on the streets. And having a police record and a "deviant" label makes it hard to escape from the life into a "legitimate" line of work. Prostitution

thus becomes a "revolving door" crime in which arrests lead to repeat offenses and then to more arrests.

In addition to the harm they do to prostitutes, antiprostitution laws are also seen by some as an invasion of both clients' and prostitutes' right to privacy, an inappropriate use of criminal law. Like the consumption of alcohol or marijuana, prostitution falls in the fuzzy area of the law known as "victimless" or "consensual" crime. In such behaviors no one regards himself or herself as the victim at the time of the crime. Complaints are instead filed by the police. The assumption seems to be that society as a whole is hurt by the behavior.

Even if it were appropriate for our government to try to stamp out behaviors some people define as immoral, antiprostitution laws do not seem to meet that goal. Since there continue to be plenty of interested buyers, prostitution has not disappeared despite energetic efforts to get rid of it. In Atlanta, for example, a crackdown on prostitution in the streets and in bathhouses simply forced it into new disguises: nude lounges, nude encounter sessions, nude modeling studios, nude mud-wrestling rooms. Meanwhile, the "hooker-to-cop" ratio rose to six to one, higher even than in nineteenth-century days when prostitution was permitted within a patrolled area of the city (Bode 1978).

In addition to being ineffective, antiprostitution efforts are expensive. Court costs alone run from $500 to $1100 for each prostitution arrest. Taxpayers must shell out an additional $20 to $40 each day a prostitute is held in jail (Milner 1979). San Francisco spends over $2 million a year on arrests, defense, prosecution, and imprisonment of the prostitutes its twenty vice officers pick up

(Lynch and Neckes 1978). Critics point out that this money might be far better spent if it were channeled into programs to help prostitutes escape the life by training them for other jobs.

Reform Efforts

Claiming that both they and our society have been abused by antiprostitution laws, some organizations are now demanding different legal treatment of the profession. In 1973 the National Organization for Women declared its support for dropping antiprostitution laws. During the same year the American Civil Liberties Union set up a Sexual Privacy Project to attack laws that prohibit certain sexual activities between consenting adults, such as homosexual behaviors and prostitution. Also in 1973 Margo St. James established COYOTE—an acronym for "Call Off Your Old Tired Ethics" now known as The National Task Force on Prostitution. This group unites prostitutes and feminists in fighting for an end to laws controlling female sexuality. Its first target is antiprostitution statutes, but its long-range goal is to free women to enjoy their own sexuality and that of their partners (Withers and James 1977). Attendance at COYOTE's annual Hookers' Ball is now so respectable that tickets can be purchased through Ticketron.

Such groups cite national surveys indicating that 75 to 85 percent of the population approves of treating prostitution in some noncriminal way. They have found that the major barrier to change is the power structure that benefits from the present outlaw status of the profession. This power structure includes organized crime figures, hotel owners, politicians who use prostitution "cleanups" to win votes, and local police who receive sexual favors and inside tips about local politicians, businesspeople, and criminals in return for ignoring prostitutes' activities (Nielson 1979). To force changes past this entrenched power structure, some prostitutes are now threatening to reveal the names of prominent lawmakers who have been their customers. Some are also demanding jury trials as expensive, court-jamming deterrents to prostitution arrests (Koughan 1979).

Legalization. Several alternatives to the present illegal status of prostitution have been suggested.

The first is to declare prostitution a legal profession and then subject it to governmental controls. Prostitutes would be required to register with local officials, satisfy age requirements, check in weekly for VD tests, pay taxes on their income, and work only in licensed brothels. Such a system, it is claimed, would have many advantages. It would supposedly (1) eliminate the dangers of association with the criminal world, (2) get prostitution off the streets so that no one would be offended, (3) keep STD in check, (4) provide funds for local government in the form of extra business taxes, (5) prevent teenage prostitution, and (6) eliminate the exploitative pimp.

Legalization has been tried in Germany. Prostitutes are housed in large dormitories. Customers take their pick from closed-circuit TV displays. The government even helps pay for visits if doctors or psychiatrists prescribe them as therapy. *Coyote Howls* notes, "It's probably better than Valium" ("Prostitution Therapy" 1978, p. 12).

But despite its proposed benefits, legalization has not proved satisfactory to either customers or prostitutes. German men have avoided the large government brothels because they are antiseptic, impersonal, and too open for the discreet encounters married men seek (Milner 1979). Many customers have turned back to illegal street prostitutes, and the international traffic bringing them in continues (Barry 1979).

Decriminalization. Because legalization can be as restrictive as the present system is abusive, reform groups are advocating decriminalization. This proposal means removing prostitution from criminal codes as much as possible, on the grounds that all private sexual behaviors are outside the jurisdiction of the law. The only controls that might be used could deal with age, tax, STD, and advertising concerns. To avoid victimization of persons considered too young to consent to selling sexual services, the age of legal consent to prostitution could be set at eighteen. Prostitutes could be expected to report their income to the IRS, just like other self-employed people. Licenses might be required or offered as options to those who have had sex-therapy and STD training and who take regular STD exams. Advertising could be limited to small signs or discreet magazine ads. Only prosti-

Some people believe that prostitutes' hustling and explicitly sexual movies are an invasion of their privacy—that they have a right not to be exposed to sexual come-ons. To accommodate their wishes, erotic movie houses and working prostitutes could be allowed to operate only within specific nonresidential areas.

tutes who are actually bothering people by public solicitation might be fined and then only when a complaint is filed by someone not working for the police department. Prostitution activities could be limited to certain nonresidential areas if desired (James 1976b; Stevens 1977).

Broader Reforms. Although decriminalization proposals are being pushed for local and national adoption, they are seen as only a temporary solution. An end to the exploitative, stigmatized nature of the profession would require major social reforms. Priscilla Alexander (1979) of The National Task Force on Prostitution believes that to attack the problems forcing people into prostitution, government would have to dramatically increase services to victims of incest and child abuse. Education for sound job opportunities would have to be provided for all children. Humane, nonsexist, candid sex education programs would be needed throughout the school years. And unequal sexual and economic treatment of women and minorities would have to be ended. Only then would the needs of men who now buy or sell sex be met through more rewarding jobs and personal relationships. Ideally, prostitution would then exist as a respected form of therapy offered by those who freely choose the profession.

Summary

Sex appeal sells everything from books and clothes to partners. Some in our society would limit the commercialization of sex on the grounds that such selling is obscene, violence causing, and/or sexist. Nevertheless, the selling of sex continues to flourish, including the ancient trade of prostitution. Prostitutes operate as a loosely organized network that also includes peripheral figures ranging from pimps and madams to local officials who are paid to look the other way.

Types of prostitutes include call girls, house prostitutes, streetwalkers, "massage" parlor employees, bar "girls," strippers, lesbian prostitutes, homosexual and heterosexual male prostitutes, and child prostitutes. Most in the lower echelons come from chaotic low-income homes, but call girls and massage-parlor workers may be well educated and relatively well heeled. Many use various tactics to avoid the social stigma of the prostitute label. Those who visit prostitutes tend to be middle-aged, middle-class married men; since male pursuit of sex is regarded as normal, these customers are less often charged with illegal behavior than the women who serve them. Attempts to stamp out prostitution have been attacked as discriminatory and have not worked well. Reform possibilities include legalization of prostitution, decriminalization of consensual paid sex, or the broad reform of social conditions that lead prostitutes and their clients to sell and buy sex.

14

Enhancing Sexual Health

When my old lady and I first started therapy, I didn't want to go. I didn't think our sex was that bad, but she dragged me there. My idea was, how can you change things by just talking about them? Well, we've been at it about three months and I really do some things different now. I'm noticing her more, like when she's upset, or has something on her mind, or hasn't come. Actually, in some ways it's better than when we first got married. At first I didn't like being told to love her up more—a man's got his pride, you know. But she sure smiles more now, and it's better for me, too.   A 28-year-old married factory worker

I think that I could really accept myself if it weren't for my grimacing. Sometimes my strange faces make me feel like I'm in a horror show.

All of my life I have been told that I can control my shaking if I just keep calm. Sometimes it works, but it is hard to make love or just be myself when I have to think about keeping calm. Why is shaking so wrong?

Do you know how demoralizing it is to call someone up for a date and be asked if I am sick, or drunk, or retarded? I'm learning to despise my own voice.

I'm ashamed to admit this, but it is painful for me to be sitting here looking at all of you in this room. I have always avoided people with cerebral palsy. They remind me too much of myself.

[Rousso 1982, p. 83]

Sometimes while Ginger is making her last bathroom stop, I just try to totally relax under the covers. I'll start with different parts of my body—sometimes the toes, sometimes the hands or the shoulder—wherever the tensions from the day's busyness need to flow out. Often I'll start with my face muscles and eyes to try to let all the tension go and then go to all the rest of my body. I find that this relaxation is better than most anything else, even a warm bath, because I pay attention to the slightest sensations. By the time Ginger comes to bed I'm completely ready for her. The day's concerns are put aside and I can focus on our lovemaking. Sometimes I do the same thing at my office desk, trying to keep my body free of anxieties in the face of daily crises. It has made me a calmer person and my sex life is much better.

A 24-year-old cohabiting male journalist

Given the inevitable accidents, illnesses, and hurts of life, the sensual and erotic capacities of the human mind and body are a blessing. Whatever our economic status, race, physical condition, sexual orientation, or intellectual level, the delights and joys of sex are available to enhance personal health and to enrich relationships. A sex-positive society would promote and celebrate such pleasures for reasons of societal and individual health.

But ours is not yet a sex-positive society. It seems easier for us to imagine sexual problems than sexual health, for our society is not geared to encouraging the latter. Consequently, many of us suffer sexual anxieties and other problems needlessly. We need not, however, be passive victims or collaborate with our own sexual suppression. We have both the power and the right to help ourselves or to seek support or assistance from various health professionals.

Professional help for sexual health involves a maze of overlapping disciplines. Some are based on a medical model (treating physical illness), some are based on a therapeutic model (helping troubled relationships), and some are based on a broader, holistic health view of sex.

In this chapter we'll look at present and emerging models for professional sexual health care, opportunities for self-help, and growing awareness of ways that physically disabled people can enjoy sex. In the chapters that follow, we'll examine other sex-related health issues: sexually transmitted diseases, conception, pregnancy, and conception control. Although all of these issues have traditionally been considered things we go to doctors for, they cannot be understood in medical terms alone. Consequently, we'll look not only at the physiological factors involved but also at what these issues mean to us as sexual people.

SEXUAL SELF-HELP

Much of the responsibility for our sexual well-being rests with us as individuals. There seems to be a growing awareness of this fact and a willingness to do something about it. For instance, in 1980 the magazine *Medical Self Care* asserted:

In addition to feeling good, massage can relax, invigorate, and help us get in touch with our own body's sensations.

There's a quiet revolution underway. One that's taking many aspects of medical care out of the ivory towers and stainless-steel examining rooms and putting responsibility for one's own health in the hands of the individual . . . Can you do a breast or testicular self-exam? Why the hell not? . . . It's not enough for your doctor to stop playing God. You've got to get up off your knees.   [*Medical Self Care* 1980, p. 43]

Taking responsibility for our own sexual health means, among other things, regarding medical personnel as resources to be used and chosen carefully. Women, men, and children do not have to patiently suffer unresponsive and autocratic medical personnel. We can be consumers shopping for quality patient services; we need not be completely dependent clients of physicians. There are useful guidelines for choosing practitioners in helping professions, there are referral groups such as women's centers and self-help clinics in many cities, and there are friends to consult about their experiences. The right to understand is part of any good health care or treatment.

Taking at least partial responsibility for our own sexual health also involves learning more about our bodies as well as our sexual choices. Sexuality education in the form of self-help books and other materials is available to everyone. Individuals or couples can do a great deal for personal and relational growth by informing themselves and giving sensitive thought and discussion to their options. Unless relationships have degenerated to the point of noncommunication, some couples with sexual problems can enjoy experimenting with solutions of their own. *Therapy without therapists* is often possible when friends and sexual partners help as sources of feedback, information, advice, and role models. Becoming more aware of our own and our partners' feelings can help us make sexual decisions that are personally satisfying rather than, as sex educators Robert Meyners and Claire Wooster (1979, p. 4) put it, "grasp[ing] frantically at all worn-out roles that serve no useful purpose . . . [or] stumbl[ing] blindly into some sexual revolution of which [we] are the victim rather than the beneficiary."

Sexual self-help can also include the physical aspects of sexual health. To fully enjoy our sexuality, we can keep ourselves in exuberant good health by eating, sleeping, and exercising well. Sex

Awareness for Sexual Health: The TSS Example

One of the primary ways in which we each can assume responsibility for our own sexual health is through awareness—awareness of our own body, its functions, its needs, changes within it, and means to avoid unnecessary health risks to it. For example, reports of deaths due to toxic shock syndrome (TSS) are leading many women to re-evaluate the risks involved in using tampons. Toxic shock syndrome is the result of bacteria-produced toxins similar to those associated with food poisoning, the difference being that food poisoning toxins are ingested while TSS toxins are absorbed by the body.

Although there have been cases of women who don't use tampons, and even men, contracting TSS, the syndrome most often seems to be linked to tampon use. Placement of a tampon in the vagina for too long a time seems to provide conditions favorable to the growth of the toxin-producing bacteria of TSS. Use of super absorbent tampons may be especially risky, for they are left in place for longer periods of time and thus allow the bacteria to flourish.

While occurrence of TSS is quite rare—3 per 100,000 women are affected yearly, with death resulting in 8 percent of the women affected—tampon users between the ages of eighteen and twenty-nine are considered to be at highest risk (FDA 1980). The best preventive measures for TSS are knowledge of the risks involved and increased care in the use of tampons. Women should use only the least absorbent tampon needed. Changing tampons frequently or alternating tampons with napkins during menstruation may decrease the likelihood of bacterial growth. The best way to minimize the risks of using tampons is to change them as frequently as every two hours during the day and to substitute napkins in the nighttime.

The symptoms of TSS are high fever (over 102° F), vomiting, diarrhea, and a rapid drop in blood pressure that results in dizziness. A rash on the palms eventually peels similar to sunburn. These symptoms are probably caused by a strain of staphylococcus. The Centers for Disease Control in Atlanta are now involved in research concerning tampon use and TSS. For the time being women need to pay increased attention to their body's signals by taking greater care in tampon use and by discontinuing use if any of the symptoms of TSS are noticed.

itself is good exercise and is even being prescribed as a key factor in recovery from heart attacks ("Sex Said Helpful . . ." 1983). In addition, we can get to know our own bodies and pay attention to their signals.

Cervical Self-Examination

Few women are on familiar terms with their cervix, for they can't see it. But routine inspections with a plastic speculum lubricated with K-Y jelly, a long-handled mirror, and a good flashlight can reveal potential problems that should be seen by a medical practitioner. As estimated 90 to 95 percent of all women who have borne children have some form of *cervicitis* (a grab-bag term for all cervical problems) at some time between childbearing years and old age (Green 1977). These problems range from mild irritation to cancer.

Symptoms of cervicitis that can be detected without a speculum include pain with intercourse, unusual vaginal discharge, unusual bleeding from the vagina, and itching or burning sensations in the vagina. These same symptoms may result from other, sometimes related, kinds of problems—such as vaginitis or sexually transmitted diseases—but in any case they deserve careful attention.

With a speculum and directions on how to use it from a self-help source, a woman can learn what her cervix looks like when it's healthy. It should be round and pink. Its *os,* or opening to the uterus, should look like a dimple in childfree women and a slit in women who've borne children. Signs of problems include polyps, cysts, inflammation, swelling, discharge, eroded areas, or tumors. Most of these symptoms indicate rather minor, common difficulties that can be cleared up fairly easily by medical personnel.

Cervical self-examination is not a substitute for yearly checkups and Pap smears. But a woman who examines her own cervix regularly is more likely to notice abnormalities at an early stage than is a health care practitioner who sees her cervix only once a year.

Breast Self-Examination (BSE)

About one out of eleven American women will develop breast cancer, the foremost site of cancer death for this population. Men can also develop breast cancer, but this is a relatively rare occurrence resulting in about 300 male deaths annually. About 36,000 women, however, will die from breast cancer annually. Although this affliction

Figure 14-1. Some Variations in the Cervix. If a woman examines her own cervix, its opening will probably appear small and round if she has never borne children (nulliparous) or somewhat stretched and lacerated if she has borne children (multiparous). Surface irregularities—such as eversion (pushing outward of the cervical canal), erosion, or cysts—or unusual discharges should be brought to the attention of health care practitioners.

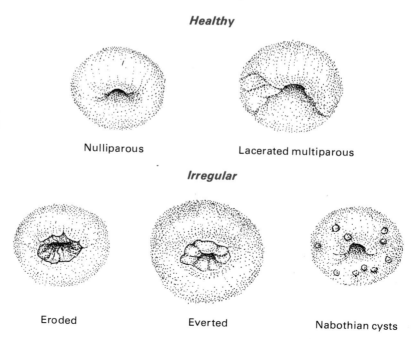

Healthy

Nulliparous   Lacerated multiparous

Irregular

Eroded   Everted   Nabothian cysts

A. Begin Your Breast Check in Front of a Mirror

 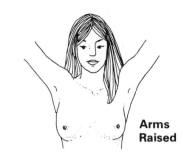 

Arms Hanging Loosely

Arms Raised

1. Look for any change in the shape or puckering of the skin or nipples, and nipple discharge or color change or hardness.

2. Turn from side to side and look for any changes since last month.

3. Press palms of hands firmly together and look for any changes.

B. Lie Down Without a Pillow

  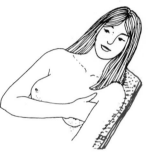

1. Place a folded towel under your left shoulder and put your left hand under your head.

2. Think of your breast as a spiral. With the flat of the fingers of the opposite hand, begin at "A" and follow the arrows around to the nipple. Feel gently, but firmly, for a lump or thickening. Also, feel under the armpit.

3. Repeat the spiral pattern with the left arm down. Check armpit again.

4. Repeat with the other breast.

5. Sit up and repeat the entire process again.

C. Sit Up and Repeat the Procedure for Both Breasts

occurs at its highest rate in women over fifty-five, it can develop at much earlier ages. Since early detection and medical action are critical, all young women are urged to practice breast self-examination (BSE) as a monthly health habit. Most lumps are not tumors or malignant, and if cancer is present in a localized stage, it can be cured or controlled (the five-year survival rate is 85 percent) (American Cancer Society 1979).

Figure 14-2.   Breast Self-Examination.   The most common cancer in women is breast cancer. Rarely fatal if caught early, it can be detected through monthly breast self-examination.

Women can detect abnormalities in their breasts at an early stage by examining them often. Since changes in the breasts occur before and during the menstrual period, it is advisable to conduct the examination about a week after menstruation or at regular one-month intervals if the menstrual cycle is irregular or prolonged. The important point is to be consistent and regular. When a woman is familiar with the consistency, texture, colors, and shapes of her own breasts, she will more certainly recognize lumps or unusual changes should they develop. Early detection and action save lives.

Testicular Self-Examination (TSE)

Although women's breast self-examination has received more publicity than self-examination for men, men too can examine themselves by checking for a developing genital disorder. Young adult males can begin the important health habit of testicular self-examination (TSE). Although only a small number of males die each year from testicular cancer (less than 500), it is a preventable fatality in many cases and it afflicts *young* men. Although most common in men aged twenty to twenty-five, the tumor is also found at earlier and later ages (American Cancer Society 1979). High school males should be taught the technique of TSE and should practice it on a routine basis. Early detection is critical.

There is some evidence that if a male was exposed prenatally to DES (diethylstilbestrol), he is more prone to undescended testicles, epididymal cysts, reproductive tract lesions, and sterility ("DES . . ." 1976). There are about 2 million DES sons, and no link has yet been established between male DES exposure and cancerous tumors. But there is a correlation of undescended testicles with testicular cancer, so it is vital for males to be responsible for knowing their own medical histories. Ironically, although a lump in the testicle may have *no* pain—which makes TSE even more necessary—a symptom of cancer of the testicles may be painful breasts and nipples. Also painful swelling or accumulation of fluid in the scrotum should be brought to the immediate attention of a urologist.

TSE is an important way for a male to discover what is normally within his scrotum. With testicular cancer apparently increasing, TSE is a self-help health practice that can save hundreds of young lives.

SEX THERAPY

Even with preventive health care sexual difficulties may occur. Because of this inevitability, a great variety of therapies have been developed to assist people in overcoming problems and reaching their sexual goals. The modern surge of rising expectations for sexual "adequacy" began with the publication of *Human Sexual Response* by William Mas-

Figure 14-3. Testicular Self-Examination. Testicles should be examined after a bath or shower. The heat from bathing causes the testicles to descend and the scrotal skin to relax, making it easier to detect anything unusual. Simply lift the testicles one at a time, gently rolling each between the thumb and the first two fingers of both hands. Feel for small lumps, especially on the front or side of the testicle. Lumps or cysts may be harmless; but if you find one, contact a health care practitioner.

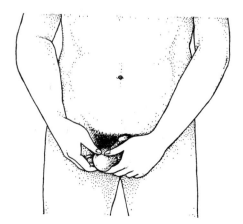

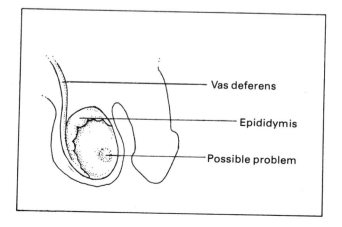

ters and Virginia Johnson in 1966. The book was a best seller even though written in turgid prose and medical language.

Although Masters and Johnson's pioneering work increased awareness and acceptance of sexuality, it also had the unintended effect of raising "performance" expectations. For instance, a young couple presented themselves for sex therapy at a major clinic a few years ago. Although they experienced satisfaction with their marriage and both had regular penis-in-vagina orgasms, they felt dissatisfied because the wife was not achieving multiple orgasms. They were accepted for a fifteen-session treatment program at a fee of $2400 (Mazur 1980). Along with the new self-permission to think and talk openly about sex came increased willingness to define oneself as sexually "dysfunctional" and to seek sex therapists' help for seeming "inadequacies" in sexual response.

Just because research indicates that something is possible in lovemaking, it doesn't mean that this is necessarily desirable as a personal goal. On the other hand, because learning, unlearning, and relearning have a major role in sexual satisfaction, sex therapists can help people enjoy a number of desired behaviors.

Sexual "Dysfunctions"

Definitions of sexual problems are not simple. As sex has become what is considered an art form, many of us have developed anxieties and confusions about sexual expectations of ourselves and others. As quickly as old sexual taboos are exorcised, we burden ourselves with new sexual fallacies.

Characteristic sexual responses that are generally thought to be dysfunctional include, in the male, *premature ejaculation* (inability to delay ejaculation), *retarded ejaculation* (taking too long to orgasm), and *impotence* or *erectile dysfunction* (inability to obtain an erection sufficient for the desired sexual activity). Female sexual dysfunctions include *vaginismus* (involuntary spasm of the muscles surrounding the vaginal opening, which makes penetration painful if not impossible), *anorgasmia* (constant or periodic lack of orgasm and of associated signs of sexual responsiveness), and *dyspareunia* (painful intercourse, not exclusively a female experience). Other sexual problems common to both women and men include *low-level desire* and *aversion to the genitalia* (one's own and/or one's partner's).

In everyday terms people often describe their sex problems as troubles with *time* ("I don't last long enough"; "It takes me too long to come"), *quantity* ("We don't do it enough"; "My partner is always after sex"), *ratio* ("I'm always left hanging"; "I can't always be as turned on as my partner"), or *quality of satisfaction* ("I have orgasm but something's missing"; "I love our cuddles and pleasuring and don't care who, or if either, has orgasm").

These conditions often involve psychosocial rather than biophysical causes. For example, a minority of impotence cases are caused by anatomical irregularities, drugs, infections, obesity, ill health, or heavy drinking; the rest stem from psychological or interpersonal factors. Premature ejaculation rarely has a physical origin; the timing of ejaculation can be brought under conscious control if the man learns to recognize the signs of inpending orgasm, relaxes fears about possible interruptions, and cares about the sexual needs of his partner. Organic causes for lack of orgasm in women—such as hormal imbalances, infections, physical abnormalities, aging, drugs, or alcohol—are implicated in only a small percentage of cases. Psychological or interpersonal factors are far more common (Higgins and Hawkins, forthcoming).

Psychological factors underlying sexual dysfunctions may include ignorance of the anatomy and physiology of sexual response, feelings of guilt or shame about one's sexuality or one's appear-

The Language of Sex

It is worthy of note that our sex-negative society has words only for sexual problems rather than for sexual joy. We speak of *dysfunction* and *dyspareunia*—terms based on Latin and Greek roots meaning diseased, difficult, or faulty. Why not also use words based on the root *eu*, which means well, pleasant, beneficial?

We could speak of *eufunction* to make it clear that there is such a thing as sexual health. And to fill the noteworthy lack in our language of any word that means great-feeling or ecstatic sex, we could use *eupareunia*.

ance, concern about lack of privacy, or fear of consequences such as getting caught, pregnant, or infected with sexually transmittable diseases. Life stresses or fatigue may dampen enthusiasm for sex.

Relationship problems are often present when sex is not fully satisfying. Issues of communication, power, trust, and respect often underlie problems in sexual functioning (McCarthy 1982). Sometimes there is a lack of affection between partners; sometimes the undercurrent is one of barely suppressed hostility or at best indifference. Sex therapists have found that for increasing numbers of married couples who are so lacking in desire for each other that they may avoid sex for months at a time, rage is a basic dynamic in these largely sexless marriages. In their annoyance with each other, people simply turn themselves off. One man described an evening in which he didn't feel like making love to his wife because he was antagonized by her leaving dirty dishes in the sink. Another night he explained,

I went into the bathroom to wash up and I saw her hair on the sink. Why does she always have to be a pig? I felt disgusted with her. Who wants to make love to such a slob? [Quoted in Botwin 1979, p. 112]

A common characteristic of sexually dissatisfied couples is that they don't spend much time enjoying each other's company. Not only do they fail to set aside time for sex, they don't even take much time to talk or play together (McCarthy 1982).

Therapies

Faced with this range of sexual difficulties and reasons why people are having problems, professional sex therapists may use a range of different approaches to helping people improve their sex lives. Five of these approaches are discussed in this section.

Masters and Johnson's treatment for sex problems usually involves two weeks of concentrated work using behavior modification strategies. At their Reproductive Biology Research Foundation in St. Louis, both members of a couple are counseled, on the assumption that both are probably involved in any problems that have developed. History taking and counseling are handled by two therapists—male and female—on the assumption

The Language of Sex

In many people's minds, male "premature ejaculation" is equivalent to the older psychoanalytic pathology of female "frigidity." Women today who do not experience orgasm no longer have to suffer that diagnostic label; they are considered "preorgasmic," which simply means they have not yet experienced a recognized orgasm. For similar reasons men should not have to suffer the sexist and drastic label of "impotency." A penis, soft or otherwise, should have nothing to do with power-potency. Why not simply refer to the situation as "pre-erectile" or "nonerectile" on this occasion?

that this combination will encourage communication between partners about what is going on and how they feel. Specific sexual tasks are assigned as "homework."

For instance, if the problem is "premature ejaculation," tasks begin with several days of "sensate focus" exercises—that is, nongenital touching in which the giving and receiving of full-body pleasure are not accompanied by expectations of orgasm or reciprocity. The person being touched is asked only to let the other know what feels good. Masters and Johnson explain:

For most women, and for many men, the sensate focus sessions represent the first opportunity they have ever had to "think and feel" sensously and at leisure without intrusion upon the experience by the demand for end-point release (own or partner's), without the need to explain their sensate preferences, without the demand for personal reassurance, or without a sense of need to rush to "return the favor." [Masters and Johnson 1970, p. 73]

Once sexual excitement can be disassociated from thoughts of orgasm, the couple is taught to use the "squeeze technique." As soon as the male reaches a full erection, the female puts strong pressure on specific points on and below the glans of his penis for a few seconds, thus stifling his urge to ejaculate. Once they've mastered this technique, they progress to nonthrusting coupling with the female on top, and then to more active thrusting. While the male is learning to identify and maintain preorgasmic levels of excitement, his partner learns how to enjoy and maximize her own sexual sensations without overstimulating him. In their 1970 book *Human Sexual Inadequcy,* Masters and Johnson claimed that 182 out of 186 couples thus treated developed adequate ejaculatory control in the male so that the female could experience orgasm at least half of the time when sexmaking included intercourse. However, such claims by this therapy team are hard to substantiate, for their research and reporting methods are questionable (Zilbergeld and Evans 1980) and their criteria for success may be so minimal as to be easily met. Sex therapy critic Bernie Zilbergeld (1983) observes that these simple training exercises may be fairly effective in treating inability to orgasm in women and premature ejaculation in men but less effective in "curing" other sexual problems.

A second model for sex therapy has been developed by Helen Singer Kaplan (1974, 1979) of the New York Hospital–Cornell Medical Center. Her approach combines Masters and Johnson's techniques of relearning with psychoanalysis. For instance, Kaplan finds that fear of both intimacy and romanticism may underlie sexual problems such as seeming lack of desire. She believes that unraveling the source of such fears may take months of psychoanalysis before partners can develop enough insight into their sexual problems to deal with them constructively. She cautions that when deep psychological stresses in a relationship are not resolved, therapy for overt sexual problems may not help much (Kaplan 1979).

A third model for sex therapy is based on the notion of high-level wellness—that is, "eufunction" rather than dysfunction. Two of its foremost practitioners are William Hartman and Marilyn Fithian of the Center for Marital and Sexual Studies in Long Beach, California. Their diagnosis of sexual functioning is based not only on psychological testing and sex history taking but also on a physical examination and a "sexological" examination to measure physical factors that affect sexual response. In the female, for instance, these factors include vaginal lubrication, blood congestion, nipple erection, strength of the pubococcygeus (PC) muscle, possible separation in the muscles of the vaginal walls, clitoral structure, and areas of sensation in the vagina. Recommendations for sexual improvement are based on people's understanding of their own patterns of response and on intimacy-enhancing exercises such as breathing together and foot caresses. Sometimes hypnosis is used to move from anxiety about sex to spontaneous enjoyment of erotic pleasures (Hartman and Fithian 1972, 1982).

A fourth therapy model is typified by Julia Heiman, Leslie LoPiccolo, and Joseph LoPiccolo's (1976) program for helping women learn to orgasm. Unlike Masters and Johnson—who treat only couples—they deal with single people who want to increase their enjoyment of sex. Their program begins with the individual. A woman, for example, first becomes familiar with her own sexual attitudes and what her genitals look like. Then she explores her body with her own hands, using

Sex Therapy as Work or as Play

A Los Angeles sex therapist, Dr. Herman Rosten, believes that many people take sex therapy too seriously. Although sex problems *are* sometimes serious, he thinks the best antidote to sexual disinterest is a lithe, playful approach to sex.

I believe that we must permit the child to awaken in the adult—especially during sex play and all of sexuality—the child who was once filled with adventure, curiosity, and creative imagination. [Rosten 1979, p. 3–4]

Many of us do not fully enjoy sex because we treat it as goal-oriented work rather than as play in which experiences are unstructured and an end in themselves. Sex therapists and sex manuals have contributed to this worklike approach to sex for they advise us to "work on" our relationships. But the task orientation and competitiveness of work do not easily blend with creative, humane sexuality. Expressions to ourselves like "Can I do it tonight? I'm working at it!" or "What still needs to be done? Oh yes, I must kiss the other ear lobe," do not lead to spontaneous, willing sharing of identities and bodies.

relaxation exercises to overcome feelings of discomfort that block sensual pleasure. She's taught how to strengthen her vaginal muscles to enhance orgasmic response and is encouraged to give herself pleasure by using fantasies, erotic literature, and vibrators to trigger arousal and orgasm. The self-pleasuring lessons also include learning to feel good about herself and giving herself permission to let go and experience the delicious sensual sensations. Once she's comfortable with arousing herself, she's then gradually introduced to sharing what she's learned with a partner, for mutual enjoyment of a variety of sexual joys.

A fifth therapy model is a comprehensive approach to sex therapy and treatment as exemplified by the Sexual Health Services (SHS) of the University of Minnesota Medical School. The principles that underlie the programs of SHS are (1) responsibility for self—"Neither partner can force the other to 'turn on,' nor can one 'give' the other an orgasm . . . our approach teaches each partner to be *responsive to* the other but *responsible for* oneself"; (2) permission to be sexual—"Many dysfunctional and dissatisfied couples require only this [guiltless] kind of permission to overcome the negative messages received during their previous socialization experiences"; (3) methods of reeducation; (4) development of increased awareness; (5) structured behavior change—"As part of their therapeutic contract, the couple in the program give over to the consultants some of the responsibility for structuring their modes of sexual expression for a specified period of time." The program lasts for three to ten weeks (Maddock 1976, pp. 57–58).

The University of Minnesota sexual enrichment and therapy programs are also based on some holistic assumptions about sexual health. According to Maddock, sexual health encompasses many factors:

(1) The conviction that one's personal and social behaviors are congruent with one's gender identity, and a sense of comfort with one's sex-role behaviors; (2) the ability to carry on effective interpersonal relationships with members of both sexes, including the potential for love and long-term commitment; (3) the capacity to respond to erotic stimulation in such a way as to make sexual activity a positive and pleasurable aspect of one's experience, including any activity that is not harmful or exploitive; (4) the judgment necessary to make rewarding decisions about one's sexual behavior which are consistent with one's overall value system and beliefs about life. [Maddock 1976, p. 355]

What is so promising and advanced about this kind of sexual health program is that it works from a framework of sexual health, takes its cues from the uniqueness and values of the individuals involved, and uses a dynamic interplay of educational and therapeutic features.

Professionals offering treatment programs such as these have been inundated with clients. The rapid and chaotic rise of the sex therapy industry in the 1970s and 1980s could not keep pace with the new quest for sexual fulfillment and the search for experienced and qualified sex educators, counselors, and therapists.

Issues of training and certification in sex therapy are lively and controversial. The major training and credential-granting agency in North America is the American Association of Sex Educators, Counselors, and Therapists (AASECT). In addition the American Psychological Association, the American Psychiatric Association, and the American Association of Marriage and Family Therapists have credential-granting programs involving sex-help training; the Institute for Advanced Study in Human Sexuality (IASHS) in San Francisco is involved not only in training and certifying sex therapists but also in research, development of educational programs, and political action for social change. Such therapy issues as group nudity, the use of erotic massage, hot tubs, surrogate partners, explicit films, body work, touching and self-disclosure from the therapist or facilitator, guided fantasy, and sexological examination will probably continue to generate controversy, research, and evaluation throughout the 1980s.

Education

Many sexual difficulties that people experience can be traced to lack of information, lack of awareness, misinformation, or unrealistic expectations about the many components of their sexuality. Educational methods and programs in human sexuality will probably improve and expand in the United States in spite of political resistance by a vocal, organized minority. Especially on the college level, where the sexual development and activity of young adults are more easily conceded by parents and where academic freedom is more supportive of the exploration of controversial topics, sexuality programs are proliferating. They range from large introductory lecture courses in sociology, biology, home economics and family relations, health education, psychology, and nursing, to workshops and presentations by women's and men's studies and centers, to paraprofessional peer sexuality education programs that train students to provide outreach, educational, and supportive counseling services to their peers (Zapka and Mazur 1977). Peer programs have also been conducted on the high school level (Carrera 1976). The steady progress of sex education in this country is due in large measure to the efforts of organizations such as the Planned Parenthood Federation of America and the Sex Information and Education Council of the United States (SIECUS).

The increasing number of academic and graduate programs in human sexuality also accelerate the professional development of sexuality education. Educators can work in institutional settings—for example, schools of medicine, social work, law, nursing, education, theology—where they can train helping professionals to deal sensitively and effectively with the sexuality concerns of their clients. They can also provide direct services to persons of all ages through community agencies or establish private practices offering enrichment programs to youth, parents, the aged, sexual minorities, or disabled persons. Sexuality educators can help couples assess the degree of severity of their sexual problems and make appropriate referrals.

Sexuality education, at its most intense level, is therapeutic as well as informative. And, most significantly, as a health promotion model it allows the prevention of sexual dysfunction and the development of an enriched quality of personal and interpersonal well-being.

HELP BASED ON THE MEDICAL MODEL

Many in the medical profession are specialists on sex-related matters such as genital disorders, contraception, problems in sexual functioning, pregnancy, and sexually transmitted diseases. In many cases seeking medical help and advice is entirely appropriate. With male sexual problems, for instance, an estimated 50 percent of cases have a physical origin ("New Approach . . ." 1982). The potential problem with doctors is that they are medical specialists and as such are usually untrained in the social psychology of sexual problems. Instead of incorporating medical observations into a holistic view of sexual expression, they may see patients in terms of organs. The problem lies equally with health care consumers who traditionally have placed responsibility for their own health in another's hands and have limited their search for help to a single doctor.

Sensitivity to sexual issues and holistic approaches to health are now being encouraged in the education of nurses. Nurse practitioners provide primary care for patients, offering not only a health assessment of the whole person, including sexuality and sexual issues, but also appropriate interventions and/or referrals to other health care professionals. Some nurses are educated as sex therapists. Even nurses who are not nurse practitioners or sex therapists may be actively engaged in teaching, counseling, and/or referring clients for all aspects of health and illness, including sexuality. In a medical setting much of the nurse's contribution to sexual health comes about in her or his day-to-day interaction with patients and their families or significant others. Often it is the nurse to whom people address questions such as, "My husband has just had a myocardial infarction. Does this mean we can never have sex again?" "When can I resume intercourse after having a baby?" "My teenage daughter is sexually active. Where can I send her for contraceptive advice?" Their education and their intimate contact with patients places nurses in a position to help people deal with the misinformation, misconceptions, and fears that are often at the root of sexual difficulties.

Specialists in Female Medicine

Physicians specializing in female disorders are called *gynecologists*. Those specializing in pregnancy and birth are called *obstetricians*. Many doctors link the two specialties, which results in the acronym OB-GYN. Accustomed to viewing sexual issues as matters of disease or reproduction, many women have turned to their OB-GYNs for all sex-related matters. In fact, they often use their OB-GYNs as a sort of general practitioner. An estimated 86 percent of women who go to OB-GYNs for a yearly genital checkup see no other kind of doctor (Burkons and Willson 1975).

By choosing an OB-GYN for all sex-related health issues, women force doctors into a role for which many are untrained. Since the sociology and psychology of sex were not part of their medical school curricula, many OB-GYNs are as uninformed, embarrassed, and perhaps rigid about sex as anyone else. In addition their medical model predisposes them to view sex from an illness, rather than wellness, perspective. Psychiatrists Malkah Notman and Carol Nadelson comment on the inadequacies in OB-GYNs' training:

Since the gynecologist-obstetrician is the physician many women turn to for primary health care, his/her

Reactions to Mastectomy

A large number of women, as part of the treatment for breast cancer, have breast tissue surgically removed. In radical mastectomy the breast and some underlying chest muscle and associated lymph nodes are removed. In simple mastectomy only the breast is removed; in lumpectomy only the lump is removed. Some doctors and women now prefer the latter two procedures as less drastic, but whether they are as effective as the radical mastectomy is controversial ("Mastectomy Study Cited" 1982).

The life-saving procedure of mastectomy is often accompanied by a great sense of loss. Women with radical mastectomies are particularly concerned about being found sexually unattractive and may find it hard to undress in front of their partners or to have sex in the nude. In addition to the blow to their self-image in a society that eroticizes breasts, half of mastectomy patients lose all or part of the erotic sensitivity of their breast. Although their general sexual capacity is undiminished, many have less sex in the first months after the operation, partly because they don't feel well, partly because they fear rejection or feel anger, and partly because their partner is afraid of hurting them and may even become temporarily impotent. To talk openly about such feelings and to share exploration of the excised area and tender massage of the affected arm can help both partners recover from the trauma of the operation (May 1981). Many women find that latex-covered, silicone-gel molded breast forms help them feel self-confident, especially in public appearances. The latex cover adheres to the skin, and the better-quality models "feel as natural to the touch as a real breast" (Kushner 1975, p. 223). But to be "restored" by a prosthetic device does not solve all emotional problems.

role has necessarily been expanded to include counseling, whether or not this is his/her original intent. The potential for a preventive approach in both physical and mental health also is important. It requires complex skills and psychological understanding that have not been part of the traditional training in obstetrics-gynecology. The full impact of gynecological treatment and procedures on an individual's self-image and sexuality must be understood. In some areas, notably pregnancy, contraceptive counseling, and sexual dysfunction, the illness model may be inappropriate. [Notman and Nadelson 1978, p. 6]

Examinations for Serious Female Disorders

Although the medical model is inadequate for many aspects of sexuality, seeing medical practitioners for prevention and treatment of physical disorders is appropriate. For women routine pelvic and breast examinations are vitally important to early detection of potentially serious problems. But many women define such examinations as "dehumanizing, degrading, and insensitive" (Green 1979, p. 32). Perhaps they react this way partly because attempts to desexualize health care practitioners' handling of areas linked with sex—through practices such as use of the drape sheet—have also limited personal contact between health care provider and patient. And to women who are uncomfortable with their sexuality, lying on a table with legs spread, feet in stirrups, and a rela-

tive stranger poking fingers and instruments into vagina and rectum and feeling their breasts may seem intrusive.

However, exposing sex-related body parts to health care practitioners for examination and/or treatment need not be defined as a debasing, embarrassing experience. Indeed, the pelvic examination is a marvelous educational opportunity when conducted by a sensitive, aware physician,

Figure 14-4. Pelvic Examination in the Female. As part of a complete pelvic checkup for a female, health care providers use a speculum to open the usually touching walls of the vagina, thereby allowing the vagina and cervix to be seen easily. (A). If a Pap smear is to be taken, a swab is inserted between the open blades and rubbed across the surface of the cervix.

Checkups also include two procedures by which the health care practitioner feels for abnormalities in structures that cannot be seen. In the bimanual pelvic examination (B), one or two fingers of one hand press organs upward from the vagina, while the other hand feels them for abnormalities by pressing down on the abdomen. In the rectovaginal examination (not shown), the health care practitioner uses one finger in the vagina and one in the rectum to feel the areas in between. Although these potentially lifesaving procedures may be slightly uncomfortable, a woman will not find them painful if she relaxes her muscles.

A. Speculum Exam

B. Bimanual Pelvic Exam

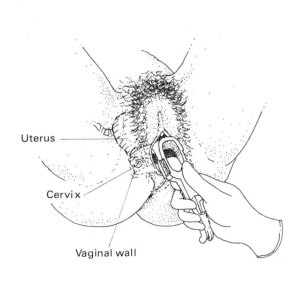

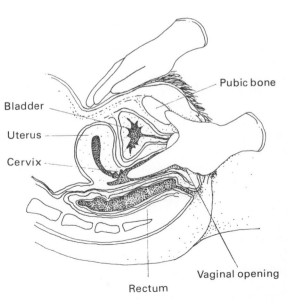

nurse practitioner, or trained paraprofessional. As the health care provider checks abdomen, breasts, clitoris, external genitalia, vagina, cervix, and rectum for possible abnormalities, the woman may watch what's going on in a mirror and learn how to examine her own genitals at home. As Diane Fordney-Settlage points out, "Bodily self-ignorance aggravates the problems of gynecological and sexual health, and the physician's authority giving permission to touch can remove at least some of this restriction" (quoted in Green 1979, p. 45).

In addition to visual and manual examinations, a *Pap smear* is also taken as a screening device for precancerous or cancerous conditions of the cervix. Pap smears can also detect certain vaginal infections. Uterine cells that collect in the vaginal fluid are picked up on a cotton swab or flat wooden stick along with cells gently scraped from the surface of the cervix. These cells are then spread on a slide and examined under a microscope to determine their degree of normality or abnormality.

According to the American College of Obstetricians and Gynecologists the Pap smear is an essential procedure that should be performed at least once a year for all women. As soon as a woman becomes sexually active, she should begin having regular Pap smears and gynecological checkups. And even if she is not sexually active, she should have the same yearly examination if she is eighteen or older. Some health practitioners recommend Pap smears every six months for women over thirty-five, women who have herpes, or women who have had problem Pap smears in the past. For females who have taken DES (diethylstilbestrol) for "morning-after" birth control or to prevent miscarriages or whose *mothers* took DES when they were pregnant, Pap smears may not be enough. A rare kind of cancer resulting from DES use—vaginal cancer—may be detected in its early stages only by *colposcopy* (visual inspection of the walls of the vagina with a lighted magnifying device).

About 7400 women die each year from cervical cancer—and most of these deaths are preventable. The American Cancer Society (1979, p. 17) claims that "if every woman had a Pap test with her regular health checkup, there would be virtually no deaths from cervical cancer." Cervical cancer rates are highest in low socioeconomic groups and among Puerto Rican immigrant and black women (American Cancer Society 1979). Cervical cancer rates also seem to be high among women who begin intercourse at an early age and/or have many sexual partners (Novak, Jones, and Jones 1975).

Specialists in Male Medicine

There has been no equivalent to the female's gynecologist for males, so men in the past have used either a general practitioner or a urologist (who specializes in the urinary tract) for help. Like the OB-GYN a urologist may have little understanding of sexuality or of healthy sexual functioning.

As men learn to be more involved in their level of wellness, it is possible that a new kind of health practitioner will emerge: the "andrologist." Journalist Sam Julty (1979, p. 346) speculates in his comprehensive guide, *Men's Bodies, Men's Selves,* that the need for specialists in male medicine who are knowledgeable in many fields—urology, reproduction, sexuality, and endocrinology (study of the effects of hormones)—may soon result in "a counterpart to the gynecologist to attend to the complex problems of the male urogenital system."

Another approach is to develop teams of specialists in various aspects of male medicine. The new Association for Male Sexual Dysfunction incorporates certified physicians in internal medicine, endocrinology and metabolism, urology, psychiatry, neurology, and vascular surgery, as well as specialists in sex therapy, marriage and family counseling, and even a sleep consultant. This group offers a comprehensive approach that takes into account all of the man's physical and psychological patterns, now thought to be the most effective way to deal with sexual problems. As examples of the range of physical causes that may be unearthed, it is currently estimated that of the thirty million American men thought to have some degree of sexual dysfunction, one and a quarter million are diabetic, six million take drugs for high blood pressure, a quarter of a million have multiple sclerosis, and many others have problems ranging from circulatory disease and hormonal abnormalities to alcoholism ("New Approach . . ." 1982).

Examinations for Serious Male Disorders

Some male genital problems are potentially life-threatening. Like some females males may be inhibited about genital examinations. The prospect of having a doctor insert a finger into their rectum is terrifying to many men, perhaps because of its taboo homosexual associations. Yet cancers of the colon, rectum, and prostate are major killers of men—and they can be detected in their early, preventable stages only by manual examinations through the rectum by a trained health care practitioner.

Recognizing—and perhaps sharing—their patients' fears, some doctors avoid conducting this essential aspect of the physical examination for middle-aged males. Consequently, men subject themselves to high risk of cancer mortality because of this sex-related aversion to contact with the anus and rectum. Men over thirty should *insist* that they receive such examinations during their yearly checkups.

The American Cancer Society (1980) estimates that more than two out of three patients might be saved by early diagnosis and prompt treatment of colorectal cancer; yet almost 53,000 people die of it each year. In 1980 an estimated 25,300 of those who died were males. Since 1940 men have been dying from this condition at about the same appalling rate. Can it really be that men would rather die than have a physician insert a finger into their rectum? The examination is simple and should be painless, unless there is cause for pain. And the slide test for blood in the feces—which is what the physician obtains on the gloved fingertip—can often be done right in the physician's office. An additional visual examination is available, the proctoscopic examination, which the American Cancer Society recommends as part of a regular checkup after the age of forty. A lighted tube is passed into the rectum and lower colon through which the doctor can inspect the walls visually.

Another rarely discussed killer of men is prostate cancer. It claims about 22,000 victims at a rate that has been relatively unchanged for the past forty years (American Cancer Society 1980). About the size of a chestnut and weighing about twenty grams, the prostate gland consists of three lobes and is wrapped around the urethra and the base of the bladder. It can be examined manually for size and firmness through the inward wall of the rectum, a procedure completed when the colorectal feces sample is obtained. Although more prostate cancer deaths occur in the over-seventy-five-year-old category than in the younger group, the prostate can be a troublesome organ for men of all ages. It is subject to acute infections and enlargement and can be responsible for a wide range of symptoms.

Figure 14-5. Rectal Examination in the Male. For a rectal examination, the male is usually asked to lean over if he is standing or to draw his knees up to his chest if he is lying down. These flexed-at-the-hip positions give the health care practitioner a better angle for feeling the structures inside. The major goals of the rectal examination are to see whether there are any masses in the rectum, to check for prostate enlargement, and to check the feces for blood. The examiner's gloved fingertip is lubricated to avoid discomfort.

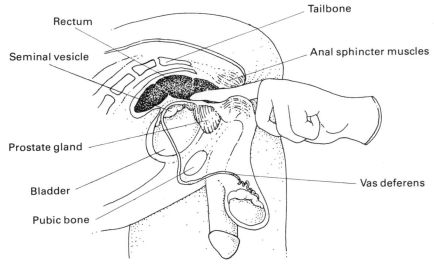

Tailbone

Rectum

Anal sphincter muscles

Seminal vesicle

Prostate gland

Bladder

Pubic bone

Vas deferens

Although most enlargements are benign, Lawrence Galton reports that autopsy findings reveal that 20 percent of men over fifty have prostate cancer; by age seventy half of the men in the United States have the beginnings of prostate cancer. Galton (1979, pp. 144–45) notes, "Unfortunately, all prostatologists agree that far too few men over forty have an annual physical examination which includes a rectal examination of the prostate. Failure to examine the prostate is perhaps the greatest omission in physical examinations."

SEXUALITY AND DISABILITY: AN ISSUE FOR EVERYBODY

Consider those who sit conspicuously in their wheelchairs with numb and paralyzed extremities, with their urine draining into plastic bags strapped to their legs. Then consider those who have other physical problems—the fat or thin, the tall or short, the deformed or weak, the bald, those with false teeth or acne, those who are too tired, too busy, or in too much discomfort to try for sexual fulfillment. If the spinal cord–injured person can become sexually successful through a process of reassessment of goals, attitudes, and abilities, others can do the same. [Mooney, Cole, and Chilgren 1975, p. xi]

Women and men with physical or learning disabilities have a great deal to teach others about what it means to be a unique female or male person. The struggle of the disabled for sexual fulfillment is an exaggerated expression of a common human goal that reflects in large images many of our expectations and assumptions about sex and sexuality.

Recognizing the Sexuality of Disabled Persons

Given our society's obsession with stereotypic Miss and Mr. America beauty and our preoccupation with orgasm counting and penis-in-vagina sex, as well as a variety of other complicatd psychological and interpersonal factors, we victimize the disabled by ignoring them or reinforcing those with low self-esteem with our negative attitudes toward their bodies. We make their struggle for self-actualization more difficult than it need be.

In spite of the enlightened federal Rehabilitation Act of 1973, and in spite of state laws setting accessibility standards for public buildings and facilities, there are critical changes that need to occur in the attitudes and beliefs of the able-bodied population.

Vincent Venditti, a college graduate confined to a wheel chair all his life with cerebral palsy, has been married ten years to a woman who is nondisabled. Reflecting on the long period of his adolescent hospitalization, he says:

The people who worked in the institution were a negative force, because they made me see myself as a sexless person. They would laugh and make sarcastic remarks about sexual matters. For instance, if I would look at a pretty girl walking by, a staff member might say, "What would you do, what could you do with that, Vinny?" Meaning that if I had the opportunity for a sexual encounter, my physical disability would prevent it from happening. They doubted my ability to handle a sexual relationship. [Davidson and Venditti 1979, p. 26]

So much remains to be accomplished in educating the general public. One study of college students' attitudes summarizes, "The data . . . indicate that among undergradute college students who appear to hold liberal and permissive attitudes toward sexuality, attitudes in the sexual revolution have not as yet embraced disabled persons" (Haring and Meyerson 1979, p. 260). The investigators conclude, "there is a need not only for sexual attitude reassessment, but also a need for knowledge if the sexual revolution is ever to arrive" (Haring and Meyerson 1979, p. 260). Through knowledge and changing attitudes, able-bodied persons can end their sexual oppression of the disabled, especially if they take the time to make personal, friendly contact with disabled persons.

In addition to the sexual health issues that the disabled reflect for everyone and the critical importance of the able-bodied's becoming aware of their oppression of the physically challenged, another reason for examining the topic is the possibility of growing in love with a disabled person or of one's lover suddenly becoming crippled or chronically debilitated.

Some experts warn physically challenged people that others may enter sexual relationships with them out of "curiosity, pity, paternalism and even sexual fetishes directed at some types of disabled persons such as amputees" (Hahn 1981, p. 229). Sifting such motivations of others involves an additional burden beyond the challenge of the disability itself. Lovers and partners of the disabled also can often use help for their own sexual health. "Sexual partners of the disabled usually need sexual counseling similar to that of the disabled," say Dorothea Glass and Frank Padrone:

Their need for information, their concerns and attitudes regarding sexuality need to be explored concurrently...Information should not be vague and diffuse but specific and to the point. There are often problems related to the partner's responsibilities as a twenty-four-hour-a-day, seven-day-a-week nurse, giving help with bathing, dressing, catheter care, bowel care, transfers, braces, wheelchair, and assisted ambulation. The question is—can this helping be a part of loving? There is a need for temporary respite, help if it is financially possible, and counseling so that the partner may have fun as well as responsibility.   [Glass and Padrone 1978, p. 47]

Intimacy and sexual pleasure are possible for all of us.

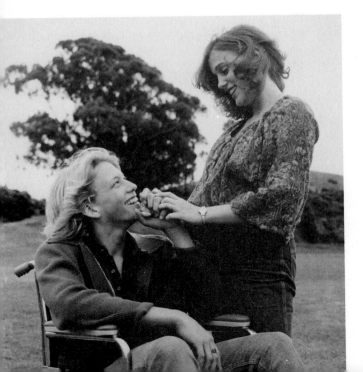

The details of such help and counseling will clearly vary, depending on the type of disability involved.

Another reason for developing a constructive philosophy and set of values toward impaired, incomplete, disfigured, or progressively debilitated bodies is to encounter our own vulnerability to accident and disease and to value life and relationships. It is sometimes said that the able-bodied are only temporarily in that condition. One skid of the motorcycle or car, one invasive virus, one wrong twist of the body while working or playing, one senseless accident for simply being in the wrong place at the right time, one more tick of a biological time bomb that explodes a hidden genetic defect, and anyone can discover how temporary able-bodiedness may be.

It is absurd to lump all conditions of disability together as if there were some breed of nonhuman "disabled" out there. A blind person has a different set of problems than a deaf person, and neither of them knows what it is like to be paralyzed and confined to a wheelchair. But disabled persons, whatever their impairments, whether congenital or acquired, have many concerns and trials in common. As one professor of social work expresses it, "Often, the sexual concerns of such clients, their partners and families, are remarkably homogeneous, particularly the psychological and social aspects of their sexuality" (Harrison 1979, p. 90). One reason for this phenomenon is the dehumanization in various guises to which they are subject. Because they have been hidden and silent for so long, the disabled are regarded as different, a kind of subhuman species. The able-bodied, by not recognizing the full humanity of disabled persons, tend to ignore their sensuous, erotic, and sexual interests and needs as well.

Seen from another perspective, "the disabled" are not necessarily handicapped in the essential human qualities of creativity, love, compassion, imagination, moral purpose, sensitivity, or sensual and erotic needs and desires. It is a tragic truth that some congenital conditions, accidents, and mental illnesses are so devastating that the individuals never unfold or recover. As equally tragic is the large number of able-bodied persons who never unfold or recover from the circumstances and stresses of their lives.

From the point of view of health as a high level of physical, mental, and social functioning, perhaps many adults in this country are operationally disabled. As it is, one out of every eleven persons in the United States is classified as handicapped (President's Commission on Employment of the Handicapped). Millions of men and women endanger their health and relationships by the abuse of food, smoking, alcohol, and/or other drugs. Such behavioral problems, with their potential life-threatening consequences, are of course theoretically reversible. They are technically curable, which distinguishes them categorically from the disabilities of spinal cord injury; mental retardation; lack of sight, hearing, or speech; rheumatoid arthritis; diabetes; stroke; muscular dystrophy; multiple sclerosis; cerebral palsy; and other degenerative diseases and terminal illnesses for which there are presently no cures.

"The disabled" must overcome as best as possible a number of assaults on their personhood and sexuality; negative body image; perceiving their own bodies as "the enemy"; lack of bowel or bladder control; spastic motion; appliances, devices, and medications; denial, rejection, or paternalistic reactions of parents, partners, or peers; outrageous social insults by strangers, even when well intentioned; awkward and sometimes incompetent treatment from health care professionals; and reliance on others, whether paid assistants, volunteers, lovers, or family members. And, for some, such as burn victims, amputees, or patients with radical internal surgery, frequent pain and more surgery lie ahead. The harsh realities of disabilities must not be glossed over. And yet, through it all, we are dealing with spirited, loving, lovable, sensual, sexy women and men—not public health statistics.

Solutions for Specific Disabilities

In addition to the general problem of not being seen as sexual by the seemingly able public, individual disabled persons have unique problems in lovemaking. For instance, for those with respiratory diseases, there is the problem of low energy levels. For those with amputations, logistics may be a problem. For the paralyzed and spinal cord injured, there may be restriction of movement and loss of sensation in some areas. For those with degenerative diseases, activities requiring physical vigor may be difficult. And for those who have urine bags draining their bladders, tubes may seem

to get in the way of sex. Nevertheless, many of these people have found—or can be helped to find—creative solutions to their desires for physical intimacy. Some specific examples follow.

Paralysis and Spinal Cord Injuries. Those with spinal cord injuries or paralysis may face challenges such as lack of sensations in their genitals, problems with bladder control, fears from partners about hurting them, and restricted physical movement. The idea that sex means male-on-top intercourse may make "sex" seem impossible in a wheelchair.

However, some paralyzed and spinal cord–injured people are exploring the phenomena of mental orgasm and sensory amplification and compensation; some use sex aids and toys and surrogate partners who understand their special needs. Of necessity their disabilities force experimentation and increased sexual awareness, with the result that the entire skin, as Ashley Montagu has asserted, becomes an erogenous zone. Elbows, noses, foreheads, and anal areas become sources of sexual delight and intimacy. Sexologists such as Milton Diamond encourage this guiltless, joyful experimentation:

Do away with the "myth" which, in essence, states that the only satisfactory means of expressing oneself sexually and achieving satisfaction is with an erect penis in a well-lubricated vagina. For the able-bodied as well as the handicapped, sexual satisfaction is possible without these practices and, in fact, may even be more satisfying. Hands, mouth, feet, any body part may be used any way to achieve satisfaction, and one means is not, a priori, to be preferred over another. [1977, p. 219]

Sexuality counseling can help spinal cord–injured persons discover and explore such options. Most such efforts have been directed toward males, partly because four out of five cord–injured persons are male. Less than half of the cord–injured women in one survey had received any kind of sexuality counseling (Zwerner 1982). But counseling alone does not automatically produce sexual happiness. Educating handicapped persons about their sexual options is not easy because most of them share the same sexual ignorance and fallacies as the general population, and they tend to resent and resist being educated for what they initially consider to be second-rate or not "real" sex. This process of reassessment is understandable because their physical limitations mandate a consideration of the options. As enlightened and healthy as the range of options may be, they are not freely chosen.

Mental Retardation.   A major shift in attitudes has occurred regarding the sexuality of the mentally handicapped. Until recently the negative consequences of their sexual activity were the primary considerations of parents, professionals, and communities. In institutions their caretakers often considered their masturbation and affectionate touching as serious problems to be prevented. By contrast, one current philosophy is to "normalize" life in all its aspects and to respect the right of the mentally handicapped to live sexually satisfying lives.

Yet much remains to be done to overcome decades of sexual repression. As in any period of social change, old fears and anxieties will continue to mingle with a desire to positively channel the sexuality inherent in every individual, whether handicapped or normal. In 1970 the United Nations passed a bill supporting the right of retarded individuals to sex education, cohabitation, and marriage. Often, though, when a retarded person expresses or acts out desires to find a mate, marry, and have children, many people continue to perceive these wishes as excessive or shocking. The mentally retarded continue to be handicapped by a lack of learned social skills thought appropriate for sex in our society and by a lack of awareness of birth control methods. In response to these needs, training workshops have been designed to increase acceptance of sexual expression by the mentally handicapped. There is a growing awareness that counseling and education on sexuality should be offered by any mental handicapped care system to residents, to their parents, and to staff.

The most appropriate, reliable, and safe form of conception control for the mentally handicapped continues to be controversial. A number of researchers claim that mildly retarded women can take the pill successfully. However, the disadvantages of the pill for the retarded exceed those for the general population. Mentally retarded women may already be taking other prescribed medication such as anticonvulsant drugs, phenothiazines, and antidepressants. The pill is best avoided if another method will work as well. Some experts consider the IUD (intrauterine device) to be most suitable for women who lack supervision and sustained motivation. One disadvantage to this method is that the device may be removed by the woman or her partner. Another drawback to the IUD is that its dislodgment may not be noticed or understood. Checkups at shorter time intervals can help ensure that the IUD remains in place. Generally, other methods such as the diaphragm, condom, and foam are considered unsuitable for the mentally retarded.

Because of its permanence, sterilization raises questions of informed consent. If the person is too severely retarded to understand the implications of sterilization, does anyone else have the right to give consent? Parents and others who request sterilization are often responding to a fear of potential rather than actual irresponsible behavior. In 1979 a New Jersey Superior Court Judge ruled that the parents of a severely retarded eighteen-year-old woman had the right to protect her from unintended pregnancies by having her sterilized. But the issues are not easily resolved ("Should Mentally Incompetent..." 1979).

Skin Problems.   People with psoriasis also face unique sexual problems. Our appearance depends considerably on the quality of our skin. Being touchable is important to sexually caress and be caressed. Psoriasis is noncontagious, but its silvery patches can cover almost any part of the body and can reach a stage where dry heavy skin layers crack, bleed, and hurt. Subsequent itching leaves powdery skin residues and scales where one undresses and sleeps. This can turn off potential sexual partners. Kathleen Coen Buckwalter (1982, p. 100) describes the sexual difficulties this condition presents, noting that "some persons may refuse to sleep in the same bed because of the scaling of their psoriatic partner."

Buckwalter concludes that there are no easy answers for the sexual issues facing people with skin disorders. One approach is to encourage social contact and not become emotionally disabled or physically inactive. Having sexual partners share ideas about cosmetics and attractive clothing may also help maintain a sexual relationship.

Blindness.   Or consider the special sex education needs of the blind. We take for granted the rich contribution of our vision to sexual stimulation and enjoyment. The blind, not having the resource of visual cues for sexual transactions, must rely on the compensation or amplification of other senses, especially the erotic quality and messages conveyed by voice and other auditory stimulation. The most natural form of sex education aid for the blind would be live, touchable, nude models, an education format that is used in Sweden. The blind acutely need to touch. We generally deny the blind this form of sex education out of our taboo against nudity and the fear that the toucher and/or the touchee might experience sensual pleasure. Is it inconceivable that we should feel anything pleasurable while studying about sex?

Need for Social Support

What do we all have to learn from an examination of issues in sexuality and disability? In a sex-negative society we are all struggling to optimize our sensual and erotic capacities in ways that promote intimacy and permit sexual satisfaction, regardless of our physical or mental inheritance or accidental or developmental condition. At a 1979 national symposium on sexuality and disability, Susan E. Knight, director of the Sex and Disability Unit, Department of Psychiatry, at the University of California in San Francisco, said:

I feel particularly sorry or empathetic for able-bodied people, especially having been disabled all my life, who feel compelled or pushed to try to live up to [sterotypic male or female sexual] images. I would like to encourage all of us, those of us who are disabled, and those who are able-bodied, to develop a sense of ourselves as unique and different people rather than as ones who have to fit into some kind of mold. All of us have the potential to have very fulfilled and enriching lives because we do dare to be different and don't try to fit into the stereotypes of how somebody thinks we should be.   [Knight 1979, p. 129]

SUMMARY

To be sexually healthy, we should pay attention not only to the personal and interpersonal matters explored earlier in this book but also to certain physical aspects of our sexuality. Part of taking responsibility for our own sexual health involves regular self-examination of our genitals and breasts.

Some of us think that we have sexual problems—that we orgasm too fast or too slow or not at all, that intercourse hurts, that we are not sufficiently interested in sex, or that we are not in sexual balance with our partners. Sometimes such problems stem from relationship issues or from our ideas of "how to have sex," in which case we may seek relationship counseling or sex therapy; sometimes they involve varying physical causes for which medical help is appropriate. The special needs of the physically challenged can help us all broaden our views of sexuality.

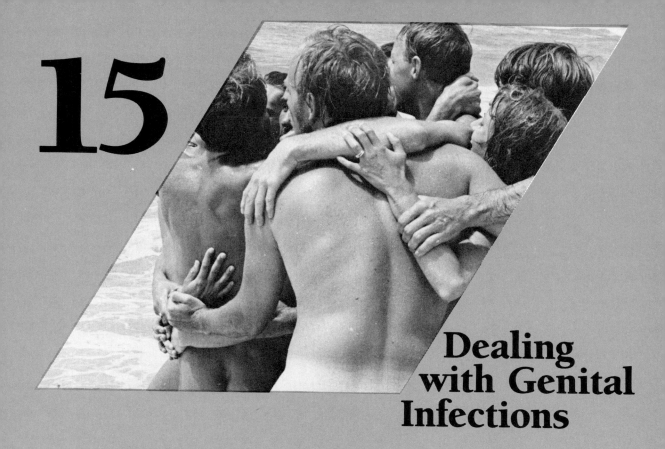

15

Dealing with Genital Infections

*M*y brother is an effortlessly attractive, personable 22-year-old. Like most budding boulevardiers, he frequents singles bars that feature a youngish crowd, extended happy hours and bargain-priced beers. But he can no longer be unconcerned about sexual experimentation.

The Herpes Scare isn't just putting-off American college seniors from sexual forays. Last month, when I was in France, middle-aged Parisian businessmen were mentioning that they've cut down their on-the-road dalliances for fear of bringing something back to the 16th Arrondissement.

As the epidemic continues, more people are bound to start wondering "Does she?" "Suppose he?" . . . and come to the conclusion, "Hell, it's not worth it."

Freudberg and Emanuel 1982, pp. 51–52*

*S*everal times, one woman has brought guys she wanted to sleep with to the [herpes] support group meetings. She insisted that her lovers be fully aware of what they might be in for, in case anything was to go wrong and they caught it. Personally, I thought she was just absolving herself of any guilt in advance. But I'm not in a position to judge. Sometimes I go to bed with a guy without telling him about it—but only when I know I'm not having an active infection.

Some people at the group criticize that attitude. One guy objected and said that he had herpes because a woman didn't think she was contagious, but she was. He felt he should have had the opportunity to make a choice for himself. But he never had that chance, and now he has something else—herpes.

I see his point. I'm not obstinate, but everyone has to make his or her own decision. I do it my way. Sometimes it's not worth the emotional pressure that's required to tell someone about it.

Carrie R., quoted in Freudberg and Emanuel 1982. 521*

I can see now that maybe going <u>only</u> to the tubs might have encouraged me not to solve problems in certain areas like intimacy and commitment and so on. . . . But that's a separate issue. Let me be totally honest with you. I still yearn to go. If they could give you a pill to prevent you from catching anything there, I'd grab it.

Tom, a 38-year-old gay male; from the authors' files

Open discussions about the risks and responsibilities involved with sexually transmitted diseases (STD) are difficult—but necessary—with both new and old partners. We have no models for dealing frankly with the possibility of genital infections. There is no script to follow. When should the subject be brought up? What should we say? Who should stock preventive measures? When should they be used? Such a script ideally should include shared responsibility and candid action before genital sex begins. In its absence we have only embarrassed silence and widespread ignorance about a series of very different sexually transmittable diseases that constitute the most serious health problems among teenagers and young adults in the United States today.

As a group sexually transmittable diseases are the most prevalent reportable communicable diseases in the United States. Only upper respiratory infections are more common than STD among teenagers and young adults. As if the spread of common gonorrhea isn't enough of a problem, *penicillin-resistant* strains are spreading. The *acquired immune deficiency syndrome* (AIDS)—initially called "gay cancer"—has spread to women, children, and heterosexual men, killing at least 40 percent of its victims, with the remainder having a very slim chance of survival beyond three years (Colen 1983; "Continuing Grim Picture" 1982). The threat of STD is no longer confined to treatable conditions—medical science's war against both old and new diseases is far from over.

The Language of Sex

Conditions discussed in this chapter are now called STD—or sexually transmitted diseases. The older term VD (for venereal disease) is being dropped because it refers to only a few conditions—mostly gonorrhea and syphilis. Today there is growing concern about a wider range of diseases that can be transmitted from one person to another by oral, anal, or manual sexual activity or even shared vibrators—not just by penis-in-vagina (venereal) sexual contact. An even more accurate label might be "sexually transmittable diseases," for some of them can be transmitted nonsexually as well as sexually.

THE MAJOR SEXUALLY TRANSMITTED DISEASES

Most STD are infections caused by bacteria or viruses. As many as twenty different diseases are primarily transmittable from one person to another during sexual activities. The most common venereal infections in this country are gonorrhea, nongonococcal urethritis (primarily *Chlamydia trachomatis*), certain vaginal infections (trichomoniasis and candidiasis), and pediculosis ("crabs"). Genital herpes, genital warts, and hepatitis B are probably more common than syphilis, but no national surveillance system for these STD has been established in the United States.

Gonorrhea

Gonorrhea, it seems, is an age-old problem. Writings from ancient China, Egypt, and Greece imply its stubborn presence in those societies, and the Old Testament describes methods of treatment and public health management for a disease with symptoms closely resembling those of gonorrhea. By A.D. 130 the cause of this common disease was so well recognized that the Greek physician Galen chose to call it gonorrhea, which means "a flow of seed."

Civilization, one might think, has had plenty of time to wipe out, or at least bring well under control, a disease that in its early stages is little more than an uncomplicated bacterial infection. And yet gonorrhea is the most common *reportable* communicable disease in the United States today. Nearly 1 million cases were reported in 1981 (Centers for Disease Control 1982). Actually, official statistics on gonorrhea probably represent less than half of the true incidence—which has been estimated to be between 2 and 2.5 million cases annually (Handsfield 1982).

What Gonorrhea Is, Who Gets It, and How. Gonorrhea, or "the clap," is an infection of the moist mucous linings of the body. Most frequently, it involves the urethra and genital organs, but the throat, anus, and eyes can be directly affected as well. In complicated cases the joints, skin, and even the heart, brain, and blood may be involved.

The cause of gonorrhea is the bacterium *Neisseria gonorrhoeae,* or the gonococcus. Not a parti-

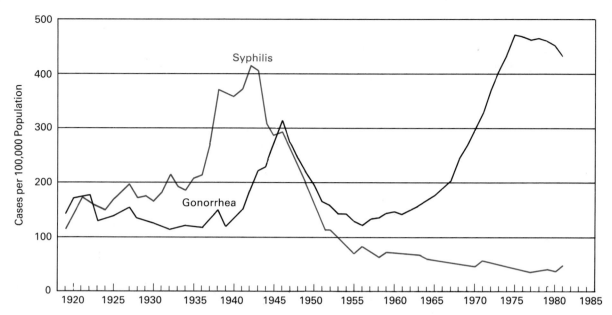

Figure 15-1. Syphilis and Gonorrhea: Reported Cases in the United States, 1919–1981. Whereas the number of reported gonorrhea cases increased during the sixties and early to mid-seventies, there has since been a slight downward trend. The number of reported syphilis cases has been dropping since the forties.

cularly hearty organism, it needs the warm, moist atmosphere of the genital area to survive. It will die outside the body within minutes. Therefore, it is difficult to "catch" gonorrhea from a toilet seat, door knob, or drinking glass; rarely can we catch it from shaking hands or kissing. Gonorrhea is almost always transmitted by intimate physical relations—usually intercourse, oral-genital sex, or anal sexual contacts—in which a genital secretion from an infected person comes into direct contact with a mucous lining of the partner.

In men the most common symptoms of gonorrhea are painful urination and discharge of thick, opaque or yellow pus from the urethra. In women the symptoms are less noticeable or are similar to other problems: abnormal bleeding from the uterus, vaginal discharge, painful or difficult urination. Oral-genital sex with someone who has gonorrhea can infect the pharynx; people sometimes experience this infection as a sore throat. Anal intercourse with an infected partner can lead to gonorrheal infection in the anus. But like throat infection, anal infection can often be detected only by specific laboratory cultures (Handsfield 1978).

The chances of catching gonorrhea from a single sexual exposure with an infected partner are high, but not 100 percent. Many people spread gonorrhea without even knowing that they have it.

Sexually active age groups account for the highest number of cases, with twenty- to twenty-four-year-olds leading and fifteen- to nineteen- and twenty-five- to twenty-nine-year-olds, respectively, not far behind (Rein 1975). More specifically, teenagers account for 25 percent of all cases, and persons thirty and under make up a whopping 90 percent (Thorn et al. 1977).

According to one study those who get gonorrhea more than once tend to be young (a mean of twenty-two years), male (62 percent), and black (82 percent); to live in poor neighborhoods; and to have dropped out before finishing high school (73 percent) (Brooks, Darrow, and Day 1978). Our own degree of risk depends on our behaviors. If we have only one or two sex partners, we are not as likely to contract gonorrhea as if we have more. And if our partners have sex only with us, we are less likely to contract gonorrhea than if they have sex with others.

In certain age groups gonorrhea among women is more prevalent and increases faster than among men. Increasing rates of gonorrhea among women probably result from the greater number of sexually active young women in the population, and the fact that many women today use oral contraceptives, intrauterine devices, and other methods of contraception that provide little or no protection against gonorrheal infections.

Women with gonorrhea often have no symptoms, or none that they or their doctors recognize as signs of gonorrhea (Handsfield 1978). Within one to seven days after contact with an infected person (but occasionally as long as one month later), men generally will have distinct symptoms: burning during urination and discharge from the urethra. Most who suffer from symptoms seek medical attention immediately, and a shot of penicillin dispatches the problem. Women, unless they have a partner who is known to be infected, may remain infected and infectious for several months and sometimes years without suspecting that they have gonorrhea ("The Sexually Transmitted Diseases" 1982).

Complications. If gonorrhea isn't detected, serious complications may occur. At least one out of every twenty-five women and many men develop some sort of complication from gonorrhea, including: disabling arthritis (when infection spreads through the body and attacks the joints), skin lesions, rheumatic fever, gallbladder disease, or perhaps even blindness, sterility, and death (McGee and Melly 1979).

The most common complication of gonorrhea is *pelvic inflammatory disease* (PID) in women. This term refers to a group of infections of the uterus and/or fallopian tubes that can be caused by gonococci or other bacteria. In half of all women whose gonorrhea goes untreated for more than eight to ten weeks, the bacteria rise from the vagina into the uterus and cause inflammation there. If the woman is menstruating, the bacteria can infect the fallopian tubes in an inflammatory condition known as salpingitis. Although salpingitis is treatable with antibiotics, 20 to 30 percent of women treated become sterile (unable to conceive babies) because of permanent blocking of the fallopian tubes by scar tissue. PID is the leading cause of sterility among young women throughout the world. In the United States alone an estimated 40,000 women now become sterile every year because of PID. Some medical experts suspect that

there are other women with PID who are able to get pregnant but who lose their babies through PID-caused complications of pregnancy (U.S. Department of Health, Education, and Welfare 1980). Symptoms of pelvic inflammatory disease may include abdominal pain, tenderness in the internal pelvic organs, painful urination, vaginal discharge, menstrual cramps that are worse than normal, abnormal bleeding, and perhaps chills and fever (Eschenbach and Holmes 1975).

Gonococcal infections can also affect the eyes, throat, respiratory tract, or anal canal of a baby as it passes through the birth canal. Many cases of stillbirth, low birth weight, and prematurity are associated with maternal gonorrhea as well (McCormack 1975).

Treatment and Prevention. With the discovery of penicillin in the 1940s, the treatment of uncomplicated gonorrhea became a simple one-shot matter. Penicillin is still used to treat gonorrhea, but other medications now seem to be as good (U.S. Department of Health, Education, and Welfare 1976b). Persons should return for follow-up tests three to five days after they have finished treatment to make certain their gonorrhea has been completely cured.

Gonorrhea is still easier to cure than a cold. Some observers worry that this ease of treatment has helped create a lack of concern about prevention. One alarming reason for emphasizing prevention rather than after-the-fact treatment: Gonorrhea is becoming more and more resistant to penicillin, and penicillin is no longer an effective cure for some strains.

Vaccines are being developed that may prove to be effective in preventing gonorrhea. Because cases of the more resistant strain have jumped from a total of less than 400 cases in 1976–79 to an annual rate of approximately 4000, reasons to be committed to vaccine research as well as to other methods of prevention have become more compelling (Ziegler 1982).

General preventive measures that we can take against many kinds of sexually transmittable diseases will be discussed in a later section. Gonorrhea is so common, however, that it warrants an additional measure: Cultures taken from the urethra (in males), cervical canal (in females); anus, and throat to check for gonorrheal bacteria should be part of the regular sexual health examinations of all sexually active people.

Nongonococcal Urethritis

The most common sexually transmittable disease is probably nongonococcal urethritis (NGU). Although no accurate statistics exist, NGU is thought to be twice as common as gonorrhea (Corsaro and Korzeniowsky 1980). Nongonococcal urethritis is exactly what it sounds like: all inflammations of the urethra in which gonorrhea infection has been ruled out. If this definition sounds a little vague, it is because research has not yet been able to identify any specific cause for the infection (it is sometimes called "nonspecific urethritis" for that reason). In fact, until its recent emergence as a widespread health problem, little research was done and misconceptions about NGU were common. Two of these beliefs were that NGU did not occur in women and that NGU was not directly linked to sexual intercourse (Cherniak and Feingold 1977). Although impeding medical progress, the latter belief had the beneficial social effect of leaving what is now recognized as a true sexually transmittable disease relatively stigma-free.

Of the two major causes of NGU—*Chlamydia trachomatis* and *Ureaplasma urealyticum*—Chlamydia is by far the most prevalent, accounting for about half of cases, with Ureaplasma causing another quarter of cases (Handsfield 1982; Corsaro and Korzeniowsky 1980). Remaining NGUs may be caused by a variety of microorganisms (Holmes and Kiviat 1978).

Since the symptoms of Chlamydia infection are less obvious than those of gonorrhea, this disease often goes undetected. Laboratory diagnosis of Chlamydia is expensive and not widely available (Handsfield 1982).

No matter what the causal agent, more is known about the diagnosis, treatment, and complications of NGU than the causes, at least in men. Most NGU research has been done on males. Although it is generally acknowledged that NGU occurs in women, its diagnosis is still largely restricted to men. At least 10 percent of men are totally asymptomatic, but they can still pass the disease to their partners (Corsaro and Korzeniowsky 1980).

The principal symptoms of NGU in men are a clear, thin, mucous discharge, frequently present only in the morning, and mild irritation on urinating. Although these symptoms are different from the thicker discharge and more painful irritation that typically characterize gonorrhea, diagnosis of NGU is primarily a diagnosis by exclusion. That is, if laboratory analysis of the discharge is negative for gonorrhea, a man with these symptoms is presumed to have NGU. Another distinction between gonorrhea and NGU that can be helpful in diagnosis is incubation period, which is usually less than a week for gonorrhea and longer for NGU (Holmes and Kiviat 1978).

Treatment of NGU, a disease once believed to be resistant to antibiotics, is with tetracycline four times a day for seven days. Although this regimen is quite successful, the Centers for Disease Control consider it an "interim recommendation": Early recurrences are common, and some patients do not improve with treatment. It may be that they reacquire NGU from sexual partners who have not sought treatment (Holmes and Kiviat 1978). Therefore it is critical that sexual partners of infected persons be treated as well (Holmes and Stamm 1979).

In women NGU may cause pelvic inflammatory disease, leading to sterility, and may pose a threat to infants during birth (Scaife 1978). From 4 to 10 percent of all pregnant women, and 25 percent of indigent, urban women have chlamydial infections (Holmes 1981). *Chlamydia trachomatis* appears to have replaced gonorrhea as the most common cause of conjunctivitis in newborns; it may also be associated with low birth weight and infant pneumonia (Chandler et al. 1977). Another frequent cause of NGU, *Ureaplasma urealyticum,* has been associated with spontaneous abortion, low birth weight, and postabortion and postdelivery fever in the mother.

NGU, like most other forms of STD, is most common in the twenty to twenty-four age group. But it differs from nearly all other common forms of STD in that cases seem to be concentrated in white, educated males of higher socioeconomic status who have relatively few sex partners. NGU may be two to nine times more common than gonorrhea in well-educated populations. The reasons for this pattern, like the medical causes of NGU, are still unclear (Holmes and Kiviat 1978).

Among men NGU is probably three times as common as gonorrhea, and its incidence has increased progressively in the last two decades (Holmes 1981).

Herpes Simplex Viruses

There is much public awareness of and concern about genital herpes, a viral infection that often results in painful blisters or sores. This infection, herpes simplex Type II, can be transmitted to sexual partners. As yet, no cure is known.

Herpes is neither new nor is it life threatening. Although herpes cold sores on the mouth (herpes Type I) have become less common over the years (herpes has been around for about 2000 years), genital herpes (herpes Type II) has become more prevalent. No precise statistics exist on the exact number of people who have genital herpes, but it is thought that at least 5 million Americans have the disease. From 200,000 to 600,000 new cases are diagnosed each year. The Centers for Disease Control report that private physicians were consulted for genital herpes nine times as frequently in 1979 as they were in 1966 (Centers for Disease Control, March 1982; Handsfield 1982).

It is not clear whether the new attention to the incidence of herpes is due to a real increase in new cases or to doctors' increased recognition of the disease. Only 1 percent of 1505 adults in a Washington Post–ABC News Poll acknowledged having had genital herpes, even though more than half said they were changing their behavior to avoid herpes ("Herpes Changes Sexual Habits . . ." 1982). Fear of herpes has apparently affected the sharp and sudden decline in the incidence of both gonorrhea and syphilis. It appears that herpes and AIDS have made people more selective in their choice of partners. Gonorrhea dropped by 6.6 percent in the first twenty-four weeks of 1983, while syphilis dropped 3 percent in the same time period (Mathews 1983).

Because genital herpes may easily be the most common STD among upper-income and college-educated people, it is easy to see why this population is so concerned about whether they will get herpes, how they can prevent it short of sexual abstinence, and how they can "cure" it if they get it. Lots of us are just plain *scared* of herpes—

"He's survived charges of fiscal irregularities, inept public service and even hints of moral turpitude, but I don't think he's going to beat that rumor of herpes."

scared of the stigma it gives us if we catch it and scared of the effects herpes would have on our intimate relationships.

Herpes is sometimes viewed as today's "scarlet letter." Moral Majority leader Jerry Falwell and ERA opponent Phyllis Schlafly emphasize herpes as "moral" punishment for those who engage in sex outside marriage. In reality, though, married persons can get herpes too; and because it often recurs after long periods of dormancy, herpes can be communicated without recent genital contact with someone who has the infection. Kissing someone who has a cold sore and later engaging in oral-genital sex with one's spouse might transmit herpes.

Just as prohibition didn't stop drinking and unplanned pregnancies haven't stopped intercourse, herpes scares are not likely to deter people from enjoying sex. Awareness of the possibility of herpes does encourage partners to talk about whether they have ever had herpes, whether they have any symptoms, and about their history of herpes if they have periodic recurrences. Several court cases are pending to determine whether herpes carriers are legally liable to inform their sexual partners before having sex.

How Do People Get Genital Herpes? What are the Symptoms?

Since Type I and Type II strains of herpes can be transmitted through oral-genital sex, either strain can cause the disease on either the mouth or the genitals. Chances of catching the infection depend on the frequency of exposure and the degree of personal resistance (Handsfield 1982). Symptoms recur in more than half of those who have been infected (Higgins and Hawkins, forthcoming).

The herpes virus is usually transmitted through direct physical contact with someone who has the infection. The disease is most contagious when the infected person either has a sore or is about to get a sore or "fever blister." The period just before the sore appears is called the *prodrome*. The prodrome occurs just before the first of a series of symptoms occurs and when viral shedding can communicate the disease even though no sore is yet evident. Prodromes vary, but recurrences of the disease can sometimes be predicted from any of the following warning signs: the sensation that something is crawling under the skin, tingling, itchiness, general fatigue, and muscular aches and pains in the lower back and legs (Freudberg and Emanuel 1982).

Some persons with herpes pay careful attention to these symptoms of possible recurrence so that they can avoid sexual contacts during such times or use a condom. Condom use is not a foolproof method of protection, however, if there are sores in areas not protected by the condom.

After coming in contact with herpes, a person may or may not get the infection. Also, it is possible to catch herpes from a partner who is asymptomatic, who may not be aware that he or she has the disease. Such carriers are probably responsible for much of the spread of herpes.

Once a person contracts herpes, painful blisters or open sores commonly develop in the genital area, sometimes accompanied by fever, headache, fatigue, and painful urination. The incubation period from contact to symptoms is usually from three to seven days and often begins with a burn-

ing or tingling sensation on the skin. The resulting sores eventually form scabs and heal. In addition to the sores and fever blisters, the lymph glands in the groin may swell and become tender. The initial infection lasts from fourteen to twenty-eight days, but the virus may remain in the body forever (U.S. Department of Health, Education, and Welfare #00-2939).

Recurrences of herpes may be spurred by tension, emotional upset, fatigue, exposure to sunlight, or (in women) menstruation. Although recurrences are of shorter duration, usually one to two weeks, and usually less severe than the original episode, they can be numerous and uncomfortable (U.S. Department of Health, Education, and Welfare #00-2797).

Concerns for Women and Children.

Watching for herpes symptoms and preventing herpes transmission is particularly important for women, in whom herpes II has been linked with cervical cancer. Patients with cervical cancer have about a five-times-higher incidence of antibodies to herpes II than women who do not have cervical cancer and are much more likely to have a history of herpes infection (U.S. Department of Health, Education, and Welfare #00-2939). Herpes II virus has also been clinically isolated from cervical tumor cells taken from women who have cervical cancer (Edwards 1978). On the basis of this evidence, some think that human cervical cancer may be a sexually transmitted disease and that herpes II may be a factor in its development.

By conscientiously having a Pap smear every six months, women who have had genital herpes can be fairly confident of the early detection and cure of any related cancer. But there are other, in some ways more threatening, risks to women from herpes II. Pregnant women with a history of herpes II have a three- to five-times-higher rate of spontaneous miscarriage than women who have never had herpes II, as well as a greater chance of premature delivery and a 40 percent chance of infecting their child during birth (Edwards 1978). Herpes II in newborns is extremely serious and frequently fatal. If an infant's entire body is infected at birth, the infant is likely to die (75 percent die in this instance). If the herpes infection is localized—to the eyes, mouth, or other areas—permanent damage often occurs to these bodily parts (Freudberg and Emanuel 1982).

Because many women don't know they have herpes, it is critical that physicians test for herpes infections during pregnancies. If the virus is found—and therefore could also be present at birth—a caesarean-section delivery is recommended.

Searching for a Cure.   Question: What's the difference between herpes and true love? Answer: Herpes is forever (or at least until someone finds a cure).

Such a joke is not something that most herpes sufferers can laugh about. The emotional and physical trauma of finding out that a herpes infection has joined them for their entire lives is extremely difficult for many to deal with.

Those who have herpes need support and accurate information about how to deal most effectively with their infection so they are not in pain and so they will not infect anyone else. Application of the antiviral ointment Acyclovir shortens and lessens the severity of an initial (primary) attack, but it does not cure herpes. This ointment has caused herpes blisters to stop shedding the virus, leaving the blisters noncontagious within twenty-four hours. If the blisters are not treated, they remain infectious for an average of two weeks. Acyclovir ointment shortens viral shedding by about three days in an initial attack, and it reduces the healing time for men with recurrent herpes but not for women (Corey et al. 1982; McLaughlin 1982). Acyclovir is now available for intravenous use as well (Higgins and Hawkins, forthcoming).

Because Acyclovir is not a cure, other methods of treatment need to be explored. Research is being conducted on various possible vaccines against herpes as well as cures.

Research results suggest that a preventive vaccine (which would also work for those who have had herpes) may soon be developed. Decreases in recurrence of herpes and a dramatically lower incidence for those who have been exposed to herpes are two positive results of recent research on herpes vaccines ("British Researchers Testing . . ." 1983; "Help Is Coming . . ." 1983).

Because there are as yet no cures for this potentially dangerous STD, herpes sufferers are banding together to support each other and to push the search for a cure and perhaps a preventive vaccine. For instance, The Herpes Resource Center, a program developed by the American Social Health Association centered in Palo Alto, California, offers members a quarterly newsletter covering herpes research, political action, educational projects, and suggestions for coping with the emotional problems of having one's social life restricted by a recurring genital disease. Herpes Anonymous groups have also sprung up around the country. Members have sex among themselves to avoid spreading the disease to noninfected people: a responsible, creative solution to a difficult situation.

Hepatitis B and Enteric Infections

In recent years the prevalence of hepatitis B (viral infection of the liver) and certain enteric, or intestinal, infections (such as shigellosis, amebiasis, and giardiasis—"gay bowel disease") in gay men has led to their classification as STD. Heterosexuals can get them too (Corey and Holmes 1980; Babb 1979).

Hepatitis B infects about 200,000 persons a year, primarily young adults. More than 10,000 are hospitalized, with an estimated annual cost of $20,000 each. An average of 250 die of the disease annually, and 6 to 10 percent of young adults with the infection are carriers (Rhinelander 1982). Carriers have a higher risk than others of developing cirrhosis of the liver or liver cancer many years after first acquiring hepatitis B (Randal 1981). The Centers for Disease Control estimate that 4000 people die from hepatitis B–related cirrhosis yearly, and more than 800 die from hepatitis B–related liver cancer (Centers for Disease Control, June 1982).

Hepatitis B is a viral infection. Medical experts once assumed that it was spread mostly through contact with the blood serum of a carrier—as in sharing of needles by drug users or in using the same needle to give shots or transfusions to many institutional patients. Semen, urine, and feces are now known to carry the disease as well. Hepatitis B can also be spread by contact with an infected partner's semen or saliva (Wright 1975). Research indicates that another form of hepatitis—hepatitis A—may be transmitted by frequent oral-rectal contact, too (Corey and Holmes 1980).

In a recent study over 6 percent of 3816 gay men examined in five STD clinics had active hepatitis B virus infections. The possibility of their ever having had the disease was related to how long they had been actively homosexual and to the number of recent male partners. Anal-genital intercourse, oral-anal intercouse ("rimming"), and rectal douching were related to Hepatitis B infections, but oral-oral contact and oral-genital contact were not (Schreeder et al. 1982).

Some people can carry hepatitis and spread it to others without knowing that they have it. Early symptoms of acute hepatitis include vague abdominal discomfort, loss of appetite, nausea, joint pain, and perhaps jaundice (U.S. Department of Health, Education, and Welfare #00-3380).

There is no recommended treatment for hepatitis B other than bed rest and a careful diet. Even though no known effective treatment exists, there is an extremely effective vaccine. At a cost of about $100, a series of three shots over a period of six months provides at least five year's protection against the disease. Screening tests are available. Such tests reveal whether a person has had hepatitis and therefore is immune to further attacks of *that type* of hepatitis (Rhinelander 1982; Randal 1981).

Seven Deadly Symptoms of AIDS

Here are the major symptoms of some of the half-dozen or so diseases that make up the killer syndrome called AIDS:

- A fever that persists for more than four or five days—or comes and goes over a long period of time
- An unplanned, unexplained weight loss of ten to twenty pounds in a few months
- General aches, pains and/or fatigue that persist steadily, or intermittently, for more than ten days
- Sore and/or swollen lymph glands for more than ten days
- The appearance of bluish or purplish spots on the skin
- Herpes sores that worsen and persist for more than four or five weeks
- Loss of sensory or motor ability; any defect in mental or neurological functioning

Consult with a physician *immediately* if you have any of these symptoms. You may have the flu. You may have infected lymph glands. But even if the odds are against your having AIDS, there are numerous other serious diseases that can cause these symptoms. All warrant medical attention (Colen 1983).

The Acquired Immune Deficiency Syndrome (AIDS)

The deadliest and most puzzling STD is acquired immune deficiency syndrome (AIDS), a disease that destroys the body's immune system. It was first discovered in the spring of 1981. By mid 1983 over 2000 cases had been diagnosed, and over 900 of these patients had died. Reports of AIDS have doubled every six months; unless the syndrome can be controlled there will be approximately 10,000 cases and 4000 deaths by 1985. Of the AIDS victims 80 to 90 percent die two years after the onset of symptoms.

At first AIDS was called the "gay plague" because it initially affected sexually active gay men. It is true that about 72 percent of the victims of AIDS are gay men, while 17 percent are intravenous drug users, 5 percent are Haitians, 1 percent are

hemophiliacs, and 6 percent have no known relevant characteristics (Centers for Disease Control, August 22, 1983).

No one knows what causes AIDS. Most victims have a shortage of "T-helper" cells, which aid "B" cells in producing antibodies against disease. Insufficient antibodies render victims easy prey to several opportunistic infections—infections that would otherwise be controlled by the body's immune system. Certain types of pneumonia, a herpes-type organism called cytomegalovirus, toxoplasmosis infection, and Kaposi's sarcoma (a rare form of skin cancer) are just some of the diseases that might result from AIDS (Colen 1983).

AIDS is thought to be transmitted by sexual contact or by direct contact with contaminated blood or blood products. Having many sexual partners without much knowledge of their disease histories increases the probability that the mysterious agent associated with AIDS will be communicated. A study by the Centers for Disease Control also found that homosexual men with AIDS were more likely than other homosexual men to have had syphilis. AIDS victims also used recreation drugs frequently, including nitrite inhalants ("poppers"), which are used by some gay men to enhance orgasm. Nitrites alone may depress the immune system. If being a highly active gay man increases one's chances of getting AIDS, so do certain sexual practices, such as oral-anal, penile-anal, and manual-anal contacts. These practices are more commonly engaged in by homosexual than heterosexual couples (Colen 1983).

AIDS is an example of a disease without definite warning. Epidemiologist Harold Jaffe has suggested that some AIDS carriers can transmit the agent when they have no symptoms at all ("CDC Speculation on AIDS" 1983).

Because AIDS apparently can be acquired through blood transfusions and by handling blood or other body fluids that are contaminated, medical technicians, doctors, nurses, and others in the medical community may be at risk of catching the disease. At this writing researchers are still seeking a cure for this puzzling disease.

Syphilis

For some the word *syphilis* still brings to mind the dreadful pattern of broken health, blindness, insanity, and death so poignantly described in Victorian novels and plays. Although these images persist, as realities they are now extremely rare: The discovery in the early 1940s that penicillin would cure syphilis is responsible for that. Yet syphilis has by no means been eliminated and remains a serious, if not so irrevocably dangerous, threat to public health. It is still the third most common reportable communicable disease (after gonorrhea and chicken pox) causing about 30,000 new infections annually (Handsfield 1982; Centers for Disease Control 1981).

Today's Syphilis. Syphilis is an infectious disease caused by the organism *Treponema pallidum*. After infection, syphilis goes through an incubation period of ten to ninety days and then, if left untreated, passes through the following stages:

1. *Primary syphilis.* The first stage is characterized by the appearance of a single, painless, firm-edged lesion, the *chancre*. It is usually found in the anal canal, on the external genitals, or on the cervix, but may occur on any part of the body including the lips, tongue, tonsils, breasts, and fingers. The chancre heals on its own in about three to six weeks, leaving a thin scar.

2. *Secondary syphilis.* After the primary chancre heals, various symptoms of the second stage may appear. These symptoms frequently include small, round, reddish *lesions* (abnormal patches of the skin, most typically on the palms of the hands and soles of the feet); broad, moist, pink lesions in the warm, moist folds of the skin; and mucous patches on the lips, tongue, pharynx, and genital mucous linings. Many patients also may experience headache, low-grade fever, weight loss, temporary baldness, and swollen lymph glands. As a rule the symptoms of secondary syphilis last about four to twelve weeks but may persist longer.

3. *Latent syphilis.* Syphilis enters the latent stage with the disappearance of the secondary lesions. During this stage there are no clinical signs of the disease, but a blood test can detect it. Latent syphilis continues throughout life or until the client enters the final, destructive stage of the disease.

4. *Late (tertiary) syphilis.* Late syphilis is a noninfectious stage marked by the onset of slowly progressive inflammatory disease of the skin, cardiovascular system, or central nervous system, and sometimes by loss of eyesight. These conditions are the ones that lead to fatal aneurysms and strokes, loss of reflexes and sensation, psychosis, and blindness in syphilis patients (Thorn et al. 1977).

Diagnosing and Treating Syphilis. Early syphilis cannot be diagnosed with certainty on the basis of clinical examination alone, no matter how thorough. Even blood tests for the presence of syphilis antibodies are of limited usefulness: Their sensitivity varies quite a bit, they may give a positive reaction because of a *past* infection, or they may not react in the early weeks of the disease (Rudolph and Duncan 1975).

A positive identification of *Treponema pallidum* through examination under a dark-field microscope is essential for an absolute diagnosis of primary and secondary syphilis—and even this technique has its problems. Accurate diagnosis by dark-field microscopy requires skills and experience with all kinds of spiral-type organisms that most physicians simply do not have. Thus laboratory diagnosis must be made at a facility with the proper resources—but *T. pallidum* must be seen *alive* to be identified, and it dies in minutes, sometimes seconds, outside the body. Obviously specimens cannot be sent to labs, so the patient must be. In many parts of the United States—and the world—this simply is not possible (Rudolph and Duncan 1975).

Part of the ability to diagnose early syphilis must be, of course, knowing when and where to look for it. The overall incidence of early syphilis is high, particularly in major metropolitan areas and among homosexual men (U.S. Department of Health, Education, and Welfare 1979c; Henderson 1977).

The most important thing to realize about syphilis epidemiology is that there has been a dramatic shift in the male/female ratio of early sypilis cases. The trend toward higher incidence in males than in females began in 1967—the year syphilis incidence began its upswing—and the change became most pronounced from 1972 to 1977, when 2.95 cases in men were reported for every single case in women (U.S. Department of Health, Education, and Welfare 1979c). Gay men now account for more than half of all cases of early syphilis (Henderson 1977; Thorn et al. 1977).

Fortunately, syphilis is easy to treat in its early stages, and late syphilis is now uncommon. For primary, secondary, or latent syphilis that has lasted less than one year, a single shot of penicillin usually wipes out the disease. When someone has had syphilis for more than a year before seeking treatment, a larger dose may be needed. Treated patients are urged to return three, six, and twelve months later for follow-up testing to make sure they've been cured (U.S. Department of Health, Education, and Welfare 1976).

If a syphilitic pregnant woman is untreated, syphilis can result in miscarriage, stillbirth, death shortly after birth, or, if the baby survives, congenital syphilis. All chance of infecting the fetus can be eliminated, however, if the mother is treated with penicillin before the sixteenth week of pregnancy.

Genital Warts

Genital warts are another common STD. Like herpes, genital warts are caused by a virus similar to one that causes a common condition that carries no stigma: skin warts. The virus for genital warts can be transmitted through intimate sexual contact. About 60 percent of the sexual partners of infected persons get warts. People who've had them once are susceptible to getting them again and should be sure that a condom is used if a partner has genital warts (Corsaro and Korzeniowsky 1980).

Like other viruses, the virus that causes warts is highly infectious, including during the period when a person has not yet developed visible warts. The incubation period is quite long—from one to six months ("The Sexually Transmitted Diseases" 1982). Those with multiple sexual partners may not be certain from which partner they contracted warts. The partner may not even know he or she has the virus, especially if the warts are not yet visible.

Warts appear on the skin of the penis and on the outer genital area of the female, but they can also grow inside the vagina, on the cervix, and in the anus. The portion of the skin on a man's penis that is most subject to pressure during intercourse is the area most likely to be invaded by warts, especially in uncircumcised men (Corsaro and Korzeniowsky 1980). Anal warts sometimes result from anal intercourse.

Genital warts are classified as either "moist" or "dry," depending on their location on the genitals. Moist warts are usually soft, pink or red, and resemble cauliflower when they appear in clusters; they are frequent and severe in pregnant women. Dry warts, which are smaller, hard, and yellow gray, resemble other common warts. Both kinds may spontaneously disappear for short periods of time in some people (Halverstadt 1972).

Although they often recur, genital warts are usually fairly easy to treat. They usually respond well to topical application of 25 percent podophylin resin (from the mandrake plant) in benzoin ointment, washed off after four hours. Usually a few such treatments will cause the warts to dry up and fall off, but the condition can persist. Persistent warts may be removed by using liquid nitrogen or dry ice or by curettage (surgical scraping), X ray, or surgery (Thorn et al. 1977; Corsaro and Korzeniowsky 1980).

Warts are best treated as soon as they appear, because they are harder to treat when they multiply and spread in clusters in different areas of skin. The warts often grow back unless they are treated effectively—usually more than once—the first time.

For unknown reasons genital warts are aggravated by birth control pills and by pregnancy. Warts can become so enlarged and extensive that they obstruct the birth canal and interfere with vaginal delivery. The real risk of genital warts during pregnancy, however, is that the virus causing the warts can be transmitted to the newborn as the infant passes through the birth canal. To avoid this risk, warts on a pregnant woman should be removed either by electrodesication (drying up) or by surgery. When warts obstruct the birth canal, a caesarean section is performed; podophyllin should not be used, for it can be absorbed to cause fetal deformities or death (Corsaro and Korzeniowsky 1980).

Vaginitis

Certain common vaginal infections are now grouped with sexually transmittable diseases because they are sometimes spread by sexual intercourse. It is normal for all women to have some degree of vaginal discharge. Although the amount and consistency vary from woman to woman, the discharge is usually clear or white, mucouslike in consistency, and most prevalent in the week or two before menstruation. It has a mild but inoffensive odor and is not irritating to the body.

Changes in the nature and amount of a woman's discharge are frequently attributable to some form of vaginitis, candidiasis, trichomoniasis, or "nonspecific" vaginitis. Although in most cases they pose little threat to patients or their sexual partners, these infections can cause much discomfort. For the most part methods of treatment are either ineffective or unsafe, and cases tend to persist and recur. Emphasis, therefore, is on prevention, alleviation of discomfort, and promotion of cure.

Millions of women in the United States suffer from some form of vaginitis every year. However, little research has been conducted on vaginitis, and

its nature and incidence are incompletely understood. Until doctors and public alike better understand the problem, it is doubtful that the three common forms of vaginitis, discussed below, will be brought under control (Rein and Chapel 1975; Pfeifer et al. 1978).

Candidiasis.   Candidiasis, also called moniliasis, is the "yeast infection" known all too well by many women. It is most common during the sexually active ages of sixteen to thirty, though there is no hard evidence that it is sexually transmitted (Rein and Chapel 1975). It seems, rather, to be brought on by changes in the body that enable *Candida albicans,* a vaginal and rectal yeast fungus, to multiply in excess of normal levels. These changes could be pregnancy, menstruation, an increase in carbohydrate level, or other conditions that lower the acidity of the vagina to a level conducive to the growth of *C. albicans.* Birth control pills do not cause candidiasis, but they are believed to aggravate the condition.

The abnormal levels of the yeast fungus usually result in a thick, white discharge resembling cottage cheese and accompanied by itchiness of the vulva. Diagnosis on the basis of these clinical signs alone is insufficient, however, and a culture should be taken to test for *C. albicans.*

Typically, yeast infection is treated with nystatin vaginal suppositories, used once or twice a day for ten days. Painting the vagina, vulva, and cervix with a 1 percent solution of gentian violet can be even more effective than the nystatin, but its messy, staining properties make it unacceptable to most patients (Rein and Chapel 1975). Boric acid suppositories placed in the vagina or vinegar douches may help as preventive measures (Boston Women's Health Book Collective 1976).

Trichomoniasis.   Trichomoniasis is caused by a one-celled parasite, *Trichomonas vaginalis,* which is found in both men and women. With close to 3 million cases estimated annually, most of them sexually transmitted, trichomoniasis is now considered by the medical profession to be a major STD. As usual incidence is highest among the sexually active and among those groups at highest risk for other STD (Rein and Chapel 1975).

Trichomoniasis infection occasionally shows

Practical Advice on the Prevention and Alleviation of Vaginal Infections

While the safety and efficacy of medical treatments for vaginitis are under debate, everything a woman can do on her own to clear up infection seems advisable. Regardless of the type of vaginitis, a cure can be helped along by following a few simple, commonsense guidelines (University of Connecticut Women's Health Clinic 1979; Boston Women's Health Book Collective 1976; Riddle 1971). Most of them will also help ward off infection or prevent it from recurring. Women are advised to:

1. *Use caution in douching.* Douching can spread infection into the uterus and remove friendly bacteria that help prevent vaginal infections. Washing away of secretions can also inhibit diagnosis of infections. But since vaginal infections are often related to too-alkaline conditions in the vagina, douching with a mildly acid solution may help restore the acidic atmosphere that the friendly bacteria need. Some women's self-help publications therefore recommend occasional gentle douching with vinegar (one to two tablespoons to one quart of warm water), or lactic acid (one teaspoon to a quart of warm water). Putting unflavored lactobacillus yogurt in the vagina sometimes helps ward off vaginal infections, too.

2. *Keep clean.* The vagina should be washed with mild soap and water. Women should wipe from front to back after going to the bathroom to avoid transferring germs from the rectum to the vagina. During a menstrual period, tampons or sanitary pads should be changed every time the woman goes to the bathroom.

3. *Avoid vaginal deodorants or deodorant tampons.* Deodorants tend to alter the natural environment of the vagina and make it more prone to infection.

4. *Avoid wearing nylon underwear, tight-fitting pants, and pantyhose.* Nylon underwear, tight-fitting pants, and pantyhose trap in moisture that seems to help harmful bacteria multiply. Loose-fitting cotton underwear and skirts allow the genital area to breathe. Underwear should never be worn to bed.

5. *Avoid vaginal sex for the duration of the infection; at all other times women should be sufficiently lubricated before intercourse.* Friction from a penis or anything else can further irritate an inflamed vagina and slow down healing; moreover, infection may spread to a male partner unless he wears a condom. A sterile, water-soluble jelly such as K-Y Jelly (not Vaseline, which irritates the vagina) may help prevent infections at other times.

6. *Communicate with their partners.* All partners should be informed of any infection, and one should not hesitate to check partners or ask them about any history of infection. When in doubt, men should use a condom.

7. *Keep their sugar and refined-carbohydrate intake low.* Diets high in sugar can change the acidity of the vagina in a way conducive to bacterial growth.

8. *Get plenty of rest and relaxation.* Fatigue and stress seem to contribute to vaginitis.

9. *If taking medication for vaginitis, take the full course of medication precisely as prescribed.* Lie down for fifteen minutes after insertion of therapeutic vaginal cream or suppositories, use external pads instead of tampons during menstruation, and soak diaphragm (if used) for thirty minutes with Betadyne scrub or 70 percent alcohol two days after medication is begun and after it is completed.

up in males as urethritis, but male carriers are more likely to have no symptoms. Trichomoniasis infection is usually more noticeable in females, but both sexes often carry it asymptomatically.

Itchiness and a yellowish-green, frothy, smelly vaginal discharge typically characterize the onset of trichomoniasis in women. It has an incubation period of about four to twenty-eight days. Symptoms frequently appear during or immediately following menstruation, when the normal acidity of the vagina is reduced by the presence of blood and the trichomonads can thrive (Rein and Chapel

1975). Acidic douches during menstruation may therefore be useful as a preventive measure.

A treatment for trichomoniasis is metronidazole (Flagyl) taken orally. To limit the spread of the disease, sexual partners should be treated simultaneously. Asymptomatic women with sustained infections should be treated for the same reason (Rein and Chapel 1975). Unfortunately, although metronidazole is quite effective, its safety is questionable (Boston Women's Health Book Collective 1976).

Nonspecific Vaginitis.   Those cases of vaginitis that cannot be attributed to *T. vaginalis* or *C. albicans* are lumped together as nonspecific vaginitis. It is now believed that many cases of nonspecific vaginitis are caused by the bacterium *Gardnerella vaginalis* or by it and some combination of other pathogens. They may be spread sexually. Although males do not get vaginitis, of course, studies show that 79 to 90 percent of male partners of women with nonspecific vaginitis carry *G. vaginalis* in their urethras asymptomatically ("Vaginitis Drug . . ." 1978; Rein and Chapel 1975).

Good News about Semen

The startling news from Germany: Semen includes an antibiotic substance that is at least as potent as penicillin! Karl Heinz Scheit and his colleagues at West Germany's Max Planck Institute for Geophysical Chemistry are continuing research on *seminalplasmin,* a protein in semen that prevents the synthesis of RNA, a chemical vital to cellular function and reproduction ("How Semen . . ." 1979).

Seminalplasmin destroys staphylococci, streptococci, bacilli, and other microbes that have plagued us. *Scheit believes that intercourse is a natural way to prevent vaginal infections* because semen protects women from microorganisms that cause vaginal infections. He also speculates that seminalplasmin may help keep the bacteria normally occuring in semen under control, thus helping to prevent infertility in men. Future research may help scientists use seminalplasmin to make other antibiotics faster working and more effective.

The abnormal discharge present with nonspecific vaginitis is usually yellowish and of thin to medium viscosity, with an unpleasant fishy smell. It may cause itching, swelling of the vaginal walls and lips, or slight abdominal discomfort in some women. To the dismay of women for whom nonspecific vaginitis is a miserable nuisance, current treatments may be ineffective.

Parasites

Some forms of STD are not really diseases at all but infestations of the genital area by parasites. The two most common are pediculosis (pubic lice or "crabs") and scabies ("mites").

A few centuries ago having "bugs" was accepted as a common bodily problem. Men and women in the highest society shaved their heads and donned wigs to alleviate itching (although the lice simply infested the wig and worked their way back to the scalp), and a French princess was taught that it was "improper to take lice . . . by the neck to kill them in company, except in the most intimate circles" (Reed and Carnrick 1976). We might do well to take our ancestors' pragmatic view of the problem. Although hygiene has so improved that bodily infestations should never again be universal, it is unlikely that they will be brought under control while the myths and misconceptions about them persist.

Crabs (Pubic Lice).   A major misconception about lice is that they are found only among poor people in squalid living conditions. Although lice are most prevalent in overcrowded areas or in facilities insufficient for keeping body and clothing clean (for example, a campground), they are found in every region of the world and may infest anyone. Crabs are extremely common on college campuses and other places where there are lots of sexually active people. Crabs appear to be more common in females than in males (probably because of the greater quantity of hair) and among young, single persons, in whom the incidence continues to rise.

The pubic or crab louse, *Phthirus pubis,* is small and turtleshaped with large claws for clasping onto the hair shaft. It is grayish white but turns more of a rust color after feeding, which it does four or five times a day on human blood.

Pubic lice are easily spread by close physical contact—usually during sexual intercourse. And crabs is one STD we *can* get from bedding, toilet seats, and an infested person's clothing (by borrowing another's clothes or trying on new clothes in a store).

The cycle of infestation, diagnosis, and treatment is simple and rarely presents complications. On contact with the human body, the louse quickly transfers itself to the short hairs of the genital area; the beard, eyebrows, and eyelashes may also be involved in transmission. The body temperature of the host provides the perfect environment for the lice. Left alone, females will live an average of thirty-five days and produce as many as fifty eggs ("nits") during that period. One male can fertilize many females, so one person may carry hundreds of eggs that will hatch in eight or nine days. The eggs, like the adults, cannot be easily washed or brushed off.

Before too many new generations of lice are born, however, most people seek medical care. Pubic lice produce an extremely uncomfortable itching that can be quite severe, especially at night; a few people also suffer from mild fever, muscle aches, or swollen cervical glands. Diagnosis is quick and easy on the basis of reported symptoms and observation: Eggs can be seen on the hair shaft, as can the parasite, either with the naked eye or under a microscope or magnifying glass. The lice are usually noticed soon after itching begins, within about two to three weeks after contracting them. They are easiest to see just after they feed on human blood and take on a rusty red color (Reed and Carnrick 1976; Corsaro and Korzeniowsky 1980).

Treatment is simple: topical gamma benzene hexachloride, marketed as Kwell or Gamene. These prescription medications are not recommended for pregnant women or small children because they are absorbed through the skin into the bloodstream.

Off the body, pubic lice can survive for up to six days. To be certain of killing lice as quickly as possible and thereby minimizing the chances of reinfection or infection of someone else, clothes and bedding can be run through a clothes dryer. A half an hour is sufficient at a temperature of 50° C or one hour at 46° C (Kraus and Glassman 1976). Rand C Spray is an over-the-counter drug for use on clothes and bedding. A final suggestion: It won't do any good to use Kwell and to sterilize clothing *unless all sexual partners do likewise.* Otherwise, they can simply "give" the lice back.

Scabies.   Scabies is another highly contagious parasitic infestation that occurs worldwide, with the majority of patients under thirty years of age. It too rose rapidly in incidence throughout the 1970s.

Scabies is caused by the mite *Sarcoptes scabiei hominis.* It is tiny, flat, and transparent white, with suckers at the ends of two of its legs. It burrows beneath the skin and uses its suckers to feed on an intercellular, lymphlike fluid but does not reach deep enough to draw any blood.

Figure 15-2. Genital Parasites. "You may think you have been sleeping alone, but. . . ." Although they often cause annoying itching, pubic lice and scabies are so small that people may be unaware of their presence.

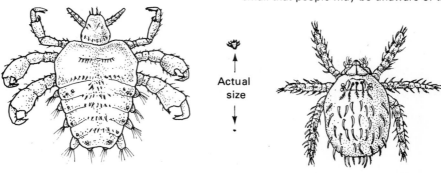

Pubic louse (crab) 2.5 mm

Actual
size

Scabies mite .3 mm

The scabies mite creates a small, wavy, hair-like and slightly elevated burrow, when it goes under the skin. The burrows can frequently be seen with a magnifying glass, particularly on the webs of the fingers where infestation is common. Scabies also infects the wrists, outer elbows, borders of the feet, armpits, buttocks, and waist area, as well as the genitals of males and nipples of females.

Like pubic lice scabies mites spread rapidly through close physical contact, bedding, and so on, and cause severe itching in the host. Also like pubic lice they are killed by applications of Kwell cream or shampoo (Reed and Carnrick 1976).

SEX-RELATED GENITAL INFECTIONS

The conditions we've examined so far are diseases or parasites that can spread from one person to another. There are other genital infections that result from the spread of ever-present bacteria from a place where they do no harm (such as the rectum) to places where they may cause trouble (the urethra, bladder, or prostate gland). Sometimes sexual activities contribute to this spread.

Cystitis

At some point in her life, nearly every woman gets cystitis, an inflammatory infection of the bladder. The symptoms are distinct: an almost constant, strong (even painful) urgency to urinate, frequently when there is no urine to pass, and a severe burning feeling as the urine is passed. Some women notice blood or an unusually strong odor when they urinate or they may have low back or abdominal pain and fever.

For a definite diagnosis of cystitis, a "clean catch" or midstream urine sample should be investigated for the presence of bacteria, usually *E. coli*. This bacterium, present in the digestive tracts of all healthy men and women, can be pushed up the female urethra to the bladder during vigorous or repeated sexual intercourse. It is for this reason, and because symptoms tend to show up within twenty-four to forty-eight hours of intercourse, that most—though certainly not all—cystitis is believed to be sexually related (nonsexual causes include use of tampons, constricted urethra, and stress).

Unlike STD such as gonorrhea, warts, herpes, and vaginitis (which have similar symptoms and can be confused with cystitis), cystitis is triggered by sexual activity but not transmitted via sex (Corsaro and Korzeniowsky 1980).

Although some women have an almost ongoing bout with cystitis, most cases are readily cleared. Usually treatment with a sulfa drug such as Gantrisin is begun at the first sign of symptoms. Frequently, the drug prescribed will contain ingredients to reduce burning during urination; the pills will turn the urine a bright red orange as a matter of course (Cherniak and Feingold 1975; Boston Women's Health Book Collective 1976).

Cystitis can even clear without treatment, but it is advisable to see a doctor. Left untreated, cystitis can spread from the bladder to cause kidney infection, a serious danger to health. Relief of symptoms can begin at home, however, by: drinking a lot of water to promote urination every hour or so; avoiding coffee, tea, alcohol, and spices, which irritate the bladder; soaking in a hot bath a few times a day; applying a hot-water bottle to painful areas; and avoiding trauma to the urethra during intercourse. Much of the advice given earlier for the prevention and alleviation of vaginitis is also applicable to cystitis, particularly the instructions about cleanliness, lubrication, and rest (Boston Women's Health Book Collective 1976; Marshall 1974). Some women find that urinating before and after intercourse and drinking cranberry juice to make the urine more acid helps to prevent cystitis.

If symptoms have not cleared up after one week of antibiotic drug treatment, another STD or other infection may be present; proper diagnosis is critical. For example, Chlamydia can cause cystitis (Corsaro and Korzeniowsky 1980). Also, women with subacute cases of gonorrhea may have the symptoms of cystitis and be treated for that, leaving the gonorrhea to multiply.

Prostatitis

The prostate is a gland surrounding the male urethra near the site of the bladder. All inflammations and infections of the gland are loosely grouped together under the name *prostatitis* (Thorn et al. 1977).

Most common are inflammations of the prostate in which no specific organisms (that is, infection) can be detected; patients also complain of low-back pain and discomfort of the testicles and the area between the scrotum and anus. Despite the absence of bacteria, patients are frequently treated with antibiotics, with varying degrees of success. Symptoms are usually treated with warm baths and prostatic massage. The latter, in giving relief to many patients, supports the theory that some cases of prostatitis are caused by congestion of the gland resulting from infrequent ejaculation. Because of the association of congestion with abstinence, this form of prostatitis is sometimes called "priest's disease" (Thorn et al. 1977; Galton 1979). One doctor's prescription for a healthy prostate is "sex three or four times a week," either with or without a partner (Sifford 1981).

There are two types of bacterial prostatitis: acute and chronic. The acute form, which typically affects young adult males, is characterized by a very tender prostate, fever, chills, and difficulty in urinating. Because it is generally attributable to one of the common urinary tract bacteria (for example, *E. coli*) or common staph bacteria, it responds well to antibiotics. In fact, since the advent of antibiotics, the incidence of acute prostatitis has greatly diminished (Thorn et al. 1977).

Chronic bacterial prostatitis is more complicated than and not as readily cured as the acute form. Symptoms vary, and infection of the bladder may add to problems experienced. Some men feel pain in their lower back or perineum. Urination may be frequent, difficult, and burning. There may be drips or discharge from the urethra. Some men have problems only during sex: lack of desire, erection problems, or ejaculations that are quick, very painful, or bloody (Galton 1979). The small numbers of bacteria that characterize chronic bacterial prostatitis can only be identified by careful quantitative bacteriologic techniques using sterile urine.

Treatment of chronic prostatitis is difficult because the prostate's low acidity prevents antibiotics from penetrating deeply enough. So far, the only treatment that has been used with fair success is sulfonamide-trimethoprim, a combination of two drugs (Septra and Bactrim). Patients may also be kept on antibiotics in order to suppress symptoms that arise when infection moves to the bladder and to keep the urine sterile (Thorn et al. 1977; Galton 1979).

PREVENTION AND CONTROL: MOSTLY A MATTER OF EFFORT

Why the continued (and growing) high incidence of STD in the United States—far higher than in other parts of the world such as Great Britain, Scandinavia, and China—and the perseverance of advanced cases of such well-known diseases as gonorrhea and syphilis? How is it that we have managed to keep once-rampant diseases such as tuberculosis, rheumatic fever, and malaria at bay but have utterly failed in doing the same with STD?

Darrow and Pauli (1983) identify moralisms that hinder progress in the control of STD: Because persons having STD are often labeled for their "improper" or "immoral" conduct, they may be denied entry into the sick role and may be treated as criminals to be punished instead of sick people to be helped. It appears that we don't really want to deal with the problem of STD. This attitude may not be conscious or admitted, but emotionally, socially, and psychologically it is there. Somehow, our feelings of fear, shame, and revulsion and our lack of knowledge and desire to know have combined to keep STD at epidemic levels in this country. It is by changes in behaviors and attitudes that STD will eventually be brought under control. Fortunately, there are practical things that everyone—from the individual, to the medical science and health care community, to the public sector—can do to bring about STD prevention and control.

Personal Action

Descriptions of various STD and statistics about their widespread occurrence frighten many of us. But rather than taking steps to avoid STD, some of us do nothing to protect ourselves. We take chances and merely hope we won't catch anything. This approach is irresponsible and dangerous. Darrow and Pauli (1983) emphasize that because health is more valued by those who don't have it, healthy people (especially teenagers and young adults) don't do much to avoid acquiring STD.

There are a number of active steps we can take to protect ourselves, our partners, and perhaps our unborn children from STD.

1. *Use of a condom.* A condom can be effective in preventing the transmission of most STD (but not crabs and scabies) if the condom is in good condition and is kept on during all phases of sexual activity (including foreplay). Despite their effectiveness, condoms are frequently rejected as a preventive measure even by those who have previously acquired an STD and are at high risk of doing so again. Notions that condoms interfere with sensory pleasure have kept people from using them. Many couples, though, still use condoms as contraceptive devices, and if interest in taking STD-preventive measures increases, condoms could play in important role in reducing the incidence of STD (Darrow and Wiesner 1975; Brecher 1975).

2. *Use of a vaginal preventive.* Although until recently a well-kept secret from the public, it has long been known that contraceptive jellies and creams kill not only sperm but also the pathogens of gonorrhea, syphilis, and some other STD as well. These preparations are quite effective when used regularly and correctly. Oral contraceptives don't offer this protection; instead, they tend to neutralize the normal acidity of the vagina, thereby encouraging the growth of certain STD organisms (Darrow 1975). More and more women are switching from the pill back to diaphragm-plus-spermicide or condom-plus-spermicide, and this trend could help reduce STD incidence (Brecher 1975). An additional benefit of the diaphragm for women: Women who use diaphragms are 40 percent less likely than other women to develop pelvic inflammatory disease (PID) ("Diaphragm Use . . ." 1982).

A lot of doubt seems to exist about the effectiveness of douching after sex in preventing STD. As a folk practice douching is still widely used, but health care practitioners usually don't recommend it as an anti-STD measure. One study even showed that sexually active people who douched regularly were *most* likely to get gonorrhea, a finding that supports the theory that douching strips the vagina

of bacteria-fighting organisms (Darrow and Wiesner 1975; University of Connecticut Women's Health Clinic 1979).

3. *Disinfection before and after sexual exposures.* Washing the genitals with soap and water both before and after sexual exposure can help prevent gonorrhea, syphilis, and possibly other STD. It seems logical that using a medicated soap would increase effectiveness of washing, but no definitive analysis has been done (Brecher 1975). This method is not practiced as often as it could be because people are unwilling to be as thorough and prompt as needed for the method to work: The entire genital area (inside also for women) must be washed, and washing must be done *immediately* before and after sex. To keep from getting STD in their throat after oral sex, some people gargle with antiseptic mouthwashes. There are no data on the effectiveness of this measure.

The genital area in men can be disinfected after sex by topical application of calomel/mercury salve, or the urethra can be cleansed with a calomel/sulfanilamide solution ("pro-kits"). These methods were used in the armed forces with high reliability—but they were mandatory, and failure to employ them carried high fines. People generally tend to find them messy and inconvenient, and as a result such methods are not widely used despite their effectiveness (Darrow 1976).

4. *Postcoital urination.* Although still a matter of debate, urinating immediately after intercourse may help prevent gonorrhea and other veneral infections. It is argued that some pathogens, including the gonococcus, do not like the acidity of urine and may be flushed out (Brecher 1975).

5. *Avoidance of sexual contact during period of infection.* Abstinence is the only method that is effective against all STD. While we are infected, it is our clear responsibility to avoid encounters that could cause transmission of the disease to someone else. To determine whether a prospective partner is infected (and therefore to be avoided), we may closely inspect his or her genitals (with somewhat less success for the female, in whom symptoms may be hidden or absent).

6. *Communication.* Many of us hesitate to bring up the subject of STD with our sex partners because we have the romantic notion that sex should be spontaneous. To do something about

STD interferes with our idea that sex should be "unplanned." But openness about STD is one of the best ways to protect ourselves and others from contracting infection. If we have an STD, we should inform all sexual contacts so they can be diagnosed and possibly treated, and we should be as cooperative as possible with health care workers. If we decide not to abstain during the period of infection, it is only fair to inform our partners so they have the option either of declining sex or of using other preventive measures.

If we suspect that a partner may have an STD, we should get up the courage to ask and, under the right circumstances, maybe even to perform a "short-arm" (close-up) inspection. If there is any doubt, we have the right to decline sex or insist on the use of a condom.

Health Care Professionals: Knowing How to Cure People Is Not Enough

Throughout the literature on epidemic STD is the suggestion, increasingly more direct, that even doctors and other health care professionals are reluctant to deal with the problem—and thus may be partly responsible for the high rate of disease (Holmes and Stilwell 1977).

Training in STD for doctors, nurses, and other health care workers is relatively superficial and tends to ignore the important sociological and prevention aspects of the diseases. With "new" STD such as AIDS, NGU, and herpes taking hold, and STD in general being recognized as one of the most complicated areas of the field of infectious diseases, improved education of health care workers should be a high priority (Holmes and Stilwell 1977; Edwards 1978).

Active tracing and treatment of partners of STD patients, follow-up, patient education, aggressive diagnostic approaches to high-risk patients (particularly pregnant women and young children at risk of sexual abuse), and more research are all needed to bring STD under control, and only health care professionals can provide these measures. But even when STD services are offered, people may not choose to take advantage of them. If health care professionals are uptight about sex or are moralistic and punitive toward potential STD patients, they will discourage people with STD from seeking medical help. It's important that caregivers have an open, realistic, unembarrassed,

nonmoralistic attitude toward sex and its consequences.

Even if medical personnel are easy to approach, some people with STD will not seek medical help. People differ in their willingness to maintain health and prevent disease. One study has shown that those who wear seat belts in automobiles, brush their teeth after meals, and don't smoke also have significantly lower rates of STD (Darrow 1976). These people may be more aware of their bodies, more interested in maintaining health, more likely to have unusual symptoms diagnosed, more likely to have the routine checkups that often uncover asymptomatic STD, and more conscientious about following treatment and test-of-cure recommendations. By contrast, other people ignore symptoms of STD, wait to see if they'll go away, or try self-cures. This approach toward health care is common among disadvantaged people whose other problems outweigh concern for taking care of what they consider relatively mild physical discomforts.

Extending the Reach of Medicine: The Long Arm of the Public Sector

One way of reaching people who cannot afford medical help or are not interested in it is through public programs financed by the government. No national problem can ever be eliminated without the support of the public sector, and the problem of STD in the United States is no exception. The public sector has a reach—through the schools and through special public screening programs and clinics—that individuals and the medical profession alone cannot hope to achieve.

Two attributes that enable the public sector to be so effective are centralization and—of course—money. Government agencies such as the Department of Health and Human Services are in a position to fund research into the many unanswered questions about STD. For instance, we know little about NGU, especially in women, even though the disease is becoming extremely common. We have little understanding of STD-resisting body mechanisms and whether they vary in individuals and in different racial groups. And funding of research on a cure for or a vaccine against both genital herpes and deadly AIDS is desperately needed.

Government agencies can also collect and

maintain data on national health patterns, communicate research findings and treatment and control procedures to state and local health agencies, support free clinics, and (perhaps most important) influence public attitudes and awareness through the mass media. But because of our society's unwillingness to deal openly with sex, funding for STD programs has been given rather low priority.

Fighting STD in the Schools.   Given that STD is not uncommon in ten- to fourteen-year-olds and that sixteen- to twenty-year-olds have an STD rate triple that of the rest of the population, fighting STD in the schools is crucial. There is a serious lack of information in young adults, even among college-aged students, making these groups the Department of Health and Human Services' prime target for STD education (Yarber 1978; Arafat and Allen 1977).

In the past programs in the schools showed little understanding of behavioral causes of STD—such as the learned notion that sex should be spontaneous, which rules out STD-preventive measures as too "planned." STD education often served only to overwhelm students with medical facts and with fear and guilt. Instead of learning to take preventive measures, students frequently turned off to the subject because they could not relate to it. Health educators, therefore, have been working on new educational strategies to make STD education more pertinent and, ultimately, more effective (Yarber 1978).

Education on the diseases themselves is, naturally, part of the strategy, but with a new focus. Emphasis is placed on preventive measures, when and where to go for treatment, the realities of STD transmission and epidemiology, and the potential complications of untreated disease. Signs and symptoms are not stressed, although one study indicated that basic symptoms are the primary impetus for teenagers to seek care, which perhaps argues for more emphasis here (Yarber 1978; Niemiec and Chen 1978).

Screening Programs and Clinics.   Even if they've learned to accept the realities of STD, people need somewhere to go for help. Over 5000 public and private medical institutions provide free or low-cost STD diagnosis and treatment. Such clinics are usually listed in the white pages of

phone books under the listings for local health departments. Publicly funded screening programs and clinics offer a unique opportunity for reaching people who either cannot or will not seek the services of private physicians. Such programs are ways of seeking out those at highest risk of contracting an STD. They thus make a valuable contribution to halting the spread of STD.

One group for whom screening and clinics have been particularly valuable and effective is gay males. In addition to their high incidence of early syphilis, they account for a large proportion of all cases of gonorrhea. As we have seen, men who have sex with each other are also at risk of contracting AIDS, hepatitis B, and various enteric infections.

A study of 4329 gay men (Darrow et al. 1981) showed that although many suffer from STD, a sizable minority of these are never checked for STD. Gay men are often reluctant to trust their problems to medical personnel who may be hostile or unsympathetic toward them; moreover, many are still concerned about exposing their homosexuality. Given the choice, they prefer community clinics staffed by gay health professionals, where they can be open and relaxed about their health problems (Merino and Richards 1977). Such clinics also are more likely to do anal and pharyngeal cultures or to check for diseases more common among gays than are other medical services.

Teenagers are another group that appears to benefit from special STD clinics that are both low cost (or no cost) and anonymous. Niemiec and Chen (1978) found that most clients (ages ten to nineteen) at such a clinic had learned about it through friends or the mass media. What they knew about STD was chiefly from these sources as well, which would argue for advertising clinic hours and locations and wide dissemination of STD information. Like homosexually active males, teenagers too wished to be treated sympathetically; girls requested "less embarrassment" when asked how a clinic could be improved (Niemiec and Chen 1978).

An even more direct approach to reaching high-risk populations is routine screening. In Atlanta, Georgia, everyone arrested for any sexual offense is offered free examinations for STD by the health department. During a three-month study, infection rates of 44.1 percent and 29.3 percent

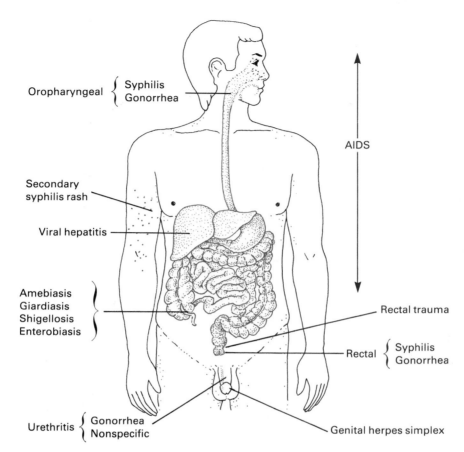

Oropharyngeal { Syphilis
               Gonorrhea

AIDS

Secondary
syphilis rash

Viral hepatitis

Amebiasis
Giardiasis
Shigellosis
Enterobiasis

Rectal trauma

Rectal { Syphilis
         Gonorrhea

Urethritis { Gonorrhea
             Nonspecific

Genital herpes simplex

Figure 15-3. Some Medical Problems Often Found in Gay Males. The diseases and medical problems shown here occur in both heterosexuals and homosexuals. However, practices such as oral-rectal and anal intercourse—which seem to be more common among homosexual males than among heterosexual males—may account for the higher incidence of some of these problems among gay males. Health care providers at gay clinics usually know to check for these conditions and can often help men discuss without embarrassment the possibility of their sexual transmission.

were found in male and female offenders, respectively. In an effort to prevent treatment failure caused by lack of follow-up, patients were counseled on prevention and the need for tests-of-cure. Local authorities believe that such active testing and treatment programs are an effective way to reach high-risk groups that would not normally seek care on their own (Conrad et al. 1979).

The prevention and control of the STD problem in the United States is neither simple nor clear-cut. Even the answer to the question of who, exactly, is responsible for controlling STD is elusive. One could say, "We all are," and that would be true—but simplistic answers to complex questions do little toward suggesting solutions. Perhaps it is more useful to look at levels and degrees of responsibility and to do so from the practical standpoint of who is *able* to do most—not the moral or ideal one of who *should*.

Looking at the STD problem in this way, we would conclude that the public sector—specifically, federal, state, and local governments—must take the primary responsibility. Only they are in a position to provide the leadership, organization, and funds for a movement to prevent and control STD in this country.

After the administrative level comes the operational one, the most demanding of all. It seems realistic to say that the *burden* of STD prevention and control lies here, with the health care professionals, who have constant opportunity to diagnose, treat, educate, and prevent.

Even with the public sector and health care professionals doing what they can, success will depend on individuals' actions for positive results. It is in this sense that the real hope for STD prevention and control lies in us.

Summary

Sexually transmittable diseases unfortunately are common—and in many cases becoming more so. Gonorrhea is the most common reportable STD; though more noticeable in men, it is often spread by women who show no symptoms. Even more common is NGU, the major cause of which is Chlamydia. The greatest public concern, however, is focused on AIDS and genital herpes, for there are as yet no cures or preventive vaccines for these diseases.

Hepatitis B can be carried by semen, urine, or feces and is more often spread by sexual than other exposures, so it has joined the list of known STD. The newest addition is AIDS, which cripples the immune system and therefore leads to death within a few years. Fortunately, a vaccine now exists to prevent hepatitis B. Unfortunately, there is no vaccine or cure for AIDS.

Syphilis—an ancient problem—is still with us. Genital warts and crabs are extremely common, as is vaginitis, which is sometimes spread sexually. Cystitis can be aggravated by sex; prostatitis can be aggravated by a lack of it.

To deal with these threats to our health, dramatic action by individuals, health care professionals, government programs, schools, and screening clinics is required.

16

Pregnancy Choices

We just had an abortion. I say "we" because both of us felt the anguish of that choice. My wife had an IUD, so we thought we were safe, but they don't always work, you know. We're both working flat-out, full-time, to support the three wonderful kids we already have. When we found out Patty was pregnant, we knew there was no way we could support another child. On top of that, we were worried that the IUD, which was still in there, might screw up the fetus. We did the best we could with our decision to get an abortion: Before the abortion, we both meditated together, explaining the situation to the soul that was trying to come through and asking it to forgive us and choose another vehicle for its life on earth. That helped us both a lot—and we feel that it understood.

I want a baby so much. I feel so alone in the world, and my baby would love me even if Rick doesn't. I have so much love inside of me—I want to take care of something, make its life happy. I know Rick wouldn't marry me, but that's okay. He thinks I'm taking the pill, but I'm not. I hope it happens soon.

Do you know how awful it feels to be unable to get pregnant? We've been trying for two years—and three doctors, and thousands of dollars of every infertility treatment you can imagine—and still nothing. Every time I get my period I cry. Sex is no fun either; I'm feeling more and more desperate because I can tell David is getting tired of trying to be so careful about when and how we do it. It seems like every other woman I see is pregnant—and I know lots of them didn't want a baby nearly as much as I do. I'm already 35—it's almost too late for us now.

Joanne's birth was fantastic! I was there for the whole thing, rubbing Sarah's back and talking her through the breathing and giving her stuff to drink. She did all the work, of course, but it was great to be there, especially when Joanne's head came through. The nurse midwife left the three of us alone after she made sure everything was okay. What a wonderful feeling to cuddle together as a family! It feels very different from just being a couple. Sure, the baby cries sometimes and all that, but having her makes us feel even closer to each other. I love Sarah more than ever; when she nurses Joanne, the love in her eyes just spreads all around.

[From the authors' files]

Contraceptives now available have made it possible to separate sex from reproduction, for the most part. Nevertheless, many people envision the possibility of pregnancy when they have intercourse. In this chapter we'll look at people's reasons for choosing or not choosing to have babies, how babies are conceived, what people do about unplanned pregnancies, and the many stages where careful decision-making can optimize pregnancy and birth. In Chapter 17, we'll examine conception control methods—ways to have sex without creating unwanted pregnancies.

Although it takes two to get pregnant, pregnancy has traditionally been viewed as a female experience. The male's involvement, other than his biological contribution to conception, has received little attention. As for the woman, pregnancy has often been treated by the medical profession as a sickness and by society at large as something she must experience in order to fulfill her feminine destiny. Such attitudes have sometimes contributed to nondecision making—for instance, "forgetting" to use contraceptives, turning over total responsibility for prenatal care to health professionals, and having boy babies routinely circumcised without questioning the practice. This inattention is unfortunate, for the many decisions or nondecisions made during the course of a pregnancy may have long-lasting effects on both parents and children.

THE BABY-MAKING DECISION

Until recently people in our culture were under tremendous pressure to marry and have children. Mass media and well-meaning relatives and friends hammered in pronatalist ("probaby") messages subtly and not so subtly: Children are a joy, and parenthood is an inevitable feature of adulthood. As a result many people unthinkingly took on a parental role.

Now, however, some people are questioning the assumption that all adults should be married parents. In part they are merely catching up with reality. The "typical" family—mother and father with children under 18—now accounts for only 30.3 percent of all U.S. households (Current Population Reports 1981). But beyond the recognition that parenthood for all is a myth that simply hasn't materialized, many people are coming to see parenthood as a choice that may not be best for everyone.

The Language of Sex

Labeling people "childless" defines them as missing or lacking something. Many people who are infertile are frustrated, even guilty and angry, at their inability to conceive and have a child. These people are the involuntarily childless. Yet many couples voluntarily choose not to have children. To call them childless places an inappropriate negative label on a choice they view as positive. Calling these couples "childfree" is a more accurate description of their "positive" choice.

The Value of Children

Some of us place high value on the anticipated rewards of having a child or children in our home: love and companionship, fun, reliving pleasant memories from our own childhood, symbolic togetherness with our mate, provision of grandchildren for our parents, extra help, proof of fertility, immortality of sorts, and contribution to the future of our society. Such values are often emphasized in romanticized depictions of family life. But expectations of finding personal fulfillment and perhaps power in parenthood may be unrealistic. For instance, the company of children is not always fun and stimulating. There's no guarantee that children will carry on our ideas or support us when we're old. There may be affection and companionship, but there are also dirty diapers and sleepless nights with crying infants, and children make heavy demands on our time and resources throughout their years at home. And as we'll see later, the stresses of parenthood may make some marriages worse rather than better.

It's hard to know ahead of time whether we will enjoy life with children. Our observations of other parents and other children tell us only a little about how we will respond to a role we've never tried and to a child we've never met. But for those who find that they truly enjoy their own children, having them around may be so rewarding that it more than makes up for any inconveniences. Sharing life with children may add a new dimension to loving.

Feelings about Parenthood

Our feelings about having children are intertwined with our feelings about being parents. Many of us

331

have been socialized to believe that only if we become parents will others view us as fully adult. Some of us believe that by having children we are fulfilling an important obligation to society. Parenthood often does make us feel that we are doing something useful and are being better persons by devoting our time to serving others. The parental role may help us feel competent, creative, successful, important, powerful, and socially accepted.

The Traditional Motherhood Mystique. Although both males and females may look for the foregoing satisfactions in parenthood, females are particularly socialized to do so. They have traditionally been taught that motherhood confirms their femininity and fulfills their biological and social destiny. The assumption has been that women not only are biologically suited for childbearing but that they also have a "maternal instinct" that naturally draws them toward children and elicits warm, caretaking behaviors. The traditional image of the mother as patient, sacrificing, endlessly loving and giving was institutionalized as the model for all women.

Ideas about "maternal instincts" are still strong among sociobiologists. They believe that there are biological explanations for why mothers are loving toward their children (Rossi 1977). But as psychoanalyst Nancy Chodorow (1978) points out in *The Reproduction of Mothering*, there is no hard evidence that women are naturally more responsive to babies than are men or children. What differences have been noted are differences in *socialization*, she claims, not differences in instinctive behaviors.

The Impact of Changing Gender Roles. We now expect women to consider developing work careers as well as the motherhood option. This change in social expectations can lead to confusion. When sociologist Kristin Luker (1978) interviewed women at a California abortion clinic, she found that many who had been socialized to some of the traditional female "virtues"—compliance, nurturing, dependence, self-effacement—were frightened by contemporary demands that they become assertive and independent. Although the traditional motherhood role has its limitations, it is comfortably familiar. Pregnancy also carries certain rights, such as the right to be passive and protected.

Willingness to abandon old sex role expectations seems strongest among the well educated. Some women in this category are rejecting motherhood totally; others recognize that there are many ways of being a mother; they are choosing motherhood but not its traditional sacrificial format. In a recent study of college students and their parents, fully 88 percent rejected the idea that women who don't want children are selfish or unnatural. About 75 percent disagreed that women's true mission is caring for men and children. And only 22 percent agreed that no child would be unwanted by a normal woman and that having babies is totally fulfilling for women (Hare-Mustin and Broderick 1979).

Men's Views. Males are somewhat slower to abandon traditional expectations about what women should do. Even well-educated men are far more likely to believe the social definitions of motherhood than are females. Males are much more likely to agree that having a baby fulfills a woman totally, that a

Men will be parents, too, and want to be involved in decisions about having children.

woman who doesn't want children is unnatural, that a truly maternal woman would not give up a baby for adoption, and that women who want respect should try to be better mothers. Males are far more likely to disagree that women who work can raise children as successfully as can women who stay at home and that women should have the right to decide whether or not to get pregnant (Hare-Mustin and Broderick 1979).

These gender differences in opinion are important, for since both partners will become parents, the decision for or against pregnancy should be a shared one. In reality this is not always the case. According to a study of childfree couples, the husband's wishes are far more likely to determine pregnancy decisions than are the wife's (Marciano 1978).

Relationship Concerns

Although the decision for or against pregnancy may not be mutually agreed on, the state of the relationship between the potential parents should be an important consideration.

It is common for pregnancy to be chosen as a means of testing a partner's commitment, of bargaining for possible marriage, or of improving an existing marriage. But such strategies do not always work. Instead of drawing partners closer, a new baby may severely strain an already shaky relationship. A peak period for divorce is during the first year after the first child is born (National Alliance for Optional Parenthood 1979). According to a survey of 2164 adults, feelings of stress are highest among those who are married with young children; stress lifts significantly after children reach the age of eighteen and begin to leave the nest (Campbell 1975).

Some who already have a good relationship hesitate to have children for fear of wrecking it. Certainly they have more time and energy to give to each other if they don't have to cope with the demands of childrearing. Voluntarily childfree women are more likely to share outside interests with their husbands, exchange stimulating ideas with them, hold calm discussions, and work on projects with them. Childfree women also have a stronger desire to continue the relationship and are happier in their marriages than in other relationships (Veevers 1980). Nevertheless, for couples with a strong relationship and good parenting skills, having children can be a lasting source of mutual joy.

Single Parenthood Considerations

Although parenthood can be stressful for two, it's sometimes easier as a shared experience than as a solo one. A woman as a single parent may find it difficult to bear all the burdens of financial support and everyday care for a child. Nevertheless, increasing numbers of women in the United States are choosing or falling into pregnancy without marriage. Births to unwed mothers doubled during the 1970s; now one in six American babies are born to unmarried women (Hoffman and Slade 1981). Many of these are sexually active teenagers who haven't used contraceptives and didn't choose abortion; among the urban poor many are said to want an affectionate bond with a baby as an antidote for their own neglect ("They Want to Be Babied. . ." 1981). As one single mother put it, "There's always someone here for me to love and who loves me" (Klein 1973, p. 163). However, motherhood increases their financial problems, and many discover that having a child alienates them from old friends who are not parents. It's also hard for them to maintain an active sex life when days are spent working and nights are the only time they can spend with their child.

Some single mothers are women who for varying reasons want the experience of motherhood without binding their lives to that of a man. Since this desire flies in the face of traditional expectations, many "illegitimate" children and their "unwed" mothers still face isolation from disapproving friends and relatives. It's difficult for some men involved in these pregnancies to accept the biological role of father with none of its traditional social rights and responsibilities. And it's hard for some of these mothers to figure out what to tell the child about his or her father. But in these times of changing gender roles and value systems, some find support rather than ostracism for their choice.

Age Considerations

Some who get pregnant are very young; some are single women in their thirties and forties who feel that they'd better have the baby they want before it's "too late." They are aware of well-publicized concerns that pregnancy is risky for older mothers. But pregnancies at the other end of the reproductive age spectrum carry considerable risks, too.

Teenage Pregnancies.   As the incidence of teenage intercourse rises all over the world, so does the incidence of teenage pregnancy. In the United States almost 30,000 babies were born in 1978 to girls younger than fifteen and over 400,000 to girls aged fifteen to seventeen ("Teenage Pregnancies on Rise . . ." 1982). Some 15 percent of teenage mothers become pregnant again within a year (Constable 1982).

Those who get pregnant as teenagers may face three difficult role transitions at the same time; adolescence, parenthood, and perhaps early marriage. The stress of these adjustments is often amplified by money problems and lost opportunities. Having to care for a baby often means dropping out of school. If they marry the father of the child, often he must drop out of school, too, to help support them. Poverty and welfare and unemployment dependency add to the strains in these marriages, and they are two or three times more likely to break up than marriages begun when both partners are twenty or older (Alan Guttmacher Institute 1976).

Teenagers are likely to be poor parents, too, for they typically have little knowledge of child development and are often impatient and irritable because of their own problems. Their children run a high risk of physical abuse or neglect, retarded development, school problems, and delinquent behaviors (McKenny, Walters, and Johnson 1979). The social

costs of teenage pregnancy are thus enormous. In economic terms alone, about half the monies disbursed by the major welfare program—Aid to Families with Dependent Children—go to households with women who bore their first child while they were still teenagers (Moore 1978).

The research on medical risks of teenage pregnancy is confusing, for effects attributed to the mother's age may instead be caused—or complicated—by poverty-related factors, such as inadequate nutrition and lack of prenatal care. Nevertheless, it appears that pregnancy is riskier for a female in her teens than in her twenties. Teenage pregnancy is also riskier for her child, who runs a high risk of premature delivery, low birth weight, and birth defects. As a result babies born to women less than sixteen years old are two to three times more likely to die than babies born to young adult women (McKenny, Walters, and Johnson 1979).

An estimated two-thirds of teenagers who get pregnant don't intend to (Alan Guttmacher Institute 1976) and are surprisingly ignorant about conception control measures. Perhaps because teenage sex is not acceptable to many adults, not enough has been done to help teenagers prevent or deal with the serious consequences of pregnancy. As we'll see in the next chapter, there has been a great reluctance to provide teenagers with contraceptive services.

Pregnancy in Older Women.   In recent years there has been a slight but growing trend among white middle-class urban women to delay childbearing until they are in their thirties. More than 5 percent of all women in the United States have their first baby after they are thirty-five; in urban areas, up to 20 percent of women are waiting this long (Schultz 1979).

According to interviews of older mothers by Terri Schultz (1979), author of *Women Can Wait: The Pleasures of Motherhood after Thirty*, these women have various reasons for waiting. Some haven't yet developed a comfortable long-term relationship with a man and are not interested in being single parents. Bonded or not, many value the professional and personal freedoms they've worked so hard to establish. They fear that becoming a mother will throw them back into the restraints of the traditional motherhood role. Others value the freedom to travel, to party, to support social causes, and

Teenage mothers may feel that their own childhood has ended prematurely. On the other hand, some who have babies outside the "normal" childbearing years are able to define and shape the experience positively.

to explore varying lifestyles and intimate relationships. Once they've done all this, they may then feel positive about having children, for they don't feel that they've missed out on life's other opportunities.

Although some women see social advantages in waiting to have children until they're ready and eager for them, the medical dangers to both mother and child increase with the mother's age. Older mothers may find the physical demands of pregnancy and childrearing more tiring than do younger mothers. Aging increases the chances that a woman will have medical difficulties that may interfere with normal growth and delivery of a fetus. Infertility increases somewhat with age, often because of *endometriosis*, the so-called career woman's disease. When the opening in the cervix has not been enlarged by childbearing, the flow of menstrual fluids through it may become clogged, causing adhesions and blocking the fallopian tubes. The chance of one kind of birth defect—Down's syndrome (formerly called mongolism)—also increases with the mother's age. The risk of having a Down's syndrome child jumps from 1 in 2500 for women under twenty to 1 in 40 for women over forty-five (Fabe and Wikler 1979).

Older pregnant women are therefore treated as high-risk patients by many health care workers. But worries about whether the fetus is normal can be allayed by special diagnostic processes coupled with elective abortion if abnormalities are found. Only one in ten middle-aged mothers actually runs a high risk of problems; her risks can be minimized through excellent nutrition, rest and exercise, training for birth, and a positive attitude (McCauley 1976).

Practical Considerations

Any woman—young or old—should think twice about becoming pregnant if there are genetic problems in her or her mate's families or if her own health is poor. In addition to the mother's health, the expense of parenthood may be a major consideration. For a middle-income family, the cost of raising a first-born child to age 22 is now about $226,000 for a boy and $247,000 for a girl (Shearer 1983). And those who need a steady paycheck—or two—just to support themselves may realistically wonder if they could afford to be away from work for a while to care for a baby.

Overpopulation Concerns

Some individuals include concern for overpopulation in their decision making. As of July 1981 the Census Bureau estimated the United States population to be 230 million. This figure is expected to peak at a middle estimate of 309 million by the year 2050 and then to begin falling slightly ("US Population ..." 1982). Birthrates in the United States now average 2.2 children per family, one point above the 2.1 zero growth rate. The birthrate is thought to have dropped because of economic hard times, delay of childbearing, and women's interest in educational and career goals. If this pattern continues, 25 to 30 percent of women may finish their childbearing years without having children (Gulino 1981).

These considerations need not convince people who really want to have children that they should not. The real problems lie in *nondecisions* that result in unwanted births. Thoughtful choices for or against parenthood could help curb the immense social problems caused by the estimated 25 to 45 percent of world births that are unwanted (Greep, Koblinsky, and Jaffe 1976).

CREATING A PREGNANCY

Whether we have babies by chance or by conscious choice, pregnancy takes the same biological course. In this section we'll examine the means by which egg and sperm unite and develop into a baby. This physiological information is important background for understanding both what it takes to create a pregnancy and, as we'll see in Chapter 17, what steps might be taken to have intercourse without creating a pregnancy. In this section we'll also look at conscious efforts—sometimes unsuccessful—to conceive and ways to know whether we've done so.

Female and Male Contributions

Chapter 2 describes the complex process by which a woman's body repeatedly prepares for pregnancy, with an ovum being released from one of the ovaries on day fourteen of each average menstrual cycle. The ovum remains viable for twelve to twenty-four hours as it is propelled through the upper fallopian tube toward the uterus.

Meanwhile, sperm cells are being produced in

Estrogen Phase

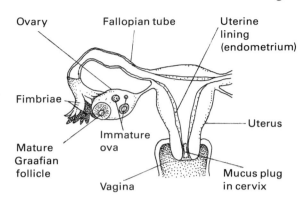

Ovary   Fallopian tube   Uterine lining (endometrium)

Fimbriae

Immature ova

Mature Graafian follicle

Vagina

Uterus

Mucus plug in cervix

Development of Graafian Follicle

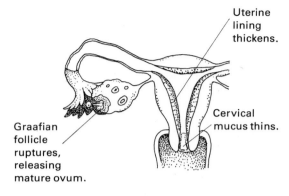

Uterine lining thickens.

Graafian follicle ruptures, releasing mature ovum.

Cervical mucus thins.

Ovulation

Progesterone Phase

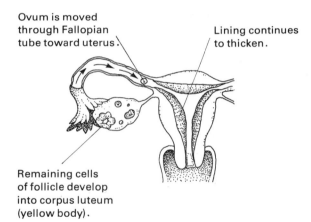

Ovum is moved through Fallopian tube toward uterus.

Lining continues to thicken.

Remaining cells of follicle develop into corpus luteum (yellow body).

Menstrual Phase

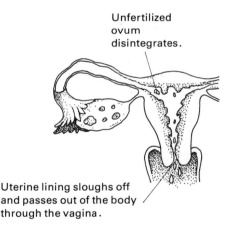

Unfertilized ovum disintegrates.

Uterine lining sloughs off and passes out of the body through the vagina.

Figure 16-1. The Menstrual Cycle. Although the days of the menstrual cycle are usually counted from the beginning of menstruation, it's easier to understand the sequence of events by starting with the estrogen phase.

the male's testicles at a tremendous rate. The average male ejaculate releases approximately 360 million sperm cells (Burt and Meeks 1975). Although numerous, sperm cells are the smallest of human cells (in contrast to the female's eggs, which are the largest). Sperm cell production begins at about twelve years of age; ejaculation of mature sperm can begin happening around age thirteen.

The male's testes are laced with tiny, convoluted tubes—the *seminiferous tubules*. Sperm production begins here. When immature sperm have assumed a long-tailed tadpolelike structure, they enter the

open space in the center of the tubes. There they are bathed in a fluid that is rich in androgens, estrogens, certain amino acids, and the B vitamin inositol.

Blood vessels feeding the area within the tubes are lined with special cells whose main function seems to be to maintain the high local concentration of androgen that is essential to sperm production. These *leydig* cells are apparently capable of synthesizing androgen from cholesterol in the bloodstream. This process seems to take place under stimulation by LH (luteinizing hormone) from the pituitary gland. Coordination of androgen supply may also be linked to FSH (follicle-stimulating hormone), just as in the female.

After their androgen bath in the seminiferous tubules, sperm cells are propelled to the long, convoluted *epididymis* attached to each testis. While the sperm are slowly pushed through the epididymis by rhythmic contractions of its walls, they mature further in preparation for their potential role in fertilizing the egg. Androgen is again somehow involved in this maturation process (Greep, Koblinsky, and Jaffe 1976). Full maturation of sperm takes a total of about sixty to seventy-two days (Diagram Group 1976). Much of this time is spent within the epididymis and nearby part of the *vas deferens*, where sperm may be stored for months until they are ejaculated.

When the male is sexually aroused to orgasm, sperm are forcefully expelled through the vas deferens into the *urethra* and out of the penis. Along the way they are joined by secretions from three small organs whose activities—like everything else in the male reproductive tract—are regulated by androgen. The *seminal vesicles* provide fluids rich in citric acid and the sugar fructose to nourish the sperm and give it energy for movement. The *prostate gland* provides a thin, watery, enzyme-rich fluid thought to aid sperm in their attempt to fertilize the egg, plus *prostaglandins*. By stimulating muscle activity in the male and female, prostaglandins may aid sperm transport toward the egg. In addition the *bulbourethral*, or *Cowper's, glands* add a small amount of lubricating, protein-rich fluids that prolong sperm life and activity. Drops of this secretion may seep from the urethral opening in the early stages of sexual excitement. Less than 10 percent by volume of the resulting solution—or *semen*—consists of sperm cells. But there may be hundreds of millions of these long-tailed cells in the ejaculated mixture. Even the preejaculatory drops of fluid from the Cowper's glands may contain enough sperm cells to cause a pregnancy.

Figure 16-2. Production and Structure of Sperm. Development of sperm cells from primitive germ cells goes on continously in a male's seminiferous tubules, one of which is represented here in cross section. Final stages of the sperm maturation process—which may take several months—take place in the epididymis.

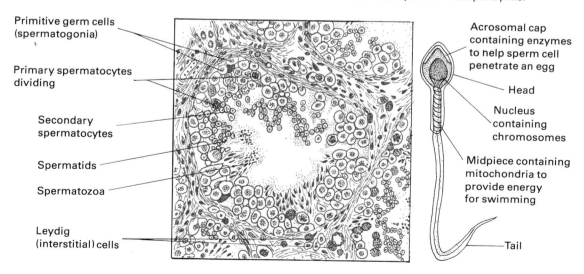

Primitive germ cells
(spermatogonia)

Primary spermatocytes
dividing

Secondary
spermatocytes

Spermatids

Spermatozoa

Leydig
(interstitial) cells

Acrosomal cap
containing enzymes
to help sperm cell
penetrate an egg

Head

Nucleus
containing
chromosomes

Midpiece containing
mitochondria to
provide energy
for swimming

Tail

**Sperm Production Within the
Seminiferous Tubules**

**Structure of a Mature Human
Sperm Cell (Spermatozoan)**

Conception

If the male's ejaculate reaches the female's vagina—even near its opening—chemical factors in the female's secretions seem to excite the sperm to vigorous movement (Greep, Koblinsky, and Jaffe 1976). Their swimming carries some of them into the opening of the cervix within ninety seconds after the male has ejaculated.

If the female is in the middle of her menstrual cycle, the normally thick, impenetrable cervical mucus will be thin and easy to penetrate. This mucus plays an important role in *conception,* or eventual union of a sperm cell with an egg cell. The alkaline mucus apparently protects the sperm from the hostile acid vaginal environment, weeds out defective sperm cells, and protects the others from cells whose job it is to engulf and digest foreign bodies. Cervical mucus may also contribute to *capacitation* of the sperm by triggering the final changes that allow it to reach and enter the egg.

Some of the sperm cells that survive the trip to the cervical canal swim into the alkaline fluid that coats the inside of the uterus. From a single ejaculation an estimated 40,000 to 50,000 sperm cells reach

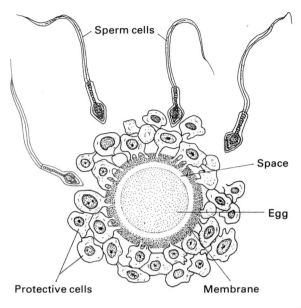

Figure 16-3.   Sperm Cells Encountering Egg. Scientists suspect that enzymes from the heads of many sperm cells may be needed to help clear a path through the egg's protective cells and membrane so that a single sperm cell can be engulfed by the egg.

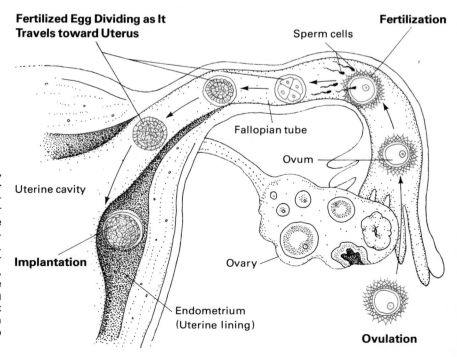

Figure 16-4. Ovulation, Fertilization, and Implantation. Fertilization generally occurs in the upper part of one fallopian tube as the ovum is slowly propelled toward the uterus. When the dividing cluster of cells reaches the uterus, it implants itself in the thickened uterine lining and continues the complex development process from cell cluster to embryo to fetus to newborn baby.

the upper end of the uterus, where many of them enter the fallopian tube that does not contain that month's egg. Only about 4000 will eventually make their way to the middle of the other fallopian tube, where an egg will be waiting or will soon arrive if it is the right time of the month for conception. Even if the egg has not yet arrived, some sperm may survive for forty-eight to seventy-two hours after entering the woman's body; these sperm may still be capable of fertilizing the egg several days after intercourse has occurred.

The journey of sperm cells toward the egg is not a competitive race but a cooperative effort. As we've seen, certain factors in the woman's secretions help the sperm mature, survive, and swim. And the sperm cells that make it to the egg may cooperate to clear a path through the mass of protective cells and the transparent membrane that surround it. In the presence of a newly ovulated egg, the cap covering the head of each sperm cell opens, releasing powerful enzymes. Of these enzymes one is thought to disperse the protective cells and another to digest a path through the membrane. One sperm cell may then swim into the space surrounding the egg, which quickly engulfs the single sperm cell. As soon as this event happens, the egg seals itself so that no other sperm can enter (Greep, Koblinsky, and Jaffe 1976).

A new life has now been created. But out of all successful unions of sperm and egg, only a fraction survive the intricate process of developing into a human baby. Almost a fifth of all pregnancies end in miscarriage. Before this bloody, observable event, almost half of all newly conceived embryos are rejected by the mother's body, apparently because they are somehow defective (Sweeney and Egan 1978). These miscarriages within the first weeks of pregnancy may go unnoticed.

Fetal Development

In viable pregnancies the united egg and sperm cells begin developing into a 6000-billion-celled human being while they are still in the fallopian tube. First the chromosomes from the egg and the head of the sperm pair up, determining the baby's gender and all the characteristics that it will inherit from its parents. Then the fertilized egg divides into two cells, each of which redivides again and again as the mass of dividing cells is propelled toward the uterus. (If the first egg division is total, two identical twins will develop; fraternal twins result when more than one egg is released and fertilized.)

Sometimes, though, the cell cluster never gets to the uterus. It begins growing inside the fallopian tube, which may eventually rupture unless surgery is performed. Women who think they may be pregnant and who feel a pain in their abdomen or shoulder or go into shock should see a doctor immediately, for they may have an *ectopic* ("misplaced") pregnancy.

In normal pregnancies the dividing egg cluster continues through the fallopian tube to the uterus. It turns into a hollow ball of cells that buries, or *implants,* itself in the soft, richly blood-fed lining. Tiny extensions from its outer layer seek blood vessels in the lining for nourishment. This area of exchange between the mother and what will be the baby is known as the *placenta.* Its thin membrane allows dissolved oxygen, food, and wastes to pass through, but blocks blood corpuscles and large molecules of protein; otherwise, the mother's body might reject the child as a foreign object.

The embryo's second week is referred to as the "fourth week" of the pregnancy. The length of pregnancy is measured not from conception (for it's hard to know when that occurred) but from the first day of the last menstrual period. During this "fourth" week, what is now called an *embryo* begins to differentiate itself into three primitive layers. From these seemingly simple layers of cells develop all the parts of the body, from heart to fingernails.

By the "fifth" week the embryo is a small dot with a spine and the beginnings of a nervous system. During the sixth week tiny buds that will become arms and legs appear.

By the eighth week the developing creature is called a *fetus.* Although it now has primitive hands and feet, it is only about one inch long. At the ten-week point it has recognizably human limbs. By twelve weeks it is three and a half inches long, with a face, separate fingers and toes, and the ability to move a bit on its own. As it floats about weightlessly within the fluid-filled *amniotic membrane,* its lifeline to the placenta is a long *umbilical cord.*

At sixteen weeks the fetus is about six inches long, with genitals that are recognizably male or female. Although it now moves vigorously, these movements usually cannot be felt until about the twentieth week. It is not until the twentieth week (five months) that many women perceive the fetus as alive. Yet despite the fact that all its organs are now working, it is still incapable of surviving outside its mother's body.

Even at twenty-four weeks, only about 3 percent of fetuses born prematurely can survive, and then only with intensive care. The chances of survival at thirty weeks are about 60 percent, at thirty-two weeks 90 percent, and at thirty-six weeks 97 percent (the normal length of pregnancy counted from the last menstrual period is forty weeks) (Ashdown-Sharp 1977). These age milestones are given moral significance, for whether the fetus looks "human," whether it has been felt as moving life, and whether it has any chance of surviving on its own are often important considerations to women thinking about abortion.

Conception Problems

Couples who want to have a baby usually stop using contraceptives, have intercourse whenever it suits them, and wait to see whether the woman misses her period. If several months go by and she is still menstruating on schedule, they may become anxious about their ability to create a pregnancy. It is not widely known that it takes an average couple four to six months to conceive. Some doctors recommend trying for about a year before seeking professional help.

When a couple discovers that they cannot conceive a child, they may experience surprise, denial, anger, isolation, guilt, or feelings of deep grief. These feelings can become an obsession. On the other hand, if resolved they may open the partners to change and growth, according to Barbara Eck Manning (1980), founder of Resolve, an organization that offers medical referrals and counseling for involuntarily childless couples.

Trying unsuccessfully to conceive may also strain the sexual relationship, especially if partners blame each other or themselves for what they regard as a lack of "masculinity" or "femininity." Even when they accept their inability to conceive as a joint problem that has nothing to do with their sexual identity, trying too hard may take the joy out of sex. On the other hand, what one woman describes as desperate and mechanical sex could instead be seen as fun and funny for a while. One infertile couple trying to conceive on schedule wanted a baby so badly that they had sex while the husband was working. His occupation: butcher. The only place they could find privacy: the deepfreeze (Sweeney and Egan 1978).

Causes of Infertility. Inability to conceive is fairly common. In the United States it affects an estimated 15 to 20 percent of all couples who are trying to have babies. Couples often assume that infertility is the woman's problem. But in about 40 percent of infertility cases, the male is the source of the problem; in another 40 percent of cases, the female's reproductive system is the cause. And in many cases both partners have fertility problems (Clark et al. 1982).

In the woman ovulation may not happen or it may happen only occasionally or with eggs of poor quality. The fallopian tubes may be blocked or defective. Fibroids in the uterus, endometriosis, cervical infections, or *pelvic inflammatory disease* (inflammation of the fallopian tubes, often from gonorrhea or unclean abortions) may cause conception problems. So may past deficiencies of iodine or folic acid in the woman's diet. Previous contraceptive use may affect fertility, too. When women who have irregular menstrual cycles take birth control pills and then stop taking them to get pregnant, ovulation may not resume for a long time. And sometimes IUD (intrauterine device) use causes pelvic inflammation (Kaufman 1978). In addition anything that interferes with intercourse—such as pain or relationship problems—will obviously decrease the chances of getting pregnant.

In the male sperm must be available in sufficient quantity and quality for conception to occur. They must also land in the woman's vagina, which may not happen if the man cannot sustain an erection or cannot ejaculate. Problems in sperm production may be caused by mumps in adulthood, severe infections, fever, sexually transmitted diseases, prostate infections, drugs, alcohol, malnutrition, or glandular deficiencies. Perhaps the most common cause of male infertility is *varicoceles,* varicose enlargement of veins in the scrotum that causes abdominal blood to pool in the scrotum, raising temperature too high for sperm. Sometimes the sperm passageway is blocked. And sometimes sperm antibodies in the male or female inhibit the sperm's activity.

Cures for Infertility. An estimated 50 to 70 percent of all childless couples eventually can have a baby (Clark et al. 1982). Sometimes the "cure" is as simple as having the woman lie on her back during intercourse and for an hour afterward, perhaps with a pillow under her hips, to encourage sperm to swim up her vagina rather than drain out. Another easy "cure" that works for some is having the man wear looser pants and take cooler baths to keep from overheating his testicles. Experimenting with the frequency of intercourse—trying it both more often and less often than usual—may help.

Gynecologists, urologists, infertility specialists, or infertility clinics can help find out what's not working and can suggest possible remedies. For instance, special hormone treatments have helped many women conceive when their own hormone feedback systems weren't working properly. Up to 20 percent of previously infertile women have reportedly conceived with the aid of a cough syrup containing guaifenesin, which seemingly thins the mucus in the cervix and dilutes sperm-destroying chemicals there (Geller 1982). Drug therapy and sometimes surgery can remove the tract-blocking tissue growths of endometriosis. New microsurgical procedures can sometimes clear fallopian tube blockage in the woman or vas deferens blockage in the man, sometimes even when the ducts have been deliberately closed off in an earlier vasectomy to prevent conception. Varicoceles likewise can be surgically corrected (Clark et al. 1982).

For some, however, years of expensive hormone treatments and operations still don't produce the longed-for pregnancy. Such couples are often described as "desperate" by the health practitioners who try to help them. One doctor commented, "When a couple wants a baby . . . they will do anything. Anything! If I told a couple to have intercourse in Macy's window at high noon, they'd do it" (Sweeney and Egan 1978, p. 24). "Anything" for some finally involves a medical procedure in which sperm is artificially injected into the vagina. The sperm may come from the husband (AIH—artificial insemination by husband) or from an anonymous donor (AID—artificial insemination by donor), either as a fresh masturbation specimen from some unseen donor or a thawed specimen from a frozen sperm bank. One service claims to offer sperm from Nobel Prize winners and other "creative, intelligent people" (Tedrick 1982, p. C16).

Despite the depersonalization of the AID procedure, both husband and wife may tend to define it negatively as "adultery" or gender role inadequacy. Some doctors try to downplay such feelings by mixing some of the husband's semen with that from the donor or advising that the couple have sex shortly before the procedure on the pretense that perhaps it will be one of the husband's sperm cells that fertilizes the egg. The woman may feel guilty over her fantasies about the anonymous donor and the man may be disturbed by feelings that his wife was "violated" with his consent and that the child is not really "his." The relationship with the child may be clouded by attempts to keep what they know about its parentage a secret. And in most states the legal rights and status of children thus conceived have not been clearly established. Despite these peculiar problems with social definitions of a medical procedure, it is widely—but quietly—used in clinics across the country to produce 6000 to 10,000 pregnancies a year ("The Anonymous Pregnancy . . ." 1979). Paid donors are carefully screened for possible genetic disorders, and according to the director of a large Los Angeles AID center, "If a husband has a good self-image, he'll readily agree to use donor sperm" (Clark et al. 1982, p. 109).

The opposite of artificial insemination of the mother with her husband's or a donor's sperm is to artificially inseminate a paid *surrogate mother* with the husband's sperm. She carries the child during the pregnancy and then turns the newborn over to the "couple" for "adoption." As in AID this option may fill the desire of a couple to have a child that is related genetically to at least one of them. However, the procedure may raise difficult emotional and legal issues for all three "parents" involved. It is also expensive. Those who use such services may pay up to $10,000 to cover legal fees and hospital costs, plus an additional $6000 to $20,000 payment to the surrogate mother (Dvorchak 1982).

Another tool available to the desperate is *in vitro* fertilization (IVF), otherwise known as "test-tube" fertilization. When the conception problem is that the woman's fallopian tubes are blocked beyond hope of surgical repair, it is now sometimes possible to remove an egg ripe for fertilization from her body and place it in a petri dish with artificially capacitated sperm from the husband. If egg and sperm unite and begin the process of cell division, the resulting cell cluster is reimplanted in the woman's uterus a few days later. This delicate procedure was first performed successfully in 1978 in England. Some people worry that this procedure tampers too much with nature or invites Frankenstein-like abuses that we don't have the wisdom to control.

Use of the drug Pergonal to coax the woman's ovaries to release several eggs, all of which are extracted and sperm treated and then inserted into the uterus, has been attacked by some religious right-to-life groups on the grounds that some cell clusters—or "lives"—are lost in the process. IVF-implanted embryos frequently abort as well. Supporters of the IVF procedure point out that even under normal circumstances, 50 percent of all natural conceptions abort spontaneously (Clark et al. 1982). The IVF procedure is expensive, often unsuccessful, and emotionally stressful, raising the potential for psychological and financial abuse of those who are obsessed with having a baby at all costs.

Pregnancy Tests

Whether pregnancy is wanted or unwanted, it's important to know as soon as possible whether conception has occurred. This information allows time for abortion decision making and early abortion procedures if this is the choice; for optimizing the baby's chances for health by being careful about drugs, food, and environmental contaminants from the beginning of the pregnancy; or for early detection of ectopic pregnancies.

The most common symptom of pregnancy is a missed menstrual period. There may also be nausea, breast tenderness, tiredness, and frequent need to urinate. None of these signs is a sure indication of pregnancy, though, so it's essential to verify the pregnancy some other way. Usually two procedures are necessary: pelvic examination for changes in the cervix and uterus plus analysis of a blood or urine sample. The first can be accurately done only by a trained health practitioner. The second can be done through a Planned Parenthood office, a women's center, a gynecology clinic, an abortion clinic, a local health department, a private gynecologist, or a home test kit.

The most accurate tests require a blood sample from the woman. *Radioimmunoassay* of the blood indicates with almost 100 percent accuracy whether she is pregnant. It can do so within seven days after conception, even before the first menstrual period is missed. Immunoassay of urine is used for routine confirmation of pregnancies in offices, clinics, or with home test kits, starting from twenty-five to twenty-eight days after conception. In addition to home or clinical chemical testing, all women should have pelvic examinations to help interpret the test results and begin pregnancy counseling or consideration of alternative reasons why a period has been delayed (Hatcher et al. 1982).

UNWANTED PREGNANCIES

If tests indicate that a woman is pregnant, she and her partner may face some serious decisions. If they have wanted and planned for a baby, they will want to provide it with a healthy fetal environment. If the pregnancy is unwanted, unplanned, or mistimed, they have some other options. They can go ahead with the pregnancy and keep the baby, go ahead with the pregnancy and give the baby up for adoption or to a temporary home, or get an abortion. Many people are faced with these choices. Demographer Christopher Tietze (1979) has estimated that there are over 2 million unintended pregnancies in the United States each year.

Having the Baby

Over 40 percent of single pregnant teenagers in the United States are presently choosing to go ahead with their pregnancies. Of these 95 percent are keeping their babies rather than putting them up for adoption (Constable 1982). There are many childless couples who are eager to adopt a baby. But even though the biological parents would like their child to have a good home, they may find it difficult to give up all rights to the child. Some would like to keep it if only circumstances were different—if they had enough money to support a child, for instance, or if they were married, or if they had a place to live. And some worry that the child may resent them for rejecting parenthood. Such feelings should be carefully weighed before any consent papers are signed. Adoptions can be arranged during the pregnancy through an adoption agency or through direct arrangements with adoptive parents, under procedures established by state laws.

An alternative for those who need time to make up their minds or reorganize their lives is putting the baby in a foster home. In this situation the government pays a foster family to care for the child. But if much time passes, there may be disagreements between the foster mother and the biological mother over how the child should be raised, and the child may be torn between the two. Also foster homes may change over the years, with possible detrimental effects on the child. Fostering is perhaps best used as a temporary solution, to be replaced as soon as possible by actual adoption or by reclaiming of the child by its biological parents.

Abortion

Another option is terminating the pregnancy. In 1973 the Supreme Court ruled in *Roe* v. *Wade* that states could not interfere with women's right to seek abortions during the first twenty-four weeks of pregnancy—before the fetus is "viable" or capable of "meaningful life outside the mother's womb." Decisions about allowing abortion of a fetus after the twenty-four-week potential-viability mark were left up to individual states, except when the mother's life was threatened by the pregnancy. In 1976 the Supreme Court further ruled that the right to choose or reject abortion belongs solely to the woman; sex partners and parents cannot override her decision. In 1983 the Supreme Court nullified most restrictions on abortions. The Court declared unconstitutional regulations requiring (1) use of hospitals rather than less expensive abortion clinics for women more than three months pregnant; (2) advising of potential abortion patients by doctors that abortion carries risks, that alternatives to abortion are available, and that the fetus is "a human life"; (3) "humane and sanitary" disposal of the aborted fetus; (4) a twenty-four-hour waiting period between signing up for an abortion and getting it; and (5) parental consent for abortion for pregnant single women under fifteen (Epstein 1983).

Despite its legality, abortion is not an easy choice. It carries slight medical risk to the mother if a decision is delayed and may be subject to conflicting social pressures concerning the rights of the mother, the rights of the father, and the rights of society and the fetus. Accordingly, few women are using abortion repeatedly as an alternative to contraception (Steinhoff et al. 1979).

The Parents' Feelings. Women who assert the right to control their own bodies generally want abortion to be available to women as an option when contraceptives fail. They point out that our society's attitudes make it especially hard for the young and the poor to obtain and use safe, effective contraceptives.

Most pregnancies that are aborted were never consciously "chosen." Typically they are described by women as accidents, and the abortion is seen as a forced response to a bad situation (Freeman 1977). But some observers claim that many women who request abortions are ambivalent about them—that they are torn between reasons for wanting to have a baby and reasons for not wanting to (Freeman 1977).

Nevertheless, Wassenberg and Nass's study (1977) of single pregnant women in Hartford, Connecticut, showed that decisions for abortion "did not involve conflicting, neurotic response patterns, but reflected fairly reasonable decision steps of women dealing with 'an accident.'" In contrast to women who chose to have their babies, those who chose abortion were more likely to be older, middle-class, and either working or going to college. They were more likely to have grown up in an intact home, to have begun intercourse at a later age, and to know about and sometimes use contraceptives. Their abortion decision seemed to be facilitated by a more liberal attitude toward women's roles and a tendency to see sex as natural and okay if both partners consent.

Women trying to decide what to do about an unplanned pregnancy also differ in how they perceive the fetus's humanity. Some consider it a human life from the moment of conception. Some think of it as a human being once it develops recognizably human features, around the tenth or twelfth week of pregnancy. To others the fetus is just an abstract idea until it begins to move during the fifth month. And still others don't define it as "human" until it's old enough to survive outside their bodies. The issue of when a fetus becomes "human" lies in the realm of philosophy; it cannot be answered by science.

According to several studies about three-quarters of males whose pregnant partners sought an abortion took responsibility for paying for the abortion, fully agreed with the abortion decision, were concerned about the woman, and continued seeing her afterward. But a significant minority of males were partly or wholly against the abortion. Many felt a sense of loss (Pfuhl 1978; Shostak 1979). Although some legislatures have been asked to grant men the right to be involved in decisions regarding abortion of children they have fathered, the few states that have passed such laws have usually seen them struck down by the courts, for to give men veto power would deny women the freedom of choice granted by the 1973 Supreme Court decision.

Social Pressures.   In addition to their own feelings, people considering abortion are often influenced by society's view of the procedure. Ever since the 1973 Supreme Court legalization of abortion, implementation of this decision has been under heavy fire from religious and right-to-life groups who define abortion as murder. They regard it as a violation of the rights of the unborn fetus. According to National Right to Life Committee spokesman Dan Donehey,

Our ultimate goal is to amend the constitution of the U.S so that all human life from conception to natural death is protected. . . . We know that, in the educational area, when people fully realize what happens to an unborn baby in an abortion, they are more apt to become pro-life.   [quoted in Foreman 1983, p. 2]

"Prochoice" groups have countered with the argument that although abortion is clearly a less acceptable choice for a woman than contraception, it should be available as a backup option for women who want to maintain control over their own fertility. They point out that women may have humane reasons for choosing abortion. For instance, the Boston Women's Health Book Collective states:

We cannot agree with [right-to-life advocates] that an unborn fetus has more rights than the pregnant woman who is carrying it. Further, many of us who choose abortion believe that the quality of life we offer our children—which includes our emotional and situational readiness for a child or another child—is as important as the life itself.   [Boston Women's Health Book Collective 1976, p. 216]

Although right-to-life groups have charged that abortion is inhumane, prochoice groups in turn charge that to give birth to an unwanted or defective child is irresponsible. Prochoice advocates believe that although no woman should be pressured into having an abortion just because she is young, poor, unmarried, or otherwise subject to social stigma, abortion should be available as an option to those who feel that it is *for them* the best solution to an unwanted situation.

Feminists see the antiabortion movement as an antifeminist backlash, an attack on efforts to achieve equality, an attempt to reduce women to their traditional barefoot and pregnant status in the patriarchal family. They see the issue of reproductive freedom as related to the wider issue of women's struggle to gain autonomy and control over their own lives.

Despite considerable publicity given to right-to-life groups, the majority of people in the United States seem to believe that women have the right to freedom of choice under certain circumstances. According to a 1980 National Opinion Survey, 90 percent approve of abortion if the woman's health is seriously endangered by the pregnancy, 83 percent if the pregnancy is a result of rape, 83 percent if there is a strong chance that the baby will be seriously defective, 52 percent if the family is poor and cannot afford any more children, 48 percent if the mother is single and does not want to marry the father, 47 percent if the woman is pregnant and does not want any more children, and 41 percent for any reason the woman might choose (Granberg and Granberg 1980).

A poll taken by the NBC News–Associated Press in 1982 showed that 75 percent of Americans were opposed to a constitutional amendment that would prohibit abortions (Foreman 1983). According to a national survey of American women by the polling organization Yankelovich, Skelly, and White, whereas 56 percent personally consider abortion morally wrong, 67 percent believe that "on the whole, . . . any woman who wants an abortion should be permitted to obtain it legally" ("Abortion: Women Speak Out" 1981, p. 47). And a 1981 ABC News–Washington Post poll found that 79 percent of American Catholics believe in abortion rights ("Catholics Speak Out for the Right to Choose Abortion" 1981).

To say the least, abortion is a politically hot

issue, and the New Right and right-to-life groups have forced some changes in public policy. For example, the June 1980 Supreme Court ruling that neither the states nor the federal government is required by the Constitution to pay for abortions for poor women spawned legislative or administrative restrictions on public funding of abortions in many states. While such actions have not made legal abortion impossible, they have made it increasingly stressful and difficult for many women.

The battle between those who favor more restrictive abortion laws and those who oppose such laws is not likely to end in the near future. The roles of religious beliefs and the law continue to conflict. The conflict is even more pronounced within some religions. For example, the Catholic church opposes abortion, but most American Catholics favor it as a woman's right. As a Catholics for Free Choice brochure argues:

The church's strong arguments against abortion and contraception are seen by many Catholics as distant abstractions, not relevant to concrete, personal situations. This has caused a gap between the actual moral decisions of Catholics, and their perception of moral principle as embodied in church teaching.   [Hurst 1981, p. 1]

Methods of Abortion.   When safe, legal abortions have not been available, women around the world who were carrying unwanted pregnancies have used a variety of home methods to try to terminate them. Some are ineffective; most are very dangerous to the mother. Legal abortion clinics instead use surgical or chemical techniques known to be relatively safe and effective. The methods used early in the pregnancy are far safer than those used to terminate more advanced pregnancies. Second-trimester abortions (those done during the middle third of a nine-month pregnancy) are three or four times riskier to the mother than first-trimester abortions (those done during the first third). Even so, abortions after the sixteenth week carry no more medical risk than does natural childbirth (Dietz 1979). Early abortions are also cheaper and less painful than later ones. It is therefore recommended that women with unwanted pregnancies make a decision and take immediate action by eight to ten weeks from the last menstrual period, at the very latest.

The *vacuum curettage* method involves slight dilation (or stretching) of the cervix under local anesthesia, allowing the fetus to be drawn out of the uterus with a small pump or syringe. It can be performed in a doctor's office, clinic, or hospital up to thirteen weeks from the last menstrual period.

The traditional *dilatation and curettage* (D and C) uses a curette (a metal loop with a long, thin handle) to reach through the dilated cervix and loosen the contents of the uterus. Because this procedure is painful, it may require local or general anesthesia and therefore hospitalization. The woman may bleed more than with vacuum curettage, and there is some risk that her uterus may be perforated or may develop an infection. But after thirteen weeks vacuum curettage is no longer an option, necessitating the use of another procedure such as the D and C. *Dilatation and evacuation* (D and E) combines the techniques of vacuum curettage and D and C and is considered particularly appropriate for abortions performed between the thirteenth and sixteenth weeks.

Labor induced by *saline* or *prostaglandin* solutions is used to abort pregnancies from sixteen to twenty-four weeks after the last menstrual period. By this time the fetus is too big to be safely removed by suction or curettage. Instead, the labor contractions and cervical dilation of a naturally occurring childbirth are induced by injecting a solution into the amniotic fluid surrounding the fetus. Prostaglandins are substances similar to hormones that appear in a normal pregnancy when birth is imminent; they seem to cause the contractions of labor. Replacement of some of the amniotic fluid with a saline (salt) solution kills the fetus and sets a natural miscarriage into motion.

In rare cases the fetus is removed through an incision in the mother's abdomen—a *hysterotomy*. Because this procedure is major surgery done with general anesthesia (which is dangerous in itself), it carries higher complication and death rates than the previous methods (Hatcher et al. 1982).

The Emotional Aftermath.   Studies of how people feel after an abortion vary. Some indicate that the major response is relief and that abortion is less likely to be followed by psychological problems than is childbirth. One such study—a survey of 320 women who had abortions—indicated that most had dealt with their negative feelings about the procedure. This majority expressed less anxiety and depression *after* the abortion than *before* it. Even the minority who regretted their decision—often because they had wanted the pregnancy—still viewed abortion as the only thing they could have done given their circumstances. Their difficulty in resolving their ambivalent feelings seemed related less to the abortion itself than to other personal problems (Freeman 1977).

Many studies indicate that for mentally healthy women, abortion may be genuinely therapeutic (Athanasiou et al. 1973). Even women who have previously seen themselves as passive victims of circumstances may develop a new awareness of their potential for active decision making. This insight, combined with contraceptive advice given by the abortion clinic and personal motivation to avoid future unplanned pregnancies, leads to greater use of contraceptives after the abortion (Freeman 1977; Athanasiou et al. 1973).

In thinking back on their abortions, most women stand behind their decision. According to the Yankelovich, Skelly, and White national survey of women, of the 9 percent who had experienced an abortion, only 8 percent thought afterwards that abortion was not the right thing for them. Most believed that their original reasons for the decision were good ones. One woman, for instance, had been brutally raped by two men and had become pregnant as a result. Her injuries from the rape were so severe that she might have died in childbirth. She explained:

It's hard to take something out of your body, but if I had had to bear the child I would have hated it. Abortion shouldn't be done merely for convenience, but I would not have been able to cope with a baby mentally. I just wanted to bury the whole episode.   [Quoted in "Abortion: Women Speak Out" 1981, p. 50]

Another woman had become pregnant while slowly recovering from a spinal fracture. Confined to a wheelchair, she thought that pregnancy at that time would have been too dangerous:

I don't have the back or the legs. I had this vision of being pregnant and falling down a flight of stairs. . . . I did go through the sadness of thinking I had killed something that would have been a person in nine months, but I owe it to myself and to the child to be in the best physical

condition so that it is a beautiful and fulfilling experience for both of us.   [Quoted in "Abortion: Women Speak Out" 1981, p. 50]

Nevertheless, abortion may be an emotionally wrenching experience, even for those who believe they made the only choice they could. Some people continue to worry about "killing the baby." Especially when ambivalence has delayed decision making until the second trimester, people may have problems accepting their decision (Kaltreider 1973).

Whether people choose pregnancy or abortion, it is important that others support their decision, for it is irrevocable. Although a mixture of pros and cons may be weighed beforehand, once the decision has been made people must continue to live with it. If the choice is to keep the pregnancy, a whole new set of choices enters the picture.

EXPERIENCING PREGNANCY

When a woman carries her baby to full term, she may experience some personal discomforts. She may

Both partners can choose to define pregnancy positively as a time of intriguing changes.

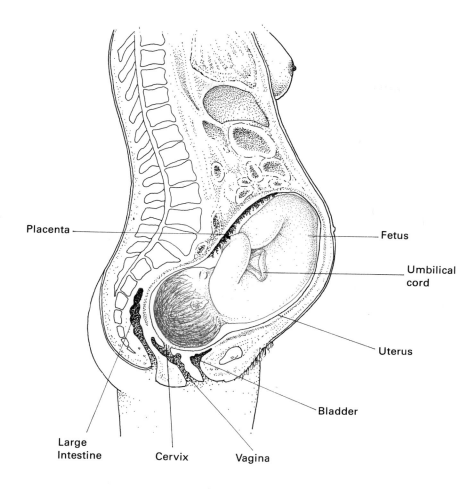

Placenta

Fetus

Umbilical
cord

Uterus

Bladder

Large
Intestine

Cervix

Vagina

Figure 16.5. Full-Term Pregnancy. A pregnant woman may experience discomforts as the fetus grows, for it may press on her intestines and bladder and pull her spine forward at the waist. Exercise minimizes such discomforts by strengthening her supporting muscles. Keeping physically fit also helps her prepare to take an active part in labor and delivery.

need to urinate more often as the swelling uterus presses on her bladder. Her breasts may enlarge and become tender as the milk glands develop. A changing chemical balance in her vagina may trigger unusual and perhaps irritating secretions. Shifting pelvic bones may pinch the sciatic nerves along the backs of her legs. Hormone changes and pressure from the fetus may cause bowel irregularity and constipation. Her body tissues may swell with retained fluids. A high acid level in her stomach, and compression of her stomach by her growing uterus may cause heartburn, nausea, vomiting, or indigestion. Hormonal shifts and the demands of the growing fetus may cause fatigue. And toward the end of her nine months' wait, she may develop backaches from leaning backwards as she walks to balance her bulging belly.

Some women experience these discomforts only mildly. They find pregnancy a truly happy time of eager anticipation and great energy. Others are thoroughly miserable. What makes the difference? And how do their male partners respond to what is basically a female experience?

The Mother's Attitudes

The psychological literature traditionally has linked problems with pregnancy to rejection of the "feminine" role. That is, women bothered by "morning sickness" symptoms such as vomiting were thought to be women who really didn't want to be mothers anyway. However, problems such as vomiting do have a physiological base. And while it's true that our mind-set strongly influences our bodily processes, women's attitudes toward being pregnant are not a simple matter of acceptance or rejection.

To begin with, women who become pregnant are already involved in life situations that they may interpret as stressful. Like nonpregnant people they vary in their ability to cope. Another factor affecting how a woman experiences her pregnancy is how she defines it. For example, women who see pregnancy and parenthood as a self-sacrificing trap may feel suffocated and alarmed by the demands the growing fetus makes on their bodies. Pregnant women's attitudes are also shaped by other people's reactions to them. Those who lack self-confidence may think that others consider them funny looking. In a culture that defines beauty as slenderness, it's hard for some women to feel okay about themselves as they get larger and larger. Their self-image is subjected to conflicting messages: Eat for two so the baby will be well nourished, but stay thin so men will love you. No matter what her attitudes, a woman has important work to do during pregnancy. This state marks the transition from childfree life to parenthood, a role change that may alter her life in many ways.

The Father's Attitudes

While the mother-to-be prepares psychologically for having a baby, the future father may feel left out unless he actively involves himself in preparations for the birth. An expectant father may also find the mother unpredictably emotional from hormonal shifts, tired and irritable because of physical problems, and unsure of her attractiveness. She may need *his* understanding and support.

Many men are actively involved in their partner's pregnancy: They marvel with her over the fetus's movements, accompany her to prepared childbirth classes, share childcare planning, and assist during labor and delivery. But even highly involved fathers may have a hard time during pregnancy, for they may worry about potential dangers to their partner and to the fetus she is carrying. Many also worry about their own "performance" during birth, for they are anxious about the risks of childbirth and want to do everything "right."

Nevertheless, men who have assisted their partners during labor and delivery have described the event as one of the most important experiences of their lives. They say they wouldn't have missed it for anything. And after the child is born, their involvement in parenting gives them something new and rewarding to share with their mate.

SEX DURING PREGNANCY

A special source of potential relationship problems during pregnancy is changes in sexual activities. Studies differ as to just what happens. Most show that frequency and/or enjoyment of intercourse tend to drop during the third trimester (Calhoun, Selby, and King 1981).

Reasons for Changing Sexual Activity

Changes in sexual patterns may stem from a number of causes, none of them well understood. For one thing a woman's estrogen, progesterone, and testosterone levels all rise dramatically during pregnancy, but researchers don't know if the new mix is likely to make her feel more sexual or less so.

As her belly begins to protrude, a woman may increasingly want to defend herself against intrusive contact—such as intercourse. "Pregnant" fathers may subtly share their partner's defensiveness about their bodies, a defensiveness that may be totally irrational. For instance, one such father admitted, "I'm nervous every time I make love to my wife because I keep thinking maybe the baby can bite me" (quoted in Bing and Colman 1977, p. 110). As the woman's belly bulges and her breasts become more tender, some intercourse positions may also become physically awkward or uncomfortable. For couples who already enjoy many forms of sex, subtracting a few intercourse positions doesn't make much difference. One caution: During oral sex air may be blown into the uterus and from there into the bloodstream, thus causing air embolism (obstruction of a blood vessel) (Bing and Colman 1977).

In addition to slight logistic problems, some people find it hard to mix ideas of sex and motherhood. Sometimes this difficulty results from a learned inability to see a large female body as sexual. As one woman put it, "I feel like a blob. I don't feel too sexy." And a male referred to his pregnant partner's belly as something he had to ignore in order to find her sexual: "She looks pretty good in clothes [as opposed to naked]. And in the dark you can't see so it's not so bad" (quoted by LaRossa 1979, p. 8). To others it doesn't seem right to be having sex with a pregnant mother. One male explained, "It just seems somehow sacrilegious" (quoted by LaRossa 1979, p. 9). Some women are so preoccupied with the pregnancy anyway that they may not be interested in their partners.

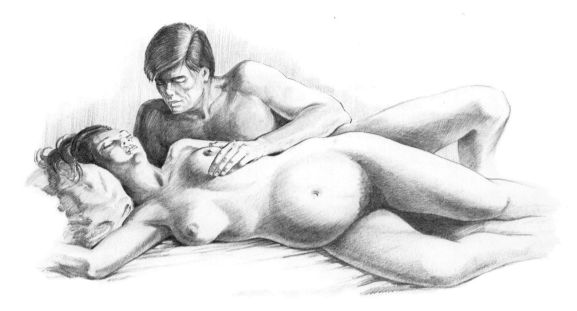

In contrast to all these possible reasons for feeling less sexual during pregnancy, some women feel *more* sexual. Masters and Johnson (1966) have found that genital blood congestion increases enormously with erotic stimulation during pregnancy.

Medical Concerns

Some men and women cut down on intercourse—or even stop entirely—during pregnancy because they are afraid they might hurt the fetus. Although there is no conclusive evidence, intercourse cannot be altogether ruled out as a cause of some miscarriages and premature deliveries. During orgasm the female's uterus contracts just as it does during labor. And the prostaglandins in semen can prolong these contractions and cause premature delivery. (Women in some cultures therefore use intercourse when their babies are due as a way to get labor started.) There is no documented evidence that intercourse will cause miscarriage by rupturing uterine tissues (Speir 1977). But sexually transmitted diseases can spread to the fetus during intercourse. And after examining the detailed records of 26,886 pregnancies, Richard Naeye (1979) found that fetal distress and infections of the amniotic fluid surrounding the fetus were more common when the mother had intercourse during the pregnancy. This finding is controversial; current advice to the pregnant couple about the safety of sex late in pregnancy

therefore varies. Naeye suggests that use of a condom or careful genital washing before intercourse may help prevent infection. Arthur Herbst (1979) suggests that until more is known, it might be wise for women who've had reproductive problems in the past or whose cervix has begun to dilate prematurely to avoid both orgasm and intercourse during the third trimester of their pregnancy.

Alternatives

Even if people decide to abstain from intercourse during part of the pregnancy, there are many other ways they can give sexual pleasure to each other. Although some women report a decrease in sexual interest, their needs for touching and affection remain high (Tolor and DiGrazia 1976). Men continue to need touching as well as reassurance that their partners will not turn their full attention to the new baby.

When people are happy about the pregnancy, instead of withdrawing from sex they may actually enjoy it more. Freedom from having to use contraception may make sex more spontaneous and fun. Women may gain a new awareness of their bodies, and their skin may take on a special glow. Their changing shape and the baby's movements may be sources of wonder and humor. And avoiding intercourse may lead to new ways of relating sexually. For instance, one couple discovered that they enjoyed dancing together in front of a mirror, with her belly sticking out and his sucked in (Bing and Colman 1977). This willingness to experiment beyond old patterns may enhance intimacy.

FACTORS AFFECTING FETAL AND MATERNAL HEALTH

Whether or not it is reasonable to worry that sex may harm the fetus, it is clearly reasonable to be concerned that what the mother ingests or is exposed to may jeopardize the fetus's health. Each year over 250,000 babies in the United States are born with birth defects of prenatal origin. Some are probably inherited, but some are seemingly caused by influences reaching the fetus through the placenta (National Foundation March of Dimes, a).

The United States also has an unusually high incidence of low-birth-weight babies: 232,000 babies weighing five and a half pounds or less are born each year. Low birth weight causes more deaths during the first year of life than any other factor and is the major cause of childhood disabilities (National Foundation March of Dimes, b). Factors known to contribute to or suspected of contributing to birth defects and/or low birth weight should therefore be taken into consideration by mothers as they make health choices during pregnancy.

Nutrition

Contrary to all social messages that it's important to be slim, women are now advised to slowly gain twenty-six to thirty pounds by eating nutritious food during their pregnancies. Their bodies must meet their own needs and supply all the nutrients needed for fetal development as well.

Requirements for protein, vitamins, and minerals increase dramatically during pregnancy. For instance, a pregnant woman needs to eat up to twice as much protein as her body normally requires. Reasons for this increased protein demand include rapid growth of fetal tissues, increase in the mother's blood volume, growth of her uterus and breasts, development of the placenta and amniotic fluid, and reserves for labor, delivery, and milk production. Malnutrition—particularly inadequacy of protein—is thought to be related to *toxemia,* a potentially serious complication of pregnancy. It is therefore recommended that pregnant women eat at least four servings of milk and milk products, four servings of protein foods, four servings of fruits and vegetables, four servings of whole-grain products, and one to three servings of fat or oil every day. Cautious use of vitamin and mineral supplements prescribed by a doctor may also be advised.

Drug Use

Many drugs mothers take can have adverse effects on their unborn babies. This warning applies not only to illegal drugs but also to over-the-counter drugs and those prescribed by doctors. For example, heavy use of aspirin or other analgesics may interfere with blood clotting in both mother and infant and may delay labor, and taking as much as one gram of vitamin C daily can be harmful (Boston Womens' Health Book Collective 1976; National Foundation March of Dimes, c). Yet according to a 1976 study by *Consumer Reports,* only 7.9 percent of women went through pregnancy with no drug prescriptions. Over a quarter of the women studied received five or more drug prescriptions during their pregnancy! Women are advised to be careful about what drugs they take—if any—while pregnant.

Drinking

Like many drugs alcohol can pass through the placenta and harm the fetus. Excessive alcohol consumption by the mother can result in a set of problems known as *fetal alcohol syndrome*—abnormal smallness (especially in the size of the head), small brain, mental deficiency, poor coordination, hyperactivity, short attention spans, behavior problems, and often heart defects. The 1 million alcoholic women of childbearing age in the United States therefore run a high risk of harming their babies. Sometimes even moderate alcohol consumption causes fetal alcohol syndrome. Pregnant women are therefore advised to think of their unborn child before choosing to drink beer, wine, or hard liquor (National Foundation March of Dimes, d).

Smoking

Pregnant women may choose to give up smoking for the sake of the fetus. Women who smoke have smaller babies, with a greater likelihood of their being born prematurely (Linn et al. 1982). Also, studies show that smoking seems to damage the babies' blood vessels, thus predisposing these children to heart attacks during adulthood. Because damage may result even if a woman stops smoking during her pregnancy, the time to stop seems to be *before* she gets pregnant ("Doctor Sees Smoking..." 1979). Stopping smoking just during pregnancy is preferable to not stopping at all ("Pregnant Woman..." 1980).

Environmental Teratogens

Many factors in the mother's environment are suspected *teratogens*—that is, substances that may cause birth defects or diseases in infants. Teratogens range from X rays to pesticides. There is a limit to what pregnant women can do to protect themselves from these toxins. Carole Spearin McCauley (1976) suggests that women can choose to avoid at least a few possible teratogens by saying no to chest or abdominal X rays during pregnancy; wearing a lead apron during dental X rays; avoiding the use of chemicals in aerosol containers; discontinuing use of hair rinses, bleaches, and dyes; and avoiding raw meat and having someone else clean the cat litter box (to avoid catching toxoplasmosis, a defect-causing disease, from the meat or droppings).

Checking the Fetus for Birth Defects

Because of their age, race, or family history, some pregnant women are thought to run a high risk of having children with certain defects. Several diagnostic procedures are now offered that can detect the development of many different kinds of birth defects long before the baby is born. If a defect is found, parents can choose to abort the pregnancy.

Amniocentesis is performed after the fourteenth week of pregnancy. A small amount of the amniotic fluid in which the fetus floats is withdrawn from the uterus with a slender needle. Laboratory tests on this fluid indicate whether the fetus has chromosomal abnormalities (including Down's syndrome) or certain amino acid disorders. Because amniocentesis also reveals the gender of the fetus, parents have a clue to whether it will inherit a family disease that only affects one gender or the other. A newer technique—*chorionic villi sampling*—offers similar information slightly earlier in the pregnancy.

In the *ultrasound* technique, soundwaves are bounced off the fetus with a scanning device. When the resulting image is displayed on a screen, specialists can tell as early as twelve weeks whether neural tube defects (such as the crippling and sometimes fatal spina bifida condition) are developing. After eighteen weeks scanning of the fetus's stomach and bladder can reveal urinary tract diseases and structural abnormalities in the stomach and esophagus ("New Pregnancy Tests..." 1976).

Hair-thin fiberoptic tubes now allow specialists to look directly at the fetus and even photograph it or draw a blood sample. This *fetoscopy* procedure allows prenatal diagnosis of certain structural defects, sickle-cell anemia (a blood problem found in some black babies), and thalassemia (a blood defect found in some babies of Mediterranean descent) (Hobbins and Mahoney 1977; Lebed, Nisenbaum, and Cope 1977).

Not all women who run a high risk of having defective children take advantage of such procedures. The tests are somewhat expensive. Some people may also be apprehensive about their dangers. With amniocentesis there is a slight chance of killing or deforming the fetus (McCauley 1976). Ultrasound is thought to be completely safe for both mother and fetus, but some observers worry that it has not been in use long enough to know whether it has any long-term ill effects (Palm 1979).

Concern has been expressed that these diagnostic procedures will be used just to select the sex of offspring—a use seen by some people as irresponsible and potentially antifemale inasmuch as male heirs are often considered more desirable. Others dislike any kind of "genetic engineering" because they think that we humans are not wise enough to be tampering with life-creating forces. And some parents believe that they have a responsibility to bear every child they conceive, defective or not.

On the other hand, there are many who believe it is irresponsible to bring defective children into this world. Many who think they are at high risk of having a defective baby would not dare to conceive without the options of fetal diagnosis and abortion of pregnancies found to be defective.

Rubella (German measles), sexually transmitted diseases, high fevers, and several rare diseases may be responsible for a variety of serious problems in the infant. Fortunately, many women are already immune to some of these; vaccines are available or being tested for some of the others.

Prenatal Medical Care

Doctors usually advise women to begin seeing health care professionals as soon as they think they are pregnant and throughout their pregnancy. This practice enables the care providers to diagnose the pregnancy, examine the mother's physical condition and blood and urine characteristics, assess her degree of risk for complications, keep track of her progress, advise her about health maintenance factors, intervene when problems threaten, and help her make arrangements for birth. Women thought to be at high risk of having defective babies may also choose fetal monitoring techniques, plus abortion if abnormalities are detected.

Prepared Childbirth Classes

A current idea is that the pregnant woman—not the doctor—should be the principal actor in pregnancy and birth scripts. Grantly Dick-Read's 1933 book *Natural Childbirth* emphasized that fear is what causes great pain during labor. He believed that this fear—and therefore much of the pain of birth—could be avoided if women knew what to expect during labor and were prepared by relaxation and exercise to meet it. French obstetrician Fernand Lamaze suggested that women could take an even more active role by responding to the stages of labor with breathing exercises they had practiced.

Prepared childbirth classes based on these ideas are now available throughout the United States. Through them pregnant women learn exercises to strengthen their pelvic floor muscles, relaxation techniques to keep other parts of their body loose while their uterine muscles work, and breathing techniques. These exercises and techniques help the woman relieve pressure on her abdomen, relax between contractions, control when necessary the urge to push the baby out, and give her something to think about other than the intense sensations of labor. She may also learn general conditioning exercises to help her carry the weight of the baby easily during pregnancy and push it out vigorously during childbirth. Women are encouraged to bring a companion (who will stay with and coach them throughout labor) to the classes to learn the techniques, too.

BIRTH DECISIONS

Giving birth can be an intensely emotional experience. For many women the final stages of labor and delivery are characterized by the same kind of breathing, vocalizations, facial expression, uterine contractions, abdominal muscle involvement, dropping away of inhibitions, extraordinary muscular strength, dulled sensory perceptions, and flood of joyful emotion as in orgasm. If the woman is physically and emotionally prepared for the birth, the exhilaration of the "pushing" stage of labor and the excitement of watching the baby appear can be an ecstatic, joyous transcending experience and a great boost to feelings of personal power.

Many people today are urging "natural" (unmedicated and awake) childbirth in nonhospital settings to make the event as personal and as meaningful as it can be. But there are some women for whom traditional hospital birth, perhaps with pain-killing drugs, remains a more appropriate choice. There is no one "right" way to have a baby. Exuberant, undrugged birth need not be seen as a performance standard—for like orgasm childbirth is not a performance but an experience.

Alternatives to hospital delivery are increasingly available. Many women still prefer to give birth with doctors, nurses, and modern technology on hand. In particular women who are thought to run a high risk of birth complications are usually advised to give birth in a hospital.

Stages of Labor and Delivery

Women typically begin labor with uterine contractions that are fifteen to twenty minutes apart and that gradually increase in strength and frequency. During this *first stage* of labor, the lengthwise muscles of the cervix are working to enlarge (*dilate*) and thin (*efface*) the opening of the cervix.

During this stage, which may last from two hours to a day or more, the health care practitioner in attendance periodically monitors the baby's life signs. When labor has advanced far enough that the

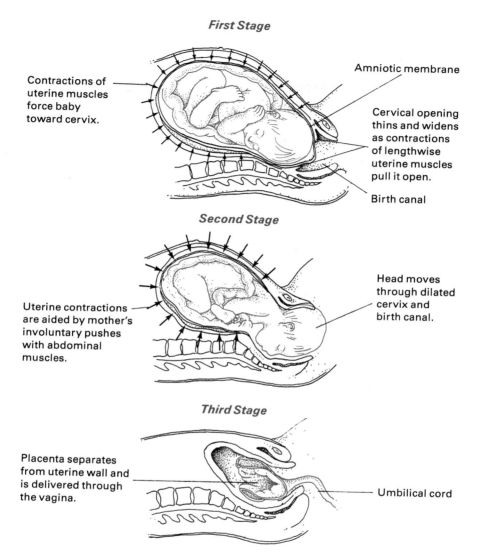

First Stage

Contractions of uterine muscles force baby toward cervix.

Amniotic membrane

Cervical opening thins and widens as contractions of lengthwise uterine muscles pull it open.

Birth canal

Second Stage

Uterine contractions are aided by mother's involuntary pushes with abdominal muscles.

Head moves through dilated cervix and birth canal.

Third Stage

Placenta separates from uterine wall and is delivered through the vagina.

Umbilical cord

baby's head begins to move through the dilated cervix into the birth canal, most women feel a tremendous involuntary urge to push, or bear down, with all their muscular strength. This period is the *second stage* of labor. It is usually much shorter than the first stage, and most women become more actively involved during this phase of the birth. Because they grimace with the strain of each push, onlookers often assume that they are in pain, when in fact such expressions may be as much the result of extreme physical and emotional concentration. Muscular, breathing, and relaxation exercises or

Figure 16-6. The Three Stages of Labor. During labor, the baby is slowly pushed toward and through the birth canal by intermittent contractions of the muscular uterus. *First stage* contractions thin and stretch the cervix in two ways: (1) by pulling it open and (2) by pushing the baby (encased in the amniotic membrane, which eventually ruptures) against it. The *second stage* of labor begins when the cervix is fully dilated to ten centimeters, large enough to allow the baby's head to pass through. At this point the mother feels the urge to push down with her abdominal muscles with each contraction. This action soon results in birth of the baby if it is in the normal position shown here. Other presentations, such as *breech* (buttocks-first) or *posterior* (head facing up rather than down), usually take longer and may require active assistance from birth attendants.

Lying on Side Increases comfort during sleep, labor, and perhaps childbirth; relieves pressure on perineum and major arteries.

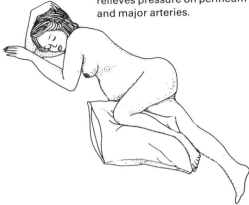

Sitting Up With heels together or legs crossed, helps to stretch the birth area; good for use throughout pregnancy and during the transition from first to second stage labor.

Squatting Opens the structures surrounding the birth canal; uses gravity to help move the baby downward during second-stage pushing.

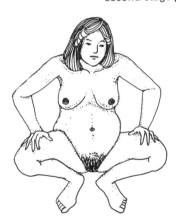

Semiseated Position

Helps to widen the pelvic structures; uses gravity to help deliver the baby; helps mother push effectively, especially if she holds her knees.

Figure 16-7. Alternative Positions for Labor and Delivery. Many pregnant women and health care practitioners are turning away from a practice that originated in seventeenth-century France: having the woman lie on her back during labor and delivery. This position puts undue pressure on important blood vessels, thereby diminishing the blood supply to the baby and parts of the mother. Women may choose instead to move around during labor; they can switch positions to stay comfortable and to actively cooperate with their body's efforts to deliver the baby. Some hospitals offer delivery tables with padded adjustable backs and footrests that allow a variety of semiupright positions; some have special birthing chairs. However, upright positions that help speed normal deliveries may cause problems in births that are already progressing very quickly.

medication can help women cope with the intensity of second stage labor.

As the woman begins to bear down, if she is in a hospital, she is typically brought to a delivery room, where she is placed on a table flat on her back with her feet held apart in stirrups. This traditional procedure is a necessity when the mother is medicated, but many hospitals have modified the procedure, for in a flat position gravity works against outward passage of the baby. If the woman is allowed to sit with her legs spread, she can push in the right direction more easily. If she squats, she can help the baby pass through by altering the position of her pelvic bones.

Accordingly, many birth settings have begun to accommodate the individual needs of the laboring woman. Depending on the progress of labor and comfort of the woman, various positions may be used throughout labor and delivery. For example, the woman may spend the early part of the second stage in a semiupright position and then, as the bearing down becomes more intense, be more comfortable lying on her side for delivery so that the baby exerts less pressure on her spine.

The second stage of labor ends when the baby is delivered and the umbilical cord is severed. During the *third stage* of labor, the placenta separates from the uterine wall. Uterine contractions continue until the placenta is expelled through the vagina, thus ending the three stages of labor.

Intervention Techniques

During the second stage of labor, the doctor may decide to make a small incision in the perineal tissue bordering the vaginal opening—an *episiotomy*—to

---

Nonviolent Childbirth

Most of us came rudely into the world. As soon as we cleared our mother's vagina, we were yanked upsidedown, spanked, and cut off from her life support system by immediate severing of our umbilical cord. After a thorough going-over by a doctor or nurse, we were perhaps fondled briefly by our mother—if she was awake for the birth—and then trundled off to a nursery with other newborns. If we could remember this experience, we might regard it as a shocking introduction to life outside the womb.

Many babies born today are being greeted more gently. Frederick Leboyer, a French obstetrician, has developed gentle techniques of delivery that are being adopted by some birth attendants in the United States. As babies are about to be born, lights are dimmed and voices hushed. Instead of being held by its heels and spanked to get its breathing started, the newborn is placed on its mother's abdomen and gently massaged. The umbilical cord is not cut until it stops pulsing. Then the baby is bathed in water warmed to body temperature.

Leboyer says these techniques are almost like making love to the baby. He recommends them as an antidote to the frightening upheavals of ejection from the womb:

Making love is the sovereign remedy for anguish: to make love is to rediscover peace and harmony. In the cataclysm of birth is it not fit that we should call upon this sovereign comfort?   [Leboyer 1975, pp. 63–64]

It is Leboyer's contention that babies who are terrified by traditional birth procedures will fear life from the start and perpetually try to protect themselves against it. By contrast to the screams of conventionally delivered babies, he claims that Leboyer babies are relaxed, alert, and sometimes even smiling. And follow-up studies show that at least in the first years of life, they continue to differ from other children. Leboyer-delivered children walk sooner, use their hands better, learn toilet training and self-feeding more easily, and show more interest in the world and other people than do children delivered by traumatic conventional methods ("Evidence of Gentler Babies" 1977).

Henry Davis, a family practitioner in Nevada who uses the gentle technique, asserts:

I'm convinced that the Leboyer method results in a better child, . . . I just can't say enough about it. These babies are so different from the others, so graceful in their movements. They seem to be reaching out instead of protecting themselves.   [Quoted in Braun 1975, p. 19]

Some physicians in this country hesitate to adopt Leboyer's methods because they fear infants won't begin to breathe properly. They think certain infants require stimulation to take their first breath, and a time delay may result in an inadequate oxygen supply reaching the brain. Also, the dimmed lights of the hospital room may prevent adequate assessment of the baby's color, which may be indicative of circulation problems. And the bath in some cases may result in a decrease in the baby's body temperature. According to one study (Nelson et al. 1980), it is the gentleness of the delivery rather than the specific techniques used that make a difference in the health of the mother and baby and in the baby's behaviors.

allow the baby's head to pass through without tearing the perineum. This procedure is sometimes necessary even though the stitched-up incision that results may cause the woman discomfort during the weeks after delivery and in rare cases even long-lasting numbness. If the doctor sews the incision too tightly—a procedure called "husband's knot" because it increases the vaginal grip on the penis—the tightness may make intercourse painful for the woman for some time. Many care providers are now avoiding the need for episiotomies by providing gentle massaging and stretching of the perineal area as the baby's head emerges.

If the baby has difficulty in coming out, the doctor may decide to use *forceps,* a metal tonglike device used to help extract the baby from the birth canal. Routine use of this procedure is becoming less common as it may cause discomfort and sometimes may damage both the mother's tissues and the baby's head. In recent years some doctors have switched to a suction-cup device—a *vacuum extractor*—applied to the baby's head.

If neither of these methods is judged adequate for a vaginal delivery and if monitoring devices indicate that the baby's life signs are slowing, the doctor may elect to deliver the baby by way of a *caesarean section*—that is, an incision in the mother's abdomen. The procedure is expensive major surgery, and the mother's recovery is much slower than in vaginal births. Nevertheless, caesarean deliveries were used for 18 percent of all births in 1980 (Cohen and Estner 1983). Controversy exists over whether the medical challenge, the increased use of fetal monitoring devices alerting physicians to fetal distress, or perhaps increased profits have made the procedure more common than it used to be.

Drugs

Several kinds of drugs may be given during labor or delivery. *Analgesics* decrease the sensation of pain. Among them are tranquilizers, narcotics, barbiturates, and general inhaled analgesics (such as ether). These drugs may help the mother relax between contractions, feel somewhat less pain from the contractions themselves, or go to sleep. But they will also be transmitted through the placenta and affect the fetus, with potentially harmful results. For instance, analgesics may seriously depress the infant's ability

to breathe and its responsiveness to cuddling and consoling (Aleksandrowicz and Aleksandrowicz 1974). Analgesics may even have negative effects on the mother. For example, tranquilizers may disrupt her ability to breathe properly during contractions and thereby cause her *more* pain (Boston Women's Health Book Collective 1976).

Anesthesia blocks pain by putting the mother to sleep (general anesthesia) or by inhibiting sensation in one part of the body (local anesthesia). General anesthesia slows down labor, so it's rarely given until birth is imminent. With local anesthesia dangers to the mother and fetus vary with location of the anesthesia. For instance, spinal anesthesia given to block sensation from the abdomen to the knees may cause a serious drop in the mother's blood pressure and, if administered improperly, may cause severe headaches and backaches after delivery. In the fetus it slows the heartbeat, decreases placental blood flow, and inhibits oxygen intake. A *pudendal block* that numbs only the vulva has the lesser effect of decreasing the newborn's oxygen intake during the first thirty minutes after birth.

Pitocin (oxytocin) may be used as well to induce or speed up labor. Sometimes there is some urgency about getting the baby out quickly. But inducing strong contractions before the mother's body is ready can be painful for her and perhaps dangerous for her baby.

Because all drugs carry risks for both mother and baby, women whose deliveries are proceeding normally without complications and who can cope with the contraction sensations would do well to avoid them. Over the past decade women and health care practitioners have become more reliant on breathing and relaxation techniques to reduce discomfort during labor and delivery.

Alternative Birth Settings

Women who think that they can cope with labor sensations on their own and who dislike the relatively impersonal nature of the traditional hospital delivery now have a number of alternative settings to choose from. In alternative birth settings many procedures used in hospitals are dispensed with as unnecessary when the mother is unmedicated and actively cooperating. Labors in these settings may be shorter, for traditional hospital routines are often so stressful to women that their labors slow down.

DOONESBURY

by Garry Trudeau

Alternative settings may also result in warmer affectional bonds among parents and children, for the mother and baby are not medicated or separated from other family members during the period after birth. Skin-to-skin cuddling during the first hours and days of the baby's life is thought to have a lasting positive effect on relationships among mother, father, and baby.

Consumer groups supporting alternative birth settings and procedures point out that hospitals and/or birth centers should be carefully analyzed before a choice is made. Many hospitals have added special beds and birthing rooms, but they are still not totally geared to a family-centered, wellness-oriented view of childbirth (Palm 1979).

Out-of-hospital birth settings should not be chosen by women who run a high risk of birth complications. These high-risk persons may include older women, teenagers, mothers who've had long labors or many babies in the past, women whose pelvic openings seem too small for the baby to squeeze through, sick women, and women with a history of placental abnormalities, premature births, and abnormal fetal positioning (Boston Women's Health Book Collective 1976). Furthermore, no woman should take on an active, independent birthing role in a nonmedical setting unless she feels quite comfortable with this decision; otherwise anxieties may hamper the progress of her labor.

Hospital-based Alternative Birth Centers.

Some hospitals now offer alternative birth centers within their own buildings. An effort is made to make the surroundings look more like a home than a hospital. Furnishings often include double beds, plants, stereos, rugs, and comfortable chairs. The mother may be kept company by anyone she chooses, including her other children if there's another adult present to watch them. Drugs are rarely used; if they are needed or if complications arise, the woman is usually transferred to the regular labor and delivery ward. Delivery takes place in the same room and the same bed. After birth the baby is left with its parents for cuddling rather than removed to a nursery. Within six to twelve hours the mother and baby usually leave for home. In Atlanta one hospital gives the new parents a candle-lit dinner with champagne before they leave.

Out-of-Hospital Birth Centers.

Birth centers outside hospitals offer a homelike atmosphere, family sharing of the birth experience, personal attention rather than routinized care, and basic nonsurgical emergency resources, without the sickness orientation of hospitals. Women are usually attended by nurse midwives, with physicians available for backup help. Women at high risk of complications or those who are not well prepared for childbirth are not admitted.

Home Births.

Some women choose to give birth at home in familiar surroundings, attended by a care provider (usually a lay midwife or nurse midwife) who stays with them throughout labor and delivery. The mother is free to walk around or use whatever positions she finds comfortable for labor and birth. No medication or intervention techniques are used. If complications develop, she is usually taken to a hospital. The care provider typically maintains a low profile, with the mother taking an active, responsible role in her own labor.

Circumcision

Increased questioning of traditional hospital practices for childbirth has also prompted a second look at routine circumcision of male babies. This operation to remove the foreskin (or *prepuce*) covering the glans of the penis is usually performed within a few days of birth. In the past parents chose circumcision either for religious reasons or on the assumption that it was a hygienic necessity. Now it appears that the latter assumption may not be true.

Some medical researchers now claim that whether the prepuce is present or absent has nothing to do with yeast infections of the penis (Davidson 1977). Cancer of the penis is statistically rare in both circumcised and uncircumcised men. It accounts for only 300 deaths a year in the United States. This cancer may be related to irritation from the smegma that collects behind the prepuce. If the prepuce is frequently rolled back and washed, smegma need not be a problem—or a reason for circumcision. And old studies that reported a relationship between noncircumcised men and cancer of the cervix in their female partners were methodologically flawed ("A Son's Rite" 1981).

If a baby is not circumcised at birth, problems such as infection of the prepuce or inability to retract it may eventually develop. These conditions may require circumcision at later ages when the operation is thought to be more painful and traumatic than at birth. And some doctors believe that circumcision should be done at birth if the opening in the foreskin is too narrow for the baby to urinate normally. However, these risks are so uncommon that in 1975 the American Academy of Pediatrics ruled that there are no valid medical reasons for routinely circumcising male infants. As they see it, the minor risks of not circumcising are outweighed by the disadvantages of potential complications from the operation (DuToit and Villet 1979).

Circumcision is performed without anesthesia (which would be dangerous for the baby) on the assumption that he doesn't feel it much. But babies undergoing circumcision often vomit, cry intensely, and then continue to have fitful sleep patterns and fussy crying for some time afterward.

Despite the fact that circumcision is no longer routinely recommended, 80 percent of American parents continue to request the procedure ("A Son's Rite" 1981). Some are skeptical of changes in medical opinion. Others choose circumcision for social and religious rather than medical reasons. Because the majority of males in the United States were circumcised at birth, some parents ask for it so their son will look like everyone else. A few believe that it's especially important for sons to look like each other or for a son to look like his father.

In spite of the persistent acceptance of circumcision by parents as a medical and social necessity, in recent years there has been a slight shift away from choosing circumcision. Parents who have had their babies delivered gently are especially likely to see circumcision as unnecessary (Chamberlain 1979). It remains for these parents and their medical advisers to put aside embarrassment about sex talk and instruct these uncircumcised boys in avoidance of health problems through careful washing.

Breast or Bottle Feeding

Another choice that goes into effect at birth is whether to give the baby milk from its mother's breasts or from a bottle. Although an estimated 95 percent of women are physically capable of breastfeeding, many choose not to. Whereas in the late 1920s about 80 percent of all first-time mothers nursed their babies, a change favoring bottle feeding occurred in the following decades (Rossi 1977).

The radical decline in breastfeeding is thought to have had several causes. One is vigorous promotion of prepared milk formulas and supplemental foods by commercial interests. Another is lack of support for breastfeeding from medical personnel.

A third reason is considered to center around a social taboo. Despite its biological function—milk production—the breast is defined as a potent sex symbol; aversion to its open use for nursing infants is often linked to general sexual embarrassment and dislike of nudity (Newton 1973). Fourth, the decline in breastfeeding is linked to the increased number of new mothers who return to work after the baby is born. Many companies find it inconvenient to provide on-site day care so that nursing mothers can breastfeed their babies every few hours.

Nevertheless, some mothers have persisted in their choice of breastfeeding. Mother's milk is more

Breastfeeding also helps the uterus return to its former shape and delays the return of menstruation (thereby augmenting, but not providing totally reliable, conception control measures). Another benefit is the emotional and sensual satisfaction it may give both mother and baby. Expectations that both mother and baby be clothed during nursing prevent spontaneous skin-to-skin loving; ideally nursing provides a time for caressing and enjoying each other, not merely an easy way of transferring milk to the baby.

Organizations such as La Leche League, a pro-breastfeeding group, have provided immeasurable support for new mothers who choose to breastfeed their babies. In 1978 the American Academy of Pediatrics recommended breastfeeding—an indication of a more positive attitude on the part of the medical community. In addition many hospitals now encourage breastfeeding by informing prospective parents of its benefits at prepared childbirth classes and by offering a number of other supportive options.

For example, some hospitals now encourage a new mother to breastfeed immediately after childbirth. Such early nursing helps stimulate production of prolactin, a hormone required for milk release. Many hospitals offer a "rooming-in" or "modified rooming-in" plan whereby a newborn spends its entire hospital stay (or selected parts) in its mother's room rather than in the nursery so that the mother may breastfeed on demand or whenever she and her baby find appropriate.

To counteract the persistent taboo on sensual touching between parents and children, a number of observers are now insisting that cuddly contact is essential to the formation of warm family bonds and the emotional and physical health of the infant (see, for instance, Montagu 1971 and Rossi 1977). Like breastfeeding, bottle feeding can also satisfy these needs, but only if the baby is lovingly held and cuddled, instead of being left alone in a crib with a propped-up bottle. Fathers may be as responsive to infants as mothers are (Chodorow 1978); bottle feeding may give them a special time for being close to their babies and for sharing parenting with the mother. Whether parents choose breast- or bottle feeding, they have the opportunity to mold in the child from birth the experience of loving as central to living.

Breastfeeding provides a time for loving and sensual joy for both mother and infant.

economical and more convenient than prepared formulas. It is highly nutritious and safe from spoilage in countries where bacterial contamination or lack of refrigeration is a problem. Advocates of breast milk further point out that it contains antibodies that help protect the baby from disease and that it has a distinct advantage if the baby shows allergic tendencies.

Summary

Those who enter pregnancy by choice rather than by accident may be influenced by many considerations: the values they place on having children and being parents, feelings about how having a child would affect their own relationship, willingness of the mother to be a single parent if she is unmarried, age factors, practical concerns about ongoing jobs and financial ability to raise a child, and concerns about population growth.

Conception, though an intricate and complex process, can occur over several days of the menstrual cycle because both sperm and egg cells remain viable within the reproductive tract for some time. Some couples experience great emotional and financial difficulty because any of a number of problems in either or both partners render their reproductive partnership infertile. In such cases medical intervention often helps create a pregnancy. By contrast, many pregnancies are unwanted. People have the choice of having the baby—and either keeping it, putting it up for adoption, or putting it in a foster home—or aborting the pregnancy. None of these choices is easy, and abortion is particularly subject to strong social pressures.

Pregnancy may be experienced in positive or negative ways. Sexual interest may decline as pregnancy progresses, but affectionate touching is often welcomed by both partners. The mother's emotions, diet, drug use, drinking, smoking, exposure to chemically harmful materials, prenatal care, and attendance—perhaps with her mate—at prepared childbirth classes all involve choices that can enhance the chances of health for her baby and herself. Before the birth careful consideration should be given to the use of drugs, new birthing techniques, and birth settings for labor and delivery, and whether to circumcise and breast- or bottle feed the baby.

17

Conception Control

Sure, using contraceptives is a bother, but I just can't get pregnant right now. We're not married, I'm going to school, and my parents would just die. So we try to be careful. We take turns using something—he buys condoms and I have a diaphragm, and I use foam with both of them. It's real important to get everything on, in, the right way, so we take time to help each other before we go too far. In fact, lots of times, putting these things on turns us on. I love the smell of his rubbers when we unroll them, and the pressure of his fingers checking to make sure my diaphragm's in straight drives me wild!

My wife used the pill for years, but I finally got tired of asking her to take all the risks. So I signed up for a vasectomy. It was a little more complicated than I expected, and I had to take it easy for about a week, but it was sure worth it. Now we both feel liberated!

I'm afraid of the pill and IUDs—I'm afraid they'd screw up my health, and I couldn't face going to a clinic to get them. Rick has condoms, but sometimes he runs out of them. Mostly we just try to keep track of my period and hope. I know there's some scientific way to figure out just when you could get pregnant, but I wouldn't mind too much if I did. Maybe then we could get married.   [From the authors' files]

In order for the human species to survive, it must reproduce. But people have been reproducing at an alarming rate. Although it took thousands of years to reach the world population mark of 1 billion, it has taken less than 200 years to quadruple that figure. The world's population is now rising by 150,000 people per day.

In many countries people are being born faster than they can be fed. On top of hunger problems, inadequately cared-for children strain society's helping services. For instance, the current epidemic of teenage pregnancies in the United States is placing a tremendous financial burden on welfare budgets. Consequently, conception is no longer an issue just between a man and a woman who engage in intercourse. It is an increasingly important social and political issue for countries all over the world.

In the United States most institutions are involved in conception control. The medical profession is intimately involved, as are the drug companies that manufacture mechanical and chemical contraceptive devices, the pharmacists and clinics that distribute them, the politicians who write and pass the laws regulating them, the government agencies (like the FDA) that police them, and the churches that sometimes prohibit them. These institutions often operate at cross-purposes. And they have failed to get at the heart of conception control: sex.

Because sex talk is still highly taboo, efforts to get people to use contraceptives when they have intercourse have been euphemistically labeled "family planning." Even literature passed out by population control advocates typically presents contraceptives as a means of limiting family size—rather than as a means of freeing people to enjoy sex without pregnancy, regardless of their marital status.

This issue is critical, for studies have shown that the way to sell the idea of contraceptives to the public is not so much to develop new contraceptives but to make more appealing the use of the ones we already have (Kantner 1979). Despite legitimate complaints that some contraceptive methods are unsafe or ineffective, some methods currently available are reasonably satisfactory on

The Language of Sex

Birth control, a term coined by Margaret Sanger, is defined as "the prevention of conception through contraception" (Guttmacher, Best, and Jaffe 1969, p. ix). This definition implies that conception and birth are synonymous, which is simply untrue. Birth is the act of bringing forth offspring: conception happens nine months earlier, when an egg is fertilized by a sperm cell, which triggers development of a baby. The methods presented in this chapter are attempts to prevent conception before it occurs or at least to block development of the early cell cluster into a fetus. Therefore it seems more accurate to call them methods of conception control.

both counts. But because talk of "family planning" has long been desexualized, we have no models for incorporating contraceptives erotically into sex and little social encouragement for distributing contraceptives to the group most likely to have sex without using anything: teenagers.

Sex-negative attitudes continue to prevent such an approach. For instance, in 1979 the director of the United States' major international population control aid program was demoted because of his advocacy of distributing condoms. The government's notion of a better idea: educating people to cut birthrates and plan family size (McCartney 1979).

In this chapter we'll focus on how various contraceptives work, how they're used, how well they prevent unintended pregnancies, what potential problems they may pose for sex or personal health, and how their use can be incorporated into sexual encounters. Such issues should be openly discussed between new as well as long-term partners. Methods are categorized as to whether they are used by the male or the female or both, are reversible or permanent, are currently available or still being researched. We'll also look at stages of contraceptive usage among young people and possibilities for reforming contraceptive services.

Table 17-1   First-Year Failure Rates of Birth Control Methods[a]

Method	Lowest Observed Failure Rate*	Failure Rate in Typical Users**
Tubal ligation	0.04	0.04
Vasectomy	0.15	0.15
Injectable progestin	0.25	0.25
Combined birth control pills	0.5	2
Progestin-only pill	1	2.5
IUD	1.5	4
Condom	2	10
Diaphragm (with spermicide)	2	10
Cervical cap	2	13
Foam, creams, jellies, and vaginal suppositories	3-5	15
Coitus interruptus	16	23
Fertility awareness techniques (basal body temperature, mucus method, calendar, and "rhythm"	2-20	20-30
Douche	—	40
Chance (no method of birth control)	90	90

*Designed to complete the sentence: "Of 100 women who start out the year using a given method, and who use it correctly and consistently, the lowest observed failure rate has been ____"

**Designed to complete the sentence: "Of 100 typical users who start out the year employing a given method, the number who will be pregnant by the end of the year will be ____"

[a]From *Contraceptive Technology 1982–1983,* by R. A. Hatcher and G. K. Stewart. Copyright © 1982 by Irvington Publishers. Reprinted by permission of the publisher.

REVERSIBLE MALE CONTRACEPTION

Traditionally, the male was responsible for conception control by using either withdrawal or the condom, two of the oldest contraceptive methods. With the advent of new methods for the female, the burden of responsibility for this concern has largely shifted from the male to the female. Nevertheless, condoms are experiencing a comeback. Since 1975, condom sales have been growing by 10 percent a year. In 1980 U.S. lovers were using over a million condoms a day (Castleman 1980)!

Ideally, men and women should share the responsibility for conception control. Around the world, one out of three people using a contraceptive method are men. An estimated 37 million use condoms, 35 million have had vasectomies, and many more practice withdrawal (Stokes 1980). The latter two methods will be discussed later in this chapter, as will research into male methods that are still in the experimental stage.

Despite the feeling of some women that they've been stuck with both the responsibility and risks of contraception, many men now are willing to share them. Condoms are second only to the pill in usage in the United States (Castleman 1980).

The Condom

The condom dates back as early as 1350 B.C., when Egyptian men wore condoms as decorative coverings for their penises. Condoms became popular for conception control and VD prevention in the eighteenth century but were outlawed by federal and state legislation by 1873 in the United States. In fact, only recently have laws banning the use of condoms been repealed throughout the United States. It wasn't until 1969 that a leading condom manufacturer's advertisement was accepted for publication in a national magazine (Brenner 1974).

Use.   A condom is a thin piece of latex rubber or animal skin shaped like the finger of a glove. It usually comes rolled up; when unrolled it measures roughly 7½ inches in length and 1⅜ inches in diameter. The condom fits over the man's erect penis to catch the sperm when he ejaculates. Thus it acts as a barrier to prevent sperm from getting to and fertilizing an egg.

The condom should be rolled onto the penis by either the man or the woman before he enters her vagina and must be left on until he withdraws.

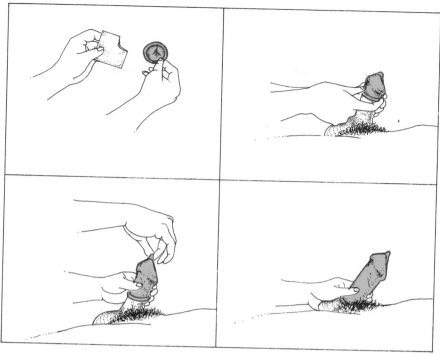

Figure 17-1. Condom Use. Condoms are sold in a variety of forms. One option is a condom with a teat at the end to make room for the semen when it's ejaculated. If a plain-ended condom is used, it should not be stretched too tight; a space of a half inch should be left between the tip of the glans and the tip of the condom to avoid possible breakage. The condom should be left sealed in its foil package until the male has an erection—it's hard to put a condom on a limp penis, and it won't fit properly once the penis has swollen anyway. Either partner can unroll the condom from the glans downward over the erect penis, squeeze the tip to release air from the space left at the end, and hold the condom against the penis to prevent spilling semen while withdrawing after intercourse.

How Effective Is Effective? —Theoretical versus Actual Use

Effectiveness may be a confusing issue because two measurements—theoretical effectiveness and actual-use effectiveness—may be applied to any method of conception control. *Theoretical effectiveness* is the statistic derived when a method is used according to instructions without any human error. *Actual-use effectiveness* is the statistic derived when a method is put to use by many people under normal circumstances. This actual-use figure includes both people who use the method without error and those who use it carelessly. The theoretical effectiveness of contraceptive methods will be higher than their actual-use effectiveness.

While he withdraws, one of them should hold the rubber ring at the end of the condom tightly to prevent spilling the contents and counteracting the contraceptive effect.

Some condoms have a "teat" on the end to catch the ejaculate. Condoms with plain ends must be unrolled so as to leave a half inch on the end for this purpose. Some condoms are prelubricated to prevent tearing and to ease insertion. Condoms that aren't prelubricated can be lubricated with K-Y jelly, spermicidal cream or jelly, or saliva. Vaseline should never be used as a lubricant, as it may irritate the vagina and cause the rubber to deteriorate.

In actual use condoms are about 90 percent effective in preventing pregnancy; their theoretical effectiveness is about 98 percent. When used in combination with a spermicidal foam in the woman, the actual-use effectiveness rate is almost as high as that of the pill (Hatcher et al. 1982).

Effects on Eroticism.   Some men claim that using a condom is "like taking a shower with a raincoat on" because it cuts down on stimulation to the penis. Modern condoms are made of very thin rubber to alleviate this complaint. Condoms made from lamb intestines, though expensive, feel more natural and increase stimulation to the penis. However, some men and women are allergic to them.

Noting that we may find caresses erotic no matter how many layers of clothing separate us from our partners, Michael Castleman points out that only "penis-preoccupied" men are bothered by the notion that condoms dull sensitivity:

Penis-preoccupied men who ignore whole-body sensuality often experience no-fun sex even if they never use a condom. But men who appreciate relaxed, whole-body lovemaking usually enjoy sensitive, problem-free sex whether they use a condom or not . . . . Lovers dull sensitivity, not rubbers . . . . Far from showering with a raincoat on, using a rubber is more like showering with a ring on one finger.   [Castleman 1980, p. 21]

People who have learned to associate the scent of a condom with sexual excitement may find even the smell of a newly opened condom a turn-on. Bringing out the package can be part of the fun, too, with either partner—or perhaps both—unrolling the rubber onto the male's penis and caressing the penis at the same time.

Condoms with special ribs to excite the vagina may be a waste of money, for women usually can't feel the ribs. But shaped condoms tapered to fit tightly behind the head of the penis stay on better than others—especially during female-on-top intercourse. A solution to the potential problem of the condom's lifting off: The male can grasp the base of the condom with his fingers, thereby providing extra stimulation for his partner's clitoris each time she thrusts.

Noncontraceptive Benefits.   Condoms can serve many useful purposes besides helping with conception control.

1. Condoms play a major role in preventing the spread of sexually transmittable diseases. When one partner has a sexually transmittable disease, using a condom during both vaginal and anal intercourse may help keep the disease from spreading to the other partner.

2. Men who suffer from premature ejaculation may find condoms helpful. Because of the decreased stimulation to the penis, a condom may help maintain an erection, delay ejaculation, and prolong intercourse.

3. In rare cases women may be allergic to their partner's sperm and/or semen. A condom can prevent these allergic reactions.

4. In some infertile couples desiring conception, antibodies have been found in the woman's body that cause her partner's sperm to stick together, rendering them ineffective to fertilize an egg. These couples may use condoms as an aid in preventing the release of sperm antigens into the vagina. This barrier lowers the amount of antibodies fighting the sperm after a few months, and conception becomes possible. These couples should stop using the condom during the woman's most fertile time.

5. Additionally, condoms may lower the anxiety some people feel about having intercourse while the woman is menstruating.

6. Finally, as Michael Castleman (1980, p. 21) points out, using a condom eliminates the perennial question, "Who's going to sleep on the wet spot?"

REVERSIBLE FEMALE CONTRACEPTION

Because women are the ones who get pregnant, they have long sought ways to prevent this often unintended outcome of sex. Some techniques have been passed on from generation to generation as folk methods to prevent pregnancy. They include douching immediately after intercourse, breastfeeding, and avoiding orgasm by the woman. These practices are unreliable in preventing conception. For instance, douching can drive some sperm further into the uterus, thereby giving them a better chance to fertilize an egg instead of washing them out. Breastfeeding may slow the return of ovulation, but because ovulation will occur before menstrual periods resume, a woman can get pregnant again before she even knows she's fertile. And conception can occur with or without the woman's orgasm.

The pill and the IUD have been in general use in the United States only since around 1960. They were hailed by many as the answers to conception control because they separated the act of conception control from the act of intercourse, thereby freeing men and women who didn't regard use of contraceptives as part of sexual fun. However, these new methods also posed problems, and sometimes they were life-threatening for some women. Many prefer to use the safer, though slightly less effective diaphragm. Other available options: cervical caps and spermicidal preparations.

The Pill

Many people once saw oral contraceptives for women as the final solution to conception control. A method had been invented to outsmart the hu-

man body: Fool the body into thinking it is already pregnant, and it will never get pregnant.

There are many different kinds of oral contraceptives. Combination birth control pills—the most commonly used kind—interfere with the menstrual cycle by introducing synthetic hormones (estrogen and progestin) into a woman's system to give her body false signals about her hormone levels. The pill introduces more estrogen into the body than it is accustomed to having at the beginning of the menstrual cycle. There is enough estrogen in the pill to block the usual hormonal message from the pituitary gland to the ovaries to begin ripening an egg. While a high level of estrogen is maintained in the body, ovulation is suppressed. The body is fooled into thinking that there is already an egg ripening, thus preventing one from actually being ripened.

Progestin, the synthetic progesterone in the pill, provides a vital backup to the elevated estrogen level. Progestin keeps the cervical mucus scanty and thick, thus acting as a barrier to any

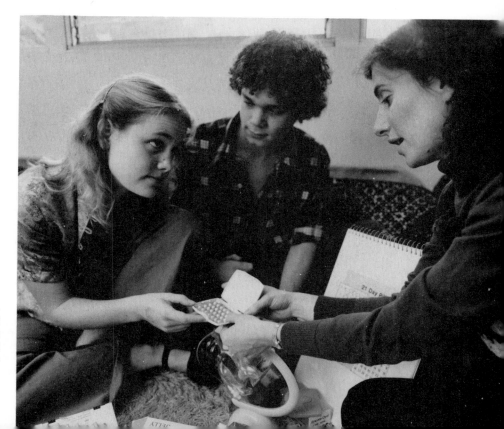

The Pill is one contraceptive method that does not have to be remembered at the time of intercourse, but one must still remember to take the pills as directed.

sperm. Even if sperm get through, progestin deters them from penetrating the cells surrounding the egg. And even if an egg has been fertilized, progestin keeps the uterine lining from developing properly, so the egg will not be able to implant on the lining of the uterus.

Because a woman who is on the pill does not ovulate, she does not have true menstruation. She has "withdrawal bleeding" brought about by withdrawal of the hormones. The lining of her uterus has been built up and thickened as a result of the hormones in the pill; when she stops taking the pill, the uterine lining, which is no longer receiving the hormonal message to prepare for pregnancy, sloughs off, thus simulating a menstrual period.

Use. The pill has been marketed in a variety of forms since it was first introduced in 1960. The *combination pill* combines estrogen and progestin in one pill for each of the twenty-one days that the pill is taken during the cycle. Sometimes an extra seven dummy pills (perhaps containing vitamins) are included in the pack so that women can get into the habit of taking one every day. Different combination pills have differing amounts of estrogen and progestin.

The *minipill,* marketed in the United States since 1973, contains small doses of progestin without any estrogen. One pill is taken every day. This progestin-only pill is slightly less effective than the combination pill, but it is also considered to be less harmful to the body. The actual long-term complications of the minipill are still being studied. ·

Pills should be taken about the same time every day so a constant hormonal level is maintained. Not taking a pill daily can return the menstrual cycle to its usual "receptive" pattern. Using backup conception control techniques at those "forgetful" periods can help avoid conception.

The high effectiveness of the pill in controlling conception accounts for much of its popularity. Actual-use effectiveness figures are about 98 percent for the combination pill. Progestin-only minipills have a slightly lower actual-use effectiveness rate, especially during the first months of use. Theoretical effectiveness of combination oral contraceptives is over 99 percent (Hatcher et al. 1982).

Potential Problems. The pill is popular, being used by about 8 million women in the United States and 50 to 100 million women in the world. Yet the pill carries potential dangers. About 40 percent of pill users have problems that range from the serious side effects of blood clotting and gallbladder problems to minor side effects such as weight gain and nausea (Hatcher et al. 1980). The side effects occur because the pill, through its hormones, influences the organ systems of the body.

Hormonal complications depend partly on the history of each woman. For example, the cardiovascular problems occur less among younger, nonsmoking women than among older women who smoke. Yet regardless of a woman's history, the estrogen in combination pills may encourage hypertension, headaches, periodic bloating, problems with fitting contact lenses, increased susceptibility to vaginitis, and a list of other side effects. Similarly, the progestin from the pill can cause side effects such as loss of hair, weight gain, breast tenderness, depression, and lower sexual desire (Hatcher et al. 1982).

Women with certain medical conditions are especially likely to develop dangerous side effects from pill use. Women with the following conditions are advised not to use the combination pill: malignancy of the breast or reproductive system (or history thereof), high blood pressure, liver dysfunctions, pregnancy, blood clots (or a history of them), severe vascular or migraine headaches, diabetes (or a strong family history of diabetes), age over thirty-five to forty (with greater risk if the woman is obese, hypertensive, a heavy smoker, diabetic, or high in cholesterol levels), undiagnosed abnormal vaginal bleeding, and sickle cell disease. There are also a number of less common conditions that make pill use unwise (Hatcher et al. 1982). Any woman considering using the pill should inform herself about all reasons that pill use may not be advisable for her.

Noncontraceptive Benefits. After years of publicity about the negative effects of pill use, new studies of currently available pills containing lower doses of estrogen and progesterone indicate that the pill is not so dangerous as was once thought and may in fact have a number of beneficial side effects. The pill is now thought to significantly *reduce* the risk of ovarian cancer, and cancer of the lining of the uterus—two benefits that may continue up to ten years after a woman stops taking the pill ("Study Cites Benefits . . ." 1982). It is also found to have a preventive effect on benign breast disease, ovarian cysts, pelvic inflammatory disease, ectopic pregnancy, iron-deficiency disease, and rheumatoid arthritis. It does not increase the risk of breast cancer. The pill also helps to lessen menstrual cramps and excessive menstrual bleeding and frees many from the pressure-inhibiting fear of pregnancy. Epidemiologist Howard W. Ory of the Centers for Disease Control concludes,

While it is quite clear that there are risks associated with pill use, they are heavily concentrated among women over 35 who smoke. But for the 90 percent of pill users who do not fall into this category, it would seem that the benefits of pill use far outweigh the risk. ["Birth Control Pill . . ." 1982, p. 2]

Intrauterine Devices

Another highly effective female contraceptive method is the intrauterine device (IUD). Because it is left in place for several years, it does not require daily remembering or interruptions to sex, which other conception control methods entail.

Use. Intrauterine devices are made of various materials and are formed into many shapes. At

Figure 17-2. Intrauterine Devices. Intrauterine devices are made of flexible plastic, sometimes with copper or progesterone added. A woman considering having an IUD inserted should discuss the pros and cons of available models with her health care practitioner beforehand. After being straightened for insertion, the IUD's "memory plastic" will resume its original shape in the uterus. Some IUDs are designed to flex somewhat within the uterus to adjust to changes in the shape of the uterine cavity.

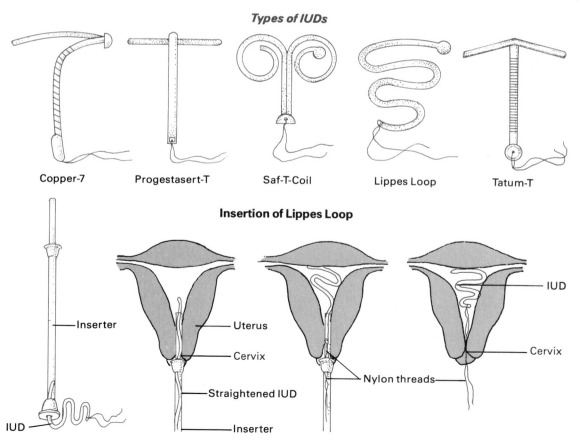

Types of IUDs

Copper-7   Progestasert-T   Saf-T-Coil   Lippes Loop   Tatum-T

Insertion of Lippes Loop

Inserter

IUD

Uterus

Cervix

Straightened IUD

Inserter

Nylon threads

IUD

Cervix

present most are made of flexible plastic so that each can be straightened out, put in an applicator, and inserted into the uterus. When the applicator is removed, the IUD returns to its normal shape. IUDs usually have one or two nylon threads attached to them, which hang down from the uterus through the cervix into the vagina. They enable the woman to check whether her IUD is in place. The IUDs themselves may contain copper or zinc; the Progestasert-T kind contains progesterone, which prevents the uterine walls from receiving an egg.

Although the effectiveness of IUDs is fairly high—90 to 96 percent effective in actual use, 97 to 99 percent effective in theory—and 60 million women throughout the world use them, the exact way in which they prevent pregnancy is not clear. But having an IUD in the uterus somehow prevents implantation of the egg into the uterine lining. It is therefore a contraceptive procedure that allows sperm to fertilize the egg but then prevents the egg from developing (Hatcher et al. 1982).

Potential Problems.   Side effects from using IUDs include increased chances of getting pelvic inflammatory disease (PID). In the United States women who use IUDs are twice as likely to develop PID as women who don't. In PID risk factors IUD use is in fifth place after having many sex partners, having intercourse more than five times a week, being under twenty-five, and being black ("PID Risk . . ." 1982).

Another concern with the IUD is the damage it does to the uterine walls or cervix. Cutting or perforation is reported in at least one per thousand users. This condition is not always easy to detect, because some cuts do not involve bleeding or even pain. Generally, symptoms of uterine perforation include pain, bleeding, and "disappearance" of the IUD strings.

Sometimes IUD strings may seem to become shorter, longer, or disappear altogether. Medical examination is important in such cases to determine whether the IUD has started to come out. Copper-7s have been particularly susceptible to string-related problems, partly because of the way they are inserted. To many clinicians, the Copper-T is a more attractive option than the Copper-7. Furthermore, if a woman does become pregnant

with an IUD either in place or partially expelled, she runs a risk of dangerous infection, spontaneous abortion, and ectopic pregnancy (Hatcher et al. 1982).

Cramping and pain often accompany the insertion of an IUD; they can also occur during IUD removal. Menstrual bleeding is often greater for IUD wearers; about 15 percent discontinue using IUDs owing to heavy menstrual bleeding or spotting at other times in their menstrual cycle. Another problem facing IUD users is spontaneous expulsion of the device, which happens in from 5 to 20 percent of users during the first year. A second contraceptive method is strongly recommended during the first three months of IUD use, because the device is most likely to be expelled during that time (Hatcher et al. 1982). Also, it is wise for women with IUDs to supplement their intake of iron for three months each year (Hatcher et al. 1982).

Judging from the known side effects, women with any of the following conditions should not have an IUD inserted: pregnancy; active pelvic infection; history of ectopic pregnancy; a single episode of pelvic infection if the woman desires a subsequent pregnancy; uterine abnormalities such as abnormal, heavy, or prolonged bleeding; cervicitis; an abnormal Pap smear; impaired response to infection; or impaired coagulation response (Hatcher et al. 1982).

The Diaphragm

Many women prefer to use a diaphragm rather than deal with risks to health. The diaphragm is a small rubber dome that holds spermicidal cream or jelly over the cervix and acts as a barrier to sperm. It ranges in size from 50 to 105 mm and comes in different rim types: coil spring, arcing spring, flat spring, and bow bend. The basic function is the same for all rim types; the different rim designs merely affect how the diaphragms are inserted. Correctly placed, the diaphragm fits inside the vagina up against the cervix. It covers the entire cervix, "hooking" behind the pubic bone in front and fitting behind the cervix in back. Diaphragms are not available over the counter, although the spermicidal creams or jellies that must be used with them are, and they must be fitted by a qualified physician or nurse practitioner.

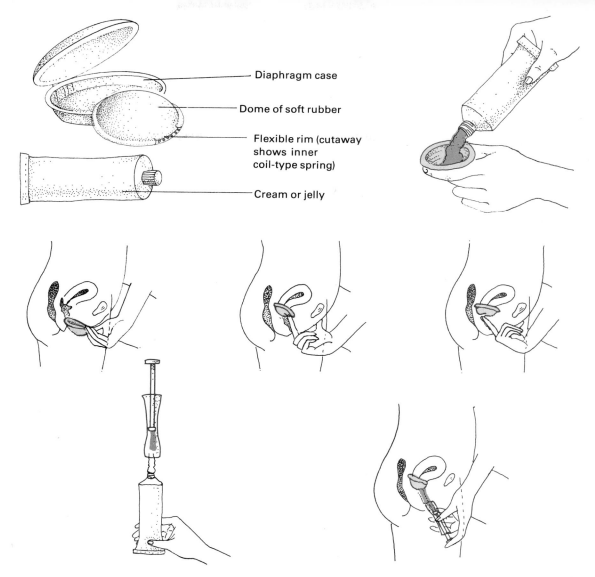

Diaphragm case

Dome of soft rubber

Flexible rim (cutaway shows inner coil-type spring)

Cream or jelly

Use. An important part of diaphram use is addition of a sperm-killing agent *(spermicide).* A table-spoonful of spermicidal cream or jelly (about three-quarters of an inch if it comes in a tube) is squeezed into the dome of the diaphragm on the side that will be against the cervix. The spermicide should be spread thoroughly to cover the entire dome. After the diaphragm is in place, additional spermicide can be inserted into the vagina with an applicator. The diaphragm should be inserted no more than two hours before intercourse and must be left in place for six to eight hours after intercourse. If intercourse occurs again within the six to eight hours, it is important to apply additional

Figure 17-3. Diaphragm Use. Before a diaphragm is inserted, a tablespoon of spermicidal cream or jelly should be squirted into the dome. Some can also be rubbed on the rim for lubrication if needed to make insertion easier, but some people think this procedure may cause the diaphragm to slip out of place. To insert the diaphragm, the woman can squat, lie down with her legs bent, or stand with one foot propped up while she or her partner squeezes the diaphragm in the center, jellyside up, and pushes it through the vagina toward the cervix. Here the vaginal walls flare, allowing the diaphragm to open. One partner should check to be sure that the diaphragm is firmly in place and that the cervix can be felt behind it. The spermicide's effectiveness declines after two hours; thus if a woman puts in her diaphragm long before she has sex, she or her partner should add more jelly or cream just before intercourse with an applicator inserted into the vagina.

371

spermicide with an applicator (*without removing the diaphragm*), because the spermicide is effective only up to six hours.

Either partner can insert the diaphragm—ahead of time or as part of sex. One of them should make sure that the diaphragm is in its proper place by reaching into the woman's vagina to feel the outline of her cervix (it should feel like the tip of her nose) through the rubber dome. The diaphragm can be removed (no less than six to eight hours after intercourse) by putting a finger or two behind the front rim and pulling down and out while bearing down with the abdominal muscles as if defecating. This procedure may take some practice, as the diaphragm may be held partially by suction, but once mastered it is quick and easy.

After use, the diaphragm should be washed with mild soap and water, rinsed, dried, and stored in its plastic container in a cool, dry place away from light. It can be dusted with cornstarch when stored. It should be checked for holes after each use. If handled and stored properly, a good-quality diaphragm can last for several years. However, doctors recommend replacing it every year or two, as the rubber may deteriorate or a woman's diaphragm size may change over time.

In a 1976 study of 2175 diaphragm users in New York, diaphragms were 98 percent effective in preventing pregnancy. These women were carefully fitted and taught how to use the method (Lane, Arleo, and Sobrero 1976). Actual-use effectiveness of diaphragms, however, usually ranges from 87 to 97.6 percent, according to various studies (Hatcher et al. 1982).

Effectiveness of the diaphragm depends largely on the effectiveness of the spermicide used with it, correct fit, proper care, and consistent use. Failure can occur 2 percent of the time even when the diaphragm is used correctly. Failure may be due to the diaphragm's slipping off of the cervix during intercourse (Boston Women's Health Book Collective 1976). Changing the size and varying the spermicide may improve effectiveness. The diaphragm should be fitted to the largest (most snug) size that the woman can tolerate (Hatcher et al. 1982). Because size may change as a woman gains or loses ten to twenty pounds, becomes pregnant, has an abortion, or for a number of other reasons, the fit should be checked regularly by a qualified clinician.

Potential Problems.   The diaphragm is probably one of the safest methods of conception control currently available. There are few side effects, and none are known to be serious or life-threatening. They are more likely a discomfort or a nuisance that will disappear if the rim type is changed or the woman stops using the diaphragm. One of these side effects is allergy or irritation from the spermicidal cream or jelly for one or both partners. This problem may be eliminated by changing spermicides. Women with allergies to latex rubber cannot use the diaphragm. Some women experience pelvic pain, cramps, and aggravation of recurrent cystitis. If change in rim types does not alleviate these problems, use of the diaphragm may have to be discontinued.

A foul-smelling vaginal discharge may result if the diaphragm is left in place too long. This problem will occur with any foreign body in the vagina and can be prevented by removing and cleaning the diaphragm every day (Hatcher et al. 1982). The same caution holds true for the two cases of toxic shock syndrome that have been linked to wearing a diaphragm for two or three days ("Diaphragm, Toxic Shock . . ." 1981). Vaginitis, too, may develop if the diaphragm is not carefully washed and dried between uses. Having two diaphragms and using them alternately allows each to dry after use (Hatcher et al. 1982).

Some people complain that diaphragm use is messy because of the spermicidal cream or jelly that must be used with it. Also, the taste of the spermicide may be offensive in oral sex. If an excess amount of spermicide is used because of repeated intercourse, the male can use a condom to reduce the need for excessive amounts of spermicide.

Noncontraceptive Benefits.   Like the condom, a diaphragm plus spermicide is thought to offer some protection against sexually transmitted diseases (Hatcher et al. 1982). Additionally, the diaphragm is useful for women who want to have intercourse during their menstrual period. By holding up to twelve hours of menstrual discharge, diaphragms prevent menstrual flow from interfering with enjoyment of intercourse (Boston Women's Health Book Collective 1976).

The diaphragm is also a good educational tool that puts women in touch (both literally and figuratively) with their bodies. For women who intensely dislike touching their genitals, using a diaphragm may be an unpleasant experience, but it may be one worth going through, for the more attuned a woman is to her body, the more likely she'll enjoy sex.

The Cervical Cap

The cervical cap, or pessary, is a small cuplike device that fits snugly over the cervix and is held in place by suction. Although highly popular in the nineteenth century, particularly in Europe, the cervical cap was gradually replaced by the larger diaphragm, which was thought to be more effective.

Recent modifications in design appear promising for revival of the cervical cap. One such modification is the development of a custom-made cap through a process similar to the fitting of dentures. Developed by Robert A. Goepp, a dentist and professor of oral surgery at the University of Chicago Medical School, this cap also contains a one-way valve allowing the downward flow of vaginal discharges but no upward flow of sperm. Preliminary results show this device to be comfortable, convenient, and effective (Seligmann 1979).

Use.   Cervical caps are made of rubber or plastic. They can be left in place for several days or can be put in and taken out as needed, like a diaphragm. Some health care practitioners advise leaving the cervical cap in place no longer than twenty-four hours at a time, in order to avoid potential inflammation of the cervix (Littman 1980). As with the diaphragm, caps must remain in place at least six to eight hours following intercourse. The cap is held in place by suction and works as a barrier method of conception control, with a small amount of a spermicide added for extra protection.

Current effectiveness data are limited. However, the Medical Committee of the Planned Parenthood Federation of America decided in 1972 that the cervical cap is "about as effective as the diaphragm" (Seaman and Seaman 1978, p. 234). The cap's effectiveness depends on its proper placement to form a suction seal, hence careful fitting and instruction in its use are essential.

Potential Problems.   Although quite popular in England, cervical caps are available in the United States only through a few health centers that have special licenses. In addition to its limited availability, the cervical cap is not suitable for women with deep cervical cysts or lacerations. It should not be fitted when a temporary infection is present but can be prescribed when the infection has cleared. Some physicians have rejected the cervical cap because of fears that it could cause erosion of the cervix (Seaman and Seaman 1978). And contrary to women's hopes that cervical caps would be a safe and effective barrier they could insert and then forget about for several days, having sex spontaneously any time during this period, current findings about toxic shock syndrome suggest that anything obstructing the normal flow of fluids from the uterus for more than several hours at a time is potentially harmful. It is not yet known whether the one-way valve type of cap alleviates this concern (Tatum and Connell Tatum 1981). Furthermore, cervical caps are harder to insert and remove correctly than diaphragms, and are no more effective (Hatcher et al. 1982).

Spermicidal Agents (Creams, Jellies, and Foams)

Spermicidal agents contain a chemical that kills sperm and an inert base—either foam, cream, or jelly—that holds the spermicide against the cervix. Its function is twofold. First, the foam, cream, or jelly acts as a mechanical barrier to sperm. Second, the spermicide acts chemically to slow down and kill sperm. Spermicidal creams and jellies are designed to work in conjunction with diaphragms or condoms, and that's how they work best. Contraceptive specialists do not recommend the use of creams or jellies without a diaphragm or condom, because used alone, creams and jellies have an actual-use effectiveness of only 70 to 78 percent (Hatcher et al. 1980). Spermicidal agents can be purchased over the counter in drugstores. They are readily available and relatively low priced.

Use.   Spermicidal foams are either inserted deep into the vagina with an applicator or placed there in the form of tablets or suppositories that melt at body temperature. Again, unless used with a condom, the actual-use effectiveness of foam is similar to that provided by creams and jellies—about 78 percent. However, when the woman uses foam and the man uses a condom, this combination is 95

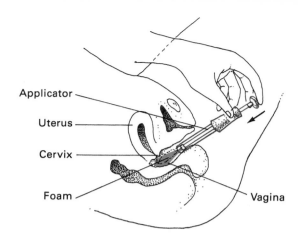

Applicator

Uterus

Cervix

Foam

Vagina

Figure 17-4. Spermicidal Agents. Either partner can insert spermicidal foam, jelly, or tablets into the woman's vagina. Here, foam from an aerosol can is used to fill a clear plastic applicator, which is then inserted deep into the woman's vagina with the tip aimed toward the small of her back. Depressing the plunger releases the foam. These chemical agents should be combined with a barrier method—such as a condom, diaphragm, or cervical cap—for maximum protection against pregnancy. The combination of foam in the woman and condom on the man is one of the most effective ways of preventing pregnancy.

percent effective (in actual use) in preventing pregnancy (Hatcher et al. 1980).

Spermicidal cream, jelly, or foam should be inserted into the vagina no more than fifteen minutes before intercourse; suppositories *must* be inserted about fifteen minutes before intercourse to fully dissolve. The spermicidal effects diminish within two hours after application, so additional applications are necessary if intercourse is repeated. The woman should not douche until at least six to eight hours after intercourse, as sperm may live for some time after they come in contact with the spermicide. Inserting the foam, cream, or jelly can be incorporated into sexmaking, with partners sharing the responsibility and the fun. Unless this is done carefully, though, the method may not work.

Potential Problems. Some creams and jellies tend to irritate the male and/or the female during intercourse. Changing to a different brand may eliminate this problem. Unfortunately, since it is generally the stronger, more effective creams and jellies that tend to irritate, when we change brands we may sacrifice some effectiveness (Boston Women's Health Book Collective 1976). Oral sex may be unpleasant when genitals are smeared with spermicides. One way around this problem is to have oral sex first and then apply the spermicide if intercourse is desired.

Noncontraceptive Benefits. Spermicides not only kill sperm but also inhibit the transmission of gonorrhea and trichomoniasis between partners and provide extra lubrication for intercourse (Hatcher et al. 1982).

AFTER-THE-FACT METHODS OF CONCEPTION CONTROL

Every time a woman has unprotected intercourse during the middle of her menstrual cycle, she has somewhere between a 2 percent and a 30 percent chance of getting pregnant (Hatcher et al. 1982). This fairly high risk leads some women to seek protection after the fact. Three methods are currently in use: the "morning-after" pill, morning-after insertion of the Copper-7 IUD, and menstrual extraction. All three methods are reportedly highly effective in preventing conception.

The Morning-After Pill

Diethylstilbestrol (DES) pills can provide conception control for a woman who has unprotected intercourse at midcycle. The FDA warns, however, that DES should be used only as an emergency measure. A woman who chooses DES must begin taking it within seventy-two hours of intercourse, 25 mg of DES twice a day for five days. This large dose of synthetic estrogen sends a hormonal message to the pituitary gland that the woman is already pregnant.

Since the morning-after pill is a massive dose of synthetic estrogen, it carries the risk of serious side effects. A woman who takes it may experience extreme nausea and vomiting. And her future children may be harmed, too. Genital abnormalities and infertility and in women, cancer, have been reported in some whose mothers were exposed to DES, which was used extensively in the past to prevent miscarriages.

Alternative morning-after pills are now available. One combines an estrogen and a progestin; two contain high doses of progestins only. It is not yet known whether these doses are harmful to the woman or to her offspring if she does become pregnant (Hatcher et al. 1982).

Morning-After Insertion of the Copper-7 IUD

Another option is insertion of a Copper-7 IUD as soon after unprotected intercourse as possible. The Copper-7 IUD is the only IUD whose after-the-fact effectiveness has been demonstrated. Other IUDs are probably equally effective, but their effectiveness hasn't been reported yet. Copper-7 IUDs probably work by preventing implantation of an egg that may have been fertilized during unprotected intercourse. If left in, the IUD will also provide future conception control. However, it also carries the complications sometimes associated with IUD use. If a woman is at high risk of PID, the IUD can be removed after she has had one or two normal menstrual periods (Hatcher et al. 1982).

Menstrual Extraction

Menstrual extraction is similar to a vacuum abortion. It is performed in a doctor's office a day or so after the woman's menstrual flow is clearly overdue. This procedure is really an early abortion that is done before a woman can know for sure that she is pregnant. For some women a menstrual extraction sidesteps the moral dilemma of deciding whether to have an abortion.

A menstrual extraction device, if marketed widely, could allow women to end their own periods as soon as they start, thereby terminating any pregnancies in the process. This practice would make other forms of conception control unnecessary. In theory, at least, women would be freed from both menstruation and pregnancy. But incomplete extractions and infections have some-

times been reported. Ellen Frankfort (1978, p. 268) warns that "at the very least, introducing foreign parts every month to a germ-free area like the uterus raises serious medical questions about infection."

SHARED METHODS

The preceding sections described male and female methods of contraception control that can work successfully when individuals practice them alone—though they can involve the cooperation of both partners. Responsibility for buying and applying the condom, diaphragm, and foam, for example, can be shared. Some people who choose these methods agree to take turns being the one to use something when they have sex. And sometimes both partners use something, such as a condom on his penis and foam in her vagina. Instead of regarding their use as a bother, partners could redefine their contraceptives as sex toys.

Aside from sharing mechanical methods of contraception control, there are three other ways in which some people actively cooperate to prevent conception: abstinence from intercourse, withdrawal, and what is sometimes known as "natural" contraception.

Abstinence from Intercourse

Abstinence can be practiced by anyone at any time. It costs nothing. It is theoretically 100 percent effective. It is free from physiological side effects. Some people choose to abstain from sex altogether at some points in their lives. Abstinence from intercourse does not necessarily mean total abstinence from sex. There are many ways to enjoy sensual pleasures and orgasm without having intercourse. Anything but intercourse may be enjoyed. For instance, oral or manual stimulation of the genitals can be as satisfying—or even more so, for some people—as intercourse. (It is important to remember that sperm that end up near the vagina can move inside and produce pregnancy even when intercourse has not occurred, so care should be taken not to let that happen.)

Withdrawal

Coitus interruptus, or withdrawal, is probably the oldest method of conception control. It costs nothing and requires no preparation and no special devices: The man simply withdraws his penis from the woman's vagina just before he ejaculates. The idea behind withdrawal is that if no sperm are ejaculated into the vagina, the woman cannot possibly get pregnant. This idea may seem reasonable and might work if sperm were released only during ejaculation. But sperm are contained in the drops of fluid that come out of the penis before ejaculation, and these sperm can fertilize an egg.

Successful withdrawal also requires considerable effort and coordination by a couple. At impending orgasm a male may plunge for deeper penetration and not be able to withdraw "in time" even if he wants to and even if the female tries to tell him, "Don't come in me!" This possibility can negate pleasure by turning participants into anxious spectators and cutting short the woman's orgasmic enjoyment.

Withdrawal has an actual-use effectiveness rate of about 77 percent (Hatcher et al. 1982). Stated differently if 100 couples used withdrawal as their only contraceptive method, 23 of the women would become pregnant by the end of one year. Withdrawal is more effective in preventing pregnancy than using nothing at all, but not much more so.

"Natural" Contraception

The term *natural contraception,* or *natural family planning,* refers to fertility awareness methods of conception control that rely on no chemicals, mechanical barriers, or synthetic hormones. Natural sex methods are based on timing abstinence from sexual intercourse during the days when a woman is most likely to be fertile. This fertile time, around ovulation, changes from woman to woman and even from month to month in the same woman, so calculating the exact time of ovulation can be tricky.

A woman can calculate her fertile (unsafe) and unfertile (safe) days by using the calendar method (rhythm), the basal body temperature method (BBT), the cervical mucus method, or the symptothermic method (a combination of the BBT and the cervical mucus methods). The rhythm method is the oldest and probably least reliable of these natural methods and is largely being replaced by

the others. These methods cost nothing, are safe to the body, and require no medical intervention. They are being adopted by some women who for religious or medical reasons are uncomfortable with other methods. They are also being used in reverse by couples who *want* to conceive, for they help indicate the woman's most fertile time. Fertility awareness can also be used with other forms of contraception to increase their effectiveness.

Rhythm.   The rhythm method is a fairly elaborate calculation that makes predictions about a woman's future menstrual cycles based on her past ones. The first day that a woman is likely to be fertile is calculated by taking the length of her shortest menstrual cycle and subtracting eighteen days from it. Likewise, by subtracting eleven days from the length of her longest cycle, she can determine the last day on which she is fertile. Using only the rhythm method for conception control, a couple must abstain from intercourse from the first fertile day to the last fertile day of the woman's cycle. The longer the time between the woman's shortest and longest cycles, the more potentially fertile days there are. Even if a woman is perfectly regular (that is, her shortest and longest cycles are equal), she will have seven unsafe days each month.

The Basal Body Temperature Method.   The basal body temperature (BBT), the lowest temperature reached by the body of a healthy person during waking hours, can be used to calculate the time of ovulation. According to this method, the BBT drops about 0.2° F just before ovulation. Somewhere between twenty-four and seventy-two hours later, there is a distinct rise in temperature, signaling the beginning of ovulation. The temperature remains elevated about 0.6° F to 0.8° F above the normal BBT. Unprotected intercourse must be avoided from the time the woman's temperature drops until her temperature has remained elevated for three consecutive days. The BBT must be determined immediately on waking every morning, before getting up and moving around, and before eating and drinking. The woman must be cautious of temperature fluctuations caused by other factors, such as sickness, use of electric blankets, or change in sleeping habits (Hatcher et al. 1980).

The Cervical Mucus Method.   Cervical mucus changes from dry after menstruation, to very slippery during ovulation, almost like raw egg white, to dry again after ovulation ends. The mucus becomes thin and slippery during ovulation to create a more friendly environment for sperm, helping them on their journey to fertilize an egg. The cervical mucus method uses these changes in the consistency of cervical mucus to predict time of ovulation and calculate unsafe and safe days. A woman can check her cervical mucus by wiping herself with toilet paper before she urinates (several times a day) and observing the changes. She must not douche, or she will wash away exactly what she is trying to observe. She must also not confuse the mucus with other vaginal discharges created by infection, seminal fluid, or sexual arousal.

The Symptothermic Method.   The symptothermic method combines the BBT and cervical mucus methods to obtain a somewhat more reliable indicator of ovulation but one that is still "relatively ineffective for preventing pregnancy," according to the World Health Organization (Hatcher et al. 1982, p. 128).

Effectiveness of "Natural" Contraception Methods.   Actual-use effectiveness figures are about 75 percent for the mucus method only, 79 percent for rhythm only, 80 percent for BBT only (Hatcher et al. 1980), and 78 to 84 percent for the symptothermic method (Hatcher et al. 1982).

Potential Problems.   The main potential problem of natural contraception is pregnancy. Natural methods should probably not be used by women who have very irregular menstrual cycles. Particularly with the rhythm method, accurate calculation of safe and unsafe times is much more difficult when based on highly irregular cycles. In addition sometimes ovulation may be *triggered* by intercourse, posing risks of pregnancy throughout the menstrual cycle. And the fact that waiting sperm may survive up to six days in the woman's reproductive tract greatly lengthens the time during which couples must abstain from intercourse. According to World Health Organization studies, most accidental pregnancies in couples using natural methods of contraception result from intercourse during the period *preceding* ovulation (Hatcher et al. 1982). Frustration may be a side effect for unimaginative couples who feel that abstinence from intercourse means total abstinence from sex.

STERILIZATION

Sterilization is a process that permanently ends fertility in a man or woman without interfering with ability to enjoy sexual intercourse. The decision to be sterilized is a serious one because it alters an important bodily function—reproduction. Even so, sterilization is an increasingly popular method of contraception control for people who have decided that they have enough children and who want to make absolutely sure that they don't have any more. Some 14 million American men and women had been sterilized by the end of 1981 ("U.S. Sterilization . . ." 1982); sterilization has become the world's most common conception control method ("Report Calls . . ." 1981).

Male Sterilization

Sterilization can be achieved through two methods in the male: castration and vasectomy. Castration is the removal of both testicles, which may render the male impotent and cause other undesirable side effects. It is only performed when a serious disease, such as cancer of the testicles or prostate, threatens life. Vasectomy, on the other hand, is a relatively minor, out-patient procedure that cuts the vas deferens, the duct that carries sperm from the testicles to the penis, thus rendering the man sterile but leaving the testicles intact so there is no subsequent physiological sexual dysfunction.

As part of the vasectomy procedure, the man's scrotum is shaved and painted with an antiseptic solution, and a local anesthetic is administered to the area. A small incision is then made into the scrotum; the vas deferens from each testicle is isolated, tied, and cut; and the incision is sutured. The complete operation takes no more than fifteen to twenty minutes, and after a brief recovery time the patient can walk out of the examination room and go home.

The man should not shower or bathe for the

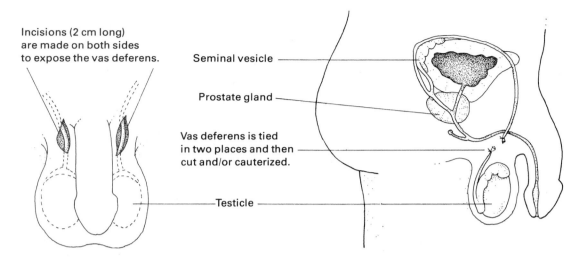

Incisions (2 cm long) are made on both sides to expose the vas deferens.

Seminal vesicle

Prostate gland

Vas deferens is tied in two places and then cut and/or cauterized.

Testicle

Figure 17-5. Vasectomy. In a vasectomy one or two small incisions are made in the upper scrotum to reveal the two vasa deferentia. These tubes are then cut and tied or cauterized to keep sperm produced in the testicles from being ejaculated through the penis. The volume of the ejaculate is diminished only slightly, because 95 percent of the seminal fluids come from the seminal vesicles and the prostate gland, which are unaffected by the operation.

first two days following the vasectomy, but baths are recommended after that time to aid in healing. He may resume sexual intercourse usually after two to three days. A second method of contraception should be used for the first two to three months after the vasectomy, as some viable sperm remain in the vas deferens after the procedure. After two negative sperm counts, usually two and three months after the vasectomy, the additional method of contraception can be eliminated. Research is being done to see whether irrigating the vas deferens with several chemical substances after vasectomy can eliminate the viable sperm. Preliminary results show immediate sterility can be achieved by using certain chemicals (Kamat, Bharucha, and Sankholkar 1978). Vasectomy is effective 99 + percent of the time. In rare cases the vas deferens reconnects, and the procedure must be performed again (Hatcher et al. 1982).

Vasectomy should be considered a permanent procedure. New techniques using microsurgery are having some success with reversing the effects of the vasectomy. This surgery is an involved process that takes more than two hours and requires several days of recuperation in the hospital. However, reattaching the vas deferens does not guarantee fertility. The success rate for pregnancy ranges between 18 and 60 percent (Hatcher et al. 1982).

Compared with other methods of contraception, physical complications from vasectomy are

infrequent, short lived, and minor. Of 843 vasectomy patients in one study, less than 6 percent reported complications (Penna, Potash, and Penna 1979). Occasionally the vas deferens will rejoin, necessitating a repeat of the surgical procedure. Commonly there is discomfort either before, during, or immediately following the first ejaculations after the operation. Infection, swelling, and inflammation are the most common side effects (Hatcher et al. 1982).

One-half to two-thirds of all men who have vasectomies develop sperm antibodies following the operation. This effect is known as an "autoimmune" response. Limited studies, mostly on animals, have linked this response after vasectomy with orchitis (an inflammation of the testes) and atherosclerosis (a disease characterized by fatty deposits in the arteries leading to the heart and brain), but a large-scale, long-term comparison of vasectomized and nonvasectomized men shows no significant differences in the incidence of cardiovascular problems or other diseases ("Longitudinal Study Supports . . ." 1983).

Some men have psychological problems with the idea of vasectomy. They may be nervous about any surgical tampering with what has been defined as a central part of their anatomy. And some have learned to define the ability to sire children as a sign of masculinity. By this definition vasectomy is an attack on their manhood. Others equate virility with fertility and fear that vasectomy will make them impotent. In reality the only effect the operation has on sex is to reduce the volume of semen slightly.

Those men who choose vasectomy typically go through a six- or seven-stage process that may take two to ten years, according to Stephen Mumford of the International Fertility Research Program. They become aware of vasectomy, discuss it with someone who's had one, decide to have no (more) children, begin to think seriously about vasectomy, reject temporary contraceptive methods as unacceptable, decide vasectomy is the best thing for them, and then perhaps get a scare when their partner misses a period or has serious side effects from using some other form of conception control ("How Men Choose . . ." 1983).

The millions of men who have undergone this operation have demonstrated their willingness to accept their share of the risks and responsibilities of conception control. But no one should be forced to have a vasectomy he doesn't want. Also, many couples may want to share in this decision because it has consequences for both in terms of childbearing.

Female Sterilization

Slightly more women than men in the United States choose to be permanently sterilized. The ratio in 1981 was 52 percent women, 48 percent men ("U.S. Sterilization . . ." 1982). Experts think that more women choose the procedure because they are the ones at risk of pregnancy and they want to be permanently protected; some men fear that having a vasectomy would hurt their sexual "performance," despite assurances to the contrary ("Why Do Females . . ." 1982). The decision nevertheless affects both in a partner relationship, and a woman may want to involve her partner in weighing the costs and benefits of permanent conception control.

There are two methods of female sterilization:

tubal ligation and hysterectomy. Tubal ligation involves tying or cutting the fallopian tubes so that mature eggs are prevented from traveling into the tubes to be fertilized. After a tubal ligation the woman will continue to have normal menstrual periods until she reaches menopause because her body is still receiving the same hormonal messages and she still has a uterus. Hysterectomy is a much more serious operation involving removal of the uterus and cervix and, in some cases, the ovaries. There is instant cessation of the menstrual period because there is no longer a uterus whose lining sloughs off monthly.

Tubal Ligation.   Tubal ligation—"having your tubes tied"—provides immediate protection from unwanted pregnancy. In most cases the woman can return home the day of the operation, and there are few complications or side effects. Between 85 and 89 percent of tubal ligations performed between 1970 and 1975 in the United States were performed on women who were married at the time of the operation. Forty-five percent of these women were younger than age thirty (Cohen 1979).

In tubal ligations each tube is tied, then cut or cauterized, making it impossible for an egg to leave the ovary and travel down the fallopian tube to be fertilized. There are several different techniques. Some, such as the culpotomy and culdoscopy, involve a vaginal entry to reach the fallopian tubes. These procedures produce no visible scars. Others, like the laparoscopy and the minilaparotomy (which can be performed under local anesthesia), utilize small abdominal incisions. Tubal ligation is almost 100 percent effective (Hatcher et al. 1982).

In a new technique awaiting federal approval, liquid silicone plugs are squirted into each fallopian tube. This inexpensive procedure can be performed in a doctor's office under local anesthesia and is theoretically reversible without surgery. However, there is as yet no evidence that the plugs can be removed, restoring fertility ("Sterilization Method" 1982).

About 1 percent of women who have had their tubes tied later ask to have the operation reversed so that they can bear children. New techniques using clips and elastic rings rather than cutting or cauterizing the tubes enhance the possibility of microsurgically reversing the process. About 10 to

Traditional Tubal Ligation

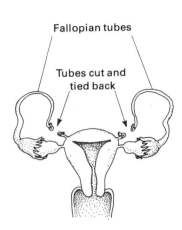

Fallopian tubes

Tubes cut and
tied back

Laparoscopy

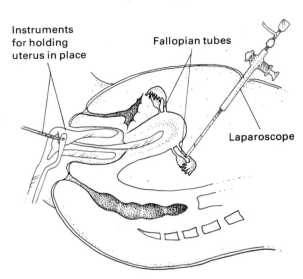

Instruments
for holding
uterus in place

Fallopian tubes

Laparoscope

Figure 17-6. Two Methods of Tubal Ligation. There are numerous surgical methods of blocking or cutting the fallopian tubes to prevent the passage of eggs from ovaries to uterus. Shown here are the traditional tubal ligation, which involves a rather large abdominal incision, and laparoscopy, done with one or two smaller incisions. In the single-incision laparascopy shown here, a lighted laparoscope is used to allow the surgeon to see the internal organs and also to introduce an instrument that cauterizes a section of each fallopian tube. Alternative methods gain access to the fallopian tubes through the vaginal wall or the uterus.

50 percent of women with operations to "untie" their tubes have been able to get pregnant (Hatcher et al. 1982). But the reversal operation is major surgery; tubal ligation is not yet easily reversed and should still be considered a permanent, voluntary decision.

The chance of complications from tubal ligation depends on the skill of the surgeon. Complications include hemorrhage, bowel trauma, and failure of the procedure to work. As with any medical procedure involving anesthesia and surgery, tubal ligation carries a slight risk of death. Short-term side effects include pain around the incision, shoulder and chest pain, and pelvic ache or discomfort. The woman is advised to leave her schedule flexible for the week following a tubal ligation to allow recovery time from the anesthesia and surgery (Hatcher et al. 1980).

Hysterectomy. The advisability of using hysterectomy, the operation that removes a woman's uterus, as a sterilization procedure is controversial. Hysterectomy has been used as a form of sterilization by some gynecologists who think that "in the woman who has completed her family, the uterus is rather a worthless organ" (S. Morgan 1978, p. 7). In women over forty, some clinicians also recommend removing the ovaries when doing a hys-

terectomy, for these "worthless organs" are viewed as potentially cancer bearing and therefore potentially dangerous. Prohysterectomy surgeons see themselves as practicing preventive medicine.

On the other side of the debate are clinicians—among them, cancer experts—who regard hysterectomy as "surgical overkill" (Larned 1978, p. 200). Compared with tubal ligations, hysterectomy incurs 10 to 100 percent greater morbidity and mortality rates and a far longer recovery period, for it is major surgery (Hatcher et al. 1982).

Besides causing major trauma to the female body, hysterectomy is an expensive operation, roughly five to seven times more expensive than a tubal ligation. Although hysterectomy is 100 percent effective in preventing pregnancy, it is such a risky and expensive procedure that women should probably get more than one medical opinion before agreeing to the operation.

Psychologically, the cessation of menstruation (an obvious result of removal of the uterus) is a sign for some women that they are no longer young and fertile. Because some women define their uterus as a badge of femininity and youth, some doctors believe that even after sterilization, the uterus should be allowed to remain intact unless a medical problem necessitates its removal.

In addition to psychological factors, some researchers argue that hysterectomy causes a lot of biological changes that may detract from sexual pleasure. For instance, the sensation of uterine contractions with orgasm is lost, and the vagina no longer balloons as high as before. If the ovaries are removed, lower estrogen levels may cause premature aging of the vagina unless synthetic estrogen is taken. And unless the vagina is carefully repaired, intercourse can be painful (S. Morgan 1978). John Perry (1980) has also found that sloppy hysterectomies may make upper orgasms impossible by destroying nerves in the tissues that seem to trigger these orgasms. On the other hand, some women find it sexually liberating to be freed from both menstruation and fear of pregnancy.

EXPERIMENTAL METHODS

In addition to the many methods of conception control already described, numerous other methods are currently being tested. If proved safe, some may soon be released for public use.

One method attracting considerable interest is *Depo-Provera* (or DMPA), an injectable drug that offers three months of contraceptive protection with a single shot of a synthetic progestogen. Its action suppresses release of the pituitary gonadotropins, thus preventing ovulation. Although Depo-Provera has been used by 10 million women for over fifteen years in eighty countries, it is presently banned in the United States because FDA-mandated tests with dogs and monkeys showed that the injection increased the incidence of breast and uterine cancer in these animals. The Upjohn Company, which makes the drug, argues that these test results are not relevant to human health because dogs and monkeys have the opposite reactions to progesterone as humans: Whereas dogs tend to develop abnormal breast tissue and monkeys develop endometrial deposits in the presence of progesterone, this same drug actually prevents breast disease and is used in the treatment of uterine cancer in humans (The Upjohn Company 1983).

Because Depo-Provera contains no estrogen, it has none of the estrogen-related side effects of estrogen-containing oral contraceptives. In countries where it has long been used, rates of cancer are not increased among women receiving the shot. Side effects that have been noted include weight gain, diminished sex drive, irregular menstruation, and sometimes a complete halt of menstrual bleeding ("Effective, but How Safe?" 1983).

Another chemical approach to contraception has the opposite effect. It is an oral dose of antiprogesterone that brings on menstruation, expelling that month's egg whether it has been fertilized or not. The pill, called *RU-486*, is taken only two to four days a month, lessening the amount of chemicals ingested by the woman. Developed by a French and Swiss team, RU-486 does not yet appear to have dangerous side effects for either animals or humans. But because it triggers what amounts to an early abortion if conception has taken place, it has been attacked on moral grounds by the Roman Catholic church ("New Birth Control Pill . . ." 1982).

Also under study are *contraceptive implants*, small capsules inserted under the skin of a woman's arm that slowly release a contraceptive hormone. One being tested by the International Committee for Contraception Research is levonorgestrel, a progestin. Expected to cost $20 or less, the implant can be inserted in five minutes under local anesthesia, providing protection from pregnancy for five to seven years. The effect can be reversed by removal of the tiny capsule when pregnancy is desired. Found both safe and highly effective in seven years of testing, the implant nevertheless seems to cause weight gains and irregular or prolonged menstrual periods in some women ("Another Birth-Control Method" 1982).

Vaginal sponges are disposable, spermicide-saturated sponges to be inserted high in the vagina, posing a mechanical and chemical barrier to sperm. Sponges are thought to be only 86 to 92 percent effective in preventing pregnancy. They were released for over-the-counter sale in the latter part of 1983 (LaFleche 1983).

Whereas the new methods discussed thus far have all been applied to the women, research is ongoing to determine reversible chemical ways of blocking fertility in the male. *Gossypol,* an extract of cottonseed oil, is a Chinese pill that apparently blocks or greatly reduces the production of sperm. According to Chinese researchers, the gossypol pill is theoretically 99.8 percent effective in preventing pregnancy. Side effects noted in 1 to 3 percent of the Chinese men included nausea, digestive disturbances, a decrease in appetite, and weight gain or loss (McLaughlin 1979). The safety of the drug has not yet been established in the United States.

Finally, an approach that holds promise of contraception for both sexes is use of *peptides,* synthetic hormonal proteins instead of the synthetic versions of steroid hormones now used in oral contraceptives. Research is being conducted on the use of *LRF,* or luteinizing hormone-releasing factor (also known as LRHR). Bombarding the pituitary gland with super doses of LRF confuses its normal feedback system and ultimately results in suppression of sperm development in males or inhibition of ovulation in women. The substance may, however, decrease sexual capacity (Clark et al. 1983). And some consumer health and feminist groups oppose the use of any such drugs for contraception. Barbara Seaman, for example, argues that "nothing hormonal that interferes with the menstrual cycle will ever be fully safe" ("Female Phase Fazer . . ." 1982, p. 21).

STAGES IN EARLY CONTRACEPTIVE USE

Although the contraceptive methods now available are far from perfect, some are relatively safe and effective. Why, then, do so many young people fail to use them—and consequently create pregnancies?

Studies of teenagers show that they know about contraceptives and have access to them. However, a 1979 national sample of teenagers shows that they are having more sex with *less effective* contraceptive protection and *more* pregnancies (Zelnik and Kantner 1980). Surveys of sexually active young people show that use of contraceptives is not significantly affected by parents' input, religion, or personality. It seems that the strongest factor influencing contraceptive use is simply *whether partners have discussed it.* (Delamater and Maccorquodale 1978; Thompson and Spanier 1978). Talking about contraceptives requires awareness and acceptance of the probability that intercourse will occur. The likelihood that people will talk openly about contraceptives changes over their early sexual career.

In interviewing 52 sexually active young women (half of whom had just had abortions), Warren Miller (1980) found that they passed through four rather distinct stages in contraceptive use: abstinence, risk taking, use of nonprescription methods, and then use of prescription methods. In the first—sheer abstinence—partners avoid pregnancy by avoiding intercourse. The subject of contraception doesn't come up during this period, for partners are at no risk of creating a pregnancy.

Risk Taking

The second stage in contraceptive use is the beginning of intercourse. Even though pregnancy is now a clear risk, many people start having intercourse without using anything. This risk taking is most common among the youngest sexmakers. Although there was a dramatic increase in use of contraceptives by teenagers during the 1970s, almost half of the fifteen- and sixteen-year-olds having intercourse for the first time still didn't use

The most important factor in successful contraception is discussing it ahead of time.

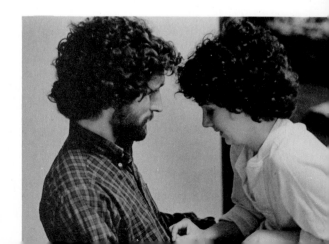

What Is the Risk of Pregnancy?

Every time a female has intercourse without using any contraceptive method, she runs a 2 to 30 percent chance of getting pregnant, depending on where she is in her menstrual cycle. If she is sexually active for a year without using anything, there's an 80 to 90 percent likelihood that she'll get pregnant (Hatcher et al. 1980; Boston Women's Health Book Collective 1976).

People's luck varies. Warren Miller found that of 11 young women he interviewed who'd just had an abortion and who had sex with a single partner: one got pregnant on her first intercourse; one, the second time she had intercourse; one, the third time; one, two weeks after she started having intercourse; one, three months after intercourse started; four, about six months after intercourse started; and one, after one year of occasional intercourse; one, three years after beginning intercourse (after a two-year separation from her partner) [Miller 1980, pp. 211–38].

anything (Zelnik and Kantner 1977). Nonuse of contraceptives continues into the college years. In one study 36 percent of college students were still using contraceptives only sporadically or not at all (Maxwell et al. 1977). Typical explanations for taking chances: People didn't expect intercourse to "happen," they thought sex should be spontaneous, they thought it was a "safe" time for the female, they didn't know where to get contraceptives, or they didn't care whether the female got pregnant (Reichelt 1979; Finkel and Finkel 1975; Maxwell et al. 1977).

Behind these superficial explanations for unprotected intercourse, people may have more complicated reasons for taking chances. Kristin Luker (1975) found that rapid social changes increase the odds that females will risk intercourse without contraception. One of today's social forces in transition is changes in the role of courtship. As sex per se loses its power as a bargaining chip for marriage, some females have developed the notion that *pregnancy* might be a way to force their partner into a commitment.

Second, we are witnessing gradual changes from traditional scripts for sex to newer ones. Dur-

ing this transition period, some people are doing things sexually that conflict with values they learned earlier. Their ambivalence about what they are doing may result in unwillingness to define themselves as sexually active—and thus they avoid contraceptives.

Third, changing contraceptive technology has prompted the notion that the most effective conception control techniques are those applied to the female. So much attention has been given to the pill and the IUD that many people are unaware that a shared method—condom plus foam—is one of the most powerful contraceptives available.

Some women's subtle resentment over their unshared responsibility, their unwillingness to define themselves as sexual, and their feeling that pregnancy might have some benefits make it likely that they won't do anything about contraception. At the same time males may feel that they are helpless to stop their partner's risk taking (Luker 1975).

These choices are not rational. They are the confused results of rapid, multiple social transitions. Females who don't become pregnant during this chance-taking stage are no different from those who do become pregnant—they're just luckier (Miller 1980).

Use of Nonprescription Methods

Miller (1980) found that females typically began having intercourse without consistent use of contraceptives—until they were alarmed by a pregnancy scare: a delayed menstrual period. This situation had one of three results: (1) actual pregnancy; (2) relief when the period finally started and a false feeling of safety, which led to more risk taking; or (3) open talk and information gathering for the first time.

When people do begin using contraceptives, their earliest use usually involves methods that are applied to the male and/or don't require a doctor's prescription (to avoid social embarrassment). Condoms or withdrawal methods are most common; sometimes the female tries the rhythm method or foam (Fox 1977; Maxwell et al. 1977). Male methods may be more prominent at this point because females are reluctant to make a psychological commitment to sexuality. Socialized not to choose sex for themselves, women are unlikely to assert their sexuality actively by seeing a doctor to get a prescription method. Young sexually active females with a high level of sex guilt are more embarrassed about going to a birth control clinic and less likely to read up on contraceptive methods on their own than are women with low sex guilt (Herold and Goodwin 1981b).

Whether the male or the female tries using something at this point, he or she may not use it all the time. Conception control is hard to stick with when people are impulsive, present-oriented, and trying to rationalize or suppress ambivalence about what they're doing—common characteristics of this stage (Miller 1980).

Prescription Methods

The growing sense that intercourse is inevitable and that one might as well accept it and do something about it leads to a new stage in contraceptive use: typically a switch to doctor-prescribed methods applied to the female. Most of the women in Miller's survey took this step only within the context of a long-term relationship. They seemed to define it as a sign of commitment and sexual availability to their partner (Miller 1980). At this point use of the pill jumps to 50 percent, while use of condoms, withdrawal, rhythm, or "nothing" drops off sharply (Maxwell et al. 1977).

Pill use brings new problems for some females. If they live at home, they may be distressed at having to hide their pills from disapproving parents. And motivation to take one every day may be dependent on ups and downs in their feelings about their partner(s). If things aren't going well in their relationships, they may stop taking the pills temporarily, thus making themselves vulnerable to pregnancy again.

Although female methods seem most common at this point, who assumes responsibility for contraception depends on dominance patterns in the relationship and gender role attitudes. Often the male tries to control the female's use of contraceptives by ordering her to get foam, pills, or a diaphragm or even by keeping track of her menstrual cycle. Alternately, the male may use contraceptive measures himself. Either way, within this context the female is merely a passive participant in contraception. If she counts on her partner to withdraw in time, to use a condom, or to know when her "safe" time is, she may wind up pregnant (Miller 1980).

It's interesting that attitudes about gender roles affect responsibility taking in exactly opposite ways for males and females. A study of 683 midwestern university students revealed that males' sense of personal responsibility for contraception is highest among men with traditional gender role attitudes. By contrast, women who take active responsibility for contraception are likely to have nontraditional gender role attitudes and a strong sense of personal control over what happens to them (Fox 1977).

IMPROVING CONTRACEPTIVE SERVICES

What can society do about this interplay of social factors that predisposes some people to contraceptive risk taking? Kristin Luker (1975) recommends, for one thing, an aggressive community outreach program. Newspapers, radio, and TV could be flooded with public service announcements about the statistical chances of getting pregnant (many teenagers don't know how easy it is) and where to get and how to use nonprescription methods of conception control. For many years family planning and population groups have in fact urged an end to the current ban on TV and radio commercials for nonprescription conception control methods. With methods like condoms selling well anyway, companies have little financial incentive to use additional advertising, and a majority of adults are reportedly opposed to such ads ("Contraceptive Commercials . . ." 1983).

Second, Luker recommends an improved system of contraceptive clinics. She believes that these clinics should be widely available on a drop-in rather than appointment basis, so that people can get help whenever they're motivated to do so. She recommends that contraceptives be provided free of charge or on a sliding scale based on people's ability to pay. This approach would cost society a lot less than subsidizing the results of unintended pregnancies. For instance, in 1978 it was estimated that at $66 per client per year, it would take only $112 million "to provide modern birth control services for every sexually active teenager at risk of an unintended pregnancy who is not currently receiving them" (Moore 1978, p. 235), compared with billions in welfare payments and abortions for teenage pregnancies. Nearly a million unplanned births and 1.4 million abortions were prevented by the use of existing birth control clinics by teenagers in the 1970s (Forrest, Hermalin, and Henshaw 1981).

Why haven't such programs been expanded? Perhaps a major barrier to distributing contraceptive tools and information is the notion that this service will encourage teenagers to have more sex with more people. Data don't support this idea. Surveys of teenagers using contraceptive clinics show that the majority started intercourse *before* beginning to use contraceptives, and that those who seek contraceptive help do not increase their number of partners. They may have sex a little more often because they feel safer from pregnancy, but *92 percent* of clinic clients in one study had only one partner (Reichelt 1979; Nahmanovici, Racinet, and Salvat 1978).

It's quite possible to argue that instead of "corrupting" young people, contraceptive services may help them make more mature sexual decisions. Maturity in this sense means being aware of contraceptive techniques, accepting ourselves as sexually active people, recognizing that pregnancy is a likely outcome of intercourse.

As Emily Mudd and her associates at the University of Pennsylvania (1978) point out, our social environment does not promote clear consideration of these factors. We have a good bit of freedom to experiment with sex, but little information about the statistical likelihood of pregnancy and little encouragement to acknowledge our sexuality openly. And as we saw in Chapter 16, parenthood is often romanticized; its problems and the alternatives to parenthood receive little positive publicity. By encouraging talk about these issues and use of contraceptives in sexual relationships, we could help each other avoid risk-taking nondecisions and begin to assert mature control over our own sexual choices.

Summary

Population control is both a global and a personal issue. Until recently methods of preventing unwanted pregnancy have concentrated on females, but many men have shown their willingness to share with their partners the risks and responsibilities of conception control. The major reversible male method now in use is the condom, which is safe and effective if used carefully, particularly when combined with use of spermicide by the female.

Reversible methods now used by females include oral contraceptives, IUDs, diaphragms, cervical caps, and spermicides. All have potential problems, but most are also found to have noncontraceptive benefits as well as varying degrees of effectiveness in preventing conception. When intercourse occurs during the woman's fertile period without any contraceptive protection, she still has the option of using one of the "morning-after" methods of preventing pregnancy: a morning-after pill of synthetic hormones, insertion of a copper IUD, or menstrual extraction.

Some couples choose methods that require shared cooperation and no chemical risks. These include outright abstinence from intercourse, withdrawal, and fertility awareness calculations with abstinence from intercourse during days the woman is potentially fertile. A more permanent and effective alternative is sterilization—either of the male, by vasectomy, or the female, by some form of tubal ligation. The use of hysterectomy for contraceptive purposes is questionable.

"New" methods currently under testing include the Depo-Provera shot, the RU-486 pill, contraceptive implants, vaginal sponges saturated with spermicides, the gossypol pill for men, and doses of LRF for either sex.

Although teenagers know about contraceptives, and can get them, they don't always use them when they begin having intercourse. Stages leading to use of effective methods are abstinence, risk taking, using nonprescription methods, and then using prescription methods. Some in our society want to expand services making contraceptives available to the young; some would limit services in hopes of limiting teenage sex. Studies suggest that limiting access to contraceptive services would not decrease the incidence of teenage sex but would instead raise the number of unplanned pregnancies.

Post-script

Positive Sexual Choices Today and Tomorrow

As we look toward the late 1980s and beyond, some of us will do well to take closer stock of our sexual choices—what makes them meaningful and satisfying, and what weakens them. The issues and information explored in this book can be a basis for reexamining how we express our sexuality.

Taking stock includes reevaluating what it means to be female and male and straight, bi, gay, or lesbian. We can choose to try harder to share and cooperate rather than continuing to compete and outmaneuver each other in a way that leaves women and men each other's victims. Women can choose to become more sexually assertive and more creative in exercising their imaginations to initiate fantastic sex, and men can choose to become more sensitive and less aggressive.

To be more comfortable with their sexuality, women can choose to reject the victim image that many have taken on, and can replace it with a positive, self-confident image. But women won't be able to change unless men cooperate and change, too. Men will need to reject their long-rewarded aggression with each other and with women, open-

ing as whole, feeling individuals. Partners will need to make it comfortable for them to do so. Sexual relationships will then become more fun, more friendly, and more deeply satisfying.

In exploring our options, we may not find a rational basis for the separation of friendship and romance. Sex can be pleasurable within a range of relationship choices. For some of us sex is best as shared with one special person at a time, while for others sex is best as friendship, love, and fun with interested and interesting partners. For some celibacy is a positive option.

Desire can become a positive word describing both individual and couple satisfactions. Lust needn't get bad press. Love needn't mean possessing another. The recent emphasis on fighting pornography has largely ignored positive alternatives to exploitative sex in the media. We can choose to create a new genre of erotic art and literature that will turn on women as much as men without objectifying either sex. We can learn to accept and relish our sensual and erotic selves without viewing sexual pleasure as a way to put down the other sex. If we are to become a sex-positive society—sexually aware rather than sexually obsessed—we will have to become individual ripples combining to make waves of jubilant sexual pleasure.

Although it might seem that we can all freely choose how to live our sexual lives, the state of the economy and the resulting social and political pressures affect our choices more than we would like to acknowledge. For one thing it is hard to develop and grow in an intimate relationship when we are struggling to survive in our jobs. Because sex has often been viewed as work (the entire "adequacy" emphasis of many sex therapists and educators), it is hard to find a place for pleasure in a society that has no time or energy for it. Sex can become another task—another performance in an already arduous day unless we choose to approach it differently.

For a positive sexual society to emerge, we can choose to defuse groups that deny our choices. Such groups have every right to be selective about sex *in their own lives*—but not in our lives. We have a human right to make our own sexual choices as long as we don't exploit other human beings. This means that groups lacking power and status—the aged, women, low-income groups, teenagers, and those who are physically or mentally challenged—deserve the right to make sexual choices that are not repressively controlled by others.

The future won't take care of itself. One approach is to chip away at the violence and exploitation we encourage as a society. We have to share to shape the future—to develop friendships between nations and between individuals. We can support and participate in research, education, and more effective programs in sex-related areas. And in our own relationships we can have a kind of sexual honesty that is refreshing.

We don't need to wait until the year 2000 to regret what we could have done to change our sexual world. To transform our sex-negative society into a sex-positive society, we can take some risks and try out new choices now. We can choose to *get in touch,* rather than *fearing to touch* each other. We can choose to discuss and reevaluate our sexual ethics in open dialogue so we can reappraise our choices, look within ourselves, relate, and enjoy each other with more care and joy than we have ever experienced or imagined.

Appendixes

A / A Brief Look at Sex Research

Throughout this book sex research has been cited as one way of "knowing" about our sexuality. As with research on any social behavior, sex research varies in quality, methods of data collection, and the ability to generalize findings.

Sex research (or sexology) is conducted by sociologists, psychologists, biologists, psychiatrists, and others trained to carry out scientific analyses of sexual conduct. Although space hasn't allowed a full presentation of all the methods, samples, contributions, and flaws of each study cited, this appendix provides a general orientation to sex research.

ASKING ABOUT SEX

First it is important to clarify what sex research is. Most sex research is self-reported data obtained either from questionnaires (filled out in groups or through the mail) or from interviews. Kinsey and his colleagues utilized the interview method to tease out a description of sexual behavior over a person's sexual career. Others have included in interview and questionnaire studies questions about the *meaning* of sex. The trend is to delve more deeply into *why* people engage in sex rather than merely describing how many do so. Explanations of our sexual choices necessitate a conceptual orientation. Theoretical explanations evolve from interviews where the complexities of our choices can be probed. The so-called major or big studies haven't included much on the meanings and situational implications of sex. Bigger is not always better. The forced-choice format (similar to objective tests in college) with structured attitude scales and a total preconception of possible responses limits sex surveys to a scratch-the-surface sketch.

Magazine surveys such as the *Playboy, Ladies Home Journal, Cosmopolitan, Redbook* and *Psychology Today* studies (Petersen et al. 1983; Frank and Enos, 1983; Wolfe 1982; Tavris and Sadd 1975; Athanasiou, Shaver, and Tavris 1970) give us benchmarks to compare with other large sample studies such as the Kinsey (1948, 1953) interviews and the Hunt (1974) group-administered questionnaire study. Magazine surveys sometimes claim larger samples than they actually *use* in the data analysis—a prime example being the *Cosmopolitan* survey, where Linda Wolfe claimed to "reveal the sexual behavior of 106,000 *Cosmopolitan* readers" but where she only used 10,000 readers for her conclusions.

Surveys tell us a little about a lot of people, but even large-scale samples aren't without bias. It's difficult to know how accurate they are when generalizations are made to include those not located and those who refuse to be studied. The response rate (those who choose to participate out of all those asked to do so) hasn't been very high in much sex research with volunteer "subjects." There are several reasons why people refuse to be researched. Some see research as an invasion of their privacy, others don't want to take the time, and still others don't (or can't) acknowledge their sexual choices to themselves, let alone to a researcher.

Surveys give us a rough idea of what "average" people do and what their attitudes are, but responses are often colored by what's socially desirable. Because of such biases, researchers may falsely conclude that people *really* act as they *say* they act. That is not to say that interviews are without bias, but interviews usually result in a more complete picture of our sexual lives than do questionnaires. Questionnaires are quicker, cheaper, and easier to administer and analyze than interviews, but in-depth interviews are usually worth the added time, expense, and energy.

Whether questionnaires or interviews are better depends on the goals of a study, the skills of available interviewers, and the available support for the research. Questionnaires and interviews complement each other, with each method adding information about our sexuality. People remain anonymous in most questionnaire studies, but well-trained and sensitive interviewers are often able to gain the trust of people by assuring the confidentiality of all data. Gaining trust and cooperation isn't easy, but a greater openness about sex makes valid interviews more likely.

Lengthy and/or repeated interviews with the same people may be accomplished with more ease if those interviewed are paid for their time. But even with financial payments, some refuse to be studied. Those who refuse may be sexually more conservative than those with no qualms about discussing their sex lives with a stranger. The results of studies may be biased in a liberal or conservative direction, depending on the age, social class, gender, and other social and personal factors of the sample.

In addition to questionnaire and interview studies, self-report data is gathered in clinical-therapy settings where intervention and research occur simultaneously. Case histories are reported from clinical interviews as well as from nonclinical, in-depth interviews. Since clinicians are usually trained more in therapy skills than in research techniques, there is some potential for biased interpretations of their research, including unfounded inferences extended to those not in therapy. This isn't to say that clinicians cannot offer hypotheses and qualified observations. Such tentative conclusions can be tested on nonclinical samples that are representative of more people than those in therapy.

Some clinicians have contributed to sex research and theory. Freud is a prime example. Many of Freud's insights were based on his patients, his family, and himself. But such an introspective approach needn't be taken as gospel or as universally accurate. If sex researchers don't qualify potential sample biases, time and methods of data collection, and analysis procedures, persons who read their reports must do so.

Sometimes the goals of a study are to obtain a lot of information about a few people. These goals are consistent with case studies and in-depth interviews. But whether we ask a lot about a few or a little about a lot, self-reports don't *prove* causal relationships between sexual choices and personality and social variables. We can *infer* causal relationships and we can identify the strength of relationship (correlation) between variables (such as how religious we are and what our sexual choices are), but we cannot control variables or the causal order of variables (what causes what) from one-shot self-report research.

Although science is concerned with causal relationships and the prediction of future events, the meaning of these events and a reasonable explanation of their complexities are also of scientific (and humanistic) interest. Some researchers are more concerned with statistical accuracy than they are with the relevance of their data to our dilemmas, feelings, and choices. Although controlled experimental studies that identify causal relationships may enlighten our choices, they may also be irrelevant to them.

OBSERVING SEXUAL BEHAVIOR

Sex researchers observe people in both public and private places—where sexual negotiations occur and where the researchers study ongoing sexual acts (as have Masters and Johnson 1966 and Perry and Whipple 1980). The observation of others in the field, whether public or private, is necessary for a comprehensive view of sexuality. If we depend totally on self-report data, it's difficult to label sex research a *behavioral science*.

Some anthropologists, sociologists, and psychologists have observed sexual negotiations and actual sexual acts in the field (as in cocktail lounges or singles bars) as well as in what usually are defined as private places (such as restrooms and hotel rooms). With a few exceptions observations of people in sexual negotiations, flirtations, or actual sexual acts involving touching, kissing, and genital stimulation have been notably absent. Exceptions are controversial; examples include studies such as Laud Humphreys's *Tearoom Trade*

(1970), where he observed male homosexual acts in public restrooms (and later interviewed some of the same men after disguising himself and tracing the men to their homes by taking their car license numbers), and Martha Stein's *Lovers, Friends, and Slaves* (1974), where she observed call girls' negotiations and sexual acts with male clients who didn't know she was observing.

In another departure from traditional methods, Jack Douglas, Paul Rasmussen, and Carol Ann Flanagan (1977) observed and interviewed people who enjoyed the sun, surf, and casual sex on a California nude beach. These researchers teased out the everyday interactions that often resulted in sex with strangers and acquaintances. A holistic grasp of sexual choices was obtained through the combined use of interviews and participant observations where the researchers mingled with others on the nude beach.

The creative use of public and private observations hasn't been supported by funding agencies and conventionally trained social scientists. Debates over whether observations without "informed consent" (a DHEW-imposed rule for research, whether funded by the government or not, as long as such research occurs at a university or other institution receiving any DHEW funds) are ethical are common among sex researchers, politicians, governmental officials, funding agencies, and the public. Ambiguities as to what constitutes harm to research subjects, whether social benefits outweigh potential psychological or other risks to people, and the right to confidentiality are interpreted and applied to specific studies by university and governmental human subjects committees. No research is supposed to be done without the approval of these committees.

Observational studies are sometimes limited more than self-report studies by strict adherence to DHEW human subjects rules, but self-report research has also been heavily curtailed by these medically and biologically based "guidelines." As an editorial in *The Nation* asserted:

H.E.W. internal memorandums state quite frankly that universities will use the review board to kill politically sensitive research. . . .

In failing to distinguish between medical injections or LSD experiments and survey research or *interview procedures customary in the social sciences, the proposed guidelines mark a truly terrifying extension of federal power in American life.* [*The Nation*, May 31, 1980, p. 645]

It may be a long time before society deals with the protection of researchers as well as of persons studied. One concerned group of academics is involved with an active campaign to change the human subjects procedures so that research can be conducted without undue and unfair limitations (Committee of Concern about Institutional Review Board Practices). This committee is a kind of lobby for ethical and fair guidelines for research.

If social scientists and investigative journalists (such as Myron Farber, a writer for the *New York Times*, who was jailed for refusing to reveal the confidential source for a story) must continually fear a subpoena to appear before a grand jury and reveal confidential data, little controversial research will occur, especially when people in the upper social classes are to be researched. No one has attempted a large-scale study of the sexual behavior and related conduct of the upper classes. Among other things, covert observations by those who work for the upper class, as well as informal interviews (if they could be accomplished), might yield empirically based conclusions that expose punitive sexual controls imposed by the powerful on the powerless. Although such research could lead to lawsuits (invasion-of-privacy statutes have never been tested with sex research), the probability of suits would be minimized if the identities of those studied were carefully kept anonymous.

Experimental research has also been used to study sexual response. Such experiments usually include some self-report measures as well as the physiological measurement of arousal. Sometimes audio- and/or videotapes are also taken in the laboratory. Although it's easier to control variables so that outside influences don't directly affect comparisons between "experimental groups" exposed to specific stimuli or experiences and "control groups" not exposed, the artificiality of experiments often limits generalizations beyond the laboratory.

Using more than one method is a step toward higher-quality research, but another step that would add to the current one-shot data collection practice is a longitudinal view of sex. Following the same people over a period of years gives us a better understanding of the process of making sexual choices, including the variables that affect choices in particular situations. Some questionnaire studies (such as Jessor and Jessor 1975) have followed people for a few years, but it would be more helpful to follow people for longer periods, and to include more questions on choices and what they mean.

FINDING ANSWERS ABOUT SEX

The questions researchers ask depend on their disciplinary training (sociology, psychology, biology, medicine, child development and family relations, health education, and so on) as well as on the priorities of funding agencies and of academia and the personal interests and biases of researchers.

The questions researchers have asked need not limit what could be asked. But if researchers continue to follow the old pose-hypotheses-and-develop-a-theory-before-you-collect-data approach, little experientially based theory will result. A sex-positive orientation to sex research includes an openness to what is happening. This orientation replaces the still common preconceived this-is-what-probably-is-happening-so-I'll-give-out-a-questionnaire-to-my-class-with-responses-I-expect-to-find approach.

The recent recognition of qualitative sociology, influenced in part from cultural anthropology, offers a legitimate complement to the hard-science, heavily quantitative (statistical) approach and provides hope that scientists will use more than one method.

Sex researchers often rely heavily on traditional theories about behavior. For example, an overreliance on role theory to define expected and actual sexual choices fails to recognize choices that are not rigidly scripted into roles such as "the sexual role" often referred to in marriage and family literature (Nye 1976). And although some researchers assume otherwise, much of our sexual behavior is irrational and unpredictable. We can't trace all of our sexual choices to theories of causation.

More emphasis on our feelings and emotions and their relationship to our choices would provide a deeper grasp of our sexual lives. We need to study sex as it is—not just tie it to the family or to social and personal problems. A sex-positive approach requires extending beyond the limitations of biological and medical models for doing research and collecting more data on what sex *means* in a variety of contexts. As sociologist-sex researcher Jack Douglas observes:

Sociologists and other social scientists have almost never tried to look closely at sex, except in the form of deviance, changing sexual mores, and changing family patterns (divorce). All of these are in various ways the outcomes, or symptoms, of the revolt of sexual feeling, of the growing insistence on expressing, gratifying, fulfilling, and increasing sexual feeling. We have almost no sociology of sex, but a wasteland of the sociology of the pale reflections of sex. (Indeed, most of the sociology of marriage and the family is so rationally symbolic as to be ludicrous. There are literally textbooks in this field that include "indexes of marital compatibility.")   [Douglas and Johnson 1977, pp. 20–30]*

THE FUTURE OF SEX RESEARCH

Just as sex researchers have "jumped on the band wagon" and studied whatever seems in vogue (premarital sex was once "in" to study, then came extramarital sex, and most recently incest), it is likely that the media will still lead the way with exposures of "new" trends or fads. Long after these trends become common knowledge, sex researchers will claim they have discovered something new. The questionnaire or brief-interview approach to the latest controversy is consistent with a sex-negative approach to research and isn't likely to cease anytime soon.

The distant future (after the twentieth century) *may* be more sex-positive—with research that is more humanistic and relevant to the real world. This means that we'll fill more voids with

* From Jack Douglas, "Existential Sociology," in Jack Douglas and John M. Johnson, eds., *Existential Sociology* (Cambridge and New York: Cambridge University Press, 1977). Reprinted by permission.

knowledge from empirically based theories that are relevant to education, therapy, social policy, and intelligent media portrayals.

A sex-positive approach to sex research could be facilitated by laws protecting researchers and the persons they study from public identification and harassment. Public and private funding agencies, university human subjects committees, and sex researchers must face the challenge to do studies with more of a reality orientation. This approach assumes that the purpose of sex research is to facilitate more *joyful sex* rather than to control or punish those who attempt to enjoy sex.

Our sexual choices can be wiser and more joyful if we make them on the basis of sound information. The availability of research and the popularization of research findings through the media depend on First Amendment freedoms as well as on more freedom to do research. Without these freedoms sex will be left to the dark corners of what can aptly be called the secret society. Contrary to the opinions of some, exposing myths and creating new knowledge won't take the fun out of sex. We're all our own sex researchers when it comes to our sexual choices!

B/ The Yellow Pages for Informed Sexual Choices

This final section is intended as a resource list for students who wish to pursue a special interest, problem, or service. The resources included are not intended to be exhaustive. They are included because they in some way complement the sex-positive themes in *Sexual Choices*. (Note: Addresses may change; these are the most current addresses at press time.)

SPECIAL INTEREST GROUPS

Elysium
814 Robinson Road
Topanga, CA 90290
—A clothing-optional resort and educational facility, based on the belief that "There is an essential wholesomeness in the human body and all of its functions"; offers classes in yoga, massage, and body/self-image, as well as workshops and playshops dealing with singleness, sensory awakening, creativity, love, personal identity, and group support.

National Androgyny Center
P.O. Box 7429
San Diego, CA 92107
—Is focused on an internal balance between feminine and masculine characteristics for people regardless of their sexual (or gender) preferences; publishes *Androgyny Review*.

National Federation of Parents and Friends of Gays
5715 Sixteenth Street, N.W.
Washington, DC 20011
—Offers support groups across the country to gays and their heterosexual friends and family members.

National Gay Task Force
80 Fifth Avenue, Suite 1601
New York, NY 10011
—Offers information and support to lesbian and gay people, or those interested in personal and social issues affecting same-sex intimacies.

National Organization for Women
425 Thirteenth Street, N.W., Suite 1048
Washington, DC 20004
—An information and action group promoting equality between the sexes; offers a newsletter, meetings and conferences concerning issues such as sexual abuse, abortion, and lesbianism.

The Naturists
P.O. Box 132
Oshkosh, WI 54902
—Offers literature on clothes-optional recreational spots around the world; supports legal, lobbying, and educational activities to protect and publicize the clothes-optional lifestyle for those who choose it.

Sex and Disability Unit
Human Sexuality Program
University of California
814 Mission Street, Second Floor
San Francisco, CA 94103
—Provides services for persons concerned about the effect of physical limitations and social stigma on sexual and interpersonal aspects of living. Sexual health services include professional and community education, training, counseling, consultation, and research.

Sexual Freedom League
P.O. Box 0105
College Grove Station
San Diego, CA 92115
—A group of people, mostly in Southern California, interested in sexual freedom; offers a monthly newsletter and weekly parties.

Lifestyles Inc.
2742 West Orangethorpe—Suite A
Fullerton, CA 92633
—Coordinates and validates swing clubs throughout North America, sponsors annual lifestyle conferences with academic and popular presentations, publishes a newsletter.

Zero Population Growth
1346 Connecticut Avenue, N.W.
Washington, DC 20036
—An information and action group with the intent of raising issues to discourage population increases.

SEXUAL AIDS

The following catalogue services sell vibrators, massage oils and lotions, books and other materials for educational and entertainment purposes. Since each service changes what they offer from time to time, interested readers should write for the latest catalogue.

Eve's Garden
119 West Fifty-Seventh Street
New York, NY 10019

Good Vibrations
3416 Twenty-Second Street
San Francisco, CA 94110

Lawrence Research Group
(The Xandria Collection)
1245 Sixteenth Street
San Francisco, CA 94107

Multi-Media Resource Center
1525 Franklin Street
San Francisco, CA 94109

CONTRACEPTION, PREGNANCY, INFERTILITY, AND HEALTH SERVICES

American Society for Psychoprophylaxis in Obstetrics
1523 L Street, N.W.
Washington, DC 20005
—A national organization that certifies childbirth educators with the Lamaze method.

Emory University Planning Program
67 Peachtree Park Drive, N.E., Suite 115
Atlanta, GA 30309
—Offers family planning information for consumers and health care providers.

International Childbirth Education Association
P.O. Box 20048
Milwaukee, WI 55420
—Deals with all facets of childbearing, including pregnancy, birth, conception control, familying in early stages, caesarean births, and teenage pregnancies; offers educational literature and referrals to classes in local areas.

LaLeche International, Inc.
9616 Minneapolis Avenue
Franklin Park, IL 60123
—Offers information on breastfeeding, with local support groups.

National Abortion Rights Action League
825 Fifteenth Street, N.W.
Washington, DC 20005
—An activist group concerned with the freedom to choose abortion.

National Alliance for Optional Parenthood
2010 Massachusetts Avenue, N.W.
Washington, DC 20036
—An information and activist organization concerned with the legitimacy of remaining childfree in the desire that every child be wanted and cared for.

National Association of Parents and Professionals for Safe Alternatives in Childbirth
Route 3, Box 23A
Marble Hill, MO 63764
—Deals primarily with alternatives to hospital birth, including home and birthing centers (maternity centers); offers referrals to local sources.

National Clearing House for Family Planning Information
P.O. Box 2225
Rockville, MD 20852
—Offers a bulletin on the latest resources on contraception, sex education, nutrition, and related areas.

National Women's Health Network
224 Seventh Street, S.E.
Washington, DC 20003

—A feminist health advocacy and resource group concerned with women's health issues such as maternal and child health during pregnancy and birth, safe conception control, abortion, breast cancer, and toxic shock syndrome; offers addresses of local women's health services, including clinics offering cervical caps.

Planned Parenthood Federation of America
810 Seventh Avenue
New York, NY 10019

—Offers pelvic and breast examinations, Pap smears, and STD testing at local centers; provides birth control information and counseling, pregnancy tests, referrals to infertility clinics, and sterilization information.

Resolve, Incorporated
P.O. Box 474
Belmont, MA 02178

—A national, nonprofit organization offering infertility counseling, referral, and support groups.

Society for the Protection of the Unborn through Nutrition
17 North Wabash Avenue, Suite 603
Chicago, IL 60602

—Offers literature promoting better nutrition for pregnant women.

SEXUALLY TRANSMITTED DISEASES

Centers for Disease Control
Attention: Technical
Information Services
Atlanta, GA 30333

—Offers literature and references for those writing papers or otherwise in need of specific information on particular sexually transmitted diseases.

Gay Men's Health Crisis Hotline
212-685-4952

—Offers information and help dealing with gay health, including AIDS.

Herpes Resource Center
American Social Health Association
P.O. Box 100
Palo Alto, CA 94302

—Offers free information about herpes (send self-addressed, stamped envelope); publishes *The Helper,* a quarterly journal about herpes.

New Day Introductions
P.O. Box 267
Framingham, MA 01701

—A national social organization formed exclusively to help people with herpes meet new friends; confidential service.

VD National Hotline
260 Sheridan Avenue
Palo Alto, CA 94306
1-800-227-8922

—Provides toll-free telephone information about VD, as well as names of over 5000 free or low-cost clinics in the continental United States; offers services seven days a week.

SEXUAL ABUSE AND HARASSMENT

Men Against Rape
P.O. Box 2126
Santa Cruz, CA 95063

—Offers support and counseling to men who are close to rape victims, who have been sexually assaulted themselves, or who are in the process of transcending their sex role training; challenges images of sexism and violence. Similar groups are developing in other cities.

National Rape Information Clearing House
National Center for the Prevention and Control of Rape
5600 Fishers Lane
Rockville, MD 20857

—Conducts and facilitates public information; develops and publishes training materials for programs designed to prevent and control rape; reports research findings; and improves communication between those working in the area of sexual assault.

Working Women's Institute
593 Park Avenue
New York, NY 10021
—A national research, resource, and educational center focused on sexual harassment on the job; includes national information and referrals, speakers and workshops, crisis counseling, a legal backup center, technical assistance and training, and research and evaluation.

MEDIA

Down There Press
P.O. Box 2086
Burlingame, CA 94010
—A progressive and sex-positive agency for unusual publications for women, men, and children; such as *I Am My Lover; Men Loving Themselves; The Sensuous Coloring Book; Good Vibrations: The Complete Women's Guide to Vibrators;* and playbooks about sex for men, women, and children.

Ed-U-Press
P.O. Box 583
Fayetteville, NY 13066
—A mail-order press with books, casette tapes, and pamphlets on sex education for children, teens, and young adults; provides material for handicapped persons.

Focus International, Inc.
1776 Broadway
New York, NY 10019
—Sells and rents sex education films, slides, and video materials.

Multi-Media Resource Center
1525 Franklin Street
San Francisco, CA 94109
—Contains up-to-date information on human sexuality in a readable and interesting style.

PROFESSIONAL ASSOCIATIONS

The following organizations offer a variety of opportunities for professionals involved with research education, and therapy:

American Association of Sex Educators, Counselors and Therapists
One East Wacker Drive,
Suite 2700
Chicago, IL 60601

**Association of Sexologists
(The Institute for Advanced Study of Human Sexuality)**
1523 Franklin Street
San Francisco, CA 94109

International Academy of Sex Research
c/o Dr. Heino Meyer-Bahlburg
722 West 168th Sreet
New York, NY 10032

Sex Information and Education Council of the United States
84 Fifth Avenue
New York, NY 10011

Society for the Scientific Study of Sex
P.O. Box 29795
Philadelphia, PA 19117

"Abortion: Women Speak Out." 1981. *Life*, November, 45–54.

Ackroyd, Peter. 1979. *Dressing Up*. New York: Simon and Schuster.

Adams, Bert, and Ronald Cromwell. 1978. "Morning and Night People in the Family: A Preliminary Statement." *Family Coordinator* 27, no. 1 (January):5–14.

Adams, David B., Alice Ross Gold, and Anne D. Burt. 1978. "Rise in Female-Initiated Sexual Activities at Ovulation and Its Suppression by Oral Contraceptives." *New England Journal of Medicine* 299, no. 21 (November):1145–50.

Adams, Junis. 1979. "What's New with Office Romance?" *Cosmopolitan*, December, pp. 294–99, 350.

Adams, Margaret. 1976. *Single Blessedness*. New York: Basic Books.

Africano, Lillian. 1979. "Results of the *Forum* Masturbation Survey." *Forum*, March, pp. 35–39.

Alan Guttmacher Institute. 1976. *11 Million Teenagers: What Can Be Done about the Epidemic of Adolescent Pregnancies in the U.S.?* New York: Planned Parenthood Federation of America.

Alderman, Jeffrey D. 1981. ABC News–Washington Post Poll, survey no. 0034, aired June 8.

Aleksandrowicz, Malca K., and Dov R. Aleksandrowicz. 1974. "Obstetrical Pain-relieving Drugs as Predictors of Infant Behavior Variability." *Child Development* 45, no. 4 (December):935–45.

Alexander, Priscilla. 1979. "National Decriminalization a Must as Hypocritical, Sexist Vigilante Groups Spring to Action across the U.S." *NTFP News*, September–October, pp. 1, 7.

Allen, Donald M. 1980. "Young Male Prostitutes: A Psychosocial Study." *Archives of Sexual Behavior* 9, no. 5 (October):399–426.

Allon, Natallie, and Diane Fishel. 1979. "Singles Bars." In Natallie Allon, ed., *Urban Life Styles*. Dubuque, Iowa: William C. Brown.

"America Shapes Up." 1981. *Time*, November 2, pp. 94–106.

American Cancer Society. 1979. *Cancer Facts and Figures 1980*. New York.

————. 1980. "TSE."

Amir, Menachem. 1971. *Patterns in Forcible Rape*. Chicago: University of Chicago Press.

Amonker, R. G. 1980. "What Do Teens Know about the Facts of Life?" *Journal of School Health* 50, no. 9 (November):527–30.

"The Anonymous Pregnancy: Psychological Implications of A.I.D." 1979. *Sexuality Today*, October 1, p. 3.

"Another Birth-Control Method." 1982. *Parade Magazine*, November 21, p. 10.

Arafat, Ibtihaj, and Donald E. Allen. 1977. "Venereal Disease: College Students' Knowledge and Attitudes." *Journal of Sex Research* 13, no. 3 (August):223–30.

Arafat, Ibtihaj, and Wayne L. Cotton. 1974. "Masturbation Practices of Males and Females." *Journal of Sex Research* 10, no. 4 (November):293–307.

Ard, Ben N. 1977. "Sex in Lasting Marriages: A Longitudinal Study." *Journal of Sex Research* 13, no. 4 (November):274–5.

Armstrong, Louise. 1978. *Kiss Daddy Goodnight, A Speakout on Incest*. New York: Hawthorne.

Ashdown-Sharp, Patricia. 1977. *A Guide to Pregnancy and Parenthood for Women on Their Own*. New York: Vintage Books/Random House.

Athanasiou, Robert. 1979. Personal communication, April 23. Used by permission.

————. 1980. "A Review of Research on Pornography." In Benjamin B. Wolman and John Money, eds., *Handbook of Human Sexuality*. Englewood Cliffs, N.J.: Prentice-Hall.

————, P. Shaver, and Carol Tavris. 1970. "Sex." *Psychology Today*, January, pp. 37–52.

————, Wallace Oppel, Leslie Michelson, Thomas Unger, and Mary Yager. 1973. "Psychiatric Sequelae to Term Birth and Induced Early and Late Abortion: A Longitudinal Study." *Family Planning Perspectives* 5, no. 4 (Fall):227–36.

Atkinson, Maxine, and Jacqueline Boles. 1977. "Prostitution as an Ecology of Confidence Games: The Scripted Behavior of Prostitutes and Vice Officers." In Clifton D. Bryant, ed., *Sexual Deviancy in Social Context*. New York: New Viewpoint/Franklin Watts.

Atwater, Lynn. 1982. *The Extramarital Connection: Sex, Intimacy, and Identity*. New York: Irvington Publishers.

Axelson, Cathy. 1981. "Lesbian Chorus." *Valley Advocate*, December 16, pp. 1, 6–18a.

Ayres, Toni. 1979. Personal communication, April 6. Used by permission.

Babb, R. R. 1979. "Sexually Transmitted Infections in Homosexual Men." *Postgraduate Medicine* 65, no. 3 (March):215–18.

Baker, Elizabeth R. 1981. "Menstrual Dysfunction and Hormonal Status in Athletic Women: A Review." *Fertility and Sterility* 36, no. 6 (December):691–96.

———, Rajesh S. Mathur, Robert F. Kirk, and H. Oliver Williamson. 1981. "Female Runners and Secondary Amenorrhea." *Fertility and Sterility* 36, no. 2 (August):183–87.

Balswick, Jack O., and James A. Anderson. 1969. "Role Definition in the Unarranged Date." *Journal of Marriage and the Family* 31, no. 4 (November):776–78.

Barclay, Andrew M. 1969. "The Effect of Hostility on Physiological and Fantasy Response." *Journal of Personality* 37, no. 4 (December):651–67.

Barrett, Karen. 1982. "Date Rape." *Ms.*, September, pp. 48–51, 130.

Barry, Kathleen. 1979. "International Exposé: Terror and Coercion—The Female Sexual Slave Trade." *Ms.*, November, pp. 62–63, 75–85.

Bart, Pauline. 1978. "Avoiding Rape: A Comparative Study." Paper presented at the meeting of the International Sociological Association. Uppsala, Sweden, August.

———. 1981. "A Study of Women Who Both Were Raped and Avoided Rape." *Journal of Social Issues* 37, no. 4:123–138.

———, and Margaret Jozsa. 1979. "Dirty Books, Dirty Films, and Dirty Data," revised. Paper read at Feminist Perspectives in Pornography Conference. San Francisco.

Bar-Tal, Daniel, and Leonard Saxe. 1976. "Physical Attractiveness and Its Relationship to Sex-Role Stereotyping." *Sex Roles* 2, no. 2 (June):123–33.

Baumrind, Diana. 1982. "Are Androgynous Individuals More Effective Persons and Parents?" *Child Development* 53:44–75.

Beach, Frank A. 1977. "Hormonal Control of Sex-Related Behavior." In Frank A. Beach, ed., *Human Sexuality in Four Perspectives*. Baltimore, Md.: Johns Hopkins University Press.

Beauvoir, de, Simone. 1973. *The Coming of Age*. New York: Warner Books.

Bech, Barbara. 1982. "Men's Underwear: A Brief Look." *Boston Globe*, December 18, p. 13.

———, and Martin S. Weinberg. 1978. *Homosexualities: A Study of Diversity among Men and Women*. New York: Simon and Schuster.

Bell, Alan P., Martin S. Weinberg, and Sue Kiefer Hammersmith. 1981. *Sexual Preference*. Bloomington, Ind.: Indiana University Press.

Bell, Robert R., and Kathleen Coughey. 1980. "Premarital Sexual Experience among College Females, 1958, 1968, and 1978." *Family Relations* 29 (July):353–57.

Bell, Ruth Davidson. 1978. "The Middle Years." In Boston Women's Health Book Collective, *Ourselves and Our Children: A Book by and for Parents*. New York: Random House.

Benjamin, Harry. 1967. "Transvestism and Transsexualism in the Male and Female." *Journal of Sex Research* 3, no. 2 (May):107–27.

Bennett, Susan M., and Winifred B. Dickinson. 1980. "Student-Parent Rapport and Parent Involvement in Sex, Birth Control, and Venereal Disease Education." *Journal of Sex Research* 16, no. 3 (May):114–30.

Benson, Donna J. and Gregg E. Thomson. 1982. "Sexual Harassment on a University Campus: The Confluence of Authority Relations, Sexual Interest, and Gender Stratification." *Social Problems* 29 (February):236–51.

Berezin, Martin A. 1976. "Normal Psychology of the Aging Process, Revisited—1. Sex and Old Age: A Further Review of the Literature." *Journal of Geriatric Psychiatry* 9:189–209.

Berger, David G., and Morton G. Wenger. 1973. "The Ideology of Virginity." *Journal of Marriage and the Family* 35, no. 4 (November):666–76.

Berk, Bernard. 1977. "Face-saving at the Singles Dance." *Social Problems* 24, no. 5 (June):119–31.

Bermant, Gordon, and Julian M. Davidson. 1974. *Biological Bases of Sexual Behavior*. New York: Harper & Row.

Bernard, Jessie. 1972. *The Future of Marriage*. New York: World.

Berscheid, Ellen, Elaine Walster, and George Bohrnstedt. 1973. "Body Image—The Happy American Body: A Survey Report." *Psychology Today*, November, pp. 119–31.

Bieber, Irving. 1962. *Homosexuality: A Psychoanalytic Study*. New York: Basic Books.

Bing, Elisabeth, and Libby Colman. 1977. *Making Love During Pregnancy*. New York: Bantam.

Birke, Lynda I. A. 1982. "Is Homosexuality Determined?" In Noretta Koertge, ed., *Nature and Causes of Homosexuality*. New York: Harnorth Press.

"Birth Control Pill Helps Fight Arthritis, Cancer." 1982. *Willimantic Chronicle* (UPI), August 18, p. 2.

Bixler, Ray H. 1982. "Sibling Incest in the Royal Families of Egypt, Peru, and Hawaii." *Journal of Sex Research* 18, no. 3 (August):264–81.

Blank, Joani. 1979. Personal communication, March 13. Used by permission.

Blount, John, and Jacqueline Boles. 1981. "Structural Determinants of Sexual Harassment and Its Psychological and Physical Consequences." Paper presented at Eastern Economic Association.

Blumstein, Phillip, and Pepper Schwartz. 1975. "The Acquisition of Sexual Identity: The Bisexual Case." Unpublished.

————. 1977. "Bisexuality: Some Social Psychological Issues." *Journal of Social Issues* 33, no. 2 (Spring): 30–45.

————. 1983. *American Couples: Money, Work, Sex.* New York: William Morrow and Company.

Bode, Ken. 1978. "New Life for the Oldest Profession." *New Republic*, July 8 and 15, pp. 21–25.

Bohlen, Joseph G., James P. Held, and Margaret Oliver Sanderson. 1980. "The Male Orgasm: Pelvic Contractions Measured by Anal Probe." *Archives of Sexual Behavior* 9, no. 6:503–21.

Boles, Jacqueline. 1980. Personal communication, April. Used by permission.

————, and Albeno P. Garbin. 1974. "The Strip Club and Stripper: Customer Patterns of Interaction." *Sociology and Social Research* 58, no. 2 (January):136–44.

Bonen, Areud, Angelo N. Belcastro, William Y. Ling, and Allan A. Simpson. 1981. "Profiles of Selected Hormones During Menstrual Cycles of Female Athletes." *Journal of Applied Physiology* 50, no. 3:545–51.

Boston Women's Health Book Collective. 1976. *Our Bodies, Ourselves.* 2d ed. New York: Simon & Schuster.

Botwin, Carol. 1979. "Is There Sex After Marriage?" *The New York Times Magazine.* September 16, pp. 108–12.

Bower, Donald W. 1975. "A Description and Analysis of a Cohabiting Sample in America." Masters thesis, University of Arizona, Tucson.

Boyar, Robert M., and James Aiman. 1982. "The 24-hour Secretory Pattern of LH and the response to LHRH in transsexual men." *Archives of Sexual Behavior* 11, no. 2 (April):157–69.

Bozett, Frederick. 1981. "Gay Fathers." *Alternative Lifestyles* 4 (February):90–108.

Brashear, Diane B. 1979. "Honk! If You Masturbate!" In Manfred F. DeMartino, ed., *Human Autoerotic Practices.* New York: Human Sciences Press.

Braun, Jonathan. 1975. "Born with a Smile Instead of a Slap: The Struggle for Acceptance of a New Birth Technique." *Parade*, November 23, pp. 17, 19.

Brecher, Edward M. 1969. *The Sex Researchers.* Boston: Little, Brown.

————. 1975. "Prevention of the Sexually Transmitted Diseases." *Journal of Sex Research* 2, no. 4 (November): 318–28.

————. 1980. Personal communication, January 13. Used by permission.

Brenner, Lewis R. 1974. "Condommunication." In Myron H. Redford, Gordon W. Duncan, and Denis J. Prager, eds., *The Condom: Increasing Utilization in the United States.* San Francisco: San Francisco Press.

Briddell, Dan W., et al. 1978. "Effects of Alcohol and Cognitive Set on Sexual Arousal to Deviant Stimuli." *Journal of Abnormal Psychology* 87, no. 4 (August):418–30.

Briedis, Catherine. 1975. "Marginal Deviants: Teenage Girls Experience Community Response to Premarital Sex and Pregnancy." *Social Problems* 22, no. 4 (April):480–92.

Brissett, Dennis. 1972. Comment on Gerhard Neubeck's "The Myriad Motives for Sex." *Sexual Behavior* 2, no. 7 (July):55.

————. 1978. "Toward an Interactionist Understanding of Heavy Drinking." *Pacific Sociological Review* 21, no. 1 (January):3–20.

"British Researchers Testing a Herpes Vaccine." 1983. *Boston Globe* (June 14), p. 3.

Brooks, George F., William W. Darrow, and Janet A. Day. 1978. "Repeated Gonorrhea: An Analysis of Importance and Risk Factors." *Journal of Infectious Diseases* 137, no. 2 (February):161–69.

Brooks-Gunn, Jeanne, and Diane N. Ruble. 1980. "The Menstrual Attitude Questionnaire." *Psychosomatic Medicine* 42, no. 5 (September):503–12.

Brown, Rita Mae. 1973. *Rubyfruit Jungle.* New York: Daughters Publishing.

Brownmiller, Susan. 1975. "The Real Spoils of War." *Ms.*, December, pp. 82–85.

————. 1976. *Against Our Will: Men, Women, and Rape.* New York: Bantam.

Bryan, James H. 1972. "Apprenticeships in Prostitution." In Robert P. Bell and Michael Gordon, eds., *The Social Dimension of Human Sexuality.* Boston: Little, Brown.

Buchwald, Art. 1978. "No Divorce for Singles." Los Angeles Times Syndicate.

Buckwalter, Kathleen Coen. 1982. "The Influence of Skin Disorders on Sexual Expression." *Sexuality and Disability* 5, no. 2 (Summer):98–106.

Buffum, John. 1982. "Pharmacosexology: The Effects of Drugs on Sexual Function—A Review." *Journal of Psychoactive Drugs* 14, nos. 1–2:5–45.

Bullough, Vern. 1975. "Sex and the Medical Model." *Journal of Sex Research* 11, no. 4 (November):291–303.

Burgess, Ann Wolbert, and Lynda Lytle Holmstrom. 1974. *Rape: Victims of Crisis*. Bowie, Md.: Robert J. Brady.

————. 1976. "Coping Behavior of the Rape Victim." *American Journal of Psychiatry* 133, no. 4 (April):413–18.

————. 1979. *Rape Crisis and Recovery*. Bowie, Md.: R. J. Brady.

Burke, Peter J., and Judy C. Tully. 1977. "The Measurement of Role Identity." *Social Forces* 55, no. 4 (June):881–97.

Burkons, D. M., and J. B. Willson. 1975. "Is the Obstetrician-Gynecologist a Specialist or a Primary Care Physician to Women?" *American Journal of Obstetrics and Gynecology* 121, no. 6 (March):808–16.

Burt, John J., and Linda Brown Meeks. 1975. *Education for Sexuality*. Philadelphia: Saunders.

Butler, Robert N. 1978 "Psychological Aspects of Reproductive Aging." In E. L. Schneider, ed., *The Aging Reproductive System*. New York: Raven Press.

————, and Myrna I. Lewis. 1976. *Sex after Sixty*. New York: Harper & Row.

Buunk, Bram. 1982. "Strategies of Jealousy: Styles of Coping with Extramarital Involvement of the Spouse." *Family Relations* 31, (January):13–18.

————. 1980. "Extramarital Sex in the Netherlands: Motivations in Social and Marital Context." *Alternative Lifestyles* 3, no. 1 (February):11–39.

Byrne, Donn, and John Lamberth. 1971. "The Effect of Erotic Stimuli on Sex Arousal, Evaluative Responses, and Subsequent Behavior." In *Technical Report of the Commission on Obscenity and Pornography* 8. Washington, D.C.: Government Printing Office.

————, Jeffrey D. Fisher, John Lamberth, and Herman E. Mitchell. 1974. "Evaluations of Erotica: Facts or Feelings?" *Journal of Personality and Social Psychology* 29, no. 1 (January):111–16.

Caldwell, Mayta A., and Letitia Anne Peplau. 1979. "The Balance of Power in Lesbian Relationships." Preliminary draft, February.

Calhoun, A. W. 1945. *A Social History of the American Family*. 3 vols. New York: Barnes and Noble Books.

Calhoun, Laurence G., James W. Selby, and H. Elizabeth King. 1981. "The Influence of Pregnancy on Sexuality: A Review of Current Evidence." *The Journal of Sex Research* 17, no. 2:139–151.

Campbell, Angus. 1975. "The American Way of Mating: Marriage Si, Children Only Maybe." *Psychology Today*, May, pp. 37–43.

Caplow, Theodore, Howard M. Bahr, Bruce A. Chadwick, Reuben Hill, and Margaret Holmes Williamson. 1982. *Middletown Families: Fifty Years of Change and Continuity*. Minneapolis: University of Minnesota Press.

Carrera, Michael. 1976. "Peer Group Sex Information." *Journal of Research and Development in Education* 10, no. 1 (Fall):50–56.

Castleman, Michael. 1980. "The Condom Comeback." *New Roots*, January–February, pp. 21–24.

"Catholics Speak Out for the Right to Choose Abortion." 1981. Brochure, Catholics for Free Choice.

Cavan, Sherri. 1976. "Talking about Sex by Not Talking about Sex." In Jacqueline P. Wiseman, ed., *The Social Psychology of Sex*. New York: Harper & Row.

Centers for Disease Control. 1981. "Communicable Diseases—Number of Reported Cases, United States, Calendar Year 1981." Atlanta, Ga.

————. 1982. *Morbidity and Mortality Weekly Report* 31, no. 11 (March):138–48.

————. 1982. *Morbidity and Mortality Weekly Report* 31, June 25, 317–28.

————. 1982. "Sexually Transmitted Disease (STD) Statistical Letter." August, tables 1–36.

————. 1983. "Acquired Immunodeficiency Syndrome (AIDS): Weekly Surveillance Report." August 22.

"CDC Speculation on AIDS." 1983. *Boston Globe*, January 7, 17.

Centers, Richard. 1975. *Sexual Attraction and Love*. Springfield, Ill.: Charles C Thomas.

Chamberlain, Tony. 1979. "Circumcision: Is It Necessary?" *Boston Globe*, August 29, pp. 63, 67.

Chandler, J. W., E. R. Alexander, and T. A. Pheiffer. 1977. "Ophthalmia Neonatorum Associated with Maternal Chlamydial Infections." *Transactions*, March–April, pp. 302–8. American Academy of Opthamology and Otolaryngology.

Cherniak, D., and A. Feingold. 1972, 1975, 1977. *VD Handbook*. Montreal: Montreal Health Press.

Chess, Stella, Alexander Thomas, and Martha Cameron. 1976. "Sexual Attitudes and Behavior Patterns in a Middle-Class Adolescent Population." *American Journal of Orthopsychiatry* 46, no. 4 (October):689–701.

Chodorow, Nancy. 1978. *The Reproduction of Mothering: Psychoanalysis and the Sociology of Gender*. Berkeley and Los Angeles: University of California Press.

Chopra, G. S. 1969. "Man and Marijuana." *International Journal of Addictions* 4:215–47.

Clanton, Gordon. 1979. "A Conversation with Albert Ellis." *Alternative Lifestyles* 2, no. 2 (May):243–53.

————, and Lynn Smith. 1977. *Jealousy.* Englewood Cliffs, N. J.: Prentice-Hall.

Clark, Matt, with Mary Lord, Timothy Nater, and Deborah Witherspoon. 1983. "The Depo-Provera Debate." *Newsweek*, January 24, 70.

————, with Deborah Witherspoon, Pamela Abramson, Daniel Shapiro, Sandra Gary, and Marsha Zabarsky. 1982. "Infertility: New Cures, New Hope." *Newsweek*, December 6, 102–10.

Clarke, Juanne. 1978. "The Unmarried Marrieds: The Meaning of the Relationship." In J. Ross Eshleman and Juanne Clarke, eds., *Intimacy, Commitment, and Marriage.* Boston: Allyn and Bacon.

Clayton, R., and H. Voss. 1977. "Shacking Up: Cohabitation in the 1970s." *Journal of Marriage and the Family* 39, no. 2 (May):273–83.

Clement, Dory, et al. 1979. *Sexual Assault Hurts.* Storrs, Conn.: Storrs-Willimantic Rape Crisis Center.

Clifford, Ruth. 1978. "Development of Masturbation in College Women." *Archives of Sexual Behavior* 7, no. 6 (December):559–73.

Cohen, Joel B. 1979. "Contraceptive Tubal Sterilization Rate Increases More Then Twice During the Period 1970–1976. *Family Planning Perspectives* 11, no. 4 (July–August) :253–55.

Cohen, Nancy Wainer, and Lois J. Estner. 1983. *Silent Knife.* South Hadley, Mass.: Bergin and Garvey.

Cohen, Stanley, and Laurie Taylor. 1976. *Escape Attempts: The Theory and Practice of Resistance to Everyday Life.* Harmondsworth, Middlesex, England: Penguin.

Cole, Charles L. 1979. Personal communication to Roger Libby, August 1.

Cole, Charles L., and Stephen L. Goettsch. 1981. "Self-Disclosure and Relationship Quality: A Study among Nonmarital Cohabiting Couples." *Alternative Lifestyles* 4, no. 4 (November):428–66.

Coleman, Emily, and Betty Edwards. 1979. *Brief Encounters.* Garden City, N. Y.: Doubleday.

Colen, B. D. 1983. "Is There Death after Sex?" *Rolling Stone*, February 3, 17–20.

Comfort, Alex. 1967. *The Anxiety Makers.* London: Thomas Nelson.

————. 1972. *The Joy of Sex: A Cordon Bleu Guide to Lovemaking.* New York: Crown.

Commission on Obscenity and Pornography. 1970. *The Report of the Commission on Obscenity and Pornography.* New York: Bantam.

Conrad et al. 1979. *Sexual Offenders and Sexually Transmitted Diseases.* Atlanta, Ga.: Center for Disease Control.

Constable, Pamela. 1982. "More Teens Keeping Their Babies without Husbands, Jobs, Income." *Boston Globe*, December 13, pp. 1, 16.

Consumer Reports. 1976. *The Medicine Show.* New York: Consumer's Union.

"Continuing Grim Picture of AIDS Victims, Numbers Doubling Every Six Months." 1982. *Sexuality Today*, December 13, p. 1.

"Contraceptive Commercials—Still a Long Way Off." 1983. *Sexuality Today* 6, no. 11 (January):4.

Cook, Kevin, Arthur Kretchmer, Barbara Nellis, Janet L'ever, and Rosanna Hertz. 1983. "The Playboy Readers' Sex Survey—Part 3." *Playboy,* May, pp. 126–28ff.

Cook, Mark, and Robert McHenry. 1978. *Sexual Attraction.* Elmsford, N. Y.: Pergamon Press.

Corea, Gena. 1977. *The Hidden Malpractice: How American Medicine Mistreats Women.* New York: Harcourt Brace Jovanovich.

Corey, Lawrence, and King K. Holmes. 1980. "Sexual Transmission of Hepatitis B in Homosexual Men." *New England Journal of Medicine* 302, no. 8 (February):435–38.

Corey, Lawrence, A. J. Nahmias, M. E. Guiman, J. K. Beneletti, C. W. Critchlow, and K. K. Holmes. 1982. "A Trial of Topical Acyclovir in Genital Herpes Simplex Virus Infections." *New England Journal of Medicine* 306 (June):1313–19.

Corsaro, Maria, and Carole Korzeniowsky. 1980. *STD: A Commonsense Guide to Sexually Transmitted Diseases.* New York: Holt, Rinehart and Winston.

Corzine, Jay, and Richard Kirby. 1977. "Cruising the Truckers." *Urban Life* 6, no. 2 (July):171–76.

"Cosmetics: Kiss and Sell." 1978. *Time*, December 11, pp. 86–96.

Cottle, Thomas J. 1979. "Trying on Adult Masks." *Psychology Today*, February, pp. 40–44.

Courtright, John A., and Stanley J. Baran. 1980. "The Acquisition of Sexual Information by Young People." *Journalism Quarterly* 57, no. 1 (Spring):107–14.

Crosby, John F. 1981. *Sexual Autonomy: Toward a Humanistic Ethic.* Springfield, Ill.: Charles C Thomas.

Crouch, Stanley. 1982. "Gay Pride, Gay Prejudice." *Village Voice*, August 27, pp. 1, 13–19.

Crouse, Bryant Bernhardt, and Albert Mehrabian. 1977. "Affiliation of Opposite-Sexed Strangers." *Journal of Research in Personality* 11, no. 1 (March):38–47.

————. 1980. "A Statistical Portrait of Women in the United States: 1978." Series P-23, no. 100.

————. 1981a. Population Characteristics. Series P-20, no. 371. U.S. Department of Commerce, Bureau of the Census, March.

————. 1981b. Population Characteristics. Series P-20, no. 367. U.S. Department of Commerce, Bureau of the Census, October.

————. 1982a. Population Characteristics. Series P-20, no. 372. U.S. Department of Commerce, Bureau of the Census, June.

————. 1982b. Population Characteristics. Series P-20, no. 374. U.S. Department of Commerce, Bureau of the Census, September.

Cutler, Winnifred Berg, Celso Ramon Garcia, and Abba M. Krieger. 1980. "Sporadic Sexual Behavior and Menstrual Cycle Length in Women." *Hormones and Behavior* 14:163–172.

Dank, Barry M. 1971. "Coming Out in the Gay World." *Psychiatry* 34 (May):180–97.

Darrow, William W. 1976. "Social and Behavioral Aspects of the Sexually Transmitted Diseases." In Sol Gordon and Roger W. Libby, eds., *Sexuality Today and Tomorrow*. North Scituate, Mass.: Duxbury Press.

————. 1979. Personal communication, October 24.

————. 1983. Personal communication, September 1.

————, and Mary Louise Pauli. 1983. "Health Behavior and Sexually Transmitted Diseases." In King K. Holmes, Per-Anders Mardh, P. Frederick Sparling, and Paul J. Wiesner, eds., *Sexually Transmitted Diseases*. New York: McGraw-Hill.

————, and P. J. Wiesner. 1975. "Personal Prophylaxis for Venereal Diseases." *Journal of the American Medical Association* 233, no. 5 (August):444–46.

————, D. Barrett, K. Jay and A. Young. 1981. "The Gay Report on Sexually Transmitted Diseases." *American Journal of Public Health* 71:1004–1011.

Davenport, William H. 1977. "Sex in Cross-Cultural Perspective." In Frank A. Beach, ed., *Human Sexuality in Four Perspectives*. Baltimore, Md.: Johns Hopkins University Press.

Davidson, Albert, and Vincent Venditti. 1979. "Two Clients' Views." *Sexuality and Disability* 2, no. 1 (Spring):23–27.

Davidson, Fiona. 1977. "Yeasts and Circumcision in the Male." *British Journal of Venereal Diseases* 553:121–22.

Davis, Alan J. 1977. "Sexual Assaults in the Philadelphia Prison System and Sheriff's Vans." In Clifton D. Bryant, ed., *Sexual Deviancy in Social Context*. New York: New Viewpoints\Franklin Watts.

Degler, Carl N. 1980. *At Odds: Women and the Family in America from the Revolution to the Present*. New York: Oxford University Press.

de Groat, William C., and August M. Booth. 1980. "Physiology of Male Sexual Function." *Annals of Internal Medicine* 92, pt. 2:329–31.

Delamater, John, and Patricia Maccorquodale. 1978. "Premarital Contraceptive Use: A Test of Two Models." *Journal of Marriage and the Family* 40, no. 2 (May):235–47.

Delin, Bart. 1978. *The Sex Offender*. Boston: Beacon Press.

DeMartino, Manfred F. 1974. *Sex and the Intelligent Woman*. New York: Springer Publishing.

Demos, Catherine. 1979. Personal communication to Roger W. Libby, October. Used by permission.

DeMott, Benjamin. 1980. "The Pro-Incest Lobby." *Psychology Today*, March, pp. 11–16.

Denfield, D. 1974. "Dropouts from Swinging: The Marriage Counselor as Informant." In J. R. Smith and L. R. Smith, eds., *Beyond Monogamy*. Baltimore, Md.: Johns Hopkins University Press.

Densmore, Dana. 1970a. "On Celibacy." In Leslie Tanner, ed., *Voices from Liberation*. New York: Signet.

————. 1970b. "Independence from the Sex Revolution." In Anne Koedt and Shulamith Firestone, eds., *Notes from the Third Year: Women's Liberation*. P.O. Box AA, Old Chelsea Station, New York, N. Y. 10011.

"DES: Potential Risk for Men, Too?" 1976. *Medical World News*, January 26, pp. 99–100.

Diagram Group. 1976. *Man's Body—An Owner's Manual*. New York: Paddington Press.

Diamond, Milton. 1977. "Sexuality and the Handicapped." In Robert P. Marinelli and Arthur E. DellOrto, eds., *Psychological and Social Impact of Physical Disability*. New York: Springer Publishing.

"Diaphragm, Toxic Shock Linked." 1981. *Boston Globe*, December 24, 8.

"Diaphragm Use Is Said to Lower Risk of Disease." 1982. AP, *Boston Globe*, July 9, p. 3.

Dick-Read, Grantly. 1933. *Natural Childbirth*. London: Heinemann Publishers.

Diepold, John Jr., and Richard David Young. 1979. "Empirical Studies of Adolescent Sexual Behavior: A Critical Review." *Adolescence* 14, no. 53 (Spring):45–64.

Dietz, Jean. 1979. "How Safe Are Abortions?" *Boston Globe*, April 29, B1-B2.

Dion, K. I., Ellen Berscheid, and Elaine Walster, 1972. "What Is Beautiful Is Good." *Journal of Personality and Social Psychology* 24, no. 3 (December):285–90.

Dixon, Katherine N., L. Eugene Arnold, and Kenneth Calestro. 1978. "Father-Son Incest: Underreported Psychiatric Problem?" *American Journal of Psychiatry* 135, no. 7 (July):835–38.

"Doctor Sees Smoking Symptoms in Children." 1979. UPI, *Willimantic Chronicle*, October 20.

Dodson, Betty. 1974. *Liberating Masturbation: A Meditation on Self-Love*. New York: Betty Dodson.

Dominican Sisters. 1978. "The Celibate Experience." *Women* 5 (3):35.

Douglas, Jack D., and John Johnson, eds. 1977. *Existential Sociology*. Cambridge and New York: Cambridge University Press.

Douglas, Jack D., Paul K. Rasmussen, with Carol Ann Flanagan. 1977. *The Nude Beach*. Beverly Hills, Calif.: Sage.

Dressel, Paula L., and W. Ray Avant. 1978. "Neogamy and Older Persons: An Examination of Alternatives for Intimacy in the Later Years." *Alternative Lifestyles* 1, no. 1 (February):13–70.

DuToit, D. F., and W. T. Villet. 1979. "Gangrene of the Penis after Circumcision." *South African Medical Journal* 55, no. 13 (March):521–22.

Dutton, Donald G., and Arthur P. Aron. 1974. "Some Evidence for Heightened Sexual Attraction under Conditions of High Anxiety." *Journal of Personality and Social Psychology* 30, no. 4 (October):510–17.

Dvorchak, Bob. 1982. "Surrogate Birthing Grows, but Raises Many Questions." *Hartford Courant*, December 26, p. C21.

Dyer, Wayne W. 1976. *Your Erroneous Zones*. New York: Avon Books.

Easton, Dorothy M. 1977. "Hartman and Fithian Research Update." *MMRC Guide*, Fall. San Francisco: Multi-Media Resource Center.

Edwards, John N., and Alan Booth. 1976. "The Cessation of Marital Intercourse." *American Journal of Psychiatry* 133, no. 11 (November):1333–36.

Edwards, Martha Shatley. 1978. "Venereal Herpes: A Nursing Overview." *Journal of Obstetric, Gynecologic and Neonatal Nursing* 7, no. 5 (September–October):7–14.

"Effective, but How Safe?" 1983. *Time*, January 24, p. 67.

Egan, Stephanie. 1982. "Juggling More than One Lover." *Cosmopolitan*, December, pp. 114–16, 120.

Eibl-Eibesfeldt, Irenäus. 1970. *Ethology—The Biology of Behavior*. New York: Holt, Rinehart and Winston.

Ellis, Albert. 1962. *The American Sexual Tragedy*. New York: Lyle Stuart.

Ellis, Havelock. 1942. Vol. 1. *Studies in the Psychology of Sex*. New York: Random House. (First published 1905).

"Enforcement of Prostitution Laws Expensive." 1979. *Coyote Howls* 6, no. 1 (Spring):4.

Epstein, Aaron. 1983. "High Court Nullifies Abortion Restrictions." *Boston Globe*, July 16, p. 1.

Erickson, Barbara. 1977. Master's thesis. San Diego State University, San Diego, Calif.

Eschenbach, David A., and King K. Holmes. 1975. "Acute Pelvic Inflammatory Disease: Current Concepts of Pathogenesis, Etiology, and Management." *Clinical Obstetrics and Gynecology* 18, no. 1 (March):35–56.

Esser, Doug. 1982. "When Wooing, Reject Macho." *Amherst Bulletin*, June 2, p. 33.

Evans, Ian M., and Larry A. Distiller. 1979. "Effects of Luteinizing Hormone-Releasing Hormone on Sexual Arousal in Normal Men." *Archives of Sexual Behavior*, 8, no. 5:385–95.

"Evidence of Gentler Babies." 1977. *New York Times*, January 30, p. E7.

Exner, John E., Jr., Joyce Wylie, Antonnia Leura, and Tracey Parrill. 1977. "Some Psychological Characteristics of Prostitutes." *Journal of Personality Assessment* 41, no. 5 (October):474–85.

Fabe, Marilyn, and Norma Wikler. 1979. *Up against the Clock*. New York: Random House.

Faderman, Lillian. 1981. *Surpassing the Love of Men*. New York: William Morrow.

"The Fanatical Abortion Fight." *Time*, July 9, pp. 26–27.

Faraday, Ann. 1974. *The Dream Game*. New York: Harper & Row.

Fast, Julius. 1977. *The Body Language of Sex, Power, and Aggression*. New York: Harcourt Brace Jovanovich.

Fasteau, Marc Feigen. 1974. *The Male Machine*. New York: McGraw-Hill.

Fearing, Franklin. 1954. "An Examination of the Conceptions of Benjamin Whorf in the Light of Theories of Perception and Cognition." In Harry Hoijer, ed., *Language in Culture*. Chicago: University of Chicago Press.

Fee, Elizabeth. 1978. "Women and Health Care: A Comparison of Theories." In Claudia Dreifus, ed., *Seizing Our Bodies*. New York: Vintage Books/Random House.

Feldman, Carole. 1979. "N. J. Code to Legalize Sex at 13." *Boston Globe*, April 24, pp. 1, 20.

Felstein, Ivor. 1970. *Sex in Later Life*. Middlesex, England: Penguin.

"Female Phase Fazer: New Birth Control?" 1982. *Science News* 121 (January 9):21.

Ferrarini, Elizabeth. 1982. "Finding a Mate—Computer Style." *Cosmopolitan*, September, pp. 148–52.

Ferrell, Mary Z., William L. Tolone, and Robert H. Walsh. 1977. "Maturational and Societal Changes in the Sexual Double-Standard: A Panel Analysis (1967–1971; 1970–1974)." *Journal of Marriage and the Family*, 39, no. 2 (May):255–71.

Finger, Frank W. 1975. "Changes in Sex Practices and Beliefs of Male College Students during Thirty Years." *Journal of Sex Research* 11, no. 4 (November):304–17.

Finkel, Madelon Lubin, and David J. Finkel. 1975. "Sexual and Contraceptive Knowledge, Attitudes and Behavior of Male Adolescents." *Family Planning Perspectives* 7, no. 6 (November–December):256–60.

Finkelhor, David. 1979. "Social Forces in the Formulation of the Problem of Sexual Abuse." In *Sexually Victimized Children,* edited by David Finkelhor. New York: Free Press.

———. 1980. "Sex among Siblings: A Survey on Prevalence, Variety, and Effects." *Archives of Sexual Behavior* 9, no. 3 (June):171–94.

———, and Kersti Yelo. 1982. "Forced Sex in Marriage: A Preliminary Research Report." *Crime and Delinquency,* July, pp. 459–79.

Firestone, Ross (ed.). 1975. *The Book of Men.* New York: Stonehill Publishing.

Firestone, Shulamith. 1972. *The Dialectic of Sex: The Case for Feminist Revolution.* New York: Morrow

Fisher, Seymour. 1973. *The Female Orgasm.* New York: Basic Books.

Fisher, William A., and Donn Byrne. 1978. "Sex Differences in Response to Erotical Love vs. Lust." *Journal of Personality and Social Psychology* 36, no. 2 (February):117–25.

Fleming, Karl, and Anne T. Fleming. 1975. *The First Time.* New York: Berkley Medallion Books.

Florescu, John M. 1979. "Brother, Sister Plead Guilty in Incest Case." *Boston Globe,* August 2, p. 20.

Ford, Clellan S., and Frank A. Beach. 1951. *Patterns of Sexual Behavior.* New York: Ace Books.

Foreman, Judy. 1979. "Rape Is Emerging from the Shadows." *Boston Globe,* April 9, p. 25.

———. 1983. "Ten Years after Supreme Court Decision, Abortion Debate Goes On." *Boston Globe,* January 21, p. 2.

Forrest, Jacqueline Darroch, Albert I. Hermalin, and Stanley K. Henshaw. 1981. "The Impact of Family Planning Clinic Programs on Adolescent Pregnancy." *Family Planning Perspectives* 13, no. 3 (May/June):109–16.

Foster, Arthur Lee. 1979. "Relationships between Age and Sexual Activity in Married Men." *Journal of Sex Education and Therapy* 5, no. 5 (Summer):21–26.

Fox, Greer Litton. 1977. " 'Nice Girl': Social Control of Women through a Value Construct." *Signs* 2, no. 4 (Summer):805–17.

Fox, J. Robin. 1968. "Contexts for Early Learning Experiences." In Kent Geiger, ed., *Comparative Perspectives on Marriage and the Family.* Boston: Little, Brown.

Frank, Ellen, and Sondra Forsyth Enos. 1983. "The Love Life of the American Wife." *Ladies' Home Journal,* February, pp. 71–73, 116–19.

Frankfort, Ellen. 1978. "Vaginal Politics." In Claudia Dreifus, ed., *Seizing Our Bodies: The Politics of Women's Health.* New York: Vintage Books/Random House.

Freedman, Mark. 1975. "Far from Illness: Homosexuals May Be Healthier than Straights." *Psychology Today,* March, p. 30.

Freeman, Ellen W. 1977. "Influence of Personality Attributes on Abortion Experiences." *American Journal of Orthopsychiatry* 47, no. 3 (July):503–13.

Freudberg, Frank, and E. Stephen Emanuel. 1982. *Herpes: A Complete Guide to Relief and Reassurance.* Philadelphia: Running Press.

Friday, Nancy. 1973. *My Secret Garden: Women's Sexual Fantasies.* New York: Pocket Books.

———. 1980. *Men in Love.* New York: Dell.

Friedrichs, David O. 1972. "The Body Taboo." *Sexual Behavior* 2, no. 3 (March):64–72.

Friend, Richard A. 1980. "GAYging: Adjustment and the Older Gay Male." *Alternative Lifestyles* 3, no. 2 (May):231–48.

Fullerton, Gail Putney. 1972. Comment on Gerhard Neubeck's "The Myriad Motives for Sex." *Sexual Behavior* 2, no. 7 (July):52–53.

"G Spot/Female Ejaculation Researchers Vindicated by New Research." 1983. *Sexuality Today* 6, no. 11 (May):1, 3.

Gagnon, John H. 1973. "Scripts and the Coordination of Sexual Conduct." Nebraska Symposium on Motivation, University of Nebraska, Lincoln.

———, and William Simon. 1973. *Sexual Conduct: The Social Sources of Human Sexuality.* Chicago: Aldine.

"Gallup Poll on Gay Rights: Approval with Reservations." *San Francisco Chronicle,* July 18, pp. 1, 18.

Galton, Lawrence. 1979. *The Complete Medical, Fitness and Health Guide for Men.* New York: Simon & Schuster.

———. 1980. "VD: Outbreak of a New Variety." *Parade,* February 24, p. 16.

Ganong, William F. 1981. *Review of Medical Physiology.* Los Altos, Calif.: Large Medical Publications.

Gawin, Frank H. 1978. "Pharmacologic Enhancement of the Erotic: Implications of an Expanded Definition of Aphrodisiacs." *Journal of Sex Research* 14, no. 2 (May):107–17.

"The Gay World's Leather Fringe." 1980. *Time,* March 24, pp. 74–75.

Gebhard, Paul H. 1970. "Postmarital Coitus among Widows and Divorcees." In Paul Bohannon, ed., *Divorce and After.* New York: Doubleday.

————. 1977. "The Acquisition of Basic Sex Information." *Journal of Sex Research* 13, no. 3 (August):148–69.

————, et al. 1965. *Sex Offenders: An Analysis of Types*. New York: Harper & Row.

Gecas, Victor, and Roger W. Libby. 1976. "Sexual Behavior as Symbolic Interaction." *Journal of Sex Research* 12, no. 1 (February):33–49.

Geller, Andrew. 1982. "Physician Uses Cough Syrup to Treat Female Infertility." *Hartford Courant*, July 29, p. A12.

Gelles, Richard J. 1977. "Power, Sex, and Violence: The Case of Marital Rape." *Family Coordinator* 26, no. 4 (October):339–47.

Gerstel, Naomi R. 1979. "Marital Alternatives and the Regulation of Sex." *Alternative Lifestyles* 2, no. 2 (May):145–76.

Gilmartin, Brian. 1977. "Swinging: Who Gets Involved and How?" In Roger W. Libby and Robert N. Whitehurst, eds., *Marriage and Alternatives: Exploring Intimate Relationships*, Glenview, Ill.: Scott, Foresman.

————. 1978. *The Gilmartin Report*. Secaucus, N. J.: Citadel Press.

Ginsburg, Kenneth N. 1977. "The 'Meat-Rack': A Study of the Male Homosexual Prostitute." In Clifton D. Bryant, ed., *Sexual Deviancy in Social Context*. New York: New Viewpoints/Franklin Watts.

Gittelson, Natalie. 1979. "Co-ed Dorms." *McCall's*, September, pp. 14, 19, 24, 158.

Glass, Dorothea D., and Frank J. Padrone. 1978. "Sexual Adjustment in the Handicapped." *Journal of Rehabilitation* 44, no. 1 (January–February–March):43–47.

Glenn, Norval D., and Charles N. Weaver. 1979. "Attitudes toward Premarital, Extramarital, and Homosexual Relations in the U.S. in the 1970s." *Journal of Sex Research* 15, no. 2 (May):108–19.

Gold, Alice Ross, and David B. Adams. 1981. "Motivational Factors Affecting Fluctuations of Female Sexual Activity at Menstruation." *Psychology of Women Quarterly* 5, no. 5 (supplement):670–80.

Goldberg, Carole. 1979. "The Dating Game—Those 'Personals'." *New Haven Advocate*, February 7, p. 42.

Goldfarb, Barbara, and Roger W. Libby. 1984. "Mothers and Children Alone." *Alternative Lifestyles*, forthcoming.

Goldman, Ronald, and Juliette Goldman. 1982. *Children's Sexual Thinking*. London: Routledge and Kegan Paul.

Goldsen, R. 1978. Letter to the editors of *Human Behavior*, February, pp. 7–8.

Goodman, Hal. 1982. "Assertiveness Breeds Attempt." *Psychology Today*, December, p. 75.

Gordon, David Cole. 1968. *Self-Love*. New York: Verity House.

Gordon, G. G., K. Altman, A. L. Southren, E. Rubin, and C. S. Lieber. 1976. "Effect of Alcohol (Ethanol) Administration on Sex-Hormone Metabolism in Normal Men." *New England Journal of Medicine* 295, no. 15 (October):793–97.

Gordon, Sol. 1981. "The Case for a Moral Sex Education in the Schools." *The Journal of School Health* 51, no. 4:214–18.

Granberg, Donald, and Beth Wellman Granberg. 1980. "Abortion Attitudes, 1965–1980: Trends and Determinants." *Family Planning Perspectives* 12, no. 5 (September:October):250–61.

Green, Richard. 1978. "Sexual Identity of 37 Children Raised by Homosexual or Transsexual Parents." *American Journal of Psychiatry* 135, no. 6 (June):692–97.

————. 1979. *Human Sexuality: A Health Practitioner's Text*. 2d ed. Baltimore, Md.:Williams & Wilkins.

Green, Thomas A. 1977. *Gynecology: Essentials of Clinical Practice*. Boston: Little, Brown.

Greenberg, Judith B. 1979. "Single-Parenting and Intimacy: A Comparison of Mothers and Fathers." *Alternative Lifestyles* 2, no. 3 (August):308–31.

Greene, Gail. 1964. *Sex and the College Girl*. New York: Dial Press:Delacorte.

Greenhouse, Herbert B. 1974. "Penile Erections during Dreams." In Ralph L. Woods and Herbert B. Greenhouse, eds., *The New World of Dreams*. New York: Macmillan.

Greep, Roy. O., Marjorie A. Koblinsky, and Frederick S. Jaffe. 1976. *Reproduction and Human Welfare: A Challenge to Research*. Cambridge, Mass.: MIT Press.

Griffin, Susan. 1977. "Rape—The All-American Crime." In Duncan Chappell, Robley Geis, and Gilbert Geis, eds., *Forcible Rape*. New York: Columbia University Press.

————. 1979. *Rape: The Power of Consciousness*. New York: Harper & Row.

Gross, Leonard. 1982. "The Passion Cycle." *Mademoiselle*, May, p. 99.

Groth, A. Nicholas. 1979. *Men Who Rape*. New York: Plenum Press.

————, and H. Jean Birnbaum. 1978. "Adult Sexual Orientation and Attraction to Underage Persons." *Archives of Sexual Behavior* 7, no. 3 (May):175–81.

Gulino, Denis G. 1981. "Study Says More Women Staying Childless." *Boston Sunday Globe*, February 8, p. 12.

Gutheil, Thomas G., and Nicholas C. Avery. 1977. "Multiple Overt Incest as Family Defense against Loss." *Family Process* 16, no. 1 (March):105–16.

Guttmacher, Alan F., Winfield Best, and Frederick S. Jaffe. 1969. *Birth Control and Love*. New York: Macmillan.

Hagan, Richard, and Joseph D'Agostine. 1982 "New Study Warns Cigarettes May Cut Sex Drive." *Sexuality Today*, July 19, p. 3.

Hageman, Mary Jeanette Clement. 1979a. "Male Heterosexual Prostitution." Expanded version of a paper presented to the annual meeting of the American Sociological Association, San Francisco. Used by permission.

————. 1979b. Personal communication. November.

Hahn, Harlan. 1981. "The Social Component of Sexuality and Disability: Some Problems and Proposals." *Sexuality and Disability* 4, no. 4 (Winter):220–33.

Halikas, J., R. Weller, and C. Morse. 1982. "Effects of Marijuana Use on Sexual Performance." *Journal of Psychoactive Drugs* 14:1–2.

Hall, Elizabeth. 1980. "Acting One's Age: New Rules for Old," interview with Bernice Neugarten. *Psychology Today*, April, pp. 62–82.

Halverstadt, Donald B. 1972. "Venereal Warts." *Medical Aspects of Human Sexuality* 6, no. 6 (June):12–21.

Hamilton, Eleanor. 1978. *Sex with Love: A Guide for Young People*. Boston: Beacon Press.

Hammond, Charles B., and Wayne S. Maxson. 1982. "Current Status of Estrogen Therapy for the Menopause." *Fertility and Sterility* 37, no. 1 (January):5–25.

Handsfield, H. Hunter. 1982. "Sexually Transmitted Diseases." *Hospital Practice*, January, pp. 99–116.

————. 1978. "Gonorrhea and Nongonococcal Urethritis—Recent Advances." Symposium on Infectious Diseases. *Medical Clinics of North America* 62, no. 5 (September):925–43.

Hare-Mustin, Rachel T., and Patricia C. Broderick. 1979. "The Myth of Motherhood: A Study of Attitudes toward Motherhood." *Psychology of Women Quarterly* 4, no. 1 (Fall):114–28.

Haring, Marilyn, and Lee Meyerson. 1979. "Attitudes of College Students toward Sexual Behavior of Disabled Persons." *Archives of Physical Medicine and Rehabilitation* 60, no. 6 (June):257–60.

Hariton, Barbara E. 1973. "The Sexual Fantasies of Women." In *Psychology Today*, eds., *The Female Experience*. Del Mar, Calif.:Communications/Research/Machines.

————, and Jerome L. Singer. 1974. "Women's Fantasies during Sexual Intercourse." *Journal of Consulting and Clinical Psychology* 42, no. 3 (June):319.

Harris, Bertha. 1978. Quoted in "The Joy of Gay Sex." *Sexuality Today*, January 30, p. 2.

Harrison, Barbara Grizzuti. 1975. "The Sexual Awakening of Women Over 35." *McCall's*, May, p. 26.

Harrison, Deanne. 1979. In Dale Kunkel, ed., *Sexual Issues in Social Work*. Honolulu: University of Hawaii, School of Social Work.

Harry, Joseph, and Robert Lovely. 1979. "Gay Marriages and Communities of Sexual Orientation." *Alternative Lifestyles* 2, no. 2 (May):177–200.

Hartmann, Heidi I., and Ellen Ross. 1978. "Comment on 'On Writing the History of Rape'." *Signs* 3, no. 4 (Summer):931–35.

Hartman, William E., and Marilyn A. Fithian. 1972. *Treatment of Sexual Dysfunction*. Long Beach, Calif.: Center for Marital and Sexual Studies.

————. 1979. Basic Lecture Series, IASHS. San Francisco, October.

Hatcher, Robert A., et al. 1980 and 1981. *Contraceptive Technology, 1978–79*. 10th ed. New York: Irvington Publishers.

————. 1982. *Contraceptive Technology 1982–1983*. New York: Irvington Publishers.

Hatfield, Elaine, Sue Sprecher, and Jane Traupmann. 1978. "Men's and Women's Reactions to Sexually Explicit Films: A Serendipitous Finding." *Archives of Sexual Behavior* 7, no. 6 (November):583–92.

Hayes, Andrea. 1979. "An Exploratory Study into the Influence of Feminism on Female Sexual Scripts." Senior honors thesis, University of Massachusetts, Amherst.

Heath, R. G. 1972. "Pleasure and Brain Activity in Man." *Journal of Nervous and Mental Disorders* 154:3–18.

Heim, Nikolaus, and Carolyn J. Hursch. 1979. "Castration for Sex Offenders: Treatment or Punishment? A Review and Critique of Recent European Literature." *Archives of Sexual Behavior* 8, no. 3 (May):281–304.

Heiman, Julia R. 1975. "Women's Sexual Arousal—The Physiology of Erotica." *Psychology Today*, April, pp. 91–94.

————. 1977. "A Psychophysiological Exploration of Sexual Arousal Patterns in Females and Males." *Psychophysiology* 14, no. 3 (March):266–74.

————, Leslie LoPiccolo, and Joseph LoPiccolo. 1976. *Becoming Orgasmic: A Sexual Growth Program for Women*. Englewoods Cliffs, N.J.: Prentice-Hall.

"Help Is Coming for Herpes." 1983. *Time*, June 27, p. 63.

Henderson, R. H. 1977. "Control of Sexually Transmitted Diseases in the United States—A Federal Perspective." *British Journal of Venereal Diseases* 53:211–15.

Hendrick, Shirley Smith. 1982. " 'Cinderella' Success Stories Obscure Real Picture." *National Business Employment Weekly*, *The Wall Street Journal*, October 17, pp. 13–14.

Henig, Robin Marantz. 1982. "Dispelling Menstrual Myths." *New York Times Magazine*, March 7, pp. 64–79.

Henley, Nancy M. 1977. *Body Politics.* Englewood Cliffs, N.J.: Prentice-Hall.

Herbst, Arthur L. 1979. "Coitus and the Fetus." *New England Journal of Medicine* 301, no. 22 (November):1235–36.

Herold, Edward S., and Marilyn Shirley Goodwin. 1981a. "Adamant Virgins, Potential Nonvirgins and Nonvirgins." *The Journal of Sex Research* 17, no. 2 (May):97–113.

————. 1981b. "Premarital Sexual Guilt and Contraceptive Attitudes and Behavior." *Family Relations,* April, pp. 247–53.

"Herpes Changes Sexual Habits, Poll Concludes." 1982. *Boston Globe,* October 12, p. 3.

Herrell, James M. 1975. "Sex Differences in Emotional Responses to 'Erotic Literature'." *Journal of Consulting and Clinical Psychology* 43, no. 6 (December): 921.

Hess, Eckhard H. 1975. *The Tell-Tale Eye: How Your Eyes Reveal Hidden Thoughts and Emotions.* New York: Van Nostrand Reinhold.

Higgins, Loretta P., and Joellen W. Hawkins. Forthcoming *Human Sexuality Across the Life Span: Implications for Nursing Practice.* Monterey, Calif.: Wadsworth Health Sciences.

Hill, Charles, Zick Rubin, and Letitia Anne Peplau. 1979. "Breakups before Marriage: The End of 103 Affairs." In George Levinger and Oliver Moles, eds., *Divorce and Separation.* New York: Basic Books.

Hindelang, Michael J., and Bruce J. Davis. 1977. "Forcible Rape in the United States: A Statistical Profile." In Duncan Chappell, Robley Geis, and Gilbert Geis, eds., *Forcible Rape: The Crime, the Victim, and the Offender.* New York: Columbia University Press.

Hines, Melissa. 1982. "Prenatal Gonadal Hormones and Sex Differences in Human Behavior." *Psychological Bulletin* 92, no. 1 (July):56–80.

Hite, Shere. 1976. *The Hite Report: A Nationwide Study of Female Sexuality.* New York: Macmillan.

————. 1981. *The Hite Report on Male Sexuality.* New York: Ballantine.

Hobbins, John C., and Maurice J. Mahoney. 1977. "Fetoscopy in Continuing Pregnancies." *American Journal of Obstetrics and Gynecology* 129, no. 4 (October):440–41.

Hoffman, Eva, and Margot Slade. 1981. "A Case against Family Court." *The New York Times,* November 1, n.p.

Hollister, L. E. 1975. "The Mystique of Social Drugs and Sex." In M. Sandler and D.L. Gessa, eds., *Sexual Behavior: Pharmacology and Biochemistry.* New York: Raven Press.

Holmes, King K. 1981. "The Chlamydia Epidemic." *Journal of American Medical Association* 245 (May 1):1718–23.

————, and Walter E. Stamm. 1979. "Chlamydial Genital Infections: A Growing Problem." *Hospital Practice,* October, pp. 105–17.

Holmes, K. K., and M. D. Kiviat. 1978. "Urethritis." In W. Harrison, ed., *Campbell's Urology.* Philadelphia: Saunders.

Holmes, K. K., and G. A. Stilwell. 1977. "Gonococcal Infection." In P.H. Hoeprich, ed., *Infectious Diseases.* 2d ed. Hagerstown, Md.: Harper.

Holmstrom, Lynda Lytle, and Ann Wolbert Burgess. 1978. *The Victim of Rape.* New York: Wiley.

Hoon, Peter W., John P. Wincze, and Emily Franck Hoon. 1977. "A Test of Reciprocal Inhibition: Are Anxiety and Sexual Arousal in Women Mutually Inhibitory?" *Journal of Abnormal Psychology* 86, no. 1 (February):65–74.

Hooper, Anne. 1979. "How to Give Your Man an Erotic Massage." *Forum,* February, pp. 59–61.

Hoppe, Arthur. 1979. "A New Sex Fad." *San Francisco Chronicle,* October 10, p. 57.

Horn, Marilyn J. 1975. *The Second Skin: An Interdisciplinary Study of Clothing.* Boston: Houghton Mifflin.

Horn, Patrice D., and Jack C. Horn. 1982. *Sex in the Office.* Reading, Mass.: Addison-Wesley.

"How College Men and Women Feel Now about Sex, Dating, and Marriage." 1980. *Glamour* (August), pp. 190–91, 295.

"How Gay Is Gay? Homosexual Men and Women Are Making Progress toward Equality." 1979. *Time,* April 23.

"How Men Choose Vasectomy." 1983. *Sexuality Today* 6, no. 12 (January 10):1.

"How Semen Kills Germs." 1979. *Newsweek,* October 1, p. 40.

How to Be Happy Though Married. 1885. London: T. Fisher Unwin.

Howard, Michael C., and Patrick C. McKim. 1983. *Contemporary Cultural Anthropology.* Boston: Little, Brown.

Huang, L. 1974. "Research with Unmarried Cohabiting Couples, Including Non-Exclusive Sexual Relations." Unpublished manuscript, Illinois State University, Normal.

Huber, Joan, John Gagnon, Suzanne Keller, Ronald Lawson, Patricia Miller, and William Simon. 1982. "Report of the American Sociological Association's Task Group on Homosexuality." *American Sociologist* 17, no. 3 (August):164–180.

Humphreys, Laud. 1970. *Tearoom Trade: Impersonal Sex in Public Places.* Chicago: Aldine.

Hunt, Morton. 1974. *Sexual Behavior in the 1970s.* Chicago: Playboy Press.

————, and Bernice Hunt. 1977. *The Divorce Experience*. New York: Signet.

Hursch, Carolyn J. 1977. *The Trouble with Rape*. Chicago: Nelson-Hall Publishers.

Hurst, Jane. 1981. *The History of Abortion in the Catholic Church: The Untold Story*. Catholics for Free Choice. Washington, D.C.

Huston, Ted L., and George Levinger. 1978. "Interpersonal Attraction and Relationships." *Annual Review of Psychology* 29:115–56.

"I Never Set Out to Rape Anybody. . . ." 1972. *Ms.*, December, pp. 22–23.

"Insanity, Produced by Masturbation." 1835. *Boston Medical and Surgical Journal* 12:109–11.

James, Jennifer. 1976a. "Motivations for Entrance into Prostitution." In Laura Crites, ed., *The Female Offender*. Lexington, Mass.: Lexington Books.

————. 1976b. "Prostitution: Arguments for Change." In Sol Gordon and Roger W. Libby, eds., *Sexuality Today and Tomorrow*. North Scituate, Mass.: Duxbury Press.

————. 1977a. "Answers to the 20 Questions Most Frequently Asked about Prostitution." In Jennifer James, *The Politics of Prostitution*. 2d ed. Seattle, Wash.: Social Research Associates.

————. 1977b. "Women as Sexual Criminals and Victims." In Judith Long Laws and Pepper Schwartz, eds., *Sexual Scripts*. Hinsdale, Ill.: Dryden Press.

————. 1980. "Self-Destructive Behaviors and Adaptive Strategies in Female Prostitutes." In Norman L. Farberow, ed., *The Many Faces of Suicide: Indirect Self-Destructive Behaviors*. New York: McGraw-Hill.

Janus, Samuel S., and Barbara E. Bess. 1981. "Latency: Fact or Fiction?" In Larry L. Constantine and Floyd M. Martinson, eds., *Children and Sex: New Findings, New Perspectives*. Boston: Little, Brown.

Jardine, Jack Owen. 1979. "Turn Your Man into a Lover (Who's So Good It's Downright Sinful)." *Playgirl*, April, pp. 55–56.

Jennings, M. Anne. 1976. "The Victim as Criminal: A Consideration of California's Prostitution Law." *California Law Review* 64(5):1235–84.

Jesser, Clinton J. 1978. "Male Responses to Direct Verbal Sexual Initiatives of Females." *Journal of Sex Research* 14, no. 2 (May):118–28.

Jessor, Richard, Francis Costa, Lee Jessor, and John E. Donovan. 1983. "Time of First Intercourse: A Prospective Study." *Journal of Personality and Social Psychology* 44, no. 3:608–26.

Jessor, Shirley L., and Richard Jessor. 1975. "Transition from Virginity to Nonvirginity among Youth: A Social-Psychological Study over Time." *Developmental Psychology* 11, no. 4 (July):473–84.

Jones, Hardin B., and Helen C. Jones. 1977. *Sensual Drugs*. New York: Cambridge University Press.

Jong, Erica. 1973. *Fear of Flying*. New York: New American Library.

————. 1977. *How to Save Your Own Life*. New York: New American Library.

"The Joy of Running in Regular Cycles." 1980. *Science News* 118 (July 5):6.

"Judicial System Found Remiss in Identifying Teen Offenders." 1979. *Sexuality Today*, June 11, pp. 1–2.

Julty, Sam. 1979. *Men's Bodies, Men's Selves*. New York: Simon & Schuster.

Kaas, Merrie Jean. 1978. "Sexual Expression of the Elderly in Nursing Homes," *Gerontologist* 1, no. 4 (August):372–78.

Kaltreider, N. B. 1973. "Emotional Patterns Related to Delay in Decision to Seek Legal Abortion." *California Medicine* 118, no. 23:23–27.

Kamat, D. S., E. K. Bharucha, and P. C. Sankholkar. 1978. "Immediate Sterility after Vasectomy with the Use of 0.1% Ethacridine Lactate." *Journal of Postgraduate Medicine* 24, no. 4 (October):218–20.

Kantner, John F. 1979. "From Here to 2000: A Look at the Population Problem." *Johns Hopkins Medical Journal* 144, no. 1 (January):18–24.

Kaplan, Helen Singer. 1974. *The New Sex Therapy*. New York: Bunner/Mazel.

————. 1979. *Disorders of Sexual Desire*. New York: Simon & Schuster.

Karagianis, Maria. 1979. "Overhaul of Rape Laws Pushed." *Boston Globe*, August 8, p. 17.

Kaufman, Michael. 1973. "Spare Ribs: The Conception of Women in the Middle Ages and the Renaissance." *Soundings* 56, no. 2 (Summer):139–63.

Kaufman, Sherwin A. 1978. *You Can Have a Baby*. Nashville, Tenn.: Thomas Nelson.

Kavanaugh, Dorriet, ed. 1978. *Listen to Us! The Children's Express Report*. New York: Workman Publishing.

Kegel, Arnold H. 1952. "Sexual Functions of the Pubococcygeus Muscle." *Western Journal of Surgery* 60:521–24.

Kelly, Jim. 1977. "The Aging Male Homosexual: Myth and Reality." *Gerontologist* 17, no. 4 (August):328–32.

Kenney, Michael. 1979. "A Rape Suspect the Experts May Have 'Misjudged'." *Boston Globe*, May 4.

Kent, Rosemary. 1975. "Should You Sleep with Your Boss?" *Harper's Bazaar*, November, p. 147.

Kerckhoff, Richard K. 1976. "Marriage and Middle Age." *Family Coordinator* 25, no. 1 (January):5–12.

Kerr, Carmen. 1977. *Sex for Women Who Want to Have Fun and Loving Relationships with Equals.* New York: Grove Press.

Kimmel, Douglas C. 1978. "Adult Development and Aging: A Gay Perspective." *Journal of Social Issues* 34, no. 3 (Summer):114–30.

Kinsey, Alfred C., Wardell B. Pomeroy, and Clyde E. Martin. 1948. *Sexual Behavior in the Human Male.* Philadelphia: Saunders.

Kinsey, Alfred C., Wardell B. Pomeroy, Clyde E. Martin, and Paul H. Gebhard. 1953. *Sexual Behavior in the Human Female.* Philadelphia: Saunders.

Kirsch, Felix M. 1930. *Sex Education and Training in Chastity.* New York: Benziger Brothers.

Kirtley, Donald D. 1975. *The Psychology of Blindness.* Chicago: Nelson-Hall.

Klein, Carole. 1973. *The Single Parent Experience.* New York: Walker.

Klein, Fred. 1978. *The Bisexual Option: A Concept of One Hundred Percent Intimacy.* New York: Arbor House.

Klemesrud, Judy. 1978. "The Year of the Lusty Woman." *Esquire,* December 19, pp. 33–36.

Kline-Graber, Georgia, and Benjamin Graber. 1978. "Diagnosis and Treatment Procedures of Pubococcygeal Deficiencies in Women." In Joseph LoPiccolo and Leslie LoPiccolo, eds., *Handbook of Sex Therapy.* New York: Plenum.

Knapp, Jacquelyn, and Robert N. Whitehurst. 1977. "Sexually Open Marriage and Relationships: Issues and Prospects." In Roger W. Libby and Robert N. Whitehurst, ed., *Marriage and Alternatives; Exploring Intimate Relationships.* Glenview, Ill.: Scott, Foresman.

Knight, Michael. 1977. "Darien Begins a Crackdown on Prostitutes Who Solicit Truck Drivers by CB Radios." *New York Times,* July 16, p. 25.

Knight, Susan E. 1979. "Future Issues for Consumers and Practitioners." Sexuality and Disability: A National Symposium. San Francisco, University of California.

Koff, Wayne C. 1974. "Marijuana and Sexual Activity." *Journal of Sex Research* 10, no. 3 (August):194–204.

Kohlenberg, Robert J. 1974. "Directed Masturbation and the Treatment of Primary Orgasmic Dysfunction." *Archives of Sexual Behavior* 3, no. 4 (July):349–56.

Kohn, Jane Burgess, and Willard K. Kohn. 1978. *The Widower.* Boston: Beacon Press.

Komarovsky, Mirra. 1976. *Dilemmas of Masculinity: A Study of College Youth.* New York: Norton.

Konner, M. 1982. *The Tangled Wing.* New York: Holt, Rinehart and Winston.

Kopay, David, and Perry Deane Young. 1977. *The David Kopay Story.* New York: Arbor House Publishing Co.

Koughan, Martin. 1979. "In Union, Prostitutes Seek Strength." *Boston Globe.*

Kraus, S. J., and L. H. Glassman. 1976. "The Crab Louse—Review of Physiology and Study of Anatomy as Seen by the Scanning Electron Microscope." *Journal of the American Venereal Disease Association* 2, no. 4 (June):12–18.

Kreston, Jo-Ann, and Claudia S. Bepko. 1980. "The Problem of Fusion in the Lesbian Relationship." *Family Process* 19, no 3 (September):277–89.

Kushner, Rose. 1975. *Breast Cancer.* New York: Harcourt Brace Jovanovich.

Ladas, Alice Kahn, Beverly Whipple, and John D. Perry. 1982.*The G Spot and Recent Discoveries about Human Sexuality.* New York: Holt, Rinehart and Winston.

LaFleche, Ellen. 1983. "New Contraceptive Available Soon." *Amherst Bulletin,* July 20, pp. 14–15.

Lane, M., R. Arleo, and A.J. Sobrero. 1976. "Successful Use of the Diaphragm and Jelly in a Young Population: Report of a Clinical Study." *Family Planning Perspectives* 8, no. 2 (March-April):81–86.

Laner, Mary Riege, Roy H. Laner, and C. Eddie Palmer. 1978. "Permissive Attitudes toward Sexual Behaviors: A Clarification of Theoretical Explanations." *Journal of Sex Research* 14, no. 3 (August):137–44.

Langfeldt, Thore. 1981a. "Childhood Masturbation: Individual and Social Organization." In Larry L. Constantine and Floyd M. Martinson, eds., *Children and Sex: New Findings, New Perspectives.* Boston: Little, Brown.

———. 1981b. "Processes in Sexual Development." In Larry L. Constantine and Floyd M. Martinson, eds., *Children and Sex: New Findings, New Perspectives.* Boston: Little, Brown.

LaPlante, Marcia N., Naomi McCormick, and Gary G. Brannigan. 1981. "Living the Sexual Script: College Students' Views of Influence in Sexual Encounters." *Journal of Sex Research* 16, no. 4 (November):338–55.

Larned, Deborah. 1978. "The Epidemic in Unnecessary Hysterectomies." In Claudia Dreifus, ed., *Seizing Our Bodies.* New York: Vintage Books/Random House.

LaRossa, Ralph. 1979. "Sex during Pregnancy and Marital Stress." Unpublished paper.

Larsen, Knud S., Michael Reed, and Susan Hoffman. 1980. "Attitudes of Heterosexuals toward Homosexuality: A Likert-Type Scale and Construct Validity." *Journal of Sex Research* 16 (August):245–57.

Latham, Mary. 1972. "Selling Celibacy." *Women* 3(1):24–25.

LaTorre, R. A., and Karen Kear. 1977. "Attitudes toward Sex in the Aged." *Archives of Sexual Behavior* 6, no. 3 (May):203–13.

Lebed, Marc, Harvey Nisenbaum, and Stan Cope. 1977. "Letter to the Editor: Prenatal Diagnosis with Fetoscopy," *New England Journal of Medicine* 297, no. 17 (October 27):949–50.

Leblanc, Gloria. 1980. Personal communication, January. Used by permission.

Leboyer, Frederick. 1975. *Birth without Violence.* New York: Knopf.

Lee, John Alan. 1979. "The Social Organization of Sexual Risk." *Alternative Lifestyles* 2, no. 1 (February):69–101.

LeMasters, E. E. 1975. *Blue-Collar Aristocrats: Life-Styles at a Working-Class Tavern.* Madison: University of Wisconsin Press.

Lemere, Frederick, and James W. Smith. 1973. "Alcohol-Induced Sexual Impotence." *American Journal of Psychiatry* 130, no. 2 (February):212–13.

Leo, John. 1979. "Homosexuality: Tolerance vs. Approval." *Time,* January 8, pp. 48, 51.

Leonard, George. 1982. "The End of Sex." *Esquire,* December, pp. 70–80. Adapted from George Leonard, *The End of Sex.* New York: Houghton Mifflin, forthcoming.

Lever, Janet, and Pepper Schwartz. 1976. "The Weekend System: The Mixer." In Jacqueline P. Wiseman, ed., *The Social Psychology of Sex.* New York: Harper & Row.

Levin, R. J. 1975. "Facets of Female Behavior Supporting the Social Script Model of Human Sexuality." *Journal of Sex Research* 11, no. 4 (November):348–52.

Levitt, Eugene E., and Albert D. Klassen. 1973. "Public Attitudes toward Sexual Behaviors: The Latest Investigation of the Institute for Sex Research." Paper presented at the annual convention of the American Orthopsychiatric Association, New York City.

Lewinsohn, Richard. 1958. *A History of Sexual Customs.* New York: Harper & Row.

Lewis, Dio. 1874. *Chastity; or, Our Secret Sins.* Philadelphia: George Maclean & Co.

Lewis, Robert A., Ellen B. Kozac, Robert M. Mildardo, and Wayne A. Grosnick. 1981. "Commitment in Same-Sex Love Relationships." *Alternative Lifestyles* 4, (February):22–43.

Libby, Roger W., and John Carlson. 1973. "Premarital Sexual Decision-Making in the Dyad." *Archives of Sexual Behavior* 2, no. 4 (December):365–79.

———, and Gilbert D. Nass. 1971. "Parental Views on Teenage Sexual Behavior." *Journal of Sex Research* 7, no. 3 (August):226–36.

———, and Murray A. Straus. 1980. "Make Love Not War? Sex, Sexual Meanings, and Violence in a Sample of University Students." *Archives of Sexual Behavior* 9, no. 2 (April):133–49.

———, Alan C. Acock, and David C. Payne. 1974. "Configurations of Parental Preferences Concerning Sources of Sex Education for Adolescents." *Adolescence* 9, no. 33 (Spring):73–80.

Lief, Harold I. 1977. "Sexual Survey #4: Current Thinking on Homosexuality." *Medical Aspects of Human Sexuality* 11, no. 11 (November):110–11.

———. 1981. "Sexuality and Sexual Health." In Harold I. Lief, ed., *Sexual Problems in Medical Practice.* Monroe, Wis.: American Medical Association.

Linn, Shai, Stephen C. Schoenbaum, Richard R. Monson, Bernard Rosner, Phillip G. Stubblefield, and Kenneth J. Ryan. 1982. "No Association between Coffee Consumption and Adverse Outcomes of Pregnancy." *New England Journal of Medicine* 306, no. 3 (January 21):141–44.

Littman, Karel Joyce. 1980. "Contraceptions: The Cervical Cap." *Ms.,* October, pp. 91–95.

Longcope, Kay. 1979. "Fear of Becoming a Gay's Haven Splits Residents of Bellows Falls." *Boston Globe,* May 24, pp. 19, 25.

"Longitudinal Study Supports Safety of Vasectomy." 1983. *Sexuality Today* 6, no. 12 (January 10):1.

Long Laws, Judith, and Pepper Schwartz. 1977. *Sexual Scripts: The Social Construction of Female Sexuality.* Hinsdale, Ill.: Dryden Press.

LoPiccolo, Joseph, and W. Charles Lobitz. 1972. "The Role of Masturbation in the Treatment of Orgasmic Dysfunction." *Archives of Sexual Behavior* 2, no. 2 (December):163–71.

Lowenthal, Marjorie Fiske, and David Chiriboga. 1972. "Transition to the Empty Nest." *Archives of Genetic Psychiatry* 26, no. 1 (January):8–14.

Lowry, Thomas. 1982. "Participants Call Brachioprotic Eroticism 'Mystic Experience.'" *Sexuality Today* 5 (April 12):1.

Lubenow, Gerald C., Pamela Abramson, and Patricia King. 1982. "Gays and Lesbians on Campus." *Newsweek,* April 5, pp. 75–77.

Luker Kristin. 1975 and 1978. *Taking Chances: Abortion and the Decision Not to Contracept.* Berkeley and Los Angeles: University of California Press.

Lynch, Theresea, and Marilyn Neckes. 1978. *The Cost-Effectiveness of Enforcing Prostitution Laws.* San Francisco: Unitarian Universalist Service Committee.

Lyons, Richard D. 1973. "Psychiatrists in a Shift, Declare Homosexuality No Mental Illness." *New York Times,* December 16, p. 1ff.

Maccoby, Eleanor Emmons, and Carol Nagy Jacklin. 1974. *The Psychology of Sex Differences.* Stanford, Calif.: Stanford University Press.

McCaghy, Charles H., and James K. Skipper, Jr. 1969. "Lesbian Behavior as an Adaptation to the Occupation of Stripping." *Social Problems* 17, no. 2 (Fall): 262–70.

McCarthy, Barry. 1978. "Men's First Intercourse." *Medical Aspects of Human Sexuality* 12, no. 7 (July):65.

———. 1982. "Sexual Dysfunctions and Dissatisfactions among Middle-Year Couples." *Journal of Sex Education and Therapy* 8, no. 2 (Fall/Winter):9–16.

McCartney, James. 1979. "U.S. Birth Control Official Is Told He'll Be Demoted." *Boston Globe,* June 5, p. 20.

McCauley, Carole Spearin. 1976. *Pregnancy after 35.* New York: Pocket Books.

McCormack, William M. 1975. "Management of Sexually Transmissible Infections during Pregnancy." *Clinical Obstetrics and Gynecology* 18, no. 1 (March): 57–71.

McCormick, Naomi. 1979a. Personal communication, March 30. Used by permission.

———. 1979b. "Come-ons and Put-offs: Unmarried Students' Strategies for Having and Avoiding Sexual Intercourse." *Psychology of Women Quarterly* 4, no. 2 (Winter):194–211.

MacDonald, A. P., Jr. 1976. "Homophobia: Its Roots and Meanings." *Homosexual Counseling Journal* 3 (1): 23–33.

———. 1982. "Research on Sexual Orientation: A Bridge That Touches Both Shores but Doesn't Meet in the Middle." *Journal of Sex Education and Therapy* 8:9–13.

McDonald, Gerald W. 1980. "Parental Power and Adolescents' Parental Identification: A Reexamination." *Journal of Marriage and the Family* 42, no. 2 (May):289–96.

McGee, Z. A., and M. A. Melly. 1979. "Gonorrhea in 1979: Update on Diagnosis and Treatment." *Consultant,* April, pp. 36–43.

McIlvenna, Ted. 1979. Personal communication, May 15.

McKain, Walter C. 1969. *Retirement Marriage.* Storrs: University of Connecticut.

McKenny, Patricia, Lynda Henley Walters, and Carolyn Johnson. 1979. "Adolescent Pregnancy: A Review of the Literature." *Family Coordinator* 28, no. 1 (January):17–28.

MacKinnon, Catherine. 1979. *Sexual Harassment of Working Women.* New Haven, Conn.: Yale University Press.

Macklin, E. 1978. "Review of Research on Nonmarital Cohabitation in the United States." In Bernard Murstein, ed., *Exploring Intimate Life Styles.* New York: Springer Publishing.

McLaughlin, Loretta. 1979. "Chinese May Be Using Male Contraceptive Soon." *Boston Sunday Globe,* April 15, p. 22.

———. 1982. "Pill for Herpes Effective in Studies." *Boston Globe,* October 3, p. 4.

———. 1983. "Brain Cancer Is Found in 3 AIDS Victims." *Boston Globe,* January 6, p. 13.

MacNamara, Donald E. J., and Edward Sagarin. 1977. *Sex, Crime, and the Law.* New York: Free Press.

Macy's ad. 1982. *The New York Times,* December 12, p. 15.

Maddock, James W. 1976. "Sexual Health: An Enrichment and Treatment Program." In David Olson, ed., *Treating Relationships.* Lake Mills, Iowa: Graphic Publishing.

Mahoney, E. R. 1980. "Religiosity and Sexual Behavior among Heterosexual College Students." *Journal of Sex Research* 16, no. 1 (May):97–113.

Malatesta, Victor J., Robert H. Pollack, W. A. Wilbanks, and Henry E. Adams. 1979. "Alcohol Effects on the Orgasmic-Ejaculatory Response in Human Males." *The Journal of Sex Research* 15, no. 2 (May):101–107.

Malatesta, Victor J., Robert H. Pollack, Terri D. Crotty, and Lelon J. Peacock. 1982. "Acute Alcohol Intoxication and Female Orgasmic Response," *The Journal of Sex Research* 18, no. 1 (February):1–17.

"Man Convicted of Raping Previous Sex Partner." 1979. *Sexuality Today,* April 16, p. 1.

Manning, Barbara Eck. 1980. "The Emotional Needs of Infertile Couples." *Fertility and Sterility* 34, no. 4:313–19.

Marciano, Teresa Donati. 1978. "Male Pressure in the Decision to Remain Childfree." *Alternative Lifestyles* 1, no. 1 (February):95–112.

Marcus, Irwin M., and John J. Francis, eds. 1975. *Masturbation from Infancy to Senescence.* New York: International University Press.

Marino, Thomas M. 1979. "Resensitizing Men: A Male Perspective." *Personnel and Guidance Journal* 58, no. 2 (October):102–105.

Marshall, Donald S. 1971. "Too Much in Mangaia." *Psychology Today,* February, pp. 43–44ff.

Marshall, S. 1974. "Cystitis and Urethritis in Women Related to Sexual Activity." *Medical Aspects of Human Sexuality* 8, no. 5 (May):165–76.

Martin, Clyde E. 1981. "Factors Affecting Sexual Functioning in 60–79-Year-Old Married Males." *Archives of Sexual Behavior* 10, no. 2 (April):399–420.

Martin, Del, and Phyllis Lyon. 1972. *Lesbian/Woman.* San Francisco: Glide.

Martinson, Floyd M. 1966. *Sexual Knowledge, Values, and Behavior Patterns.* Report based on a study conducted by the Department of Sociology, Gustavus Adolphus College, St. Peter, Minn.

————. 1981. "Eroticism in Infancy and Childhood." In Larry L. Constantine and Floyd M. Martinson, eds., *Children and Sex: New Findings, New Perspectives.* Boston: Little, Brown.

Maslow, A. H. 1942. "Self-Esteem (Dominance-Feeling) and Sexuality in Women." *Journal of Social Psychology* 16, no. 3 (November):259–94.

"Mastectomy Study Cited." 1982. *Boston Globe,* September 17, p. 8.

Masters, William H., and Virginia E. Johnson. 1966. *Human Sexual Response.* Boston: Little, Brown.

————. 1970. *Human Sexual Inadequacy.* Boston: Little, Brown.

————. 1979. *Homosexuality in Perspective.* Boston: Little, Brown.

————, with Robert J. Levin. 1975. *The Pleasure Bond.* Boston: Little, Brown.

Mathews, Jay. 1983. "Reported Cases of VD Decline." *Boston Globe,* July 2, p. 13.

Mathis, James L. 1977. Commentary on Barbara E. O'Connell, "Women's Reactions to 'Wolf Whistles' and Lewd Remarks." *Medical Aspects of Human Sexuality* 11, no. 10 (October):646–66.

Maxwell, Joseph W., et al. 1977. "Factors Influencing Contraceptive Behavior of Single College Students." *Journal of Sex and Marital Therapy* 3, no. 4 (Winter):265–73.

May, Harold J. 1981. "Integration of Sexual Counseling and Family Therapy with Surgical Treatment of Breast Cancer." *Family Relations* 30 (April):291–95.

Maynard, Joyce. 1978. "Coming of Age with Judy Blume." *New York Times Magazine,* December 3, pp. 806–92.

Mazur, Ronald. 1973. *Open-Ended Marriage.* Boston: Beacon Press.

————. 1980. Personal communication, February.

Mead, Margaret. 1935. *Sex and Temperament in Three Primitive Societies.* New York: Morrow.

Medical Self Care. 1980. Advertisement in *New Roots,* January–February, p. 43.

Medical World News. 1979. October 29, p. 48.

Medora, Niulfer, and John C. Woodward. 1982. "Premarital Sexual Opinions of Undergraduate Students at a Midwestern University." *Adolescence* 27, no. 65 (Spring):213–24.

Meiselman, Karin C. 1979. *Incest.* San Francisco: Jossey-Bass.

"Men's Fragrances: The Sexual Message." 1979. *Harper's Bazaar,* April, p. 152.

Mercer, G. William, and Paul M. Kohn. 1979. "Gender Differences in the Integration of Conservatism, Sex Urge, and Sexual Behaviors among College Students." *Journal of Sex Research* 15, no. 2 (May):129–42.

Merino, Hernando L., and Jeff B. Richards. 1977. "An Innovative Program of Venereal Disease Casefinding, Treatment, and Education for a Population of Gay Men." *Sexually Transmitted Diseases* 4, no. 2 (April–June):50–52.

Merry, Sally Engle. 1980. "Manipulating Anonymity: Streetwalkers' Strategies for Safety in the City." *Ethnos* 45, no. III-IV:157–75.

Meyer-Bahlberg, Heino F. L. 1977. "Sex Hormones and Male Homosexuality in Comparative Perspective." *Archives of Sexual Behavior* 6, no. 4 (July):297–325.

Meyners, Robert, and Claire Wooster. 1979. *Sexual Style: Facing and Making Choices about Sex.* New York: Harcourt Brace Jovanovich.

Michael, Richard P. 1975. "Hormones and Sexual Behavior in the Female." *Hospital Practice* 10, no. 12 (December):69–76.

Miller, Brian. 1979. "Social Construction of an Alternative Family Reality: Lifestyles of Gay Fathers." In M. Levine, ed., *Gay Men: The Sociology of Male Homosexuality.* New York: Harper & Row. Used by permission.

Miller, Patricia Y., and William Simon. 1979. "The Development of Sexuality in Adolescence." In Joseph Adelson, ed., *Handbook of Adolescence.* New York: Wiley.

Miller, Warren B. 1980. "Sexual and Contraceptive Behavior in Young Unmarried Women." In David D. Youngs and Anke A. Ehrhardt, eds., *Psychomatic Obstetrics and Gynecology.* New York: Appleton-Century-Crofts.

Miller, William R., and Harold I. Lief. 1976. "Masturbatory Attitudes, Knowledge, and Experience: Data from the Sex Knowledge and Attitude Test (SKAT)." *Archives of Sexual Behavior* 5, no. 5 (September):447–67.

Milner, Richard. 1979. "Should Prostitution Be Decriminalized?" *Penthouse Forum,* April, pp. 55–58.

Minnigerode, Fred A., and Marcy R. Adelman. 1978. "Elderly Homosexual Men and Women: Report on a Pilot Study." *Family Coordinator* 27, no. 4 (October):451–56.

Minutes of the General Assembly of the United Presbyterian Church, U.S.A. 1970. Philadelphia: Office of the General Assembly.

Mirin, Steven M., Roger E. Meyer, Jack H. Mendelson, and James Ellingboe. 1980. "Opiate Use and Sexual Function." *American Journal of Psychiatry,* (August):909–15.

Moffett, Robert K. 1974. *Tantric Sex.* New York: Berkley Publishing.

Moller, Herbert. 1959. "The Social Causations of the Courtly Love Complex." *Comparative Studies in Society and History* 1 (January):137–63.

Monagan, Charles. 1979. "Sugar in the Morning." *Connecticut,* April. pp. 44–50.

Money, John, and Anke A. Ehrhardt. 1972. *Man and Woman, Boy and Girl.* Baltimore, Md.: Johns Hopkins University Press.

Montagu, Ashley. 1971. *Touching: The Human Significance of the Skin.* New York: Columbia University Press.

Mooney, Thomas O., Theodore M. Cole, and Richard A. Chilgren. 1975. *Sexual Options for Paraplegics and Quadriplegics.* Boston: Little, Brown.

Moore, Kristin A. 1978. "Teenage Childbirth and Welfare Dependency." *Family Planning Perspectives* 10, no. 4 (July–August):233–35.

"More Bare Breasts, Less of a Sensation." 1978. *Boston Globe,* August 17, p. 23.

Morgan, Robin. 1978. "How to Run the Pornographers Out of Town." *Ms.,* November, pp. 55, 78–80.

Morgan, Susanne. 1978. "Sexuality after Hysterectomy and Castration." *Women and Health: Issues in Women's Health Care* 3, no. 1 (January–February):5–9.

Morin, Jack. 1981. *Anal Pleasure and Health.* Burlingame, Calif.: Down There Press.

Morin, Stephen F., and Ellen M. Garfinkle. 1978. "Male Homophobia." *Journal of Social Issues* 34, no. 1 (February):29–47.

Morris, Jan. 1975. *Conundrum.* New York: New American Library.

Mosher, Donald L. 1973. "Sex Differences, Sex Experience, Sex Guilt, and Explicitly Sexual Films." *Journal of Social Issues* 29 (3):95–112.

——. 1980. "Three Dimensions of Depth of Involvement in Human Sexual Response." *The Journal of Sex Research* 16, no. 1 (February):1–42.

Mudd, Emily H., et al. 1978. "Adolescent Health Services and Contraceptive Use." *American Journal of Orthopsychiatry* 48, no. 3 (July):495–504.

Munich, Adrine. 1978. "Seduction in Academe." *Psychology Today,* February, pp. 82–84, 108.

Naeye, Richard L. 1979. "Coitus and Associated Amniotic-Fluid Infections." *New England Journal of Medicine* 301, no. 22 (November):1986–2000.

Nahmanovici, Charles, Claude Racinet, and Jacques Salvat. 1978. "Number of Sex Partners Not Increased by Giving Contraception to Teens." *Family Planning Perspectives* 10, no. 6 (November–December):368.

The Nation. 1980. "HEW on the Line." May 31, p. 645.

National Alliance for Optional Parenthood. 1979. "Optional Parenthood." Washington, D.C.

National Center for the Prevention and Control of Rape. 1979. *Rape and Older Women: A Guide to Prevention and Protection.* Rockville, Md.: National Institute of Mental Health.

National Foundation March of Dimes. a. *All about the March of Dimes.*

——. b. *Leaders Alert Bulletin* 29.

——. c. *Drugs, Alcohol, Tobacco Abuse during Pregnancy.*

——. d. *Pregnant? Before You Drink, Think . . .*

Naturists. 1982. Brochure. P.O. Box 132, Oskhosh, Wis. 54902.

Nelson, Joan A. 1981. "The Impact of Incest: Factors in Self-Evaluation." In Larry L. Constantine and Floyd M. Martinson, eds., *Children and Sex: New Findings, New Perspectives.* Boston: Little, Brown.

Nelson, N. M., M. W. Enkin, S. Saigal, K. J. Bennett, R. Milner, and O. L. Sackett. 1980. "A Randomized Clinical Trial of the Leboyer Approach to Childbirth." *New England Journal of Medicine* 302, no. 12:655–60.

Neubeck, Gerhard. 1972. "The Myriad Motives for Sex." *Sexual Behavior* 2, no.7 (July):51–56.

"New Approach to Treating Male Sexual Dysfunction." 1982. *Sexuality Today* 5, no. 19:3–4.

"New Birth Control Pill Developed." 1982. AP, *Boston Globe,* April 21, p. 5.

"New Pregnancy Tests Could Wipe Out Birth Defects." 1976. UPI, *Willimantic Chronicle,* June 3, p. 7.

"New Study Reports Resistance Effective in Interrupting Rape Attempts." 1982. *Sexuality Today,* November 29, p. 3.

Newton, Niles. 1973. "Interrelationships between Sexual Responsiveness, Birth, and Breast-Feeding." In Joseph Zubin and John Money, eds., *Contemporary Sexual Behavior: Critical Issues in the 1970s.* Baltimore, Md.: Johns Hopkins University Press.

Nguyen, Tuan, Richard Heslin, and Michele L. Nguyen. 1975. "The Meanings of Touch: Sex Differences." *Journal of Communication* 25, no. 2 (Spring):92–103.

"Nick Groth on Sexual Assault of Children." 1982. *Sexuality Today,* June 4.

Nielson, Gary. 1979. "Screwing the System." *Valley Advocate,* November 14, pp. 12A–14A.

Niemiec, M. A., and S. C. Chen. 1978. "Seeking Clinic Care for Veneral Disease: A Study of Teenagers." *Journal of School Health* 48, no. 1 (January):680–85.

Nobile, P. 1982a. "Penis Size: The Difference between Blacks and Whites." *Forum,* August, pp. 21–28.

Nobile, P. 1982b. "Women's Penis Preferences." *Forum,* September, pp. 23–28.

Notman, Malkah T., and Carol C. Nadelson, eds. 1978. *The Woman Patient: Sexual and Reproductive Aspects of Women's Health Care,* vol. 1., New York: Plenum.

Novak, Edmund R., Georgeanna Seagar Jones, and Howard W. Jones. 1975. *Gynecology.* Baltimore, Md.: Williams & Wilkins.

"NYC Teen Survey Demonstrates Need for Sex Education." 1982. *Sexuality Today* 6, no. 1 (October 25):1.

Nye, F. Ivan. 1976. *Role Structure and Analysis of the Family.* Beverly Hills, Calif.: Sage.

O'Connell, Barbara E. 1977. "Women's Reactions to 'Wolf Whistles' and Lewd Remarks." *Medical Aspects of Human Sexuality* 11, no. 10 (October):58–64.

"The Older Rape Victim and Her Assailant." 1979. *Sexuality Today,* March 26, pp. 1–2.

Olds, James. 1956. "Pleasure Centers in the Brain." *Scientific American* 195 (4):105–16.

O'Neill, Nena, and George O'Neill. 1972. *Open Marriage.* New York: Avon.

Osborn, Candice A., and Robert H. Pollack. 1977. "The Effects of Two Types of Erotic Literature on Physiological and Verbal Measures of Female Sexual Arousal." *Journal of Sex Research* 13, no. 4 (November):250–56.

Otto, Herbert A., and Roberta Otto. 1972. *Total Sex.* New York: Peter H. Wyden.

Palm, Kathleen. 1979. "The Childbirth Revolution." *Hartford Advocate,* November 14, pp. 6, 12, 13.

Palmore, Erdman. 1981. *Social Patterns in Normal Aging: Findings from the Duke Longitudinal Study.* Durham, N.C.: Duke University Press.

Parcel, Guy S., and David Luttman. 1981. "Evaluation of a Sex Education Course for Young Adolescents." *Family Relations* 30 (January):55–60.

Parr, D. 1976. "Sexual Aspects of Drug Abuse in Narcotic Addicts." *British Journal of Addiction* 71:261–68.

Payne, David C. 1970. "Sex Education and the Sexual Education of Adolescents." In Ellis D. Evans, ed., *Adolescents.* Hinsdale, Ill.: Dryden Press.

Penna, Ronald M., Joel Potash, and Sharlene M. Penna. 1979. "Elective Vasectomy: A Study of 843 Patients." *Journal of Family Practice* 8 (4):857–58.

Peplau, Letitia Anne. 1981. "What Homosexuals Want." *Psychology Today,* March, pp. 28–38.

————, and Susan D. Cochran. 1979. "Attachment and Autonomy in Gay Men's Relationships." Draft under review, January.

————, Zick Rubin, and Charles T. Hill. 1977. "Sexual Intimacy in Dating Relationships." *Journal of Social Issues* 33, no. 2 (Spring):86–109.

Peplau, Letitia Anne, Susan Cochran, Karen Rook, and Christine Padesky. 1978. "Loving Women: Attachment and Autonomy in Lesbian Relationships." *Journal of Social Issues* 34, no. 3 (Summer):7–27.

Perry, John. 1979. Personal communication, May 10.

————. 1980. Personal communication, April 1.

————, and Beverly Whipple. 1980. "Diagnostic, Therapeutic, and Research Applications of the Vaginal Myograph." Synopsis of presentation made at annual meeting of American Association of Sex Educators, Counselors, and Therapists. Washington, D.C., March 6.

————, and Beverly Whipple. 1981. "The Varieties of Female Orgasm and Female Ejaculation." *SIECUS Report,* May–July.

Persky, Harold, Harold I. Lief, Dorothy Strauss, William R. Miller, and Charles P. O'Brien. 1978. "Plasma Testosterone Level and Sexual Behavior of Couples." *Archives of Sexual Behavior* 7, no. 3 (May):157–73.

Petersen, James R., Arthur Kretchmer, Barbara Nellis, Janet Lever, and Rosanna Hertz. 1983a. "The Playboy Readers' Sex Survey, Part One." *Playboy,* January, pp. 108, 241–50.

————. 1983b. "The Playboy Readers' Sex Survey, Part Two." *Playboy,* March, pp. 90–92, 178–84.

Pfeifer, Terrence A., et al. 1978. "Nonspecific Vaginitis. Role of *Haemophilus vaginitis* and Treatment with Metronidazole." *New England Journal of Medicine* 298, no. 26. (June 19):1429–34.

Pfeiffer, Eric. 1975. "Sexual Behavior." In John G. Howells, ed., *Modern Perspectives in the Psychiatry of Old Age.* New York: Brunner/Mazel.

————, Adriaan Verwoerdt, and Hsioh-Shan Wang. 1970. "Sexual Behavior in Aged Men and Women." In Erdman Palmore ed., *Normal Aging.* Durham, N.C. Duke University Press.

————, Adriaan Verwoerdt and Glenn C. Davis. 1972. "Sexual Behavior in Middle Life." *American Journal of Psychiatry* 128, no. 10 (April):82–87.

Pfuhl, Erdwin H., Jr. 1978. "The Unwed Father: A 'Non-Deviant' Rule Breaker." *Sociological Quarterly* 19 (Winter):113–28.

Phelps, Linda. 1975. "Female Sexual Alienation." In Jo Freeman, ed., *Women: A Feminist Perspective.* Palo Alto, Calif.: Mayfield.

"PID Risk Increased Sharply among IUD Users." 1982. *Family Planning Perspectives* 13, no. 4 (July/August):182–83.

Pietropinto, Anthony, and Jacqueline Simenauer. 1977. *Beyond the Male Myth.* New York: New American Library.

Pinhas, Valerie. 1980. Personal communication, February.

Pomeroy, Wardell B. 1968. *Boys and Sex.* New York: Delacorte Press.

————. 1969. *Girls and Sex.* New York: Delacorte Press.

————. 1975. Interviewed in Julius Fast and Hall

Wells, *Bisexual Living.* New York: M. Evans.

—————. 1978. "A New Look at Incest." *The Best of Forum,* pp. 92–97.

Potter, Jessie. 1982. Lecture notes from "Touch Is as Vital as Food." National Institute for Human Relationships, Oak Lawn, Ill., October.

Potterat, John J., Richard Rothenberg, and Donald C. Bross. 1979. "Gonorrhea in Street Prostitutes: Epidemiologic and Legal Implications." *Sexually Transmitted Diseases* 6, no. 2 (June):58–63.

Potterat, John J., et al. 1979. "Becoming a Prostitute: A Case-Controlled, Pilot Study of Female Gonorrhea Patients in Colorado Springs, Colorado, 1976–77." Paper presented at the annual meeting of the Society for the Study of Social Problems. Boston, August.

Prager, Emily, with Edward Claflin. 1976. "Prostitution: Conversation with People in 'The Life'." *Viva,* November, pp. 100–07.

"Pregnant Women and Smoking." 1980. *Forum,* February, pp. 9–10.

Prescott, James W. 1975. "Body Pleasure and the Origins of Violence." *Futurist,* April, pp. 64–74.

The President's Commission on Employment of the Handicapped, Washington, D.C.

Preterm Institute. 1975. *Exploring Human Sexuality.* Cambridge, Mass.: Schenkman.

"Prostitution Therapy." 1978. *Coyote Howls* 5, no. 2 (Summer):12.

"Public Perceptions of Gays: Few Changes in Past 5 Years." 1982. *Sexuality Today,* December 6, p. 1.

Purifoy, Frances E., Lambert H. Koopmans, and Darrel M. Mayes. 1981. "Age Differences in Serum Androgen Levels in Normal Adult Males." *Human Biology* 53, no. 4 (December):499–511.

Quinn, Robert E. 1977. "Coping with Cupid: The Formation, Impact and Management of Romantic Relationships in Organizations." *Administrative Science Quarterly* 22 (March):30–45.

Rada, Richard T. 1975. "Alcoholism and Forcible Rape." *American Journal of Psychiatry* 132, no. 4 (April):444–46.

—————. 1978. *Clinical Aspects of the Rapist.* New York: Grune & Stratton.

Randal, Judith. 1981. "Hepatitis-B Vaccine Gets Approval from FDA." *Boston Globe,* November 17, p. 3.

"Rape and Sexual Dysfunction." 1977. *Sexuality Today,* November 14, p. 1.

"Rape Education for School Children." 1978. *Sexuality Today,* February 27, p. 1.

Raphael, Sharon M., and Mina K. Robinson. 1980. "The Older Lesbian: Love Relationships and Friendship Patterns." *Alternative Lifestyles* 3, no. 2 (May):207–30.

"The Rapist as Sexual Ignoramus." 1978. *Sexuality Today,* March 13, pp. 2–3.

Rasmussen, Paul K., and Lauren L. Kuhn. 1976. "The New Masseuse: Play for Pay." *Urban Life* 5, no. 3 (October):271–92.

Raymond, Janice G. 1979. *The Transsexual Empire: The Making of the She-Male.* Boston: Beacon Press.

Reed and Carnrick, 1976. *Lice and Scabies: From Infestation to Disinfestation.* Kenilworth, N.J.: Reed & Carnrick.

Reich, Wilhelm. 1968. *The Function of the Orgasm.* London: Panther Books.

Reichelt, Paul A. 1979. "Coital and Contraceptive Behavior of Female Adolescents." *Archives of Sexual Behavior* 8, no. 2 (March):159–71.

Reid, Robert L., and S.S.C. Yen. 1981. "Premenstrual Syndrome." *American Journal of Obstetrics and Gynecology* 139:85–97.

Rein, Michael F. 1975. "Gonorrhea." *Practice of Medicine,* vol. 3. East Norwalk, Conn.: Appleton-Century-Crofts.

—————, and T.A. Chapel. 1975. "Trichomoniasis, Candidiasis, and the Minor Veneral Diseases." *Clinical Obstetrics and Gynecology* 18, no. 1 (March): 73–87.

Reis, Harry T., Ladd Wheeler, Nancy Spiegel, Michael H. Kernis, John Nezlek, and Michael Perri. 1982. "Physical Attractiveness in Social Interaction: II. Why Does Appearance Affect Social Experience?" *Journal of Personality and Social Psychology,* 43, no. 5:979–96.

Reiss, Ira L. 1981. "Some Observations on Ideology and Sexuality in America." *Journal of Marriage and the Family* 43, no. 2 (May):271–83.

—————, and Frank F. Furstenberg, Jr. 1981. "Sociology and Human Sexuality." In Harold I. Lief, ed., *Sexual Problems in Medical Practice.* Monroe, Wis.: American Medical Association.

Reitz, Rosetta. 1977. *Menopause: A Positive Approach.* New York: Penguin.

Renshaw, Domeena C. 1978. "Rape." *Journal of Sex Education and Therapy* 4, no. 2 (Winter):11–14.

"Report Calls Sterilization Top Birth Control Method." 1981. AP, *Boston Globe,* April 29, p. 11.

"Researcher Confirms: 'Our Culture Supports Rape'." 1978. *Sexuality Today,* December 4, pp. 1–2.

"A Revolution in Rape." 1979. *Time,* April 2, p. 50.

Rhinelander, David H. 1982. "Study Suggests Limit on Hepatitis Program." *Hartford Courant,* September 9, p. C3.

Richardson, Lauren Walum. 1979. " 'The Other Woman': The End of the Long Affair." *Alternative Lifestyles* 2, no. 4 (November):397–414.

Riddle, Dorothy. 1971. *What the Doctor Forgot to Tell You (or How to Survive Vaginal and Urinary Infections)*. Pittsburgh, Pa.: Know.

Ritter, Bruce. 1978. "Good Kids on Mean." *Human Ecology Forum* 8, no. 4 (Spring):10–11.

————, with Bob Weinstein. 1979. "The Tragedy of Teenage Prostitution." *Senior Scholastic* 3, no. 2 (February 8):20–21.

Robbins, Mina B., and Gordon D. Jensen. 1978. "Multiple Orgasm in Males." *Journal of Sex Research* 14, no. 1 (February):21–26.

Roberts, Elizabeth J. 1981. "Sexuality and Social Policy: The Unwritten Curriculum." In Elizabeth Roberts, ed., *Childhood Sexual Learning: The Unwritten Curriculum*. Cambridge, Mass.: Ballinger.

————, David Kline, and John Gagnon. 1978. *Family Life and Sexual Learning*. Cambridge, Mass.: Project on Human Sexual Development, Population Education.

Robinson, Ira E., and Davor Jedlicka. 1982. "Change in Sexual Attitudes and Behavior of College Students from 1965 to 1980: A Research Note." *Journal of Marriage and the Family* 44, no. 1 (February):237–40.

Rock, Maxine. 1979. "A Very Private Torment." *Atlanta*, March p. 45.

"Role Reversal." 1982. *Time*, August 2, p. 19.

Rose, Sara. 1978. "Ode to Your Cock." In Charleen Swansea and Barbara Campbell, eds., *Love Stories by New Women*. Charlotte, N.C.: Red Clay Books.

Rosenberg, Jack Lee. 1973. *Total Orgasm*. New York and Berkeley, Calif.:Random House/Bookworks.

Rosenthal, Kristine M., and Harry F. Keshet. 1978a. "The Impact of Childcare Responsibilities on the Part-time or Single Fathers." *Alternative Lifestyles* 1, no. 4 (November):465–92.

————. 1978b. "The Not-Quite Stepmother." *Psychology Today*, July, pp. 82–88.

Rossi, Alice S. 1977. "A Biosocial Perspective on Parenting." *Daedalus* 106, no. 2 (Spring):1–31.

Rossi, William A. 1976. *The Sex Life of the Foot and Shoe*. New York: Saturday Review Press/Dutton.

Rosten, Herman. 1979. "Bring Humor Back into Sex Therapy." *Sexuality Today*, October 15, pp. 3–4.

Rousso, Harilyn. 1982. "Special Considerations in Counseling Clients with Cerebral Palsy." *Sexuality and Disability* 5, no. 2 (Summer):78–88.

Rowland, Kay F., and Stephen N. Haynes. 1978. "A Sexual Enhancement Program for Elderly Couples." *Journal of Sex and Marital Therapy* 4 (Summer).

Rubin, Arline. 1983. "Sexually Open Versus Sexually Exclusive Marriage: A Comparison." *Alternative Lifestyles*, forthcoming.

Rubin, Lillian Breslow. 1976. *Worlds of Pain*. New York: Basic Books.

Rubin, Zick. 1973. *Liking and Loving*. New York: Holt, Rinehart and Winston.

Rudolph, Andrew H., and W.C. Duncan. 1975. "Syphilis—Diagnosis and Treatment." *Clinical Obstetrics and Gynecolgy* 18, no. 1 (March):163–81.

Russell, Diana E. 1982. *Rape in Marriage*. New York: Macmillan.

Saflios-Rothschild, Constantina. 1977. *Love, Sex, and Sex-Roles*. Englewood Cliffs, N.J.: Prentice-Hall.

Sagarin, Edward. 1977a. "Doing, Being, and the Tyranny of the Label." *Et cetera*, March, pp. 71–77.

————. 1977b. "Incest." *Journal of Sex Research*. 13, no. 2 (May):126–35.

Sage, Wayne. 1972. "The Homosexuality Hang-Up." *Human Behavior* 1 (November–December):56–61.

Saghir, Marcel T., and Eli Robins. 1973. *Male and Female Homosexuality*. Baltimore, Md.: William & Wilkins.

Santa Cruz Men Against Rape. 1983. Brochures. Santa Cruz, Calif.

Santini, Rosemarie. 1976. *The Secret Fire: A New View of Women and Passion*. Chicago: Playboy Press.

Scaife, W.M. 1978. "New VD Strain Worries Doctors." *Morning Union*, November 10, p. 14C.

Schaefer, Leah Cahan. 1973. *Women and Sex*. New York: Random House.

Schäfer, Siegrid. 1976. "Sexual and Social Problems of Lesbians." *Journal of Sex Research* 12, no. 1 (February):50–69.

————. 1977. "Sociosexual Behavior in Homosexuals." *Archives of Sexual Behavior* 6, no. 5 (September):355–64.

Schneider, Elizabeth M., Susan B. Jordan, and Cristina C. Arguedas. 1978. *Representation of Women Who Defend Themselves in Response to Physical or Sexual Assault*. New York: Center for Constitutional Rights.

Schram, Donna. 1978. *Forcible Rape: Final Project Report*. Washington, D.C.: National Institute of Law Enforcement and Criminal Justice, Law Enforcement Assistance Administration. U.S. Department of Justice.

Schreeder, Marshall, et al. 1982. "Hepatitis B in Homosexual Men: Prevalence of Infection and Factors Related to Transmission." *Journal of Infectious Diseases*, 146 (July):7–15.

Schreiner-Engel, Patricia, Raul C. Schiavi, Harry Smith, and Daniel White. 1981. "Sexual Arousability and the Menstrual Cycle." *Psychosomatic Medicine* 43, no. 3 (June):199–214.

Schultz, Terri. 1979. *Women Can Wait: The Pleasures of Motherhood after 30.* Garden City, N.J.: Doubleday.

Schwartz, Pepper. 1977a. "Female Sexuality and Monogamy." In Roger W. Libby and Robert N. Whitehurst, eds., *Marriage and Alternatives: Exploring Intimate Relationships.* Glenview, Ill.: Scott, Foresman.

————. 1977b. "Sexual Life-Styles." In Judith Long Laws and Pepper Schwartz, eds., *Sexual Scripts.* New York: Dryden Press/Holt, Rinehart and Winston.

Schwartz, Tony. 1981. "The TV Pornography Boom." *New York Times Magazine,* September 13, pp. 44, 120–36.

Seaman, Barbara. 1973. "Notes from 'The Female Orgasm'." *Ms.,* May, pp. 35–38.

————, and Gideon Seaman. 1978. *Women and the Crisis in Sex Hormones.* New York: Bantam.

Seligmann, Jean. 1979. "A Contraceptive Device Updated." *Newsweek,* September 3, p. 69.

"Sex and the Married Woman." 1983. *Time,* January 31, p. 80.

"Sex Said Helpful to People Recovering from Heart Attacks." 1983. *Daily Hampshire Gazette,* January 13, p. 8.

"Sexual Harassment on Federal Jobs Called Costly." 1981. UPI, *New York Times,* May 3, p. 63.

"Sexual Harassment Policy." 1982. University of Massachusetts, November 16, pp. 1–7.

"The Sexually Transmitted Diseases." 1982. Department of Public Health, Commonwealth of Massachusetts, pp. 1–50.

Shah, Diane K., Linda Walters, and Tony Clifton.1979. "Lesbian Mothers," *Newsweek,* February 12, p. 61.

Shames, Richard, and Chuck Sterin.1978. *Healing with Mind Power,* Emmaus, Pa.: Rodale Press.

Shea, Robert. 1980. "Women at War." *Playboy,* February, pp. 87–88ff.

Shearer, Lloyd. 1983. "The High Cost of Children." *Parade's Special Intelligence Report,* May.

Sheehan, Nancy, 1980. Personal communication, January.

Sheleff, Leon S. 1976. "Victimology, Criminal Law, and Conflict Resolution." Paper presented at the Second International Symposium on Victimology, Boston, September, p. 12.

Sherfey, Mary Jane. 1972. *The Nature and Evolution of Female Sexuality.* New York: Random House.

Shope, David E. 1971. "Sexual Responsiveness in Single Girls." In James M. Henslin, ed., *Studies in the Sociology of Sex.* New York: Appleton-Century-Crofts.

Shornack, Lawrence L., and Ellen McRoberts Shornack. 1982. "The New Sex Education and the Sexual Revolution: A Critical View." *Family Relations* 31, no. 4 (October):531–44.

Shorter, Edward. 1977. "On Writing the History of Rape." *Signs* 3, no. 2 (Winter):471–82.

Shostak, Arthur B. 1979. "Abortion as Fatherhood Lost: Problems and Reforms." *Family Coordinator* 28, no. 4 (October):569–74.

"Should Mentally Incompetent Individuals Be Sterilized?" 1979. *Sexuality Today.* December 17, pp. 1–2.

Shulman, Alix Kates. 1973. *Memoirs of an Ex-prom Queen.* New York: Bantam.

Siegel, Alberta E. 1977. "Communicating with the Next Generation." In Leonard L. Sellers and William L. Rivers, eds., *Mass Media Issues.* Englewood Cliffs, N.J.: Prentice-Hall.

Siegelman, Marvin. 1978. "Psychological Adjustment of Homosexual and Heterosexual Men: A Cross-National Replication." *Archives of Sexual Behavior,* 7, no. 1 (January):1–11.

Sifford, Darrell. 1981. "Every Man's Prostate Primer." *Boston Globe,* February 24, p. 58.

Sigell, L. T., F. T. Kapp, G. A. Fusaro, E. D. Nelson, and R. S. Falck. 1978. "Popping and Snorting Volatile Nitrites: A Current Fad for Getting High." *American Journal of Psychiatry* 135:1216–18.

Sigusch, Volkmar, Eberhard Schorsch, Martin Dannecker, and Gunter Schmidt. 1982. "Official Statement by the German Society for Sex Research on the Research of Prof. Dr. Günter Dörner on the Subject of Homosexuality." *Archives of Sexual Behavior* II, no. 5 (October):445–49.

Silber, Sherman J. 1981. *The Male from Infancy to Old Age.* New York: Charles Scribner's Sons.

Simmons, Roberta G., Dale A. Blyth, Edward F. Van Cleave, and Diane Mitsch Bush. 1979. *American Sociological Review* 44 (December):948–67.

Simpson, Mary, and Thomas Schill. 1977. "Patrons of Massage Parlors: Some Facts and Figures." *Archives of Sexual Behavior* 6, no. 6 (November):521–25.

Singer, Barry. 1980. Personal communication.

————. 1982a. Personal communication.

————. 1982b. "Conversation with Robert McGinley." *Alternative Lifestyles* 5, no. 2 (Winter):69–78.

Singer, Irving. 1974. *The Goals of Human Sexuality.* New York: Schocken Books.

Singer, Josephine, and Irving Singer. 1972. "Types of Female Orgasm." *Journal of Sex Research* 8, no. 4 (November):255–67.

Sipress, Alan. 1982. "Catholic Gays Claim Diocese Ignores Them." *Boston Globe,* August 29, pp. 21, 25.

Skipper, James K., and Gilbert D. Nass. 1966. "Dating Behavior: A Framework for Analysis and an Illustration." *Journal of Marriage and the Family* 23, no. 4 (November):412–21.

Skipper, James K., and Charles H. McCaghy. 1978. "Teasing, Flashing, and Visual Sex: Stripping for a Living." In James Henslin and Edward Sagarin, eds., *Sociology of Sex.* New York: Schocken Books.

Slater, Philip. 1977. *Footholds: Understanding the Shifting Family and Sexual Tensions in Our Culture.* New York: Dutton.

Smith, D. E., M. E. Buxton, and G. Dammann. 1979. "Amphetamine Abuse and Sexual Dysfunction: Clinical and Research Considerations." In D. E. Smith, ed., *Amphetamine Use, Misuse, and Abuse.* Cambridge, Mass.: G. K. Hall.

Smith, Don D. 1976. "The Social Content of Pornography." *Journal of Communications* 26, no. 1 (Winter):16–24.

"Some Happenings in the Homosexual Community." 1978. *Sexuality Today,* July 17.

"A Son's Rite." 1981. *Time.* August 31, p. 57.

Sorensen, Robert C. 1973. *Adolescent Sexuality in Contemporary America.* New York: World.

Spada, James. 1979. *The Spada Report.* New York: New American Library.

Spanier, Graham B. 1977. "Sources of Sex Information and Premarital Sexual Behavior." *Journal of Sex Research* 13, no. 2 (May):73–88.

————. 1983. "Married and Unmarried Cohabitation in the United States: 1980." *Journal of Marriage and the Family* 45, no. 2 (May):277–88.

Speir, Betty Ruth. 1977. "Coitus during Pregnancy Not Apt to Rupture Uterine Tissues." *Medical Aspects of Human Sexuality* 11, no. 8 (August):90, 118.

Speizer, Jeanne Jacobs. 1978. "The Teenage Years." In Boston Women's Health Book Collective *Ourselves and Our Children: A Book by and for Parents.* New York: Random House.

Speroff, Leon, Robert H. Glass, and Nathan G. Kose, 1978. *Clinical Gynecologic Endocrinology and Fertility.* 2d ed. Baltimore Md.: Williams & Wilkins.

Spitz, Rene A. 1975. "Authority and Masturbation: Some Remarks on a Bibliographical Investigation." In Irwin M. Marcus and John J. Francis, eds., *Masturbation from Infancy to Senescence.* New York: International University Press.

Sprey, Jetse. 1971. "On the Management of Conflict in Families." *Journal of Marriage and the Family* 33, no. 4 (November):722–31.

Stecich, Marianne. 1977. "The Marital Rape Exemption." *New York University Law Review* 52 (May):306–23.

Steffl, Bernita M., and James J. Kelly, 1979. "Teaching Learning about Sexuality and Aging." *Educational Gerontology. An International Quarterly* 4:377–88.

Stein, Martha L. 1974. *Lovers, Friends, Slaves . . . The Nine Male Sexual Types.* New York: Berkley Publishing/Putnam's.

Steinem, Gloria. 1978. "Erotica and Pornography: A Clear and Present Difference." *Ms.,* November, pp. 53–57ff.

————. 1981. "In the Middle of the Backlash, Some Cheerful Words About Men." *Ms.,* June, pp. 43–45.

Steinhoff, Patricia G., Roy G. Smith, James A. Palmore, Milton Diamond, C. S. Chung. 1979. "Women Who Obtain Repeat Abortions: A Study Based on Record Linkage." *Family Planning Perspectives* 11, no. 1 (January–February):30–38.

Stephan, Walter, Ellen Berscheid, and Elaine Walster. 1971. "Sexual Arousal and Heterosexual Perception." *Journal of Personality and Social Psychology* 20, no. 1 (October):93–101.

"Sterilization Method." 1982. *Boston Globe,* November 27, p. 6.

Stevens, Nancy. 1977. "What Is Prostitution?" *Playgirl,* January, pp. 33, 54, 79, 128.

Stokes, Bruce. 1980. *Worldwatch Paper 41: Men and Family Planning.* Washington, D.C.: Worldwatch Institute.

Stoller, Robert J. 1976. *Sex and Gender: The Transsexual Experience,* vol. 2. New York: Jason Aronson.

Streib, Gordon F. 1978. "An Alternative Family Form for Older Persons: Need and Social Context." *Family Coordinator* 27, no. 4 (October):413–20.

————, and Mary Anne Hilker. 1980. "The Cooperative 'Family' as an Alternative Lifestyle for the Elderly." *Alternative Lifestyles* 3, no. 2 (May):167–85.

"Study Cites Benefit of Pill." 1982. AP, *Boston Globe,* July 30, p. 6.

Sue, David. 1979. "Erotic Fantasies of College Students during Coitus." *Journal of Sex Research* 15, no. 4 (November):299–305.

Summers, Darryl. 1982. "Juvenile Male Prostitutes: Runaways Become 'Situational Hustlers.'" *Sexuality Today,* March 8, p. 1.

Suppe, Frederick. 1979. "The Bell/Weinberg Study and Future Priorities for Research on Homosexuality." *ASS Symposium on Paradigms and Prejudices in Research on Homosexuality.* Houston, Texas, January 5.

Sussman, N. 1976. "Sex and Sexuality in History." In B. Sadock, H. Kaplan, and A. Freedman (eds.), *The Sexual Experience.* Baltimore: Williams and Wilkins.

Sweeney, William J., III. 1978. As told to Jacqueline Nardi Egan, "New Arrival: The Test-Tube Baby." *Family Health* 10, no. 12 (December):22–24.

Symonds, Carolyn L. , Maureen J. Mendoza, and William C. Harrell. 1981. "Forbidden Sexual Behavior among Kin: A Study of Self-Selected Respondents." In Larry L. Constantine and Floyd M. Martinson, eds., *Children and Sex: New Findings, New Perspectives.* Boston: Little, Brown.

Symonds, Donald. 1979. *The Evolution of Human Sexuality.* New York: Oxford.

Tanner, Donna M. 1978. *The Lesbian Couple.* Lexington, Mass.: Lexington Books.

Tatum, Howard J., and Elizabeth B. Connell-Tatum. 1981. "Barrier Contraception: A Compromise Overview." *Fertility and Sterility* 36, no. 1 (July):1–12.

Tavris, Carol. 1976. "Good News about Sex." *New York*, December 6, pp. 51–57.

———. 1977. "The Sexual Lives of Women Over 60." *Ms.*, July, pp. 62–65.

———, and Susan Sadd. 1975. *The Redbook Report on Female Sexuality*, New York: Dell.

———, and Susan Sadd. 1977. *The Redbook Report on Female Sexuality*, 2d ed. New York: Dell.

Taylor, G. Rattray. 1970. *Sex in History*. New York: Harper & Row.

Tedrick, Dan. 1982. "Bank of Sperm from 'Intelligent' Men Produces First Baby." *Hartford Courant*, May 25, p. C16.

"Teenage Pregnancies on Rise, Panel Told." 1982. AP, *Boston Globe*, October 20, p. 10.

Thamm, Robert. 1975. *Beyond Marriage and the Nuclear Family*. San Francisco: Canfield Press.

Therman, Eeva. 1980. *Human Chromosomes: Structure, Behavior, Effects*. New York: Springer-Verlag.

Thevenin, Tine. 1976. *The Family Bed*. P.O. Box 16004, Minneapolis, Minn. 55416: Tine Thevenin.

"They Want to Be Babied Themselves." 1981. Editorial in the *New York Times*, November 1, p. 20E.

Thompson, James S., and Margaret W. Thompson. 1980. *Genetics in Medicine*. Philadelphia: Saunders.

Thompson, Linda, and Graham B. Spanier. 1978. "Influence of Parents, Peers, and Partners on the Contraceptive Use of College Men and Women." *Journal of Marriage and the Family* 40, no. 3 (August):481–91.

Thorn, George W., Raymond D. Adams, Eugene Braunwald, Kurt J. Isselbacher, and Robert G. Petersdorf. 1977. *Harrison's Principles of Internal Medicine* 8th ed. New York: McGraw-Hill.

Thornburg, Hershel D. 1981. "Adolescent Sources of Information on Sex." *Journal of School Health* 51 (April):274–77.

Tiefer, Lenore. 1978. "The Context and Consequences of Contemporary Sex Research: Feminist Perspective." In T. E. McGill, et al., eds., *Sexual Behavior*. New York: Plenum.

Tietze, Christopher. 1979. "Unintended Pregnancies in the United States, 1970–1972." *Family Planning Perspectives* 11 (May–June):186–88.

Tolor, Alexander, and Paul V. DiGrazia. 1976. "Sexual Attitudes and Behavior Patterns During and Following Pregnancy." *Archives of Sexual Behavior* 5, no. 6 (November):539–51.

Toomey, Beverly G., and Nancy J. Beran. 1979. "The Lesbian Looking-Glass: Rejection or Reinforcement?" Paper presented at the annual meeting of the Society for the Scientific Study of Social Problems. August.

Tripp, C. A. 1976. *The Homosexual Matrix*. New York: New American Library.

Trippett, Frank. 1980. "Looking Askance at Ageism." *Time*, March 24, p. 88.

Udry, J. R., and N. Morris. 1968. "Distribution of Coitus in the Menstrual Cycle." *Nature* (London) 220, no. 5167 (November):593.

"Understanding 'Transition' Phase, an Aid to Curing Dysfunction." 1981. Sexuality Today, December 7, p. 3.

Uniform Crime Reports. 1982. *Crime in the United States*. U.S. Department of Justice, August 26.

University of Connecticut Women's Health Clinic. 1979. Student handout on vaginal discharges.

University of Massachusetts Policy, November 16, 1982.

"Unwed Couples Tripled, U.S. Says." 1983. *Boston Globe*, July 5, p. 5.

The Upjohn Company. 1983. "Depo-Provera Summary." *US*. 1979. January 9, p. 8.

U.S. Department of Health, Education, and Welfare/Public Health Service/Center for Disease Control. 1976. *Recommended Treatment Schedules for Syphilis, 1976*. Pamphlet no. 98–478.

———. 1978. Publication no. (OHDS) 72-2006.

———. 1979c. *STD Fact Sheet*, 34th ed.

———. 1980. *International Symposium on Pelvic Inflammatory Disease*. Atlanta, Ga., April 1–3.

———. *#00-2797. Herpes Simplex Type 2.*

———. *#00-2939. Herpes Genital Infection.*

———. *#00-3380. Sexually Transmitted Diseases Summary.*

U.S. Food and Drug Administration. 1980. *FDA Drug Bulletin* 10, no. 2, July.

"U.S. Sterilization Nears 14 Million Mark." 1982. *Sexuality Today*, December 13, p. 4.

Usher, Carolyn E., and Stephen R. McConnell. 1980. "House-Sharing: A Way to Intimacy?" *Alternative Lifestyles* 3, no. 2 (May):149–67.

"Vaginitis Drug Stirs Safety-Efficacy Debate." 1978. *Medical World News*, August 7, p. 29.

Van Wyk, Paul H. 1982. "Relationship of Time Spent on Masturbation Assignments with Orgasmic Outcome in Preorgasmic Women's Groups." *Journal of Sex Research* 18, no. 1 (February):33–40.

Veevers, Jean E. 1980. *Childless by Choice*. Toronto: Buttersworths.

Vinick, Barbara H. 1978. "Remarriage in Old Age." *Family Coordinator* 27, no. 4 (October):359–63.

Voeller, Bruce, and James Walters. 1978. "Gay Fathers." *Family Coodinator* 27, no. 2 (April):149–57.

Wagner, Carol A. 1980. "Sexuality of American Adolescents." *Adolescence* 15 (Fall):576–80.

Wallerstein, Edward. 1980. *Circumcision: An American Health Fallacy.* New York: Springer.

Walsh, Robert H., and Wilbert M. Leonard. 1974. "Usage of Terms for Sexual Intercourse by Men and Women." *Archives of Sexual Behavior* 3, no. 4 (July):373–76.

Walster, Elaine, and G. William Walster. 1978. *A New Look at Love.* Reading, Mass.: Addison-Wesley.

Warren, Carol A. B. 1974. *Identity and Community in the Gay World.* New York: Wiley.

Wasow, Mona, and Martin B. Loeb. 1979. "Sexuality in Nursing Homes." *Journal of the American Geriatrics Society* 27, no. 3 (February):73–79.

Wassenberg, Theresa F. 1982. The Breakup of the Intimate, Non-Marital Dyad: An Exchange and Attributional Analysis. Ph.D. dissertation, University of Connecticut.

———, and Gilbert D. Nass. 1977. "Abortion or Single Parenthood? Analysis of the Pre-Term and Prenatal Pathways." Unpublished report.

Watson, Mary Ann, and Flint Whitlock. 1982. *Breaking the Bonds: The Realities of Sexually Open Relationships.* Denver: Tudor House.

Webster, Paula. 1982. "Going All the Way . . . to Pleasure." *Ms.,* July/August, pp. 260–63.

Weinberg, Martin. 1965. "Sexual Modesty, Social Meanings and the Nudist Camp." *Social Problems* 12 (Winter):311–18.

Weinberg, Thomas S. 1978. "Sadism and Masochism." *Bulletin of the American Academy of Psychiatry and the Law* 6, no. 4 (September):284–95.

———, and Gerhard Falk. 1978. "Sadists and Masochists: The Social Organization of Sexual Violence." Paper presented at the annual meeting of the Society for the Study of Social Problems. September 2–4.

Weis, David.L., and Michael Slosnerick. 1981. "Attitudes toward Sexual and Nonsexual Extramarital Involvements among a Sample of College Students." *Journal of Marriage and the Family* 43 (May):349–58.

Weiss, Robert S. 1979. *Going It Alone: The Family Life and Social Situation of the Single Parent.* New York: Basic Books.

Wesson, D. R. 1982. "Use of Cocaine by Masseuses." *Journal of Psychoactive Drugs* 14 (1–2):75–77.

Whitam, Frederick L. 1977. "The Homosexual Role: A Reconsideration." *Journal of Sex Research* 13, no. 1 (February):1–11.

———, and Mary Jo Dizon. 1979. "Occupational Choice and Sexual Orientation in Cross-Cultural Perspective." *International Journal of Sociology.*

White, Diane. 1979. "Altogether, a Strange Experience." *Boston Globe.* December 15, p. 10.

White, David. 1981. "Pursuit of the Ultimate Aphrodisiac." *Psychology Today,* September, pp. 9–12.

White, Gregory L. 1981. "Jealousy and Partner's Perceived Motives for Attraction to a Rival." *Social Psychology Quarterly* 44, no. 1 (March):24–30.

———, Sanford Fishbein, and Jeffrey Rutstein. 1981. "Passionate Love and the Misattribution of Arousal." *Journal of Personality and Social Psychology* 41, no. 1:56–62.

"Why Do Females, Not Males, Seek Sterilization?" 1982. *Sexuality Today* 6, nos. 9–10 (December 20–27):4.

Williams, Robert H., ed. 1981. *Textbook of Endocrinology.* 6th ed. Philadelphia: W. B. Saunders.

Willis, Ellen. 1979a. Column in *The Village Voice,* October 15, p. 8.

———. 1979b. Column in *The Village Voice,* November 12, p. 8.

———. 1980. Personal communication, August 4.

Wilson, G. Terence, David M. Lawson, and David B. Abrams. 1978. "Effects of Alcohol on Sexual Arousal in Male Alcoholics." *Journal of Abnormal Psychology* 87, no. 6 (December):609–16.

Wilson, John. 1965. Logic and Sexual Morality. New York: Penguin.

Wilson, Paul R. 1978. *The Other Side of Rape.* St. Lucia, Australia. University of Queensland Press.

Wilson, W. Cody. 1975. "The Distribution of Selected Sexual Attitudes and Behaviors among the Adult Population of the United States." *Journal of Sex Research* 11, no. 1 (February):46–64.

Withers, Jean, and Jennifer James. 1977. "Three Organizations Working to Change Prostitution Laws: N.O.W., A.C.L.U., and C.O.Y.O.T.E." In Jennifer James, *The Politics of Prostitution,* 2d ed. Seattle, Wash.: Social Research Associates.

Wolf, Deborah Goleman, 1979. *The Lesbian Community.* Berkeley and Los Angeles: University of California Press.

Wolfe, Linda. 1981. *The Cosmo Report.* New York: Arbor House.

———. 1982. "The Next Sexual Hype—'The G Spot.'" *New York Magazine,* July 19, pp. 37–39.

Woods, Nancy Fugate. 1975. *Human Sexuality in Health and Illness.* St. Louis, Mo.:Mosby.

Wright, Richard A. 1975. "Hepatitis B and the HBsAg Carrier: An Outbreak Related to Sexual Contact." *Journal of the American Medical Association* 232, no. 7 (May):717–21.

Wyatt, Joseph, and Chere Stewart-Newman. 1982. "The Educationally Oriented Adult: Attitudes toward Sex Education." *Journal of Sex Education and Therapy* 8, no. 1 (Spring):22–25.

Yaffê, Maurice, and Edward C. Nelson, eds. 1982. *The Influence of Pornography on Behavior.* London: Academic Press.

Yalom, Marilyn, Suzanne Estler, and Wenda Brewster. 1982. "Changes in Female Sexuality: A Study of Mother/Daughter Communication and Generational Differences." *Psychology of Women Quarterly* 7, no. 2 (Winter):141–54.

Yarber, W. L. 1978. "New Directions on Venereal Disease Education." *Family Coordinator* 27, no. 2 (April):121–25.

"You Can't Steal Love, Court Says." 1982. AP, UPI, *Milwaukee Journal,* July 18, p. 2.

"Youth for Sale on the Streets." 1977. *Time,* November 28, p. 23.

Zapka, Jane, and Ronald Mazur. 1977. "Peer Sex Education Training and Evaluation." *American Journal of Public Health* 67, no. 5 (May):450–54.

Zelnik, Melvin, and John F. Kantner. 1977. "Sexual and Contraceptive Experience of Young Unmarried Women in the United States, 1976 and 1971." *Family Planning Perspectives* 9, no. 2 (March–April):55–71.

———. 1980. "Sexual Activity, Contraceptive Use and Pregnancy among Metropolitan-Area Teenagers: 1971–1979." *Family Planning Perspectives* 12, no. 5 (September–October):230–37.

Zelnick, Melvin, and Young J. Kim. 1982. "Sex Education and Its Association with Teenage Sexual Activity, Pregnancy and Contraceptive Use." *Family Planning Perspectives* 14, no. 3 (May–June):117–26.

Zelnick, Melvin, Young J. Kim, and John F. Kantner. 1979. "Probabilities of Intercourse and Conception among U.S. Teenage Women, 1971 and 1976." *Family Planning Perspectives* 11, no. 3 (May–June):177–83.

Ziegler, Bette, and Jane Seskin. 1979. *Sexuality Today.*

Ziegler, Dan. 1982. "Promising Gonorrhea Vaccine May Be Tested on Volunteers." *Hartford Courant,* August 12, p. A9.

Zilbergeld, Bernie. 1978. *Male Sexuality: A Guide to Sexual Fulfillment.* Boston: Little, Brown.

———. 1983. Interviewed by Philip Nobile in *Forum,* June, pp. 14–24.

———, and Michael Evans. 1980. "The Inadequacy of Masters and Johnson." *Psychology Today,* August, pp. 29–43.

Zimbardo, Philip G. 1977. *Shyness.* Reading, Mass.: Addison-Wesley.

Zuckerman, Marvin. 1978. "The Search for High Sensation." *Psychology Today,* February, pp. 38–46, 96–99.

Zwerner, Janna. 1982. "Yes We Have Troubles but Nobody's Listening: Sexual Issues of Women with Spinal Cord Injury." *Sexuality and Disability* 5, no. 3 (Fall):158–71.